Toward a New
Council of Florence

'On the Peace of Faith'
and Other Works by Nicolaus of Cusa

Toward a New Council of Florence

'On the Peace of Faith'
and Other Works by
Nicolaus of Cusa

Translated and with an
Introduction by
William F. Wertz, Jr.

SCHILLER INSTITUTE, INC.
Washington, D.C. 1993

© 1993 Schiller Institute, Inc.
ISBN: 0-9621095-8-4
Library of Congress Catalogue Card Number: 92-85238
SIB 93-001

Front and back cover photos from *Nikolaus von Kues,
1401-1464: Leben und Werk im Bild,* by Dr. Helmut
Gestrich, Cusanus-Gesellschaft, Bernkastel-Kues,
Germany.

Cover design: World Composition, Inc.
Book design: World Composition, Inc.
Editor: Marianna Wertz

Please direct all inquiries to the publisher:
Schiller Institute, Inc.
P.O. Box 66082
Washington, D.C. 20035-6082

To
My wife Marianna

Contents

Preface

Most of the works by Nicolaus of Cusa in this volume have never been translated into English before. To my knowledge, the only exceptions are *On the Not-Other*, *On the Peace of Faith*, *An Examination of the Koran*, and *On the Gift of the Father of Lights*. Therefore, what is unique about this volume is first, that it contains translations of twelve works of Cusanus previously unavailable to an English-speaking readership; second, that it contains new translations of three other important works of Cusanus and of the prologues to a fourth; and finally, that it makes all of these translations available in one inexpensive paperback volume.

As should be clear from the title of this volume, my purpose in translating these works and making them as widely available as possible is not academic. It is my firm belief, and the belief of the Schiller Institute, that the writings of Nicolaus of Cusa can contribute significantly to resolving the crisis facing humanity today.

The circumstances under which I translated these works were indeed extraordinary. I was first introduced to the works of Nicolaus of Cusa by Helga Zepp-LaRouche, the founder of the Schiller Institute, in the late 1970's. Throughout the 1970's and 1980's, Mrs. LaRouche and her husband, Lyndon H. LaRouche, Jr., continuously emphasized the importance of Nicolaus of Cusa, both as the founder of modern science and as a political and religious thinker. At their suggestion, during the 1980's I immersed myself in reading all of the writings then available in English translation.

On January 27, 1989, Mr. LaRouche and several of his

political associates, including myself, were unjustly imprisoned, after being falsely convicted of conspiracy to commit mail fraud. The real reason for our imprisonment was that we had incurred the wrath of powerful political enemies inside and outside of the U.S. government, because of our fight for a policy of world peace based upon economic development.

On May 5, 1989, Helga Zepp–LaRouche delivered a speech, entitled "Nicolaus of Cusa and the Council of Florence," to a conference in Rome, Italy, sponsored by the Schiller Institute to commemorate the 550th anniversary of the Council of Florence. Inspired by her presentation, I decided to put my time in prison to good use by translating those works of Cusanus to which I could gain access and which had not yet been translated into English.

It is my hope that the broader circulation through this volume of the works of Nicolaus of Cusa, the man who contributed more than anyone else to the launching of the European Renaissance of the fifteenth century, might help to catalyze a renaissance of the human spirit today. In particular, it is my hope that this book will contribute to the building of an international coalition for world peace and development, based upon respect for all human beings as created *in the living image of God.*

I wish to express my gratitude to several people who have helped me in preparing this volume. I would like to thank Helga Zepp-LaRouche and Lyndon H. LaRouche, Jr., for having introduced me to the work of Cusanus and for sharing with me their appreciation of his importance. I am grateful to Jonathan Tennenbaum for initially suggesting that I translate *On Conjectures.* And most of all, I am indebted to my wife Marianna, whose love helped to sustain me during my imprisonment and encouraged me to persevere in this endeavor.

Toward a New Council of Florence 'On the Peace of Faith' and Other Works by Nicolaus of Cusa

Today, in the midst of the second Great Depression of the twentieth century, the world is rife with political and religious conflict. It might even be said that the world is currently experiencing a spreading brushfire of local wars which cumulatively could flare up into World War III. Religious warfare has broken out on the Indian subcontinent between Hindus and Muslims. In the Middle East, Christians have been assassinated and brutalized by Muslims in Lebanon, and Jews have massacred Palestinian Muslims in Jerusalem. The military forces of the United States of America waged war against the nation of Iraq. Serbia has conducted a genocidal war against both Christian Croatia and Muslim Bosnia. Warfare is either already taking place or threatening to break out between various nations of the former Soviet Union. And throughout Ibero-America narco-terrorist gangs like the Sendero Luminoso are waging genocidal war against the very existence of Christian civilization.

In the aftermath of the liberation of the nations of Eastern Europe and the former Soviet Union from governments based upon Marxist atheistic materialism, the liberal capitalist governments of the United States and Great Britain are attempting to create a new global imperial order. However, this new "Pax Americana," based on a Malthusian conception of man, rather than producing true peace, can only produce a New Age of

North-South conflict and genocide, as the liberal capitalist economy itself collapses in depression.

The situation thus described is similar in many respects to that which existed during the lifetime of Nicolaus of Cusa in the fifteenth century. At that time Christian Europe was threatened by the expansion of the Ottoman Empire. In 1438 the Pope called for a crusade to defend Europe from the advancing Ottoman Turks. The crusade was finally organized in 1444, after the Council of Florence had succeeded in reuniting the Roman Catholic and the Eastern Orthodox Churches in 1439. However, after Christian forces were defeated at Varna, the Western Christian world was so weakened that in 1453 Constantinople fell to the Turks.

In that same year, 1453, Nicolaus of Cusa wrote *On the Peace of Faith,* in an effort to lay a true basis for ending religious warfare and establishing global peace. The ecumenical principles he enunciated in this work were an extension of the same principles he had fought for earlier, in 1439 at the Council of Florence, which was convoked for the purpose of reuniting Christendom.

In the recent period of world history a misguided conception of ecumenicism has been advocated directly opposite to that pursued by Cusanus at the Council of Florence and in all of his writings, including especially *On the Peace of Faith.*

The primary basis for peace among diverse religions and peoples, Cusanus rightly recognized, was respect for the sovereignty and sanctity of the individual as *imago viva Dei,* i.e., in the living image of God. As Christ taught, all laws can be subsumed by two: love of God and love of one's fellow man, including one's enemy. As St. John says, God is love. Therefore, man, as in the living image of God, must adhere to the law of charity in respect to his fellow man.

The critical concept which Nicolaus of Cusa puts forward both in *On the Peace of Faith* and in *On Learned Ignorance* is that of "formed faith." According to St. Thomas Aquinas, who employs this same expression in the *Summa Theologica,* the concept of "formed faith" derives from St. Ambrose, who maintained that love is the form of all virtues. Thus, Cusanus, in the tradition of Sts. Ambrose, Augustine and Aquinas, maintains, as the Apostle Paul wrote, that man is not justified by works of the law, but rather by faith alone. However, the faith which justifies must be formed by works of charity, otherwise, as St. James wrote, it is formless and dead. (James 2:17)

This concept of faith formed by works of charity is expressed theologically by the notion of the *Filioque*. The word *Filioque* is Latin for *and the Son*. The Nicene Creed proclaims that the Holy Spirit proceeds both from the Father *and the Son*. However, since the schism of 1055 A.D., the Eastern Orthodox Churches had rejected the phrase *and the Son,* or *Filioque,* as a Western innovation.

At the Council of Florence in 1439, due primarily to the historical research and argument of Cusanus, representatives of both the Greek and Russian Orthodox Churches were convinced that the *Filioque* was essential to the Christian faith. It was the concept of the *Filioque* and everything implied by it that was the basis not only of Cusanus' effort to reunite Christendom, but also of his effort to establish ecumenical peace among disparate religions. Virtually every one of Cusanus' writings is an exploration and elaboration of the implications of the concept of the *Filioque* and the related concept of the Trinity, in opposition to Aristotelian gnosticism.

Unfortunately, the reunification achieved at Florence was short-lived. When the Russian Orthodox religious leaders returned to Russia they were denounced for having agreed to belief in the *Filioque* and their agreement was repudiated. The ensuing split was in no way an invalidation of the approach taken by the Council under Cusanus' intellectual leadership. Unification of Christianity is not possible without the concept of the *Filioque,* because such unity would not be Christianity and in fact would deny that man is *imago viva Dei*.

In fact, the denial of the *Filioque* concept is reflective of an anti-Christian world outlook characteristic of Oriental, autocratic societies, in which the ruler governs on the basis not of reason and love but of arbitrary, irrational whim, and in which the ruled are regarded as obedient serfs, virtually beasts of burden, subject to the ruler's caprice. In such societies the idea that man, through imitation of Christ, who is the Word or Logos, is capable of creative reason and love, is regarded in itself to be a threat to the established order.

Ironically, the essential problem facing the former Soviet Union today is the fact that the Russian Orthodox Church repudiated the agreement of its representatives, who participated in the Council of Florence, to accept the *Filioque*. It is no exaggeration to say that the problem with the Soviet economy today, which will not be solved by the introduction of so-called "free market" economics of the liberal capitalist variety, is the lack of the individual creativity reflected explicitly in the *Filioque* concept.

The fact that the Russian Orthodox leaders who attended the Council of Florence accepted the *Filioque* as part of their credo is proof that, on the basis of reason, there is no obstacle to the Russian Orthodox Church accepting the *Filioque* today. There is no inherent obstacle in Russian Orthodoxy to the notion that man, through imitation of Christ, who is the Logos, is capable of creative reason and love. The only obstacle today to acceptance of the *Filioque* concept is the outlook of an oligarchical political establishment, which is threatened by republican freedom. However, that establishment is doomed to self-destruction by its own continued suppression of the individual creativity of its citizenry. The only solution to the economic and political crisis in the East is finally, after over half a millennium, to rehabilitate those Orthodox leaders who correctly accepted the *Filioque* and to renounce the crime of their persecution.

The crisis of liberal capitalism in the West is equally as severe as that which led to the discrediting of Marxism in the East. As any number of papal encyclicals, including *Centesimus Annus,* have correctly argued, liberal capitalism with its cultist worship of the invisible hand of the "free market" is philosophically as materialist as Marxism. How else can one explain the commitment of Great Britain and the United States in particular to policies which violate the very idea of the sanctity of life? Why is it that the Anglo-American establishment advocates and is implementing a Malthusian policy of genocidal population reduction on a global scale? Why is it that the Anglo-Americans are implementing a monetary policy through the International Monetary Fund and World Bank, which values the potential for development of the human species in the Southern Hemisphere of this globe less than the collection of debt based on usury? Why are they so resistant to calls for debt moratoria and for peace founded on economic development?

The reality is that the economic and social policies of particularly the Anglo-Americans in the West are increasingly divorced from Christian morality. This is reflected in the fact that many Protestant churches in the West, in pursuit of a false ecumenical unity with the Russian Orthodox Church, have either abandoned, or have signaled their willingness to abandon, the *Filioque* concept.

The Church of England has been in the forefront of the current drive to eliminate the *Filioque* from the Nicene Creed. In doing so, it has lent itself to efforts on the part of an Anglo-American oligarchy, which in recent years has publicly organized support for a Malthusian "New Age of Aquarius" to replace the fundamental values of Christianity. The British royal family, particularly Prince Philip, have explicitly attacked the Christian and Jewish belief that "God created man in his own image . . . and said unto them, Be fruitful and multiply and replenish the earth and subdue it and have dominion over . . . every living thing that moveth upon the earth." (Gen 1:27-28) This belief, which is related to the notion of the *Filioque,* is seen correctly by Prince Philip and his allies in the Church of England as the major cultural obstacle to a new imperial order. Thus the Church of England today, as well as those Protestant churches which are moving to eliminate the *Filioque,* are serving the interests of today's oligarchy in the West, just as surely as those Russian Orthodox Church leaders who repudiated the *Filioque* concept after the Council of Florence in 1439 were serving their oligarchical masters.

What is needed today if human civilization is to survive and progress is a revival of the initiative taken by Nicolaus of Cusa beginning over 500 years ago, to establish global peace based on the development of the divine potential of the human species for the exercise of reason and the expression of charity. Without such an effort, the world in the immediate period ahead will be increasingly plagued by depression, disease, starvation and war.

Although the problems in the world today are more complex than during the fifteenth century, the fundamental solutions advanced by Cusanus in his writings remain valid. Therefore, in the interest of helping to launch a global cultural offensive in behalf of world peace, this author has undertaken the translation of a number of important works by Cusanus, most of which have not appeared before in English translation.

By reading already existing translations of such works by Cusanus as *The Catholic Concordance* (1434), *On Learned Ignorance* (1440), *In Defense of Learned Ignorance* (1449), *The Layman: About Mind* (1450), *The Vision of God* (1453), *On Actual-Potential* (1460), and *On the Game of the Spheres* (1463), in combination with the translations now made available by this author, the reader can study for himself the mind of one of the most profound and influential writers in the history of Western Civilization.

The works translated by this author and their dates of composition are as follows: *On Conjectures* (1440), *On the Hidden God* (1444), *On Searching for God* (1445), *On the Filiation of God* (1445), *On the Gift of the Father of Lights* (1446), *On Genesis* (1447), *On the Peace of Faith* (1453), *On the Theological Complement Represented in the Mathematical Complements* (1453), *On Beryllus* (1458), *On the Origin* (1459), *On Equality* (1459), *Prologues to an Examination of the Koran* (1461), *On the Not-Other* (1462), *On the Hunt for Wisdom* (1463), *Compendium* (1464) and *On the Summit of Vision* (1464). These translations are based on the Latin texts and accompanying German translations, which were published in three volumes in the years 1964, 1966 and 1967 on the occasion of the 500th anniversary of the death of Nicolaus of Cusa in 1464, by the Herder & Co. publishing house in Vienna, Austria.

Cusanus' Life

Before discussing the contents of Cusanus' philosophy as expressed in these works, it is useful to situate his ideas in the context of his life's work. As abstract as Cusanus' philosophy may at first appear to some readers, as his biography documents, Cusanus' entire life, from 1401 to 1464, far from an Aristotelian recluse, was that of an apostolic missionary, who worked tirelessly on a global scale to achieve peace based upon the development of the divine potential for reason and love in all men.

Nicolaus was born in 1401 in the city of Kues, opposite the city of Bernkastel on the Mosel River in the diocese of Trier, Germany, the son of a boatman by the name of Johann Krebs. In his very early years it is reported that he received educational training from the Brothers of the Common Life in Deventer, Holland, where Thomas à Kempis studied 20 years earlier and where Erasmus of Rotterdam also later studied. In 1416 the still very young cleric Nicolaus attended the University of Heidelberg, which he left in 1417 with a bachelor's degree in philosophy, in order to begin the study of canon law in Padua, Italy. He completed this study and in 1423, at the age of 22, received a doctorate degree. In 1425, he returned to Germany and enrolled at the University of Cologne, where he studied philosophy and theology, in order to be ordained as a priest. During this period he was the student of Heymericus de Campo, who introduced him to the philosophy of Albertus Magnus, through whom he also became acquainted with the writings of both Raymund Lull and Dionysius the Areopagite. In 1426, he became secretary to the Archbishop of Trier, Otto of Ziegenhain, and in 1427, deacon of the Church of St. Florin in Koblenz.

In 1430, the Archbishop died, and a struggle ensued over his replacement. An election was held, the results of which were contested and appealed to the Pope, who named the Bishop of Speyer as the new Archbishop. In 1432, one of the original contestants, Ulrich von Manderscheid, represented by Nicolaus of Cusa, brought his claim to the Council of Basel, which had begun in July 1431. Although Cusanus was eventually to lose this case, shortly after arriving in Basel, he was incorporated into the Council and made a member of the Committee on the Faith. During the course of 1433, as a member of the Committee on the Faith, he wrote *The Catholic Concordance,* which he submitted to the Council at the end of 1433 or the beginning of 1434.

In this book, the central, revolutionary thesis which Nicolaus developed is, that since by nature all men are created equal in power and freedom, and are endowed by God with reason, all authority over them can only be established by election. Since all legislation is based on natural law, and natural law is based on reason, all legislation, to be valid, must be rooted in the reason of man. Therefore, all legitimate governance and all true religious and political peace can only come from the agreement and consent of the people, and not from any coercive law. To quote Nicolaus: "All legitimate authority arises from elective concordance and free submission."

Cusanus, however, was not unaware of the dangers of pure democracy. Since, in his view, "the number of fools is infinite," in order to avoid a situation in which ignorance might outweigh the vote of the wise and the majority might become tyrannical, he insisted that true freedom must be subject to reason. Universal harmony involves diversity and difference, he argued, but does not endure unless the governed are joined in "rational harmony with the Word."

Both in *The Catholic Concordance* and in *On Learned Ignorance* Cusanus poses the solution to conflict in terms of the relationship between the "one and the many." According to Cusanus, universal concordance derives from the "many" rational creatures adhering to the "One," who is Jesus or the Word. There can be no union among the many, to the extent that the individual abandons adherence to the Word. No creature exists in himself and apart from union with the Word, and yet this union does not deny the sovereign existence and role of the individual. As Cusanus writes, each member of the one body exists with his own role and does not lose his freedom on account of being in union with the Word. In fact, the many are only truly free to the extent that they rise to the level of the intellect.

Interestingly, Cusanus bases his concept of the consent of the governed upon the example of the Virgin Mary, who gave birth to Christ "by her own free consent when she said 'Be it done unto me according to thy word.' "

Nicolaus initially hoped the Council would contribute to Christian unity based upon the principles elaborated in *The Catholic Concordance*. However, when the Council itself became a source of division, due to its heretical insistence upon its own supremacy over the Pope, and opposed the suggestion of Pope Eugene IV and the Eastern Orthodox Church that an ecumenical council be held in an Italian city for the purpose of achieving reunification, Cusanus left the Council and took the side of Pope Eugene IV. In the spring of 1437, Nicolaus, with two others, was sent by Pope Eugene IV to Constantinople as envoy to the Greek Emperor and the Patriarch. In November of that year he sailed back with them and 28 archbishops of the Eastern Church. The Pope then met them at the Council of Florence to discuss reunion. Eugene dissolved the Council of Basel, which had elected the anti-Pope, Amadeus, Duke of Savoy, who called himself Felix V.

For ten years Cusanus worked with Eugene IV, and after his death in 1447, with his successor Nicolaus V, to overcome the neutrality which the German princes maintained between the Pope and the anti-Pope. His mission finally succeeded in 1448, when Vienna signed a concordat with the Curia and Nicolaus V was recognized as the legitimate Pope.

Cusanus had been appointed Cardinal secretly by Pope Eugene IV, who, however, died before the appointment was made public. On March 5, 1449 it was announced that Eugene's successor, Nicolaus V, had elevated Cusanus anew to the Presbyter of Cardinals with the title of St. Peter in Chains. In that same year, in which the anti-Pope Amadeus gave up the title of Pope, Pope Nicolaus V confirmed Nicolaus of Cusa in the Archdeaconry of Brabant and named him Bishop of Brixen. Nicolaus of Cusa himself is reported to have received numerous votes for the papacy in the conclave which selected Nicolaus V.

At the end of 1450 Pope Nicolaus V sent Cusanus as legate to Germany, Bohemia, and the adjacent countries. His mandate was to work for peace and reform of doctrine and morals, to hold provincial councils, visit monasteries, and raise contributions for the crusade against the Turks. The legation lasted until 1452, during which time he preached extensively in his native German tongue and attempted to implement deep-seated reforms.

Cusanus has been portrayed falsely by the neo-Kantian Ernst Cassirer in his book, *The Individual and the Cosmos in Renaissance Philosophy,* as having broken completely with existing Church doctrine. To the contrary, in his effort to reform the Church in Germany during this period, Cusanus ordered all parish priests to have a copy of St. Thomas Aquinas' *Summa of the Articles of the Faith and of the Sacraments of the Church.*

The Pope also wished to send him to England to try to bring about peace between England and France, but this legation never materialized. Therefore, in March 1452 he set out for Brixen, which he found to be in a bad state of affairs. In 1453, 1455, and 1457, Nicolaus held diocesan synods at Brixen. From the first he was in conflict with Archduke Sigismund over his episcopal dues and temporal powers. In a long struggle between Cusanus and Verena of Stuben, an abbess who refused any reform of her convent for ladies of noble Tyrolean families, the Archduke supported the abbess; though deposed by Papal Bull in 1454, she only resigned in 1459.

In 1458, Nicolaus was in Rome for the conclave which

elected an old friend of his, Aeneas Sylvius Piccolomini, Pope Pius II. In 1460, the conflict with Sigismund finally resulted in a rupture and Nicolaus left the diocese for good, after the Archduke had imprisoned him, robbed him, and threatened his life. Pope Pius II laid the district under an interdict, as his predecessor Calixtus III had also done.

In 1460, Nicolaus was appointed the General Vicar of Rome by Pope Pius II, in whose absence Cusanus governed the papal states. In this position, he convened a Reform Synod and wrote a proposal for General Reform of the Church.

Nicolaus' death occurred on August 11, 1464 at Todi in Umbria, while on the way to confer with the Pope at Ancona. He was buried at the Church of St. Peter in Chains in Rome.

As can be seen from this brief biography, Nicolaus of Cusa was not accidentally given the title of St. Peter in Chains. Like St. Peter, Nicolaus was in a very real sense the rock upon which the Church and Western civilization were revitalized during the fifteenth century. Every one of his political-ecclesiastical deployments was critically designed to ensure the survival and renewal of Christianity in the face of both external and internal threats. If his efforts at reforming the Church, epitomized by his legation to Germany, Bohemia, and adjacent countries, and his endeavors in Brixen, had been successful, the schismatic Reformation of the following century would not have occurred. Necessary reform would have occurred within a unified Church on the highest theological level.

Influence on Science

What is not immediately reflected in this biographical sketch of Cusanus is the profound influence his thinking has had on the development of modern science, and thus not only on man's spiritual life, but also upon the simultaneously necessary increase in man's capacity to exercise dominion over nature. Cusanus' scientific method, which is explicitly in the tradition of Plato and those two great Christian theologians who employed Plato's method, St. Augustine and Dionysius the Areopagite, had an indisputable influence upon such seminal scientific minds as Leonardo da Vinci (1452-1591), Johannes Kepler (1571-1630), Gottfried Wilhelm Leibniz (1646-1716) and Georg Cantor (1845-1918).

As will be seen in his writings, Cusanus' primary service to the development of modern science was to revive the Socratic method of Plato from the improved Christian standpoint of St. Augustine, and in the course thereof, to free the human mind from the gnostic restraints imposed upon it by entrenched Aristotelianism. Lawfully, this service was directly related again to the issue of the *Filioque*. Aristotle's method, in contrast to the Christian version of the Socratic method of Plato, denies that the human mind can participate in divinity. It therefore denies that man, through the exercise of his creative reason, is in the living image of God. It denies that through imitation of Christ man can become an adoptive son of God. It denies that creative reason, as distinct from deductive logical rationality, even exists for man. By challenging the hegemony of the Aristotelian method in theology and science, Cusanus personally laid the basis for the fifteenth-century scientific and artistic renaissance, which began in Italy and spread throughout the rest of Europe, including into those countries in which Cusanus had been papal legate.

Contrary to the anti-religious, rationalist view which has come to dominate since especially the Enlightenment, for Cusanus as for St. Augustine before him, there is no conflict between faith and reason. Indeed, in *On the Filiation of God,* Cusanus argues as follows:

> Who indeed does not believe, does not ascend at all, but rather, judges himself not able to ascend, whilst he himself obstructs the way; indeed one attains nothing without faith, which places the wanderer on his way at the beginning. Therefore, the power of our soul is able to climb upwards to the perfection of the intellect only insofar as it believes. Therefore, the ascent to the filiation of God is not prohibited, if faith is present.

Proceeding from this standpoint, Cusanus catalyzed a revolution against the Aristotelian philosophy prevalent in his day, which was obstructing the development of modern science. The primary polemic of both *On Learned Ignorance* and its companion piece, *On Conjectures,* was against the Aristotelian "law of contradiction," which denied the "coincidence of opposites" in the Divine Mind. The fact that Cusanus' concept of the "coincidence of opposites" was an attack on Aristotelianism was immediately recognized by John Wenck, who attacked *On Learned Ignorance* in a book entitled *On Unknown Learning*. Wenck, a professor of theology at the University of Heidelberg, accused Cusanus of destroying the "fundamental principle of all knowledge: viz., the principle that it is impossible both to be and not to be the same thing, as we read in *Metaphysics*. But this man cares little for the sayings of Aristotle." Wenck attributed Cusanus' method to "a meagerness of instruction in logic" and insisted that Cusanus' notion of the coincidence of opposites "destroys Aristotle's entire doctrine."

In 1449, Cusanus wrote *A Defense of Learned Ignorance*, in which he pointed out that Wenck was an apologist for the condemned Council of Basel and an adherent of the Aristotelian sect. In his response to Wenck, he wrote as follows: "But the Aristotelian sect now prevails. This sect regards as heresy the method of the coincidence of opposites. Yet, the endorsement of this method is the beginning of the ascent unto mystical theology. Hence, this method, which is completely tasteless to those nourished in this sect, is pushed far from them, as being contrary to their undertaking. Hence, it would be comparable to a miracle— just as would be the transformation of the sect—for them to reject Aristotle and to leap higher."

Two related examples will suffice to demonstrate the magnitude of Cusanus' revolutionary influence on the development of modern science: his work in cosmology and his contribution to the development of the notion of the transfinite.

Cusanus versus Aristotle

The cosmology of Aristotle, which prevailed in the scientific world for centuries, entailed the following fundamental assumptions: 1) the universe is spherical, has a center and a circumference, and is therefore a vast but finite structure; 2) the earth lies at the center of the universe and is itself immobile, since the heavenly bodies revolve in uniform circular motion around the center and therefore around the earth; and 3) the heavenly bodies are essentially different from phenomena in the sublunar region of the earth.

Nicolaus of Cusa, on the other hand, hypothesized that the universe is neither finite, in the sense of being a bounded aggregate of finite objects, nor is it absolutely infinite, since only God is such. In *On Learned Ignorance* he thus writes: "And although the universe is not infinite, it cannot be conceived as finite; for it lacks the boundaries within which it is enclosed." Thus, according to Cusanus, the universe is not bounded by a fixed circumference as Aristotle believed. Rather it consists of a boundless multitude of "monadic unities" or, to use a concept developed in the nineteenth century by Georg Cantor, it is transfinite.

Moreover, Cusanus argued that there can be neither absolute rest nor absolute motion in the universe. Therefore, the earth cannot be immobile. On this same basis he also concluded that there can be no fixed center in the universe and no fixed circumference of the universe. Every part of the universe must be in motion. Cusanus also pointed in the direction of elliptical orbits by disputing that the motions of the heavenly bodies are perfectly circular: "Rather, though the matter appears to us to be otherwise, neither the sun nor the moon nor the earth nor any sphere by its motion can describe a true circle, since none of these is moved around a fixed point."

Thus the universe, according to Cusanus, is not geocentric, as Aristotle had argued. In *On Learned Ignorance,* Cusanus hypothesizes that "the earth is moved." He also entertains the idea that the earth and the other planets rotate around the sun, as is clear from a drawing he made, which portrays the sun surrounded by the planets. However, he does not make the sun the center of the universe as a whole. Rather he argues, "Hence, the world-machine will have its center everywhere and its circumference nowhere, so to speak; for God, who is everywhere and nowhere, is its circumference and center."

Hence it is also clear that the Aristotelian division of the universe into sublunar and supralunar regions is not tenable in the face of Cusanus' cosmological argument.

Cusanus' work in this area was extraordinarily significant in helping to lay the basis for the Age of Exploration and Christopher Columbus' discovery of the New World, less than thirty years after Cusanus' death in 1464. Cusanus' contribution to Columbus' discovery and evangelization of the Americas was mediated directly through two of Cusanus' closest associates—the Italian scientist Paolo Toscanelli and Ferdinand Martin, the Canon of Lisbon, Portugal. Both appear as participants in dialogues written by Cusanus. Toscanelli is Cusanus' interlocutor in *The Dialogue on the Quadrature of the Circle,* and Martin is one of several participants identified in *On the Not-Other.* Both individuals witnessed Cusanus' last will and testament on Aug. 6, 1464. Also, a relative Ferdinand's, Antonio Martin, the Bishop of Oporto, had accompanied Cusanus in his mission to Constantinople in 1437.

When Columbus was in Portugal, he learned that Toscanelli had written letters to Ferdinand Martin about a westward voyage to the Orient. With Martin as intermediary, Columbus then engaged in a direct correspondence with Toscanelli. In 1480, Columbus received a letter from Toscanelli which included a map and the scientific information required for such a voyage. Columbus is known to have carried this navigational map with him during his successful voyage in 1492.

In addition to the profound impact that Cusanus' philosophical outlook had on the development of modern science in the fifteenth and sixteenth centuries, it also played an important role in contributing to the development of the conception of the transfinite by Georg Cantor in the late nineteenth century. In his *Foundations of a General Theory of Manifolds* (1883), Cantor writes in a revealing footnote, that he derived his revolutionary notion of the transfinite from Plato and Nicolaus of Cusa.

First, Cantor notes that in the *Philebus* dialogue, Plato posits two principles, namely, that of the infinite or unlimited, and that of the finite or the limit. Plato takes the infinite as unterminated, but nevertheless able to be terminated or defined by the finite or the limit, which as form defines and terminates the formless infinite. However, Plato additionally argues in the *Philebus* that there is also an infinite or unlimited sequence of such finite limits or forms.

The transfinite conception, which Cantor derives from this conception of Plato, of a mixture of the finite and infinite in the form of an unlimited family of limits limiting the unlimited, he also finds in Cusanus. As Cantor writes in the same footnote, "Similarly I find points of contact for my conceptions in the philosophy of Nicolaus Cusanus."

For example, in *On the Origin,* Cusanus writes as follows:

And if someone examines more subtly, then the position of the Melian is not so absurd as Aristotle portrays it. For in every consideration one sees nothing other than infinity, namely, a defining infinity and a definable infinity. The defining infinity is the end, which has no end; it is the origin subsisting through itself, which enfolds every end. And it is God before every entity. And the definable infinity, on the contrary, is the being free of every terminus and every definable definition through the infinite end. And it is after every entity.

Therefore, when the infinite first defines the second, then the finite entity arises from the infinite origin, that is, from the first, which is more than the entity, because it precedes it. It does not arise from the second, since the latter is after the entity.

In the first infinite everything definable exists as actuality, in the second infinite everything definable exists in respect to the omnipotence of the first.

It is these finite infinities or, as Cusanus also calls them in *On the Origin,* "monadic unities," which arise when the defining infinity defines the definable infinity, which Cantor calls transfinite. In this way the universe, which is created out of nothing by God, is not itself the Absolute Infinite, nor is it finite in the sense that Aristotle says the universe is a bounded aggregate of finite objects, but rather the universe is *transfinite;* it is a boundless or negentropic multitude of monadic unities, which are derived from the absolute Infinite One, who is God.

In *On Learned Ignorance,* Nicolaus of Cusa writes that "every created thing is, as it were, a finite infinite. . . ." This distinction between the Creator, who is absolutely infinite, and the creature as a finite infinite, is the same as that made by St. Thomas Aquinas in *Summa Theologica* between God as absolutely infinite and His creatures as "relatively infinite." As Aquinas says, God's creatures do not have a univocal relationship to Him. The caused is not the same as the Cause. However, the creature does have an "analogical" relationship to his Creator. Therefore, although a created thing is finite, it is simultaneously infinite.

This concept of the creature as a finite or contracted infinite, or to use Aquinas' term, a relative infinite, is the theological basis of Georg Cantor's concept of the transfinite and is in total opposition to the Aristotelian view that no creature, including man, participates in any way in God's infinity.

Although John Wenck accused Cusanus of pantheism, nothing could be further from the truth. As we shall see as we explore his ideas in more depth, Cusanus follows St. Paul in asserting that God is "all in all" (1 Cor 15:28), in the sense that everything that exists owes its existence to its cause. But at the same time, Cusanus maintains that God is "nothing of everything." God precedes the universe, which He calls into existence out of nothing, and therefore is not the universe itself, but rather transcends it.

Cusanus addresses this issue directly in *On the Not-Other:*

> For since everything is ordered to God or the Not-other
> and in no way to the other, which is after Him, the universe
> is not to be regarded as though the end of the universe; for
> then God were the universe. Since, however, the universe
> is ordered to its origin—through order the universe indeed
> shows itself as being from God—it is ordered to Him as to
> the Order of the order in everything.

In *On the Origin,* Cusanus makes the same point in a different way. He argues that only the infinite and eternal is auto-hypostatic or self-subsisting, for this alone is indivisible and nothing can be added to it. However, everything finite, which admits of addition or subtraction, is not auto-hypostatic or self-subsisting, but rather from an older cause. Therefore, God is the necessary One exalted above everything finite, the "Hypostasis of all hypostases." Thus neither the universe, as pantheism asserts, nor the human species, as gnostics like Ludwig Feuerbach (1804-72) and the secular humanists maintain, is self-subsisting. Only God is auto-hypostatic and everything created owes its subsistence to its necessary origin, God. Without God nothing, including the transfinitely ordered universe, remains. As Cusanus writes in *On the Origin:* "Entity has from the One, what it is. If one sublates the One, then nothing remains."

In fact, it is Aristotle, whose arguments are pantheistic. As Cusanus points out in *On the Hunt for Wisdom,* the Peripatetics believed that the universe, and with it time and motion, exist from the beginning and therefore are not made by God. Cusanus writes as follows:

> Aristotle, however, denies that the potential-to-become has a beginning; thus he does not believe that motion and time have been made, having been deceived by the following reasoning: The world, which has become, could become, and the potential-to-become does not become actual without motion. Thus he concluded that motion and time have not been made. If he had paid attention to the fact that the eternal is before the potential-to-become as actuality, he would not have denied that the potential-to-become originated from that which precedes it.

According to Cusanus, Aristotle made a number of related errors. First, as Cusanus argues in *On Beryllus,* God "is absolute and superexalted, since He is not a contracted origin such as nature, which acts out of necessity, but rather is the origin of nature itself, which is therefore supernatural and free, because He creates everything through His will." Aristotle, on the other hand, believed, according to Cusanus, that "the Composer-Intellect made everything out of the necessity of nature." But, as Cusanus writes, God "does not act as nature or a necessary instrument through the command of a superior, but rather through the free will, which is also His essence." If man, who is in the living image of God, is free and not merely an instrument of nature, then God Himself must be free. If He is not, if He must act out of necessity as an instrument of nature, then man does not have free will.

Second, as Cusanus maintains in *On Beryllus,* since Aristotle denies that contradictory opposites coincide in God, who precedes duality, "he misplaced the beginning of forms in matter." Moreover, Aristotle believed that, although God administers the heavens, "the heavens exist only for the sake of this world. . . ." According to Cusanus, Aristotle did not attend to the fact that the heavens "are not created as the end of the earthly world, but rather for the laud of the Creator."

Finally, in *On Beryllus* Cusanus points out, in respect to Aristotle in particular and all pagan philosophers in general, that they lack the Christian concept of love or charity. He writes as follows:

> . . . if one examines it acutely, then it is a question of that connection, of which I speak. But he has thus neither known nor named it. And for this reason, all philosophers have not attained to the spirit, which is the principle of connection and, according to our perfected theology, the third person in the divinity. . . .

We shall have occasion to return to Cusanus' polemic against Aristotle in the course of what follows. However, having introduced the reader to Cusanus' fundamental differences with Aristotelianism, the best way to give the reader a comprehensive picture of Cusanus' most important conceptions is to review the "ten fields of wisdom" as he discusses them in *On the Hunt for Wisdom*. Cusanus wrote this piece in 1463, one year before he died, in order "to leave to posterity, briefly summed up, my huntings for wisdom." As he writes in this work, "I regard ten fields especially suited for the hunt for wisdom. The first I call learned ignorance; the second actual-potential; the third the not-other; the fourth I designate the field of light; the fifth the field of laud; the sixth the field of unity; the seventh the field of equality; the eighth the field of connection; the ninth the field of termini; and the tenth the field of order."

Each of the ten names which Cusanus employs to characterize the fields in which he carries out his hunt for wisdom is a metaphorical expression, either for the method by which one can obtain a mental vision of God, who is Himself invisible, or a metaphorical name for God Himself, who is ultimately nameless.

On Learned Ignorance

As Cusanus argues in his seminal book *On Learned Ignorance,* and reports as well in *On Conjectures,* which was written in the same year, "the truth in its precision is unattainable." Since everything which is known can be known better, nothing is known just as it is knowable. Therefore, as one does not know God, who precedes everything and is the cause of all things, neither is the quiddity of all things known as it is knowable. Thus a positive assertion of the true, if it be articulated by men, is always only a conjecture, which can always be rendered better or less imperfect, "for the apprehension of the true can always be enlarged, but never exhausted." Therefore, the better one knows that one comprehends the incomprehensible only incomprehensibly, the more learned one is. Or, as Paul wrote to the Corinthians: "The wisdom of this world is foolishness with God." (1 Cor 3:19)

Moreover, the intellect would not be content with itself, if it were the image of a Creator who is so small and imperfect that He could be comprehended. As Cusanus writes, "He rejoices more, who finds an infinite and innumerable, incomprehensible and inexhaustible treasure, than he who discovers a finite, numerable, comprehensible one."

It is important to note, however, that in contrast to the Aristotelians, who argue that since God is infinite and incomprehensible and man finite, man cannot participate in the divine, Cusanus does not see the incomprehensibility of God as incompatible with man's participation in divinity by becoming an adoptive son of God. In *On the Filiation of God,* Cusanus writes: "Perhaps you are struck by what you have frequently heard: God is incomprehensible and the filiation, which is the apprehension of the truth, which is God, cannot be attained." Cusanus goes on to say that, although God is not attained as He is, nevertheless, in the purity of the intellectual spirit man can participate in God in the similitude through which He communicates Himself. As Cusanus writes in *On Beryllus,* "the Truth, which is what it can be, is imparticipable; but in its similitude, which can be received to a greater or lesser degree, according to the disposition of the recipient, it is communicable."

In *On Learned Ignorance,* Nicolaus of Cusa employs the example of the impossibility of squaring a circle to demonstrate why it is that the human intellect can never know God as He is (see Figue 1). If one inscribes a polygon representing the human intellect within a circle representing the Truth itself, no matter how many times one multiplies the number of sides of the polygon, the polygon will never attain to identity with the circle. On the surface the polygon may appear to be becoming more and more like the circle, however, in reality, as more sides are added, the number of locations where the polygon is discontinuous with the circle will increase. The reason this is the case is that the circle

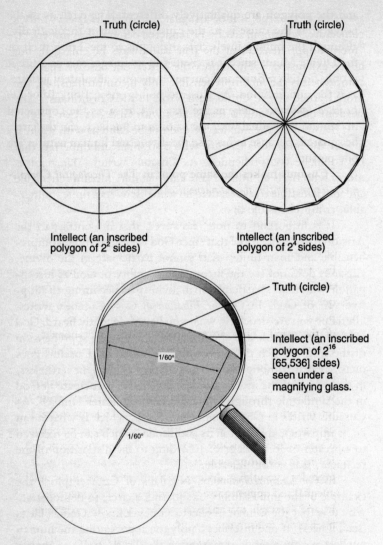

FIGURE 1   *As Cusanus writes in* On Learned Ignorance, *Book I, Chapter 3,* "a noncircle [cannot measure] a circle, whose being is something indivisible. Hence, the intellect, which is not truth, never comprehends truth so precisely that truth cannot be comprehended infinitely more precisely. For the intellect is to truth as [an inscribed] polygon to [the inscribing] circle. The more angles the inscribed polygon has, the more similar it is to the circle. However, even if the number of its angles is increased ad infinitum, the polygon never becomes equal [to the circle] unless it is resolved into an identity with the circle."

and the polygon are qualitatively different. The circle is to the polygon as the cause is to the caused. To put it theologically, although the human intellect is analogous to the Truth itself or the Divine Mind, since it is created in its image, as a creature it is only finitely infinite and can never become absolutely infinite, as is the mind of God. As Cusanus points out in Book III of *On Learned Ignorance,* only in the case of Christ, as the contracted maximum individual with the maximum intellect, can the circle be squared, because in his case the divine and human natures are one person.

Cusanus makes the same point in *The Theological Complement Represented in the Mathematical Complements*:

> Indeed, those who sought after the quadrature of the circle presupposed the coincidence of the square and circle in equality, which is certainly not possible in the sensible. For there is no square which is not unequal in relation to every circle which can be given in the material. Consequently, they did not see this equality, which they presupposed, with the eyes of the flesh, but rather with those of the mind. They attempted to show it in rationality. However, since rationality does not admit the coincidence of opposites, they were unsuccessful. However, they should have sought the coincidence intellectually in that circle which is equal to every polygon, and also is of equal circumference with another and diverse polygon. Then they would have attained their intent. From this is elicited that its being is not actually knowable, as it cannot be known except by means of the infinite intellect, which is infinite equality. It precedes everything diverse and different and other and unequal and opposite and whatever else denotes inequality. In and through this infinite intellect alone is everything intelligible measured.

Despite the fact that the human intellect can never become equal to the Divine Mind, man can become an adoptive son of God to the extent that he rises above sense perception and discursive reasoning, i.e., above inductive and deductive logic to the level of the intellect, which Cusanus describes as mental vision or intuition. One achieves the state of learned ignorance, by learning that one is ignorant of the Truth itself, insofar as one locates truth in the mere perception of physical objects or in that form of rationality, the hereditary principle of which is the Aristotelian "law of contradiction." For this reason, Nicolaus of Cusa writes in his *A Defense of Learned Ignorance,* that "learned ignorance pertains to the intellect."

A further insight into Cusanus' concept of learned ignorance can be obtained from his essay *On Searching for God.* In this essay Cusanus demonstrates that God is to everything as vision is to the visible. As he writes, we see objects in the region of the visible by means of color. However, vision itself has no color. If vision itself were colored, its vision would be distorted by its own color. On the other hand, the world of color does not know vision because it attains nothing that is not colored. Thus color is not perceived from itself, but rather from a higher cause, i.e., vision.

Next, Cusanus suggests that we ascend from vision to hearing, taste, smell, and touch. Clearly, there must be a higher cause than vision or any of the senses, which is capable of distinguishing between those finite objects perceived by the senses. This higher cause, according to Cusanus, is "rationality." However, rationality is only capable of judging that which is perceived by the senses based on the "law of contradiction." It itself is incapable of conceiving the infinite, where that which appears to it as contradictory actually coincides. Therefore, one must proceed higher to the intellect, which is above everything rational and therefore sees the compatibility of contradictories. As Cusanus writes, "the rational is apprehended through the intellect, however, the intellect is not found in the region of the rational; the intellect is as the eye and the rational as the colors." Finally, since the intellect itself is created, one must proceed above the intellectual region to God, who is infinitely anterior to all intellectual wisdom.

For Nicolaus of Cusa, learned ignorance is the means by which one rises to the level of the intellect. Since the intellect is not found in the region of the rational, the Aristotelian who limits the human mind to the region of rationality or discursive reason will tend to define Cusanus' notion of the intellect as mystical or irrational.

But for Cusanus, it is only by rising to the level of the

intellect that man becomes an adoptive son of God and thus Godlike, or deiform. As opposed to the religious fundamentalist who believes that St. Paul's description of himself as "raptured" to the "third heaven" (2 Cor 12:2-4) is an entirely emotional and therefore irrational experience, Cusanus insists in both *On Conjectures* and in *On the Vision of God* that the "third heaven" or "Paradise" into which Paul was "raptured" is located beyond the sensible and rational regions in the intellectual region, which he describes as the third heaven, from which state of mind one can indeed see God, not in the sense of physical sight, but rather in the sense of mental vision. As Cusanus writes, to enter Paradise one must vanquish the lofty rational spirit of logic and ascend to the third or intellectual heaven where the truth shines clearly as it is. Only in the third heaven are we able to possess the kingdom of Truth as true sons.

Actual-Potential

According to Nicolaus of Cusa, in addition to the ten fields there are three regions of wisdom: the eternal, the perpetual, and the temporal. The actual-potential is eternal, the potential-to-become is perpetual, and that which becomes actual is temporal.

According to Cusanus, "everything which has become or becomes, since it neither has become nor becomes without the potential-to-become, has one absolute origin; this is the origin and the cause of the potential-to-become and it is that eternal, which precedes the potential-to-become, and is the absolute and the uncontractible origin, since it is everything which it can be. . . ."

Thus, God, who is everything that He can be (in Him potentiality is actuality), is the inception and cause of the potential-to-become of all things, and the Former of all formable forms. As such, He precedes all potential-to-become and is its terminus. The potential-to-become is created out of nothing by God, who is the actual-potential. Therefore, the potential-to-become is created, but does not cease, rather it remains for all time and is perpetual, because it precedes everything that has become actual, which is temporal.

As Cusanus stresses, since the potential-to-become cannot bring itself into actuality—for production comes from actuality—actuality exists before passive potentiality. Therefore, God is the purest actuality. He is the Creator of the potential-to-become of the universe, which Cusanus describes as the "archetypal world in the eternal mind of God." And He makes everything that has become or becomes through the potential-to-become. Everything that follows the potential-to-become, so that it becomes actual, is only actual insofar as it imitates the actuality of the actual-potential.

As Cusanus writes in *On Actual-Potential,* "all things that exist after Him exist with their possibility and their actuality distinct. And hence God alone is what [He] is able to be; but no creature whatsoever is what it is able to be, since possibility and actuality are identical only in the Beginning."

In the epilogue of *On The Hunt for Wisdom,* Cusanus writes as follows:

> Since nothing has become that had not been able to become and nothing can make itself, it follows that the potential is threefold, namely, the potential-to-make, the potential-to-become, and the potential-to-have-become.
>
> Before the potential-to-have-become is the potential-to-become, before the potential-to-become is the potential-to-make. The origin and terminus of the potential-to-become is the potential-to-make. The potential-to-have-become has been made through the potential-to-make from the potential-to-become.
>
> The potential-to-make, since it is before the potential-to-become, has neither been created nor can it become something other. It is therefore everything that it can be. Therefore, it cannot be greater and this we call the maximum, nor smaller and this we call the minimum, nor can it be other. Therefore, it is the efficient, formal or exemplary, and final cause of everything, since it is the terminus and end of the potential-to-become and for that reason also of the potential-to-have-become. Therefore, everything which can become and which has become is previously in the potential-to-make as in the efficient, formal, and final cause, and the potential-to-make is in everything as the absolute cause in the caused.

Introduction

The implications of Cusanus' conception of God as actual-potential are severalfold.

First, God, who is eternal, is ontologically transfinite in respect to the universe and everything that arises in it.

Second, the universe as a whole, or the potential-to-become, is created, but does not cease. Therefore, the universe as a whole is not entropic, but rather, as the perpetual similitude of the eternal, it is negentropic. As Cusanus writes elsewhere in *On the Hunt for Wisdom,* "At all events, it is most certain that the whole world can never cease."

Third, God as actual-potential stands before every distinction, including the distinction between actuality and potentiality, the distinction of being and not-being, etc. Therefore, God is not to be found in the ambit of the logical principle that something either is or is not. He excels the logical law of contradiction, subsuming contradictory opposites. Therefore, the human mind, which desires to see God, must employ creative reason to search for the truth, which is above the appearance of contradictory opposites, rather than limit its hunt to the ambit of logical rationality.

And fourth, Cusanus suggests that the method appropriate to discovering the Truth itself is isoperimetric, i.e., that God is simultaneously the maximum and the minimum. In *On the Hunt for Wisdom,* Cusanus derives this maximum–minimum principle from Dionysius the Areopagite, who in the ninth chapter of *On Divine Names* says that the eternal first cause is both inaugmentable and irreducible, in contrast to passive potentiality, which is subject to both growth and diminution. As Cusanus writes, "I take . . . the inaugmentable and the irreducible, and hasten with them to the hunt and I say that the inaugmentable cannot be greater; therefore, it is the maximum. The irreducible cannot be smaller; it is therefore the minimum. Hence, because it is equally the maximum and minimum, it is in no way smaller, since it is the maximum, and in no way greater, since it is the minimum, but rather the most precise, formal and exemplary cause and measure of everything great or small."

As Cusanus points out in *On Actual-Potential,* if one applies the concept actual-potential to a line, one recognizes that the line, which is what it can be, is simultaneously maximal and minimal. "For since the line is what it is able to be: it cannot be greater,

25

and thus it is seen to be maximal; nor can it be lesser, and thus it is seen to be minimal." Thus by applying the concept of actual-potential to a line, one ascends to an infinite line which enfolds all figures which can be made from a line.

In a later work, *On the Summit of Vision,* written in the last year of his life, Cusanus concluded that God, for whom we search, were better named the potential-itself. In *On the Summit of Vision,* Cusanus says the following:

> You will see below that the potential-itself, in respect to which nothing can be more powerful or earlier or better, names more aptly that without which nothing can be, live, or understand than the actual-potential or some other designation; for if it can be named at all, then it is better named the potential-itself, beyond which nothing can be more perfect. And I do not believe that there can be another name which were clearer, truer, and easier.

For Cusanus the potential-itself is a more precise way of designating what he had earlier designated by means of the term actual-potential. In fact, the concept of the potential-itself is already present in his essay *On Actual-Potential,* where he says that the compound expression "actual-potential" (*posse est*) means that the potential-itself (*ipsum posse*) exists. In the same essay, Cusanus also states that the "potential-itself is actually the most perfect potentiality." Cusanus thus makes a distinction between the potential-itself, which as God is absolute potentiality, and the potential-to-be, the potential-to-live, and the potential-to-understand, which are created potentialities. Therefore, as Cusanus stresses, "To the potential-itself nothing can be added, since it is the potential of every potential."

The Not-other

That which precedes the potential-to-become, the actual-potential, or, as Cusanus later referred to it, the potential-itself, also precedes that which is other. Since the other is after the actual-potential, the actual-potential cannot become another. Therefore, it cannot be defined through another, but rather must define itself and everything other. Cusanus therefore concluded that the actual-potential must be designated as the Not-other. According to Cusanus, Dionysius the Areopagite came closer than anyone else to the concept of the Not-other, and considered knowledge of the Not-other as "perfect ignorance, since it is the knowledge of that which is beyond everything which is known."

Cusanus explains the "negative theology" reflected in his concept of the "Not-other" in the first book of *On Learned Ignorance*. There he states that without negative theology, "God would not be worshipped as the infinite God but, rather, as a creature. And such worship is idolatry; it ascribes to the image that which befits only the reality itself." The biblical basis for the concept of God as Not-other is St. Paul's statement that God is "above all principality and power and virtue and dominion and every name that is named, not only in this world, but also in that which is to come." (Eph 1:21)

The essential point that Cusanus makes in his tetralogue *On the Not-Other,* as well as in his dialogue *On the Hidden God,* is that God is infinite. Therefore, He excels everything finite, including any name which we as finite creatures choose to apply to Him.

In his concept of "negative theology," Cusanus is very much influenced by Dionysius the Areopagite, so much so that he quotes extensively from Dionysius' writings, which were newly translated in 1439 by Ambrogio Traversari, a Florentine monk who worked closely with Cusanus to convene the Council of Florence in 1439. Dionysius was long thought to have been the member of the Court of Areopagus referred to in Acts 17:34 as a convert of St. Paul. However, by Cusanus' time it was realized that Dionysius was more likely a pseudonym adopted by a later writer. Before Cusanus, Dionysius' writings had had a significant influence on such traditional church doctors as St. Albert the Great, St. Thomas Aquinas, and St. Bonaventura.

Cusanus was also significantly influenced by Proclus' *Commentary on the Parmenides,* which is referred to at the beginning of *On the Not-Other,* as well as in *On the Origin* and other locations. Although Cusanus reportedly had access to several of Plato's original writings, including the *Republic,* the *Phaedo,* the *Apology,* the *Crito,* the *Meno* and the *Phaedrus,* there is no evidence that he was able to study Plato's *Parmenides* directly. As a result, he had to rely on Proclus' commentary, from which he extracted the core of Plato's ideas, while explicitly rejecting Proclus' pagan notion that there is a multitude of gods, which Proclus calls "henads," consequent to the one God.

In the beginning of *On the Not-Other,* Cusanus develops his concept of the Not-other as uniquely capable of defining itself and everything other. In respect to itself, the Not-other is not other than the Not-other. Thus, the Not-other defines itself as preceding everything other. Furthermore, in defining itself the Not-other is necessarily triune. As Cusanus explains:

> If, therefore, the same repeated three times is the definition of the first, as you see, then it is in fact triune and this for no other reason than that it defines itself. For it were not the first, if it did not define itself. If, however, it defines itself, it appears as threefold.

In this way, Cusanus establishes that the Christian notion of God as Father, Son, and Holy Spirit, which, as we shall see, he also represents conceptually as unity, equality, and connection, is the only valid concept of the origin of the universe. His concept of the Not-other also explains the fact that the Holy Spirit proceeds both from the Father and the Son (*Filioque*):

> Indeed, when the first Origin, signified through the Not-other, defines itself, then the Not-other arises in the definitive motion out of the Not-other, and from the Not-other and the arising Not-other the definition is concluded in the Not-other.

At the same time, the definition of the other necessarily presupposes the Not-other, just as an effect presupposes its cause. Cusanus defines everything other as follows: The other is not other than the other.

Cusanus' concept of the Not-other thus involves what appears to be a contradiction from the standpoint of discursive reason. On the one hand, God transcends everything other, or as Cusanus writes, He is "nothing of everything." On the other hand, since everything owes its existence to God, He is "everything in everything." Again Cusanus relies for his conception upon St. Paul, who wrote that God "is before all things, and in

Him all things hold together" (Col 1:17) and that God is "all in all." (1 Cor 15:28) While the Creator is not the same as His creature, He is also not so far removed that He is something other. As St. Paul said: "God is not far from us, for we are in Him and we are moved." (Acts 17:27-28)

The moral significance of this concept is made explicit by Cusanus in *On Learned Ignorance* where he writes as follows:

> And then whoever in this life receives any one of those who are Christ's receives Christ; and what is done to one of the least of these is done to Christ. . . . And whoever rejoices in Heaven over the least one rejoices over Christ and sees in each one Jesus, through whom he sees Blessed God. Thus, through His Son, our God will be all things in all things.

Although, as Cusanus stresses, the Not-other is not the name of God, it nonetheless leads us to Him, just as St. Paul argued that "Ever since the creation of the world, His invisible attributes of eternal power and divinity have been able to be understood and perceived in what He has made." (Rom 1:20) The Not-other transcends and is before everything other, and yet since the Not-other is the invisible cause of everything other in the visible domain, when we see the other we see not only the other but also the Not-other. As Cusanus writes: "Indeed, that seeing, which I refer to God, is not a visible-seeing, but rather a seeing of the invisible in the visible." Seen from this standpoint, as Cusanus says, the creature is the revelation of the Creator defining Himself.

In this context Cusanus launches into another attack on Aristotle. In searching for the substance of things, Aristotle realized that the quiddity of things was not something other. But he failed to grasp that that sought after is not other than the Not-other. Therefore, he only found the other from the other. The reason he fails is that Aristotle's method is based solely on rationality, which cannot advance to that which precedes it. As Cusanus' interlocutor, Ferdinand Martin, says in *On the Not-Other:*

> That philosopher regarded it as most certain, that every affirmative assertion contradicts a negative one and that

both cannot simultaneously be said of the same thing, inasmuch as they are contradictions.

However, the Not-other and the other do not contradict themselves as contradiction. The Not-other, since it defines and precedes it, does not stand in opposition to the other. Rather it stands as the cause to the effect. As Cusanus stresses, the fact that the Not-other is the other of the other and is not opposed to the other "is a secret with which there is no comparison."

In contrast to Aristotle's logical rationality, Cusanus once again points to a higher mental capacity, the intellect, which is capable of seeing beyond mere rationality to the coincidence of opposites. The Not-other, as Cusanus says in *On the Not-Other*, is the concept which he "sought for many years by means of the coincidence of opposites."

The Light

According to Cusanus, all things which are, live, and think are not other than the varied receptions of the light of the Not-other. In *On the Gift of the Father of Lights*, Cusanus refers to God as the Father of Lights based upon the words of St. James: "Every best gift and every perfect gift is from above, from the Father of Light." (James 1:17) Also in *On Equality* he refers to His Son, Jesus Christ, as the light of men. Seen from this standpoint, all things, whether they are, live, or think, are appearances or lights of God the Father generated through His Son, the Word. Thus God, in order to manifest Himself, makes various lights descend from Himself, which are called theophanies. Through these theophanies He makes known the wealth of His glory.

This generation, which occurs voluntarily, since it has no other cause than that of God's goodness, occurs in the Word of Truth, His only-begotten Son, who, as the Nicene Creed states, is "Light from Light." Every creature is therefore a manifestation of the Father, since it participates in the manifestation of the Son, albeit variously and contractedly. Thus, some creatures manifest Him more obscurely, others more clearly, according to the variety of the theophanies.

In his (unfortunately) influential book, *The Individual and the Cosmos in Renaissance Philosophy,* Ernst Cassirer went so far in his distortion of Cusanus' theology as to suggest, that Cusanus so deemphasized the importance of man's original sin as to break from St. Augustine's writings against the heretical Pelagian view that man can achieve wisdom without divine grace. Nothing could be further from the truth than Cassirer's self-serving representation of Cusanus' views.

In *On the Gift of the Father of Lights,* Cusanus states that the Apostle James, in saying that "every best gift and every perfect gift is from above, from the Father of Lights," had two objectives in mind. First, he wanted to exclude the errors of those who "assert God is the cause of evil." And second, he wanted to exclude the error of those who "have the presumption to assume man can come to apprehension of wisdom by himself, without the gift of grace or the assistance of the Father." Cusanus then goes on to identify precisely this second error as the actual cause of evil.

> Of this kind was the sin of the most presumptuous separated rational spirit, Lucifer, who attempted from his power to ascend to similitude with the highest. And likewise it was the sin of the incorporated rational spirit of the parents, who hoped by means of the nutritive power of the sensible tree's fruit to come to the perfection of knowledge of the gods. For we are taught that this actuality—that we apprehend wisdom, which is the living light and the glorious rest of our spirit—can come neither from us nor from the inferior sensible vegetation; it comes rather from the Father and the Giver of forms, who alone perfects.

Man is able, with the help of divine grace, to attain the filiation of God through the achievement of wisdom. However, the perfection of man is not attained from the Father in the descent of generation, but rather in the ascent, whereby his intellectual power is perfected in the Spirit, which proceeds from the Father and the Son. The Spirit brings it about that every creature ascends through perfection to God, as far as the condition of its nature allows it.

In respect to man, each of us is created in the living image of God and therefore has the capacity to participate in divinity (*capax Dei*). We receive this capacity in the descent of generation.

During our lives we must then strive to perfect ourselves so as to become Godlike, or deiform. This ascent, which Cusanus otherwise refers to as becoming adopted sons of God, can only be achieved through the grace of God.

Unlike the philosophers of the eighteenth-century Enlightenment, who glorified the independent powers of human rationality, Cusanus insists that man's intellectual potential is only led to perfection by the divine illumination of faith. Only when the intellect is illuminated by the light of faith does it ascend beyond rationality to the apprehension of the truth: as Cusanus writes, "because it is led by this light to believe it can attain the truth." Or as Christ says, "I came into the world as light, so that everyone who believes in me might not remain in darkness." (John 12:46)

Our intellectual spirit is granted many lights with which to advance to the font of light. As Cusanus argues in *On the Gift of the Father of Lights,* man sees that there are various creatures and in this variety he is illuminated, so that he advances to the essential light of creatures.

> For when he sees that one creature without vital motion is, another lives, another ratiocinates, then he is immediately illuminated and knows that the absolute essence of creatures does not thus exist, live, or ratiocinate. If indeed life belonged to the essence of creatures, then the non-living creature would not exist. If ratiocination belonged to the essence of creatures, then a stone or a tree were no creature.
>
> He therefore understands that nothing of everything, which is apprehended in the variety of creatures, belongs to the essence. Since, therefore, every creature is something in contraction, the essence of everything is not something, but rather nothing of everything in an uncontracted manner. Thus you see the variety of forms. Therefore, the essence is nothing of this kind.

Thus we, who are the sons of the light, come to apprehend the paternal light of our lives by perfecting our intellectual power. This is achieved by ascending from the variety of theophanies to the Father of Lights by means of divine illumination. Thus it is that Christ says, "I am the light of the world: He that followeth

me shall not walk in darkness, but shall have the light of life."
(John 8:12)

Laud

Since God created everything and "saw that it was very good,"
everything lauds God through its very being. All that the creature
has is from God, who is everything in everything. Since God is
the definition defining Himself and everything, the fact that all
creatures are good, great, true, etc. is because He is good, etc.
Everything created is good, etc. through reception of His gift of
light. Therefore, those qualities which are lauded in and by all
creatures are derived from God. By lauding those qualities which
are derived from God we are in fact lauding God.

According to Cusanus, everything lauds God through its
very being. But man, who is, lives, and thinks, participates more
than all other visible creatures in God's laud. His life therefore
consists of giving back to God what he, in order to be, has
received.

Idolatry, in which the laud meant for God is bestowed on
a creature, is therefore, according to Cusanus, an insanity. In the
eighteenth century the philosopher Ludwig Feuerbach expressed
this insanity in its extreme, when he claimed that the human
species is self-subsisting and that man merely projects those positive qualities, such as goodness, etc., which are those of his
species, upon a non-existing God. In opposition to this madness,
which was also adopted by Karl Marx, it need merely be said
that the human species has not created itself and only God is
auto-hypostatic. If a creature is lauded, this laud is not meant for
it but rather for its composer in it. As Dionysius the Areopagite
holds, "visible beauty is an image of invisible grace." If we are
good, beautiful, etc., it is only because we have received these
qualities from the Father of Lights, who is thus the good, the
beautiful, etc. that is in us.

However, Cusanus stresses that laud of God is not accomplished merely by uttering the words "Praise the Lord!" Rather,
it is unutterable. As Cusanus writes, "As they love Him, so they
laud Him also, and the more they laud Him, the more laud do
they themselves achieve and come ever nearer to the infinitely
laudable, even though they never attain equality with Him."

To laud God, according to Cusanus, as it was for his fellow Brother of the Common Life Thomas à Kempis, is to imitate Christ by laying aside love of self and love of this world and taking up his cross. As Cusanus writes in *On the The Hunt for Wisdom:*

> . . . those who have achieved perfection laud God in the highest and lay aside what could impede this laud, such as self-love and love of this world, and put themselves aside, in that they enter into the religious faith, which mortifies the impeding love of self and the world. They imitate the teacher of truth, the Word of God incarnate, who in laud of God taught to take upon oneself voluntarily through word and example the most terrible of all terrors, namely, the most disgraceful death. Following him, an infinite num- ber of martyrs have achieved immortal life through death and today most religious aspire by dying to the world and becoming free for these lauds of God to be perfect praisers of God.

If man, who has free will, decides in favor of vice and the opposite of the laudable, he is not laudable, but rather contrary to himself and God, who is in him. If man elects with divine grace to laud God by aligning his free will to the laudable, he is thus laudable by election, as well as by nature. Whoever always lauds God becomes constantly more perfect and becomes always more similar to God. The more he lauds God the more similar he becomes to divine laudability, which, as Cusanus points out, Plato rightly said is the end of man.

Unity

Nicolaus of Cusa's influence on Gottfried Wilhelm Leibniz is seen most clearly in Cusanus' treatment of unity. In his seminal work entitled *Monadology*, Leibniz hypothesizes that God is the original or primitive One and, as such, He is the origin of all existence, which takes the form of a multitude of derivative monads, each of which is indivisible. These monads are produced through fulgurations from the divinity. They are likenesses of the original One and differ from one another in proportion to their reception of His light.

According to Cusanus, unity is prior to all multitude and, even though the Not-other precedes unity, if unity is conceived negatively as the not-many, it has the same significance as the Not-other. For this reason, Cusanus points to the fact that, according to Proclus, "Plato believes it (unity) abides in negation." Moreover, Cusanus reports that Dionysius the Areopagite says, that "the negations, which, as privations that show excellence, are pregnant affirmations, are truer than simple affirmations." In *On the Origin,* Cusanus therefore writes, "The not-many as origin of everything enfolds everything—just as negation is called pregnant with affirmation."

In the *On the Hunt for Wisdom,* Cusanus proceeds to argue that the One, which is not-many, is the cause of everything singular and is the singularity of everything singular. It is the most singular cause of all singular things. Moreover, since the singular has been singularized from an eternal cause, it can never be resolved into the not-singular. Thus the singular is indivisible.

> Because every singular thing is good, the singular never desists from the good. Thus, the singular entity never ceases to be this, since everything actual is a singular entity and however much a singular body is divided, it always remains a singular body.

Therefore, all variety is not in respect to the singular, but rather in respect to that which is accidental to the singular.

According to Cusanus, everything is singular because its potential-to-become is singular:

> . . . the potential-to-become is singular. Therefore, everything is singular, which was or is made, because it derives from the potential-to-become. Therefore, the imitable singularity is the potential-to-become itself, in whose potential to be singular every singular thing is enfolded and from which it is unfolded.

However, although the singularity of all creatures derives from the singularity of the potential-to-become, the potential-to-become is itself created by the very first One. Thus, all created monadic unities or singularities are nothing other than similitudes of the eternal light of the Absolute One.

Cusanus thus adopts from Plato, both directly and indirectly through Proclus, the distinction between the Absolute One or God and the one universe which He has created. The one universe is posterior to the Absolute One and subsists through participation in the prior. If the Absolute One were removed, the one universe would cease to exist.

In opposition to Aristotle, who believed that the One and entity are coextensive, Cusanus, as should be clear from the above, argues that entity or being, life, and intellect are merely derivative modes of the very first Monad. Those who criticize Leibniz's *Monadology,* such as Leonhard Euler (1707-83), all make the same mistake, assuming falsely that monadic unities are extensive and therefore infinitely divisible. This error is based upon Aristotle's erroneous assertion that both time and motion are eternal and that material existence is therefore coextensive with the Absolute One. However, as Cusanus stresses, the Absolute One precedes the potential-to-become and the constitution of the physical universe. Therefore, the One is not the universe, even taken as a whole; the One is the most singular cause of all singular things, including the universe as a whole. Moreover, as Cusanus stresses, the very idea of quantitative extension is a concept of deductive, logical rationality and presupposes matter as primary.

Equality

As referenced earlier in numerous locations, Cusanus represents the Christian conception of the triune God or the Trinity of Father, Son, and Holy Spirit in terms of unity, equality, and connection. As he writes in *On the Peace of Faith,* "Those who worship God ought to adore Him as the origin of the universe; in this one universe, however, there is a plurality of parts, inequality, and separation." The origin of plurality is unity; the origin of inequality, the equality of unity; and the origin of separation or distinction, connection of unity and equality. Therefore, the origin of the universe must be threefold and singular.

This way of representing the Trinity is not entirely original to Cusanus. In the *Summa Theologica* Part I, Q. 39, art. 8, St. Thomas Aquinas reports that St. Augustine wrote in *Christian Doctrine:* "Unity is in the Father, equality in the Son, and in the Holy Spirit is the concord of equality and unity."

In *On the Origin,* Cusanus also represents the triune God as the Origin without origin, the Origin originated from the Origin, and the Origin originated from both. This representation is an elaboration of St. Thomas Aquinas' own use of the terms "Origin without an origin" and "Origin from an Origin" to describe God the Father and the Son in the aforementioned location. Using a temporal analogy, Cusanus compares the Origin without origin to paternity, the Origin originated from the Origin to filiation, and the Origin originated from both to the connection of love between father and son. However, in eternity these three aspects of the one Origin are not numerically divisible, because the One is not extensive and precedes all number. Thus unity, equality, and connection are not other, since they are the Not-other, which precedes the potential-to-become and the other. As said above, the Not-other is not other than the Not-other.

Like St. Augustine in his work *The Trinity,* Cusanus in *On Equality* argues that the human intellective soul, since it is created in the image of God, is the similitude of eternity. Therefore, by examining itself, the human intellect can see its origin as through a mirror.

Moreover, since it is the similitude of the triune God, who defines Himself and everything, the universe as a whole and everything in it are similitudes of the human intellect. Therefore, as Cusanus puts it, the human intellective soul sees the "knowable extrinsic through the consubstantial intrinsic. . . . The more it moves towards the other, in order to know it, the more it enters into itself, in order to know itself." Thus the intellective soul comes to know the universe through itself. This implies that the laws of the human intellect are the same as the laws of the universe.

As the similitude of eternity, the intellective soul of man is timeless time. Since it is merely a similitude, the soul is not eternity. Therefore, it is time. However, in its work the intellect frees itself of all otherness and is therefore timeless. As such, it sees itself as timeless triune time, as equally past, present, and future.

According to Cusanus, "the soul, which is timeless time, sees the past and future as present and names the past memory, the present intellect, and the future will." The intellectual memory generates from itself the intellect or the word and the will or love proceeds from both. According to Cusanus, "This consideration of timeless time makes manifest that the soul is the similitude of eternity and that it understands everything through itself as through the similitude of eternity." What the soul finds in itself, namely, the triunity of memory, intellect, and will, and the equality of past, present, and future in timeless time, is an image of the eternal triune God. Thus, just as the intellective soul is in itself memory, intellect, and will, so the triune God is the Father or intellectual memory, the Son, or the Word, of the intellectual memory, and the Holy Spirit, or the will, which is love.

Just as in *On the Origin* Cusanus makes the point that the Word is the Origin, so in *On Equality* he writes that "equality is the name of the first and eternal Origin." Thus, "equality generates from itself the Word, which is its equality. From both proceeds the connection which is equality. This connection we name the spirit or love, since from the generating and the generated equality, only equality can proceed, which is called connection or love." Cusanus continues as follows:

> . . . if it is designated as absolute, then equality is charity. Therefore, the intellectual charity generates from itself the concept of its essence, which can be nothing except the charity of charity, and from both nothing can proceed except charity, which is the connection of both.

Since absolute equality is before otherness, there are not three numerically equal things, but rather three hypostases of equality. Although no two completely equal things are found in the universe, because a plurality of things cannot participate in equality equally, nevertheless the quiddity of everything that is, is equality. Everything is only true insofar as it participates, albeit variedly, in the unity of equality.

Cusanus concludes therefore that, "although unity appears

to be the father of equality, nevertheless absolute equality enfolds unity. For that which is equal is in one mode. In unity one sees nothing except equality."

Without equality the universe could not exist, because it would be totally incoherent and arbitrary. Therefore, the human intellect must conclude that everything is from, through, and in equality. That is nothing other than to say that nothing has been made by God without the Logos, which is the Word. If this were not the case, the universe were not made rationally. As Cusanus says, "To say this of God, the wisest, were a blasphemy."

Citing the Gospel of St. John, "In the beginning was the Word and the Word was with God and the Word was God. . . . All things were made by Him and without Him was not any thing made that was made," Cusanus concludes, "Indeed, the pure intellect is never without its notion. Likewise the eternal God the Father was never without this consubstantial Son."

Thus those who argue against the *Filioque* concept are arguing, contrary to the Gospel of St. John, against not only the consubstantiality of the Son, but also against the rational coherence of the universe and the capacity of men as adoptive sons of God and co-heirs with Christ of immortal life to know and do the will of God themselves through the work of charity.

Connection

As we have indicated in the above, the third person of the triune God is the connection of love, which proceeds from unity and the equality generated from it. Although Cusanus generally refers to connection as love, in various locations he also refers to it as will, desire, or joy. However, there is no contradiction between these various expressions. Love is the will of God, it is His desire and His joy. As St. John writes in his first epistle: "God is love." (1 John 4:8)

It is this notion of the Holy Spirit as the connection of love, which distinguishes Christianity from all of the pre-Christian philosophers. In *On Beryllus* Cusanus writes: "All philosophers have not attained to the spirit, which is the principle of connection and, according to our perfected theology, the third person in the divinity." In *On the Hunt for Wisdom,* Cusanus writes similarly: "Few philosophers recognized this. They appear not to have grasped the principle of connection, without which nothing subsists and all intellectual nature must do without happiness. Because they lacked it, they did not attain wisdom."

In his book *The Trinity,* St. Augustine describes the triune God as three aspects of love—the loving, the lovable, and the love proceeding from both, which connects and unites the two. Cusanus adopts this conception and argues that love is the spirit diffused throughout the universe, which connects everything. It is the spirit by means of which every creature participates in the order of the universe.

In respect to the love of God, the foremost of the commandments, Cusanus writes as follows in *On Conjectures:*

> . . . God, who is the infinite connection, may not be loved as some sort of contracted lovable, but rather as most absolute infinite love. In this love therefore, with which God is loved, the simplest unity and infinite justice must exist. It is also necessary, that every love with which God is loved, is smaller than that with which he can be loved. You also know that to love God is the same as to be loved by God; for God is charity. Therefore, the more someone loves God, the more he participates in divinity.

Who can honestly argue that this spirit, the Holy Spirit of charity, does not proceed both from the Father and the Son? Not only did God so love the world that He gave it His only begotten Son, but also Christ so loved God and his fellow man, that he submitted willfully to God's will and laid down his life to redeem him. As Christ says: "This is my commandment: Love one another as I love you. No one has greater love than this, to lay down one's life for one's friends." (John 15:12-13)

In this context, Cusanus writes in *On Conjectures:*

> When a law recedes from unity and connection, it cannot be just. This law, "what you wish to be done to you, do to others," describes the equality of unity. If you want to be just, it is necessary for you to do nothing other than not to recede from that equality, in which unity and connection exist.

In *On the Peace of Faith,* Cusanus affirms that faith alone justifies the assumption of man into eternal life. In *On Searching for God,* he adds:

> . . . not some virtue nor even divine service nor law nor instruction justifies. . . . A virtuous life, observation of the commandments . . . and all the rest . . . accompany everyone who seeks correctly divine life and eternal wisdom. If they are not with him, then it is manifest that he finds himself not on the path, but rather outside it. The indications that someone is not off the path but rather on the right one, we can obtain from works, which accompany those proceeding correctly.

Similarly in *On the Peace of Faith* Cusanus has Paul say: "It is impossible that someone please God without faith. However, it must be a formed faith, for without works it is dead." When the Tartar asks, "What are these works?" Paul replies:

> If you believe in God, you keep His commandments. For how would you believe God is God, if you were not to take care to fulfill that which He prescribes? . . . The divine commandments are very brief and are all well known and common in every nation, for the light that reveals them to us is created along with the rational soul. For within us God says to love Him, from whom we received being, and to do nothing to another, except that which we wish done to us. Love is therefore the fulfillment of the law of God and all laws are reduced to this.

Thus to deny the *Filioque* concept, to deny that the connection of love proceeds from the Father and the Son, and that man participates in divinity by imitating Christ through works of love, is to have a faith which is dead, it is to be off the path that leads to eternal life and joy, it is to deny the will and spirit and law of God, which is the work of charity. Positively expressed, however, to believe in the *Filioque* concept in one's heart and to testify to that belief in one's works is the basis for establishing a just peace among men. Such peace is "unity in the equality of love."

Terminus

According to Cusanus, the end or terminus of the potential-to-become and everything that has become or becomes, does not follow the potential-to-become, but rather precedes it. Thus the terminus of the creatable is the creating Creator, who is the actual-potential or the infinite terminus.

The infinite terminus is interminable because it has no beginning and no end. No other terminus precedes the infinite terminus or the divine Mind. There is no terminus of the terminus. It is the terminus, which terminates or defines itself and everything other. Therefore, it is the beginning, the middle and the end of everything terminable. It lies before every terminus of that which can become and therefore determines the universe as a whole and defines every individual. It is the completely interminable terminus of the potential-to-become, which bears in itself the terminus or definition of everything which can become.

As Cusanus argues in *On the Hunt for Wisdom,* the terminus of the potential-to-become of everything is the potential-to-make of everything. "Everything which can become and which has become is previously in the potential-to-make as in the efficient, formal and final cause, and the potential-to-make itself is in everything as the absolute cause in the caused."

Since no external necessity defines the infinite terminus, but rather it defines itself, the infinite terminus or eternal mind is free and it creates the potential-to-become of everything, according to its will. However, since its will is never without the Word or Logos, everything is terminated not arbitrarily, but rather in the wisest manner. The variety of terminated things is based only upon their varied participation in the most simple exemplar or infinite terminus.

As the divine Mind is the interminable Terminus of all termini, the Form of all forms and the Essence of all essences, so the human intellective soul, which is the similitude of eternity, is in its own manner also an interminable terminus. The human mind is free to establish termini for all things in its conception. If it proposes to do something, it first determines it in itself. Thus "it is the terminus of all its works and," according to Cusanus, "nothing of everything that it makes places a terminus on it itself, beyond which it could make nothing more." Although our mind is not the origin or terminus of things and thus does not determine their essences, it is the origin and interminable terminus of its own notions and actions upon the universe. As such it has an endless capacity for concept formation.

As Cusanus writes in *On Equality,*

> The soul sees the terminus in everything terminated and since there is no terminus of the terminus, it sees itself without otherness as unterminated notional terminus. And thus it sees that it is neither extended nor divisible, therefore also not corruptible.

Since the infinite terminus is the terminus of everything including the human mind, which is its similitude, the end of the human intellect is to assimilate the intelligible and thus to attain the infinite terminus in itself and in everything creatable. In this way the human intellective soul comes to apprehend the infinite terminus, which is the Essence of its essence, as interminable notional terminus.

Order

In the tenth and final field of *On the Hunt for Wisdom,* Cusanus cites Dionysius, who argues that in our search for God, we find Him not in His own nature, which is incomprehensible, but rather "we climb from the most ordered disposition" of the universe produced by Him "by means of a path and order, to that which transcends everything, in the most eminent privation and in the cause of all things."

God is thus the Order of everything ordered and one sees the Author of order in the terminus of that which can be ordered. Even though the world is varied, since no two things are equal, it pleased the Creator to order the variety such that the orderability, which is absolute beauty, is reflected in everything. Citing the human body, Cusanus points out that "the proportion of every single member to the other and to the whole is ordered by the Creator of all things, who has created man beautiful. It is that proportion, without which the one form of the whole and of its parts to the whole would never appear beautiful and ordered."

Cusanus argues that order was in the simplest beginning of

things, since from the essence of order comes the beginning, the middle, and the end. Therefore, nothing can exist without order and beauty. Because the origin is order, the originated have order.

Referring back to the Trinity, Cusanus writes,

> I now see that whence the beginning without beginning and the beginning from the beginning and the beginning proceeding from both arises, so also will the originated without prior origination and the originated from the originated and the originated proceeding from both arise.
>
> The originated without prior origination is the essence, the originated from the originated is the power, and the originated proceeding from both is the action.
>
> These are to be found in all things, so that everything participates in the divine order and this entire world consists of the intellectual, the vital, and the existing.

In his work *On Genesis,* Cusanus establishes that the generative principle of the universe is self-similar. Specifically, Cusanus describes the cause of all things as the Absolute Same. The Absolute Same stands before and beyond all diversity and opposition, which follow the Absolute Same. Therefore, everything which is identical with itself, and other in respect to the other, is not the Absolute Same. That a thing is the same as itself the Same effects; that a thing is another from another is because it is not the Absolute Same, the Form of every form.

Creation or genesis can be described as the assimilation of the Absolute Same, which by effecting the same, calls the nothing to itself. When the Absolute Same calls the not-same to itself, the assimilation arises in the many, which participate in the same variedly. Therefore, variety arises in the process of the Same effecting the same. Hence there is order in the variety, which is participation of the same in variety and harmony.

Cusanus cites as further evidence of the order and beauty of creation the fact that man, as the highest of sensible nature and the lowest of intelligible nature, is the connection between the inferior temporal and the superior perpetual. But what is more, if we become like our mediator Jesus Christ, which occurs through faith and love, we can be released from the connection with the mortal and resurrected to the life of the immortal spirit. As Cusanus writes in *On the Hunt for Wisdom,* "What is more beautiful than this marvelous order or regeneration, through which we attain to the resurrection of life?" What greater evidence is there that order rather than disorder prevails in the universe, than that the dead can attain to resurrection of life, insofar as they do not deviate from the ordered path which leads us to God, for whose sake and in whose image we were born?

Imago Viva Dei

Having thus traversed the ten fields of Cusanus' *On the Hunt for Wisdom,* only one question remains to be discussed, before returning in conclusion to the question of how to establish world peace. That question, which is directly related to the *Filioque,* is, in what manner man is in the living image of God and how does this conception of man differ from the view held by the followers of Aristotle.

The idea that man is in the living image of God is the critical one distinguishing Judeo-Christian humanism from all forms of Aristotelianism. This notion was initially expressed in Genesis, where God said, "Let us make man in our image, after our likeness." (Gen 1:26) This conception of man is developed further in the New Testament, where it is reported that Jesus Christ is the Son of God and that those who believe in him and imitate him in their heart and works can also achieve the filiation of God. Through such faith and love man can achieve eternal life and accomplish miracles. As Christ says to his disciples, "Amen, amen, I say to you, whoever believes in me will do the works that I do, and will do greater ones than these. . . ."(John 14:12)

Because the Aristotelian believes that God is infinite and man finite and that the finite never attains to the infinite, he necessarily denies that Christ is God-man and that man can participate in divinity through imitation of Christ. He denies that man, as Cusanus says in *On Learned Ignorance,* is a finite or contracted infinite, or as St. Thomas says in *Summa Theologica,* a "relative infinite." Aristotelianism is thus the philosophical basis for gnosticism, which denies the divinity of Christ and therefore the very idea that man has the capacity to become increasingly Christlike, or deiform.

Cusanus, on the other hand, conceives of man as capable of becoming an adoptive son of God, insofar as he employs his God-given intellectual capacity in imitation of his Creator. Thus in *On Beryllus,* he tells his readers to pay attention to the utterance of Hermes Trismegistus to the effect that "man is a second God." Cusanus writes as follows:

> For just as God is the creator of real entities and of natural forms, man is the creator of rational entities and artificial forms. These are nothing other than similitudes of his intellect, just as the creatures of God are similitudes of the divine Intellect. Therefore, man has intellect, which is a similitude of the divine Intellect, in creating.
>
> Therefore, he creates similitudes of the similitudes of the divine Intellect, so the extrinsic artificial figures are similitudes of intrinsic natural forms. Hence he measures his intellect through the power of his works and from this he measures the divine Intellect, as the truth is measured through its image.

In *On the Filiation of God,* Cusanus writes similarly:

> . . . just as God is the actual essence of all things, so is the intellect, separated and united in itself vitally and reflexively, a living similitude of God. Therefore, as God Himself is the essence of all things, so the intellect, the similitude of God, is the similitude of all things. However, cognition is effected through similitude. However, since the intellect is an intellectual living similitude of God, it knows, when it knows itself, everything in itself as the one. However, it then knows itself, when it intuits itself in God, just as it is; this then is the case, when God is in it, it itself.
>
> Therefore, to know everything is nothing other than to see oneself as the similitude of God, which is the filiation.

Finally, in *On Conjectures,* Cusanus says the following:

> Man is indeed god, but not absolutely, since he is man; he is therefore a human god. Man is also the world, but not everything contractedly, since he is man. Man is therefore

46

a microcosm or a human world. The region of humanity therefore embraces God and the whole world in its human potentiality. Man can therefore be a human god and just as he can be god in a human way, so can he also be a human angel, a human animal, a human lion or bear or anything else. Within the potentiality of humanity everything indeed exists in its mode.

In humanity everything is therefore unfolded in a human way, as in the universe in a universal manner, because it exists as a human world. Everything then is enfolded in it in a human manner, since it is a human god. For humanity is unity, which is also infinity contracted humanly.

Thus, in contrast to Aristotelian gnosticism, which insists upon the finitude of the human mind, the Christian view, which is the scientific view, sees the human mind as a "contracted infinity" (neither absolutely infinite nor merely finite), or, as indicated earlier, "an interminable notional terminus," insofar as it is in the living image of God. This is precisely the point made by Georg Cantor in his *Foundations of a General Theory of Manifolds.* Cantor argues against those who deny the possibility of the transfinite on the basis of the Aristotelian view that the human mind is finite:

> Human understanding must also be granted the predicate "infinite" in certain respects. As limited as human nature may in fact be, much of the infinite nonetheless adheres to it, and I even think that if it were not in many respects infinite itself, the strong confidence and certainty regarding the existence of the absolute, about which we are all in agreement, could not be explained. (*Foundations,* Section 5)

The Aristotelian view of the human mind as finite, in contrast to the Christian view of the human mind as a "contracted infinite," is reflected in the fact that Aristotelians, including such philosophers as Immanuel Kant, deny the existence of creative human intelligence as distinct from rationality or deductive logic. In his work *On Conjectures,* Cusanus argues, like Plato before him, that "creative intelligence" exists and that such intelligence is precisely that which distinguishes man from animals. Cusanus writes in *On Conjectures* as follows:

> Conjectures must go forth from our minds as the real world does from infinite divine reason. . . . The human mind is therefore the form of the conjectural world, as the divine is that of the real.

Moreover, since the divine Mind is triune, Cusanus argues that number is the "prime exemplar of things in the mind of the Composer," and that the triunity is impressed upon the mind of man. Therefore man, who is distinct from animals in that he can count, proceeds in his conjectures "from the rational numbers of his mind to the real ineffable numbers of the divine Mind." As Georg Cantor wrote in his *Foundations,* the human mind "has an unlimited, inherent capacity for step-wise formation of whole number classes . . . whose powers are of ascending strength."

Cusanus conjectures, based upon the numerical image elicited from the human mind, that the unity of the mind consists of four unities. The first is the simplest mind of God, the second is intelligence or creative intellect, the third is the rational soul, characterized by deductive logic, and the fourth is the body. Moreover, the mind comprehends the first divinely as truth, the second intellectually as true, the third rationally as verisimilar, and the fourth corporeally in confusion. God is thus the form of the human intellect, the intellect the form of the rational soul, and the soul the form of the body. Cusanus represents this transfinite ordering of unities numerically in terms of a simple unity, a second root unity, a third quadratic unity, and a fourth cubic unity.

In the first absolute unity the mind of God is absolved of all plurality. Therefore, God, as super-simple origin and as Not-other, precedes every opposition. The intellect, which descends from the simplest unity, is not preceded by oppositions, but arises at the same time with opposition, in that it is composed from the One and the other. Therefore, in the intellect the oppositions are themselves undivided and indissolubly coupled. Hence in the intellect, oppositions are compatible. However, the rational soul, which is preceded by the intellect, judges oppositions to be irreconcilable. It is governed by the law of contradiction.

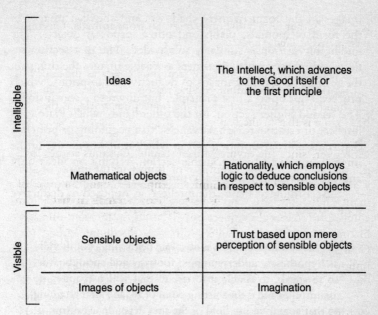

FIGURE 2. *Plato's Divided Line of Human Mentation*

Finally, in the corporeal sphere, the senses perceive but do not distinguish. The senses only affirm that something perceptible exists, but not if it is this or that.

As Cusanus points out, most modern theologians, in speaking of God, subjugate Him to the rules of rationality. Thus those who argue against the triunity of God do so from the standpoint of the rules of rationality, which assert that three persons cannot be one. Thus, according to Cusanus, "the philosophers and theologians who only engage in ratiocination through the erection of its first principle (the law of contradiction) have themselves closed the thither-bearing path."

This latter point is the central polemic that Cusanus wages in *On Conjectures.* In so doing, Cusanus aligns himself with Plato as against Aristotle.

In Book VI of the *Republic,* Plato represents the unities of the mind in terms of a line, which is divided into two sections, the visible and the intelligible (see Figure 2). The visible section of the line is subdivided, to reflect at the lowest level visible images in the form of mere shadows, and above it images in the form of animals, plants and other corporeal objects. The intelligible section is similarly subdivided. The first section reflects rationality, which considers as visible images the things in the former division by means of deductive assumptions, which proceed "not up to a first principle, but down to a conclusion." The second higher section, on the other hand, which Plato calls intellect or creative reason, advances "to a beginning or principle that transcends assumption and in which it makes no use of the images employed by the visible section, relying on ideas only and progressing systematically through ideas."

According to Plato, the intellect, as opposed to deductive logic, treats

> . . . its assumptions not as absolute beginnings but literally as hypotheses, underpinnings, footings and springboards, so to speak, to enable it to rise to that which requires no assumption and is the starting point of all, and after attaining to that again, taking hold of the first dependencies from it, so to proceed downward to the conclusion, making no use whatsoever of any object of sense, but only of pure ideas moving on through ideas to ideas and ending with ideas.

As Cusanus points out in numerous locations, Aristotle, in contrast to Plato, bases his entire philosophy on deductive logic or rationality and actually denies the very existence of the intellect, which employs the method of conjecture, or, as Plato says, hypothesis, to rise above the axiomatic assumptions which constrain rationality to the domain of finite sensible objects.

In Chapter I of Part II of *On Conjectures,* Cusanus points out that rationality

> . . . denies an unfolding of opposites and affirms their unattainability. . . . Therefore, this is the root of all assertions of rationality, namely, that the coincidence of opposites is unattainable. Hence, every number is either even or odd . . . [otherwise] it would require the coincidence of even and odd. . . . Everything that one demonstrates to be true is from it, because were it not so, the coincidence

of opposites would be introduced and that would mean abandoning rationality.

Since rationality, or deductive logic, is based upon the principle that the coincidence of contradictory opposites must be avoided, he who fails to challenge this assumption "excludes the infinite" from his apprehension. Since the intellect of man, which is a similitude of the absolute infinite, is itself a "contracted infinite," like Aristotle, he must deny that which sets mankind apart from and above all other species, the creative intellect of the sovereign individual. Finally, he fails to grasp what Cusanus describes as the ultimate perfection of the intellect: "It ascends continuously through the theophany descending to it, to approximation and assimilation with the divine and infinite unity, which is the infinite life, the truth and the repose of the intellect."

On the Peace of Faith

In a very real sense then, the primary philosophical obstacle to establishing global peace among men is nothing other than the Aristotelian gnostic denial of the fact that man is in the living image of God and that, as expressed in the concept of the *Filioque,* the Holy Spirit of charity proceeds not only from the Father and the Son, but also from those who are adoptive sons of God through their imitation of the Son. Thus the first step that must be taken on the road to establishing peace among men is to repudiate the Aristotelian view that man is indistinguishable from the beast.

This is most efficiently accomplished by defending the concept of the *Filioque* as the true basis of a new ecumenical movement in the tradition of the Council of Florence. Such a movement must not only defend the *Filioque* as dogma; it must also reflect the *Filioque* in action. It must launch a global offensive to replace what Pope John Paul II has referred to as the "structures of sin" with a just new world order among sovereign nation-states based upon an economic policy consonant with the idea of man as in the living image of God.

Just such a concept was put forward in celebration of Easter in 1967 by Pope Paul VI in his famous encyclical entitled "Populorum Progressio" or "On the Development of Peoples." It is in this encyclical that Pope Paul VI said that "Development is the new name for peace" and called upon all men of good will to become "the apostles of a development which is good and genuine, which is not wealth that is self-centered and sought for its own sake, but rather an economy which is put at the service of man, the bread which is daily distributed to all, as a source of brotherhood and a sign of Providence."

The example of recent events in Eastern Europe and elsewhere suggests that Christianity has a central role to play in establishing peace on earth. Although Christianity does not exercise temporal power, it can and must be responsible for providing spiritual guidance to the nations and peoples of the world, including those of other religions.

Despite the fact that different religions have received their commandments through the hands of various prophets, Cusanus points out through the person of Paul that the divine commandments are known universally, because they are innate in the human intellect. In each of us reason or the Word, who is God, says to love Him and do nothing to another except that which we wish done to us. Therefore, love is the fulfillment of the law and all laws are reduced to it.

Faith in the one God and adherence in one's actions to the law of love are thus the unique basis for establishing concord among religions and, through their spiritual unity, "a community of principle" among the sovereign nation-states of the world. Such a community of principle among nation-states, each dedicated to assisting the sovereign individual citizen to actualize his divine potential as a "contracted infinite," is thus rigorously defined triunely as "unity in the equality of love."

Such a concept of an ecumenical alliance in behalf of peace based upon development has nothing to do, however, with religious relativism. In his book *the Individual and the Cosmos in Renaissance Philosophy*, Ernst Cassirer so completely distorted the content of Cusanus' *On the Peace of Faith* as to suggest that Cusanus was advocating some form of "universal religion." Cassirer even went so far as to write that for Cusanus, "There is no form of faith so low, so abominable, that it cannot find its relative justification. . . . Even polytheism is not excluded." He even suggests that Cusanus reduces the content of faith to mere conjecture and that, as a result, for Cusanus there is no longer any universally binding orthodoxy.

Nothing could be further from the truth. The approach taken by Cusanus in *On the Peace of Faith* and in *An Examination of the Koran* is just the opposite. Cusanus systematically argues that the beliefs of all people presuppose the truths of Christianity. In *On the Peace of Faith,* the Word of God, Peter, and Paul demonstrate in a dialogue with representatives of diverse peoples from throughout the world, that the love of wisdom among philosophers presupposes the existence of one God; that the nature of the created universe and of the human mind presupposes the Trinity; and that the belief in the immortality of the soul and eternal life shared by all peoples presupposes some highest man in whom human nature is united to the divine, i.e., Jesus Christ.

In *An Examination of the Koran,* Cusanus argues that Mohammed was in reality a Nestorian Christian. Nestorius had been condemned by universal Church councils in the third and fourth centuries for having held that Christ was not the Son of God, but rather only a man who had received God's grace. It was to counter this particular form of gnosticism that the same councils gave the Virgin Mary the name *Theotokos,* or the Mother of God. Cusanus' ecumenicism did not prevent him from recommending at the end of this work that the Sultan mandate faith in the Virgin Mary as the *Theotokos.*

Thus for Cusanus there is no contradiction between social action and doctrine, because the very possibility of establishing peace on earth derives directly from Jesus Christ himself, who is equality or justice itself. As Cusanus writes in *On Learned Ignorance,* through Christ's love the many are united "by means of a most perfect union—the numerical distinctness of each being preserved. Because of this union the following statement of Christ's is true: 'Whatever you have done to one of the least of my brethren, you have done to me.' "

As Cusanus points out in *On Conjectures,* man participates in the divine nature in the unity, which is the light of intelligence, in equality, which is the light of justice, and in connection, which is the light of love. Since, as he stresses in *On Equality,* absolute equality subsumes unity and such equality is charity, the basis of a peaceful world order must be equality, or justice. Moreover, as Cusanus writes, "Justice is founded on the rule, 'what you wish to be done to you, do to the other.' "

Finally, Cusanus emphasizes that, since with the removal of equality, or justice, nothing remains, one must conclude that everything is from it, through it, and in it. Therefore, there is no durable, peaceful order in the world unless it be founded upon justice among men.

This must necessarily be reflected not only in respect to the political-legal rights of man, but also in respect to the right of man to share the benefits of economic development. The peoples of Eastern Europe, as with racial minorities in the U.S. as a result of the civil rights movement, have gained a degree of political freedom, but for that freedom fully to reflect justice, it must also take the form of freedom from poverty. Similarly in the Third World today, many peoples have juridically gained their freedom from colonialism, but continue to be exploited economically through neo-colonialism. The absence of equality or justice in the economic sphere is thus a continuing seed of disorder. Since equality is the Hypostasis of all hypostases, the Order of all order, and without it nothing remains, then unless the relations among nations on this planet be based on economic justice, peace cannot be achieved.

In *On the Peace of Faith,* Cusanus points out that most men are compelled to lead laborious lives in servile subjugation. Since the majority of men are thus distracted by corporeal cares and duties, only a few have the time and leisure necessary to employ the freedom of their will and to gain knowledge of themselves. It is therefore incumbent upon those few to reject both self-love and love of the world, so that they can devote their lives to creating the just conditions under which the multitude of humanity can be freed from both political and economic tyranny.

As St. John writes, "If anyone says, 'I love God,' but hates his brother, he is a liar; for whoever does not love a brother whom he has seen cannot love God whom he has not seen." (2 John 4:20) To love God is to love the invisible God who is in one's fellow man. To be just is nothing other than not to deviate in one's actions from the equality of love.

In *On the Filiation of God,* Cusanus describes what is required of each of us to become adoptive sons of God and co-heirs with Christ of eternal life. He writes as follows:

Filiation therefore is the ablation of all otherness and diversity and the resolution of everything into one, which is also the transfusion of the one into everything. And this is the *theosis* itself. . . . Therefore, you must elevate yourself in profound meditation beyond all contrarieties, figures, locations, times, images, and contractions, beyond otherness, disjunctions, conjunctions, affirmations, and negations, because through the transcendence of all proportions, comparisons, and ratiocinations into the pure, intellectual life, as the son of life, you are transformed into life.

In *On Searching for God,* Cusanus writes that "God loves who loves Him." Since God is everything in everything, by loving even the least among our brothers, who, as a "contracted infinite," is in the living image of God, we indeed love God. We love God in our fellow man. If we fail to give food to the hungry, to give drink to the thirsty, to clothe the naked, to welcome the stranger, to care for the ill, or to visit the prisoner, we, like the goats in Christ's parable, are not on the path to God, but rather outside it.

Indeed, as Cusanus concludes, the purpose for which we have come into the world is to search for God, to adhere to Him and to find peace in Him. For, as Christ said, "I am the way, the truth, and the life and no man comes unto the Father but by me." (John 14:6) Thus, as Cusanus emphasizes in reference to the *Filioque,* "and all this occurs in man through the Holy Spirit, which proceeds from the Father and the Son, which is the spirit of the Son and also the charity of God."

WILLIAM F. WERTZ, JR.
October 29, 1992

On Conjectures

(1 4 4 0)
First Part

To his honored teacher, the God-beloved, most reverend Father, Lord Julian, most worthy Cardinal of the Holy Apostolic Chair, N.C.

I.

Given the current opportunity, I wish to set forth my conception concerning conjectures. Although I know that it is obscured by the faultiness of human inventions in general and by the insufficiency of my obtuse mental power in particular, nevertheless, I have confidently laid it out to you, dear Father, who are most erudite in all letters, so that it can receive the purification possible through your almost divinely illuminating, wonderfully resplendent, amply tested intellect. For I know that this new formula for investigation of the arts cannot perish in its coarseness, if through its acceptance the most renowned man of all will deign to make it worthy with his correcting file. Therefore, with your most ornate authority give courage to those seeking access to the highest on this short and most clear pathway.

II.

Since in my prior booklet, *On Learned Ignorance*, you have intuited much more profoundly and clearly than I myself have in my endeavor, that the precision of the truth is unattainable, it follows that every human positive assertion of the true is a conjecture;

for the augmentation of the apprehension of the true is not exhaustible. Now, if our actual knowledge stands in no proportion to the greatest knowledge attainable for men, the fall of our weak power of apprehension from the purity of truth down into uncertainty makes our positions concerning the true into conjectures.

Therefore, the unity of the unattainable truth is known through conjectural otherness and the conjecture of otherness is known in the simplest unity of the truth. Later we shall intuit a notion of this more clearly. However, since a creative intelligence of finite actuality does not exist in the other except otherwise, so that there remains a difference between all conjecturers, nothing will be able to remain completely certain, except that the diverse conjectures of diverse men are steps toward the same inapprehensible truth, nevertheless they are improportionate to one another, and indeed such, that no one can ever conceive the meaning of one faultlessly, even if the one is perhaps closer than the other. Hence, accept these inventions, which I bring forth here, elicited through not a little reflection from the possibility of my small mental powers, as my conjectures, which are perhaps vastly unequal to greater intellectual flashes. If I also fear that they are despised by many on account of the ineptitude of my representation, I would like to prepare them, as it were, like a meal, which is not completely unsuited to be transformed by higher minds into clearer intellectualities. For, whoever will attempt to elicit some spiritual nourishment here through diligent mastication and frequent rumination, will find comfort and refreshment, even if this meal appears at first crude and, on account of its newness, rather offensive.

Since, however, the light of experience is lacking to the younger, there should be a certain palpable guide, which entices the appearance of the hidden, so that it is elevated stepwise to the more unknown. In order to more conveniently elucidate the secret of my conjectures, I shall therefore first, through a rational progression well known to all, construct examples and models of the concept, through which our discourse can attain to the universal art of conjecturing. In the second place, I shall then elicit certain flowery annotations, and in adding a fruitful, practical application in some most welcome solutions, I will take care to refresh the souls, which are famished for the truth.

III.
Whence the Origin of Conjectures

Conjectures must go forth from our minds as the real world does from infinite divine reason. For, since the human mind, the lofty similitude of God, participates, as far as it can, in the fecundity of the creatrix nature, it exserts the rational from itself, as the image of omnipotent form, in the similitude of real entities. The human mind is therefore the form of the conjectural world, as the divine is that of the real. Therefore, just as that absolute divine Entity is all that which is in everything which is, so also the unity of the human mind is the entity of its conjectures.

However, God does everything for His own sake, so that He is the intellectual beginning and equally the end of everything; thus the unfolding of the rational world, which issues forth from our enfolding mind, exists for the sake of the fabricatrix herself. Indeed, the more subtly the mind is contemplated in the world unfolded by the mind, the more abundant the fruit it produces in its interior. The mind's end is infinite rationality; only in infinite rationality will the mind intuit itself as it is, since infinite rationality alone is the measure for all rational things. The closer we are elevated to assimilation with it, the more deeply we penetrate into our mind, whose unique vital center it is. For this reason, we aspire with natural desire for perfecting knowledge.

However, that you come to apprehend my intention and accept the mind as the origin of conjectures, you must consider that, because the first beginning of all things and also of our mind has appeared as triune, there is one origin of the multitude, inequality, and division of things, from whose absolute unity flows forth the multitude, from whose equality the inequality, and from whose connection the division. Likewise our mind, which conceives only an intellectual nature as creatrix, regards itself as the triune origin of its rational art.

For rationality alone is the measure of multitude, magnitude, and composition, so that if it were sublated, nothing of these would subsist; just as if infinite Entity be denied, the entity of all things is equally denied. For this reason, unity of the mind enfolds all multitude in itself, its equality all magnitude, and its connection composition. Therefore, from the power of its enfolding unity, the mind as triune origin first unfolds multitude, the multitude then engenders inequality and magnitude. For this reason, our mind hunts in the primordial multitude for the magnitudes or perfections, which are varied and unequal, as integrated in a prime exemplar. Then it proceeds from both to composition. Therefore, our mind is the distinctive, proportionative and compositive origin.

IV.
The Symbolic Exemplar of
Things Is Number

The natural, sprouting origin of the rational art is number; indeed, beings which possess no intellect, such as animals, do not count. Number is nothing other than unfolded rationality. So much, indeed, is number shown to be the beginning of those things which are attained by rationality, that with its sublation, nothing remains at all, as is proven by rationality. And if rationality unfolds number and employs it in constituting conjectures, that is not other than if rationality employs itself and forms everything in its highest natural similitude, just as God, as infinite mind, in His coeternal Word imparts being to things. There cannot be anything prior to number, for everything other affirms that it necessarily existed from it.

Indeed, everything that issues forth from the simplest unity is composed in its mode. However, no composition can be understood without number; for the plurality of parts and simultaneously their diversity and the proportion of their composability are from it. Also substance, quantity, whiteness, blackness, etc. were not distinct things without otherness; what it is, it is through number. But number is composed out of itself. The ternary, for example, should be conceived as composed out of three in combination. Otherwise the ternary were no more than if you imagined the wall, roof, and foundation of a house separately and you wished to conceive the form of the house. Therefore, one should not imagine them separately, but rather as composed simultaneously, and then the combination of three will be not other than the ternary. It is, therefore, composed out of itself.

The first contracted opposition must likewise be contracted out of itself, which is impossible outside of number. Therefore, every number is composed out of oppositions, which are different and stand in a proportion to one another, such that they are this number itself. The even number is opposed to the odd. And every number, whether even or odd, exists from the even and the odd, i.e., from itself. The quaternary is composed from the odd ternary and the even quaternary. However, that it appears combined out of two binaries should not be referred to the quaternary's essence, but rather to its quantity. However, how can anything be conceived more similar to our mind than number? Is not the unity of the ternary the ternary? Is not the equality of the ternary the ternary? Thus, the connection of the ternary is also the ternary.

The essence of number is therefore the prime exemplar of the mind. For indeed, one finds impressed in it from the first the trinity or the unitrinity, contracted in plurality. In that we conjecture symbolically from the rational numbers of our mind in respect to the real ineffable numbers of the divine Mind, we indeed say that number is the prime exemplar of things in the mind of the Composer, just as the number arising from our rationality is the exemplar of the imaginal world.

V.
On Natural Progression

To contemplate the nature of number is more acutely useful to you, the more deeply you attempt to investigate the rest in its similitude. At first, however, concern yourself with its progression, and you shall confirm that it is accomplished by the quaternary. Indeed, one, two, three and four added together produce ten, which unfolds the natural power of simple unity. Now from this same ten, which is the second unity, the quadratic unfolding of the root is achieved through a similar quaternary progression: 10, 20, 30, and 40 added together are one hundred, which is the square of the denary root. Likewise, the hundred exserts the thousand as unity through the same movement: 100, 200, 300, and 400 added together are one thousand. Yet do not proceed further on this path, as if something still remained.

However, not only after the ten—as with eleven, where after the ten a regression to unity occurs—but also in a similar

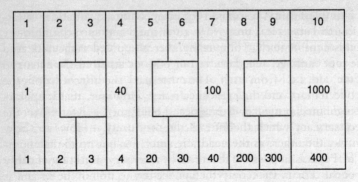

FIGURE I

manner after the thousand, the repetition is not denied; in the natural influx, there are therefore no more than ten numbers, which are contained in a quaternary progression. And beyond the one thousand, the sum of the cube of the denary root, there is no variation in the repetition, since this arises through the triply repeated quaternary progression in the denary order. Consider also, that the quaternary, the unfolding of unity, contains the power of the total number. For the general unity is distinguished through four unities, which are represented in suitable order: the first is the simplest; the second has only added the zero figure to the order, as it corresponds to the second unity; the third adds two of this nature; the fourth three, so one obtains 1, 10, 100, 1000, all of which, although undoubted by all, I have reduced to a visible formula suitable to our purpose (see Figure 1).

VI.
On the Four Unities

The mind, supposing of itself that it embraces everything, examines and comprehends everything, concludes that it is in everything and everything is in it, such that it affirms that there can be nothing that is outside it and escapes its gaze. Thus it contemplates its own unity, which is its entity, in the numerical similitude elicited from itself, as in an image natural and peculiar to it.

It acquires this unity from number as quadruple; for there

is a simplest unity, a second root unity, a third quadratic unity, a fourth cubic total unity. Thus the mind intuits the simplest unity at the beginning of number, thereafter the denary unity as the root of the second, then the unity of one hundred, the square of ten, and finally the unity of one thousand, the cube of ten. For between the diverse and opposite unities, the simple and the total, a single precise median cannot occur; but rather, at least two are necessary, of which the one, as the root unity, inclines to the simple, the other, as the quadratic unity, inclines to the total.

For it is impossible that there be a simple connection of the unequal. For indeed, only the connection of infinite unity and equality can be simple. Therefore, the mind contemplates its whole entity in these quadruply distinct unities, so that it sees that the first one is the most simple mind prior to everything, as the Creator, a second proceeds directly from the first as the root of the others, a third proceeding from this root is inclined toward the fourth, which does not admit further progress on account of its gross solidity.

These mental unities it expresses in vocal signs: the first, highest, and simplest mind it calls God; the second, the root, which has no root before itself, it calls intelligence; the third, the quadratic contraction of intelligence, it calls rational soul; however, the last, the total, which is gross, unfolded, and unfolds nothing further, is conjectured to be body. However, everything in God is God, in the intelligence is intellect, in the rational soul is soul, in the body is body. This means nothing other than that the mind embraces everything either divinely, intellectually, rationally, or corporeally. It does so divinely insofar as the thing is the truth; intellectually, insofar as the thing is not the truth itself, but is true; rationally, insofar as it is verisimilar; corporeally, insofar as it abandons verisimilitude and enters into confusion.

The first unity is completely absolute; the last, on the contrary, abandons all absolution and is contracted as far as possible; the second is more absolute and less contracted; the third is less absolute and more contracted. As intelligence is not completely divine or absolute, so also the rational soul is not completely without participation in divinity, so that in a wonderful reciprocal progression, the divine and absolute unity descending stepwise to intelligence and rationality, and the contracted sensible unity ascending through rationality to intelligence, the mind equally distinguishes and connects everything.

VII.
On the Prime Unity

Let the utility of what I say make you still more attentive; for I will attempt to lead the great and the hidden into the light. First, if number is conceived as the exemplar of things, it appears that that divine unity precedes and enfolds everything. For, in preceding all multitude, it also comes before all diversity, otherness, opposition, inequality, division, and everything other that accompanies multitude. Unity is indeed neither binary nor ternary, etc., although it is all those which are ternary, quaternary, and other numbers. If the species of things are distinguished as numbers, then the absolute unity is of no species; it has no name and no shape, although it is everything in everything. It is the unity of every plurality. Indeed, it is the unity of the plurality of genera, species, substances, accidents, in general of everything created, the one measure of all measure, the one equality of everything equal and unequal, the connection of everything united and divided, as unity in its simplicity enfolds, unfolds, and connects not only every even but also every odd number.

Intuit the infinite power of unity with a profound mind; it is indeed infinitely greater than any number that could be given. Indeed, there is no number, however great, in which the power of unity would come to rest. Since for every possible number through the unity of unity a greater one can be had without end, it is established through the inexhaustible power of the one alone to be omnipotent. Concerning this you have already heard much in the preceding and you see that one could always say much more about it. For indeed, those things which can be expressed, are numbers of not unfoldable unity or numeral figures of invariable truth, which is the more clearly intuited, the more absolutely and unitively it is conceived. For, whoever conceives absolute unity and only itself, sees that it is ineffable. With respect to what should the one rather than the other name be allotted to it? If you segregate everything other and consider it alone; if you understand that it never was, nor is, nor can become something other; if you disregard every plurality and you advance to the simplest unity itself, so that you establish that it is no more simple than not-simple, no more one than not-one, you have thus penetrated all secrets, there is no doubt, no impediment.

Contemplate, therefore, the unity of your mind through this absolution from all plurality, and you will see that its life in its absolute unity, in which it is everything, is not corruptible. The certitude of this absolute unity is, however, most precise, so that the mind effects everything in it and through it. Every inquisitive and investigative mind inquires only in its light, and there can be no question which does not suppose it. Does not the question "whether something exists" presuppose entity, the question "what it is," the quiddity, the question "why," the cause, the question "wherefore," the end? Therefore, that which is supposed in every doubt must be most certain. Therefore, absolute Unity, because it is the Entity of all entities, the Quiddity of all quiddities, the Cause of all causes, the End of all ends, cannot be drawn into doubt, but rather the plurality of doubts exists after it.

Observe therefore, Father Julian, how clear and concise theology is, even though inexplicable with words, since to every question which can be formed about God, one can at first respond: You see that every question about Him is inept. For every question admits in respect to that asked, that only one of two oppositions can be verified, or that in respect to this question something other is to be affirmed or to be denied than in respect to the other question. But to believe that of absolute Unity is most absurd.

Neither one of two oppositions is affirmed, nor is the one affirmed rather than the other. However, if you wish to satisfy the question affirmatively, then deduce the absolute presupposition, so that, if it is asked "whether He exists," the response given is entity, which is presupposed as being itself. Likewise, to the question, "what He is," you respond quiddity, etc. In the question, "whether God is man," entity and humanity are presupposed. Hence, it could be said that He is the entity through which humanity exists. Likewise, to the question, "whether God is an angel," it is asserted that He is the absolute entity of angelicality, etc.

However, since every affirmation opposes a negation, it is

believed that this aforementioned answer cannot be the most precise; from this you observe that the First infinitely precedes every opposition, since nothing can approach it, that is not it itself. A conjecture concerning this First, which admits an affirmation to which a negation is opposed, or which prefers a negation as if it were truer than the affirmation, is therefore not the truest. Although it appears to be truer, that God is nothing of all that can be conceived and said, than that He is something thereof, this negation, which an affirmation opposes, nevertheless does not attain precision.

A concept of the truth which rejects both oppositions, the disjunctive and simultaneously the copulative, is therefore more absolute. To the question, "whether God exists," no more infinite response can be given than that He neither is, nor is not, and also that He neither simultaneously is and is not. That is the one, higher, simpler, more absolute, more conformal response to every question concerning the first, simplest, ineffable entity. This most subtle, conjectural response is the same to all questions. But it is only conjectural, since a most precise answer both for rationality as well as for the intellect remains ineffable and unattainable.

VIII.
On the Second Unity

This unity is the intellectual. However, since everything which is not First descends from the most absolute and cannot be understood otherwise than as advancing toward otherness, this unity will not be the simplest, as the First, but rather is composed intellectually. However, the composition is from the One and the other, that is, it is from opposites, as rationality states. Nevertheless, this unity is not from opposites otherwise than that it befits it to be a simple root. Therefore, the opposites do not anticipate it, such that it is from those which precede it, but rather they arise simultaneously with it, just as number must be composed intellectually.

Therefore, in their root simplicity the opposites themselves are coupled undividedly and indissolubly. Indeed, the unity of ten has no root; for no unity precedes it except the First, through whose multiplication it arises. It takes its origin only from the First, which every opposition follows. Its beginning is thus involved in no diversity. Therefore, everything that in the subsequent progresses to division is in this root unity undivided, just as the divisive, opposite differences, which are divided up in the species, are enfolded in the general root of the species; however, the connection is simpler and earlier than every disjunction.

Therefore, you see that questions which suppose that one of two oppositions can be denied and only the other affirmed of this entity, are raised improperly; for all that can be affirmed of the intelligence has no incompatible opposition. For the intellectual being is higher and simpler than that mode of being which is incompatible with not-being. Hence, that intellectual unity is, so to speak, the enfolding root of those oppositions which in their unfolding are incompatible. Indeed, those oppositions which are incompatible in their unfolded, quadratic, rational unity, are enfolded in it. For rationality, motion is incompatibly opposed to rest; but as infinite motion coincides with rest in the First, so here, in its closest similitude, they do not exclude one another, but rather are compatible; for rest is not opposed to the motion of intelligence such that, while it is moved, it does not at the same time rest. For this intellectual motion is simpler than rationality can measure. The same is true of rest and of everything else.

Therefore, conceive this as acutely as you can! For as I recall, in my previous exposition, *On Learned Ignorance,* I have spoken often of God in an intellectual manner through the combination of contradictories in simple unity; just now, however, in the aforesaid I have unfolded my intent in the divine manner. The negation of disjunctive and copulative oppositions is improportionately simpler than their combination. One must speak differently concerning God, if one speaks in the divine manner, according to the concept of the first absolute Unity, than if one speaks about Him according to this intellectual unity and in a still much lower manner according to rationality. This unity, however, which is improportionate to the First, does not escape completely from the composition of opposites, but rather in it the opposites have not yet abandoned compatible concordance.

Hence, since all questions which proceed from investigative rationality are all that they are from intelligence, no question can be formed concerning intelligence in which it is not already reflected as presupposed. For if rationality investigates intelligence, which it comprehends with no sensible signs, how could it begin this investigation, if the light of intelligence did not incite its illumination? Intelligence is therefore related to rationality as God himself is to intelligence. Therefore, if you want to respond conjecturally to questions raised concerning it, pay attention to the presupposition and respond with it itself. Therefore, to the question, "whether there is intelligence," say that it is the entity which is presupposed by the investigative rationality, by which rationality takes its own entity as from its root. To the question, "what it is," say equally that it is the presupposed intellectual quiddity, upon which the quiddity of rationality depends, etc.

The root unity is therefore certain, although it is not certitude itself, as is the First, and it exists and is presupposed in all rationality as the root is in the quadratic. If you undertake to direct the investigation to the intellectual truth, it is necessary that you have the benefit of intellectual terms which have no incompatible opposition, since incompatibility cannot be of the nature of that intellectual unity. Hence, the usual terms, which are rational entities, do not attain to intelligence. Indeed, the intelligence neither stands, nor is it moved, nor does it rest, nor is it in a location; it is neither form, nor substance, nor accident in that mode, which these terms, imposed by rationality, indicate.

For just as intellect is the root of rationality, so are its terms the intellectual roots of the rational. Hence, rationality is the intellectual word, in which it is reflected as in an image. The root of vocal terms is therefore intellectual speech. It is known to you, however, that the unity of simple rationality enfolds the rational concepts of motion and rest, of curvature and straightness and of other oppositions. If, therefore, the rational concepts of oppositions are compatible with one another in the simplicity of the more absolute unity of rationality, and if rationality is the speech of intelligence, then it will be manifest to you that the enfolding of oppositions of the intellectual unity is not reflected in the usual terms of rationality, but rather in the unity of rationality itself.

Therefore, if it is asked, "whether the intelligence be extensive," one could answer in a related conjecture, spoken by means of rationality, that it is in no other way extensive than the rational concept of "extensive" indicates, for this term "extensive" is not intellectual, but rather is the rational concept of "extensive." Likewise one must say to the question, "whether it be in a location," that it is in a location, just as the rational concept of "location" indicates. For the location of intelligence is the rational concept of "location." Just as the square is the container of the root, so indeed is rationality itself substance, that is, since the rational concept of "substance" flows from it, etc. Intelligence is therefore nothing of that which can be said or named; but rather is the origin of the rational concepts of everything, just as God is the origin of intelligence.

Consider these things with diligent assiduousness and if your mind is then deeply penetrated, that which is difficult for many will become manifest to you with the pleasure of intellectual sweetness, which excels incomparably all sensible loveliness.

IX.
On the Third Unity

The soul is not improperly understood as the number of intelligence, which quadratically unfolds. For just as the intelligence is the number of supersimple unity, the unity of intelligence is counted in the soul, while it is multiply contracted. However, because the unity of intelligence is unfolded in the soul, the intelligence is reflected in the soul as in its own image. God is the light of the intelligence, since He is its unity; thus the intelligence is indeed the light of the soul, since it is its unity.

Attend to this more attentively, because in this way the corporeal form exists as the number of the unity of the soul. We intuit the power or the unity of the soul not in itself, but rather sensibly in its corporeal unfolding. Thus we intuit the intelligence not in itself, but rather in the soul, and the first, simplest, most absolute unity not itself as it is, but rather in the intelligence, as in a number and in a sign. God is therefore the form of intelligence, intelligence the form of the soul, the soul the form of the body. Therefore, since all bodies are the number of the soul, the power of its unity correctly occurs to you as great.

Therefore, do not consider rationality as the root of cubic bodies, but rather as the means through which the intellectual root descends into the body; for it is the instrument of the intellect and thus the origin or the instrumental root of corporeality. The unity of one hundred represents the soul, the unity of one thousand the body. However, the thousand arises from the conveyance of the ten into the hundred, that is, from the multiplication of the intelligence by the soul. Therefore, since the soul is reflected in all corporeal things as the instrumental root, it will not be difficult for you to hunt it down in all its sensible signs, since it is the form impressed upon them by the intelligence like a seal in wax.

Therefore, everything which is perceived through hearing bears its character. You grasp that all questions which you hear raised concerning it are marked by it. Hence, they all presuppose the rationality of the soul, for the question, "whether it exists," pertains to rationality, and likewise all others. Therefore, it cannot be doubted, "whether it exists," since without it no doubt could be raised. If someone asked, "whether the soul be extensive," you should say, it is not extensive corporeally, but rather extensive as the number of the intelligence is, for, since it is the unity of sensible things, everything sensibly diverse is one in it. Therefore, sensible or corporeal quantity or quality, and likewise concerning every single sensibility, are such, that the rationality of the soul is the unity of them all, from which unity they proceed. The sensibly diverse, otherwise and opposite, have one rationality, whose varied contraction effects the variety of sensible things.

The judgments of the soul are therefore like numbers, of which the one is even and the other odd, and the same is never at the same time even and odd. For this reason, the soul does not judge opposites to be compatible in its own rationality, since its judgment is its number; and if you consider more acutely, then the number of every unity is in a mode conformed to its unity. For the number of every unity is perfected through ten; the number of the simplest unity attains to ten through the simplest number. What, therefore, in the first unity is the simplest unity itself, in its numerical unfolding is found to be diverse and distinctly other. Thus, intelligences, which are the number of the simplest and absolute unity, indeed participate intellectually in the nature of number in the order related to the First. One finds, therefore, intellectual difference, opposition, otherness, and whatever else befits number, but these are unity in the absolute unity. Likewise, the diversities, othernesses, and oppositions of the square in rationality are intellectual unity. And the sensible and corporeal oppositions and othernesses of the cube are unity in rationality. You must proceed on this path in your investigations, if you want to attain to truer conjectures.

X.
On the Final Unity

This unity, which is represented by the thousand, is sensible and corporeal. For this reason it is indeed the final, because it is the unfolding of unities. Also it enfolds nothing in itself, such that it advances in number, just as the First, which enfolds everything in itself, does not follow a number. This sensible unity is solid and is completely composed, just as the thousand.

In order to obtain a concept of these unities, conceive them as different, just as if the first were the unity of the simplest point, the second that of the simple line, the third that of the simple surface, the fourth that of the simple body. After this you will know more clearly that the unity of the simplest point is all that which is in the unity of the line, of the surface, and of the body. But, the unity of the line is all that which is in the unity of the surface and of the body; and likewise, the unity of surface is all that which is in the unity of the body. The three first unities are not sensible and distinguishable except by means of the mind, which alone conceives the point, the line, and the surface separately; the senses on the other hand only attain the corporeal. Now you are able to examine our ineptitude clearly, when we endeavor to measure the mental by means of the sensible, when we strive to represent the trinity of the surface with a gross body. We act ineptly, if we endeavor to represent the simplicity of the line by means of a body. However, we act most ineptly, when we clothe the indivisible, most absolute point with corporeal form. Therefore, we only ineptly sketch the subtle theological and intelligential forms by means of these corporeal, sensible forms or by means of these sensible literal traditions.

The sense of the soul perceives the sensible, and there is nothing sensible unless the unity of the senses exists. But this sensation is confused and gross, remote from all distinction. For the senses perceive and do not distinguish. Every distinction is indeed from rationality, for rationality is the unity of sensible number. Therefore, if the white is distinguished from the black by means of the senses, the warm from the cold, the acute from the obtuse, this sensible thing from that one, this descends from the property of rationality. For this reason, the senses as such also do not negate; for negation belongs to distinction. The senses only affirm that something sensible exists, but not that it is this or that. So rationality makes use of the senses as an instrument, in order to distinguish the sensible, but it is rationality itself which in the senses distinguishes the sensible.

Observe, Father Julian, how every negation and not-being is alien to the region of sensible things; on the contrary, every affirmation is far removed from the region of the supreme unity. In the regions of the median unities both are permitted: enfolding in the second, unfolding in the third. In this lowest unity there are only words of the present time; in the first, supreme unity, there are only timeless words; in the second, enfolding, words of the present and not-present; in the third, unfolding, words of the present or not-present.

If you adapt your terms to the unities about which you intend to inquire, you will effect truer conjectures. Indeed, if one asks concerning God, "whether He has been yesterday," through the fact that words are absolved from time in the divine, you easily conceive the response: since "to have been" indeed embraces being and becoming and is timeless, then it corresponds to eternity. However, if this question is formulated in respect to intelligence, if "to have been" enfolds the present and not-present, it could correspond to the eternal, falling very near to and proceeding from eternity, etc. Thus, even if you speak of one unity just as of the other, you must adapt your mode of speaking to it, so that when we as rational men speak about God we subject Him to the rules of rationality; we affirm one thing of God, we deny another, and we apply contradictory oppositions disjunctively. And this is the method of almost all modern theologies, which speak of God in accordance with rationality. Through this method we allow much in the school of rationality that we know is denied according to the region of simple unity.

Rationality resolves everything into multitude and magnitude; the origin of multitude, however, is unity and that of magnitude the trinity, just as the triangle in respect to polygons. According to the method of rationality, therefore, the origin of everything is one and three; not as if unity and trinity were plural, since the origin of plurality is unity, but rather as they are a unity, which is a trinity. The intelligence, however, which observes the ineptitude of rational words, rejects these terms. It conceives God beyond that which is signified by these terms, as the origin enfolding them. And because it sees its concept to be deficient in the radiated light of divinity, it affirms that God must be understood beyond every enfolding and unfolding, and that He, as He is, cannot be conceived. We act in a similar manner in respect to intelligence, when we discuss it with ratiocination.

If we elevate sensible things in this way to rationality or to intelligence or to the first most absolute Unity, then we must speak of them according to the rules of that region; if we absolve the unity of a stone from all sensible, rational, or intellectual plurality and return to infinite simplicity, then nothing further is affirmable concerning it. It is then no more stone than not-stone, but rather it is everything, etc.

And you understand this without scrupulosity, if you observe that the absolute unity of the stone is no more stone than not-stone, and that there is one absolute Unity of everything, which is God. Hence, just as the absolute Unity of this sensible and rational stone is God, so is its intellectual unity intelligence. It is clear from this by which rules conjectures concerning it are then to be made.

I beseech you to observe one thing more: how the sensible unity, to which no path lies open for advancing further, regresses upwards, for with the descent of rationality to the senses, the senses return to rationality. And pay attention to the progression in this regression. For the senses return to rationality, rationality to the intelligence, the intelligence to God, where beginning and consummation are in perfect circulation. Therefore, the sensible number returns to the beginning of its unity, in order to be able to attain to intelligence through it and through intelligence to God, the End of ends. The end of sensible things is the soul or rationality. The sensible life therefore deviates from the path of the regression and of the end, if it estranges itself from the unity of rationality; just so rationality deviates, if it digresses too far from the unity of the intelligence; likewise also the intelligence, if it turns elsewhere from the absolute Unity which is the Truth. That is sufficient said for the moment.

XI.
On Unity and Otherness

As far as the unrefined nature of my mental power permitted, I have unfolded some foundations of my conjectures from the ordering of numbers. Now I want to add still one more, which, contained in the same root, should always be incorporated in the mind.

It is established that every number is constituted out of unity and otherness, the unity advancing to otherness and otherness regressing to unity, so that it is limited in this reciprocal progression and subsists in actuality as it is. It can also not be that the unity of one number is completely equal to the unity of another, since a precise equality is impossible in everything finite. Unity and otherness are therefore varied in every number. The odd number appears to have more of unity than the even number, because the former cannot be divided into equal parts and the latter can be. Therefore, since every number is one out of unity and otherness, so there will be numbers in which the unity prevails over the otherness, and others in which the otherness appears to absorb the unity.

No one doubts, however, that the root numbers are simpler than the quadratic and the cubic. For it is certain that the simple root numbers, which issue forth from no other preceding root than from simple unity, have much unity and little of otherness; indeed, in them no otherness appears in respect to all the other numbers, whose roots they represent. If some otherness exists in them on account of their egression from the first simplest unity, this is conceived correctly to exist only in respect to the infinite simplicity of the First. In the quadratic numbers, on the other hand, there is necessarily more otherness, since they arise from the multiplication of the root. Multiplication is, however, a departure from the simplicity of unity. But you see that they still bear much of unity, because they enfold in themselves the cubic number, which proceeds from them. The cubic, however, contains little of simple unity and much of otherness, divisibility, and multiplicity.

On the basis of this example which I have given, conjecture that the universe and all worlds and everything that is in them are constituted out of unity and otherness, in reciprocal progressions, and indeed in a varied and diverse manner. For you have indeed heard that the unity and otherness of the supreme heaven are simpler, intellectual, and radical, those of the middle heaven are median, and those of the lowest heaven are sensible and solid. The intellectual numbers are indeed simple, and they are the simple essences of rational and sensible numbers. From them arise the rational numbers, which are proportional; for only rationality attains the nature of proportions; thereafter the sensible, more solid number.

However, the unity of the intellectual number, as is the trinity, is indivisible and unmultiplicable. For there cannot be more than one trinity; however, it is established most clearly that the rational proportion of the triple can be pluralized and in the sensible contraction multiplied. However, it is clear that the trinity is much more enfolding than the proportion of the triple. For it enfolds everything trine and triply intelligible or numerable, without which there could not be a triple proportion. Since, therefore, the triple proportion does not concur with its essence, but rather conversely, its essence indeed embraces everything trine, whether it was triple or not, its enfolding is the maximum. The triple also enfolds many triple numbers and everything triplicable, but three enfolds nothing. For if I count a, b, c and say "three," then I unfold number. According to this or another similitude more acceptable to you, form more suitable terms and figures, in order to gain access to the diverse numbers of these diverse worlds, which you nevertheless recognize in the superior world, if you know that the intellectual numbers are ineffable sensibly.

Since you have now attained to the point that by conjecturing you see, that everything is constituted from unity and otherness, conceive unity as a kind of formal light and as a similitude of the first unity, otherness, however, as a shadow and a recession

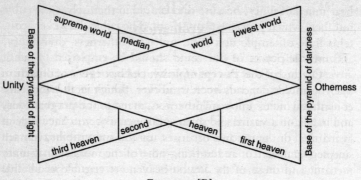

FIGURE 2 [P]

from the simplest First and as gross matter. And let the pyramid of light proceed into the darkness and the pyramid of darkness into the light, and lead everything that can be investigated, back to this figure, so that through a sensible guide you can direct your conjecture to the concealed. In order to make it easy for you in an example, behold the universe reduced in the figure here above (see Figure 2).

Observe that God, who is unity, is, as it were, the basis of light. The basis of darkness, however, is nothing. However, we conjecture that between God and nothing falls every creature. Hence the supreme world abounds in light, as you perceive visually; nevertheless, it is not free of darkness, although the darkness, on account of the simplicity of this supreme world, appears to be absorbed in light. In the lowest world darkness rules, although it is not entirely without light; nevertheless, the figure demonstrates that this light is more latent than eminent in the darkness. In the middle world, however, the habitude is also median. If you wish to inquire into the interstices of the orderings and choirs, do this through the subdivisions.

That this figurative sign not lead you to false phantasmata, I would like to admonish you always to bear in mind these frequently repeated words; for neither light nor darkness should be conjectured in respect to the other worlds, as you see them in the sensible world. If you always hold firmly to this, then in all inquiries utilize this figure, which I will name P in the following, since it is paradigmatic.

XII.
Explication

The whole power of our mind should be employed in subtle investigation of the concept of unity, because every multitude of the cognizable depends upon its notion, which in all knowledge is all that which is known. However, attend to the fact that every multitude of its names is, so to speak, a number of the unity of its name. For the rational nature of unity is indivisibility in itself and segregation from everything other; hence we say that unity is named through many attributes of its strength. For all that which indicates a certain indivisibility, distinction, and connection befits unity. However, the figure enfolds everything of this kind through unity, the oppositions through otherness.

Therefore, the progression of indivisibility to divisibility is not other than the descent of unity to otherness; it is likewise for the progression from incorruptibility to corruptibility, from immortality to mortality, from immutability to mutability, from immobility to mobility, and likewise for everything similar. For the same reason, it is likewise for the transition from form to the formable, because the form is distinctive, therefore it is unity; distinction progresses to the indistinct or continuous, the special to the confused, light to darkness, the subtle to the gross, spirit to body, etc. Likewise, actuality descends to potentiality, the whole to the part, the universal to the particular, the species to the individual, love to the lovable, art to the artful, and in this manner everything connecting or enfolding to the enfolded. It is not possible to find oppositions, of which the one is not as unity in respect to the other.

If, therefore, you direct your view to Figure P, then you will see through the descent of unity into otherness and the regression of otherness into unity, how in the supreme heaven, everything that there is of otherness, advances to unity itself: divisibility to indivisibility, darkness to light, grossness to subtlety, the composite to the simple, the mortal to the immortal, the mutable to the immutable, the feminine to the masculine, the potential to the actual, the imperfect or the part to the whole, etc. It is to the contrary in the lowest world, where indivisibility degenerates to divisibility. For the unity of indivisible form follows divisible nature, so that every part of water is water, every part of earth earth. Stability is here in instability, immortality in mortality, actuality in potentiality, masculinity in femininity, etc. In the middle world, however, the habitude is median.

If you reflect upon this diligently in your mind, you shall intuit the greatest, and to many the most concealed, things in the clearest light and be led to the greatest secrets of nature. You shall also intuit in the variations of terms in the one and the other world, how in the inferior world stability is in instability and generally unity is in otherness; for here its unity, which has passed over into otherness, is not to be unity, but rather otherness. The contrary is the case in the supreme world, where this otherness is not to be otherness, but rather unity. However, Figure P shows here that every possible thing in one world is different in this; indeed, unity is absorbed differently in otherness in the one or conversely; it exists differently according to more or less in the other. Therefore, one does not come to a simply maximum or minimum.

The less, therefore, the formal unity passes over into otherness, the more noble it is, since it is more one; the animal form is more one than the vegetative; therefore, the form of an animal does not follow the division of the animal, as it sometimes accompanies the division of the vegetative and still more that of the mineral, and maximally that of the elements. You also see why one must come necessarily to a not-stone in the division of a stone, and this so much the more swiftly, the more perfect is the stone, etc., and that if a progression into infinity is not to occur, one must necessarily come to what are called elements, concerning which we shall speak below.

However, it is necessary in order to investigate anything particular by means of Figure P, that you conceive unity in its perfection and imagine according to it the intensity of the light and the grossness of the darkness, great or small, so that according to how it falls in the universe, you can have a more singular notion of everything in respect to all others. From what you have heard, however, conjecture the gradations of unities, so that you affirm that as greater, which is more indivisible and more united.

For the unity of the whole uniting all parts is greater than that of the unitable parts. For the less a unity is in actuality and the more it is in potentiality, the more alterable it is. A uniting unity is more perfect than a unitable unity, and the more conditions of unity you see concur in the unity of something, the more perfect it is. For unity indicates the rational nature of the origin and the end of that which it unites in itself. Therefore, the unity of the soul is more perfect than the unity of the body, because the end of the unity of the body is the unity of the soul, on which the corporeal depends as on its origin; for if the soul were ablated, its unity would perish and be dissolved. We see, however, that some unities are more in the potentiality of unitability, others more in actuality, so that, therefore, one cannot come to a simply maximum or minimum in the things which admit more or less, nor do we actually attain the determinate, demonstrably lowest, and minimal elementary unities, although rationality believes that they exist and that they are reciprocally unitable, subsisting only in continuous unitability. In them the unity is in continuous alteration. Nor does one come by means of rationality to the actually maximum elementary unities, where the potentiality of unitability is in perfect actuality, expecting no other union.

Observe therefore, that you must conceive with the intellect alone beyond rationality, in order to assert that a progression into the infinite and simultaneously an achievement of an actual maximum and minimum is not possible; for one cannot know which earth is only element, since no earth which is not an element can be given, which is not distinct from all other earth. The same is true of water; there is indeed no water that does not differ in the gradation of the elements in its species from the other.

Therefore, neither the actually minimum nor maximum is knowable; look at quantity. For if in respect to every given number there can be given one greater, it is known that there can be no infinitely great number, and simultaneously, that no given number is the maximum. Thus also, if everything extensive is divisible into ever more divisible parts, it is known that one can neither come to infinite parts, nor to a minimum part. Hence, although the senses believe something is a minimum part, rationality, nevertheless, says that it is further divisible and not the minimum. Likewise the intellect knows, that that is still divisible which rationality deems to be the minimum. Therefore, everything that can be given is greater than the minimum and smaller than the maximum, but without this procession running into the infinite.

Only this negative knowledge brings unattainable precision to you; for although it appears to rationality, that one must necessarily come yonder to a maximum, where an infinite step-wise ascent is prohibited, the intelligence nevertheless sees through the negation of precision, that it is truer that nothing that can be given is precisely the maximum, in the class of things which admits something greater.

So great, therefore, is the power of the simple intellectual nature, that it embraces that which rationality divides as oppositions. Indeed, rationality, which does not attain to a number without proportion and which admits an actual maximum, conjectures that it has a path from the known to the unknown. The intellect, on the other hand, which observes the weakness of rationality, rejects these conjectures and affirms those numbers are equally proportional and improportionate, so that precision, which is the blessed God, of all and of each singular thing is equally hidden. Rationality, however, is in some measure the precision of the senses; for rationality unites the sensible numbers in its precision, and the sensible things are measured through rational precision; but that is not a simply true, but rather a rationally true, measure. The precision of the rational, however, is the intellect, which is the true measure. However, the highest precision of intellect is truth itself, which is God.

Note this most attentively. The progression from unity to otherness is simultaneously a regression from otherness to unity. Observe this most diligently, if you would like to intuit unity in otherness intellectually. For, that the soul is in the body means, that it passes over into the body, such that corporeal unity enters into it; it is likewise in respect to the form; the more one and the more perfect a form has been, the more its progression is a regression to otherness. In the simple intellect conceive that the progression is coupled with the regression, if you care to attain to those secrets which are more truly attained beyond rationality, which divides the progression from the regression, alone in the pure intellect, which enfolds the oppositions into one. The philosophers and theologians, who only engage in ratiocination, through the positing of its first principle, have hitherto shut themselves off from the path leading to it.

XIII.
Nothing Intelligible Is Understood As It Is

Because unity is unity means that it is precisely, and as it is, it is established for you sufficiently and most clearly that unity is incommunicable, inexplicable and, as it is, unattainable identity. For just as every entity is in its own entity as it is, so it is in another otherwise. If you are attentive, you will easily apprehend this.

Indeed, the circle, as it is an entity of rationality, is attained as it is, in its own rational entity. For when you conceive the figure in which all lines from the center to the circumference are equal, then you attain in this rational concept the circle as it is an entity of rationality, but outside of its own rationality you attain it as it is a sensible thing. As it is in another, it is indeed otherwise. It is therefore not possible, that a circle outside of rationality is as it is in rationality. Therefore, a sensible circle participates in the unity of the rational circle in otherness.

Therefore, that precision of the circle as it is, remains incommunicable, for it is not multiplied except in otherness. For no sensible circle can be given, in which the lines leading from the center to the circumference are precisely equal; indeed, no one line can be given, which is equal to another in everything just as it is. Therefore, there is no circle which is seen so precise, that there could not always be one more precise than it. Although it is communicated just as it is, not otherwise than as it is, in the other, nevertheless, it cannot be participated in except otherwise. Therefore, it is not, as it is, imparticipable on account of a deficiency, but rather because it is participated in in another, hence otherwise.

Pay total attention to this, so that you penetrate into the variety of conjectures. You perceive that you can understand nothing intelligible as it is, if you admit that your intellect is some other thing than the intelligible. For the intelligible is understood as it is only in its own intellect, whose entity it is; however, otherwise in every other. Nothing is attained, therefore, as it is, except in its own truth, through which it is. Therefore, only in divine intellect, through which every entity exists, is the truth of all things attained as it is, in other intellects otherwise and variedly.

Also the intellect of a thing as it is, is not attainable in another, just as the circle, as it is here on this sensible pavement, can only be otherwise elsewhere.

Therefore, inexplicable identity is unfolded in otherness variedly and differently, and variety itself is enfolded concordantly in the unity of identity. Indeed, vision is participated in differently in various seeings, and the variety of visible things is enfolded concordantly in the unity of the sense of sight; just as the diversity of seeings is contained concordantly in the unity of absolute vision. And since the divine Mind is the most absolute precision of all, it happens that every created mind participates in it differently in the otherness of variation, while that ineffable Mind itself endures as imparticipable, and the condition of those participating in it brings this about.

However, the minds do not receive the ray of divine light in themselves, as though by nature they came before this participation, but rather the participation in the intellectual, incommunicable, most actual light, is their quiddity. The actuality of our intelligence exists therefore in the participation in the divine Intellect. However, because this most actual power cannot be received except in the variety of otherness, which is conceived rather as a kind of concurrent potentiality, hence it happens that minds, which participate, participate in the otherness of the most actual intellect, as if in that actuality which, related to this divine Intellect, is otherness or potentiality.

Therefore, all our intelligence exists out of participation in the divine actuality in the variety of potentiality. To be able to understand the truth as it is in actuality befits created minds, just as it is peculiar to our God to be that actuality, which is participated in variedly in created minds in potentiality. The more deiform, therefore, an intelligence is, the closer its potentiality is to the actuality as it is; however, the more obscure, the more distant.

Hence, it is participated in in near, remote, and the most remote potentiality, variedly and differently. That summit is neither inaccessible, and so one must approach it as if one could not reach it, nor if one has approached it should one believe that one has actually apprehended it; but rather it is more, that one can indeed always come nearer, while it remains always unattainable as it is. Indeed, time advances thus towards eternal duration, to which, although it continuously approaches it, it could never be equivalent.

You see now that the positive assertions of the wise are only conjectures. For when you, Father, personally behold with your clearest sight the face of the highest priest, of our most holy lord and Pope Eugene IV, you conceive a positive assertion of it, which you affirm as precise according to your sense of sight. However, when you turn to the root, from which the discrimination of the senses emanates, I mean to rationality, then you understand that the sense of sight participates in the power of discrimination in organic, contracted otherness. For this reason, you intuit the defect of falling away from precision, since you do not contemplate the face as it is, but rather in otherness according to your visual angle, which is different from that of all living beings.

Therefore, conjecture is a positive assertion, which participates in the truth as it is in otherness. However, as the senses experience their otherness in the unity of rationality and form conjectures in absolving sensible assertions of the unity of precision, so does rationality discover in its root unity, namely, in the light of intelligence, its otherness and the falling away from precision into conjecture; and thus intelligence itself, as the next potentiality, rejoices to be able to conjecture in the divine unity in its clearest mode.

Whoever holds fast to this, can effect the conjecture of participation through this method. For, since everything participable is participated in only in otherness, it must be participated in in the quaternary; indeed, unity advances from itself into otherness, and everything which is participated in in otherness subsists through the quaternary. It can be received neither as maximal, nor minimal, nor equal. Since the simplicity of unity is not participated in simply as it is, but rather in another manner, this occurs, so to speak, in a certain composition or a falling away from this simplicity, that is, it is participated in in the otherness of simplicity. The simplicity therefore is not participated in as a part, since it is simplicity; but rather in the manner in which the simple is participable, as the whole itself. However, because the simplicity of unity cannot be communicated maximally, minimally, and equally (so indeed, as it is, it is participated in through coincidence, as this was revealed in *Learned Ignorance*), the simplicity of unity must then be participated in in a certain quaternary, which falls away from the maximum, minimum, and equality.

Therefore, unity is not participated in as it is enfolding simplicity, nor as it is unfolding otherness, but rather as its unfolding and alterable participability. It is understood through a certain coincidence as a certain mode of the power of enfolding imparticipable unity.

In accordance with the configuration appearing below (see Figure 3), I say that: A, the simple enfolding unity, is imparticipable, as it is; it is also imparticipable in the manner of B or C, namely maximally or minimally or corresponding to a higher or inferior gradation of its power. It is also imparticipable in the manner of D, E, or F, that is, maximally, minimally, or equally or corresponding to a superior, inferior, or median gradation. Nor is it participable as in G, H, I, or K, as if in four simple distinct modes of being, namely, the superior, the inferior, and the two median, or also in the maximal, minimal, greater, or lesser manner. For if indeed it were participated in so distinctly, as though according to certain parts of its power, then it were not participated in in that more perfect manner, in which the totality of simple unity could be participated in, but rather deficiently. It is therefore not participable according to any gradations distinct from itself, since simplicity is not distinguishable. Nor is it participable so that those four are regressively three, for example, so that G, H, I, K appear drawn back from their quaternary otherness to the ternary D, E, F. Nor so that they appear more united in the binary B, C, but rather so that in the unity A, a sort of fourfold power subsisting in the unity of substance is considered. For only here does unity, which is imparticipable, coincide with participability, and indeed so that everything which participates differently can only in quaternary otherness attain the unity that is imparticipable in another manner. This will become clearer in what is said below.

The great power of the art of conjecture becomes evident

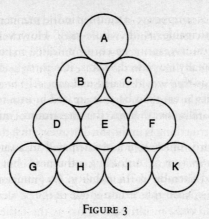

FIGURE 3

to you in this way, if you observe the unfolding of the denary in an enfolding manner. The art through which the truth itself is investigated is indeed most brief; although it can be written with three lines in the enfolding of its simple unity, nevertheless it can neither be communicated nor participated in without the otherness of modes; hence you may excuse me for its reiteration.

XIV.
On the Three Worlds

After these perhaps unsuitable representations, conceive that a supreme world is constituted through the theophanical descent of the first divine unity into the denary and the regression from the unity of the denary to the first. This supreme world can also be called, if you will, the third heaven. Through a like descent from the second unity into the third and an ascent of the third into the second you constitute another world, which can also be called the second heaven. However, conjecture a third world through the descent of the third unity into the fourth and the reascent of the fourth into the third.

The universe will therefore consist of a central most spiritual world, a circumferential most gross world, and a median world. The center of the first world is God, the center of the second is intelligence, the center of the third is rationality. Sensibility is, as it were, the grossest cortex of the third world and is only circumferential. The first center of indivisible entity, which holds everything in everything, is central everywhere; sensibility always forms the extremity. Everything is in the first, everything in the second, everything in the third world, in its own manner. The entity of every single thing is the center or that most absolute unity.

Therefore, since this unity is the truth of each and every thing, every true thing is in the third heaven, such that it emanates from its truth immediately and unmixedly, as the father in his sons. It is in the second heaven, such that it is in more remote similitude to the truth, as the father in his grandsons. It is in the lowest heaven, such that it lies in the remotest shadows, where it is concealed only in ultimate signs, as the father in the most distant consanguinity of his descendants. However, God is our Father and origin; we have the image of His true filiation only in the third heaven, the central unity of which is truth itself; only there will we be able to possess the kingdom of truth as true sons. Hence, this is the intellectual heaven, where the truth shines clearly as it is. The light of this truth in the second rational heaven, shaded in by rationality, assumes opinionative variety; however, in the inferior heaven it becomes confused by the densest grossness.

XV.
On Three Times Three Times Three Distinctions

A further conjecture leads me to think, that each of the already named worlds of the universe contains in itself a series of numbers, so that each is perfect in its manner, although all the numbers of the first and supreme heaven are in proportion to the others the simplest and most formal, just as the ten simple digits, which are extended stepwise up to the thousand. The numbers of the second heaven retain this unit of measurement, but are grosser, less lucid, and formal, as if the ten articulations hastened stepwise up to the thousand. Those of the lowest, however, are shaded in with much darkness and are more material, so that the proportion of their unity to the first is as 100 to 1 and to the second is as 100 to 10.

If you ponder the habitude of each of the worlds previously set forth, you see how the circle of the world is triply distinguished through three numerical progressions, so that thus in the universe there are nine unities descending stepwise from the first simplest unity. However, in order that the quaternary be completed in this distinction, which alone represents the complement of the investigations, we are forced to the conjecture, that the progressions, through which one unity attains to another, are to be counted four times separately, so that we observe, finally, in each world three times three distinctions, and thus arrive in the universe at the cube of three, as the figure written below shows you (see Figure 4).

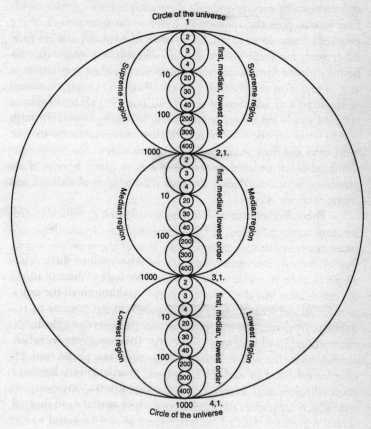

FIGURE 4

XVI.

Great mysteries, which are certainly hidden from most, will become known to you if, as the matter demands, you consider the figure with your mind's eye.

Every number is comprehended by the number ten. Every progression is completed by the quaternary. Therefore, 4 times 10 is 40. Hence, you find 40 circles, both the great as well as the small, all collected into one. Hence, this progression 1, 3, 9, 27, since it yields 40, is not unsuitably praised. For as 1, 2, 3, 4 is the most ordered progression of all numbers, than which none more ordered can be given—indeed, the multiplication of two yields four just as does the addition of unity to three; therefore, the 4 proceeds from them in the most ordered manner; and no four other such numbers can be found—likewise no progression is better ordered for 4 times 10, namely for 40, than that which is 1, 3, 9, 27. You can confirm this as follows: Through reciprocal subtraction and addition of these four numbers all numbers are attained singly up to 40, just as in the first progression through combination of the four numbers all numbers arise up to ten. You may confirm that yourself in both cases. No other four numbers of an ordered progression can be given besides these numbers, which combined, through their reciprocal addition and subtraction satisfy each.

Thereafter consider, that the simple unity, which in this location represents God, is contiguous to four circles: the maximum, namely, that of the universe, that of the supreme world, that of the supreme order, and that of the supreme choir. Thus all participate stepwise in its light and its entity: first of all the universe, after this the supreme world, next the supreme order, in the final and fourth location the supreme choir. You see consequently, how one choir communicates the received light to the other choir, until it comes to the last. It is especially to be observed, how that which is found in the universe, is also found in every world and in each of its orders, however, in a different, more absolute and more contracted manner. For the unity of ten, which represents the intelligence, the unity of one hundred, which represents the soul, and the unity of one thousand, which represents the body, is otherwise in the supreme world, namely, according to the high, simple, and noble nature of this world, otherwise in the middle, otherwise in the lowest, shadow world, and in the same supreme world it is different in the supreme order and in the subsequent ones; for you see, that the lowest in the superior coincides with the supreme in the inferior in all things.

The senses of the superior world are indeed simpler than the intelligence of the median one, and the senses of a superior order are more perfect than the intellect of the subsequent one. The nine unities of ten, the nine unities of one hundred and the nine unities of one thousand, which you find in the 27 minor circles, are therefore related to one another according to the progressional numbers, always taking their beginning from the absolute unity. And then you will experience, how the progression is completed in each world. For if the first ten of the superior world is as 2, the second as 3, and the third as 4, the progression is complete. If in the second world the first ten is as 20, the second as 30, the third as 40, then this progression is complete. Thus, the progression is complete, if in the third lowest world the first ten is as 200, the second as 300, the third as 400.

Hence, you will see likewise concerning the other unities, if you conceive them, how the unity of intelligence of the inferior world is not of the nature of the superior or median world, but rather falls from its simplicity, corresponding to the numerical proportion presented; just as the school of grammar judges an intelligent man one way, the school of mathematics another, and that of theology yet another. Likewise, the judgments concerning these necessarily vary indeed according to the varied judgments of the diverse worlds. The judgment of the inferior world is one thing if it attends singularly to itself, another if its habitude towards the superior is considered.

Whoever, therefore, wants to distinguish the proportional measure of conjectures must take heed, that he knows both to distinguish and to consider that which is distinguished both in itself singularly and in regard to the other, in order that he first denies, then affirms according to the habitudes. If, for example, it is asked, whether the nature of an inferior world has intelligence, then you see that one must say, that intelligence is found there contracted according to this world, but intelligence is not found according to the habitudes of a higher world, etc. For one world does not count or speak or do something as another does; for example, intelligences are not counted as stones or animals, they also do not speak as men; but rather each world employs its own manner.

SECOND PART

I.

Although I have now presented all the fundamentals of my conjectures in more detail than is necessary for your most acute mind, nevertheless, it appears to me to be necessary to make comprehensible the simplicity and identity of the concept in the variety of the many othernesses, for the sake of slower minds, who will perhaps occasionally read this. Hence I want to explain in part what I have said in practical application, so that when you see one and the same shine forth in varied ways, you will easily deduce everything through the art of conjecture. However, since our whole endeavor is most fervent, to experience in ourselves the knowledge of the true, I want to present some preliminary explanations of universal knowledge, so that you can finally acquire the art of hunting down knowledge of yourself at least conjecturally, since all precision remains hidden from us.

However, all things are that which they are, through participation in the One. In everything, and indeed in each in its mode, this One shines forth; participation in it is the being equally of all and of each individual. Hence, you need to have no other mode of consideration, than that in the diversity of the things investigated by you, you seek the identity, or in the otherness the unity; for then you will intuit, so to speak, the modes of absolute unity in the otherness of contracted entities. Also all figures should be of use in the manner applied in investigating everything.

The variety of the modes, which arises from the diversity of things, can be conceived such that absolute Unity indeed represents the mode of absolute Necessity, which is received in the otherness of things variously, so that each entity or each unity is indeed a mode of necessity. As sensible vision is a certain mode of the necessity of that vision, which is absolute Necessity, so also is rational vision a certain mode and intellectual vision a certain mode. But divine vision is a mode which is participated in variously; it is absolute Necessity itself. In relationship to every other vision this absolute vision is identical. Its mode, therefore, is the same in the search for the truth of each one.

But if you propose to observe rationally the diversity of the one from the other, which exists as a result of the otherness of the mode of participation, you should not hesitate to avail yourself of the unity of the mode variously, in order to investigate sensible vision sensibly, rational vision rationally, intellectual vision intellectually in the figures. The Figure P will indeed help you in respect to each and all; in respect to the sensible, if you take the sensible unity as light and sensible otherness as shadow; in respect to the rational, if you name the discursive or rational unity light; it will similarly help in respect to the intellectual, if you take the intellectual unity as light. If you want to form a conjecture of the participation, then proceed in the same way, supposing the mode from the vision which you want to investigate.

It is likewise in the figure of the universe. If you suppose the circle of the universe as the universe of those which participate in absolute vision, then you intuit clearly all the variety of intellectual, rational, and sensible vision. If you only have interest in the intellectual, then in making the larger circle into that of the universe of intellectual vision, you will behold what you seek. It is likewise with the rational, which you consider rationally, and with the sensible, which you consider sensibly. With this art you can investigate not only vision, but rather everything in general, so that diversity is observed in identity and identity in diversity. But you must always be attentive, so that you be not seduced by the deception of inept words, but rather use them in the appropriate modes, as you heard from these few preliminary remarks, and you will gain not a little fruit.

It is also necessary that you ceaselessly disclose that foundation of unattainable precision; if a sensible, rational, or intellectual precision occurs to you, you must accept this as a contracted kind of precision, whose otherness you will intuit only when you ascend to the more absolute unity of this contraction. For rationality indeed says to you, 2 plus 3 are precisely 5, because this cannot be denied according to the judgment of rationality; nevertheless, if you look toward the unity of rationality, namely to the intellect, where the number five is not greater than the number two or the number three, you will find neither the one even and the other odd, nor the one great and the other small; since there, you see every number of rationality in the simplest absolute unity, the proposition that 2 plus 3 are 5 will not be true except in the heaven of rationality. Precision is therefore found only contractedly in the rational rationally, just as in the senses sensibly.

If you assert that the other is completely incompatibly opposed to the one, then you affirm a truth as precise on the path of rationality, which lacks precision intellectually. Thus also, if you assert that the understanding of intelligence is something other than its will, etc., then you express something true intellectually, but not divinely, where understanding and willing are not different from one another. Precision is therefore only attained as other, as if all precision participated in the absolute Truth, which is God, in otherness, just as all being participates in absolute Entity.

Pay attention, I entreat, to the profound root in all scientific inquiries: All that which is shown to be precise on the path of rationality, is so, because it is from the heaven of rationality; the same is true of the senses and also of the intellect. For since rationality is the otherness of the enfolding unity of intelligence, the intelligence is only in rationality in altered participation. Rationality therefore denies an enfolding of opposites and affirms their unattainability, just as the senses deny the rational generic unity of many sensible things. For vision cannot affirm of the nature of a sensible thing, that it is resonant or sweet. Therefore, this is the root of all assertions of rationality, namely, that the coincidence of opposites is unattainable. Hence, every number is either even or odd, hence comes the order of number, its progression, its proportion. Hence, the proportion of the diameter to the side is irrational, because it would require the coincidence of even and odd. Hence, the diameter of the circle is improportionate to the circumference, because rationality does not attain the coincidence of such different things.[1]

---

1. The following alternative wording appears in a different version of the Latin text: "Hence, a rectilinear polygon is improportionate to the circle, because rationality does not attain the coincidence of the curve and the straight line."

In order to say much most briefly: In mathematics one can know nothing from another root. Everything that one demonstrates to be true is from it, because were it not so, the coincidence of opposites would be introduced and that would mean abandoning rationality. So everything which is shown from this to be unobtainable through rationality, is so because knowledge thereof would bring with it the coincidence of opposites. And because this principle shines forth in mathematics, its proofs are the most rational and the truest according to rationality. And rationality is delighted by these just as in the unfolding of its own power, where it intuits itself participating in intelligence in otherness. Hence, even without an instructor, these sciences are easy to many people, whose rationality is neither excessively absorbed in intelligence, nor is contracted in the shadows of sensible things.

Because the otherness of rationality is at the same time the unity of the senses, it obviously enfolds and unfolds the sensible othernesses. Hence it runs from the enfolding to the unfolding, seeking the same logically or rationally in diversity. In a syllogistical conclusion the same is in the premises as in the conclusions, however enfolding is in the major term, unfolding in the conclusion and in a middle mode in the minor term. However, where the conclusion is enfolding, the major term is unfolding. An enfolding power is therefore in rationality, because it is the unity of the sensible othernesses. And at the same time an unfolding power, because it is at the same time the otherness of the unity of the intellect and the unity of sensible things. The heaven of rationality therefore embraces the coincidence of enfolding and unfolding. Hence rational enfolding and unfolding are not opposites of the kind which coincide only in the intellectual unity. In the divine enfolding everything coincides without distinction; in the intellectual enfolding contradictory opposites are compatible; in the rational, contrary, as the opposite distinctions in the genus.

From this observe how when you count, rationality advances to the coincidence of enfolding and unfolding; for through counting you unfold unity and enfold plurality in the unity of any number. For, when you count ten, you have unfolded the most known enfolding unity decimally and enfolded the unknown plurality in the unity of ten. In rationality there is therefore a certain coincidence of opposites, which cannot be attained in sensible things. However, since the senses cannot attain this coincidence of contrary opposites and the precision of rationality, all things subsist, as they are, sensibly. If it were otherwise, they would bring the coincidence with them.

II.

He who turns his attention to the aforesaid, obtains fruitful conjectures. For if he finds in the unfolding of the rational inventions only rationality as the cause, he will extend the powers of its multiplicity in the varied otherness of its unity. For if you apprehend with rationality, that every triangle has three angles equal to two right angles, and if you see that the cause of this apprehension is not other than rationality itself, then you have found the way to the profundity of rationality. You must understand this thus: Rationality, because it is rationality, judges in this way, because it is necessarily so in the heaven of rationality.

For, if it be true that the triangle does not have three angles precisely equal to two right angles, then this is so either through the coincidence of unity and plurality, or trinity and unity, or right and not-right angles, or other very opposite things, and then it is the language of the intellectual world; or it is so because there is neither a precise right angle, nor two precisely equal, nor three angles which are precisely equal to two—then that is the language of the sensible world, which falls away from rational equality in sensible otherness. Hence, from this you see most clearly, that rationality enfolds the truth in itself rationally and that there is no other cause of apprehension except that it is rationality and not intelligence or the senses.

If one says that every quantity can be divided into always further divisible parts according to proportional parts, then rationality necessarily concurs. For, if it were not true, then rationality would admit the coincidence of contradictory opposites, which cannot possibly occur according to the judgment of rationality.

Therefore, consider that rationality is itself alone the cause of all rational arts, and you see that it alone is the root cause of all things which are attained through it. If one therefore asks you: Why in all triangles two sides joined together are greater than the third, or why the square of the diameter of a square is twice as large as the square of the side, or why the square of the side opposite the right angle is equal to the squares of the two other sides, you will answer: This is necessary according to the method of rationality, because if it were not so, the coincidence of contradictory opposites would follow. If one asks: Why a section of a circle from the smaller chord opposite the diameter and the arc is improportionate to the circle, you answer likewise: Because otherwise the coincidence of contradictory opposites would follow. Therefore, to know that everything can be reduced to this principle, "the coincidence of contradictory opposites must be avoided," is sufficient for all the arts which can be investigated with rationality.

I once attempted to affirm that the proportion between the diameter and circumference of the circle[1] is unattainable and inadmissable, because the aforementioned coincidence must be avoided. In this attempt I immediately saw what is to be affirmed geometrically and what is to be denied. For, in the conceptions of thinkers and in all the demonstrations of Euclid or of whomever, I found in the variety of figures this unique principle. Who does not see that this proportion[2] could be attained, if the two sides of a triangle joined together could be equal to the third? For, if any chord is smaller than the arc to which it stretches and if the chord of a smaller arc is more similar to its arc than the chord of a larger one, then it is obvious, that the coincidence of the chord and the arc[3] would result, if one admitted that the two chords of the middle arcs were equal to the chord of the whole arc. One would come necessarily to the same conclusion, if any given arc were not divisible through the middle.

If this frequently named coincidence is to be avoided, it is therefore necessary that the two sides of the triangle joined together be greater than the third and that every quantity be always divisible by proportional parts; you will discover this easily in all

---

1. The following alternative wording appears in a different version of the Latin text: ". . . the quadrature of the circle by means of rationality . . ."
2. The following alternative wording appears in a different version of the Latin text: ". . . the quadrature of the circle . . ."
3. The following alternative wording appears in a different version of the Latin text: ". . . the quadrature of the circle and the coincidence of straight line and the curve . . ."

geometrical demonstrations. I will try once, as time is given me, to unfold this root of mathematics, in order to reduce this knowledge in this way to a certain sufficiency.

If you scrutinize the causes of harmony, you will find that otherness cannot subsist other than in unity. However, since otherness is a diminution of unity, harmony is the combination of unity and otherness. Necessarily the simple of unity advances to the double through multiplication with itself. Therefore, the combination of the simple and the double, through the descent of the simple and the ascent of the double to the one, must necessarily be the first harmonic combination; accordingly, the combination of the double and the triple is the second, and the combination of the triple and the quadruple is the third. And, because unity is unfolded in the quaternary, it is also so in every harmony.

All harmony therefore rests in these numbers 1, 2, 3, 4 and their combinations. The cause of every harmony arises therefore from the necessity of this rational progression. However, the fact that the precision of semi-tone remains hidden to rationality, is because one cannot attain it without the coincidence of the even and odd. You see that sensible combinations are unfoldings so to speak of rational unity, whence the harmonic rational unity; when it is closely contracted in the combination of sensible things, rationality takes delight in it just as though in its own work or in its close similitude.

However, because its precision cannot be unfolded, the harmonic unity is unfolded variedly in the variety of sensible things, so that it, which can be unfolded in nothing precisely as it is, is unfolded variedly in varied things. A rational perusal of the science which is called dialectics, leads likewise to a definite necessity of rationality. For, if the unfolding unity, which is also universality, is unfolded in otherness, the unfolding unknown is attained rationally from the enfolding known. Otherwise intelligence were not in rationality rationally, and unity were not in number numerically or in otherness in the mode of otherness, and there would be nothing of everything. It is therefore necessary according to the method of rationality, that many things be in the one genus generically and in the one species specifically and in an inferior species still more specifically, and that the species be in individuals individually and the individual be in the species universally.

Rationality, however, unfolds this unique discursive art in fourfold otherness. Hence, it speaks of four quantities of propositions, of four modifications, of four syllogistic figures, etc. Logic is nothing other than the art in which the power of rationality is unfolded. Whoever is naturally strong in rationality is therefore vigorous in this art. Moreover, a speaker who wants to imprint his concept on his listeners, utilizes rationality in order to change their minds. Indeed, he knows that it is good for the reception, if the word is adorned in the suitable proportion, and so that it is animated by rationality, he forms a quaternary of causes and contracts them within the circle of the universe.

He sees three heavens. In the supreme heaven he speaks of the matter according to the necessity of justice, in the second he shows the utility of his concern so that it is deliberated upon accordingly, in the third and lowest he demonstrates that it is also honorable. And to this end, he finds the suitable loci, in order to proceed clearly and orderly from the enfolding to the unfolding.

If you wish to assemble a more detailed treatment by means of these aforementioned principles of conjecture, then refer back to the figure of the universe, and take the maximum circle as rationality, and elicit from it the most lucid, more brilliant and more abstract rational art; the lowest more adumbral; and the median rational arts. If you inquire into mathematics, do the same, so that you constitute one as it were intellectual, another as it were sensible, and a median as it were rational; likewise with arithmetic, likewise with geometry, and likewise with music. If you wish to know more about music in itself, then take the circle of the universe as the rational nature of music; and you will intuit a music as it were more intellectually abstract, another as it were sensible, and a third as it were rational. You can effect the miraculous in all these things, if you devote yourself to them with diligent meditation.

If you wish, you can also deal with sensible, rational, and intellectual logic, likewise with rhetoric and with grammar. You will see miraculous things. Although the rational power is participated in in all the arts, nevertheless, if you apply the higher part of rationality to some rational art, it will be as it were intellectual in respect to this same art, if it is animated with an inferior power of rationality.

This is now sufficiently treated. I will add yet some other generalities from the power of our art, suitable to our purpose.

III.
On Difference and Agreement

The human mind investigates by means of rationality; in that it excludes the infinite from every circle of its apprehension, it says there could be no thing that is infinitely different from any other thing, and that every possible difference is smaller than an infinite difference, and an infinite difference is no more difference than agreement. It conceives of agreement correspondingly. Everything therefore agrees and differs with everything, but this is impossible in precisely the same manner; for this precision is detached from the universe.

Therefore, if you see that in the sensible world this is true according to the nature of this world, then it will be clear to you that every sensible thing has a certain universal agreement with every other in a universal way, and with the one more than with the other. Conceive of the agreement, moreover, as unity, however, the difference as otherness, and observe in the Figure P the reciprocal progression of one to the other. The greater therefore the agreement, the smaller is the difference and vice versa. In the quaternary, however, the agreement proceeds to difference. And if you would extend this progression up to the cube of three, then you will attain the distinctions more clearly.

Every sensible thing therefore has a certain most universal agreement with every other sensible thing and a most specific difference. And between them lie two middle terms, of which the one, because of its generality, is drawn to the universal; the other on account of its specific nature is contracted to the most specific. Hence, the union of all sensible things occurs in a kind of universal nature common to all in a universal way.

Another union is not so universal, but general to many, another one is more specific, and the ultimate union is most specific. Therefore, every sensible thing, insofar as this is something existing singularly, agrees with all and none, differs from all and none.

In order to see this, your conjecture, in the figure of the universe, make the center point of each of the minimum circles into something singular. As the center point, it differentiates itself from everything. However, as a point inside the circuit of the universe, namely, contained by the larger circle, it is in universal agreement with everything included inside this orbit, in general agreement, however, with those which after this are enclosed in the subsequent larger circle. After these, however, it is in more specific agreement with those which the more contracted circle includes, in most specific agreement, however, with those which the most contracted circle binds together. Singularity therefore singularizes everything, specificity specializes, generality generalizes, universality universalizes. Indeed, all things universal, general, and specific in you, Julian, julianize, just as harmony lutinizes in the lute, zitherizes in the zither, etc. In another this is not possible as in you.

However, that which in you, Julian, is to julianize, is in all men to humanize, in all animals to animalize, etc. If you want to advance to more discrete concordances, then resolve the most contracted circle in the universal, and thus you will intuit, that you agree in a universal way with the universe of men. Generally, however, with those whom the fifth climate zone intercepts, more specifically with those who live to the west and most specifically with the Italians. Now resolve this most contracted circle in the universal one, and you will see that you belong universally to the Italians, generally to the Latins, specifically to the Romans, and more specifically to the family of Cesarini, from which you were born.

All this you will attain in each particular from the transmitted principles in the relatively truest conjecture according to the grades of difference and agreement, if you observe that you make use proportionally of sensible things in the sensible, rational things in the rational, and intellectual things in the intellectual according to the given rules.

IV.
On the Elements

From this and the foregoing you conceive the conjecture regarding the elements sufficiently and clearly. If indeed a certain universal agreement of all things indicates, that a first and most universal nature common to all dwells in all things, then we conjecture that this is elemental in a universal way. If, however, it has become obvious that in the sensible world all sensible things come together in a kind of community in the most general nature, then we conjecture that it is a general element. And it is likewise in respect to the more specific and most specific. However, after I have given the necessary attention to everything of which I want to treat, I name as element the unity of every region which is absorbed in the continuous otherness of the same, so that it cannot subsist simply in itself, because of the purity of its actuality or of its unity. Something arising from the elements can therefore not be resolved into simple elements, since the resolution cannot achieve the simple, and the simple element lacks the power to subsist in actuality. Elicit the distinction of elements from the generally distinguishing figure.

For the totality of elements is threefold: radical, quadratic, cubic. The elements of one are indeed more intellectual, the other more rational, the other more sensible. For that which the sense takes first of all for an element, rationality demonstrates to be something arising from the element, and what appears to rationality as simple, the intelligence comprehends as composed. Therefore, it is with the different gradations of elements as with the point, line, and surface. The sensible world attains nothing simpler than the surface, the rational world however places the simple line before the surface; the intellectual world, however, prefers the indivisible point to the line. Likewise we see the elements of one as simple letters, another as syllables, and another as words: that arising from the elements, however, is speech. Among the letters themselves we intuit again a threefold differentiating distinction, just as with the syllables and words. Therefore, pay attention to how, according to the judgment of rationality, everything sensible which can be given, nevertheless always remains a composition from elements, even though the one sensible thing comes closer to the simplicity of the elements than the other. Likewise, according to the assertion of the intellect, rationality does not obtain the pure element, nor does the intellect, according to the judgment of the simplest divinity.

Rationality forms four prime elements, which are resolvable and unitable with one another circularly; for if the progression of unity to otherness subsists in the quaternary, the descent of unity and the reversion of otherness will be a quaternary. If we conceive of the elements as points, because they cannot be resolved into something prior, then we are easily led to know in an infallible ascent, that three elements cannot suffice for the constitution of a solid whole, and that a combination of each with each is not possible according to the quaternary; we know this from the fact that each line, whether long or short, can be divided into lines, which themselves can always be further divided up, and this division cannot arrive at the point; hence no more points are contained potentially in one line than in any other.

It will therefore be impossible to divide the point from the line, since it is neither part of the line, nor does it contain unity for its subsistence. For the same reason, also the simple line cannot be constituted separate from the surface, and also the surface cannot be detached from the body. For neither of these two could succeed without separation of the point from the line. It is clear, however, that a line falls between two points. Two points are therefore bound to one another through a line; three points, however, through a simple surface, which is enclosed by three lines; four points, however, are held fast by a body in mutual combination. In the quinary such a connection, in which each point has been tied to another, is not possible, as you can experience in all figures.

If therefore the first surface, which nevertheless cannot subsist in itself, needs three points, four points are sufficient, which for the four surfaces are necessary for the solidity of the first body. One conjectures that four elements are necessary for the composition of the perfect. It is certain that everything which now transcends the quaternary of points, is not the first solid body, but rather is composed from the first, just as in a quadrangular surface, which requires four points and can be resolved in a triangular one, the first, triangular one, which cannot be traced back to a prior one, is the principle of multiangular figures.

Therefore, from four elements you will not elicit more than six lines, and from these no more than four surfaces, as you can intuit, if you wish, visibly in the tetrahedron, which possesses four points, six lines, and four triangular surfaces. Hence there are four prime elements, from which six arise and by means of which then four again. You see that this all must come together for the composition of a perfect, or solid, actually subsisting body, as the tetrahedron, which is the first solid figure, reveals. The progression of the four prime elements into the prime composition arising from these constitutes the most imperfect entity of this region, so that its unity dwells in flux and constant mutability.

However, since the prime elements must be such that they can combine with one another, it is certain that they are unequal and diverse. Hence one thing arises if the one unified the rest, another if they are unified in another. Each of the elements therefore can enfold in itself the three others, as in the cone of a three-sided pyramid, such that the unity of one is the actuality of the other elements, and thus a composition arises peculiar to each element.

Hence there are four prime compositions. In the simpler, brighter, and more unified element, the three others, constricted in the sensible region, have the name fire; contracted in the grosser and darker element, they bear the name earth; in the middle, which approaches lucidity, they are called air; in the lower, denser region, they receive the appellation water. But those things which commonly are called elements, are these four most general things, which have arisen first from the elements and which enfold in themselves the more specific combinations.

V.
How the Element Is in That Which Has Arisen from It

However, in order that in a conjecture you may receive help in understanding how the element exists in that which has arisen from it, look at the first figure (see Figure 4). For if you imagine the universe as fire or air, water or earth in the larger circle, then you will intuit that the circles of the other three elements are contained in it; and also, that the other three elements are in the air of the fire, etc., and this process does not go beyond the quaternary. Therefore, one comes from the universal to the specific in a quaternary progression. Therefore, the one element has enfolded in itself three universally, the three have nine in themselves generally, the nine have 27 enfolded in themselves specifically. The cube of the ternary is therefore the unfolding of the species unity of each element. The species, however, enfolds its specific elements, just as the Latin language, taken as a species, possesses its specific elementary letters. Hence, just as a Latin speech consists of most universal, general, more specific, and finally most specific contracted Latin letters, which, although they are only a few, nevertheless are of inexhaustible power, so everything sensible is, as it were, like a perfect speech.

The unfolding of each individual species is therefore inexhaustible and not unfoldable. For the power of the force of its unity embraces the number, which can never be ended in time, just as the unity of the Latin language embraces the number of unspeakably many speeches. You have heard that the infinite coincides with unity. Thus the infinite of individuals is the specific unity. Thus everything which is smaller than the infinite, is also smaller than its unity. No number can therefore be as large as the force of the specific unity. Therefore, the universality of the elements ascends to the most specific as the point to the body, by means of the line and the surface, or as the letters to speech by means of syllables and words, as potentiality to actuality. And that which has arisen from the elements descends in the most specific way to the most universal element, without which it cannot subsist, just as actuality into possibility. For the individual is, as it were, the end of the flux of the elements and the beginning of their reflux; the most general is, as it were, the beginning of their flux and the end of their reflux. The most specific force, however, contracts the generality of the elements in the circumference of its region, and it causes the once contracted to flow out, in order that it turn back to generality. According to this similitude the ocean is called the universal mother of rivers; through the general water courses, it is ultimately contracted in the fountainhead in a most specific manner, where the rivulet originates; and finally the rivulet turns back to the ocean. Thus according to this similitude one must imagine the universal element as the ocean and the most specific as the fountainhead. However, it is sufficiently evident to you that no science can attain the precise composition of the elements, since it is impossible for two things to be able to participate equally in the nature of the elements. Likewise the proportion of the difference of the one and the other is in no manner knowable. Since, therefore, science does not attain the point, knowledge of the gradations of the elements runs together with ignorance, such that in more confused and more general knowledge the ignorance is smaller, in the more singular, however, as a result of presumption, the deficiency is greater. Thus you see that the medicinal science, like every other which relies upon measurements, cannot evade conjecture.

VI.
Explanation

In order to apprehend the true intellectually, you may not ignore what I have often repeated. For you must understand unity as simultaneously participable and not participable; then you will gain the capacity to understand what is said. Unity is not participable in its precise simplicity. Since, however, there is no multitude without participation in it, it is indeed not so as it is, yet is participable in otherness. For this reason rationality intuits participability of unity in otherness.

However, when unity proceeds to otherness, it comes to rest in the quaternary. The quaternary is therefore participable unity. Everything which participates in unity must hence participate in it in the quaternary. Therefore, corporeal unity is participable not otherwise than in quaternary otherness, the unity of the original not otherwise than in the quaternary otherness of the original, the unity of color not otherwise than in quaternary otherness. It is likewise with the unity of the truth, which is participable only in the quaternary otherness, of that which one can call similitude or unfolding.

Actuality is unity, which can only be participated in in otherness, therefore actuality is not participated in except in potentiality, since this is its otherness. Divinity is absolute actuality, which is participated in in the supreme creatures in the supreme potentiality, which is to understand; in the median creatures in the median potentiality, which is to live; in the lowest in the lowest, which is to be. And even the unity of a tone or of a taste or of an odor or of anything sensible is not otherwise than fourfold in the manner explained in the first part. Therefore, the participable unfolding of unity is resolved into the quaternary.

Hence we conjecture four elements of all participable unities which are found differently in every participating thing. Everything which can be given that participates in the unity of color, participates in it in quaternary otherness. It is likewise for taste, for odor and all others; there can therefore be no color, except in quaternary otherness. However, because there can be no color in simple unity, each possible color emanates quadruply from the simple; it is the same for all elements, since neither their simple combination, nor anything whatever is participable in its simplicity.

Unity is, however, a certain precision, which is not participable except in otherness. Hence the precision of vision is not communicable without otherness. Therefore, the certitude which is in vision, is in no way participable without otherness. Therefore, the simplicity of certitude is not participable, as it is in vision, through a representation either of hearing or of any other sense. The precision of color, as it is perceived through vision, can be communicated to a blind person through no speech. Also the sight of the city, Rome, or of any other form cannot be communicated in its precision to someone who does not see. You see that the true is imparticipable other than in otherness. Therefore, the one true name of each thing is necessarily imparticipable and ineffable as it is. Effable names therefore participate in the true, only intellectual name in otherness in the rational ground or cause, because rationality is the otherness of intellectual unity. Therefore, according to some cause or rational ground, for example the material, *homo* signifies men, because he is from the earth, *humus*. However, in this cause the three other elemental causes must be included in their mode for the constitution of the quaternary, although this cause seems to stand out. You can see clearly enough on the basis of yourself, that this argument, that he is man because he is from the earth, does not suffice. Therefore, participation in unity takes its point of origin in quaternary otherness.

However, it is certain that every unity which is thus participable, can be participated in this side of the infinite and beyond every possible number. For the unity of your countenance, Julian, is participable in the otherness of similitude beyond every possible number, however on this side of the infinite; indeed, the number of eyes cannot be given without their being able to participate in this itself in the otherness of the similitude, although progression to the infinite is prohibited. The same is true of the unity of the voice, which as you see is participated in by innumerable ears, etc. Therefore, we come from the multitude of things participating in some unity to the general elementation of this quaternary otherness; since we know that the many participate in the one in different ways, we see that the difference arises from the fourfoldness. Everything colored must therefore be differentiated in color, but the differences can be resolved into the four elemental colors, in which every color participates variously. The same is true of all sensible and all natural and artificial things.

Indeed, participation in the unity of grammatical art cannot occur without the elemental othernesses. For every grammatical speech participates in the unity of this art in elements. Thus every art has its elements. The variety of the multitude of the arts admonishes us to investigate the fourfold elemental participation of all the arts. Thus the variety of the multitude of the sensible, rational and intellectual things shows, that there are four elements of sensible, rational and intellectual nature. This, together with that which was mentioned before, may suffice for the generality of the art of conjecture, so far as it relates to the root of the elements.

However, if you wish to go into the particularity of the elements, you must utilize the rules proportional to the regions. For just as you conjecture that in the sensible world the sensible elements are fire, air, water, earth, so in the rational nature conceive of them as rational elements, so that rationality is, as it were, fire-like, air-like, water-like and earth-like and that all rationality participates in the unity of rationality in these rational elements. Likewise, in the intellectual region conceive of the intellectual elements symbolically. And so that you can form conjectures, imagine the elements, as it were, as the four unities

1, 10, 100, 1000; for the unities of the elements of the same one must be differentiated. However, how the one is participated in in quadruple unity, is presented sufficiently in the foregoing. The unity is participated in, as it were, in the simplicity of simple, tenfold, hundredfold, and thousandfold unity in variously different ways by everything which has arisen from the elements, so that, as it were, the imparticipable simple is participated in through its help. You see now, on the basis of the similitude of the unities, that you must conjecture the subtle and the gross and two middle elements in the sensible world sensibly, in the rational rationally, in the intellectual intellectually.

You must concentrate totally here, Julian. For the absolute Unity itself, which is also the super-ineffable Truth as it is, remains imparticipable. The being of intelligence, however, is to understand, that is indeed to participate in the truth. This, however, is not participable as it is, but rather remains eternal and most absolute infinity. It is also not participable in the otherness of our rationality, since our rationality is the otherness of intelligence. Therefore, we participate in it in the intellectual otherness above all rationality. Spiritual intelligences participate, therefore, in an ineffable manner in the absolute truth in intellectual otherness by means of four intellectual elements in variously different ways, just as the unity of that thus-participating intelligence is participated in in the variety of rational souls by means of rational elements, and the unity of rationality is participated in in the otherness of sensible things by means of sensible elements in varied ways, as for example the rational concept of the triangle in the various sensible triangles.

And because it is necessary that those things which participate in unity in otherness participate variously, the one participates in unity more perfectly and more nearly, the others, however, more otherwise and more remotely. That participation will be beautiful in which the force of unity shines forth in otherness more harmoniously and more unitedly. Thus the visible color is more pleasant to the sight, in which the variety of its colors shines forth in the unity, and the ear is pleased to hear the variety of sounds in unity or harmony. The same is true of all the senses, rationality and intelligence.

Therefore, this joy is ineffable, when someone attains the unity of infinite truth in the variety of intelligibly true things.

For, he sees intellectually in the otherness of visible things the unity of all beauty, he hears intellectually the unity of all harmony, he tastes the unity of the sweetness of everything delectable, he apprehends the unity of the causes and rational bases of all things; he embraces everything in the truth, which he alone loves, with intellectual joy.

VII.
On the Senary, Septenary and Denary

A progression which returns circularly to itself, is counted by means of the senary. A progression, however, which does not return to itself, but rather leads to another, to a likeness, is subsequent to the senary and is counted by means of the septenary. However, then two progressions are necessary, which are measured by means of the denary. Look at this seriatim.

That unity coincides with infinity intellectually, you have already seen. Absolute Unity coincides therefore with absolute Infinity, the intellectual with the intellectual, the rational with the rational, just as the sensible unity coincides with the sensible infinity. Every unity exists as imparticipable, indivisible, and incorruptible. Absolute Unity therefore is not participable except in intellectual otherness; the intellectual is not except in rational otherness, the rational is not except in sensible otherness. God, who is absolute Unity, can therefore not be attained except intellectually, intelligence cannot be attained except rationally, and rationality cannot be attained except sensibly. Thus absolute Unity descends into intellectual infinity, intellectual unity into rational infinity, and rational unity into sensible infinity; sensible unity, however, ascends into rational infinity, rational unity into intellectual infinity, and intellectual unity into the absolute, superdivine infinity.

Herein rationality counts the senary. For the beginning of this flux and the end of the reflux coincide in the absolute Unity, which is the absolute Infinity; likewise the end of the flux and the beginning of the reflux coincide in sensible unity; the two middle terms are doubled; thus six are yielded at the same time. Consider this cycle in the figure (see Figure 5).

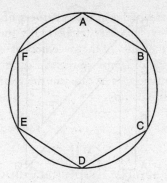

Let *A* be the absolute Unity, *B* the intellectual unity, *C* the rational unity, *D* the sensible unity, *E* the rational unity, *F* the intellectual unity. Indeed, just as the radial chords inscribed by the circumference return completed in themselves, so the descent and ascent circle in the senary.

However, you must take notice of the fact that for the light to descend is nothing other than for the darkness to ascend, if you would embrace the truth. Indeed, that God is in the world is nothing other than that the world is in God; for the actual to proceed to the potential is nothing other than for the potential to come to the actual; for the point to ascend to corporeality is nothing other than for corporeality to descend to the point; for darkness to rise into the light is nothing other than for the light to descend into the darkness; for the potential of matter to proceed to the actuality of the form is nothing other than for the actual form to descend to the potential matter. Therefore, with intellectual acumen couple the ascent with the descent, so that you conjecture more truly. Through this intelligence conceive the perfectional cycle of the senary, so that you can intuit how the measure of perpetuity is ascribed to the senary, and how to progress from the most universal to the most specific is to return from the most specific to the most universal.

The septenary number of the progressions proceeds, however, from the senary, as time and succession proceed from perpetuity, which you find in the nature of generative and corruptible things. For while from the seed the tree comes forth and

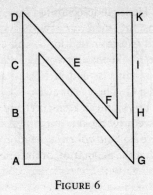

FIGURE 6

from the tree the seed, the septenary embraces both. The seed first ascends to the sprout, then to the shrub and finally to the tree, the tree descends to the branch, to the sprout and to the fruit or to the seed; this latter seed is, however, according to the number an other one than the first.

Since, therefore, the end does not here coincide in number with the first, but the end of the efflux coincides with the beginning of the reflux, so the septenary arises directly and then the denary (see Figure 6). For if *A* is the seed, *D* the tree, *G* another seed, *K* another tree, then *A* progresses through *B* and *C* to *D*, but *D* through *E* and *F* to *G*, and the septenary is concluded; but *G* ascends through *H* and *I* to *K*. Thus the full denary arises. The individual contraction of the species in the seed *A* is corruptible in itself, however, in the species incorruptible, since it has endeavored to preserve itself in the power of the species, which is contracted in it. Wishing to resolve itself again in the species, it gives up the individualization in the seed, in order to be able to elicit a likeness of itself by means of the species.

Therefore, it ascends in a quaternary progression to the tree, since without this means it cannot multiply itself in its specific similitude. Therefore, *G* aims to produce *G*, and because it cannot accomplish that without ascent toward *D*, it ascends toward *D*, in order to arrive thus at its aim. However, *D* is the existing tree, which sees that it cannot preserve itself except in a similar tree; it therefore strives toward *K*. However, it cannot attain K without G. Hence it descends to G, in order to be able to attain K by this means. In A therefore a twofold appetite is coupled: a natural one, which is terminated in G; and an accidental one, which ends in D. In D likewise a twofold appetite is coupled: a natural one, which obtains its end in K; and an accidental one, which is terminated in G. There is likewise in G a natural appetite that is imparted to it by A, and an accidental one, that is impressed on it by D. So you see how the one appetite stimulates and leads the other, so that there is an unbroken succession of generation and corruption, and so that the generation of the one is the corruption of the other. However, you observe that you cannot come to knowledge of these facts, except from two seeds and two trees, which are four things. You must therefore simultaneously fold together in your intellect the progression A, D, G and D, G, K, in order to adduce in an uninterruptible succession the coincidence of the end of one and the origin of the other.

You observe from this fact how, according to the aforesaid, the unity of the seed, which is imparticipable in itself, obtains participability in otherness, namely in the tree. Also, the unity of the tree, in itself imparticipable, obtains participability in the otherness of the seed. The unity, therefore, of the unity of the seed is its species contracted individually in this seed; this species unity, detached from its individual contraction, is received in the tree; since its power is unlimited, many seeds can participate in it. Therefore, according to the specific power of the seed, the general nutriment, and according to the nature of the tree, the location and circumstances, a plurality of seeds and their perfection is specified.

I have spoken here of the seed and the tree. However, strive to exhaust the universality, so that you may form conjectures accordingly with regard to minerals, plants, animals and all sensible things. Also utilize this figure symbolically with regard to the rational and the intellectual. For from the seed of admiration arises the rational tree, which produces similar fruits for admiration, and this tree of rationality thus erects a tree of rationality similar to itself through the admiration elicited by it. Correspondingly, the intellectual tree proceeds from the seminal beginning of a demonstration, which exserts the seminal beginning from itself, through which an intellectual again ascends.

VIII.
On the Difference of Individual Things

It is sufficiently well known to you that in sensible things the seeds and similarly the trees are individuals. You see also that in animals, which are like trees, some are masculine, others are feminine; likewise some seeds must also be masculine and others feminine. Therefore, if you imagine the Figure P (page 76), where the descending light signifies actuality and the shadow potentiality, the species will show you that in the species the actuality absorbs the potentiality and vice versa, and that accordingly the individuals participate in its nature. If, in order to be more specific, the actuality is resolved into Figure P, then the light will be the masculinity of actuality, and the shadow its femininity; it is likewise in regard to potentiality.

However, it is necessary to differentiate both the masculine as well as feminine. For no masculine individual can be found which agrees precisely in its masculinity with another, and there can also be none that is the maximum masculine. Therefore, in all masculinity femininity is absorbed in different ways. Hence, we also see, that in masculine animals, feminine characteristics, for example the indications of breasts, appear. Likewise seeds also act in a contrary manner. Every individual absorbs the other in its singular individualization, as in your individual masculinity femininity is absorbed; just as the seed, from which a being of masculine seed came into actuality, has overcome femininity, so femininity in its manner absorbs masculinity. The masculine seed contracts the feminine in itself and in its potentiality embraces the actual masculine and feminine. It is the opposite in regard to the feminine seed.

We know that these individuals participate in the species in varied ways. Some participate more perfectly in the species as seeds, some as trees. The more ignoble and potential a species is, the more perfectly the seeds participate in its nature. The more noble and perfect, formal and actual a species is, the more do the trees participate in its nature, and where the trees participate in it more perfectly, that species is more perfect which is more masculine, and where the seeds participate more perfectly, that species is more perfect which is more feminine. Hence the pear tree is more noble than the pear and the masculine lion more noble than the lioness and the seed of the lion. It is the reverse, however, with wheat, where the seed is better than the chaff, etc. Where the tree participates more in the conditions of the incorruptible species, since it produces the fruit from itself and nevertheless retains the power to produce further fruits, the tree participates more in the perfection of the species. However, where the seed contracts the nature of the incorruptible species more, and the power of the tree is exhausted with its production, because it has passed over entirely into the seed, as with grains of wheat, white wheat, oats and the like, the grain or the seed is more perfect, and indeed so much the more noble, the more feminine. No seed, however, can be found, which is so feminine and so much in potentiality, that it could not be more in potentiality; likewise no tree is in such perfect actuality, that it could not be still more so.

Therefore, all possible individual things participate in these differences variedly and differently. Indeed, the tree participates in the nature of the seed more as sapling and less as the stem, the child participates in the nature of the seed more in childhood than in youth. However, the perfect tree, which participates in the nature of the species more perfectly, because it proceeds from the potentiality of the seed to the actuality, will produce, in that it holds fast to the unfolded nature of the seed, a fruit in the likeness of this seed. And because the tree is, as it were, an extended channel for the power of the seed, so it digests the sap in itself and specifies it according to its extended nature. It specifies perfectly, if the power of the seed was perfect and perfectly extended, and if its nutriment was perfect and perfectly specifiable. Both must therefore be observed.

Hence, we see, that a grain in rich soil, on account of the noble nutriment, yields grains which are more perfect than it itself, although this only occurs successively, since in the first year they are not yet so perfect as in the following. On the other hand, we see that the best grain in infertile soil yields ignoble fruit, although not so ignoble as another, less noble grain. Hence, successively, a noble grain, on account of the disproportion between the nutriment and its nobility, becomes similar to the ignoble one. Therefore, based on the diversity of nutriment and location, the individuals must necessarily vary.

Also pay attention to the fact that, although the nutriment is specified and its potentiality is absorbed in the formal power of the species, its nature nevertheless cannot be fully and totally absorbed by all, as you see, when a pear shoot is grafted to an apple tree. Namely, the sap made specific to apples in the trunk of the apple tree is formed specific to pears in the grafted pear shoot, and it is individualized in a pear. Nevertheless, this pear is not entirely free of the nature of the apple, although this is concealed in the pear and occurs less, the stronger the power of the shoot. In the course of time, the specific power of the pear branch successively diminishes and it manifests more of the nature of the apple. The same is true in respect to location; a German in Italy is more German in the first year than in the second; for the location successively characterizes the one transplanted into this location according to the strength of the local nature. As we experience this sensibly in the sensible world, so also rationally in the rational world, as for example, in morals and customs and in the doctrines of rationality, which are, as it were, alimentation. Also in the intellectual world you should pay heed to this intellectually.

IX.
On the Different Modes of Being

From this you can sufficiently conjecture my intention and, if you want, you can conceive both the difference of conjectures as well as that of conjecturers in a kind of general art. For just as the confused sensible are other than the verisimilar rational, and these other than the true intellectual, the conjecturers are also different. Some run hither and thither in confused sensibility, some ratiocinate from principles, some are free for intellectual abstraction.

The conjectural unity, which proceeds to the conjecturable, has its four elements, namely, subtlety, grossness, and two middle elements. Indeed, in the most acute subtlety the conjecture proceeds as it were like fire upwards, and intuits the mode of being of things in a kind of absolute Unity or Necessity. Through earthly or gross conjecturing one forms a dark mode of being in possibility. One effects two other modes of being: One of them approaches to absolute Necessity; it is this mode, without which a true thing cannot be understood. And this is the mode of the second necessity or consequence. Indeed, if one presupposes that the truth of humanity is necessary, then that follows necessarily; without that it cannot be.

The other essential mode is closer to possibility and lies above the latter, but underneath the aforementioned. It has less necessity and more possibility, since it is an actual mode of being.

You can see that in Figure P, where unity is necessity, otherness is possibility, and everything, according to what you have heard, can be reduced to the same.

Therefore, a conjecturer hunts down the variety of modes of being very easily with the figural art, and indeed by the fact that he sees the one mode is taken up in the other and absorbed. And he differentiates and assembles the variety of the participants in these modes of being, in order to conceive the same thing in the dark possibility corresponding to this mode of being and in actuality corresponding to another mode of being. And likewise he also attains the modes of conjecturing and the variety of the conjecturers who participate in these modes. He also attains the mode of duration, so that the mode of duration which belongs to the mode of being of absolute Necessity, is one, and another that which belongs to the mode of possibility. Infinite duration indeed belongs to absolute Necessity. For what is necessary simply, cannot be other. It does not therefore proceed to otherness; hence it is absolute Eternity. The possible mode of being, however, is only in otherness. The actual has some stability and much possibility; the second necessity has much stability and little otherness. Therefore, he distinguishes the modes of being of motion and finally he contracts these and similar modes of being, so that one conjectures them sensibly in the sensible world, rationally in the rational world, intellectually in the intellectual world.

Also one conjectures that these modes of being of the three domains are connected with one another, so that the universe is one. Hence he admits the highest sensible necessity as rational possibility, and affirms that the highest and necessary rationality is the intellectual possibility. Thus he sees that the four modes of being are resolved into the denary, which is the universal number.

X.
On the Differences of Beings Composed Out of the Soul and the Body

Look at Figure P (page 76) and let unity be the soul, but otherness, the body. Corporeality proceeds upwards into spirituality, the spirit proceeds downwards into corporeality. Because the descent of the spirit is the ascent of the body, you must combine both, in order to conceive the difference of bodies from the difference of souls and likewise to conjecture the difference of this soul from the body.

Indeed, that the human soul causes its body to differ from the bodies of other living creatures, ensues likewise from the fact that such a body requires a different spirit. The Platonic-being of Plato is different from all men, and this difference arises equally from the unity of the soul as from the otherness of the body. Therefore, whoever wishes to investigate the disposition of souls by means of the sensible, as for example physiognomy, intuits the body and hunts down the difference of the spirit based upon the differences and agreements of the same with other men and living creatures. Hence it is that we experience ourselves as weak in the flesh but willing in mind.

The progressive motion of animals, according to which animals are differentiated from vegetation, must be referred not only to the needs of the body, but also those of the soul. For an animal changes not only its location in order to gather necessary nutriment, but also in order to perfect the operation of its soul. One animal surpasses another not only in flying, in running, or in industry, because the preservation of its condition requires this, but also because its spirit asks for this. Thus man is not provided with greater rationality, so that he knows to sow, to plant, to conduct business, to build houses, to weave, to cook and the like for the sake of his corporeal needs, but rather the Supreme Maker instituted it such that this rational nature would descend into the body, so that the body would ascend to the rational; for the sensible body is subject to rationality and the body does not need these things except for the sake of the spirit. Indeed, as the body seems to desire such a rational nature on account of its needs, so also this subtle spirit requires such a noble body, because it needs these things. The spirit does not otherwise exist for the sake of the body, than that the body exists for the sake of the spirit; indeed, the spirit returns above itself. Therefore, every sensible creature is differentiated from every other, whereby the difference connected with it arises from the difference of the spirit and the body. However, every spirit necessarily differentiates itself from every other spirit, and every body from every other body.

However, there is no difference without agreement. Hence every spirit must at the same time agree with and differ from every other. This cannot occur equally. It agrees more with the one, less with the other, but in simplicity with none maximally or minimally. Therefore, since every spirit is different from every other spirit, such that it always differentiates itself less through the difference, which can always be smaller, without however proceeding to infinity, it differentiates itself in an improportionate proportion, such that the proportion between one spiritual nature and another can always be more proportional, without a progression into infinity occurring. Precision in the difference of proportions is therefore unattainable. A spirit therefore agrees with another spirit in an agreeing difference; hence a darker spirit is to a more lucid spirit according to Figure P; for the unity of the spirit progresses into otherness and the spiritual otherness regresses into unity.

In the supremely noblest spirits the dark, sensible otherness is absorbed in intellectual clarity. In the inferior spirits, on the contrary, the spiritual unity, which can be called intellectual, is absorbed in spiritual otherness. Hence the vegetative spirit conceals in its darkness the intellectual; and certain signs of it appear in the branches as support, in the leaves and in the skin as protection of the fruit. Nevertheless, we experience more intellectual signs among animals, where the spirit is clearer; for we experience the signs of intellectual vigor more clearly and nearly in the senses, still more in the imagination and more amply in rationality. Among those living creatures endowed with ratiocination there are again clearer signs of providence among men than among the creatures. Hence we conjecture here a more lucid intelligence. We thus affirm that in the intelligent spirits the sensible nature is concealed and absorbed in intellectual light. However, we conceive that the rationality of the soul is the mean between the lowest and the supreme part of the soul, and that therefore in certain creatures it participates more in the superior nature of intellectual unity, in others, on the other hand, more in the inferior otherness.

Hence we said that in the inferior world everything is according to the nature of this world; in the median world medianly; and in the supreme supremely, namely, according to the mode of its nature. The sense which is in plants, through which they sense the most intense cold and excelling heat, is of a vegetative nature. The sense of animals is of an animal nature; the sense in intelligent beings is of the intellectual nature. The same is true for rationality and the intellect. The intellectual subtlety in plants, through which a plant puts forth branches in order to gain support for its weight, is of a vegetative nature. The intellectual subtlety in animals, through which they hunt and attend to gains for their future needs, is of an animal nature. In the supreme, however, the intellectual subtlety is wisdom, which leads to the truth itself. In its manner every spirit therefore participates in the elements of the spiritual nature, just as the body participates in those of the corporeal. These are most manifest to you in the frequently stated, since there is one method for all progressions.

If among all living creatures you let unity be the soul and the body be otherness, then conceive that what you see in the body in a corporeal and unfolded manner, is in the soul in the manner of the soul as in an enfolding power, and indeed as in the power of the unity of the same unfolded corporeal nature. In your body you see that the head, hands, and feet differ in their tasks according to the gradation of their nobility; likewise imagine in the soul the intellect in effect as head, rationality as hands, and the senses as feet; indeed, just as the body walks and is conveyed with corporeal feet, so the soul itself also proceeds with the senses in the manner of the soul to sensible things, and it employs rationality as hands and the intellect as a power, which unifies the senses, so that the intellect is the head and the more noble part in the soul.

The intellect in the ambit of intellectual power is as the eyes in the head. Through such symbolic hunting ascend from the unfolding of corporeal nature to the power of the soul and conceive the power of the soul of each living creature enfolded contractedly, so that you conjecture the unfolded variety of the body. Conceive that the soul of a lion possesses in effect an intellectual head, rational hands, and sensible feet, according to the contraction of its unity, which is leoninity, just as we affirm that this is the case in man humanly, etc.

You can deduce the universal distinction of the body from our figure by means of the same rational deliberation, according to which you can deduce everything. For if you let the corporeal subtlety be the unity of light, and the grossness be otherness, you will easily intuit what you seek. Likewise, if you will hunt down the variety of compositions, then take the unity of the light as well-harmonized, optimally compacted, and unified, and take otherness as variable, not compacted, and as disharmony rather than harmony. If you will investigate the spiritual body or the corporeal spirit, then you also observe, that between the luminous spirit, which descends into the dark body, and the returning corporeal grossness, fall two median connections, the one more spiritual, the other one, however, more corporeal.

But also the former, which is nearer to the spirit, does not give up all corporeal latitude; hence one could call it spiritual body. The other, more depressed one, nearer to corporeal grossness, which, however, does not give up all spiritual latitude, may be called the corporeal spirit. And thus you consider three gradations of the descending spirit and three of the ascending body, from which in its manner the universe and everything which is in it exist. Indeed, we experience that there is a soul or a certain spiritual nature in living creatures. We experience that the corporeal spirit, which is included in the arteries, is the vehicle of the connection of the soul. We experience that there is a certain light or a corporeal spirit, through which the power of the soul operates in the body and in the sensible, so that the power of the soul is attached to the body with its help, in order to carry on its activities. This descent of the connection of the soul is also the ascent of the body, because the latter is made so subtle, that it is more suitably united with the spirit. However, all sensible things participate in their manner in that which in the one sensible thing is found clearer and more incorruptible, in the other obscurer and more corruptible, according to the general and specific differences and agreements.

XI.
On Life

If you want to intuit life in its differences, be it of form or spirit or something else, then resolve it first in Figure P on the basis of the unity of the light and the otherness of darkness. And thus you see that noble life, in whose clear unity all otherness is absorbed. However, you intuit another, whose unity is enveloped in the otherness of the fluxible and instable darkness. And if you take life itself in the universal figure as the universe, then you can distinguish three lives radically, quadratically, and cubically. Hence, through this method you attain conjecturally an incorruptible life, one that is alterable yet more incorruptible, and one that is more alterable and corruptible, and their subdivisions. However, because between the life in which the victory of otherness induces the corruptibility and dissolubility of unity, and the life in which the victory of unity produces incorruptibility, there can be no identical middle, which would be neither corruptible nor incorruptible, it is nevertheless with respect to the nature of the aforesaid differences, just as we have most frequently said.

So that the inferior life is united with the superior in the unity of the universe, it will be necessary that the superior be conjoined with the inferior. Therefore, this one composition, existing from the life in which unity triumphs, and from the life in which otherness triumphs, proceeds to otherness according to the conditions of the inferior and is therefore enveloped with corruptibility, according to the nature of the superior; however, it also approaches the unity of incorruptibility. It is therefore certain, that such a composition exists from corruptible and incorruptible life and this differently among the participants in this connection. The death of such is therefore not other than the death of another mortal. For because of the flux of otherness it strives towards dispersion. The stable unity of incorruptible life therefore remains, when the alterable unity falls away from the harmonic root of its unity. However, the intellectual life, elevated to incorruptible truth, does not know to move towards corruptible otherness. Therefore, the lowest specific gradation of this nature, which is little in actuality and almost as if in potentiality, possesses a certain participability in connection with fluxible life, indeed not such that it would furnish fluxible life the vigor of stability, but rather such that it is moved rationally as the consequence of its connection with it through admiration of sensible things, and in dormant potentiality it is awakened and excited to actuality.

It is not possible to multiply this specific gradation of the connection of both lives, so that there were several species of this connection, although it is necessary that the individuals participate in this species in varied ways. The indissoluble life is therefore the intellectual; but the dissoluble is the sensible; the median, however, which is nearer to the intellectual, is rational, noble and intellectual, which one can also call the intellectual sense; the rational, however, which approaches the senses, is ignoble or imaginative, and one can call it the sensible intellect. Therefore, the superior rationality, which participates in the intellect, is connected with the inferior rationality of the sensible nature in the human species. Through such a conjecture you can attain that which a discourse on life can hunt down.

XII.
On Nature and Art

Nature is unity, art otherness, because it is the similitude of nature. God, in intellectual language, is at the same time absolute nature and art, although it is the truth that He is neither nature, nor art, nor both. However, since precision is unattainable, we are admonished to believe that there can be nothing which is only nature or art: Indeed, everything participates in both in its manner. One easily conceives that the intelligence, insofar as it emanates from divine rationality, participates in art. However, insofar as it exserts art from itself, we see it as nature. Indeed, art is, as it were, the imitation of nature. That some things are indeed natural sensible things, others artificial things, is obvious. But it is not possible that the natural sensible things are destitute of art, and likewise the artificial sensible things cannot be without nature. Language proceeds from art, which is based upon nature, so that the one language is more natural than the other, another, however, less natural. To ratiocinate is also natural for man, however, not without art. Hence the one is without doubt more capable than the other in the art of ratiocinating. For, as in language, which cannot be possessed without art, the natural unity of rationality shines forth, so that from the language everyone, who and howsoever he may be, is known in his rationality and nature, so the art of him who ratiocinates manifests itself also in rationality.

If you want to investigate the differences of nature and art and the connection of both, then return to the frequently revealed guidance of the figure. Nature indeed consists of masculine unity and feminine otherness. In intellectual masculinity femininity is absorbed. It is therefore fertilized unitively in itself. In vegetative femininity otherness determines the masculine nature in itself; hence it fructifies unfoldedly. The nature of animals distinguishes the sexes, the man generates in the woman, the woman gives birth externally. In intelligent beings nature engenders intellectual fruit, in animals animal fruit, in vegetation vegetative fruit. The sensible nature obeys the rational, the rational the intellectual, the intellectual the divine. The sensibly formable thing obeys the rational art, the rational the intellectual, the intellectual the divine. As all nature is contracted sensibly in a sensible thing, so the formability is also contracted sensibly in a sensible thing, rationally in a rational thing.

Rationality is the unity of nature and of sensible art. Through the unity of rationality the sensible multitude of individuals is specified; just as also through the unity of rationality, which exists, for example, in the one art of shoe-making, innumerable shoes are produced. The unity of rationality therefore enfolds in itself the multitude of all natural and artificial sensible things. Therefore, it exserts from itself the rationality of natural and artificial things. The rationality of artificial things, however, is ordered to the end of the natural things. For the beginning and end of artificial things is nature. Therefore, the rational art, as for example to speak, to weave, to sow, to cook, etc., is ordered to the end of sensible nature, just as the art of intelligence is ordered to the end of rational nature.

XIII.
On the Intellectual Nature

Universal nature, as the circle of the universe, at first enfolds in itself the orbits of the three regions and natures—the intellectual, the rational and the sensible. The intellectual region, which absorbs the alterable darknesses in itself, is of the masculine, subtle, most unified, and most noble nature. The nature of the intelligence is neither extended, nor does the intellectual motion belong to the quantitative genus, except intellectually or virtually, so that simplicity, indivisibility and whatever else belongs to intellectual unity are not opposed to it. Indeed, its movement in otherness means nothing other than that otherness comes to unity more absolutely. For its unity descends into the intelligible rational, just as the intelligible ascends to the unity of the intellect. For it is the origin and the end of the intelligible rational, just as its origin and end is absolute unity. To attain union with the latter according to its intellectual nature is to strive upward and to repose in this motion, just as rationality rests in the intelligence, to which it cannot ascend, except through the descent of the intelligence and the emission of its participated light. Thus you should not conceive the rational quality of the nature of the intellect, but rather the rational altered similitude.

For the intellect has nothing adventitious, which succumbs to rationality or the senses; also, the intelligible nature is not localizable other than intellectually, indeed it is localizable such that it is also location. And indeed, this means it cannot be shown to be in a location through rationality or the senses. Therefore, it is not everywhere and nowhere absolutely, as God, but rather it is everywhere and nowhere in an intellectually contracted manner, just as humanity, which is contracted specifically, is everywhere and nowhere in this region of the species. So also our soul is everywhere and nowhere according to the contraction of the body; for it is in every part of this its region and nowhere. For it is in no part of the body such that it is in one location rather than in another. For as universals are in the intellect and their location is called intellect, so must this be understood according to the often repeated rule, namely, that the intellect is in the universals such that the latter are in it, as for example the president is in his realm, such that the realm is in him. The intelligent nature therefore is not movable, except from location to location in the manner in which it can be in a location.

Therefore, the intelligible nature moves intellectually in its realm, which is determined to it. And indeed this is a movement with which rest concurs, since it is an obeyer of the truth; as for example the movement of the president's command is compatible with the rest on the throne of the ruler. Indeed, intelligent beings are moved, as if resting in the center of their contraction or their realm, and we conceive this movement as that of judging. For intelligence is the judge of rationality, and it is said to be moved when it selects the one because it is truer and rejects the other, and when it illuminates and induces those who ratiocinate.

Intelligent beings must therefore be conceived as universal powers and as the rulers of rational contractions, and indeed, if they were to take the place of the sun in their regions, such that, as in this sensible world through the vigor of the sensible sun the eyes come sensibly to a judgment concerning the beautiful or ugly, in the rational world the intelligence provides vigor to the cognition of the true. However, the infinite God is the sun of intelligent beings, the intelligent beings in turn, as varied contracted lights, are that of rationality. In varied ways we see that rationality is contracted in the vegetative and animal beings according to their diverse genera and species, and from hence we conjecture that there are diverse ruling intelligent beings.

However, intelligent beings are not numerable through a rational number as sensible things, rather their intellectual number, which is indeterminable and unrepresentable through rationality, is as the light of rationality and rational number. For, just as unity is numerable through no number, but rather itself counts all numbers, so also intelligence is not discernible through rationality, but rather only through the most absolute and most divine unity itself. Where being counted and counting, distinction and non–distinction tend toward coincidence, admittance is precluded to rationality.

In similitude to that which has often been stated, derive from the figure in a conjecture, that the variety of intelligent beings participate variously in the singlemost truth theophanically with diversity of mediation, so that some, as if intellectual, are more mediate and most elevated from all potentiality to actuality, others are as if intelligible and nearer to mastery, finally others come nearer to rational potentiality, so that they require doctrinal elevation.

And if you also want to fabricate conjectures concerning the darker spirits of this region, whose intelligence slumbering in the otherness of dark ignorance is crucified, which sunken rather in servile custody and in sensibly submerged rationality receive the deceptive incitements of their veiled intelligence, so that the perpetual is absorbed in corruptibility, the light in darkness; and concerning the different natures of these demonic spirits, and indeed how there are in the intellectual region more sensible spirits as it were, which live in sensible temptations and mingle with the inferior, and how there are others in the middle location, who as rational intelligences are the rulers of the spheres and their movements, but which are not under the command of the superior spirits, which are more nearly inflamed by divine illumination, then achieve this yourself from the aforesaid by means of symbolic measurement.

However, I would like you always to be most attentive not to fall into the view that these presiding spiritual services, which they skillfully expend as envoys of the highest and maximum Ruler of the universe to the species, nations, language groups, congregations, realms and churches, have been assumed by them only for our sake, as it were, but rather they do this for our sake and for the sake of others, over whom they preside, so that they constitute themselves as the end; thus the angelic spirits exist for our sake, just as we exist for their sake. For, if it seems to some who live under the rule of a king, that the royal care exists on their account, the king, if he reflects this in himself, makes himself no less the end of his care and the well-being of the people. Also, the obedience of the people and the diligence of the prince were not voluntary, if the people and the ruler did not conjecture that they would receive compensation respectively for their subjection or for his labor. Hence the natural ruler, who penetrates the law of the truth, combines these causes as much as possible into one, so that he believes that his own well-being also lies in the well-being of the people. May that, briefly summarized, so far as it was possible in this location, be sufficient said concerning the nature of the intellectual spirit.

XIV.
On Man

In the common way conceive man from the unity of the light of human nature and the otherness of corporeal darkness and, in order to unfold him more distinctly, resolve him into the previous figure. You will intuit distinctly three regions in him: a lowest, a middle and a supreme, and these are differentiated thrice triply. You will conjecture that the more ignoble corporeal parts are at one time constantly fluctuating, but then gradually more stable and more formal and most noble. Subsequently conceive in a similar ascent the more spiritual nature of the body, with which the sensitive power is mixed; divide this into gradations, so that you can come to the more subtle from the more obtuse.

Also add the nine distinctions of the noble soul. You see the nine corporeal differences of the three orderings of man, which absorb in themselves the sensitive light, so that they are content with vegetative life. Then you see nine mixed, where the sensitive power, which is mixed with the sensible and corporeal, is vigorous. Finally you see nine nobler differences, where corporeal shadow is absorbed in the discriminative spirit. However, the corporeal nature climbs upward stepwise to the sensitive, and indeed such that its ultimate ordering nearly coincides with the sensitive. Accordingly the sensitive is ennobled into the discriminative.

However, every sensation arises from an encounter. Hence, as many sensations are caused through an encounter with contingencies, so are others incited stepwise by more distant objects. Therefore, the sense of smell, which is effected in its organ, is also stimulated by distant objects on account of its nobler nature, so that a sensation arises. The hearing is stimulated by still more distant objects. However, the sense of vision excels all the other senses, so that it is incited to sensation by more distant objects.

The imagination, with its more absolute liberty, transcends the contraction of the senses in the quantity of mass, time, form and location, apprehends more and less than the sensitive nature, embraces that which is nearer, more distant and even absent, however, it does not abandon the genus of sensible things.

Rationality, however, also surpasses the imagination, for

example, it sees that the antipodes cannot fall away any more than we can, since the weight moves toward the center, which lies between them and us. However, the imagination does not attain that. It is therefore obvious, that rationality surpasses the imagination and that it attains everything more truly and unrestrictedly.

The intellect, however, is to the rationality as the power of unity is to the finite number, so that nothing of its power can entirely escape.

Marvelous is this work of God, in which the discriminative power ascends stepwise from the center of the senses up to the supreme intellectual nature, through certain steps and organic rivulets, in which the ligaments of the most subtle corporeal spirit are constantly illuminated and simplified, on account of the victory of the power of the soul, until one reaches the inner cell of rational power. After this one comes to the supreme order of intellectual power, as if by way of the brook to the unbounded sea, where we conjecture there are choirs of knowledge, intelligence, and the simplest intellectuality.

Since the unity of humanity is contracted in a human way, it seems to enfold everything according to the nature of this contraction. For the power of its unity embraces the universe and encloses it inside the boundaries of its region, such that nothing of all of its potentiality escapes, because it conjectures that everything is attained with the senses, rationality, or the intellect and that it enfolds these capabilities in its unity, when it sees itself and supposes it can advance to everything in a human way. Man is indeed god, but not absolutely, since he is man; he is therefore a human god. Man is also the world, but not everything contractedly, since he is man. Man is therefore a microcosm or a human world. The region of humanity therefore embraces God and the whole world in its human potentiality. Man can therefore be a human god and just as he can be god in a human way, so can he also be a human angel, a human animal, a human lion or bear or anything else. Within the potentiality of humanity everything indeed exists in its mode.

In humanity everything is therefore unfolded in a human way, as in the universe in a universal manner, because it exists as a human world. Everything then is enfolded in it in a human manner, since it is a human god. For humanity is unity, which is also infinity contracted humanly. However, because it is the condition of unity to unfold entity from itself, since it is the entity which enfolds entity in its simplicity; hence humanity has the power to unfold everything within the circumference of its region, to exsert everything from the potentiality of the center. However, it is the condition of unity to constitute itself as the end of the unfoldings, since it is infinity.

Therefore, there is no other end of the creative activity of humanity than humanity. When it creates, it does not go outside of itself, but rather when it unfolds its power, it comes to itself. Nor does it effect something new, but rather all that it creates through unfolding, it experiences to have existed in itself. Indeed, we said that the universe exists in it in a human way. Indeed, as the power of humanity is able to advance to everything in a human manner, so can the universe enter into it. That this wonderful power traverses and proceeds to everything, is not other than that it enfolds the universe in it in a human way.

However, you have heard, Father Julian, concerning the absolute triune Origin, the Creator of the universe, how He is the omnipotent Creator, because He is the absolute Unity or Entity, in whom exist infinite equality and connection. And because He is the infinite equality, in which unity and connection exist, He is therefore the ruler, orderer and governor of the universe. Because He is the infinite connection, in which unity and equality exist, He is therefore the preserver of the universe.

Affirm that in the same way one must conjecture contractedly about humanity. It is indeed the contracted origin of its creation, order, government, and preservation, because it is the unity, in which equality and connection exist. It is the equality, in which unity and connection exist. It is the connection, in which unity and equality exist, insofar as you reduce the terms in their significance to the contraction of humanity. In the power of humanity man creates in the superior sensible part, that is, in that of the phantasy, similitudes or images of sensible things, since he is the unity, in which equality and connection exist.

He orders and locates these created images, because he is equality, in which unity and connection exist. Thereafter, he retains them in memory, because he is the connection, in which unity and equality exist. In the intellectual region he acts intellectually through creating, ordering, and preserving and likewise in the middle, rational region. However, he refers this entirely back to himself, so that he can understand, govern, and preserve himself; and thus man approaches deiformity, where everything rests in eternal peace.

XV.
On the Same

If you, however, propose to put forth the agreements and differences of the totality of men by means of your conjectures, then pay attention to the figure of the universe, and let the human species be contracted in the larger circle. Then you see in the species of humanity such men, who are contemplative and more abstract and are occupied principally in conversation with the intellectual and eternal, as it were, in the supreme heaven of humanity; and they are as the intellect of this species and have time for speculation concerning the true. Then there are others as the rationality of this species, who stand ahead of the inferior, as it were, sensible men. The first are the wise, the clearest and purest lights, who bear the effigy of the spiritual, incorruptible world. The last are the sensible, who follow concupiscence and voluptuousness like animals. The median participate in the influence of clarity from the superior and stand ahead of the inferior. Hence in the unity of the species the multitude of men come to participate in these three parts in a general manner in respect to the entire species.

Furthermore, you intuit in the part of religion or of contemplation three, more specific, different parts, since the one is a certain multitude of men, who participate therein in a lofty and noble manner above all rationality and all the senses, a second, however, is that which contracts it into a certain rationality, a lowest, which contracts it into sensibility.

And since, as you see in this way, a specific religion is inherent in all men by nature, which promises a higher, immortal end, it is participated in by the inhabitants of this world in varied ways, as you find in the universe. Therefore, the first, more abstract men, who participate in religion in the intellectual above all rationality and all the senses, expect a life which in its excellence surpasses all capacity of rationality and the senses. The second, however, which lead felicity back under the boundary of rationality, establish their end in the cognition and enjoyment of things. The third see it completely absurdly, in sensible delectation. Therefore, the first are distinguished triply, just as are the second and the third.

Intuit stepwise in this way the most general agreement and difference of all men; in the third heaven in regard to religion, in the second in regard to dominion, in the lowest in regard to subjection. However, these parts, which are derived from the species, although they persist in their generality everywhere incessantly, nevertheless undergo mutation in their specificity, since the precision of the truth can be achieved by us only in conjecture. In varied otherness, therefore, the intellectual unity of that religion is received and in the fluxible multitude that of the ruler of the second heaven is received fluxibly. So also the ruler's unity, which is also called the unity of the rational species, persists unstably in the fluxible multitude of the sensible subjects in the varied otherness of its mode.

Notice also, that although a religion or government appears stable for some time in a nation of this world, nevertheless this is not precisely the case. Indeed, the Rhine River has seemed to flow stably for a long time, yet it never remains in the same condition. Now it is more turbulent, now clearer, now swelling, now declining. Thus one can truly say, that it was already larger and smaller and that it has gone gradually from larger to smaller, nevertheless it is certain that it was never precisely as it is now. Thus religion also flows unstably between spirituality and temporality. The same is true of governing: It perseveres in suspension between greater and less obedience.

You can also hunt down conjecturally the variety of all the inhabitants of this world as regards condition, figure, vices and virtues, subtlety and grossness, by constituting the circle of the universe of inhabitants, which encompasses the north, south, east and west horizon, and establishing the higher world in the south, the inferior in the north, and the median in the middle. Therefore, there is an ascent of the human species from the north to the south and a descent from the south to the north. Thus all men who participate in the horizon in the supreme heaven are more vigorous in the intellect, those who participate in the middle heaven, more in rationality, those who participate in the lowest, more in the senses. In those northern regions, therefore, the intellect is more immersed in possibility and sensibility, so that they are, as it were, sensible men. In the middle region the intellect is vigorous in rationality, in the third region more abstract. Hence in Indian and Egyptian regions, the intellectual religions and the abstract mathematical arts predominate. In Greece, Africa, and Rome dialectic, rhetoric, and jurisprudence are vigorous. In the other, more northern regions the sensible mechanical arts. Nevertheless, all regions must possess people experienced in all these arts in their manner, so that the one nature of the one species is participated in variously in all.

In the same way if you turn your investigations to the corporeal disposition of men, then pay attention to Figure P. If you investigate the color of man, then make the north point the unity of light, the south that of darkness, and you will see, that the white men are in the north region, the black men in the south, however, you will see that those in the middle have a median mode. If you investigate the condition in this way, then you see that the middle are better conditioned, since the extremes there are brought quite harmoniously and concordantly to a certain combination in unity. In the northern you see an excess of coldness and undigested moisture. In the southern you see a lack thereof and an abundance of dryness, and you see that warmth thrives more in the interior through its contraction towards the center than in the colder regions, and in the warmer regions more in the extremes.

From this you can conjecture according to the difference of location concerning nutriment and instrument, habitations and customs, corporeal powers, infirmities and defects, the variety of form and stature. Thus if you conjecturally investigate the faults and virtues of peoples, then look at the same. For humanity, which begins its ascent to the Antarctic at the Arctic Pole, reaches the height and the end of its ascent under the equinoctial. However it ascends from this world to another. Therefore, it proceeds just like man, first in the age of growth, then in that of standstill, finally in that of decline.

Hence the habitude of men who occupy the inferior gradation and who inhabit the third part of the world and the first part of the ascent of the world, is to that of the others, as the habitude of that man in the period of life, in which he still exserts the powers of the body from potentiality to actuality, namely, between the age of a child and of a man. The northern regions therefore participate variedly in the faults which are characteristic of this time and similarly differently in the virtues of this period of life. The ones are indeed nearer to manhood, the others nearer to childhood; among them some people, the more eastern, are more austere, more masculine and more dexterous; the others, the more western, are more feminine, loquacious, reckless, pious and inconstant. Likewise, the middle peoples participate in the faults and virtues of this period of life between the age of adulthood and old age variedly and differently as regards east and west. The more southern, however, have faults and virtues which correspond to the time between old age and decrepitude.

Sufficient has been said concerning these comparisons. You can seek more distinct particulars from this yourself, if you wish.

XVI.
On the Human Soul

First, conceive from that which has been frequently said, the universe as from unity and otherness, and resolve that one universe into three regions, as the large figure shows you.

Say that to the first region the simple intelligent beings belong, in which the otherness of darkness is absorbed in the brightness of the light. Conceive that to the lowest region those natures belong, which through their corporeality have altered the light. Call the middle natures, if you wish, souls. The souls abide, indeed, in the middle, so that through them the descent of intelligence into the inferior region and the reflux of the inferior to the superior region occurs.

The first paradigmatic figure shows you, however, that the extremes are united, namely, that the supreme nature of the soul coincides with the lowest of the intellectual and its lowest with the supreme of the corporeal. Therefore, if you wish to investigate more distinctly the differences of souls, then make the large circle now into the universe of souls and in this universe observe three divisions: the radical, quadratic and the cubic. However, conceive intelligence of this universe as the simple unity, just as God is the unity of everything universally. You will intuit in all clarity, that the intelligence is united with all souls through a kind of universal conjunction, which is represented through the maximum circle; furthermore, you will intuit that it is united in a general manner with the souls of the first region, in a more specific way with the supreme order, but most specifically with the supreme choir, which is called the human species.

Every soul, therefore, participates in the unity of intelligence in otherness, the one more clearly, the other more obscurely, however, only the supreme souls are united with it in the most specific union. And this is the participation, through which the supreme of the inferior comes into coincidence with the lowest of the superior. That animals participate more clearly in intelligence than do plants, is brought about through the medium of the soul. However, the animal as genus has several species, which proceed in an ordered manner as the numbers from the unity of the genus. Of these that species is nobler and loftier, which is nearer to unity.

Therefore, the soul of the most perfect animal species, which advances to unity with the intellectual nature, also virtually enfolds in itself the other powers of all souls, as if in the genus of metal the species of gold is more perfect through its power and embraces all other metallic species; and in the genus of the ruling, the authority of the king unites in itself that of all dukes, counts, and other inferior rulers. Hence all the species of living beings unfold the united power of the human soul according to numerical progression and contract their nature in varied difference, the ones in a clearer, the others in a more obscure rationality. Nevertheless, no species is able to achieve equality precisely. However, since the human soul is the lowest intellectual nature, it is in potentiality intellectually; the intellectual potentiality, however, is the light of rationality.

Therefore, conceive the human soul according to Figure P, as from intellectual unity and sensible otherness. Therefore, if the light of intelligence descends into the sensual shadows and the senses ascend to the intellect in three steps, two arise in the middle, which I suppose to have the name of rationality. The superior part of this rationality, which is found closely connected to the intellect, is the apprehensive; the inferior, however, is the fantastic or imaginative; if one wishes, one can designate them with other names.

These are, as it were, the four elements of the human soul. However, the intellect descends in our soul to the senses so that the sensible things can ascend to it. The sensible thing ascends to the intellect, so that the intelligence can descend to it. The descent of the intellect to the sensible thing is indeed the same as the ascent of the sensible thing to the intellect. For something visible is not attained through the sense of vision, if the intention of the intellectual vigor is absent.

We experience that when, intent upon something else, we do not discern something transient. Indeed, the senses apprehend a sensible thing, which ascends to them, confusedly; however, this sensation is not formed and distinguished without the intellect, which descends to us through the medium of rationality; we also do not attain a sensible thing as such without the senses. Indeed, a blind person does not attain sensible colors. However, the intellect, which in respect to the intellectual region is in potentiality, is in respect to the inferior regions more in actuality. It is therefore in the sensible world in actuality. For in vision it actually apprehends the visible, in hearing the audible. In the senses, however, it is the senses, in the imagination, imagination, in rationality, rationality.

Indeed, the soul is nothing other than a noble and simple, unified power. Every part of its power, however, is verified by the whole. For since the sensitive and imaginative power of our soul is in the soul, it is the soul, as also the ducal power or the power of the count is royal power in the king, and as the royal power is ducal power in the duke. Since the soul is the vivification of the body, it is the vivification of the foot in the foot, and the vivification of the hand in the hand. And since the vivification of the soul is the soul itself, it is the corporeal unity of uniting otherness. Hence it is in every part as unity in number.

As the power of one who throws a stone upward elevates the heavy stone, and indeed such that the latter hastens downward in its cessation, so does the power of the soul move the body, and death is nothing other than the cessation of the vivifying power. Therefore, the soul is the vision in vision and the hearing in hearing.

Therefore, because the intellect is in the senses in actuality, dormant rationality is aroused through astonishment, so that it hastens to the verisimilar. Thereupon, the intelligence is struck, so that more detached from the dormant potentiality it may rise more vigilantly to cognition of the true. For it depicts the sensibly perceived in phantasy, and if it seeks their rationality, it advances to the actuality of the understood and to the knowledge of the true. Indeed, it unites the othernesses of the sensibly perceived in phantasy, it unites then the variety of the othernesses of phantasmata in rationality, and finally it unites the varied otherness of rationality in its simple intellectual unity. The unity of the intellect descends to the otherness of rationality, the unity of rationality to the otherness of the imagination, the unity of the imagination to the otherness of the senses.

Enfold, therefore, the ascent with the descent intellectually, so that you apprehend. It is indeed not the intention of the intellect to become the senses, but rather to become perfect and actual intellect; but because it cannot be constituted in actuality in another way, it becomes the senses, so that it can by this means proceed from potentiality to actuality. Thus the intellect returns above itself, in that it completes a circular motion; just as a noble man, who has the potential of military service, however, because of his poverty cannot conduct this in actuality, submits for a time, in order to gain the means by which he can bring himself to the actuality of military service.

The wealthy and more noble intelligent beings do not require the senses, since they are indeed as burning, inconsumable, and ever growing fires, which to burn do not require a wind, which stimulates them from outside through a sensible blast into flaring up. For they exist in actuality, although in a different manner. However, since our intellectual portion is, as it were, the spark of a fire concealed under the green wood, it requires this. And do not believe that we men, who are vigorous in the senses, attain something which is hidden from intelligent beings.

The latter attain intellectually, that which we attain with the senses sensibly. Indeed, if someone speaks a Roman dialect, I attain the voice by means of hearing, however, you attain the thought also in the voice; an intelligent being, however, intuits the thought without speech; I attain the thought non-rationally, you rationally, the angel intellectually. Therefore, that which is sought is attained more truly and perfectly by means of intellectual intuition than by means of sensible hearing.

Just as you have heard that the intellect, in order to perfect itself, descends and returns in complete reversion to itself, observe this also in respect to the senses. For in order to perfect their sensitive life, they proceed upward to the intellect. They are connected therefore to two appetites, a natural and an accidental, which are fulfilled in reciprocal circular motion. Since, however, the perfection of the intellect is to actually understand—the potentiality to understand is perfected, when it advances to actuality—thus the intellect, which forms the intelligible from itself, which proceeds to the intellect, is the fecundity of itself. For the descent of the intellect to the sensible species is their ascent from contracted conditions to more absolute simplicities. The more deeply it therefore immerses itself in them, the more these species are absorbed in its light, so that finally the intelligible otherness, resolved into the unity of the intellect, rests in its end.

The unity of the intellect is therefore all the more complete, the more it advances from potentiality to actuality. And the more powerful the fire is in actuality, the more rapidly it causes the ignitible to proceed from potentiality to actuality. To transform the ignitible into fire, is nothing other than that the fire pours itself out in the ignitible. The intellect is in us, as it were, the seed of an intellectual fire, which is placed in the rational ignitible as in its matter. Therefore, as color is not visible except in the unity of light, since color is the otherness of light, but otherness is not attainable except in unity, so also phantasmata are not intelligible except in the light of rationality: for phantasmata are the othernesses of the unity of rationality. Therefore, the nearer the phantasmata are to the unity of rationality, the more intelligible they are, just as color is more visible which is nearer to the light. Therefore, as the flame, since it is absorbed in the light, is visible through itself, and we in its illumination intuit the alterations of the light, for example, colors, so concepts are also absorbed in the light of rationality, so that they are understood through themselves and render other, more obscure, things intelligible, as is established in the principles known through themselves.

Rationality, therefore, is conveyed into the intellect

through itself, as light is into vision, and the intellect descends through itself into rationality, as the sense of vision proceeds to the light. That means that the rationality, which is intelligible through itself, is the intellect, which descends into it. However, as unity proceeds through itself to number, so rationality proceeds to phantasmata. And just as number is not attained except through unity, so the intellect does not apprehend the phantasmata except by means of rationality.

Therefore, observe that unity is unattainable through itself, otherwise precision, the infinite, and the unattainable would be attained through rationality, which is impossible. Therefore, unity is not attained except by means of otherness; for example, unity of the species by means of the otherness of individuals and the unity of the genus by means of the diversity of the species.

For the same reason otherness is also not attained through itself. Hence, otherness is not attained except by means of unity. For the individual is not attained except by means of the species, nor the species except by means of the genus, nor color except by means of light, nor sound except by means of air, since sound is otherness to the quiet of air. Also pain, which is otherness, is not perceived except in the unity of the continuity or the complexion. Indeed, if the unity of the continuity is dissolved and altered or the harmonic unity of the complexion is attacked by some otherness, a disharmony is sensed in the unity.

And because it is established that the intellect is the unity of rationality, which participates in it in otherness, the intellect, which exists before otherness, is neither subject to time, which arises from rationality, nor to corruptibility, since it is the more absolute unity of rational otherness. Its nature is therefore not corruptible, since it precedes rationality. However, where unity absorbs otherness, there is immortality. Hence, that rational higher nature, which absorbs the otherness of phantasmata in the light of its unity and which itself is concealed in the light of the immortal intellect, is also immortal, just as the light, which cannot be obscured.

Indeed, as the light, insofar as it is in itself, cannot be invisible, so the pure rationality cannot be unintelligible. And this is its life and its perfection. And herein you can hunt down the difference between human and animal rationality. Why is the human rationality absorbed in the immortality of the intellectual life, which is an enduring knowledge? Because it is always intelligible through itself, as the light is visible through itself. The othernesses of the light, as for example colors, are, however, not visible through themselves; also the othernesses of rationality, which exist in the other species of animals, are not so, hence they are corruptible and alterable.

However, since a man who was blind for a long time and then begins to see, experiences this for the first time in light, the light is the otherness of the spirit of vision, and the sense of vision does not apprehend its unity except by means of otherness. That light which pours forth into the eye and by means of which he apprehends that he sees, is another light from the light of the spirit of vision. If, therefore, the strength of the light of the spirit of vision absorbs the visible light in itself, the visible passes over into the sense of vision. If, however, the otherness of visible light through its strength absorbs the debility of the spirit of vision, the unity of the power of sight passes over into otherness and division.

I believe we must conjecture in the same way concerning the power of the intellect and the light of rationality. For rationality is the otherness of intellectual unity and if its power were not strong, it would be absorbed frequently in the otherness of rationality, so that one would hold opinion as true intellect. Thus also, the otherness of phantasmata often absorbs rationality, so that a man judges that which he imagines as shown him by rationality. Thus also, occasionally the otherness of the senses absorbs the unity of the power of phantasy, so that he judges that which he attains with the senses to be that which he imagines; for example, a child, who possesses a still unformed power of phantasy, holds a woman, whom it sees, for its mother, whom it imagines. Likewise it is also accustomed to approaching others, who are weak in this power.

Therefore, the intellect, which is the unity of rationality, is combined with the body by means of just this rationality; for the corporeal nature cannot participate in the intellectual except in otherness; and since it is maximally distant from the latter, it requires intermediary steps. Therefore, the corporeal nature participates in the intellectual in the otherness of the light of rationality by means of the vegetative and sensual. The sensible, however, ascends through the corporeal organs to rationality itself, which adheres to the brain in a most tenuous and most spiritual spirit.

The otherness, however, which is taken up into rationality, is taken into the intellect, free of all organs, by means of the unity of this rationality, which is itself the otherness of the intellect. And because this ascent of rationality is the descent of the intellect, the absolute intellect, when it hunts in rational otherness, embraces the truths as they have been elevated upwards from the phantasmata.

Hence, if it takes its origin from the sensible things, it cannot be absolutely true, but rather only in a certain respect; for in rationality it is true according to rationality, in the imagination according to the imagination, in the senses according to the senses. However, if it intuits things more abstractly and outside of every otherness of rationality in its simple intellectual nature, it embraces them outside the phantasmata in the clarity of the truth.

Indeed, the intellect is the otherness of infinite Unity. Therefore, the greater the extent to which the intellect abstracts from its otherness, in order to be more able to ascend to the most simple unity, the more perfect and lofty it is. For since all otherness is not attainable except in unity, the intellect, which is otherness, since it is not the most absolute divine Intellect, but rather the human intellect, cannot intuit itself, except in the most divine unity, as it is.

For the intellect can attain neither itself nor anything else intelligible as it is, except in that truth which is the infinite Unity of all; nor can it intuit this infinite Unity except in intellectual otherness. Therefore, the intellect does not in itself intuit that unity as it is, but rather as it is humanly understood. And through the infinite Unity, which it thus understands in otherness, it elevates itself, in order to proceed more absolutely to it as it is, from the true to the truth, eternity, and infinity. And that is the ultimate perfection of the intellect, since it ascends continuously through the theophany descending to it, to an approximation of assimilation with the divine and infinite unity, which is the infinite life and the truth and the repose of the intellect.

However, the intellect is of so subtle a nature, that it, as it were, intuits the sphere in the indivisible center point. When it is contracted in rationality, it intuits the sphere in that rationality in which all lines from the center to the circumference are equal. When it intuits it in phantasy, then it imagines it round and corporeal. The sense of vision, however, cannot intuit the sphere, rather only a part of it, but it is attained through rationality, which composes part with part.

As the intellectual truth is therefore in its precision unattainable through rationality, so the truth of rationality is uncontractible sensibly. For a defect must always exist in otherness. Unity can therefore not be found in otherness otherwise than with a falling off of precision and equality. For otherwise it were not otherness, if it were precise equality. Hence the rational concept of the circle is not the true intellectual circle; for the circle is not judged by it as true intellectually, because the lines from its center to the circumference are equal. Rather this is a rational definition of the intellectual circle, which is to the true circle as the sign to the designated, as otherness to its unity, as the composed to the simple, as the unfolding to the enfolding, as the contracted to the absolute.

According to the method of rationality the circle in its contracted being cannot be other, but it exists intelligibly in its more absolute unity without the otherness of lines and circumference. However, as rationality in the unity of the intellect can offer *a priori* proof, so our intellectual cognition cannot be truer, than if in absolute Unity, which is the Truth, every otherness were intuited as absolutely and precisely as this is conceded through a divine gift, not as otherness, but rather as unity. This can only occur with complete precision through the divine Intellect, which is absolute precision itself. Indeed, it alone is all that which understands in every intellect and is understood in every intelligible thing.

Therefore, this intellectual cognition in its actual perfection is to the others as the body to the surface, the line, and the point, but in its subtlety as the point to the line, the surface, and the body. It embraces the true simultaneously, punctually, subtly, and perfectly. Rational cognition is more contracted and more perfect as the surface, subtle as the line. Imaginative cognition, which is more contracted, is perfect as the line and gross as the surface. Finally, sensitive cognition is individually most contracted, it is most imperfect as the point and most gross as the body.

These cognitions are varied diversely corresponding to the variety of the organs and spirits, the power of distinction and the variety of unity, through which one comes to otherness. If a diaphanous medium, through which the otherness of light ascends to vision, is altered by red or another color, then the thing seen appears of this color, since it is indeed not attained in the simple unity, that is, in the pure light, but rather in a light which is altered in a diaphanous medium, for example, in beryllus, a glass, a flame, a colored or altered ray of light. Thus the intellect does not attain pure phantasmata, if rationality has not been pure and free, since rationality is the unity of otherness of the phantasmata. If rationality is corrupted or altered, then its judgment is also corrupted, as we see it when rationality is bound to authority. For it is then altered and contracted from its purity, and its judgment is correspondingly corrupt. Hence a correct judgment is lacking to a passionate person, in whom the light of rationality is contracted and altered, as in a sense of taste, which through a corrupt flow of saliva judges sweetness corruptly, namely, as bitter, etc.

XVII.
On Self Knowledge

From the following, which I will now reveal to you abundantly, you can easily elicit a summary conjectural knowledge of yourself.

First, Father Julian, you do not doubt that you are a human. It is not in doubt that human is named from humanity, just as white is from whiteness. You see clearly, that humanity is a unity, which is participable in otherness, so far as you see that I am a human and indeed another from you and single individuals. You observe in the otherness of humanity and leoninity and equinity, that humanity, which is contractible individually in otherness, is the otherness of a more absolute Unity. You see the most absolute and therefore entirely uncontractible first unity or entity, in which one participates uncontractibly in varied otherness.

In order to help you with a visible example, imagine to

yourself that the simplest unity of this visible world is the uncontractible light, in whose otherness of participation all visible things are that which they are. The color of this light is therefore the altered participation. The circle of the universe is therefore the ambit of color. However, color cannot exist except contractedly, since its unity, in that it falls away from the absolute, is contracted in otherness. Observe therefore three regions of the contraction of color with their nine boundary differences. The contraction of color of the supreme region results in such a way, that the participation of the more absolute light conceals the shadowy othernesses in clear resplendence. However, the condition in the last region is contrary to this. The participation in the light is absorbed when it enters into the darkness. The middle region is accordingly in a median way.

Intuit these regions more distinctly in three-times-three distinctions. In the same way, Julian, if you now let divinity be the light, humanity be color, and the universe be the visible world, then seek yourself in the figure and see whether you are in the supreme, middle, or lowest region. I believe that you contract humanity in the supreme region and in the noble species of this supreme region, in clearer participation in divine light. On this open-lying road everyone can make a conjecture concerning himself through comparison with the other men.

However, as soon as you have found yourself in the order of those, who contract humanity through participation in the most absolute Unity, then notice that your humanity embraces your whole being and you participate in the divinity in its contraction. However, the divinity is infinite unity, equality, and connection, and indeed such that equality and connection are in the unity, unity and connection in the equality, unity and equality in the connection.

Therefore, make your contracted humanity, in which you participate in divinity itself, into the circle of the universe, and consider in respect to the regions and their subdivisions in succession, how in the supreme nature of your humanity you participate in divinity in the supreme way, in the lowest in the lowest way, and in the middle in the median way. Indeed, in the nobler nature you participate in it according to the conditions of its region, that is, intellectually, in the middle nature rationally, in the lowest sensibly, according as these regions fall in the circle of your contracted humanity.

To participate intellectually in the light of divinity, is to participate in the unity, in which equality and connection exist. Therefore, this is the intellectual being, which is to understand. Hence you participate in the divinity in the light of intelligence, in order to know that you possess intelligence through a gift from above and that through that unity, in which equality and connection exist, it is greater intellectually, the more it has become one. Therefore, in unity the intelligence is great, likewise in the equality of unity and in the connection of both, however, it is greatest in the unity, in which equality and connection exist. In the same way you participate in divinity intellectually in the equality, in which unity and connection exist, and that is in the light of justice. Therefore, the more you participate intellectually in the absolute equality, in which unity and connection exist, the more deiform you are. You also participate in divinity in the connection, in which unity and equality exist. That is, however, the light of love.

Therefore, the more you participate intellectually in the love, in which unity and equality exist, the more divine will you be corresponding to the intellectual and higher nature of your humanity.

In all this, however, pay heed that you utilize the terms according to the rules presented. If I have spoken in terms concerning divinity, then you must transfer them to its nature. Likewise, if I have revealed a concept to you about the intellectual region, then you must adapt the terms to the laws of this region. After this turn to the other regions in the same way, so that you can see in your rational part, when your rationality participates in divinity in its manner. For that in which the intellect participates intellectually, rationality in its manner and likewise the senses, according to the conditions of their nature, also participate.

You see now, Julian, that when your unity participates variedly in contracted humanity in the triune light in the three regions, and when you participate in the supreme nobility of your nature in the supreme unity or entity, which is in the intellectual power, and in the supreme equality, which is in the power of comparison and judgment, and also in the supreme connection, which is the power of connecting or loving, you participate supremely, that is, intellectually. Likewise, you participate in the triune power in the middle region medianly; therefore, you see that you participate contractedly in the power of being or discerning rationally, of comparing or judging rationally, and of connecting or loving; thus also corresponding to the lowest region in the power of being or sensing sensibly, of comparing or judging sensibly, and of connecting or loving sensibly. These participated powers are enfolded in the power of your humanity.

However, because in the participation in unity or entity, equality, and connection, which are in this unity, are simultaneously participated in, the power of the equality and connection in the participated unity of your intellect is the being of the intellect, that is, the power of understanding and the power of connecting or loving, which proceeds from the intellect and its intellection. Indeed, the intellect loves its understanding, and the love of the intellect supposes the intellect and the understanding. In their manner the same can be said of rationality and the senses.

Therefore, you know, Father Julian, that you participate in that power which bears in itself the nature of equality and connection, so that your intellect participates thus in its way in the divine being, and it can understand and embrace the intellect in its equality, so that your understanding is nothing other than the equality of the participated unity of your intellect. Therefore, in the equality or the similitude of the intellectually participated divine light, you know that you have attained the power of understanding as also of ratiocinating and of knowing. However, since the more perfectly unity is participated in, the greater the equality and connection have become in it, understanding and connecting cannot be increased without the perfection of the unity of the intellect. The intellect is therefore inclined to understanding and loving, in order to perfect its nature, and likewise rationality to ratiocination and the senses to sensible perception.

From this it follows, that the intellect concerns itself with the discovery of the intellectual arts, which are speculations, so that it can help itself with them and to avail itself of them for its nourishment, preservation, perfection, and adornment. It exserts these speculative sciences from the intellectually participated light. Likewise, rationality elicits the ratiocinative arts from the rationally participated light, and also the senses extract the sensible arts from the sensibly participated light for nourishment, preservation, perfection, and adornment of its sensible nature. Do not neglect what you have often heard, that you conceive through the participation in the divine light in rationality after the intellect and through its mediation, and likewise in the senses through rationality.

However, you see, Father Julian, how you are a similitude of God. The humanity contracted in you is indeed triune, for it is unity or entity contracted individually, in which equality and connection exist; through the entity of humanity you are man, and indeed such that in this entity the equality of entity, justice or order, and connection or love exist. For everything that is in you is ordered most justly in this unity according to the equality of unity.

For it is manifest, that all members have the justice and order of the equality of your one entity; the corporeal members are ordered in respect to the body, the body to the vital soul, the vital soul to the sensible, the sensible to the rational, the rational to the intellectual, and everything to the unity of your humanity. And as this just order is in unity, so is the loving connection also in unity. For connection is in entity, so that everything is one man. For as soon as connection ceases to be in unity, your one human being similarly will necessarily come to an end.

It is now perfectly well known to you in yourself that no contracted being whatsoever can exist other than through the unity, in which equality and connection exist. In yourself you therefore come to cognizance of everything, so that you know that everything participates variedly in the most absolute Triunity. Also you elicit from yourself the order of the universe in unity, so that you see justice not otherwise than in the order, which is in unity. For it is not unjust, but rather most equitable, that your head is above and in it are the brain, the eyes, the ears, and that the rest are arranged in steps and the feet are below; for above and below and this entire order of members resolved into unity cannot be otherwise than the most equitable. This order is therefore most equitable and most just, which exists in unity. However, that order which tends to division and otherness is most unjust and contrary to divinity.

You elicit, of course, from yourself, that this connection of love, which is in unity, is the firmest, for you see that love, or connection, indicates unity. For love unites the loving with the lovable. However, the love or the natural connection, with which your head is united with your body, is no other love than that which proceeds from unity and equality. They are therefore connected to unity from the root of your entity and the equality of order. You see therefore that the divine love is no participating connection, which is outside of the one and the order to the one. Nothing of the universe therefore may be loved, except in the unity and the order of the universe. No man may be loved, except in the unity and order of humanity. Also man may not be loved generally, except in the unity and order of animality, etc.

From yourself you are able, therefore, to intuit the election, which is deiform; for you see that God, who is the infinite connection, may not be loved as some sort of contracted lovable, but rather as most absolute, infinite love. In this love, therefore, with which God is loved, the simplest unity and infinite justice must exist. It is also necessary, that every love with which God is loved, is smaller than that with which he can be loved. You also know that to love God is the same as to be loved by God; for God is charity. Therefore, the more someone loves God, the more he participates in divinity.

Thus you see also, that through participation in the divine light, that which contains unity and connection in itself is just and equitable. When a law recedes from unity and connection, it cannot be just. This law, "what you wish to be done to you, do to others," describes the equality of unity. If you want to be just, it is necessary for you to do nothing other than not to recede from that equality, in which unity and connection exist. Then in unity and love you will equally endure adversity, poverty and wealth, honor and blame, and you will wander neither to the right nor to the left, but rather you will be most secure in the middle of equality.

Nothing grave and adverse will be able to happen to you, if you understand all that which appears adverse to the senses and embrace it as something which is to be endured in the equality of the unity of being and loving, since this means, to participate in divinity in a noble and felicitous manner. You see, however, that in this already-mentioned equality all moral power is enfolded, and that there can be no virtue except in participation in this equality.

You are able to a greater degree than I to contemplate in yourself the participated triune light of divinity, to which you have already through a just life removed yourself from the distracting things of the world in order to foster justice. And I would not have presumed to reveal these, my conjectural ineptitudes, to you, if I had not known that you would receive them due to the oft-mentioned law of equality in the unity of love.

On the Hidden God
A Dialogue of Two Men
The One a Gentile,
The Other a Christian

(1 4 4 4)

And the GENTILE says: I see you bowed down full of reverence shedding not false, but rather heartfelt, tears of love. I wish to know who are you?

CHRISTIAN: I am a Christian.

GENTILE: Whom do you adore?

CHRISTIAN: God.

GENTILE: Who is the God whom you adore?

CHRISTIAN: I do not know.

GENTILE: How can you so earnestly adore, what you do not know?

CHRISTIAN: Because I do not know, I adore.

GENTILE: I find it astonishing, that a man is affected by something that he does not know.

CHRISTIAN: It is even more astonishing, that a man is affected by something that he thinks he knows.

GENTILE: Why so?

CHRISTIAN: Because he knows that which he believes he knows less than that which he knows he does not know.

GENTILE: I beseech you to explain!

CHRISTIAN: Whoever thinks he knows something, although one can know nothing, seems insane to me.

GENTILE: It seems to me rather that you are entirely lacking in rationality, if you say that one can know nothing.

CHRISTIAN: I understand by knowledge apprehension of the truth. Whoever says that he knows, says he has apprehended the truth.

GENTILE: I believe the same.

CHRISTIAN: Then how can one apprehend the truth except through it itself? For it is not apprehended, if the apprehending comes first and the apprehended afterwards.

GENTILE: I do not understand why the truth cannot be apprehended except through itself.

CHRISTIAN: Do you believe that it can be apprehended in another way and in something other?

GENTILE: I think so.

CHRISTIAN: You are clearly in error; there is no truth outside of the truth, no circle outside of circularity, no man outside of humanity. Therefore, truth is not found outside of the truth, neither otherwise nor in something other.

GENTILE: How then is it known to me what a man is, what a stone is, and everything else of which I have knowledge?

CHRISTIAN: You know nothing of these, but only believe that you have knowledge. For if I questioned you about the quiddity of that which you think you know, you would affirm that you cannot express the actual truth of man or the stone. But that you know the man is not a stone, comes not from the knowledge through which you knew the man and the stone and their difference, but rather comes from their accidents, from the diversity of their actions and shapes, upon which, when you discern them, you impose diverse names.

GENTILE: Is there one or are there several truths?

CHRISTIAN: There is only one: for there is only one unity and truth coincides with unity, because it is true that there is only one unity. Just as only one unity is found in number, so only one truth is found in the many. And thus whoever does not attain unity, will always be ignorant of number, and whoever does not attain truth in unity, can know nothing truly.

And although he believes he truly knows, he nevertheless easily experiences, that that which he believes he knows, can be known more truly. For instance the visible can be seen more truly than it is seen by you; it will indeed be more truly seen by more acute eyes. Hence it is not seen by you as the visible is in truth. It is the same with hearing and the other senses. However, since everything which is known, but not with that knowledge with which it can be known, is not known in truth, but rather otherwise and in another way (however, since otherwise and in another way from the way which is the truth, the truth is not known), he is insane, who believes he knows something in truth and is ignorant of the truth. Is not the blind man judged to be insane, who believes he knows the distinctions of color, when he is ignorant of colors?

GENTILE: Which man then is knowing, if one can know nothing?

CHRISTIAN: One is appraised to be knowing, who knows his ignorance, and only he will revere the truth, who knows that he can apprehend nothing without it, neither being, nor living, nor understanding.

GENTILE: Perhaps it is that which attracts you to adoration, namely the desire to be in the truth.

CHRISTIAN: Exactly this, which you say. For I worship God, not him whom you gentiles falsely name and think you know, but rather God Himself, who is the ineffable truth itself.

GENTILE: Now since you, brother, worship the God who is truth, and since we do not intend to worship a God who is not God in truth, I ask you, what is the difference between you and us?

CHRISTIAN: There are many differences, but the greatest one of these is that we worship the absolute, unmixed, eternal, and ineffable truth itself; you, however, do not worship it as it is absolute in itself, but rather as it is in its actions, not absolute unity, but rather unity in number and multitude. And you are in error, for the truth, which is God, is not communicable to another.

GENTILE: I ask you, brother, to lead me to it, so that I can understand that which you know about your God. Answer me: What do you know about the God whom you adore?

CHRISTIAN: I know that everything which I know is not God, and that everything I conceive is no comparison to Him, but rather He excels it.

GENTILE: Therefore God is nothing.

CHRISTIAN: He is not nothing, for even this nothing has the name nothing.

GENTILE: If He is not nothing, is He therefore something?

CHRISTIAN: He is also not something, for something is not everything. However, God is not something rather than everything.

GENTILE: Astonishingly, you affirm the God, whom you adore, is neither nothing, nor something; that no rationality comprehends.

CHRISTIAN: God is above nothing and something. The nothing obeys Him, so that it becomes something. And this is His omnipotence, through which power He exceeds everything which is or is not, and that which is and that which is not obeys Him in like manner. For He causes not-being to pass over into being, and being into not-being. Therefore, He is nothing of those things which are under Him and which His omnipotence precedes. And since everything comes from Him, one can no more call Him this than that.

GENTILE: Can He not be named at all?

CHRISTIAN: What is named is small. He, whose magnitude cannot be conceived, remains ineffable.

GENTILE: Is He therefore ineffable?

CHRISTIAN: He is not ineffable, but rather above everything effable, since He is the cause of everything nameable. How could He, who gives a name to the others, Himself remain without a name?

GENTILE: Therefore He is both effable and ineffable.

CHRISTIAN: This neither. For God is not the root of contradiction, but rather He is the simplicity prior to every root. Hence one can also not say that He is effable and ineffable.

GENTILE: What then do you say concerning Him?

CHRISTIAN: That He is neither named nor not named, nor named and not named, but rather that everything which can be said, disjunctive and copulative, in agreement or contradiction on account of the excellence of His infinity, does not correspond to Him. He is the one origin before any formable cogitation concerning Him.

GENTILE: Therefore God does not correspond to being.

CHRISTIAN: You speak correctly.

GENTILE: He is therefore nothing!

CHRISTIAN: He is neither nothing nor is He not, nor is He and is He not, rather He is the font and the origin of all principles of being and not-being.

GENTILE: Is God the font of the principles of being and not-being?

CHRISTIAN: No.

GENTILE: But you have just stated this.

CHRISTIAN: I have said the truth, when I said it and now say the truth, when I deny it. For if there are principles of being and not-being, then God precedes them. But not-being does not have as its principle not-being, but rather being. For not-being needs a principle, in order to be. Therefore, being is the principle of not-being, because not-being does not exist without it.

GENTILE: Is God not truth?

CHRISTIAN: No, rather He precedes all truth.

GENTILE: Is He something other than the truth?

CHRISTIAN: No, for otherness does not befit Him; rather He is infinitely more excellent than everything that is conceived and named by us as truth.

GENTILE: Do you not name God God?

CHRISTIAN: We name Him thus.

GENTILE: Are you speaking truly or falsely?

CHRISTIAN: Neither the one nor both. For we do not say the true, if we say that this is His name, and we do not say something false, for it is not false that it is His name. And we also do not say the true and the false, for His simplicity precedes everything nameable and not nameable.

GENTILE: Why do you name Him God, although you are ignorant of His name?

CHRISTIAN: On account of the similitude to perfection.

GENTILE: I beseech you to explain.

CHRISTIAN: The name God (*Deus*) comes from *theoro,* which means I see. For God is in our domain as vision is in the domain of color. Color can only be attained through vision, and so that any color whatsoever could be attained, the center of vision is without color. In the domain of color, therefore, vision is not found that is without color. Hence in regard to the domain of color vision is nothing rather than something. For the domain of color does not attain being outside its domain, but rather asserts that everything which is, is inside its domain. And there it does not find vision. Vision, which exists without color, is therefore unnameable in the domain of color, since the name of no color corresponds to it. But vision gives every color its name through distinction. Hence all denomination in the domain of color depends on vision, and yet we have discovered that the name of Him, from whom all names exist, is nothing rather than something. Therefore, God is to everything, as sight is to the visible.

GENTILE: What you have said pleases me. I understand clearly that in the domain of all creatures, neither God nor His name is to be found. And that God escapes every conception rather than be affirmed as something, since as something that does not possess the condition of a creature, He cannot be found in the domain of creatures. Also one does not find the not-composed in the domain of the composed. And all names which are named, are names of composition. However, the composed is not from itself, but rather from that which precedes all composition. And although the domain of the composed and everything composed are through this that which they are, nevertheless, since it is not composed, it is unknown in the domain of the composed. Therefore, may God, hidden from the eyes of all of the wise men of this world, be praised in eternity.

On Searching for God

(1 4 4 5)

I want to satisfy your desire as well as I can, venerable Brother
in Christ, and attempt to repeat briefly and clearly in writing,
what I endeavored to explain at the Epiphany festival to the
people concerning the rational ground of the name of God. May
we both be stimulated thereby in our meditation and may the
inner man be transformed in the intellectual ascent of the light
gradually into light, until he comes through the light of glory
into clear knowledge and enters into the joy of his Lord.

I.

First, dear Brother: You know well that Paul, who reports of
himself, he had been transported into the third heaven all the way
to the view of secrets, proclaimed the truth on the Areopagus to
the men, who then dedicated themselves in Athens to the most
highly praised study of philosophy. As introduction to his theme,
he stated he wanted to bring them the Good News of that unknown God, to whom the Gentiles had consecrated an altar there.
And as he commenced to explicate this, he began with how God
had created all in one man; He has indulged them a definite time
to be in this world to search for God, if they are able by chance
to attain and find Him. He added thereto that He is not very
distant from anyone, since in Him we indeed are, live, and
are moved. Thereupon the Apostle repudiated idolatry and said

thereof, that nothing can be in the cogitation of man, which were similar to the divine.

As often as I read the Acts of the Apostles, I admire this train of thought. Paul indeed wanted to reveal the unknown God to the philosophers and then affirms of Him, that no human intellect can conceive Him. Therefore, God is revealed therein, that one knows that every intellect is too small to make itself a figuration or concept of Him. However, he names him God, or in Greek, *theos*.

If, therefore, man has come into the world to search for God and, if he has found Him, to adhere to Him and to find repose in adhering to Him—man cannot search for Him and attain Him in this sensible and corporeal world, since God is spirit rather than body, and cannot be attained in intellectual abstraction, since one is able to conceive nothing similar to God, as he asserts—how can one, therefore, search for Him in order to find Him? One thing is certain: If this world were not helpful to the seeker, man were sent into this world to search for Him in vain. Therefore, this world must assist the seeker and he must also know, that neither in the world nor in everything which man conceives is something similar to God.

We now want to see if the name *theos* or *deus* offers us assistance thereto. Indeed, the name *theos* is not the name of God, who excels every conception. Indeed, what cannot be conceived, remains ineffable. To make effable is indeed to express an intrinsic concept through vocal and other figurative signs externally. Therefore, if one conceives no similitude of a thing, then its name is unknown. Therefore, *theos* is the name of God only insofar as He is sought by man in this world. Therefore, the seeker of God may consider attentively, how in this name *theos* a path is enfolded on which God is found, so that one can attain Him. *Theos* comes from *theoro,* which means "I see" and "I run." Therefore, the seeker must run by means of vision, in order to be able to advance to the all-seeing *theos*. Therefore, vision bears in itself a similitude of the path on which the seeker should proceed. We must therefore extend the nature of sensible vision before the eye of intellectual vision and form from it a ladder for the ascent.

Our vision is generated from a lucid and clear spirit descending from the brain above into the organ of the eye and, as soon as the extrinsic light concurs, a colored object multiplying the similitude of its species in it. Therefore, in the region of the visible nothing is found except color. However, vision is not from the region of the visible, but is constituted beyond everything visible; since it does not belong to the region of colors, vision has no color, and, in order to be able to see all colors, it is not contracted to something, and so that its judgment is free and true, it has no more of one color than of another, and so that its power is in relation to all colors, it is restricted through no color. Vision is not mixed with colors, so that its vision is true.

Through an experiment we demonstrate that vision is deceived through a colored medium, through glass or a transparent stone or something other. Vision is so pure and free from every blemish of the visible, that in comparison with it everything visible is darkness and corporeal density, in comparison to the spirit of vision.

However, if we intuit the world of the visible with the intellect and ask if knowledge of vision is found in it, then it becomes apparent that all this world of color does not know vision, because it attains nothing not-colored. And if we then said, there is vision and yet it is nothing colored, then this world of the visible will want to make of it a figure of similitude, yet in all its concepts will find nothing similar to vision, since its concept is impossible without color. And if inside the ambit of its region it finds neither vision nor something similar or configurable to it, it cannot attain vision; indeed it is not even able to attain that vision is something at all. For outside of color it attains nothing, but rather judges that everything not-colored is not something.

Therefore, of all the names which can be named in this region, no name befits vision; neither the name of whiteness nor of blackness, nor that of all mixed colors; for it is neither whiteness and not-whiteness copulatively nor blackness and not-blackness copulatively. Therefore, whether the region of the sensible denotes all names singularly and disjunctively, or whether it considers the names of contrary colors copulatively or the copulation of all nameable names, it attains nothing of the name and essence of vision.

If someone now stated that color is not distinguished and perceived from itself, but rather from a higher cause, i.e., vision, and if he then asked all visible things if this is true and how they conceive this cause, then they will respond: that presupposed, which has given them names, is—just as is vision—the best and most beautiful according to what can be conceived. However, if they prepare themselves to form a concept of this best and most beautiful, then they return to color, without which a concept cannot be formed. For this reason they say it is more beautiful than every white color, for in the region of color the white color is not so beautiful that it could not be still more beautiful, and not so lucid and resplendent, that it could not be still more lucid. Therefore, all visible things would not claim as their king some color of their region, which is actually among the visible things of this region, but rather would say, he is the highest possible beauty of the most lucid and perfect color.

Such and many similar things, dear Brother, you see as most true. Therefore, ascend now from vision to hearing in a similar manner, and to taste, smell, and touch, thereupon to the universal sense, which stands above every other sense, as hearing above the audible, taste above the tasteable, smell above the smellable, and touch above the tangible.

From there proceed higher to the intellect, which is above everything intelligible, which is above everything rational. Indeed, the rational is apprehended through the intellect, however, the intellect is not found in the region of the rational; the intellect is as the eye and the rational as the colors. If you would, extend your consideration; thus you will apprehend how the intellect is as it were a free vision, namely, a true and simple judge of all rationality, in which there is no mixture with the species of the rational. Therefore, its judgment of rationality is clear and intuitive in the variety of the region of rationality. In respect to knowledge of rationality, the intellect judges this necessary, that possible, this contingent, that impossible, this demonstrative, that sophistical and apparent, this commonplace, etc., just as vision judges this color as white, that as not-white but rather black, this as more white than black, etc.

Nowhere in the entire region of rationality does one attain the intellect. However, if this world or the universe wanted to portray its king, commander, and judge, then it would say he is the terminus or ultimate perfection of rationality. But the intellectual natures can likewise not deny that a king is placed over them. And just as the visible natures assert of this king placed over them that he is the ultimate perfection of everything visible, so the intellectual natures, which view the true intuitively, also affirm their king is the ultimate perfection of the intuition of all things. They name Him *theos* or God, the speculation, as it were, or the intuition in the complement of its all-seeing perfection.

Nevertheless, nothing is found in the entire region of intellectual powers, to which the King is similar, nor is there a concept which is similar to Him in the entire intellectual region. Rather, He is above everything which is conceived or understood; His name, although it names and discerns everything intelligible, is not intelligible. And His nature is infinitely anterior to all intellectual wisdom in altitude, simplicity, strength, power, beauty, and goodness; everything which dwells in the intellectual nature is in comparison with Him shadow and impotence, grossness and meager wisdom; and one could extend such comparisons infinitely.

You are therefore able to run on this path, on which God is found above all vision, hearing, taste, touch, smell, speech, sense, rationality, and intellect. It is found as none of these, but rather above everything as God of gods and King of all kings. Indeed, the King of the world of the intellect is the King of kings and Lord of lords in the universe. For He is the king of the intellectual nature, which has dominion in the rational nature; the rational in turn rules in the sensible and the sensible rules in the world of sensible things, over which vision, hearing, taste, feeling, smell preside as kings. All these kings discern, speculate, and theorize up to the King of kings and the Lord of lords, who is the speculation, and God or *theos* Himself, in whose power all kings stand and from whom all kings have that which they have: power to rule, beauty, entity, loveliness, joy, life, and everything good.

From this it follows that in the realm of the greatest and highest king all attractiveness of visible forms, the variety of colors, pleasing proportions, the resplendence of carbuncles, the greenness of meadows, the brightness of gold and whatever delights the sight, in which the sight reposes and takes delight as if in the thesaurus of its realm, have no value in the curia of the great King, because they belong to the lowest litter of the curia. Likewise the concordant resonance of all voices and that sweet harmony in the realm of hearing, the indescribable variety of all instruments, the melody of those golden organs, the songs of nightingales, and sirens and all the other exquisite riches of the king from the realm of hearing are as though dregs, which adhere to the pavement in the curia of the greatest and best King of kings. Likewise every sweet and sour, bitter and pleasant, taste of paradise apples, of the most delicious fruits, of the grapes of Engaddi, of the wine of Cyprus, of the honey of Attica, the grain and oil and everything which India and the woods and water of this whole world present as refreshment and offer for pleasant taste, are of little moment in the palace of that most powerful ruler of the world. The pleasant smell of perfume, frankincense and myrrh, musk and everything emitting an odor, which dwells in the realm of olfaction—all this is not regarded as something precious in the great palace of the highest King, and still less all that which through its softness delights the sense of touch. If indeed the sense of touch of the king seems extensive and its realm extended throughout the world, it is, however, hardly a point, nearly imperceptible, in respect to the realm of the Ruler of the universe.

That king appears great, who commands these kings already named, and whose vassals they are; he is the universal sense, which enfolds in his power all the power of those already named. And yet he is a purchased slave and the lowest servant in the realm of the all-seeing and all-containing King.

In incomparable altitude above all the already named, the intellectual nature has obtained its realm. All the previously named and described realms are dependent on its power; it presides over them dominantly.

However, the kings of the intellectual nature are of the family of the highest commander and they enjoy being ascribed to his military. Their wish is nothing other than to be able to obtain any available position in the court of the ruler, in which they can be refreshed in intellectual intuition by Him, who is called *theos*. And everything which is in the previously named universal realm, does not concern them, for it is nothing in comparison to the good, which they know in their ruler; in Him everything is in complement, in itself divine and exceedingly good; all that which is found in the other kings is not only imperfect, outside themselves and in shadow or image, but rather also contracted at an incomparable and improportionate distance.

Therefore, the color, which is perceived in the realm of the visible by vision, does not see, but rather is only visible. It lacks life, vital motion, and perfection, such as the stem of a plant or subsistent forms have. But the senses, which are in the realm of the universal sense, the particular senses, have a nature which in the vitality and cognition of the sensible spirit enfolds in itself the form of the sensible world. Therefore, there is not less in the realm of the senses than in the realm of the sensible.

However, everything which is unfolded in the realm of the sensible is enfolded and vital in the realm of the senses in a more vigorous and perfect mode. For the realm of the sensible reposes in them. Likewise that which belongs to the realm of the senses is in a much clearer and more perfect mode in that realm, in which it is intellectually. Indeed, in the intellectual being of the intellectual realm, color has an incorruptible nature and differs through its perfection from the color of the sensible world, just as the perpetual from the corruptible, and the intellectual life from death, and light from shadow.

But in the realm of the Almighty, where the realm is king, where everything that is in all realms is the King Himself; where color is not sensible or intellectual but rather divine color, indeed God Himself; where everything which in the sensible world is without motion and life, and everything which has vegetative, sensible, rational, or intellectual life is the divine life, which is the immortality, in which God alone dwells and where in Him everything is He Himself; there the delight of all joys, which we drink up through the eyes, ears, taste, touch, smell, sense, life, motion, rationality, and intelligence, is the divine, infinite, and inexpressible delight and the repose of all delight and delectation; for God is the *theos,* speculation and running, which sees everything, is everything, runs through everything. Everything looks to Him as to its King; at His command everything is moved and runs, and every running to the end of repose is a running to Him. Therefore, everything is *theos,* the beginning, from which everything flows out, the middle, in which we are moved, and the end, to which everything flows back.

Therefore, on this path, my brother, endeavor to search for

God in the most diligent speculation. If He is sought in the right manner, it is impossible not to find Him, who is everywhere. And He is then sought correctly and according to His name, if He is sought to the end that His laud, according to His name, fulfills our earthly nature up to the limit of its power.

II.

But now, turning to the second part of our inquiry, we want to see in what manner we are led in a stepwise ascent to the indicated theory—indeed we are not moved to the completely unknown, and in order to inquire into this, we want to look back again at vision.

First we state: A double light concurs, so that vision detects the visible discretely. For it is not the spirit of vision which imposes the name of colors, but rather the spirit of its father, who is in it. The spirit, which descends through the optical nerves from the brain into the eye, is struck by the obviation of the species opposite it and a confused sensation arises. The vital power is astonished by this sensation and endeavors to discern it. Therefore, the spirit which is in the eye does not discern it, but rather a higher spirit in it effects this distinction. We could demonstrate this to ourselves as true through an everyday experiment. Frequently we do not detect the transient—although its species is multiplied in the eye—since we do not perceive it when we do not attend to the others, and if several men speak, we understand only him, to whom we have turned our attention.

This demonstrates to us that the spirit which is in the sense attains the operation of its activity through a higher light, namely, that of rationality. If, therefore, the eye says this is red and this is blue, then the eye does not speak but rather the spirit of its father speaks in it; namely this vital spirit, whose eye this is.

But although the attention of him who wants to see is present, the color is still not on that account visible; for that it is necessary that the visible be made visible by the other light of an illuminant. Indeed, in shadow and darkness the visible does not have the aptitude to be seen. Its adaptation occurs through the light which illuminates it. Thus the visible is only apt to be seen in the light, because it is not able to enter the eye by itself, and for this reason it is necessary that it be illuminated; for it is the nature of the light to enter into the eye by itself. Then, therefore, if the visible is in the light, which has the power to enter into the eye by itself, it can enter the eye. However, color is not in the light as in another, but rather as in its origin, for color is nothing other than the terminus of the light in the diaphanous, as we experience it in the rainbow. Indeed, according as the ray of sun is terminated in a rain cloud in different ways, a different color is generated.

Color, manifested in its origin, namely, in the light, is therefore visible, because the extrinsic light and the spirit of sight communicate in clarity. The light, which illuminates the visible, penetrates a similar light and brings the opposing species of color to sight.

On this basis, Brother, prepare yourself a course, on which to inquire how the unknown God presides over all that through which we are moved to Him. For although it is already certain for you, that a vital spirit discerns in the spirit of the eye, and the light makes the visible apt to be seen, nevertheless, vision detects neither the spirit itself nor the light. Indeed, the light does not belong to the region of colors, since it is not colored. Consequently, it is not to be found in the entire region where the eye holds sway. Therefore, the light is unknown to the eye and nevertheless is delectable to vision.

Therefore, as rationality, which discerns the visible in the eye, is a distinguishing spirit, so it is an intellectual spirit, which in rationality understands, and it is a divine spirit, which illuminates the intellect. However, the distinguishing light of the soul in the eye, ear, tongue, nose, and in the nerve, which governs the sense of touch, is one light received in various organs variedly, in order, according to the variety of organs, to discern variedly the things which are of the sensible world. And the light itself is beginning, middle, and end of the senses. For the senses are only for the purpose of distinguishing the sensible and they are only from that spirit and are moved in no other. In it also all the senses live. Indeed, the life of vision is to see, the life of hearing to hear, and the more perfect this life is, the more discrete it is. Indeed, the vision which discerns the visible more perfectly is more perfect, and the same is the case for the hearing.

Therefore, life and perfection, joy and repose and whatever all the senses desire, lie in the distinguishing spirit, and from it they have everything that they have. Even if the organs lose in power and the life in them decreases in activity, it does not decrease in the distinguishing spirit, from which they receive the same life, when the fault or infirmity is removed.

In like manner, conceive the same about the intellect, which is the light of distinguishing rationality, and from it elevate yourself to God, who is the light of the intellect. And if you run thus through that which you have discovered in vision, you will discover how our God, blessed be He in eternity, is everything which is in everything which is, just as the distinguishing light in the senses and the intellectual in the rational, and that it is He Himself, from whom the creature has that which it is, from whom it has life and motion, and that all our cognition is in His light, so that it is not we who know but rather He in us. And if we ascend to cognition of Him Himself, then although He is unknown to us, nevertheless we are moved in nothing other than in His light, which enters into our spirit, so that we advance to Him in His light. Therefore, as being is dependent on Him, so also is being known. Just as the being of color depends on corporeal light, so the cognition of color depends on this light, as we have already said above.

Therefore, we must attend to the fact that wonderful God created the light among His works. In its simplicity it excels all the other corporeal things, so that it is the middle between spiritual and corporeal nature, through which this corporeal world ascends, as it were, through its simplicity into the spiritual world. Indeed, it brings the forms into vision, so that the form of the sensible world ascends to rationality and the intellect, and through the intellect attains its end in God. Thus the world itself also enters into being, so that this corporeal world is what it is through participation in light; and one regards the corporeal things in the corporeal genus as more perfect, the more they participate in light, as we experience it stepwise with the elements. Also a creature that has the spirit of life is the more perfect, the more it participates in the light of life. Thus a creature of intellectual life is the more perfect, the greater its participation is in the intellectual light of life.

However, God cannot be participated in and He is the infinite light, which shines in everything, just as the distinguishing light in the senses. However, the varied termination of this light, in which nothing can participate and which cannot be mixed, shows varied creatures, just as the termination of corporeal light shows various colors in the diaphanous, although the light itself remains unmixable.

III.

I do not doubt, Brother, that you are able to advance from these explanations in clarity and to apprehend that as color is only visible through the medium of light, that is to say, as color can ascend only in the light of its origin to repose and to its end, so our intellectual nature can only attain the felicity of repose in the light of its intellectual origin. And vision does not discern, but rather the distinguishing spirit in it discerns; thus also in our intellect, which is illuminated by the divine light of its origin according to its aptitude to let it enter, we shall not know or live through ourselves in intellectual life, but rather God will live in us in infinite life. And this is that eternal felicity, where the eternal intellectual life, that excels every concept of living creatures in inexpressible joy, lives in us in strictest unity, just as the distinguishing rationality lives in our most perfect senses and the intellect lives in the clearest rationality.

It is already apparent to us, that through the motion of the light of His grace, we are drawn to the unknown God, who cannot be detected otherwise than if He manifests Himself. And He wants to be sought. And He wants to give light to the seekers, without which they cannot seek Him. He wants to be sought, and He also wants to be apprehended, for He wants to reveal and manifest Himself to the seekers. Therefore, He is sought with the desire to be apprehended and He is sought theoretically, with the running leading the runner to the repose of motion, when He is sought with maximum desire. Hence, one proceeds correctly towards attaining wisdom, only if He is sought with maximum desire. And when He is sought thus, He is sought on the correct path, where without doubt He will be found through the manifestation of Himself. No other path is given us than this one and in all the teachings of the saints, who attained wisdom, no other is bequeathed to us.

Therefore, they all erred, the proud, the presumptuous, who regarded themselves as wise, who trusted in their own genius, who in ascending arrogance deemed themselves to be similar to the highest, who arrogated to themselves the knowledge of the gods; they closed off to themselves the path to wisdom, because they believed it to be no other than that which they measured with their own intellect; they passed away in their vanities, they embraced the tree of knowledge and did not apprehend the tree of life. Therefore, to the philosophers who did not honor God, there was no other end, than to perish in their vanity.

Those, however, who saw that one cannot attain wisdom and perennial intellectual life, unless it be given through the gift of grace, and that the goodness of the Almighty God is so great that He hears those who invoke His name, and they gain salvation, became humble, acknowledging that they are ignorant, and directed their life as the life of one desiring eternal wisdom. And that is the life of the virtuous, who proceed in the desire for the other life, which is commended by the saints.

There is no other tradition of the holy prophets and those who obtained the grace of divine light in this life, than that everyone who wishes to attain the intellectual life and immortal divine wisdom, first must believe that God exists and that He is the Giver of all goods; that one must live in fear of Him and advance in His love; that one must in all humility implore Him for immortal life and, so as to be worthy of attaining it, must embrace everything which is ordered to this immortal life in deepest devoutness and the most sincere worship.

Now you see, Brother, that not some virtue nor cult nor law nor instruction justifies us, so that we deserve to obtain this most excellent gift. But a virtuous life, observation of the commandments, sensible devotion, mortification of the flesh, contempt for the world, and all the rest of this kind accompany everyone who seeks correctly divine life and eternal wisdom. If they are not with him, then it is manifest that he is not on the path, but rather outside of it.

However, the indications that someone is not off the path but rather is on the path, we can obtain from the works which accompany those proceeding correctly. Whoever endeavors with the greatest desire to apprehend eternal wisdom places nothing before it in his love; takes care not to offend it; affirms that, in comparison to it, everything else is nothing; also regards everything else as nothing and spurns it. To please the loved wisdom he adapts his whole effort to it, knowing that he cannot please it if he clings to the other, corruptible prudence of the world or sensible delectation. Therefore, abandoning everything, he hastens freely in the fervor of his love. As the deer desires the font of water, so does such a soul desire God. Thus, we merit the incomparable thesaurus of glory not through works which we accomplish, but rather God loves who love Him; for He is charity and love and gives Himself to souls, so that they enjoy this best good in eternity.

Now you see, Brother, to what purpose you have come into this world, as we have already mentioned in the introduction, namely, in order to search for God. You see that *theos* means for the seekers, how one can seek Him on a certain path. If you walk on this, then it will be your path and it will be well known to you; you will delight in it on account of its loveliness and the fecundity of its fruits, which are found all around it. Therefore, exercise yourself by multiplying your action and theoretical ascension and you will find the pastures, which augment and strengthen you on your path, and which inflame you more from day to day in desire.

For our intellectual spirit has the power of fire in itself. For no other purpose is it sent by God to the earth than that it glow and grow into a flame. When it is excited by admiration, then it grows, just as if the wind entering into a fire excited its potential to actuality. If we apprehend the works of God, we marvel at eternal wisdom. And through the extrinsic wind, which proceeds from works and creatures of such varied powers and operations, we are incited so that our desire grows into love of the Creator and attains to the intuition of His wisdom, which has ordered everything wonderfully.

If we turn our view to the minimum grain of mustard seed and intuit its strength and power with the eye of the intellect, then we find a vestige, which excites us in admiration of our God. For although its body is so small, nevertheless its power is without limit. In this granule is a large tree with leaves and little branches and many other seeds, in which similarly is the same power beyond all number. Thus I see in the intellect the power of the grain of the mustard seed; if it should be unfolded as actuality, this sensible world would not suffice thereto; not even ten or a thousand, indeed not even so many worlds as one could enumerate.

Who is not seized by admiration, when he reconsiders this, especially when one adds that the intellect of man embraces all the power of the grain of seed and apprehends this as true, and thus excels in its capacity of apprehension all that of the whole sensible world, and not only of this one, but rather of infinitely many worlds? And so our intellective power embraces every corporeal and measurable nature.

What magnitude therefore is in our intellect! If, therefore, the merely punctual magnitude of the intellectual spirit embraces every possible sensible and corporeal magnitude with infinitely greater capacity of apprehension, how great then is the Lord! And how laudable is He, whose magnitude is infinitely more excellent than the magnitude of the intellect! And just because He is so great, everything is in comparison to Him nothing and can be in Him nothing other than God Himself. Blessed be He in eternity! You could likewise ascend through a similar ascent from the power of a millet seed, just as from the power of every vegetative and animal seed, and no seed has less power than the grain of mustard seed. And there are infinitely many such seeds. Oh how great is our God! He is the actuality of every potentiality, for He is the end of every potentiality; not only the potentiality which is contracted to a grain of mustard seed or millet seed or a grain of corn or to the seed of our father Adam or to others, and thus to infinity!

But because, in all these, immeasurable strength and power is contracted according to their genus, absolute potentiality, which is also infinite actuality, is in God without contraction. What man would not be astounded by the power of God, if he seeks thus? Who would not be inflamed to the highest ardor and fear and love for the Almighty? Who can observe the power of the minimum scintilla of fire without being filled with admiration for God beyond everything that can be said? If the power of a scintilla, insomuch as it is in actuality—for in order to be actual, the scintilla is obtained from potentiality by means of the motion and striking of iron against the flint—is so great, that it is in its power to resolve everything into its nature and to place all fire in potentiality into actuality, wheresoever it is in this world, although there were infinitely many worlds, oh, how great is the power of our God, who is a Fire that consumes fire! And if you turn yourself, Brother, to the nature and conditions of fire (there are twenty-four, as the highest contemplator of divine things, Dionysius, explains in the hierarchy of the angels), then you have a wonderful path for seeking and finding God. Look there and you will be astonished.

IV.

But if you search for another path to the wisdom of our Master, then take heed. For with the eye of the intellect you apprehend that in a small piece of wood, in this most minute stone, in a piece of ore or gold, in a grain of mustard seed or millet all the artificial corporeal forms are in potentiality. Indeed you doubt not that in each of them the circle, triangle, tetragon, sphere, cube, and whatsoever else geometry names is included; thereby also the forms of all animals, all fruits, all flowers, leaves, trees, and the similitude of all forms, which are in this world and could be in infinite worlds.

Therefore, if that one is already a great artist, who knows how to educe from a small piece of wood the face of a king or of a queen, an ant or a camel, how great then is the mastery which can form as actuality everything which is in all potentiality? Therefore, God, who is able to produce from the most minute piece of matter the similitude of all forms which can be in this world and in infinitely many worlds, is of admirable subtlety.

Still more wonderful, however, is the power and knowledge of Him who has created the grain of millet itself and has placed this strength in it. And truly stupendous is the mastery of that wisdom, which knows how to excite all possible forms in the grain of seed, not in accidental similitude, but rather in essential truth. Beyond all intellect, however, is the indescribable stupor over the fact that it not only knows how to excite living men from the stones, but rather also men from nothing, and to call into being that which is, as well as that which is not. And since it is certain that all created arts only attain something in something, i.e., some similitude, which is not without defect, namely, in something created—for example a statue in the material of iron, which is somehow similar to a man—who then is this Master, who produces not a similitude with a defect, but rather the true essence without some material from which it is brought into being?

On such paths we advance to God in vehement admiration, and then the spirit glows with desire to find Him completely securely, and it is consumed in loving longing, that ultimate salvation be shown it.

V.

Finally, there is still a way to search for God, in yourself, which is the ablation of terminations. For when an artist seeks the face of the king in a piece of wood, then he discards all other terminations besides the face itself. Through the concept of his faith he sees in the wood the face, which he seeks to make visibly present to the eye. For the face, which through faith exists in the present for the mind in the intellectual concept, is in the future for the eye.

If, therefore, you conceive that God is better than can be conceived, then you discard everything that is terminated or contracted. You discard the body, in that you say that God is not body, therefore, is not terminated through quantity, location, form, or situation. You discard the senses, which are also terminated: You do not see through a mountain, nor into the hidden depths of the earth, nor in the clarity of the sun; for hearing and the other senses it is the same. Indeed, they all are terminated in potentiality and power. Therefore, they are not God. You discard the universal sense, fantasy and imagination, for they do not exceed corporeal nature. Indeed, the imagination does not attain the incorporeal. You discard rationality, for it frequently fails and does not attain everything. If you wish to know why this is a man, why that is a stone, you do not attain the rational ground in all the works of God. The power of rationality is slight; therefore, God is not rationality. You discard also the intellect, for the intellect itself, although it embraces everything, is terminated in its power. It is not able to attain perfectly the quiddity of a thing in its purity, and in everything which it attains, it sees that it were attainable in a more perfect mode. God is therefore also not intellect.

But if you search further, you find in yourself nothing

similar to God, but rather you affirm that God stands above all this as cause, origin, and the light of life of your intellective soul.

You will be happy to have found Him above everything which belongs to your interior, as a font of goodness, from which everything flows out to you which you have. You turn yourself to Him, from day to day you enter into Him more deeply, you abandon everything which is turned towards the outside, so that you are found on that path on which God is found, so that you are able to apprehend Him after this life in truth. This He would grant you and me; He, who gives Himself abundantly to those who love Him. Blessed be He in eternity. Amen.

On the Filiation of God

(1 4 4 5)

*Dedicated by Nicolaus of Cusa to the devout priest and
fellow brother Conrad of Wartberg, Canon of the Maifeld
Monastery.*

The fervor of your study has finally compelled me to respond
to your frequent reminders. You seem indeed to demand
from me that I conjecture concerning the filiation of God, of
which it is made public by the most lofty theologian John that it
is given us by the eternal ray of light; he indeed says: "But to all
who receive Him, He gave the power to become sons of God,
to them who believe in His name." Therefore, my truly venerable
fellow brother, receive that which occurs to me, however, on
the condition that you do not intend me to add something to that
which you have already read in my earlier conceptions. For in
my inner heart nothing remained that I had not entrusted to those
writings, which express my general conjectures of whatever
kind. Probably you will experience it yourself in that which I
wish to say.

I.

I, however, as I will say in summary, think that the filiation of
God is to be judged not other than deification, which is called
theosis in Greek. The *theosis,* which is also wont to be called
the knowledge of God and of the Word, or intuitive vision,
represents, which you know yourself, the ultimate perfection.
This sentence of the theologian John I indeed judge thus: The
Logos or the eternal rational ground, which was in the beginning

God with God, gave man rational light, when it gave the Spirit over to him, to lead him to its similitude. Thereafter it declared, through various admonitions of the seeing prophets and finally through the Word, which appeared in the world, that the light of rationality is the spirit of life and that in this our rational spirit, if we have received the Divine Word, the power of filiation arises in the believing.

This exceedingly wonderful participation in the divine power means that our rational spirit has this power in its intellectual force, as if the intellect itself were a divine seed, whose power in the believing is able to ascend so high that it extends to the *theosis* itself, that is, to the ultimate perfection of the intellect, that is, to the apprehension of the truth; of a truth which is not obscured as in this sensible world in figures and enigmas and various otherness, but rather as it is intellectually visible in itself. And this is the sufficiency itself, which our intellectual power, which is actualized among the believing through the excitation of the Divine Word, has from God. Who indeed does not believe, does not ascend at all, but rather, judges himself not able to ascend, whilst he himself obstructs the way; indeed one attains nothing without faith, which places the wanderer on his way at the beginning. Therefore, the power of our soul is able to climb upwards to the perfection of the intellect only insofar as it believes. Therefore, the ascent to the filiation of God is not prohibited, if faith is present.

And since filiation is the ultimate of every power, our intellectual power can also not be exhausted this side of the *theosis,* nor does it attain in any steps that which is its highest perfection, this side of that repose of the filiation of perpetual light and of the life of everlasting joy. I believe, however, that this deification goes beyond every mode of intuition. For nothing in this world, be it howsoever high and elevated, can enter the heart of man, his mind or intellect, without remaining inside this mode of contraction; thus no concept of joy, of gladness, of truth, of essence, of power, of self-intuition, or of any other can be without this restrictive mode; and this mode will be retracted to phantasmata in every single diverse thing, according to the condition of this world. Yet if we are absolved of this world, then we are also freed from these obscured modes; then also our intellect to its felicity is liberated from these impeding modes and obtains in its intellectual light the divine life, in which, although without the contracted enigmas of the sensible world, it is elevated to the intuition of truth.

Nevertheless, this intuition will not be without the measure of this world. Indeed, the theologian asserts, the light of the rational ground has the power to obtain for all who receive and believe the Word, the filiation of God. Therefore, the filiation will be in many sons, who participate in it in various ways. For, since everything existing must necessarily be in another otherwise, the multitude participates in unity variously in varied otherness. Therefore, the filiation of the many will not be without measure; and this mode can perhaps be called participation in adoption. However, the filiation of the only-begotten Son exists without measure in identity with the nature of the Father; it is the superabsolute filiation, in which and through which all sons by adoption obtain filiation.

II.

Now you seem to wish that I lead you to some mode, where you can see what that ineffable joy of filiation is. Indeed, you do not expect that what surpasses every mind could be expressed sufficiently, especially since we, who must occupy ourselves with conjectures, are not able to spring over the modes of enigmas. Nevertheless, I am afraid that it will be criticized as presumptuous audacity, if I take upon myself as a sinful man the task of the purest mind. The great wish to please you, however, does not permit me to be silent. Therefore, accept most briefly what I now conjecture.

I do not believe that we become sons of God such that we are then something other than now. Rather, we shall then be in another mode, that which we now are in this mode. Indeed, the intellectual power, which receives the actual divine light through which it is vivified, through faith, attracts its continuous influx, so that it matures to a perfect man. Virility, however, is not of the world of puerility, where man is still growing up, but rather of the world of perfection. The boy is the same as the man. But the filiation does not appear in the boy, who is counted as the servant, but rather in adulthood, when he rules in common with the father. He is the same, who now is in school in order to advance, and who after this obtains mastery. Here we study, there we are master.

However, we study, as the theologian asserts, in the mode that we receive the Word of the rational ground from the Master, in whom we believe, because He is the truthful Master and teaches us correctly; we trust that we can advance and, because we receive His Word and believe, we will be teachable by God. And thereby arises in us the capability to obtain the mastery, which is filiation.

First the painter teaches the student to inscribe many particular figures with his stylus and then finally he is transferred from the school over to mastery. However, mastery is the assumption of particular knowledge over to the universal art, and between the two there is no proportion. In this world we study by means of the senses, which attain to only the particular. We are transferred from the sensible world of particular things to the universal art, which is in the intellectual world. Indeed, the universal is in the intellect and belongs to the intellectual domain. In this world our study is occupied with various particular objects, as with various books. In the intellectual world, there is only one object for the intellect, namely, the truth itself, in which it possesses universal mastery. For the intellect seeks nothing in this world by means of the senses in the various particular objects, except its life and the nourishment of its life, namely, the truth, which is the life of the intellect.

And this is the mastery which it seeks in the study of this world, namely, to know the truth, indeed to have mastery of the truth, indeed to be the master of truth, indeed to be the art itself of truth, but it does not find the art itself, but rather those particulars, which represent works of art. However, it is transferred from the school of this world into the domain of mastery and is made the master or the art of the works of this world.

Therefore, the study of life and perfection and every motion of the intellect will come to rest, when it discovers itself to be in the domain where the master of all workable works is, namely, the Son of God, that Word, through which the heavens are formed and every creature, and that it is similar to him. Indeed, when that art is in it, then the filiation of God is in it; indeed it itself is that divine Art, in which and through which everything is; indeed it itself is God and everything, in that manner in which it has acquired mastery. You will perceive this through attentive meditation.

Knowledge in its universal reception embraces everything knowable, namely, God and everything that is. However, a learned scribe, who has obtained mastery of universal knowledge, has a thesaurus from which he can bring forth the new and the old. Therefore, his intellect embraces God and everything according to the mode of mastery, so that nothing escapes from it or is outside it, so that in it everything is this intellect itself. Thus the same is true in another learned scribe in his manner, etc. Therefore, the more diligent someone has been in the school of this sensible world in the exercise of intellectual study in the light of the Word of the Divine Master, the more perfectly he will achieve mastery.

Therefore, if the mastery which we seek and in which lies the felicity of our intellectual life, is concerned with the true and the eternal, and if our intellectual spirit should result in perfect mastery, in order to possess eternally in itself the most delectable intellectual life, then its study should not adhere to the temporal shadows of the sensible world, but should use them only perfunctorily for its intellectual study, just as the boys in the school use the material and sensible writings. For their study is not concerned with the material figures of the letters, but rather with their rational significance.

Likewise they also use the vocal speeches, in which they are instructed, intellectually and not sensibly, so that through the vocal signs they advance to the mind of the master. Those, however, who delight rather in the signs, do not advance to mastery in philosophy, but rather degenerate as the ignorant into writers, painters, speakers, singers, or players of the cithara.

Through such an example, we who aspire to the filiation of God are admonished not to adhere to the sensible things, which are only enigmatic signs of the true, but rather on account of our infirmity to use them without the adhesion of their pollution, as if through them the master of truth were speaking and they were books, which contain the expression of his mind. And then we shall contemplate in the sensible the intellectual, and in an improportionate comparison of the transitory and the fluid temporal, whose being is unstable flux, ascend to the eternal, where all succession is carried away into the fixed permanence of repose, and we shall be free in the contemplation of the true, just, and joyful life. We separate ourselves from every defilement dragging us down, so that, absolved of this, in the ardent desire and striving for that life, we can attain mastery and enter into that life.

This is the joy of the Lord, which no one can take away, when we experience through the intellectual taste that we have attained incorruptible life. And this is that highest delectation, as if with the soundest sense we taste the food of life, which we hungrily desire. A sick person, who suffers from an illness of the palate, eats the most savory food; however, since the vitality of his sense of taste does not sense the sweetness of the taste, he lives in misery, fatigue, grief, and labor and it is a punishment for him to masticate food. However, whoever longs for food with a pure and healthy palate, eats with joy and delight. With this, although very remote similitude, one can represent the uninterrupted joy of the sons of God, because the intellectual life, as a result of its incorruptible nature, is not only not corrupted in annihilation, but rather lives in the intellectual taste; through it the man whom the pure truth eternally revives, senses that he lives in the true intellectual life.

III.

Perhaps you are struck by what you have frequently heard: God is incomprehensible and the filiation, which is the apprehension of the truth, which is God, cannot be attained.

I think you have understood sufficiently that the truth cannot be comprehended in another except otherwise. However, since those modes of theophany are intellectual, God—although He is not attained as He is—nevertheless is intuited without any enigmatic phantasmata in the purity of the intellectual spirit, and this is for the intellect a clear and facial vision. This mode of appearance of absolute Truth—because it is the ultimate vital felicity of the intellect thus enjoying the truth—is God, without whom the intellect cannot be fruitful. I would like you to attend to how the coming to rest of all intellectual motion is the truth opposite it; outside the domain of truth no intellectual vestige is found, and also, according to the judgment of the intellect, nothing can exist outside the heaven of the truth. However, if, as we have developed it in our other books, you distinguish most subtly, then the truth is not God as He triumphs in Himself, but rather it is a mode of God, through which He can communicate Himself in the eternal life of the intellect. For God triumphing in Himself cannot be understood or known, is neither truth nor life, nor is He; but rather He precedes everything intelligible as the one simplest origin. Since He thus surpasses every intellect, He is not found in the region or heaven of the intellect, nor can He be attained by the intellect, since He is outside its heaven. Because God can only be attained negatively outside the intellectual region, we attain Him on the road of fruition in the truth of being and life, in the empyreal Heaven itself, namely, in the highest rapture of our spirit in peace and repose, when the spirit is satisfied in the appearance of the glory of God.

And therein lies the highest intellectual joy: to know that His beginning, His middle, and His end excel every height of apprehension, and to intuit Him in His own object, namely in the pure truth. And this means that one apprehends Him Himself in the truth, in such excellent glory that one understands that nothing can be outside Him, but rather everything is in Him He Himself.

A similitude should help you: Without doubt it is not unknown to you that forms of equal size in straight mirrors appear smaller in curved ones. Now if we conceive the highest resplendence of our origin, of glorious God, in which God Himself appears, it would be the mirror of truth, without blemish, completely straight, unbounded, and most perfect; all creatures would be His contracted and differently curved mirror. Among them the intellectual natures are the living, clearer, and straighter mirrors. Of these, since they are living and intellectual and free, conceive that they can curve, straighten, and purify themselves.

I therefore say: The one mirror-clarity shines forth variedly in these universal mirror-reflections and in the first, completely straight, mirror-clarity all mirrors shine forth just as they are. One can see this in material mirrors, whose fronts are turned in a circle towards one another. However, in all others, the contracted and curved, they do not appear as they are, but rather according to the condition of the receiving mirror, i.e., diminished, because the mirror receiving it recedes from straightness.

Therefore, when one has translated any intellectual, living

mirror into the first straight mirror of the truth, in which everything, just as it is, shines forth truthfully without defect, then
this mirror of the truth transfuses itself with all the mirrors which
it has received, into the intellectual, living mirror, and the latter
intellectual kind receives that mirror-ray of the mirror of truth,
which the truth of all mirrors holds in itself. However, it receives
in its own mode, in the one true moment of eternity, the living
mirror, like a living eye, which receives the reflecting light of
the first mirror and therefore sees itself in the same mirror of
truth, just as it is, and sees in itself everything in its own determined mode. The simpler, more absolute, clearer, purer,
straighter, more just, and true it has been, the more limpid,
joyous, and true it will contemplate in itself the glory of God and
everything.

In that first mirror of the truth, therefore, which can also
be called the Word, Logos, or Son of God, the intellectual mirror
acquires filiation, so that it is everything in everything and everything in Him, and His kingship is the possession of God and
everything in a life of glory!

Therefore, Brother, remove the quantitative contractions
of the sensible mirror and absolve your concept of time and place
and everything sensible, while you elevate yourself to the rational
mirror-clarity, where our mind observes the truth in the clarity
of rationality. We inquire into the hiding places of doubt in
the clarity of the rational mirror and know that as true, which
rationality shows us.

Now transfer the just-presented paradigm to the intellectual
domain, so that you can elevate yourself through such a device
nearer to observation of the filiation of God. For in a secretive
intuition you are able to taste in advance that the filiation is
nothing other than that translation from the shady vestiges of
images to union with the infinite rational ground, in which and
through which the spirit lives and knows itself to live; and indeed,
so that it sees that nothing lives outside God, and that only all
that lives, which is in Him He Himself. And it knows that
God has such an exuberance of life that everything lives in Him
eternally; indeed so that something does not present life to Him,
but rather He Himself is the life of the living.

God will be for it not other, nor diverse or distinct from
His spirit; also divine rationality will be no other and the Word

of God and the Spirit of God nothing other. For every otherness and diversity is far inferior to filiation. Indeed, the purest intellect makes everything intelligible into intellect, since everything intelligible in the intellect is intellect itself. Therefore, everything true is true and intelligible through the truth itself. Therefore, the truth alone is the intelligibility of everything intelligible. Therefore, the abstracted and most pure intellect makes the truth of everything intelligible into intellect, so that it lives in the intellectual life, which is to understand. It will therefore be intellect, when in it the truth itself is intellect, always understanding and living. And because it understands the truth, which in it is it itself, it will understand nothing that is other from itself. Indeed, outside of the intelligible nothing is understood. However, everything intelligible in the intellect is intellect. Therefore, it remains nothing except the pure intellect, which corresponds to itself and which is not able to understand that outside of the intelligible something more can exist.

Because it is so, the intellect knows neither that other intelligible, nor will its understanding be something other, rather the one understanding and that which is understood and the actuality itself, which is the understanding, are in the unity of essence. The truth will not be something other from the intellect, and the life in which it lives will be nothing other from the living intellect, according to all the force and nature of the intellectual vigor, which embraces everything corresponding to itself and transforms everything into itself, because everything in it is it itself.

Filiation, therefore, is the ablation of all otherness and diversity, and the resolution of everything into one, which is also the transfusion of the one into everything. And this is the *theosis* itself. For God is the One, in which everything is as one—and which is also the transfusion of the One into everything, so that everything is that which it is—and since in the intellectual intuition the being-one, in which everything is, and the being-everything, in which the One is, coincide, then we are rightly deified, because we are exalted to this, so that in the One in which everything is, and in everything in which the One is, we are He Himself. However, do not believe that these locutions are precisely correct. For the ineffable is not attained by locutions.

Therefore, you must elevate yourself in profound meditation beyond all contrarieties, figures, locations, times, images, and contractions, beyond othernesses, disjunctions, conjunctions, affirmations, and negations, because through the transcendence of all proportions, comparisons, and ratiocinations into the pure, intellectual life, as the son of life, you are transformed into life. And these are for the moment my conjectures about *theosis,* although they are very remote. You can conjecture yourself according to your abilities, how one can describe its highest profundity, and that one must ascend beyond all rationality, in simple purity, to something which is high above everything which can be explained with any signs. This is enough said concerning this.

IV.

However, since it is surely your wish that I reveal to you a concept of the path on which I conjecture to advance in the flux of this time in the study of filiation, I will attempt to explain this, just as it occurs to me. I am of the opinion that the school of resolution frees us from the various involutions, if we reflect upon the One and the modes of the One. Certainly the One, absolved of all considerations, which is the beginning, the middle, and the end of everything, indeed everything in everything and nothing in nothing, is not in any manner coordinated with intelligible, rational, and sensible entities, as I have explained it elsewhere in *On Learned Ignorance;* for neither in the ascent nor in the descent of things is one able ever to attain to the simple maximum. It always remains super-exalted above every order and every grade. Nevertheless, although it remains unattainable, it is the One, which is attained in everything attainable.

It will, therefore, simultaneously be the One which is everything, and the unattainable One, which is attained in everything; as if someone names the monad innumerable which nevertheless is every number and is counted as the innumerable monad in every number. Indeed, every number cannot be other than the monad. The denary has everything which it is from the monad, without which the denary were not one number and not the denary. That it is the denary, it has completely from the monad. It is not other from the monad and it is nothing that receives something from it, as if some being besides the monad could befit it, but everything which it is, is the monad. Nevertheless, the denary number does not count the monad, but it remains innumerable for the denary as also for every other number, for the innumerable monad is exalted above every other number. And since the six is not the seven, these two numbers will be diverse, although the monad of the six and the monad of the seven are not other. In them nothing is found except the one monad in variety.

Therefore, the monad, which is the origin of number, cannot be found in number; rather unity is in the number numerably and in the monad innumerably. There is no coordination or proportion of the numerable to the innumerable, of the absolute to the modally contracted.

Thus it is good if you conjecture that that One, the origin of everything, although it is the origin of everything effable, is ineffable. Therefore, everything which can be expressed does not express the ineffable and yet every elocution expresses the ineffable. For it is the One itself, the father or generator of the Word; all that which is verbalized in every word, is signified in every sign, etc.

In order to guide you with another example: The intellect of the master is unattainable through everything in the rational and sensible domains. This intellect is moved from the plentitude of mastery and power or goodness, in order to unite the other to its own similitude. It generates from itself the mental word, which is the simple and perfect word of the master or the perfect art of the master itself. He wants this art to inspire the minds of his students. However, since it is only able to enter into the mind through sensible signs, he inhales the air and forms from it the voice, which he variedly gives form to and expresses, in order thus to elevate the minds of the students to equality with the mind of the master. However, all the words of the master cannot show the author of the words, namely, the intellect, except through the mental concept or the intellectual Word itself, which is an image of the intellect.

In such an expression of the teaching of the master, the master's affection shines forth, which shines out variously in his delivery according to the various modes of expression. So that the word bear fruit, the affection of the master appears in the signification of the words as concept, the mastery itself also shines forth, from which it emanates fruitfully and masterfully. But all the modes of delivery do not attain to affection, for it is so great that it cannot be sufficiently expressed; and all the modes of speech do not attain to the concept, which is of inexpressible fecundity, since it is the art of mastery. Neither speech nor delivery is able with all possible modes to express intellectual mastery, although nothing other presents itself and is signified in every speech than its own manifestation, with the end of transformation into similar mastery.

In such a similitude, our Triune Origin created in His goodness this sensible world, for the sake of the intellectual spirit; He made its material as though a voice, in which He made the mental word shine forth variedly, so that all sensible things are utterances of various expressions unfolded by God, the Father, through His Son, the Word, in the spirit of the universe to the end, that through sensible signs the teaching of the highest mastery is transfused into human minds and transforms them completely to similar mastery. This total sensible world exists for the sake of the intellectual, and man is the end of the sensible creatures, and glorious God the beginning, middle, and end of all his actions.

Therefore, the study of those who strive after the filiation of God, aims at knowing that everything effable comes from the ineffable, not-coordinated, and superexalted, and that this ineffable has its place beyond everything intellectual and is the beginning, middle, and end of everything intelligible, and that the One is in a not-communicable way the font of intelligible entity and all that which is this, just as the mental word is the font of the vocal word and all that which is and is signified by a vocal word without mixture or partition of itself. For the mind cannot be participated in or attained in any way through a vocal word.

However, the intellectual word is the intellectual reception of the ineffable word. Every word, therefore, which is freed from all sensible contraction, remains intellectual. The intellectual, however, has intellectually from the ineffable what it is. However, if the ineffable is named through the intellect, then that occurs in an absolute manner, since the intellectual mode is absolute in respect to the sensible contractions.

Therefore, the ineffable cannot be named or attained in any manner. Neither the name, the absolute, nor entity, deity, goodness, truth, power, nor anything else, therefore, names

God, the unnameable, but rather they express the unnameable God in various intellectual modes. However, in this way the ineffable is effable, the not-communicable communicable, the beyond-all-measure measurable.

God is therefore the origin beyond the One and its measure, who in the One and in the mode of the One exhibits Himself as communicable. Therefore, I conjecture that the study, with which we attempt to ascend in this world to filiation, can perhaps also exist in something other; that our observation be occupied with the One and the mode of the One.

V.

So that you taste what I intend speaking more contractedly in an example, apply the One and its mode to something, about which you have experienced that it is in everything and is vigorous. We experience, however, that a certain power is inherent in all things. Therefore, free the power by means of the intellect, so that you consider its force in the absolute mode. The absolute power will therefore be a certain maximum size, coordinated with everything which has in itself all grades and modes of power in the universal height, and in the unity of intellectual simplicity, and which has in itself the highest modes, in which the superexcellent, ineffable, and completely unattainable cause of all power is intellectually attained. For God is not the power, but the Lord of the power.

It is further to be attended to that God, who exists beyond everything absolute and contracted, is not attained through even the highest absolution, just as He is, but rather only in the absolute mode. In this absolute mode the intellectual natures participate intellectually in what cannot be participated in; thus they are powers which are elevated above all contraction of power, according as power itself is overshadowed in the sensible world.

However, this absolution of the powers has modes. Indeed, without a mode the absolution is not participable. The absolution of power in the variety of modes shows various participating powers. There are, therefore, various intellectual spirits, which participate in power in various modes of absolution, so that all absolute spirits, which participate in the one power variedly, are not other than the absolute power participated in in various modes.

Already you see how great the potency of the spirit is, for it is a power which is exalted above all power in the sensible world. Therefore, in the potency of its power all the power of heaven and of those things which are under it is enfolded, so that every power which is in them is a certain unfolding of the power of the intellectual spirit. However, in the variety of the modes this sensible world participates sensibly in that one power, in which the intellectual world participates intellectually. The absolute power of the intellectual world is contracted in the sensible world in the various modes of participation; heavenly in the heaven, animatedly in animate souls, vitally in the living, vegetatively in vegetation, minerally in minerals, etc.

If you pay attention, you will therefore find in everything its power and its mode. It is therefore the One, which is everything in all things, which participate in it in their own mode. You can make the same conjectures concerning entity, goodness, and truth, as concerning power. For entity is that one, in which everything participates that is. It is correspondingly the case with goodness and truth. Therefore, the most prudent legislator, Moses, says God has created the universe and formed man, as if God were the creative and formative power, although He is beyond all this. But he endeavors to indicate how through participation in His power—in the manner that one can participate in it variously—everything advances into being. Likewise he says: God has seen that everything is good. Thereby he shows that God is the font of goodness, from which arise the various goods according to the mode in which one can participate variously in it. There is therefore nothing except the One, in which one cannot participate without the mode.

In order to sufficiently disclose that which I conjecture to you: the One is that which all theologians and philosophers endeavored to express in a variety of ways. The One is the realm of heaven, of which there is one similitude, which can only be unfolded in the variety of modes, as the master of truth has shown. What Zeno, what Parmenides, what Plato, and whatever others have said concerning the truth is not in each case an other, but rather they all looked at the One and expressed it in various modes. Although these modes of expression appear contrary and incompatible with one another, they nonetheless strive for nothing other than in their own mode—the one affirmatively, the other negatively, still another doubtfully—to unfold the One that is unattainably beyond all contrariety.

Indeed, the one theology is the affirmative, which affirms everything concerning the One; the negative is that one, which denies everything concerning the One; the doubtful, which neither denies nor affirms; the disjunctive, which affirms the one, denies the other; and the copulative, which affirmatively connects the opposites, or negatively, copulatively rejects thoroughly the opposites. Thus, all possible modes of expression are under the one theology in the endeavor to express the ineffable in some way.

Therefore, this is the path of study of those who strive after *theosis;* in the diversity of all possible modes to turn towards the One itself. Indeed, as soon as each one who strives after it, considers subtly and attends to how this One, the cause of everything, cannot not be expressed in every expression, just as the Word cannot not be spoken in every speech, whether he now says he spoke or whether he does not say he spoke, then it is manifest to him that the power of the ineffable embraces everything expressible, and that nothing can be said, in which it does not shine forth in its own manner as the cause of all saying and said.

Therefore, one who is truthfully occupied with theology will find nothing, in all the variety of conjectures, which perturbs him. For him, he who asserts there is nothing at all says no less than he who asserts everything is which is seen. He who asserts God is everything speaks no more truly than he who asserts He is nothing or is not, for he knows that God is ineffably beyond all affirmation and negation, whatever someone says, and also that, that which each says of Him, is not other than a certain mode, in which someone speaks concerning the ineffable; just as the two species, man and the ass, express the genus of animality in various modes—the human species indeed rationally, that of the ass irrationally. According to the expression of the human species, rationality seems to befit animality, according to the expression of the ass, irrationality.

However, whoever looks to the genus as such and sees how it is exalted above these differences, and that, therefore, none of the differences befits it, observes that the expression of the human species is a certain differential mode of the genus exalted above differences; the same is true for the species of the ass. Hence these contrary expressions of the contrary differential modes form no impediment for those who intuit the one superexalted genus.

Whoever strives for the filiation of God should not neglect, that in this school of the sensible world the One, which is everything, is sought in the variety of modes, but if mastery is achieved, then everything is known in the heaven of pure intelligence in the One. However, how it occurs, you should conjecture from the foregoing.

For the mind is not moved to apprehension on the path of ratiocinative reflection by reception through the senses, but rather the mind participates intellectually in the absolute power and indeed such that, according to the exuberant power of its nature, it is a kind of notion of everything intelligible. In this world it endeavors to elevate the potency of this power to actuality through sensible incitement. If, however, this power is later actualized through ratiocination and is freed thereby from the vivification of the body, in which it communicates itself, then it turns back to itself unitively in the living intellect and experiences itself as the power, which exists as the actual notion of things.

Indeed, just as God is the actual essence of all things, so is the intellect, separated and united in itself, vitally and reflexively, a living similitude of God. Therefore, as God Himself is the essence of all things, so the intellect, the similitude of God, is the similitude of all things. However, cognition is effected through similitude. However, since the intellect is an intellectual living similitude of God, it knows, when it knows itself, everything in itself as the One. However, it then knows itself, when it intuits itself in God, just as it is; this then is the case, when God is in it, it itself.

Therefore, to know everything is nothing other than to see oneself as the similitude of God, which is the filiation. Therefore, everything is intuited in one simple cognitive intuition. However, here it seeks the One in the variety of modes. Therefore, it is also such that the intellectual power, which expands itself rationally and sensibly in this world for the sake of its hunt, collects itself again, as soon as it transfers itself from this world. Indeed, the intellectual powers, which are participated in in the sensible and ratiocinative organs, return to their intellectual center, in order to live in the intellectual life in the unity from which they have emanated.

It can now be sufficiently clear to you, how according to my conjectures the intellectual nature in an intellectual mode is the totality of things. While it abides in the schools of this world, it seeks to place its potentiality into actuality and assimilates particular forms. From its power, with which it bears in itself the totality of things intellectually according to potentiality, it causes the knowledge of this and that thing to develop, whilst it assimilates the known things as actuality. Later, however, this assimilative potentiality, which here was only actualized in particular things, is transferred entirely into actuality and the perfect art of mastery, when it knows itself in the intelligible heaven as the similitude of all things. Then the intellect as actuality is the intellectual totality of all things, because it is the distinguishing notion of everything.

Nevertheless, the intellect then does not intuit anything outside of the intelligible heaven of its repose and its life. Indeed, it does not see the temporal temporally in the unstable succession, but rather in the indivisible present. For the present or the now, which enfolds all time, is not of this sensible world, but rather of the intellectual world, since it cannot be attained by the senses. Thus the intellect also in no way intuits quantity in extended, divisible corporeality, but rather in the indivisible point, in which the intellectual enfolding of all continuous quantity exists. Nor does it intuit the otherness of things in the variety of numbers, but rather in the simple monad, which enfolds every number intellectually.

The intellect therefore perceives everything intellectually beyond every sensible, distracting, and overshadowing mode. It does not intuit the entire sensible world in a sensible mode, but rather in a truer, that is an intellectual, mode. Indeed, this cognition is therefore called perfect intuition; for between the cognition of that world and this sensible world almost the same difference exists as between the knowledge which one receives through vision and that which one receives through hearing. Therefore, as much as that cognition, which is generated through vision, is more certain and clearer than that which is effected by the same thing through hearing, by so much and much more the intuitive cognition of the other world excels that which belongs to this world; thus the knowledge of the *wherefore* can be called the intuitive cognition, since the knowing reflects upon the rational ground of the thing, and the knowledge of the *that* can be called the cognition acquired from hearing.

Therefore, kindly receive, I entreat you, that which I have written down quickly and deficiently concerning your question, so far as time has permitted me. If God will provide me with something more excellent in another time, it shall not remain concealed from you. Now farewell, my well-beloved fellow brother, and let me participate in your prayers, so that we, translated away from here, obtain the filiation of God in His only-begotten Son, Jesus Christ, who is always blest.

On the Gift of the Father of Lights

(1 4 4 6)

Nicolaus of Cusa to the Reverend Father Gerard, Bishop of Solon.

Although the obscurity of my mental power is already known to you, Father, from earlier, you have nevertheless attempted to find light in it through a skillful investigation. Indeed, when in the collection of plants the words of the Apostle James— "Every best gift and every perfect gift is from above, from the Father of lights"—occurred to you, you demanded that I write down any conjectures as to the meaning of this text. I know, Father, that you have firmly in memory, what was transmitted by the most learned theologians, whereas I have only read a few of these writings. Hence I correctly would have to be ashamed of myself, if I were ignorant of the sincerity of your mind. Therefore, read and receive the interpretations which I realize.

I.

It was, as I believe, the intention of the most blessed Apostle to bring us on the easy road to everything desired. Every intellectual spirit desires to know. For to understand is the life of the intellect and this itself is its desired being. However, he who does not know his light, is not able to ascend to the apprehension of wisdom. Indeed, whoever needs something, needs that which he lacks. Therefore, the needy must know himself as needy and hasten avidly to that by which his need can be supplied. If, therefore, he who needs wisdom demands it from him whose treasuries are the plentitude of wisdom, and who, while empty-ing them still augments them—whose tenacity is the most lavish effusion—then he cannot not attain the wisdom, which infuses itself in the mind of the seeker. That is the loftiest proof of the wise Philo, who in his endeavor to laud wisdom, shows that it joins itself with the mind of the seeker.

To demand, however, is with earnest faith to seek in un-doubting hope for the attainment. Whoever advances in an ardent course toward wisdom, which he does not know, him it encoun-ters as an honored mother. However, the Apostle, who wants to exclude all error, shows from whom the wisdom, the light for the path and the lamp for our feet, the rational ground and the life of the soul should be requested, by saying: Every best gift and every perfect gift is from above. For if all that which is, insofar as it is considered good, that it wishes to be nothing other than itself, and indeed in the best possible way in which its nature contains the condition, then all that power, which knows itself to be from the best, knows that it exists in the best way. It knows, therefore, that its being, whose corruption or mutation to another being outside of its own species it wants at no time, is not given it by anything other which is not high above everything in the height of all the best.

For the human intellect does not believe that its nature could be given it by anything whose goodness is not the highest, high above everything good; also no entity would come to rest in its given nature, if this had been given it by a diminished and created good. However, because it has obtained its being from the best and the greatest Master—there is none better than He—every-thing which is finds its rest in its specific nature, as in the best from the best. Every natural gift, in all that which is, is the best, according to the judgment of all who are and who rest in their being as in the best. Therefore, it comes from above, from the infinite Omnipotence, which has such art and wisdom, that it is the most sufficient formative power of everything.

But because not every given nature actually attains the degree of perfection possible for its species, but rather one knows that every individual contraction of the species—except in the one, our Lord Jesus Christ—is distant from the ultimate perfec-tion of the activity of potentiality, the intellect, whose potential-ity embraces everything that is not its Creator, requires therefor that it be actualized as apprehension, the gift of grace of Him who has created it. The rational creature has in itself the discerning light of rationality; yet it is as the eye of the night owl, weak and obscured by many shadows in this sensible body. Therefore, it is actualized through the afflation of the spirit of the divine Word, and its darknesses are illuminated. Through the word of the teacher the student is illuminated, when the rational power of the student is led stepwise to actuality through the gift of the illuminated rationality of the master, which enters through the verbal spirit.

But all this actualizing illumination, which is a gift from above, descends from the Father of all gifts, which gifts are lights or theophanies. Solomon, according to the nature of his soul, had obtained the best gift from God. Nevertheless, his soul was not better on account of this gift than the soul of another man, but rather according to the gift of illumination he obtained this soul, whose intellectual power for actual apprehension ascended above that of all the Jewish kings who had preceded him. Whilst he requested this gift of wisdom from above, from the Father of lights, it descended to him.

We see that the power of the seed, which is given by the Father of lights, namely, the sun, is not brought into actuality, unless this is given by Him. For no tree develops from the potentiality of the seed, unless the sun, whose gift it is that this power is in the seed, gives this. The Apostle, therefore, wanted to exclude the errors of those who assert God is the cause of evil, as well as of those who have the presumption to assume man can come to apprehension of wisdom from himself, without the gift of grace or the assistance of the Father. Of this kind was the sin of the most presumptuous separated rational spirit, Lucifer, who attempted from his power to ascend to similitude with the highest. And likewise it was the sin of the incorporated rational spirit of the parents, who hoped by means of the nutritive power of the sensible tree's fruit to come to the perfection of knowledge of the gods. For we are taught that this actuality—that we apprehend wisdom, which is the living light and the glorious rest of our spirit—can come neither from us nor from the inferior sensible vegetation; it comes rather from the Father and the Giver of forms, who alone perfects.

He also enervated the errors of the others, who neglected

the Father of lights and requested assistance from Minerva, Apollo, Jupiter and the other gods, whilst he shows thereby that the position of all the gentiles asserts that there is no other Creator than the one infinite God of gods, that from Him alone must be requested every perfective gift and not from those gods which were deified on account of His power. The faculty of giving is not theirs, who have nothing from themselves that they have not received from the Father of all, since they possess nothing which is their own. For every gift, through whosesoever assistance it is participated in, is the gift of the Father, of whom everything is that is and from whom it must necessarily descend. All our intercessors, who have obtained possession of wisdom, therefore, request that light be given by the Father of lights. They do not give, rather He alone, who is giver and gift. This the Apostle appears to want, who calls us to constant prayer in the firmest faith without any hesitation and in the hoped-for certitude of attainment, for our Father gives affluently and without delay. So much is thus said concerning the Apostle's sentence.

II.

Now we wish to further admire the wonderful light, which is latent in the words of the Apostle, and I shall attempt, as it presents itself, to lay bare the proper meaning of the words. He says: "Every best gift," etc. From this every creature seems in a certain manner to be god. God alone is indeed the maximum good or the best. Therefore, if the creature is the best gift, every creature, since it is very good, seems to be a given god. Nothing can indeed be given, which is not subjected to His power. Indeed, that which is given must be in the power of the giver. However, the good is in the power of the good. The best, however, is nothing other than the One, simple, impartible, because it is the best. It can, therefore, give nothing other than itself.

The best is the diffusion of itself, but not in parts, because the best can only be the best. For it is all that which it can be. Its being is therefore its optimality and its eternity. It therefore communicates itself without diminution. Therefore, it appears that God and the creature are the same, i.e., God according to the mode of the giver, creature according to the mode of the gift. There will, therefore, only be one, which according to the diversity of modes obtains different names. Therefore, this same will be eternally according to the mode of the giver and temporally according to the mode of the gift, and it will be Creator and created, etc.

Without doubt this mode of expression lacks precision, yet we seek comprehension of the truth. The philosophers say it is the form, which gives being to the thing. This expression lacks precision. For it is not the thing to which the form gives being, because then nothing were except through the form. The thing therefore obtains being not from the form. For then it were, before it were. Nevertheless the form gives being to the thing, i.e., the form is the being itself in every thing that is, so that the being given to the thing is the form, which gives being. God, however, is the absolute Form of being, and that is the apostolic testimony in this location, since all being of everything is given by the Father.

But the form gives being. God, therefore, is the universal Form of being, who gives everything being. However, because the form gives being to every particular thing, that is to say that the form is itself the being of the thing, God, who gives this being, is called correctly by many the Giver of forms. Therefore, God is not the form of the earth, of water, of air, or of the aether, or any other thing whatsoever, but rather He is the absolute Form of the form of the earth or the air. Therefore, God is not the earth or something other, but rather the earth is earth, and the air is air, and the aether aether, and man man, each through its form. For the form of each is the descent from the universal Form, so that the form of the earth is its form and not that of something other, etc.

With admirable subtlety the Apostle expresses that to us in the following words: "The best gift descends," just as if he said: The Giver of forms gives no other from Himself, but rather His gift is the best and is His absolute and universally maximum optimality. However, it cannot be received just as it is given, since the reception of the given occurs in the descent. The infinite is, therefore, received finitely, the universal in the particular, and the absolute contractedly. However, since this reception falls from the truth of the communicating itself, it verges toward similitude and image, so that it is not the truth, but rather the similitude of the Giver. For in the other it can only be received otherwise.

Your face, which multiplies the equality of its superficial disposition, is received variously in the mirror, according to whichever mirror is receiving it; it will be diverse: in the one clearer, because the reception of the mirror is clearer, in the other more obscure; but in none at any time just as the face itself is. For it must be received otherwise in the other.

Only one mirror is without blemish, namely God Himself, in whom it is received just as it is, since this mirror is not other from something that is, but rather is that which is in all that which is, because He is the universal Form of being.

Many examples assist us in apprehending the aforesaid. For the light is, as it were, a universal form of all visible being, i.e., of every color. Color is indeed a contracted reception of light and the light is not mixed with the things, but rather it is received descendingly according to some degree of the descent. The termination of the light in the shining is the color, which is according to one mode red, according to another blue. And all being of color is given through the descending light, so that the light is all that there is in all colors, whose nature it is to pour forth purely from its goodness. And although it gives itself, by communicating itself purely, nevertheless the variety of color arises from its varied descending reception. Also the color is not the light, but rather it is in such contracted similitude received light, which is as the form of light to the form of color.

Thus God, the infinite Light, is as the universal Form of being to the forms of creatures. Thus the substantial form of Socrates is a one, simple, and impartible form, complete in the whole and in every part, through which Socrates, and everything which is Socrates, is. That the hand of Socrates is indeed that of Socrates and not that of another, it has from the form of Socrates. But because the hand does not receive the form of Socrates with that simplicity which is the form of Socrates, but rather in the particular descent, namely, as such a member, the hand of Socrates is not Socrates. The same is true also for the other members.

Our soul is the universal distinguishing power for discerning, and it is one and simple, complete in the whole and in every organ, so that all the distinguishing power is given in the eye of the soul, which gives itself to vision. But the eye receives the soul only in the descent, because it does not receive it as the universal distinguishing power. For this reason, the eye does not discern between the audible and tasteable, but rather only receives the universal power contractedly, in order to discern the visible. The eye is not the seeing or distinguishing soul, although everything which in it discerns, is a gift of the soul. It is likewise with hearing, etc.

The substantial form universally gives the substantial being. This being is received descendingly, i.e. quantitatively, qualitatively, respectively, actively, passively, situationally, habitually, locationally, and temporally. Indeed, simple unity is received in nine modes, so that everything is thus numerated in the denary. However, because through quantity it is not received purely and substantially, but rather descendingly and in such contraction, quantity is not the substance, although all being of quantity is given by substance, so that everything which is in quantity is not other from substance and the quantity is the quantity of substance. And it is likewise with other accidents.

From this our intellect can help itself and penetrate somewhat into the apostolic reading, so that it may be able to see how God is the universal Form of being of all forms; the latter do not receive specific form in the descent universally and absolutely, just as it is and gives itself, but rather receive it in specific contraction. Angelicality receives the universal form of being corresponding to that descent which is called angelicality. Humanity contracts the universal form of being according to that descent which is called humanity. Leoninity participates according to that descent in the absolute form. And although God is thus everything in everything, humanity is nevertheless not God, although one can accept the expression of Hermes Trismegistus, insofar as he is understood correctly: that God is named with the name of all things and all things with the name of God; so that man can be called a god made human and this world, as Plato also wished it, a sensible god. And because He, who has done everything for His own sake, is Himself the end of His work, He gave Himself as the sensible world, so that the sensible world, as His descending reception, which diverges in sensible steps, exists on account of Himself and attains goodness sensibly, and the infinite Light lights the sensible sensibly—just as it lights the living vitally, the rational rationally, and the intelligent intellectually. And this is thus said about this.

III.

Moreover, I observe how cautiously the Apostle expresses it, that every creature is in the Giver eternal and eternity itself. For the omnipotence of the Giver coincides with eternity itself; indeed, omnipotence could always give. Therefore, every gift was in eternity with the Father, from whom it descended, when it is received. Indeed, the Giver gave always and eternally, but it was not received except in the descent from eternity. However, such a descent is the contraction of eternity into duration, which has a beginning.

One understands this easily, if one considers how the plurality of things descends from the eternal rational ground. But plurality is number. And this same, which is for rationality to ratiocinate or enumerate, is for the Creator to create. Number, which descends from the rational ground, has an origin, namely unity. But it has no end, since it is not possible to give a number beyond which no other can be given.

Number is therefore the originated eternity, and the absolute rational ground the absolute eternity. Indeed, the rational ground is the cause, and the absolute rational ground denies it is originated or caused, since it is the absolute cause. The creature descends therefore from the eternity, in which it has always been.

However, because the given eternity was received only contractedly, this eternity without origin exists as received in the manner of the originated. The world therefore has no origin, as far as the eternity in it is its entire being. However, because eternity is received only in the manner of the originated in the descent of the world, the world is not the absolute eternity, but rather the eternity contracted in the manner of the originated.

The eternity of the world is therefore originated and the eternal world is made; the world, which is with the Father eternally, and the one that was made through the descent from the Father, is not other, but rather it is the same world, which is without origin and which is received in the manner of the originated through the descent into its own being. It is with the Father and is not transmutable, but remains the same as the Father in perpetual stability, in highest clarity and without all vicissitude of shadows. But, as it is received in the descent from the Father into its own being, it is transmutable in the vicissitude of the shadows and unstably fluid, just as if the world were a transmutable god in the vicissitude of the shadows, and the world, intransmutable and without all vicissitude of the shadows, were the eternal God.

These are intelligible modes of speech, without all precision, although in the mode of communicating the intelligence, with which one conceives God and the world, they approach precision. He speaks more precisely, however, about the ineffable God, who affirms of Him, that He dwells beyond all affirmation and negation, beyond all positing and denying, beyond all opposition, transmutation, and intransmutation in the light inaccessible to intelligence. I have spoken extensively about this elsewhere.

And because to speak in this manner about the ineffable God is to employ a speech which is beyond all speech and silence, where silence is speech, such a speech is not of this world, but rather belongs to the eternal realm. Just as we communicate our intelligence in this world, the Apostle denies that transmutation and vicissitude of shadows befit God the Father, for He is the eternal light, in which there is not any darkness.

IV.

Now it still remains for us to ponder that passage, where the Apostle says God is the Father of lights. He does not say that He is the light, but rather the Father of lights. And he does not say that He is darkness, whom he affirms as the Father of lights. Rather He is the font of light. We affirm that which comes to our knowledge, to be. However, what in no way appears to us, we do not apprehend that it is. All things are appearances or lights of some kind. However, because the Father and the font of light are one, all things are appearances of the one God, who, although He is one, nevertheless can only appear in variety. For how could infinite power appear otherwise than in variety?

If a teacher has an adept, potent and active intellect, then it can appear only in the variety of numerous rational conclusions.

The various rational and syllogistical lights, therefore, descend from such an intellect, which is the Father of lights, so that it thus manifests itself. Unity, the simple origin of number, is of the greatest and of incomprehensible power, and the appearance of this power appears only in the variety of the numbers descending from this power. The power of the simplest point is incomprehensible; it is observed only in the quantities descending from the most simple point as in various lights. The simplest power of the present is incomprehensible; it can only be detected in temporal succession.

However, everything according to number is in unity, everything according to quantity is in the point, everything according to temporal succession is in the now of the present, and everything according to everything is what it is or was or can be in the infinite power of omnipotence. In an absolute manner our God is the infinite power, which is wholly in actuality; when it wants to manifest itself on the basis of the nature of goodness, it makes various lights descend from itself, which are called theophanies. In all these lights it makes known the wealth of glory of its light.

But this generation, which occurs voluntarily, since it has no other cause than that of its goodness, occurs in the Word of truth. The Word of truth is the absolute rational ground or art or the rational ground, which can be called the light of all rational grounds. In this light, which is not only the Word but the only-begotten Son and the highest appearance of the Father, the Father of lights has voluntarily generated all descending appearances, so that thus all lights of appearance are enfolded in the highest power in the fortitude of the union of appearances; just as every unfoldable filiation whatsoever is in an abstract filiation, and everything somehow unfoldable through art is in the most universal art, and every discerning light is in the absolute rational ground or the absolute distinction.

However, He generated us in that Word of eternal art and appearance, so that when we receive the light of His manifestation, which is the infinite Word, in the descent, in the manner in which it can be received by us in the descent, we are a certain beginning of His creation. Therefore, the reception in the descent of the manifestation of the Father in the Word gives the beginning of creation. Through this we are indeed a certain beginning of His creation, because we receive in our manner the Word of truth, in which He has generated us.

It is satisfactorily shown above, that the reception in the descent brings it about that the eternal and universal light effects the beginning of particular creatures, so that in this way a creature arises, which has its first beginning in the Word of truth. We are therefore the genus of God, since He has generated us. Yet He generated us all in the one Son, who is the Word of truth, in whom He caused us to have a certain beginning of His creation.

Just as in the Word or rational ground or art of humanity all men are generated, so that they have received through the generation of humanity that they are a certain beginning of the being of particular men, everything which is truthful is generated in the generation of universal truth, so that it is a certain beginning of the generating creation.

Therefore, everything which is, is only insofar as it is true. The false indeed is not. Therefore, it is eternally generated in the eternal generation of the truth itself, and as such it is the eternal power of the truth. It receives from the truth that, when it appears in temporal succession, it is a certain beginning of the creation of the generating Father; just as the branch of the tree, which, as I now see, begins to grow in the tree, previously generated in the seed, was not branch but rather seed. The truth of the branch was indeed in the truth of the rational ground of the seed. The truth of the seed is therefore the truth of the branch. The truth of power therefore contains the beginning of some being, i.e., a branch which is, as it were, the creature of the seed, from whose power it proceeds. Therefore, the truth of the branch, which was generated always with the seed in the truth of the seed, appears now and through its appearance shows the power of the seed of the Father.

Thus we see clearly how, according to the absolute Omnipotence and the infinite Light, the Son is in the divine the true manifestation of the Father. But every creature is a manifestation of the Father, since it participates in the manifestation of the Son variedly and contractedly; some creatures manifest Him more obscurely, others more clearly according to the variety of the theophanies or appearances of God.

V.

Now I want to add something concerning the gifts of illumination, which we must not omit. The gifts of the one, perfect divine Spirit are various. Indeed God, who is the purest actuality, is also the infinite perfection. In the descent He is not attained as He is, but rather in the manner of potentiality. Indeed, in the descent of generation the perfection of man is not attained from the Father, but rather man is in potentiality in the seed of the Father; and also the tree is not received in the fruit, which descends from it, but rather the tree is in potentiality in the seed.

Therefore, as the Father generated everything in the Word of truth, so everything is perfected in the Spirit, which proceeds from the Father and the Son. For the Spirit fulfills, i.e., it leads the circle of the world, and everything which has the knowledge of the Word, to perfection. All are in the Father in the manner of the Father, in the Son in the manner of the Son, in the Holy Spirit in the manner of perfection. In the Father all have being, in the Son power, in the Holy Spirit activity. God, the Father, is everything in everything; God, the Son, enables everything in everything; God, the Spirit, effects everything in everything.

From being and potential proceeds the work. However, the Spirit works the perfection of being in the existing, the perfection of life in the living, and the perfection of knowledge in the thinking. The one Spirit, who is blessed God, works all this so that every creature, as far as the condition of its nature allows it, ascends nearer through perfection to deification, i.e., to the terminus of its repose. The shadowed and corporeal being finds its repose in the living, the living in the intellectual, the intellectual in the truth, which is God, so that in this way every corporeal being, by means of that which lives and the latter through the intellectual, flows back to the origin.

However, the intellectual being is that through which the inferior flows from God and flows back to God. Therefore, the intellectual nature, according to the reception in the descent, is graded variously, just as in number the simple numeral descent is completed by the denary. However, the denary descent is the beginning of the composed number and the end of the simple number and it is also another unity. Therefore, there are ten grades of intellectual nature; the first is abstracter and clearer, and great in the actual apprehension of God, the last, which is called the human, is immersed in corporeal shadows; it is the least in actuality, but great in potential power.

And since our intellectual spirit only attains repose, if it apprehends it with its intellectual nature—to apprehend this it has indeed received intellectual being—the perfecting Spirit grants it many lights, so that it can attain to actuality from the power of its potentiality.

Indeed, whatever is created are lights, in order to actualize intellectual power, so that it advances in the light thus given it to the font of lights. Man sees that there are various creatures and in this variety he is illuminated, so that he advances to the essential light of creatures. For when he sees that one creature without vital motion is, another lives, another ratiocinates, then he is immediately illuminated and knows that the absolute Essence of creatures does not thus exist, live, or ratiocinate. If indeed life belonged to the essence of creatures, then the non-living creature would not exist. If ratiocination belonged to the essence of creatures, then a stone or a tree were no creature.

He therefore understands that nothing of everything, which is apprehended in the variety of creatures, belongs to the essence. Since, therefore, every creature is something in contraction, the essence of everything is not something, but rather nothing of everything in an uncontracted manner. Thus you see the variety of forms. Therefore, the essence is nothing of this kind.

Some creatures are large, others are small, others higher, others lower, some were, others will be, some here, others there, and it is thus with all nameable variety. The essence is therefore not extended or large or small or in a higher or lower location or in a past or future time, etc.

You see that many things come together in the elemental genus, many in the vegetative, many in the sensitive genus, and that these genera are varied. The essence is therefore not something of them. You see that there are many diverse species under the genera, thus for example, in the genus of animals the species of man, of the lion, of the horse, etc. The essence of the genus of animals is, therefore, not some species of all but rather none of those species.

You see that there are various men; that the one was, the other will be, that the one is young, the other is old, that the one is German, the other French, the one masculine, the other feminine, the one large, the other small, the one blind, the other seeing, the one white, the other black; and it is thus with everything, since in everything that one can consider, there is variety. Everything sensible, visible, tangible, etc. is, therefore, not of the essence of man.

Humanity therefore is nothing of that which can be apprehended in every possible man; rather humanity is the simplest essence, which receives the generic essence specifically, in which, as in simple power, is all that which is participated in individually in the variety of men. Humanity is therefore the father of lights of various men; the same essence of Plato is in humanity beyond all sensible and temporal habitude, and in Plato in sensible and temporal habitude. And it is thus with everything.

Therefore, the essences of the sensible are insensibly in the species, and the specific essences without specification in the genera, and the essences of the genera without generality are in the absolute Essence, which is blessed God.

There are also other lights, which are infused through divine illumination, which lead the intellectual potential to perfection; such is the light of faith, through which the intellect is illuminated, so that it ascends beyond rationality to the apprehension of the truth. And because it is led by this light to believe it can attain the truth—which it nevertheless is not able to attain with the assistance of rationality, which is, as it were, its instrument—and thus in an endeavor given it by the Divinity leaves its infirmity and blindness, on account of which it is wont to rely upon the staff of rationality and, strengthened in the Word of faith, can go alone, it is led in undoubting hope, out of firm faith, to obtain the promised, that it apprehends it rapidly in the loving course. And that is the illumination of the Apostle, who announces without hesitation, that he who believes and requests will obtain wisdom.

Our intellectual power possesses the ineffable riches of the light in potentiality. But since they are in potentiality, we are ignorant that we possess them, until they are revealed to us through the intellectual light existing in actuality, and the way is shown to lead them into actuality.

Thus in the little field of the pauper many riches are in potentiality, which if he knows that they are there and seeks them in the appropriate manner, he will find. For yonder is wool and bread and wine and meat, etc., that he desires and does not see with his eyes. But rationality grants him the light of revelation, so that he knows that they are there and that he elicits wool from the lamb, milk from the cow, wine from the grapevine, and bread from the grain. And the various experienced farmers manifest the light of knowledge given them for the good cultivation of the field. In this light the farmer advances in faith and obtains the fruit of sensible life.

In a similar way all things of the intellectual field are in potentiality. These yield the intellectual life, insofar as it is correctly cultivated and its powers are expressed through the necessary exercises and modes. And for its cultivation various illuminations transmitted to us are found by those, who diligently occupy themselves with this intellectual culture. As for example the men who, devoted to the virtues, leave the shadows of this world and dedicate themselves to the mental light; through them the Giver of lights has revealed to us a hidden thesaurus, and the way to protect the field, as well as the laws and precepts to extirpate the noxious weeds, which do not bear the fruit of life, but rather impede and mortify the fecundity, and to plant and cultivate the tree of life in it. Such men were Moses, the prophets, the philosophers, and the apostles.

But the Word, the light of all these, has been received in the descent of the absolute Word and was not itself the Word, which is the infinite light of the Father, as far as this Word manifested itself without contraction sensibly in our Lord Jesus Christ. Generated in this Word of the truth, we are sons of the light, since He revealed that the riches of the glory of the eternal realm are among us and within us, and since He taught us that we obtain intellectual immortality through mortification of the sensible world, and since He made Himself manifest to us, so that in His light, which is the Word become flesh, we apprehend the paternal light of our life. For He Himself is the paternal light, which illuminates every man, and with His light completely fulfills that which we lack, in order to attain in Him and through Him, who is blessed eternally, the most delectable life of repose. Thanks be to God.

of the soul

Dialogue on Genesis

(1 4 4 7)

CONRAD: Often we are more delectably refreshed by less varied, although precious, dishes. Hence may it not now cause
annoyance, although you, Nicolaus, have served us things in a
generous manner, which show us a road to the imperishable food
of the soul, if I also request more tasteful nutriment.

NICOLAUS: You've known me for a long time, Conrad, and know
that I endeavor indefatigably to attain to the incomprehensible and that it gives me joy either to be stimulated by
questions or compelled by objections. Therefore, speak!

CONRAD: Many and great are the questions, which present themselves simultaneously to me. Indulge me, therefore, if I do
not set them forth in order.

NICOLAUS: It is your decision; do as it pleases you.

CONRAD: First, I do not know whether I conjecture well, that the
investigations of all the sages are terminated in one Origin.
When one has come from the lake over the river to the font,
one stands still. For the end has no end and the beginning
no beginning. However, where there is the coincidence
of beginning and end, there the middle must necessarily
coincide. However, this appears to be the same in which
everything is the Same itself. The prophet David says of it:
"In the beginning You have founded the earth and the
heavens are the work of Your hands. They shall perish,

You, however, are the same." Tell me if I conjecture correctly.

NICOLAUS: That is most certain; but I await what you are driving at.

CONRAD: I am astonished at how the Same itself is the cause of all things, which are so diverse and contrary. The endeavor of my investigation is aimed at the genesis of the universe and I wished very much to hear from you concerning it as briefly and easily as possible.

NICOLAUS: How should I, the most foolish of all, make clear in an easily understandable compendium, a matter which all before me deserted as the most difficult and most inexplicable?

CONRAD: How well I know, on the basis of your teaching, that nothing is attainable or expressible as it is—in the case of genesis, the divine Moses and many others have spoken variously and have set forth the difficulty through a variety of conjectures—nevertheless I hope to be able to hear something about it that strengthens me.

NICOLAUS: All who spoke about genesis, as you assert, expressed the same in varied ways. Why, therefore, are you astonished that the cause of diverse things is the same?

CONRAD: Because the same seems to be born capable of effecting the same.

NICOLAUS: You assert correctly. And hence it is, that everything is from the absolute Same that which it is and in the mode in which it is.

CONRAD: If you do not explain that more clearly, I will not understand it.

NICOLAUS: First, you know, Conrad, that one becomes knowledgeable through attentive consideration.

CONRAD: I admit that only on the basis of attentive consideration is there a difference between knowledge and ignorance.

NICOLAUS: Therefore, turn your attention to the absolute Same and immediately you will see, that the absolute Same is eternal, because it is the same. The absolute Same can indeed not be from another. For if, as you say, the same is born capable of effecting the same, then also the other is capable of effecting the other. Therefore, how shall the absolute Same be from another?

CONRAD: That I understand.

NICOLAUS: Hence it is eternal, simple, interminable, infinite, inalterable, unmultiplicable, etc.

CONRAD: When I pay attention to it in attentive meditation, I cannot deny that. The Same must indeed be eternal, because it can be the same from no other. Therefore, because it is eternal it is interminable, likewise infinite and inalterable. For alterability is from the other. However, the Same in itself bespeaks inalterability and likewise unmultiplicability, not, however, multiplicability, which cannot subsist without alteration. I admit this assertion entirely, which shows itself as true.

NICOLAUS: I would also like you to attend to the fact that God is elsewhere called the One and the Same. Those who are occupied diligently with the meaning of words prefer the name *the One* to the name *the Same,* as if identity were less than the one. Everything the same is indeed one and not vice versa. They also considered entity, the eternal, and everything not-one as after the simple One; thus the Platonics above all. You, however, conceive that the Same in an absolute manner can be considered beyond the same in name. It is this of which the prophet speaks; since it is the absolute Same itself, which stands beyond all diversity and opposition, because it is the same. Therefore, no other is the same; the ineffable Same, in which everything is the same, is nothing diverse. The universal and the particular are in the Same the same; unity and infinity are in the Same the same. It is likewise with potentiality and actuality, likewise with essence and being. Indeed, in the absolute Same even being and not-being must be the Same itself.

CONRAD: When I consider this attentively it is revealed to me clearly. Indeed, many name the same, who say that a thing is; similarly they name the same, if they say that it is not. Therefore, I understand the absolute Same as that in which the opposition, which the same does not admit, cannot be found, so that everything other, diverse, opposite, composite, contracted, general, special, etc. of this kind follows the absolute Same at a great distance.

NICOLAUS: You grasp it well, Conrad. For if we say the diverse is diverse, then we affirm that the diverse is the same as itself. For the diverse can only be diverse through the absolute Same, through which everything that is, is the same as itself and other from the other. But everything which is the same as itself and other from the other, is not the absolute Same, which is neither the same as, nor diverse from, the other. For how should the same as another befit the absolute Same? It is indeed not diverse. For how can diversity befit the absolute Same, which precedes all diversity and otherness?

CONRAD: I understand that you wish to say there is nothing of all entities, which is not the same as itself and other from another and that hence none such is the absolute Same, although the absolute Same is diverse from none of these entities, which are the same as themselves and diverse from others.

NICOLAUS: You conceive correctly. For the absolute Same, which we also call God, is not subject to number with every other, so that, for example, God and the heaven were many or two or other or diverse things; thus the heaven, as that which is something other from the earth, is not the absolute Same. And because the absolute Same as actuality is the Form of every formable form, there can be no form outside of the Same. That a thing is indeed the same as itself, the form effects; however, that it is other from another is because it is not the absolute Same, which is the Form of every form. The absolute Same is, therefore, the beginning, middle, and end of every form, and the absolute actuality of every potentiality is the uncontracted, not-othered Same, in which the universal does not stand in opposition to the particular, since both are after it. Indeed, the universal is the same as itself and another from the particular. It is likewise with the particular. The absolute Same is, therefore, superexalted above every intellectual universal and real particular that exists.

CONRAD: When I turn my attention to the fact, that one cannot deny that everything is the same as itself, then I see that the absolute Same is participated in by everything. For if the absolute Same were other and diverse from everything, they would not be what they are. How indeed should something be the same as itself, if the absolute Same were diverse and distinct and other from it? Likewise, if something that participates in the same were itself the Same, in which it participates, how should it be diverse from another, which also were the same as itself?

NICOLAUS: You grasp it acutely. Also the consideration of the Platonics, however subtle it may be, that the First is unparticipably superexalted, should not disturb you. Understand indeed, that the absolute One is participated in identically in the identity, of which they say that it is after the first absolute One. Indeed, it should suffice you that—however it may be participated in—everything is not the same as itself, unless it is from that, from which everything is, which is the absolute Same. And because you have already earlier often heard a lot about it from me, this may be said for more concise facility in respect to the absolute Same. I will attempt to explain the aforesaid more amply. You have said, the same is born capable of making the same. Admitting this, I conclude therefrom, that all things, as varied and diverse as they may be, on this basis are what and also how they are. You have been astonished by this. I shall endeavor to free you from this astonishment through an easy compendium.

CONRAD: Say as much as you please, if only you do it in a manner apprehensible by me, as you seem to promise.

NICOLAUS: You yourself will judge whether I have fulfilled my promise. At first you don't hesitate to accept that the same effects the same. For how could the same, by virtue of the fact that it is the same, make the diverse, since diversity in the absolute Same is the same and all diversity is much later after it. The same is, therefore, only born capable of effecting the same, i.e., making the same. Hence every thing, since it is the same as itself, effects the same, so that the intellect intellectualizes, vision visualizes, warmth warms, etc. And because the same is unmultiplicable, every identification is found in assimilation.

Therefore, the same calls the not-same into the same. And because the same is unmultiplicable and unattainable by the not-same, the not-same rises in conversion to the same. And thus it is found in assimilation; so that when the absolute Entity, which is the absolute Same, calls the not-entity to the same, since the not-entity cannot attain the unmultiplicable, absolute Entity, the not-entity is found as the arising in the conversion to the absolute Entity, i.e. in the assimilation of the same.

However, assimilation bespeaks a certain coincidence of the descent of the same to the not-same and the ascent of the not-same to the same. Therefore, the creation or genesis can be described as the assimilation of absolute Entity, since this, as the Same, by effecting the same, calls the nothing or not-entity to itself. On this basis, the saints said that the creature is the similitude and image of God.

However, since unity, which coincides with the Absolute Same, is unmultiplicable, because the same is also unity, therefore, the not-one, since it is not able to attain the unmultiplicable, absolute identity, can only be found in plurality. Therefore, when the absolute Same, which is entity and the one and the infinite, calls the not-same to itself, the assimilation arises in the many, which participate in the Same variedly. Therefore, plurality, otherness, variety, and diversity and other such arise from the fact that the Same effects the same. Hence there is also order, which is participation of the same in variety and harmony, which represents the same variedly. Everything, however varied it be, is consonant and harmonious with the same, and this consonant clamor is assimilation.

Thus, therefore, the cosmos or beauty, which is also called the world, has arisen in the clearest possible representation of the unattainable Same. Indeed, the variety of those entities which are the same as themselves and other from the other, shows the unattainable Same unattainably, since the Same shines forth in them more strongly, the greater the unattainability is unfolded in the variety of images. Indeed, the unattainability coincides with the absolute

Same. From this it is clear that I have spoken correctly: All things by virtue of this are what they are and how they are, because the Same effects the same. This perfect consequence is, therefore, the absolute Same. Therefore, all things are what they are and how they are, so that there is no rational ground or cause for all things except that the Same effects the same.

When you, however, see that innumerable things participate in this absolute rational ground, since every thing is the same as itself and has the aptitude for effecting the same and indeed all the more perfectly, the more it is the same, and when you simultaneously also perceive that every thing whatever is other from every other, then you understand easily that everything is what it is, because that which is called by the absolute Same to the unattainable Same is found in this assimilation just as it is.

You can now reduce the perfection of the gradations of entity, its powers and operations, the numbers, the weight and measure, to the same cause or to the same, in the manner in which it is given mental powers, and know that the generation, corruption, alteration and the rest of this kind are from the fact that the Same effects the same.

For if the entities—of which each is the same as itself and very opposite from the other, in order to better represent the completely clear unattainability, which coincides with the absolute Same—come together in the assimilation with the Same, so that in this way infinity or unattainability is unfolded in the maximum opposition of the participating things in the greatest possible clarity, which the condition of the participating things permits, then accordingly the things participating in the entity itself are of opposite powers.

However, since all entities are the same as themselves, these endeavor to effect the same; the warm endeavors to make warm, the cold to make cold. And since the warm calls the not-warm to identity with it and the cold the not-cold, a battle arises and from this generation and corruption and all the like: temporality, fluidity, instability, and variety of motion. Already you see the one cause of everything.

If it appears otherwise to you, then refute my words

clearly with rationality. I shall be happy to be instructed. For in order to fulfill my promise I have indeed briefly summarized the matter in question in an easy compendium and have perhaps thereby considered the matter too little, which is often the cause of an error.

CONRAD: You have done more than enough! No objection occurs to me. Indeed, when I listen to you in this train of thought, I have therein had the experience and thereby learned that one and the same unattainable illumination of learned ignorance, in everything which you have bespoken now and often earlier, shines forth to me clearly in the variety of the modes of explication, so that your explanations reflect the same art everywhere; they are indeed its assimilation, because I now have apprehended nothing other than the Same itself, which I often heard in another mode.

Indeed, the absolute Same is also the absolute maximum, which is ineffable and unattainable; and thus the ineffable is the cause of everything speakable and the unattainable the cause of everything attainable. Also, you have already made known to me that the infinite, which coincides with the absolute Same, shines forth in the innumerable multitude of particular entities in the greatest possible clarity. For, because the particular entities, of which each is the same as itself and other from the other, exceed every numerable number, but nevertheless do not attain to the unattainable infinite, the unattainability of the absolute Infinity is made clearer.

And because the absolute Same—since everything is the same as itself—is in everything, the universal, generic, or specific concordance of all things is varied; likewise also the difference, without which the concordance—on account of the unattainable—cannot be. Thus I see the eternal, which is the unattainable Same together with the absolute Same; and that there is, therefore, the innumerable variety of duration, which exceeds every rational measure, so that in this way the unattainability of the eternal Same shines forth more perfectly.

I see in sufficient clarity, that those who investigate the genesis of things could fail, if they did not consider that.

For, because they felt that the duration of the world is immeasurable for rationality, some believed that the world is eternal, although the eternal is the absolute Same, which is unattainable through all duration and whose unattainability is only all the more evident in immeasurable duration. It appears to me that the latter deceive themselves in exactly the same way as an eye, which sees some body and, although this is spherical in the part it sees, believes that it is no perfect sphere, since it cannot see that it is a sphere. Indeed, the eye cannot intuit a sphere with a single look, but as we help ourselves, by means of combinative rationality, in the apprehensibility of a sphere by means of sight, so it is also necessary that we help ourselves with the lofty intellect, which shows us that rational measure is improportionately below the eternal, so that it cannot be concluded that that is eternal, whose duration is inapprehensible with rationality. Indeed, rational measures, which attain the temporal, do not attain the things freed from the temporal, just as hearing does not attain something inaudible, although there are also those things unattainable by it.

NICOLAUS: This contribution is very good. My opinion about it you have indeed already heard elsewhere. It should now satisfy us, to have known that the absolute Same is the cause of everything, and that the absolute eternity is unattainable through all the variety of immeasurable duration, and that this unattainability of the eternal shines out in the immeasurability of the duration; that the dictum of the Peripatetics, the world was from eternity, is true, as far as they assert the eternal is unattainable through the measuring rationality; but that that of the Platonics, who say the world is generated and who see the eternal Same as the absolute origin, is truer. Nevertheless, the Platonics do not deny that the immeasurability of duration concurs with generation. Our saints expressed this as clearly as possible, when they said that the world has been made in the origin or beginning.

It is manifest that the origin or beginning of the world is not in another, but rather the absolute Same is the beginning, middle, and end of the world. And God did not give duration its beginning before the world outside of the absolute Same. Therefore, through the world everything is also what is in the world. Just as nothing which belongs to the world, just as it is, is attained other than only in the absolute Same, so also duration, just as it is, cannot be attained through any measure. For how would the same be attained through the other except otherwise? How, through the measure of the duration of the one, could the duration of the other be measured, if they were incommensurable with each other and also unknown? Indeed, only the absolute Same is the most adequate measure of everything that is in any way measurable.

CONRAD: I would easily acquiesce in everything, except the book of Moses on Genesis restrains me. For with the help of rationality, according to the account very well presented there, we can elicit the temporal measure of the beginning of the world, which does not yet amount to 7000 years, although it is read otherwise in the *Natural History* of Pliny and in many other books.

NICOLAUS: I value the scriptures of Moses highly in all respects and know, when I pay attention to the intention of the writer, that they are entirely true. For the fact that God has created the world and man after His image and indeed very well; that sin has entered the human race through man and not through the Creator; that God called man back from the evil way, which the latter has inherited not from God but rather from his first parents, with many means, with prophetic promises and gifts; that He armed him, whom He has called back, with commandments to resist corrupt inclinations; that beyond this He has given him the promise of the filiation of God in His Son, insofar as he believes and fulfills his mandate; all this I attest to and assert deeply and most constantly, when I turn towards God, whom it is suitable to deify, and indeed not because I am a Christian or am bound by a law, but rather because my rationality is forbidden to perceive otherwise.

However, where Moses expresses the mode humanly, in which all this has occurred, I believe he has expressed this elegantly, in order to express the truth in the manner in which it can be grasped by man. You know, however, that a human mode of expression was used in order to instruct men humanly. Beyond the human mode of expression he has added words in appropriate locations, so that the intelligent understand that those words, which express the mode, are a human assimilation of the unattainable divine mode.

For when he reveals that God is nothing of all that which can be seen or engraved or figured, that He is visible for men only in the vestiges, which are posterior to Him, and that He, who is infinitely powerful, does nothing in temporal periods of time, then Moses shows clearly enough that he has represented the inexpressible mode of the creation humanly.

Hence those wisemen, who say that the invisible God has created everything simultaneously, just as He wanted it, do not contradict the intention of Moses, the law-giver; as also most others do not, who have invented other modes of expression. And this he emphasizes above all by the fact that when he spoke about men, he named them Adam; this word means man and enfolds both the masculine as well as the feminine. On account of the aforesaid and much else, which can be treated more suitably elsewhere, the beginning of Genesis is entrusted by the Jews to the prudent to be preserved, so that the literal surface not offend the novice.

The prudent, however, and those experienced in theology, who know that the mode of the divine is not easily apprehensible, are not offended if an allegorical, contracted mode, more assimilated to the wont of the audience be found. Indeed, they absolve the latter, as much as it is possible for them, of that contraction, so that they see that the absolute Same effects the same. Hence they are not offended in the least by the diversity of histories, of rational grounds, of times, names, and men, the contrary flow of rivers, which are said to arise in the middle of Paradise, and everything else, although it were still more absurd. Rather, on the basis of these absurdities they hunt after still more secret mysteries, as you can find it in the written investigations of the most ingenious saints concerning this part of

Genesis, if you have read well the writings of Ambrose, "On Paradise" and "Hexaemeron," and Basil, Augustine, Jerome and others.

Although these all seem in many things to be of different points of view, nevertheless notice that these prudent men concur with one another in the principal things; although they do not all admit that the mode of Genesis is narrated literally. I accept all of their consideration in respect to the modes, as though they are various concepts of wisemen of the inexpressible mode, in that I do nothing other than to turn myself to the Same itself, which each has endeavored to portray in assimilation, and to acquiesce therein.

CONRAD: It is certainly especially pleasing to me to hear this from you concerning the origin of Genesis. For as I understand it, the intention of the law-giver was one that you affirm as completely true in the sense of all the wisemen, but you do not deny the historical representation of the mode, because you say that on account of the audience it was clothed in a human mode as history, in order to bear fruit, although man can neither conceive nor express the divine mode, except in varied assimilation. However, because our prophet David, whose words you have abundantly explained, where he speaks concerning the absolute Same, says elsewhere: "By the word of the Lord the heavens are made and by the breath of His mouth all their power," I beseech you as to whether this assimilation is in agreement; above all because it does not seem fundamentally to be very diverse from the representation of Moses.

NICOLAUS: Every philosopher has attempted to conjecture concerning the mode in which everything is from the First. However, the opinion of the more prudent philosophers is that the natural forms of things emanate from God, the purest intellect, which exists completely and most perfectly in actuality, and have arisen through the command of His will; just as the form of the house comes about in the command of the master builder, which the instruments obey. In order to express it more concisely: Through the aforesaid is shown that every agent, because it is the same as itself, effects the same. Therefore, every agent in its acting represents the creation in some similitude.

CONRAD: That is not to be doubted. But the one action is accomplished more clearly than the other. Therefore, I beseech you to guide me through a still more suitable assimilation.

NICOLAUS: Very willingly, as much as it now occurs to me. You have surely already seen how a vessel arises through the art of vitrification.

CONRAD: I have seen that.

NICOLAUS: This example can sufficiently guide you. The glassmaker collects the material. Then he adapts it in the furnace, with the help of the fire. Thereafter he takes an iron reed as help, into which the glass material is added, so that then, through the blowing of the artist, it receives the vessel form conceived in the mind of the master. The glassmaker blows his breath therein. This penetrates into the material. With the help of the breath, which moves the material according to the intention of the master, the glass vessel arises through the master from the material, which was lacking all form of a vessel. This intention forms the material so much, that a vessel arises of such a species that the material itself, which now stands under the form, no longer has the universal possibility for every form of vessel, for the universal possibility is actually made specific. But when the master proposes to make from this vessel of this species another one of another species and sees that neither this vessel nor its parts, just because they are its parts, stand in a possible relation to the vessel that he intended—any one entity is indeed whole and perfect and its parts are the parts of this whole—then he takes away the actuality of the form, through which it is held together, whilst he lets the vessel or its pieces revert to the first material; and then when the material, through resolution, is reduced to fluxibility and to universal possibility, he once again makes another vessel from it.

According to this, although distant similitude, God leads everything into being, although He does not collect the possibility of the things from anything that He has not created. If you pay attention, you will notice that nature in the sensible forms uses the warmth of the sun just as the glassmaker uses the fire, and that nature acts as the breath of the glassmaker and nature is led by the mind of the Highest Workman just as the breath of the master is led by his mind. This and many other things you can elicit.

CONRAD: You have assimilated the genesis of sensible things very well; and as if in a paradigmatic example, I see how nature is the origin of motion and how warmth is the instrument of nature; how the location is as the furnace, how warmth is as though the sword and the location the sheath. I grasp much on this basis concerning nature, which likewise is in the center. However, I entreat you, if you can, to apply a more universal similitude.

NICOLAUS: If one considers much, sufficient appropriate examples can occur to one. But I believe that among the operations known to us, teaching is a close enough assimilation of the universal mode of creation. Therefore, Moses, David and the rest of the prophets took it as an appropriate representation of the mode of creation.

In order to call the uneducated student to an identity of mastery, the learned calls the silence into voice in the similitude of his concept and the silence arises in assimilation of the concept of the master. This assimilation is the intellectual word, which is represented in the rational and this in the sensible. Therefore, the sensible arises in respect to its vocality stepwise, from silence through the confused sound to the distinct, articulated voice. For if the master teaches, then those standing more distantly hear some confused sound. The sound, therefore, represents the possibility of, or the material related to, the voice. Therefore, if the voice is called from the silence, then first the sound arises, as though the possibility of the voice, so that this possibility of the sound is neither silence nor the formed voice, but rather formable. As a result, the elements arise from the confused sound; then the combination of elements in syllables, of syllables in words, and of words in speech. And it is established that the intellectual word arises in this order in the vocation of silence stepwise to the vocal word, although the difference between earlier and later is not correctly attained by the sense of hearing.

The word thus produced by the master contains in itself a threefold order. For such a word is sensible and is attained only with sensible ears, even by those who do not know the word at all. This is the mode of bestiality. For all beasts—together with the man ignorant of the word—attain nothing other than the articulated voice.

Furthermore it is a rational word, because it is attained by those who know words. Since only rationality grasps words, the speech of the master is only attained by man and not by beasts. However, because grammarians can only attain the speech, but not the mind of the master, who attempts to explain in his speech a mathematical or theological concept, it ensues that the word of the master has existence as rational in another order.

Thereupon, because the mathematician or theologian sees the mind of the master in his word, you elicit therefrom the intellectual word of the third order, which bears the nearest similitude to the mind of the master.

As far as the vocality of the word, you also see in the master a certain power of breath, from which the various motions of the tongue, the lips, and the other instruments of speaking must proceed, so that there is a vocal word. Therein participate the movers, which are also called the Muses by the poets, of the windpipe, tongue, lips, and the jaw, which produce the breath variously, so that they are a breath, which moves the instruments of speaking variously on behalf of the same intention of the producer.

Thus the prophet assimilates the creation most appropriately with the word and the breath of the mouth. Perhaps that is also the intention of holy Moses, who similarly represents the mode of creation as that of verbal expression. Indeed, in order to compare the facility of creation with the expression of a word, he asserts: "God spoke, let there be light and there was light."

And, therefore, the ineffable, most mysterious name of God, which the Greeks, because it is written with four Hebrew characters, call the tetragrammaton, and which is also produced as Jehovah—perhaps because it is the enfolding of all vocality—is called the ineffable, since it shines forth as the font of every effable word, as though the ineffable cause, in every effable word. Indeed, it seems that one can carry out a successful search in this configuration for the entity, which emanates from the First; and indeed for everything which is offered for consideration to the one calmly and diligently attending to everything in distinction, order, motion and everything else, unless it occurs to you otherwise.

CONRAD: I do not know to whom it could seem other than a matter of greatest concern to attend to the simple and most fecund traditions of the holy prophets and to the sagacity of the philosophers. For with the help of this comprehensive similitude, I am led with great facility to intuit the beautiful order of things, namely, how the corporeal exist on account of sensible distinction, sensible distinction on account of the rational, the rational on account of the intellectual, and the intellectual on account of the true cause, which is the Creator of the universe.

   Indeed, in the previously advanced example I see most clearly that every nature serves the intellectual nature as its assimilation, so that this is a sign of the true and absolute cause and that thus every entity attains the font of its being through its mediation.

   For what does every sensible unquiet seek except distinction or rationality? What does every ratiocination seek except intellect? What does every intellect seek except the true, absolute cause? All seek the same, which is an absolute "what," whose sign is not found outside of the intellectual region. Indeed, the quiddity of the speech of the one teaching is not found except in the intellectual region, in which the true cause shines forth. If the mathematician says that every triangle has three angles, which are equal to two right angles, the student does not understand it—although he understands that it is—as long as he does not conceive the true cause. But if the cause is manifested, then he intuits the quiddity of the intellect. Thus I see the cause shine forth in the intellect.

Therefore, only the intellect has an eye for intuiting the quiddity, which it cannot intuit except in the true cause, which is the font of all desiring. And since everything desires being, the desiring is in everything which arises from the font of desiring, in which being and desiring coincide in the same. Therefore, the desiring of everything is according to its being, so that the rational desires being rationally, the sensible desires it sensibly and all the others in like manner, and this in the optimal way. Everything, therefore, desires the best, but in its own mode. One and the same is the absolute Good, to which the desiring of all shows that all are summoned.

I have joyfully taken this from your speech and it pleases me, that I can elicit through this accessible similitude many and important things about genesis and nature, but because the saints are not wanting, who compare the world to a written book, I entreat you to explain what it seems to you.

NICOLAUS: I spurn no picture, for I understand the same in every one. A written book, whose language and characters are unknown—just as if one would place some Greek book of Plato's before a German, in which Plato has described the powers of his intellect—appears to me to be an appropriate enough comparison for the world. Namely, if the German occupies himself attentively with the signs, then he could conjecture some elements from the difference and concordance of the characters and sounds from the various combinations, but in no case the quiddity itself in total or in part, except if the same were revealed to him.

Hence I conjecture the world as something in which the divine power is latent configuratively. Although one can come to the that-it-is of the elements and combinations through diligent investigation, by means of the proportions, differences, and concordances, and through diligent searching to and fro, nevertheless the investigator will find no proper name of an element, of a sound, or of a combination from itself, but rather the rationality of him who finds the things will distinguish them and give them an appropriate name. Moses expresses this beautifully, where he describes how Adam or man has imposed names on things and in the process of the history insinuates the always certain rational ground as cause of the name.

Hence various names of things are found according to the various rational grounds and also various names of the one thing on the basis of the various conjectures of rationality. This alone this book reveals to us, that He is great and exalted above everything which can be named, whose finger has written this book, and that there is no end of His magnitude, prudence and power; and that unless He reveals it Himself, nothing at all can be known; and that if the intellect does not conform to Him, it does not understand, since, unless the absolute Same is seen, the configuration of His similitude is not understood. No one can know an image of Socrates, in that he hunts for the cause of knowledge from the image, if he does not know Socrates.

Imagine the inventor of some art, for example painting. Now after him there shall be no one to whom he could bequeath it. He, however, would like to transmit his art and paints the non-configurable art of painting in a book, because he cannot bequeath it better. Will you not see various figures in this book, on the basis of which you can conjecture the wonderful and unknown art of the artist? But how can you attain with vision the art, which is the simple form of all figures, which is expressed there in everything and each single thing which has existence as the absolute quiddity of figures, if it is not visible, but rather only intelligible? Indeed, the intellect of art is lacking to you. Is not God, the Father, the font of the art of effecting the same, of that art which enfolds every art in itself and of the absolute formal quiddity of everything formable, which is also called the Son, the Word, the power or wisdom of the Father and many other names? How, therefore, can the art of essential being, which is unfolded in everything that is, be conceived by one not having the intellect of this art, since only the intellect of God, the Father, who is the art itself, has this art?

It is therefore manifest that neither in part nor in toto can anything of quiddity be attained by man. If human meditation inquires into this, then it despises its syllogistic

hunting and converts itself obediently to the revealed prophetic illuminations, and thus advances through despising
itself as if inwardly impotent to cognition and to that which
it seeks. Thus the cognition of ignorance humiliates and by
humiliating exalts and makes learned. Moses expresses this
best where he describes that the fall of man into ignorance,
which is the death of the intellect, has occurred because
man attempted through his own power to be co-equal with
God in knowledge. To attend to this will perhaps be useful
to you.

CONRAD: Indeed very, for I see this as the highest of all. And
because now so much was touched that, enfolded in the
words of the prophet, was always hidden to me, I beseech
you not to let it discourage you from adding why the
prophet says, "the heavens are formed through the Word
and the powers through his breath," since it is the absolute
Same, which effects everything in identity.

NICOLAUS: I have had the experience and have learned thereby,
that authority contributes very much to study. Indeed, if
someone receives a dictum that is disclosed as though
through divine revelation and desires with his entire effort
to see intellectually what he believes, whatever kind of
dictum it may have been, then an altogether hidden thesaurus appears, which is found there inapprehensibly. Therefore, we are led to the highest through the highest faith, as
you have heard elsewhere in *On the Filiation of God*.

Therefore, I accept through faith this expression of
the prophet as a suitable representation of the genesis of all
things and strive through the intellect to see that in similitude; nevertheless it is invisible. The prophet says:
"Through the Word of the Lord the heavens are established
and through the breath of His mouth all their power." And
where we have the expression "of the Lord," the original
Hebrew language has the ineffable name of God, concerning which I have previously said a few things and which
is pronounced as Jehovah. Therefore, he says that from
Jehovah, as though from the Father of the Word—since it
is the enfolding of all vocality, without which no word can
be uttered—comes the Word, and that, because it is "the

breath of His mouth," the breath comes from Him and the Word; just as if the mouth were the coincidence of the producing origin, of the Word and of the breath, which proceeds from both.

And this trinity is in the absolute Same, without which the same could not effect identity. Therefore, the absolute Same is the trine and one, which we experience in that it effects the same. Therefore, every agent participates in the trine and one nature, without which there were no agent. You can read about it extensively in the first book of *On Learned Ignorance,* where we have unfolded our very small intellect—which is nevertheless the best gift of God— in respect to the trinity, which many others also treated in an assimilative manner and each excellently in his own mode.

However, if we now turn again to Genesis, we state that the prophet insinuates to us, that the heavens and whatever came into being with the name, the similitude, or the rational ground of the heaven, emerged as the word of a Lord and Ruler, which is not retarded in execution; the will is its rational ground and the rational ground is its will; what He spoke, that also occurred; He commanded and it was created without the intervention of delay. After He had called the heaven into being, He breathes His power into it, so that the outside of every thing is its summons out of nothing, as if concealing and enclosing the heaven, and its inside is its turning to the Creator as a creature is expressed by God.

Whence the divine power shines forth in the power of the thing, as if breathed into the thing. And in its corre- spondence the expression of similitude with the Creator is stronger than in the correspondence of that extrinsic habitude, through which it exists as summoned out of nothing, so that in a living being one must affirm more strongly the vivifying and sentient power breathed in by God than the heaven of souls, i.e., the body, which is summoned out of nothing. We consider everything created in this way, since it is assimilation, the extrinsic, namely, the summons out of nothing, and the intrinsic, namely, participation in the true being, so that in the essence of every creature there are, as it were, these three moments: the possibility through the summons out of nothing, the actuality through participation in the divine power, and the connection of these.

Moses also expresses this elegantly, when he says: "God formed man of the dust of the earth and breathed into his face the breath of life and he became a living soul," so that he expresses in this way the earthly man, who is also called Adam, the earthly; according to the extrinsic as body, which is summoned from the dust of the earth or the nature of the elements, and according to the intrinsic as the vital power, which is from the breathing in of the divine spirit or the participation in the divine power, so that thus from this moment the living man is one true man.

Not absurdly with the name of heaven a certain specific mode can be understood, which includes the motion of the participated power; just as the syllogistic power of rationality, which is found among certain modes, is contracted specifically in its motion, so that the first figure is, as it were, the region, sphere, and heaven of that mode; and in this heaven the specific different circles, which are more contracted modes, are as in the universal mode of the first figure.

It is likewise with the other figures, so that in this way every species is a heaven, which inside its orbit contains the invisible power breathed into it, in which the inhabitants in this heaven participate variously. This participation, however, cannot occur outside its heaven, just as there cannot be the combination of a syllogism from three universal affirmations, except in the first figure. Hence every creature is moved and finds rest in its heaven, as you have heard elsewhere.

CONRAD: I have earlier and also recently heard what you have expressed, but I do not understand this last clearly. For that we men in ratiocination necessarily employ modes, as you say, occurs because syllogistic rationality requires this. Therefore, the specific modes result from combinations and in the light of rationality we see from ourselves, that the syllogistic combinations cannot be made useful otherwise. It is otherwise in God, where the will coincides with the rational ground, so that the willed is rational.

NICOLAUS: I wanted to say to you only this one thing, namely, that the heaven can be understood as the specific, finite, enclosed, and concealed mode of the assimilation of the same. I have adduced the not inappropriate example of the figure of the syllogism. You consider in one way the modes of the syllogism, which are rational in certain combinations, in others not, and in another way God, whose will is rationality. I respond to you, that I have wished the same; namely that the special mode of assimilation from God is thereby also rational.

For since the Same effects the same, one can find modes which can be concealed in certain habitudes and in their assimilation—in that they represent the same, as if led to the specific mode of representation—are called special. For the Same, since it effects the same, cannot be found outside of the assimilation. And hence as harmony has special, proportional modes, in which it can be found, and which can be participated in variously—outside of these modes of consonance or harmony we perceive dissonance—so must we also think about the same as about consonance or harmony, since the same is not inharmonious or other from these. And just as harmony requires special proportions, outside of which it cannot be found, so it is universally of the absolute Same, so that in this way the will of the same, which wants nothing other, coincides with its rational ground, since the rational ground of the same can admit nothing other.

Thus, therefore, in the absolute Same the rational ground coincides with the will, as it is represented in nature and the rational ground of harmony, so that the species of things are such species as they are, because they cannot be otherwise. If there is recession from them, then a monster or a dissonance arises and the proper species cannot be effected. To leave this species, which is just such an assimilation of the Same, is to deviate from the beautiful form of the reflection of the Same, which is absolutely the font of all beauty and good.

CONRAD: I do not know whether there is a contradiction to that
which, in my view, is established rationally. However,
because our prophet David attributes the powers and angels
to the heaven—he indeed asserts: "Praise the Lord from the
heaven, praise Him in the highest, praise you Him all His
angels, praise you Him all His powers"—say a word about
whether angels preside over this heaven now mentioned.
Then, since the already advanced night calls us to rest, I
shall cease disturbing you.

NICOLAUS: Beyond our undertaking, you introduce much and
now this, which demands space for a deeper investigation.
However, in order to satisfy you, I shall say a word about
it, namely that all motion of all rational species tends to the
absolute Same. We say that there is spiritual and rational
motion, just as if the spirit is the power exhaled from the
mouth of God, through which that motion effecting the
same, which is the power of God, and thus moves and leads
the participating to the Same, is administered incessantly.

Indeed, when we see that all lions which were and
now are, are leonine, then we conceive the sphere or region
or the heaven, which constantly embraces this specific
power and specifies and distinguishes it from another; we
set over that celestial motion an administrator-spirit, which
is, as it were, a divine power, which enfolds all that power,
which unfolds the specific motion, so that in this way the
administrator-spirit is the servant of God, the Creator, and
in that he superintends in the domain of this motion, he
performs the tasks of the rector of this legation.

If, for example, a teacher, who were rector of a school,
presides over the grammar class through the one teaching
assistant, over the rhetoric class through another, the logic
class through another, the mathematics class through yet
another, then the grammar class were the heaven of a certain
specific mode of participation in the teaching of the teacher,
who is also the rector of all, and the grammar students
are the inhabitants of this heaven, who participate in the
teaching of the rector of all, according to the specific mode
of its inhabitants, namely, the grammatical, and the intellect
of the teaching assistant were the rector and motor of this
heaven and the celestial things in this heaven.

Or, as it happens, you can find a closer comparison in yourself. For, indeed, your intellect is entirely the same as itself, for it is the sign of the absolute Same. It does not shine forth except in rationality. Indeed, various rational grounds assimilate the intellect variously; some lucidly and clearly, which are called the ostensive or demonstrative rational grounds; the others assimilate it persuasively, weakly, and obscurely—which are rhetorical rational grounds; others do it moderately. If, therefore, the intellect is exerted in effecting the same, to summon the sensible world to itself so that it arises in assimilation with it, then the intellect strives to attract it through the rational ground to itself.

And because there can be various, specific, different distinctions or rational grounds of the sensible, in which the sensible things can be elevated to assimilation with the intellect—this both in the mode of vision, as well as in the modes of hearing, tasting, smelling, or touching—a heaven of vision, a heaven of hearing, etc. arises, so that the sensible world is discerned in the visible mode; i.e., it arises to assimilation with the intellect. This occurs through the distinction, which exists visibly in vision. Therefore, the heaven of vision, which is filled by the power of vision, is governed and moved by its own peculiar, rational, and distinctive spirit, so that through this the spirit is present attentively to the eye, to enjoy the visible distinction, in which it participates in the intellect and lives delectably. You must conceive the other senses the same.

And because this material demands to be explained sufficiently and requires another more appropriate time, the discussion concerning genesis is thus now sufficient. Long ago the cock called us to rest. Farewell.

On the Peace of Faith

(1 4 5 3)

I.

News of the atrocities which have recently been perpetrated by the Turkish king in Constantinople and have now been divulged, has so inflamed a man, who once saw that region, with zeal for God, that amongst many sighs he asked the Creator of all things if in His kindness He might moderate the persecution, which raged more than usual on account of diverse religious rites. Then it occurred that after several days—indeed on account of lengthy, continuous meditation—a vision was manifested to the zealous man, from which he concluded that it would be possible, through the experience of a few wise men who are well acquainted with all the diverse practices which are observed in religions across the world, to find a unique and propitious concordance, and through this to constitute a perpetual peace in religion upon the appropriate and true course.

So that this vision might at some time come to the knowledge of those who resolve such important matters, he has written it down clearly below, as far as his memory presented it to him.

He was raptured to a certain intellectual altitude, where among those departed from life, in the council of the eminent over which the Almighty presided, the examination of this question was conducted thus. The King of Heaven and Earth said, that from the kingdom of this world sorrowful messengers have brought to Him the groans of the oppressed; that many turn their weapons against each other for the sake of religion and in their power compel men to renounce long observed doctrines or kill them.

There were very many reports of such lamentations, which came from the whole earth, and the King commanded that they be brought before the full assembly of the holy. All seemed to be known to the residents of heaven, since they had been placed from the beginning by the King of the Universe over the individual provinces and sects of the world. According to their appearance they were not men, but rather intellectual powers.

One leader, the representative of all these ambassadors, spoke the following words: Lord, King of the Universe, what has each creature, that You have not given him? It pleased You to inspire the body of man, formed from the mud of the earth, with rational spirit, so that the image of Your ineffable power would reflect in him. From one man many people have been multiplied, who occupy the surface of the dry land.

Although the intellectual spirit, which is sown in the earth and is absorbed by shadows, does not see the light and the beginning of its origin, You have nonetheless created in him all that through which he, full of wonder over that which he attains with the senses, is at some time able to elevate his mental eyes to You, the Creator of all things, and to be reunited with You in the highest charity, and thus can finally return to his origin laden with fruit.

Nevertheless You know, Lord, that a great multitude cannot exist without much diversity and that almost all are compelled to lead a laborious life full of troubles and afflictions, and in servile subjugation must be subject to the kings who rule. Hence it has occurred, that only a few men have enough leisure time to employ the freedom of their will and to gain knowledge of themselves. They are distracted by many corporeal cares and duties. Thus they cannot seek You, who are the concealed God.

For this reason You have given Your people diverse kings and seers, who are called prophets, of whom the majority instituted cults and laws corresponding to the purpose of their legation in Your name, and thus instructed the uncultivated people. They subsequently accepted these laws, as if You, the King of kings, had spoken with them face to face, and believed they heard not those men, but rather You in them.

To the various nations, however, You have sent various prophets and masters, the one for this, the other for another time.

It is a condition of earthly human nature to defend as truth lengthy custom, which is regarded as part of nature. And thus no small dissensions arise, when any community prefers its beliefs over another's.

Therefore, come to our assistance, You who alone are powerful. For this rivalry is on account of You, whom alone all venerate in all that they seem to adore. For no one desires anything in all that one seems to desire other than the Good, which You are. Also in all intellectual deliberation no one searches for something other than the true, which You are. What does the living search for other than life? What does the existing search for other than existence? You, therefore, who bestow life and existence, are that One, who seems to be sought differently in the diverse rites and is named with diverse names, since You, as You are, remain unknown and ineffable for all.

You, who are infinite power, are nothing of that which You have created, nor can the creature comprehend the concept of Your infinity, since there is no proportional relationship between the finite and the infinite.

You, omnipotent God, who are invisible to every mind, can in the manner You wish to be grasped, manifest Yourself visibly to him, to whom You wish. Conceal Yourself, therefore, no longer, Lord. Be gracious and manifest Your countenance and all people will be saved, who no longer can desert the vein of life and its too-little-tasted sweetness. No one departs from You, unless he is ignorant of You.

If You consider it worthy to act thus, the sword and the envy of hatred and every evil will cease. Everyone will know in what way there is only a single religion in the variety of rites. Indeed, one will not be able to annul this difference of rites, or in any case this will not be beneficial to do, since the diversity may bring an increase in devotion, if every region bestows the most vigilant effort upon its ceremonies, which it holds to be, as it were, the most pleasant to You, the King; however, at all events, just as You are only one—there ought to be only a single religion and a single cult of adoration of God.

Be therefore conciliatory, Lord, since Your anger is kindness and Your justice is mercy. Spare Your weak creature. Thus we, Your representatives, whom You have given to Your people as custodians and see here in this assembly, humbly entreat Your Majesty by every possible measure of our devotion.

II.

At this supplication of the archangel all the citizens of heaven inclined in the same manner towards the highest King and He, who sat upon the throne, spoke: He had sent man forth with his free will, and created him capable through this will of community with his fellow man. However, because the animal and earthly man is held down under the Prince of Darkness in ignorance and walks across the earth according to the conditions of that sensible life, which proceeds only from the world of the Prince of Darkness, and not according to the intellectual and inner man, whose life proceeds from the land of his origin, He had called the errant man back with much care and diligence through various prophets, who were seers in comparison with the others.

Finally, as all these prophets could not sufficiently overcome the Prince of Ignorance, He had sent His Word, through which He has also created time. The Word clothed itself with humanity, in order in this manner to finally illumine the docile man with free will, so that the latter would see that he would have to walk not in accordance to the outer, but rather to the inner man, if he hoped to revert one day to the sweetness of immortal life. And since His Word put on the mortal man, witness was given in his blood of the truth, that man is capable of eternal life, for the sake of which his animal and sensible life are deemed as nothing, and that that eternal life is nothing other than the deepest longing of the inner man, i.e., the truth, which alone is desired, and which, since it is eternal, nourishes the intellect eternally.

This truth, which nourishes the intellect, is nothing other than the Word itself, in which everything is enfolded and by means of which everything is unfolded. It put on human nature, so that no man would have doubt, that according to the choice of his free will in his human nature he could achieve the immortal food of truth in that man, who is also the Word.

And God added thereto: Since this has been done, what then still remains that could be done and was not done?

III.

To this question of the King of kings, the Word-Become-Flesh, who rules over all the residents of heaven, responded in the name of all: Father of Mercy! Indeed all Your works are complete and nothing remains that must be added to their completion! Nevertheless, human nature requires continual trials, so that the errors, of which there are very many in respect to Your Word, are extirpated and so the truth may constantly shine forth; this is so, because from the beginning You have decided that man would keep his free will and, since nothing in the sensible world perseveres constantly, opinions and conjectures and likewise also languages and their interpretations vary with time. Since, however, the truth is one and is impossible not to be comprehended by every free intellect, all diversity of religion ought to be brought into one orthodox faith.

This pleased the King. He called the angels hither, which preside over all the nations and languages, and commanded each to bring one experienced man to the Word-Become-Flesh. And thereupon the most eminent men of this world appeared before the countenance of the Word, as though carried aloft in a state of ecstacy. To them the Word of God spoke as follows:

The Lord, King of Heaven and Earth, heard the sighs of the murdered and the fettered and those led into servitude, who suffer thus on account of the diversity of their religions. And since all who practice or suffer such persecution, are led to it for no other reason than that they believe, thus to promote their salvation and to please their Creator, the Lord has taken pity on His people and agreed to the plan to lead all diversity of religions through mutual agreement of all men harmoniously back to a single, henceforth inviolable religion.

To fulfill this task, He entrusts to you, the elected men. From His council He gives you helping and serving angel-spirits, who may protect and guide you. As the place of assembly He designated Jerusalem, which is the most suitable therefor.

IV.

One responded to this, who was older than all others and as it appeared, was a GREEK, after he had bowed in adoration:

> We praise our God, whose mercy rules over all His works and who alone has the power to bring it about, that such a great diversity of religions would be brought together in one harmonious peace. We, who are His work, cannot disobey His direction. Nevertheless we request instruction, as to how this unity of religion can be introduced by us. For according to our persuasion, a nation will accept a faith with difficulty, which is different from that which it has hitherto defended with its blood.

The WORD responded: You will not find another faith, but rather one and the same single religion presupposed everywhere. You who are now present here, are called wise men by the sharers of your language, or at the very least philosophers or lovers of wisdom.

So it is, said the GREEK.

> If you all therefore love wisdom, do you not presuppose that this wisdom exists?

They proclaimed all at once that no one could doubt it.

The WORD continued: There can only be one wisdom. For if it were possible that there be several wisdoms, then these would have to be from one. Namely, unity is prior to all plurality.

GREEK: None of us doubts but that there is one wisdom, which we all love and on account of which we are called philosophers. Because of participation in it there are many wise men, whereas wisdom itself remains simple and undivided in itself.

WORD: You therefore all agree that the simplest wisdom is one, and that its power is ineffable. And everyone experiences that ineffable and infinite power in its unfolding. If one's view is turned towards that which is visible, and one considers that that which he sees has arisen from the power of wisdom—the same obtains for hearing and every single thing that affects the senses—then he affirms that the invisible wisdom exceeds everything.

GREEK: Also we, who practice this profession of philosophy, love the sweetness of wisdom in no other way than that of the previously tasted admiration of things, which are subject to the senses. Who would not be willing to die, in order to obtain that wisdom from which all beauty, all sweetness of life, everything desirable emanates? What power of wisdom is reflected in the frame of man: in his limbs, the order of these limbs, in the life infused in him, the harmony of the organs, in his motion, and finally in the rational spirit, which is capable of wonderful arts and is, as it were, the sign of wisdom, in which eternal wisdom, as in a close image, and truth as in a close similitude, shine forth over everything! And what is above all still more wonderful is: This reflection of wisdom comes always nearer to the truth through a vehement conversion of the spirit, until the living reflection, which comes from the shadow of the image, becomes constantly truer and more in conformity with true wisdom, even though that absolute Wisdom, just as it is, can never be attained in another. And in this manner the eternal and inexhaustible wisdom is the perpetual and imperishable food of the intellect.

WORD: You are advancing to our goal, towards which we aspire, in the correct manner. Even though you acknowledge diverse religions, you all presuppose in all of this diversity the one, which you call wisdom. But say, does not the one wisdom embrace everything that can be stated?

V.

The ITALIAN responded: Truly, there is no word outside of wisdom. The word of the wisest is in wisdom and wisdom in the word. Nothing is outside of it. The whole infinity is encompassed by wisdom.

WORD: Now if someone says, everything would be created in wisdom and another, everything would be created in the word, do they not then say the same thing or something different?

ITALIAN: Even though diversity appears in the manner of speaking, it is the same in regards to the meaning. For the Word of the Creator, in which he has created everything, can be nothing other than His wisdom.

WORD: What do you think: Is that wisdom God or a creature?

ITALIAN: Since God, the Creator, creates everything in wisdom, He Himself is necessarily the wisdom of the created wisdom. That is, prior to every creature there is wisdom, through which everything created is that which it is.

WORD: So wisdom is eternal, since it is prior to everything initiated and created.

ITALIAN: No one can deny that that, by which he understands that it is prior to everything originated, would be eternal.

WORD: It is therefore the origin.

ITALIAN: So it is.

WORD: Consequently it is also the simplest. Everything composed is originated. The composing can indeed not be after the composed.

ITALIAN: That I recognize.

WORD: Wisdom is therefore eternity.

ITALIAN: It cannot be otherwise.

WORD: It is, however, impossible, that there be several eternities, since unity is prior to all plurality.

ITALIAN: That also no one can deny.

WORD: Wisdom is therefore the one, simple and eternal God, the origin of everything.

ITALIAN: So must it be.

WORD: See, therefore, how you, the philosophers of various schools of thought, agree in the religion of the one God, whom you all presupposed in that which you as lovers of wisdom acknowledge.

VI.

At this the ARAB rose and responded: One can say nothing more clearly and truly!

WORD: If you recognize an absolute Wisdom for the reason that you are a lover of wisdom, do you then believe that there are men with vigorous intellects, who do not love wisdom?

ARAB: I believe with complete certainty, that all men naturally desire wisdom, for wisdom is the life of the intellect and this life can be maintained by means of no other food than the truth and the word of life or the intellectual bread, that is wisdom. Just as every existing thing desires all that, without which it is not able to exist, so does the intellectual life desire wisdom.

WORD: All men therefore acknowledge with you, that there is the one, absolute Wisdom, which they presuppose. This is the one God.

ARAB: So it is. And no intelligent man can advocate some other one.

WORD: There is therefore only a single religion and cult for all those who are of vigorous intellect. This is presupposed in all the diversity of rites.

ARAB: You are wisdom, since you are the Word of God. I ask you: How should those who revere several gods concur with the philosophers in reverence of a single God? For it can be established, that the philosophers have at no time felt other than that it would be impossible for there to be several gods, over which the one, superexalted God did not preside. The latter alone is the origin, from which the others have that which they have; He is more excellent by far than is the monad in number.

WORD: All who at any time worshiped several gods, presupposed the divinity to exist. They entreated it in all gods as if they participated in it. That is, as there is nothing white without whiteness, so there also are no gods without the divinity. The cult of gods therefore includes the acknowledgment of the divinity. And whoever says that there are several gods, says also that there is the one Origin, which precedes all;

similarly he who asserts that there are many sacred things, admits the sacredness of the sacred things, through the participation of which all other things are sacred. Never was a people so foolish, that it would have believed in several gods, of which each one would have been the prime cause, origin, or creator of the universe.

ARAB: I am also of this opinion. That is, one contradicts oneself, if one says there are several prime origins. Since the origin cannot be originated, because it would be originated from itself and thus would exist before it would exist, and reason does not grasp this, thus the origin is eternal. And it is not possible that there be several eternals, since unity exists prior to all plurality. Consequently, the one must be the origin and cause of the universe. Therefore, until now I have still found no people that had deviated in this from the road of truth.

WORD: If, therefore, all who venerate several gods looked to that which they presuppose, i.e., to the deity, which is the cause of all, and—as reason dictates—also assumed this latter in manifest religion, just as they worship this confusedly in all things which they name gods—the strife were dissolved.

ARAB: This were indeed not difficult. However, to terminate the worship of gods will be grievous. For the people holds as certain that it is granted support from its worship of the gods and therefore turns to these deities for its salvation.

WORD: If it were informed about its salvation, as we have done, then the people would seek salvation in that which has given existence and is itself the Savior and the infinite salvation, rather than in those who have nothing from themselves except that which is conceded to them by the Savior. However, if the people has recourse to the gods, which are regarded as sacred in the opinion of all because they lived in a deiform manner, as though to an intercessor in a state of infirmity or other necessity, or if it entreats one such in humble veneration or reverently attends to his memory, since he was a friend of God, whose life is to be imitated; then this would not contradict the single religion, so long as it dedicates the entire cult of worship to the one and only God. In this way the people could easily be satisfied.

VII.

Thereupon the INDIAN spoke: What then of statues and images?

WORD: The images which bring to our knowledge that which is conceded in the true cult of the one God, are not condemned. However, when they lead away from the cult of worship of the one God, as if something of the divinity were in the stones themselves and were attached to the statue, then, since they deceive and avert from the truth, they should deservedly be destroyed.

INDIAN: It is difficult to lead the people away from inveterate idol worship, and indeed on account of the oracles which are given by them.

WORD: Rarely are these oracles produced other than through priests, who report them as responses of the deity. For if the question has been proposed, then they give the answer pursuant to some art, i.e., in observation of the disposition of the heavens, or they form the answer, which they ascribe to the deity, by casting lots, as if heaven or Apollo or the sun had commanded them to respond. Hence it occurs that the majority of those answers are ambiguous, so that they do not openly convince by lies, or completely falsely; and if they are occasionally true, then are so accidentally. However, if a priest can conjecture well, then he issues oracles better and his answers come nearer the truth.

INDIAN: However, it is certain that frequently a spirit who is bound to a statue patently imparts an oracle.

WORD: Neither the soul of a man, nor of Apollo, nor of Aesculapius, nor of any other which is worshiped as God, but rather the evil spirit, the foe of human salvation from the inception, sometimes, however rarely, feigns through the faith placed in him by man, to be bound to a statue and to be coerced into answers, in order thus to deceive. However, after the deceit has been detected, he disappears. Therefore, today they have a mouth and do not speak. After this deception of the seducer has become known through experience in many lands, idolatry has been condemned in nearly all locations by the wiser men. And it will likewise not be difficult in the Orient to detect the deceit of idolatry and achieve the invocation of the one God, so that its inhabitants are brought into conformity with the rest of the nations of the world.

INDIAN: Since the evident deceits were detected and as a result thereof the most prudent Romans and likewise the Greeks and Arabs destroyed the idols, it is by all means to be hoped, that the idolatrous Indians will act similarly; above all, since they are wise and do not hesitate to acknowledge the necessity of religion in the worship of the one God. If they also thereby venerate their idols in their manner, they will come thus to a peaceful conclusion in respect to the adoration of the one God.

It will, however, be very difficult to achieve agreement from all sides in respect to the triune God. That is, it will appear to all that the trinity cannot be conceived without three gods. If there is a trinity in the divinity, so there will also be plurality in the deity. However, it was previously said—and in fact, it is necessarily so—that there is only one absolute Deity. Therefore, there is no plurality in the absolute Deity, but rather in the participating, who are not God in the absolute, but rather gods through participation.

WORD: God, as Creator, is three and one. As infinite He is neither three, nor one, nor anything that can be stated. The names which are attributed to God are taken from creatures, since He Himself is ineffable in Himself and is above all that can be named or stated. Those who worship God ought to adore Him as the Origin of the universe; in this one universe, however, there is a multitude of parts, inequality and separation—namely, the multitude of stars, trees, men, stones is evident to the senses—the origin of all multitude, however, is unity; therefore, the origin of multitude is the eternal unity.

In the one universe inequality of parts is found, since no part is similar to the other. However, the inequality derives from the equality of unity. Consequently, eternal equality is prior to every inequality.

In the one universe, distinction or separation of parts is found. Before every distinction, however, is the connection of unity and equality. Separation, or distinction, departs from this connection. The connection is therefore eternal.

However, there cannot be several eternals. Consequently, in the one eternity is found unity, equality of unity, and the union of unity and equality, or connection. Thus, the most simple origin of the universe is triune, since in the origin the originated must be enfolded. Everything originated, however, signifies that it is thus enfolded in its origin, and in everything originated a threefold distinction of this kind can be found in the unity of the essence. And for this reason, the simplest origin of everything will be three and one.

VIII.

CHALDEAN: Even if the sages are somehow able to grasp this, it nevertheless exceeds the comprehension of the common man. For as I understand it, it is not true that there are three gods, but rather that there is one, which one is three. Do you not wish thereby to say that that one is threefold in power?

WORD: God is the absolute power of all powers, since He is omnipotent. If there is, therefore, only one absolute power, which is the divine essence, then to name this power triune, is nothing other than to say, that God is triune. However, the divine power should not be conceived such that it would be distinguished in opposition to reality, since in God power is reality itself. The same is true of absolute potentiality, which is also power.

It appears absurd to no one, if it is said that the omnipotent divinity, who is God, would have the unity in Himself, which is entity, equality, and connection, so that in this manner the power of unity would unify or give essence to everything that has being—that is, a thing exists insofar as it is one; the one and entity can be interchanged—and so that the power of equality equalizes and gives form to everything that exists. That is, a thing is equal in that it is not more and not less than that which it is. For if it were more or less, then it would not exist. Therefore, it cannot exist without equality. Thus the power of connection unifies and binds together.

Hence in the power of unity omnipotence calls being out of non-being, so that that which was not, becomes capable of being. And it gives it form in the power of equality and binds it together in the power of connection; just as one sees in the essence of love, how love binds together the loving with the lovable.

Therefore, when man is called by omnipotence out of not-being, then unity arises as first in order, after which equality and then the connection of both. For nothing can exist, unless it is one. The one is therefore prior. And since man is called out of not-being, the unity of man arises as first in order, then the equality of this unity or entity—that is, the equality is the unfolding of form in unity, on account of which it is called the unity of man and not of the lion or some other thing. However, the equality can only arise out of the unity, for not otherness, but rather unity or identity produces equality. Finally, love or connection proceeds from unity and equality. That is, unity is not separable from equality and equality from unity. The connection or love is therefore such that, with the positing of unity equality is posited, and with the positing of unity and equality love or connection is posited.

If, therefore, no equality is found, without it being the equality of unity, and if no connection is found, without it being the connection of unity and equality, such that the connection is in unity and equality, equality is in unity and the unity is in equality, and unity and equality are in connection, then it is obvious that there can be no essential distinction in the trinity. Namely, everything that is essentially different is such that the one can be, without the other existing. However, because the trinity exists such that, with the positing of unity the equality of unity is also posited and conversely, and with the positing of unity and equality connection is also posited and conversely, it is seen not in the essence, but in the relationship, in what manner one is unity, another is equality, and another is connection.

However, a numerical distinction is essential. Indeed,

the number two differs essentially from three. With the positing of the number two, three is not posited, and the three does not follow from the existence of two. Therefore, the trinity in God is not composed, plural or numerical, but rather the simplest unity. Whoever believes therefore that God is one, does not deny that He be threefold, insofar as he understands that Trinity as not different from the simplest unity, but rather as unity itself, such that that trinity, were it not in unity, were also not the origin, which is so omnipotent that it can create the universe and each individual.

The more unified a power is, the more powerful it is; however, the more unified it is, the simpler it is. Therefore, the more powerful or stronger it is, the simpler it is. Hence if the divine essence is omnipotent, it is completely simple and threefold. For without trinity it were not the simplest, strongest, and omnipotent origin.

CHALDEAN: I am of the opinion that no one can disagree with this deliberation. However, that God had a Son and participant in His deity, this the Arabs and many with them assail.

WORD: Some name unity Father, equality Son, and connection the Holy Spirit, since those designations, even though they are not proper, nevertheless suitably designate the Trinity. For the Son is from the Father, and Love or the Spirit is from unity and equality of the Son. That is, the nature of the Father passes over in the Son into equality. Therefore, love and connection arise out of unity and equality.

And if simpler designations could be found, they were more suitable, as are, for example, unity, iddity,* and identity. These designations seem to unfold the most fecund simplicity of essence better. Also notice that there is a certain fecundity in the essence of the rational soul, that is, mind, wisdom, and love or will, since the mind exserts intellect or wisdom from itself, and from both proceeds the will or love. And this trinity in the unity of essence of the soul is the fecundity, which man possesses in his similarity

---

*The Latin *iditas* is derived from the demonstrative pronoun *id,* meaning it or that, and the suffix *itas,* meaning a state or condition. It could therefore also be translated as *itness.*

to the most fecund, uncreated Trinity. Likewise every created thing bears the image of creative power, and possesses fecundity in its manner in greater or more distant similarity to the most fecund Trinity, Creator of everything. It is therefore not so, that the creature has its being only from divine being, but rather it has its triply fecund being in its manner from the most fecund three-and-one Being. Without this fecund Being neither the world could subsist, nor would the creature exist in the best manner in which it could be.

IX.

To this the JEW responded: The Trinity, blessed above all, which no one can deny, has been explained in the best possible way. One of the prophets revealed it to us briefly, when he said, he had asked God how He, who had given others the fecundity of generation, could be sterile. And although the Jews shun the Trinity, because in their eyes it signifies plurality, they will nevertheless willingly acquiesce, as soon as they have seen that it signifies the simplest fecundity.

WORD: Also the Arabs and all wise men will easily see on the basis of these deliberations, that to deny the Trinity is to deny divine fecundity and creative power, and that to acknowledge the Trinity is to deny the plurality and community of gods. That fecundity, which is also a trinity, brings it about that it is unnecessary to have several gods, which mutually support each other in the creation of everything, for the one infinite fecundity suffices to create all that which can be created.

The Arabs can grasp the truth much better in this way, as when they say in their manner, God has essence and soul, and add thereto that He possesses word and spirit. For if one says God has a soul, then this soul cannot be understood except as the reason or word, which is God. That is, reason is nothing other than the Word. And what is the Holy Spirit of God other than the love, which is God?

Nothing is truly verified about the completely simple God, that is not He Himself. If it be true that God has the

Word, then it is also true that the Word is God. If it be true that God has spirit, then it is true that the Spirit is God. Having befits God improperly, since He Himself is everything; thus having in God is being. Therefore, the Arab does not deny that God is mind, and from this the Word or wisdom is generated, and from both the Spirit or love proceeds. This is that Trinity which was explained above and is posited by Arabs, even though most of them do not perceive that they acknowledge the Trinity.

Likewise you Jews also find in your prophets, that the heavens are formed by the Word of God and by His Spirit. In the manner in which the Arabs and Jews deny the Trinity, it must certainly be denied by all. However, in the manner in which the truth of the Trinity was unfolded above, it must necessarily be embraced by all.

X.

To this the SCYTHIAN responded: There can be no hesitancy in the adoration of the completely simple Trinity, which even now all those adore, who venerate the gods. Wise men say God is the Creator of both sexes and He is love; thereby they wish to explain the most fecund Trinity of the Creator as well as they can. Others assert that God, who is superexalted, exserts the intellect or reason from Himself. They call Him God of God, and assert that He is the Creator-God, since everything created has a cause and reason, as to why it is this and not that.

The one infinite reason of all things is therefore God. However, the reason, which is logos or word, emanates from that which produces it, such that, if the Omnipotent produces the Word, it becomes in the thing that which is enfolded in the Word; likewise if the Omnipotent says, "Let there be light," the light enfolded in the Word thus exists actually. Therefore, this Word of God is intellectual, such that a thing exists in reality, as soon as it is conceived as existing in His intellect.

They furthermore say that the spirit of connection proceeds third in order. The latter connects all to one, so that there is unity as the unity of the universe. That is, they posit a world soul or spirit, which connects everything and by means of which every creature obtains participation in the world order, in that it is a part of the universe. It is therefore necessary, that this Spirit exist in the origin of the Origin itself. Moreover, love connects. Therefore, this Spirit, whose power is diffused throughout the universe, can be called the love, which is God or charity. Thus the connection, through which the parts are connected to the one or the whole, and without which there would be no perfection, has God as its origin. In this manner one sees clearly, that all wise men touch upon something of the Trinity in unity. Therefore, when they shall hear this explanation, which we have heard, they shall rejoice and give praise.

The GAUL responded: I have also occasionally heard the following argument brandished among the learned: Eternity is either ungenerated or generated or neither ungenerated nor generated. I see that ungenerated eternity can rationally be called omnipotent Father, whereas the generated can be called Word or Son, and the neither ungenerated nor generated love or Holy Spirit, since the latter proceeds from both; it is neither ungenerated, since it is not the Father, nor generated, since it is not the Son, but rather proceeds from both.

Eternity is therefore one and it is threefold and completely simple. The one deity is threefold, the one essence is threefold, the one life is threefold, the one power is threefold, and the one strength is threefold. In this deliberation I have now progressed so far, that those things which were obscure are revealed as clearly as light, to the extent it is now granted.

However, the greatest contradiction still remains in this world, since some assert, the Word has become flesh for the redemption of all, the others, however, think otherwise; therefore it is necessary for us to be informed as to how we can attain concord in this difficulty.

WORD: The Apostle Peter has undertaken to elucidate this part of our dialogue. Listen to him. He will instruct sufficiently concerning that which is obscure to you.

XI.

And PETER appeared in their midst and began in the following
way:

PETER: All diversity of opinion regarding the incarnation of the
Word seems to be of the following variety: First we have
those who say, the Word of God is not God. This question
has previously been sufficiently answered, since the Word
of God can only be God. This Word, however, is reason.
That is, the Greeks call the Word logos, which is reason.

There is no doubt that God, the Creator of all rational
souls and spirits, has reason. However this reason of God,
as was explained above, is nothing other than God. Having
coincides in God with being. That is, that One, from whom
everything is, enfolds everything in Himself; He is everything in everything, since He is the Former of everything.
Consequently He is the Form of forms. However, the Form
of forms enfolds in Himself all formable forms.

The Word or reason, the infinite cause and the measure of all that can be, is therefore God. Therefore, those
who admit that the Word of God is incarnate or human,
must acknowledge that that man, whom they designate as
the Word of God, is also God.

At this point the PERSIAN spoke and said: Peter, the Word of God
is God. How then could God, who is immutable, become
not God, but rather a man, the Creator creature? Nearly
everyone denies that, except a few in Europe. And even if
there are a few among us, who are called Christians, they
agree with us, that it is impossible that the infinite be finite
and the eternal temporal.

PETER: This, i.e., that the eternal is temporal, I resolutely deny
together with you. However, since all of you who adhere
to Arab law, designate Christ as the Word of God—and you
do that correctly—it is necessary that you also acknowledge
Him as God.

PERSIAN: We acknowledge Him as the Word and the Spirit of
God, since among all those who are or were, no one pos-
sessed that excellence of the Word and of the Spirit of God.
Nevertheless, we do not therefore admit that He has been

God, for the latter has no participant. So that we do not fall into a plurality of gods, we deny that the former is God, but confess that he is nearest to God.

PETER: Do you believe in the human nature in Christ?

PERSIAN: We believe and affirm, that this has truly been in him and persisted.

PETER: Quite right. This nature, which is human, was not divine. And thus in everything which you see in Christ corresponding to his human nature, through which he was similar to other men, you have apprehended not Christ as God, but rather as man.

PERSIAN: So it is.

PETER: Therein no one disagrees with you. For human nature was in Christ most perfectly. Through it he was a real man and mortal just as other men. According to this nature he was not, however, the Word of God. Tell me therefore: What do you intend, if you acknowledge him as the Word of God?

PERSIAN: We do not intend nature but rather grace, that is, we intend, that he has attained this lofty grace, because God placed His Word in him.

PETER: Has God not also placed His Word in a similar manner in the other prophets? For they all spoke through the Word of the Lord and were messengers of the Word of God.

PERSIAN: So it is. However, Christ is the greatest of all prophets. Therefore, it befits him more properly to be called the Word of God than other prophets. In particular businesses and provinces several missives can contain the word of the king. However there is only one missive which contains the word of the king by which the whole kingdom is ruled, that is, because it contains the law and precept, which all must obey.

PETER: It appears that you have given us a good similitude for our purpose: The word of the king is written on various pieces of paper; however, these pieces do not change into another nature. They remain of the same nature after the inscription of the word, as they were before. Thus you say, human nature is maintained in Christ.

PERSIAN: That we do.

PETER: Very well. But notice the difference which exists between a missive and the heir of the kingdom. In the heir of the kingdom the king's own word is alive, free and unlimited, however, not in the missive.

PERSIAN: That I acknowledge. If the king sends his heir to the kingdom, then the heir bears the living and unlimited word of his father.

PETER: Is the Word not the true heir, who is neither messenger nor envoy, neither letter nor missive? And are not all the words of messengers and missives enfolded in the word of the heir? And although the heir of the kingdom is not the father, but rather the son, he is not different from the regal nature; rather he is the heir on account of this equality.

PERSIAN: I understand very well. However, there remains a difficulty: The king and his son are two. Therefore, we do not admit that God possesses a son. That is, the son would be another God than the father, just as the son of the king is another man than the father.

PETER: You impugn the similitude well. For it is not correct, if you attend to the supposited persons. However, if you remove the numerical diversity of the supposited persons and reflect on the potency, which is in the regal dignity of the father and of the son as his heir, then you see how that regal power is one both in the father and in the son; in the father it is as in the ungenerated, in the son it is as in the generated or living word of the father.

PERSIAN: Continue!

PETER: Therefore, that absolute regal power is ungenerated and generated, and the ungenerated summons to the society of connatural and generated succession one who is by his nature different, so that the different nature can simultaneously and undividedly possess the kingdom in union with its own nature. Then do not the natural and the graced or adoptive successions concur in the one inheritance?

PERSIAN: It is manifest.

PETER: Likewise filiation and adoption are also united in the one succession of the one kingdom. However, the succession of adoption does not exist in itself, but rather is supposed in the succession of filiation. Adoption, which does not succeed through its own nature, must, if it is to succeed in the existence of filiation, succeed not in itself, but rather is supposed in that which succeeds by nature. Therefore, if adoption, since it succeeds with filiation in the attainment of the completely simple and indivisible inheritance, obtains succession not from itself, but rather from filiation, the adoptive and the natural successor cannot be different, even though the nature of adoption and the natural are different.

How shall both concur in the succession of the indivisible inheritance, if the adoptive son were separated and did not subsist in the one and the same hypostacy with the natural son? We must therefore maintain, that in Christ the human nature is united to the Word or the divine nature, such that the human does not pass over into the divine, but rather adheres thus to it indissolubly, so that it is not separate in itself, but becomes a person in the divine nature; so that the human nature, which is now summoned to the succession of eternal life with the divine, can achieve immortality in the divine.

XII.

PERSIAN: I grasp that competently. However, clarify what has already been said by means of another intelligible example.

PETER: It is impossible to form precise similitudes. However, behold: Is wisdom in itself an accident or substance?

PERSIAN: As it is in itself, it is substance, however, as it occurs in another, it is an accident.

PETER: In all wise men all wisdom comes from that which is wisdom per se, since it is God.

PERSIAN: This has been demonstrated.

PETER: Is not one man wiser than another?

PERSIAN: Certainly.

PETER: Therefore, whoever is wiser, is closer to wisdom per se,

which is the absolute maximum. And whoever is less wise,
is more distant from it.

PERSIAN: That I admit.

PETER: However, according to his human nature a man can never
be so wise, that he could not be still wiser. For between
contracted wisdom, i.e., human wisdom and wisdom per
se, which is divine, maximum and infinite Wisdom, an
infinite distance always remains.

PERSIAN: That is similarly evident.

PETER: That is true in like manner of absolute Mastery and of
contracted mastery. In absolute Mastery the art is infinite,
in the contracted the art is finite. Let us therefore suppose,
that the intellect of any man possesses such mastery and
such wisdom, that it is not possible to have greater wisdom
or greater mastery. This intellect then is to such a high
degree united with wisdom per se or mastery per se, that
this union could not be greater. Would not this intellect
achieve divine strength, in the strength of the united wisdom and mastery, which are maximal and with which it is
united? And in a man who possesses such an intellect,
would not the intellectual nature of the man be united most
immediately with the divine nature or the eternal wisdom,
the Word or omnipotent Art?

PERSIAN: I acknowledge all that. However, this union would still
be one of grace.

PETER: If the union of the inferior nature with the divine were so
great, that it could not be greater, then it were united to it
in personal unity. That is, as long as the inferior nature
were not elevated into personal and hypostatic unity with
the superior, it could be greater. Therefore, as soon as the
maximum union is posited, the inferior nature subsists in
the superior, such that it adheres to it. That occurs not
through nature, but through grace. This grace, however,
is the maximum, which cannot be greater. It is not separate
from nature, since it is united with it. Therefore, even if
human nature were united with the divine by means of
grace, that grace, since it cannot be greater, would nevertheless be most immediately terminated in nature.

PERSIAN: Whatsoever you may have said, to the effect that human nature in any man can be elevated through grace to union with divine nature, the man Christ should no sooner be called God than another saint, even though he is the most sacred among men.

PETER: If you attend to the fact, that there is in Christ alone that highest height, which cannot be greater and that maximum grace, which cannot be greater and that maximum sanctity, and thus in respect to the rest; and attend to the fact, that there cannot be more than but one maximum height, which cannot be greater—the same is true of grace and sanctity—and thereafter observe, that every height of every one of the prophets, whatsoever degree it may have had, is incomparably distant from that height which cannot be greater, such that for every degree of height there can be infinitely many greater or smaller between it and the sole-highest—the same is true of grace, sanctity, prudence, wisdom, mastery, and every single thing—then you see quite clearly, that there can only be one Christ, in whom human nature is united in unity with its supposit of the divine nature.

The Arabs also acknowledge the same, although the majority do not fully consider it. The Arabs say namely, that in this world and in the future one Christ is the sole-highest and the Word of God. Even those who describe Christ as God and man, indeed say nothing other than that Christ is the sole-highest man and the Word of God.

PERSIAN: It therefore appears that the Arabs, after they have considered well that union which is necessarily present in the highest, can be led to acceptance of this belief. For the unity of God, which they endeavor to guard with maximum strength, is in no way injured through this belief, but is saved. However, tell us how one can grasp, that that human nature obtains existence not in itself, but rather is supposed through its adherence to the divine.

PETER: Take the following example, even though it is remote. A magnetic stone attracts iron upwards. And while it adheres to the air around the magnet, the nature of the iron does not subsist in its own weighty nature. Otherwise, that is, it would not hang in the air, but rather according to its own nature fall towards the center of the earth. But by adhering to the magnet, the iron subsists in the air by means of the strength of the magnet's nature, and not by means of the strength of its own nature, in virtue of which it could not be there. However, the cause whereby the nature of the iron is thus inclined toward the nature of the magnet, lies in the fact that the iron bears the similitude of the magnet's nature in itself, from which it is said to receive its origin. Therefore, if the human intellectual nature adheres most closely to the divine intellectual nature, from which it has received its being, it would adhere inseparably to it, just as to the source of its life.

PERSIAN: I understand.

PETER: There is still a large group of Arabs, who acknowledge that Christ has resuscitated the dead and created birds from clay and much else, which they expressly say Jesus Christ, as he who had the power therefor, has done. On this basis they can very easily be won over, since it cannot be denied that he has done this in the strength of the divine nature, to which the human was united suppositionally. The power of Christ, with which he commanded that that occur which is acknowledged by the Arabs to have occurred, could not be according to human nature, unless the human had been assumed in union with the divine, in whose power it lies to so command.

PERSIAN: This and much else that is described in the Koran, the Arabs affirm of Christ. However, it will be more difficult to lead the Jews than all others to faith in these things, since they expressly admit nothing regarding Christ.

PETER: In their scriptures they have everything concerning Christ. However, since they follow the literal sense, they do not want to understand. This resistance of the Jews, however, does not impede concord. That is, they are few and cannot bring the whole world into disorder with arms.

XIII.

The SYRIAN responded to this: Peter, I have heard that greater concord could be found among every religious group on the basis of their presuppositions. Tell us now, how this shall be realized in respect to this point.

PETER: I will, however, first tell me: Is not God alone eternal and immortal?

SYRIAN: I believe so, for everything besides God has originated. Because it therefore has an origin, it will also have an end corresponding to its nature.

PETER: Does not nearly every religion—that of the Jews, the Christians, the Arabs and of many other men—hold, that the mortal human nature of every man is resurrected after temporal death to everlasting life?

SYRIAN: So one believes.

PETER: Therefore, all these religions acknowledge, that human nature must be united to the divine and immortal nature. For how else would human nature pass over into immortality, if it did not adhere to the divine in inseparable union?

SYRIAN: Faith in the resurrection necessarily presupposes this.

PETER: If faith therefore holds this, then human nature is first united with the divine in some man. This occurs in that one who is the countenance of all people and the highest Messiah and Christ, as Arabs and Jews call Christ. The latter, however, who in the opinion of all is nearest to God, will be the one in whom human nature is first united with God. He is therefore the savior and mediator of all, in whom human nature, which is one and through which all men are men, is united to the divine and immortal nature, so that all men, who are of the same nature, attain resurrection from death.

SYRIAN: I understand that you would say: Faith in the resurrection from death presupposes the union of human nature with the divine, without which this faith were impossible. This is the case, so you assert, in Christ. Therefore, this faith presupposes him.

PETER: You understand correctly. From this grasp how all promises which are found among the Jews, are affirmed in the faith in the Messiah or mediator. Through him alone could and can those promises be fulfilled, as far as they concern eternal life.

SYRIAN: How is it with other religious bodies?

PETER: Similar. For all men strive and hope for nothing other than eternal life in their human nature. For this they instituted purgations of souls and sacred rites, in order to be better adapted in their nature to that eternal life. Men desire the beatitude, which is eternal life, not in another nature than their own. Man wants to be nothing but man, not an angel or another nature. He wants, however, to be a happy man, who attains the highest felicity.

This felicity is nothing other than enjoyment or the union of human life with its source, from which life itself emanates, and this is divine immortal life. However, how were this possible to man, if it were not granted to one, who shares the same nature with all to be elevated to such union, and through whom, as if through their mediator, all men could achieve the ultimate goal of their desires? And this one is the way, since he is the man through whom every man has access to God, who is the end of all their desires. It is therefore Christ, who is presupposed by all who hope to achieve ultimate felicity.

SYRIAN: This pleases me very well. For if the human intellect believes it can achieve union with wisdom, where it obtains the eternal sustenance of its life, then it presupposes that the intellect of some highest man has achieved that union in the highest measure and has attained that highest mastery, through which mastery it itself similarly hopes to come at some time to this wisdom. For if it did not believe this possible in even some highest of all men, he would hope in vain. And since the hope of all is in being able to attain at some time that felicity, on account of which every religion exists—and there is no deception in this, since this hope stems from a connate desire common to all, to which religion, which consequently is likewise connate to all, conforms—I see that this master and mediator, who possesses the summit of the perfection of human nature and dominion, is presupposed by all.

But the Jews say, to be sure, that this prince of nature, in whom all defects of all men are remedied, has not yet been born, but will one day be born.

PETER: It suffices that both Arabs, as well as Christians and others, who have borne witness in their blood, by that which the prophets have proclaimed of him, and which he himself, while he abided in the world, has effected beyond the strength of all men, testify that he has come.

XIV.

SPANIARD: There will surely be another difficulty regarding the Messiah, of whom the greater part of the world acknowledges that he has come, namely in respect to his birth, since Christians and Arabs assert that he was born of the Virgin Mary, while others hold this to be impossible.

PETER: All who believe that Christ has come, acknowledge that he was born of the Virgin Mary. For since he is the ultimate perfection of nature and the sole-highest, of which father should he then be the son? For every generating father is in the perfection of nature so far distant from the ultimate perfection of nature, that he cannot communicate to the son this ultimate perfection, beyond which there can be none higher and which is not possible except for one man. Only that father can do this, who is the Creator of nature. Therefore, the highest has no other father than Him, from whom is all paternity. Therefore, by divine strength the highest is conceived in the womb of the Virgin, and in this Virgin the highest fecundity concurred with virginity. Therefore, Christ was born to us, such that he is most connected to all men. Namely, he has Him for his Father, from whom every human father has it that he is a father. And he has her for his mother, who has joined carnally with no man, so that in this way everyone finds his nature in ultimate perfection through the closest conjunction in Christ.

TURK: A not insignificant difference still remains. Whereas the Christians assert that Christ was crucified by the Jews, there are others who deny this.

PETER: That some deny the crucifixion of Christ, but say that he still lives and will return at the time of the Anti-Christ, is due to the fact that they are ignorant of the mystery of death. And since he will come, as they assert, they believe that when he comes back, he will come back in mortal flesh, as if he could not otherwise conquer the Anti-Christ. That they deny his crucifixion by the Jews, they appear to do out of reverence for Christ, as if such men could have no power over Christ.

However, note that one must rightly give credence to those multifarious reports and the proclamation of the apostles, who have died for the truth, i.e., that Christ has died thus. Likewise, the prophets also predicted that Christ would have to be condemned to the most ignominious death, which was death on the cross.

The reason for this is the following: Sent by God the Father, Christ came, in order to announce the kingdom of heaven, and what he said of this kingdom could be confirmed in no better way than through the testimony of his blood. Therefore, in order to be most obedient to God the Father and to provide all certitude for the truth, which he announced, he has died. He took upon himself the most ignominious death, so that no man might refuse to accept the truth, in testament to which they would all know that Christ had voluntarily accepted death.

For he preached the Kingdom of Heaven and gave notice, how a man, who is capable of this kingdom, could attain it. In comparison to this kingdom, the life of this world, which is so tenaciously loved by all, is to be deemed as nothing. And so that one would know that the truth is the life of that Kingdom of Heaven, he gave up the life of this world for the truth, so that he would thus in the most perfect manner proclaim the Kingdom of Heaven, and liberate the world of the ignorance which prefers this life to the future one. He wished to sacrifice himself for the many, so that exalted thus before the eyes of all upon the cross, he would draw all to belief and clarify the Gospel, comfort the pusillanimous, and freely give himself for the redemption of the many, and do everything in the best way in which it could be done, so that man would achieve the faith of salvation, the hope of acquiring it, and the charity necessary for the fulfillment of the commands of God.

If, therefore, the Arabs would attend to the fruit of

the death of Christ, and to the fact that he saw himself as sent by God to sacrifice himself in order to fulfill the desire of his Father, and that there was nothing more glorious for Christ than to die even the most ignominious death for truth and obedience, then they would not take away the glory of the cross from Christ, through which he earned the merit of being the highest and becoming exalted above all in the glory of the Father.

If Christ further proclaimed, that men will achieve immortality after their death in the resurrection, how could the world have been able to achieve better certainty concerning it, than by means of the fact, that he himself has died of his own will, is resurrected, and appeared among the living? Namely, the world was then given ultimate certainty, when it heard that the man Christ, who had died on the cross openly and publicly, was resurrected from the dead and lives—according to the testimony of many who saw him alive and died in this testimony, in order to be faithful witnesses to his resurrection. This was the most perfect evangelization, which Christ revealed in himself, and it could not be more perfect. However, without death and resurrection it would always have been able to be more perfect.

Therefore, whoever believes that Christ has fulfilled the will of God the Father in the most perfect manner, must thereby also acknowledge all this, without which the evangelization would not have been the most perfect.

Consider further, that the Kingdom of Heaven was concealed from all until Christ. It is indeed the Gospel of Christ to proclaim this unknown kingdom to all. There was neither faith, nor hope of attaining the Kingdom of Heaven, nor could it be loved by anyone, since it was completely unknown. It was also not possible, that any man would come to that kingdom, as long as human nature had not yet been elevated to that exaltation, so that it would become a consort of the divine nature. Christ has therefore made the Kingdom of Heaven accessible to us in every way. Yet no one is able to enter Kingdom of Heaven, unless he lay aside the kingdom of this world through death. Therefore, the mortal must lay aside mortality, that is, the possibility of dying. This cannot occur except through death. Then can he put on immortality.

As mortal man, if he had not died, Christ would not yet have laid aside mortality. Likewise he would also not yet have entered the Kingdom of Heaven, in which no mortal can be. If, therefore, he, who is the first-fruit and the first born of all men, has not yet opened up the Kingdom of Heaven, our nature united with God has not been introduced into the kingdom. Thus no man could be in the Kingdom of Heaven, as long as the human nature united with God has not yet been introduced. All men who believe the Kingdom of Heaven to exist, assert the contrary. That is, all acknowledge that certain saints of their religion have achieved felicity. The faith of all, therefore, who acknowledge that there are saints in eternal glory, presupposes that Christ has died and ascended into heaven.

XV.

GERMAN: That is all very well. But I see not a few discrepancies in respect to felicity. For it is said that the Jews are promised under their law nothing but temporal things, which consist of sensuous goods. To the Arabs nothing but carnal, albeit perpetual goods have been promised under their law, which is written in the Koran. The Gospel, on the other hand, promises angelicality, i.e., that men will be similar to the angels, who have nothing of carnality.

PETER: What can one conceive in this world, for which the desire does not decrease, but rather constantly increases?

GERMAN: All temporal things die away, only the intellectual do not. Eating, drinking, luxuriating and more of the same, if they please at one time, displease at another and are unstable. However, to know and to understand and to see the truth with the eyes of the mind are always pleasant. And the older the man becomes, the more this pleases him and the more he obtains of it, the stronger becomes his appetite to possess it.

PETER: If, therefore, the desire shall be perpetual and the nourishment perpetual, the nourishment will be neither temporal nor sensible, but rather only intellectual, life. Hence, although the promise of a paradise, where there are streams of wine and honey and a multitude of virgins, is found in the law of the Koran, there are nonetheless many men in this world who abominate this. How will the latter then be happy, if they attain that there, which they do not wish to have here? It's said in the Koran, that one will find wonderfully beautiful, dark-skinned maidens, with eyes which have large, bright white eyeballs. No German would desire such a maiden in this world, even if he had surrendered to the lusts of the flesh. One must therefore understand those promises as similitudes.

At another point the Koran prohibits copulation and all other pleasures of the flesh in churches or synagogues or mosques. However, one cannot believe that the mosques are holier than paradise. How shall that be prohibited in the mosque, which is promised yonder in paradise?

In other locations the Koran says that everything is found there that we desire here, since the fulfillment of all must take place there. Thereby it reveals sufficiently what it wants to say, when it says that such things are found there. For since these things are so much desired in this world, presupposing that an equal desire exists in the other world, then they will be found exquisitely and abundantly there. For it could not express that that life is the completion of all desires other than by this similitude. Nor did it wish to express to uneducated people other, more hidden things, but rather only that which appears felicitous according to the senses, so that the people, who do not have an appetite for things of the spirit, would not despise the promises.

The whole concern of him who wrote that law, therefore, appears to have been primarily to avert the people from idolatry. And to this end he made these kinds of promises and wrote down everything. However, he did not condemn the Gospel, but rather praised it, and thereby intimated that the felicity which is promised in the Gospel would not be less than that corporeal felicity. And the intelligent and the wise men among them know that this is true. Avicenna prefers the intellectual felicity of the vision or fruition of God and the truth incomparably to the felicity described in the law of the Arabs. Nevertheless he adhered to that law. Likewise did the other wise men.

Therefore, there will be no difficulty to unite all religions. For it must be said, that that felicity is above everything that can be written or said, since it is the fulfillment of all desires, the attainment of the good in its source, and of life in immortality.

GERMAN: What then about the Jews, who do not accept the promise of the Kingdom of Heaven, but rather only the promise of temporal things?

PETER: The Jews very often take death upon themselves out of observations of the law and its sanctimony. If they did not believe that they attain felicity after death, in that they prefer zeal for the law to life, then they would not die. It is not therefore the belief of the Jews, that there is no eternal life and that they cannot attain that life. Otherwise no one would die for the law. However, the felicity, which they expect, they do not expect on the basis of works of the law, since those laws do not promise this to them, but rather on the basis of the faith which presupposes Christ, as it is found stated above.

XVI.

TATAR: I have heard much here that has been previously unknown to me. The Tatars, a numerous and simple people, who worship the one God above others, are astounded over the variety of rites which others have, who worship one and the same God with them. They deride the fact that some Christians, all Arabs and Jews are circumcised, that others are marked on their brows with a brand, others are baptized. Furthermore, there is such great diversity in respect to matrimony; the one has only one wife, another is legally married to one wife, but nevertheless has several concubines, yet another has several lawful wives. As regards sacrifice, the rites are so diverse, that one cannot even enumerate them. Among these various forms of sacrifice there is the Christian sacrifice, in which they offer bread and wine, and say it is the body and blood of Christ. That they eat and drink this sacrifice after the oblation seems most abominable. They devour what they worship. How in these cases, which moreover are varied by location and time, a union can be realized, I do not grasp. However, as long as there is not a union, the persecution will not cease. For diversity produces division and enmities, hatred and war.

Then PAUL, teacher of the peoples, commissioned by the Word, began to speak.

PAUL: It must be shown, that the salvation of the soul is granted, not on the basis of works, but rather on account of faith. For Abraham, the father of the faith of all the believing, whether they are Christians, Arabs or Jews, believed in God and he was reckoned to be justified; the soul of the just will inherit eternal life. If that is admitted, then the various kinds of rites are not disturbing, for they are instituted and received as sensible signs of the verity of faith. The signs, not the signified, assume variability.

TATAR: Explain how faith saves.

PAUL: If God promises something by virtue of His pure liberality and grace, should not He, who has the power to give everything, and who is truthful, be believed?

TATAR: Certainly so. No one who believes in Him can be deceived. And whoever does not believe in Him, would be unworthy to receive any gift of grace.

PAUL: What therefore justifies him, who attains justice?

TATAR: Not merits, or else it were not grace, but rather something owed.

PAUL: Very well stated. However, since no living being is justified in the sight of God on the basis of his works, but rather through grace, the Omnipotent gives to whomsoever He wishes, whatsoever He wishes. If, therefore, someone shall be worthy of obtaining the promise, which is issued out of pure grace, then it is necessary that he believe in God. In this therefore is he justified, since he obtains the promise only on the grounds that he believes in God, and expects that the Word of God be done.

TATAR: After God has promised, it is just that His promise be kept. Whoever believes in God is therefore justified, rather through the promise than through the faith.

PAUL: God, who promised Abraham a seed in which all would be blessed, justified Abraham, so that he attained this promise. However, had Abraham not believed in God, then he would have attained neither the justification nor the promise.

TATAR: It is so.

PAUL: Therefore, the faith in Abraham only effected that the fulfillment of the promise was just. Otherwise it would neither have been just, nor would it have been fulfilled.

TATAR: What therefore has God promised?

PAUL: God promised Abraham to give him one seed in Isaac, in whom all people would be blessed. And this promise was issued, when in accordance with the common course of nature it was impossible for Sara, his wife to conceive by him and to give birth. However, because he believed, he obtained his son, Isaac. Consequently, God tempted Abraham to offer and slay the boy Isaac, in whom the promise of the seed had been fulfilled. And Abraham obeyed God, nonetheless he believed no less in the future promise, even though it would be fulfilled after the resuscitation of his dead son. From this God found great faith in Abraham. Then Abraham was justified and the promise of the one seed, who descended from him through Isaac, was fulfilled.

TATAR: Who is this seed?

PAUL: It is Christ. In him all people attained the divine blessing.

TATAR: Which blessing is that?

PAUL: The divine blessing is the ultimate desire or felicity, which is called eternal life, and concerning which you have heard enough above.

TATAR: Do you wish to say, therefore, that God in Christ has promised us the blessing of eternal felicity?

PAUL: I wish to do just that. For this reason it is necessary to believe in God, just as Abraham has believed, so that he who so believes would be justified with the faithful Abraham in obtaining the promise in the one seed of Abraham, i.e., in Jesus Christ. This promise is the divine blessing, which enfolds every good in itself.

TATAR: Would you therefore say, that this faith alone justifies being received into eternal life?

PAUL: I wish to do that.

TATAR: How would you impart to the simple Tatars the understanding of this, so that they comprehend that it is Christ, in whom they can attain felicity?

PAUL: You have heard that not only Christians, but also Arabs, acknowledge Christ is the highest of all who have been or will be in this or a future age, and that He is the countenance of the peoples. Therefore, if the blessing of all people is in a single seed, then it can only be Christ.

TATAR: What kind of sign do you adduce for it?

PAUL: I adduce the testimony of the Arabs as well as of the Christians, that the spirit which vivifies the dead is the spirit of Christ. Therefore, if the spirit of life is in Christ, who has the power to vivify whomever he wishes, then he is that spirit, without which no one who has died can be resuscitated or any spirit can live eternally. That is, the plentitude of divinity and of grace inhabits the spirit of Christ, and from this plentitude all who shall be saved receive the grace of salvation.

TATAR: It is pleasing to have heard these things from you, the teacher of the peoples, since in conjunction with that which I have heard above they satisfy our purpose. I also see that this faith is necessary for salvation. Without it no one can be saved. But I ask you whether faith suffices?

PAUL: It is impossible that someone please God without faith. However, it must be a formed faith, for without works it is dead.

TATAR: What are these works?

PAUL: If you believe in God, you keep His commandments. For how would you believe God is God, if you were not to take care to fulfill that which He prescribes?

TATAR: It is proper to keep the commandments of God. But the Jews say they have received these commandments from Moses, the Arabs say they have them from Mohammed, and the Christians from Jesus. And there are perhaps other nations who honor their prophets, through whose hands they assert they have received the divine precepts. Therefore, how shall we arrive at concord?

PAUL: The divine commandments are very brief and are all well known and common in every nation, for the light that reveals them to us is created along with the rational soul. For within us God says to love Him, from whom we received being, and to do nothing to another, except that which we wish done to us. Love is therefore the fulfillment of the law of God and all laws are reduced to this.

TATAR: I do not doubt that both faith as well as the law of love, of which you have spoken, will be accepted by the Tatars. But I have great doubt in respect to the rites. For I do not know how they shall accept circumcision, which they deride.

PAUL: The truth of our salvation does not depend upon accepting circumcision. Indeed, circumcision does not save, and salvation exists without it. However, he who does not believe that circumcision is necessary for achieving salvation, but permits it to be done to the foreskin in order that he might be in conformity with Abraham and his successors, is not condemned on account of circumcision, if he has the faith of which we have spoken above. Thus Christ was circumcised and many Christians after Him, while hitherto the Ethiopians mentioned by St. James and others were not circumcised, as if it were a sacrament necessary to salvation. Yet how peace can be preserved among the faithful, if some are circumcised, and others not, remains a great question. If, therefore, the greater part of the world is without circumcision, one should attend to the fact that it is not a necessity, so that consequently—as I indeed judge opportune—the smaller part should adapt itself to the larger, with which it is united in faith, in order to preserve the peace. Indeed, even if for the sake of peace the larger part should conform to the smaller and accept circumcision, I would think that it should be done, so that peace might be established on the basis of mutual communication. Thus the peace would be better and firmer, if the other nations would accept faith from the Christians and the Christians would accept circumcision from the latter. However, I think that the realization of these ideas is difficult. It should therefore suffice to establish peace in faith and in the law of love, while the rites are tolerated from this time forth.

XVII.

ARMENIAN: How do you think one should regard baptism, since it is considered among Christians to be a necessary sacrament?

PAUL: Baptism is the sacrament of faith. Whoever believes some justification can be attained in Jesus Christ, also believes ablation of sins is attained through him. Every believer will manifest this cleansing, which is signified in the baptismal lotion. For baptism is nothing other than the confession of faith in the sacramental sign. He would not be a believer, who did not wish to confess his faith in the Word and in the signs which have been instituted for this by Christ. Among both Hebrews as well as Arabs there are baptismal lotions, in order to express devotion on account of religion. It will not be difficult for these to accept a lotion instituted by Christ for the profession of faith.

ARMENIAN: It appears to be necessary to accept this sacrament, since it is necessary for salvation.

PAUL: Faith is necessary for adults, who can be saved without the sacrament if they cannot obtain it. However, where they can in fact obtain it, they cannot be called believers, who do not wish to show themselves as such by means of the sacrament of regeneration.

ARMENIAN: What about children?

PAUL: They will acquiesce without difficulty to letting children be baptized. If they have undertaken on account of religion to circumcise male children on the eighth day, then the commutation of that circumcision into baptism will be agreeable. And the option will be given, whether or not to be content with baptism alone.

XVIII.

BOHEMIAN: It will be quite possible to find concord in everything that was previously stated. But it will be very difficult as regards sacrifices. For we know that the Christians cannot give up the oblation of bread and wine as the sacrament of the Eucharist, in order to please the others, since this sacrament was instituted by Christ. However, that the other nations, which do not have the practice of sacrificing in this way, will accept this mode of sacrifice, is not easy to believe, above all since they say it is insane to believe in the conversion of the bread into the flesh of Christ and of the wine into his blood and afterwards to devour the sacrament.

PAUL: This sacrament of the Eucharist represents nothing other than that we achieve by grace the refreshment of eternal life in Christ Jesus, just as in this world we are refreshed through bread and wine. If we therefore believe that Christ is the food of the mind, then we receive him under the species which feed the body. And since it is necessary to be in agreement in this faith, that we obtain nourishment of spiritual life in Christ, why then should we not show that we believe this in the sacrament of the Eucharist? It is to be hoped that in this world all men of faith will want to taste that food through faith, which will be in truth the food of our lives in the other world.

BOHEMIAN: How will one persuade all people, that in this sacrament of the Eucharist the substance of the bread is converted into the body of Christ?

PAUL: Whoever is a believer knows that the Word of God will transfer us in Jesus Christ—since nothing is impossible for God—out of the misery of this world to the filiation of God and to possession of eternal life. If we therefore believe and hope for this, then we doubt not that the Word of God can change bread into the body according to the ordination of Christ. If nature accomplishes this in animal life, how then shall the Word, through which God has created the ages, not be able to accomplish this? The necessity of faith therefore demands believing this. For if it is possible that we, the sons of Adam, who are made out of earth, are changed in Jesus Christ through the Word of God into sons of the immortal God, and we believe this and we hope for the future; and if it is possible, that we then like Jesus will be the Word of God the Father; then we must likewise believe that the transubstantiation of the bread into flesh and of the wine into blood is possible through the same Word, through which bread is bread and wine is wine, flesh is flesh and blood is blood, and through which nature converts food into the fed.

BOHEMIAN: This conversion of the substance of bread is difficult to comprehend.

PAUL: For faith it is very easy. For this is only comprehensible to the mind, which alone looks at substance as the that-it-is and not as what-it-is. For substance precedes every accident. And since consequently the substance is neither qualitative nor quantitative, and it alone is converted, so that it henceforth is no longer the substance of bread, but rather the substance of the flesh, this conversion is only spiritual, since it is totally remote from everything which is attainable by the senses. Consequently, the quantity of the flesh is not augmented by virtue of this conversion, nor is it multiplied numerically. Therefore, there is only one substance of the flesh, in which the substance of the bread is converted, even though this bread is sacrificed in diverse locations and there are many loaves, which are served in the sacrifice.

BOHEMIAN: I grasp your teaching, which is very agreeable to me; namely, as to how this sacrament is the sacrament of the nourishment of eternal life, through which nourishment we obtain the inheritance of the sons of God in Jesus Christ, the Son of God; and how there is a similitude of this in the sacrament of this Eucharist; and that it is only obtained in the mind and only tasted and grasped in faith. However, what if they do not comprehend this mystery? For the uneducated will perhaps not only abhor believing this, but also abhor accepting so great a sacrament.

PAUL: In its sensible signs this sacrament, as long as faith exists, is not of such necessity, that without it there would be no salvation. For it suffices to believe in salvation and thus to eat the food of life. Therefore, no law of necessity has been posited concerning its distribution: whether, to whom, and how often it should be given to people. If, therefore, someone who has faith, regards himself unworthy to approach the table of the highest King, then this humility is preferably to be praised. Therefore, in respect to the usage and rite of this sacrament, one will be able to establish that which appears more suitable to the leaders of the Church according to the times, as long as the faith is preserved, so that despite the diversity of rites, the peace of faith will persevere no less inviolate by means of a universal law.

XIX.

ENGLANDER: What should be done concerning the other sacraments, namely matrimony, ordination, confirmation, and extreme unction?

PAUL: One ought to take into account the infirmity of man as much as possible, unless it contravenes eternal salvation. For to demand exact conformity in everything, is rather to disturb the peace. Yet it is to be hoped, that concord can be found in matrimony and in ordination. In all nations matrimony appears to have been introduced in some way by the law of nature, so that one man possesses only one true wife. Thus also the priesthood is similarly found in all religions. Concord therefore will be easier to find in these common points. And the Christian religion is proven in the judgment of all others, to observe the most laudable purity in both sacraments.

ENGLANDER: What about fasts, ecclesiastical offices, abstinence from food and drink, the forms of prayer and other such things?

PAUL: Where no conformity in the mode can be found, as long as faith and peace are preserved, one may indulge the nations in their devotions and ceremonies. Perhaps the devotion is even augmented by virtue of the diversity, since every nation will attempt to produce its rite more splendidly with zeal and diligence, in order to outdo the others therein and thus to obtain greater merit with God and praise in the world.

    After these things had been discussed with the wise men of the nations, several books were produced of those who have written about the observances of the ancients;

in every language there were excellent authors, like, for example, Marcus Varro among the Latins, Eusebius, who has gathered together the diversity of religion among the Greeks, and many others. In their examination it became apparent, that all diversity is located more in the rites than in the worship of the one God, whom all have always from the inception presupposed and cherished in all worship, as could be found in one collection of all the writings; even if in their simplicity the people, seduced by the power of the Prince of Darkness, frequently were not mindful of what they were doing.

The concord of religions was therefore concluded in the manner described in the heaven of reason. And it was commanded by the King of kings, that the wise men return and lead the nations to the unity of the true cult and that the spiritual administrators guide them and assist them. And finally, endowed with full authority for all, they should gather together in Jerusalem as the common center and in the name of all accept the one faith and upon it establish perpetual peace, so that the Creator of all, who is praised in peace, be blessed forever.

The Theological Complement Represented in the Mathematical Complements

(1 4 5 3)

I.

I have recently written a work on mathematical complements for Pope Nicolaus V, our most worthy and learned Pontiff. However, it seemed to me, that it would not be appropriate to publish this small work, as if I had nothing to offer in my order and advanced age except to write concerning mathematics to the rector of the Church, unless I added something about the utility which it possesses transcendently for theological figures.

I will therefore attempt to work out the theological figures of that booklet, so that—as far as God will grant it—we intuit with mental vision how, in the mirror of mathematics, that truth which is sought in everything knowable shines forth not only in remote similitude, but rather, as it were, in shining propinquity.

However, it is necessary that that booklet be appended to this, if we should understand what I have said, since this complement is elicited on the basis of mathematics.

It is also necessary that he who wants to attain fruit from this, attend more to the intention than to the words. For these kinds of theological figures are better seen with the eye of the mind than they can be expressed in words.

II.

No one can ignore that the truth is attained in mathematics more certainly than in all other liberal arts. And thus we see that also those who taste geometrical instruction adhere to it in admiring love, as if a certain nourishment of the intellectual life were contained there more purely and simply.

Indeed, the geometer does not trouble himself about lines in iron, gold, or wood figures, but rather as they are in themselves, although they are not found outside the material. Therefore, he intuits the sensible figures with the sensible eye, so that he can intuit them with the mental eye as mental. Also, the mind does not see the mental less truly than the eye sees the sensible, but rather so much more truly as the mind intuits the figures in themselves absolved of material otherness. However, the exterior sense never attains them outside of otherness. Indeed, the figure receives otherness on account of the union with the material, which must necessarily be always otherwise. On that account, the triangle on this pavement is one and the one on the wall another, and the figure is present in the one in greater truth than in the other. Consequently, it is also in no material so true and precise, that it could not be still more true and precise.

Therefore, the triangle abstracted from all variable otherness, just as it is in the mind, cannot be truer; hence, the mind, which intuits the figures in itself, since it sees them free from sensible otherness, knows that it itself is free from sensible otherness. Therefore, the mind is free from sensible material and is to the mathematical figures as form. If one indeed says that those figures are forms, then the mind will be the form of forms. Therefore, the figures in the mind will be as in their form and therefore without otherness.

Therefore, whatever the mind intuits, it intuits in itself. Therefore, those which the mind intuits are indeed not in sensible otherness, but rather in itself. However, what is absolved of all otherness, is not other than the truth. For truth is not other than the lack of otherness.

However, although our mind is free of every sensible otherness, it is nevertheless not free of all otherness. The mind, which is free of every otherness except the mental, therefore sees figures absolved of every otherness. Therefore, it intuits these in the truth and not outside itself. For it intuits them mentally. Indeed, that cannot happen outside itself. Indeed, mental intuition does not occur outside the mind, just as also the senses do not attain things sensibly outside the senses, but rather attain them in the senses.

However, the mind, which intuits the inalterable in itself, since it itself is alterable, does not intuit the inalterable in its alterability. For as one says, anger impedes the soul, so that it cannot perceive the true, but rather it intuits it in its inalterability. The truth, however, is inalterability. Therefore, where the mind intuits, whatever it intuits, there is the truth of itself and every thing which it intuits. Therefore, the truth, in which the mind intuits everything, is the form of the mind. Hence the light of the truth, through which the mind is and in which it intuits itself and everything, is in the mind; just as the light is in the vision of the wolf, through which this vision is and in which the wolf sees everything which it sees. If God has created such light in its eyes for the wolf, without which he could not seek his victim at night time, so that he can make his hunt for the preservation of his life, then God also does not abandon the intellectual nature, which is nourished on account of the hunt for truth, since He has created in it that necessary light.

However, the mind does not intuit the truth itself, through which it intuits itself and everything, except that it knows that it is, but not what it is. Just as vision does not see the clarity of that solar light, through which it sees everything visible and nevertheless experiences that it does not see without it. And thus it attains the that-it-is, but in no way the what-it-is. It also attains the quantity of this light not otherwise than that it knows: It is so great that it exceeds its power. The same is true of the mind.

Hence the truth in the mind is as it were an invisible mirror, in which the mind intuits everything visible through it. However, the mirror-like simplicity is so great, that it exceeds the power and acumen of the mind. However, the more the mental power grows and becomes acute, the more certainly and clearly it intuits everything in the mirror of truth. However, the mental power grows in that speculation not other than as the scintilla which flames up in burning. And since it grasps that increase, it is transferred from potentiality through this light of truth more and more into actuality. Hence as much as that power is exhibited, it never attains to such a degree, that the light of truth could not attract it to itself still further. Thus is this speculation the most delectable and inexhaustible nourishing of the mind, through which it continuously enters more into its most joyful life.

And the speculation is the motion of the mind from the that-it-is to the what-it-is. However, since the what-it-is is infinitely distant from the that-it-is, the motion never ceases. And it is most delectable motion, because it is directed to the life of the mind. And therefore, this motion has repose in itself. Indeed, no fatigue occurs in the motion. Rather, it is more strongly inflamed. And the more rapidly the mind is moved, the more delectably it is conveyed through the light of life to its own life.

However, the motion of the mind occurs as it were simultaneously in a straight and a circular line. For it begins with the that-it-is, or faith, and advances to vision, or what-it-is. And although both are separated as if through the infinite line, nevertheless that motion seeks to be completed and to find the end and what-it-is in the origin, namely, where the that-it-is and faith are. Indeed, it seeks that coincidence, where the origin and end of motion coincide. And this motion is circular. Hence the speculative mind advances in rectilinear motion to the coincidence of that which is most distant.

The measure of the motion of the speculative and deiform mind is therefore represented in that line, in which rectitude and circularity coincide. It is therefore required that a single one be the simple measure of the straight and circular lines. However, how straight and circular lines can coincide in the unity of the simple measure and how they do it not only in the theological but also in the mathematical domain, the booklet on mathematical complements shows. This lets us assert without hesitation in theology theologically, what we affirm in mathematics mathematically.

III.

In the booklet on mathematical complements the art is treated of finding the periphery of the circle, whose measure is a straight line. And this art is attained through the coincidence of three

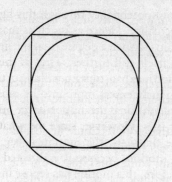

FIGURE 1

circles. Indeed, a polygon with equal sides is inscribed by a circle
and circumscribed by a circle; the periphery of the circumscribed
circle is one, that of the inscribed circle another, and that of the
polygon another (see Figure 1). However, in the circle [whose
measure is a straight line], the inscribed and circumscribed circles
are not different. Hence those three circles, the inscribed, the
circumscribed, and the isoperimetric of the polygon, coincide in
the periphery in magnitude and in all other properties of the
circle. And they are three circles such that they are one and indeed
a triune circle. This can in no way come to light unless one
reflects on the polygon. There, indeed, two circles, i.e., the
inscribed and the circumscribed, appear as different from one
another. The periphery of the polygon is greater than the periphery of the inscribed circle and smaller than that of the circumscribed. Therefore, the three different peripheries lead us to the
notion of the triune isoperimetric circle. And this trinity, which
is in all polygons with distinct peripheries, is in the circle without
all distinction as to magnitude. And the one circle is in all equal
to the others and the one does not exist outside the others.

If it is so in mathematics, then it is truer in theology. Hence
the coincidence of circular and straight lines cannot be denied
by him who intuits that the truth is inalterability. Indeed, if
inalterability is truth, then this receives neither more nor less.
Indeed, if it be true, that this piece of wood is two feet long, then
it is neither larger nor smaller. The truth is therefore infinity.
Indeed, only infinity cannot be larger or smaller.

Therefore, if one posits such a circular periphery, so that it cannot be larger, since its magnitude is without end, then it is infinite. And likewise the circular is also infinite, whose periphery is infinite. Therefore, it cannot be larger, since it has no parts. And since the larger the circle, the straighter its circumference, therefore the periphery of the infinite circle is rectilinear. Therefore, the rectilinear and circular peripheries coincide in the infinite. Infinity is therefore rectitude or absolute justice.

If we consider how a circle is described and constituted, we find that the point comes first, that from the point the line, and from the point and line the circle is unfolded. We therefore find in every circle a centerpoint, radius, and circumference. Without their simultaneous presence we do not grasp the figure as being more circle than not-circle. Therefore, if one posits the infinite circle, it is necessary that the centerpoint, radius, and circumference possess the highest equality. Indeed, the centerpoint of the infinite circle is infinite. Indeed, one cannot say that the infinite is greater than its center. Indeed, of that which cannot be smaller, such as the infinite and interminable, one cannot say that it is greater than the center. For the center is the terminus of the radial line. The terminus of the infinite is infinite. The center of the infinite circle is therefore infinite. Likewise also its radius is infinite. And similarly the circumference is also. The equality of the center, radius, and circumference of the infinite circle is therefore the highest.

And since there cannot be several infinites, since then none of them would be infinite—indeed it involves a contradiction to say that there are several infinites—the center, the radius, and circumference will be the one infinite. We see, however, that polygons are constituted from straight lines. Therefore, this infinite circle will be that with which every polygon with infinite sides coincides. And since we also see that the inscribed and circumscribed circles of the polygon are different from the periphery of the polygon, we also see that these three peripheries coincide in the isoperimetric circle and we thus see the triune circle.

Likewise in theology we find the triune infinite circle, if we consider polygons or terminated creatures. Indeed, the triune circle is that one, in which the centerpoint is the circle and the radius is the circle and the circumference is the circle. And in this the inscribed, the scribed, and the circumscribed are the same. Therefore, we do not detect the trinity of the infinite circle, if we only intuit its infinity. However, if we turn ourselves to the figures or forms which have sides, borders, and angles, then we detect that the infinite circle is triune. However, the highest equality effects that the one is in the other and that there is one infinite periphery of all.

One must diligently attend to the fact that we do not come to the truth of the equality of circular and rectilineal measure, except when we consider the isoperimetric circle as triune through the coincidence of difference in polygons. Thus the truth of anything whatsoever cannot be attained without the triune infinite. Indeed, as the circle measures every polygon and is neither greater nor smaller—since it is the triune circle, in which all difference of polygons coincides, as it was shown mathematically—so the triune infinite is also the form, truth, or the measure of everything which is not it itself. And it is the equality itself, which is also the truth of all. Indeed, it is neither greater nor smaller than everything which can be given or formed. It is rather the most adequate form of all formable forms and the actuality of every potentiality.

Indeed, whoever intuits that triune infinite and ascends from mathematical figures to the theological through the addition of infinity to the mathematical, and also absolves himself of the theological figures, in order to contemplate the triune infinite in the mind, sees—to the extent it is conceded him—that everything is enfoldedly one and in the unfolding one is everything. If one intuits that infinite without regard for the finite, then one detects neither that there are finite things, nor their truth or measure. Therefore, the creature and Creator cannot equally be seen, if one does not affirm the infinite as triune.

IV.

The ancients strove after the art of quadrature of the circle. They presupposed that this were possible. However, according to the opinion of all, equality enfolds in itself the circle as the square. Therefore, we add the infinite of equality. It is manifest to us that infinite equality will be able to be unequal in relation to no thing. For nothing of all that can be given can exceed infinite equality, since this cannot be less equal. And thus it will not be more equal in relation to the one and less equal in relation to the other. However, it is necessarily the idea, truth, or exemplar or measure of all that can receive more and less.

Indeed, everything which is not the infinite equality itself, through which alone everything equal is equal, is more equal in relation to the one than the other. And for every equality given among the diverse a greater one can always be given. Also one cannot know whether any two things are more equal to one another than two others, unless through the measure of the absolute and infinite equality. The absolute equality therefore measures all things, the straight as well as the circular, which necessarily coincide in their enfolding. And if one considers acutely: That which is presupposed in every search, is the same light which also leads to that sought.

Indeed, those who sought after the quadrature of the circle presupposed the coincidence of the square and circle in equality, which is certainly not possible in the sensible. For there is no square which is not unequal in relation to every circle which can be given in the material. Consequently, they did not see this equality, which they presupposed, with the eyes of the flesh, but rather with those of the mind. They attempted to show it in rationality. However, since rationality does not admit the coincidence of opposites, they were unsuccessful. However, they should have sought the coincidence intellectually in that circle which is equal to every polygon, and also is of equal circumference with another and diverse polygon. Then they would have attained their intent. From this is elicited that its being is not actually knowable, as it cannot be known except by means of the infinite intellect, which is infinite equality. It precedes everything diverse and different and other and unequal and opposite and whatever else denotes inequality. In and through this infinite intellect alone is everything intelligible measured.

And therein the secret is disclosed, as to how the inquirer presupposes that which he seeks, and does not presuppose it, because he seeks it. Namely, everyone who seeks knowledge supposes that there is knowledge, through which knowing is knowing. He also supposes that there is nothing knowable that would not actually be known by infinite knowledge, and that infinite knowledge is the truth, equality, and measure of all knowledge. And that everything which can be known is only known through it.

Therefore, whoever searches for knowledge is instigated by that infinite art or science. And if he walks in the light of this art instilled in him in the presupposition, he is led to that sought. And if one attends more acutely, then one notices that—when the infinite is added to a terminus, as is the case when one speaks of infinite knowledge—nothing other is involved in its addition to the terminus than that one removes the terminus, so that that which is signified through a terminated expression or a term, is intuited as infinite and interminable mentally.

And when the mind intuits thus the terminated interminably or the finite infinitely, then it sees it beyond all opposition and otherness, which is only found in the terminated. The termination can indeed not be without diversity. And, therefore, variety is found in it, which, according to that which exists as great or small, obtains its name.

If, therefore, the termination is removed, the difference passes over into concordance, the inequality into equality, the curvature into rectitude, the ignorance into knowledge, and the shadows into light. And then one sees how, after the removal of the terminus, we find the plurality of terminated things without plurality in the one, interminable and ineffable Origin.

V.

Observe further how every polygon is terminated through a certain number of angles, which are equally distant from the centerpoint, and obtains its name or term according to the number of angles, on account of which it is named polygon. Thus, for example, a polygonal figure with three angles is named by means of the term triangle. And by means of the term tetragon a figure with four angles is named, etc.

However, the more angles an equilateral polygon receives, the more similar it becomes to the circle. Indeed, if you attend to polygons, the circle has infinitely many angles. If you only consider the circle, you find no angle in it and it is unterminated and angleless. And thus the angleless and unterminated circle enfolds in itself all angular, polygonal terminations which are given and can be given. If indeed the trigon is in the tetragon and the tetragon in the pentagon, etc., then you see that all given and always giveable polygons are in the circle.

Therefore, consider attentively, how the infinite circle enfolds in itself every terminated figure or form, and not as the finite circle. For since this is the most capacious, it contains in itself the less capacious circles as the whole does the part. Indeed, the infinite circle, however, does not enfold thus, but rather as truth or equality. Indeed, no creature—as the polygon of the finite circle—has something of omnipotence, since omnipotence is impartible and does not admit more or less. The finite circle, however, since it admits more or less, cannot enfold polygons in the manner omnipotence enfolds everything terminable. And thus the mind ascends from the multiangular figure and from the circle, which enfolds all formable polygons, to the theological figures, and intuits, after it has dismissed the figures, the infinite power of the first origin, and sees the difference of the rest of the enfolded figures and their assimilation with this simple origin; it also sees that the infinite trigon is the infinite circle and the infinite tetragon is the infinite circle, etc. On this basis the infinite circle is the form of forms or the figure of figures. And it is the idea of the trigon, the tetragon, the pentagon, and the equality of the essential being of the trigon, tetragon, etc. And in the positing of the infinite circle follows that all figures are that which they are.

See how wonderful it is! While the mathematician forms a polygon, he looks to the infinite exemplar. For while he depicts the quantitatively determined trigon, he does not look to this, but rather to that trigon simply absolved of all quantity and quality, magnitude and multitude. Hence when he depicts a quantitative trigon, this does not receive its quantity from the exemplar, and he also does not intend at all to produce a quantitative trigon, but since he cannot depict the triangle which he conceives mentally, as sensible, the quantity, without which it cannot be sensible, therefore occurs accidentally. Therefore, the triangle to which he looks is neither large nor small, terminated neither through magnitude nor multitude. It is accordingly infinite. Therefore, that infinite triangle, which is the exemplar in which the mind intuits the figurative trigon, is not other from that exemplar to which the mind looks when it depicts a tetragon or pentagon or a circle.

Indeed, that circle to which the mind turns when it depicts a circle, since it is not quantitatively extended, is neither larger nor smaller than the trigon, which is not quantitatively extended, but rather it is the equality of essential being. Therefore, it is one single, infinite equality of essential being, to which I look when I depict diverse figures. Turned towards Himself, the Creator therefore creates everything, when He creates everything, since He Himself is that infinity, which is the equality of essential being.

VI.

You see more, if you consider how you depict the circle. For first you posit the punctual center. Then you extend that point in the line. Finally you draw the line beyond the point. And thus the circular line arises from the point and the straight line. Therefore, if you do this and look to the absolute equality of essential being, then you see something similar in this. For that circle, to which you look and which is ineffable or cannot be named with the names of all figures, is such that it has a centerpoint, from which the line and from which the circumference arise. However, because it is infinite, the centerpoint, line, and circumference are equality itself, as it has been treated above. Hence the centerpoint was not earlier than the line, nor were both the centerpoint and the line earlier than the circumference, since otherwise there were neither the highest equality of the centerpoint, line, and circumference, nor one infinity. Therefore, that equality in the infinite is nothing other than eternity. Therefore, the centerpoint, the line, and circumference are from the eternal. However, the line is the unfolding of the point and the circumference that of the point and line. Therefore, the centerpoint in eternity generates or unfolds eternally the consubstantial line generated from its enfolding power. And the centerpoint is together with the line the eternally unfolding connection or circumference.

If, therefore, the infinite fecundity, to which the mind looks when it depicts the circle, which it cannot depict without time and extension, is thus, then it is similar when it proposes to depict an equilateral polygon. So that the angles are equally distant from the centerpoint, it attends to representing the polygon likewise, from the centerpoint and the line, which is the equality of the distance of the centerpoint from the angles and the circumference or periphery. It therefore looks to the infinite fecundity, in order to produce that which it proposes perfectly, beautifully, agreeably, and pleasingly. Thus the Creator looks to Himself and the infinite fecundity and creates the generated or unfolded entity. And from the centerpoint and the line simultaneously proceeds the fecund essence of the creature, in which is the enfolding origin of power, which is the centerpoint or entity of the creature, which enfolds its power in itself. And the power of the entity is unfolded, which is enfolded in the centerpoint, as if in an educed line, which is the power of the entity derived from the generated or unfolded entity. And the circumference or the operation proceeds simultaneously from the centerpoint and line.

Also attend to how the centerpoint is the paternal origin, which can also be named entity in respect to the creature. And as the line is as though the origin from the origin, it is thus also equality. The origin from the origin possesses indeed the highest equality of the origin, from which it is, and the circumference is as the union or connection. For from the infinite entity and its equality proceeds the connection. Indeed, it connects equality with unity. And when the Creator looks to Himself, He creates the unity or entity or the centerpoint, and the form or equality of essential being, and the connection of both. However, the creature proceeds in similarity with the Creator from the Creator in the best possible way, which is conceded to him by the conditions of his nature. Elsewhere I have developed my concepts concerning this more extensively.

VII.

One knows from mathematics, that something cannot be called straight except according to one mode. Indeed, one straight line, whether large or small, is not more or less straight than another. Therefore, one conceives rectitude to be infinite, since it is not enclosed by quantity, nor does it admit more or less. Absolute rectitude is therefore infinite. However, curvature cannot be infinite. Therefore, the circular line of the infinite circle cannot be curved, since it is infinite. Therefore, every curvature is enclosed by the terminus of its magnitude. And curvature has no other exemplar except rectitude. Indeed, whoever would like to depict a curved line, looks in the mind to the straight and makes the former fall reflexly from the latter.

However, the curvature which is nearer to infinite rectitude is a similitude of circular curvature. Infinite rectitude is indeed the eternity, which possesses neither beginning, middle, nor end, nor quantity and quality. However, circular curvature, which is necessarily quantitatively extended and composite, has coincidence of beginning and end, and is necessarily from infinite rectitude—just as from its origin and its truth. The curvature is indeed not from itself but rather it is from that rectitude which is its measure. The straight indeed measures the curved.

Circular curvature therefore deviates from infinite rectitude in a more perfect manner than not–circular curvature, since, just as infinite rectitude, it lacks beginning, middle, and end. Thus those coincide in circular curvature and are in no way distant or different from one another. Hence circular curvature is assimilated to the infinite to a greater degree than finite rectitude, where beginning, middle, and end are distant from one another.

Indeed, infinite rectitude is on account of this infinity omnipotent and creative. Circular curvature is more similar to it, because it is more similar to the infinite than finite rectitude. We all who possess a mind are therefore affected by the circular figure, which on account of its uniformity and equality and simplicity appears to us as complete and beautiful. And this is for no other reason than that in it the Form of forms shines forth in greater propinquity than in any other figure.

Attend to how much the mind is affected by the exemplar of the circle, by infinite form and beauty, to which it alone looks. How should any creature be affected and not understand that it thus looks to the Creator, who is its love and delectation? Whoever searches for God is therefore diligent to consider that to which the mind looks, when it loves or is affected. And it turns itself to the presupposed, where it will find the ineffable sweetness of love. All that which is loved has this from the love, which is lovable absolute Love. Whoever tastes it is not forsaken.

VIII.

It should also not escape notice how the circle, if it circumvolves above the straight line, does not touch it except in the point. The circumference is indeed equally distant from the centerpoint. However, the straight tangent does not touch the circular line except in the point. Proceeding from this, one considers that that time, which revolves as if circularly, has a figure closely related to the circle, since it is constituted as if from a circular motion of the heaven. Time is indeed the measure of motion. When, therefore, time, which bears the similitude of eternity, revolves, it revolves in the manner in which a circle revolves above the straight, infinite line. Indeed, time does not subsist in itself, but rather subsists in the revolution above the infinite line or eternity. And thus time does not subsist from itself alone, nor does it have another source of its subsistence than its revolution around the point of eternity. And because it is true for every circle, whether small or large, namely, that it subsists not other than in the punctual contact with the straight or infinite line, every creature which is considered under the aspect of time, can be assimilated in its duration to a small or large circle which revolves. And no duration, whether long or short, possesses more eternity than another one. Indeed, in a single now of eternity all circles subsist and circumvolve.

And thus you notice how eternity is the subsistence of time, the measure and the meter of all duration, although it is most simple, impartible, and incommunicable to time. And you see that it is impossible that time be eternal, although the revolutions, as if circular on account of the coincidence of beginning and end, appear to have no origin. And thus it is indeed impossible that circular motion be from itself, for it is curved and reflexive. It is from the Creator, who is infinite rectitude itself and eternity. Curvature indeed presupposes its Creator, deviating from whom it is called curvature.

It is therefore not true that there is a precise circular revolution—as I have mentioned in *On Learned Ignorance*—or that the circular revolution of the sun's motion proceeds infinitely. Indeed, infinity cannot be compared to a number of circular revolutions. If we can indeed enumerate ten past revolutions, then also one hundred, one thousand and all. If someone said that not all are numerable but rather infinitely many had preceded, and then said that there would be a future revolution in a future year, then there would therefore be infinitely many plus one, which is impossible. And if it is true that the revolution of the sun will come to an end on the eleventh of March, then it is true that the revolutions of the sun have had a beginning and have been neither eternal, nor are they infinitely many.

Indeed, eternity and infinity cannot befit the motion whose measure is time, but rather only that motion whose measure is eternity; just as above we have named generation and procession in the divine the motion of infinite fecundity, whose measure is eternity.

IX.

It would not be too much for you to consider, how the capacity of the isoperimetric circle exceeds all the capacity of all formable polygons, and enfolds in itself all capacity, and is as actuality the capacity of all possible capacities. Furthermore, if a circle is given which has an equal periphery with a polygon, then it is nevertheless not equal on account of the capacity, but rather is always greater and does not desert its perfection, although it becomes equal with the periphery.

From this you can gain an insight into how the Creator—although He is the highest equality, the true measure of things, and neither larger nor smaller—nevertheless can never desist being of infinite vigor. And you have the result that perfection and enfolding are greater, the more one and simple the form is. Indeed, the circle is simpler than every formable figure. Consequently, the force of its capacity is the most perfect of all figures. Therefore, that form, which on account of its infinite simplicity is the form of all forms, is of infinite vigor.

Attend more diligently to how the finite straight line arises from the point and various polygonal figures and ultimately circles from that. The figure of the least capacity is the trigon and of the maximum capacity the circle. And the infinite isoperimetric polygons fall in the middle of the circle of less capacity and the trigon of greater capacity. However, all the polygons and the circle arise from one point. The figure is, however, the similitude of the form.

Therefore, see how the trigonal form, which is infinite, possesses its own power, which is its trigonal capacity. And thus the tetragonal form possesses its power, etc. From this you have that no form exists without its proper power. And since the polygons are named on the basis of their number of angles—so that is a trigon which has three angles, that a tetragon which has four and so forth into infinity; that, however, which gives names and distinction, is the form. The number is therefore the form. Every number, however, is from the one, in which it is enfolded.

Therefore, as the line flows from the point, so number flows from the one. And since the polygon cannot exist without line and number, the polygon is therefore contained in the potentiality of the line. For from the straight line a trigon, tetragon, pentagon, etc. can be formed. And in actuality it is not constituted unless the line, which is straight, becomes angular and joins its extremes and is formed by means of number. But the number comes only from the mind. Indeed, whoever is lacking mind cannot enumerate. The efficient cause of form is therefore the mind. Hence every form is a similitude of the mental conception, which is of infinite vigor.

The Creator therefore appears to have created two things, namely, next to nothing the point. Indeed, between the point and nothing there is nothing intermediate. The point is so near to nothing that, if you added a point to the point, no more results than if you had added nothing to nothing. And it is the other next to itself, namely, the one. It unites both, so that it is a single point. In this one point the enfolding of the universe occurred.

Therefore, the universe, which was thus educed from this one point, is conceived as if the one line were educed from the one point, so that from this line one trigon or one tetragon were made. And the ultimate, simplest, and most perfect and most similar to the Creator is the circle. If indeed one trigon cannot arise from a line without three angles, then in the form of the trigon unity and trinity coincide, namely, the unity of essence and the trinity of angles. And in the tetragon unity and the quaternary coincide, namely, the unity of essence and the quaternary of angles, etc. In the circle, however, unity and infinity coincide, namely, the unity of essence and the infinity of angles. Indeed, infinity is itself unity. The circle is indeed the whole angle. In this way it is simultaneously one and infinite.

And it is the actuality of all angles formable from the line.

From this you can elicit how the Creator of the one universe made this one universe arise in similitude from a single point, which He has created; just as our mind, which wishes to represent a figure, begins with a single point, extends it into a line, and then flexes it into angles, in order to enclose the surface and make the polygon. And since, as considered in the booklet on the mathematical complement, the line becomes the triangle through one extension, and through another greater one the tetragon, and through the maximum the circle, the circle therefore comes near to the most perfect creatures, which are most similar to their Creator, as are, for example, the higher minds.

Indeed, there is nothing more noble than the mind. However, the human mind appears similar to the origin of the universe, which is as though a single point, which, educed, is extended into a single line, in order to become the capacity of something and, for example, to become a trigon. And since the mind possesses mental life and tastes itself extended to a certain capacity, it extends itself to a greater tetragon or pentagon, etc. It can never extend itself, however, to such a capacity that it could not become still more capacious. Consequently, it constantly approaches a circular capacity, which it, however, never attains in its own power. Rather, through the grace of the Creator it is raptured from the angular capacity to the circular; just as students are raptured from reading particular books to the universal art and then to the mastery of reading all books.

Indeed, whoever reads particular writings, reads this and that in the light of the art. Finally, he perfects himself and becomes a master. And this is an appropriate figural similitude, through which you can be led to see the difference between those minds which have attained the perfection of mental capacity through a rapture into the intelligible world, and those which hunt down this capacity in the sensible world under particular sensible signs; as we experience this in mathematics in respect to the polygon and the circle.

X.

However, although the circle is the most perfect of figures, nevertheless it cannot become equal to infinite rectitude, which the infinite circle is. For from the infinitely straight something cannot arise, since it is actually everything that can be figured. Therefore, that rectitude cannot be flexed, in order to be otherwise than it is. Nor does it have extremities. Although the finite, straight line bears the similitude of the infinite straight line, nevertheless the finite, on account of its finitude and imperfection, has much of potentiality in itself. And from it figures can arise, which enclose various surfaces, although it itself is in actuality no surface. And if a figure has arisen from it, for example a trigon, then because the extremities are conjoined, no other polygon can arise from the very same line, unless after one dismisses that figure, one reverts to lineal rectitude. From this you have how form and end coincide, so that the form is not in potentiality as to form, so that from one form another could arise.

Form is indeed the terminus of motion and the actuality of potentiality and not potentiality. Therefore, the species are not transmuted. Nevertheless the one form can be in another, as for example the trigon in the tetragon, although the trigon never becomes the tetragon. Rather, that form, which is in another, is not the specific form, but rather the generic, since there cannot be a specific form except of a single thing or individual. Therefore, that form which is in another is as the general in the special, just as the vegetative is in the sensible, and in man the sensible in the rational. And as the trigon in the tetragon does not name the tetragon, but rather the tetragon is named from its ultimate form, which enfolds the trigonal form in its capacity, so the form is in the form, such that the ultimate form, which does not admit more or less and consists of a certain indivisibility, enfolds in itself or its capacity the inferior forms, which are unfolded in it only enfoldedly, not formally or actually.

Also, if correctly regarded, the form gives its terminus to the thing. Because every polygon can be formed from the line, insofar as a trigonal figure terminates this potentiality, it is a trigon. And since trigon means three angles and every polygon has angles, the substantial form is not denominated by the angles, which are common to all; the same is true of the sides and the lines, which form the periphery. The periphery, the sides, and the angles are common to all, but not the number of angles. The substantial form of the polygon is therefore denominated by number, which is special.

If, therefore, unity is posited as origin, since it terminates the thing and is thus the terminating form, number will be the substance of the thing. And it should be observed: If unity is substance, then similarly also number, since number is composed of unities. But a thing according to the order of nature has being earlier than becoming distinct, or has being earlier than being undivided from itself and divided from the other, so that the form gives being antecedently and consequently that which is undivided from itself and divided from whatsoever other follows after that, so that on account of this the thing is called one. Then the thing is called one according to that unity, which is the origin of number. And since it follows being, it is an accident. Indeed, everything which follows being is accidental to it. Therefore, the unity considered is accidental to the thing and is the origin of number. Hence numbers are not the substance of things, because they are unfolded from an accidental origin.

However unity, which is the origin, enfolds all the vigor of unity. It is in this way simultaneously the terminating origin and the creating one. In the creating one it terminates and in the terminating one it creates. Therefore, whoever looks at this coincidence sees why the Pythagoreans and the Peripatetics speak a different language, when the Pythagoreans say number is substance, and the Peripatetics it is accident. And beyond the assertion of both, you see the coincidence in number, in which simplicity and composition coincide, since its composition is from itself and is therefore simplicity, as elaborated elsewhere. Substance and accident are indeed beyond that which the Peripatetics say. Where they locate entity, there the one is located, which is convertible with entity. Therefore, one must judge otherwise concerning the number, which is from the mind, according as it is from the unity of the uncreated mind and as it is from that of the created mind.

The unity of the first number is indeed as the natural form, that of the second is as the form of art. The natural form is substantial; therefore, it is also the number of its unity. The form of art is accidental. It is the figure, since it comes after the being of the thing. Therefore, its unity is also accidental. Hence when we name the one substantial form, then we name it one from the unity, which can only be substantial. Also this unity of substantial form is nothing other than this form. Therefore, when that one form gives being, then its giving being is to terminate, to unite, to form. And since I have spoken about this in other writings often enough, this should now suffice.

XI.

It should not be overlooked that, for a given straight line, an equal circular line can be given and not vice versa. For one cannot know the second, unless one knows the first; and then one knows it proportionally, as one can find it in the already frequently cited booklet on complements.

The ancients sought the quadrature of the circle. And this inquiry presupposed that, for a given circular line, a straight line equal to it can be given. And they could never find the quadrature. If, however, they had sought the circulature of the quadrate, then perhaps they would have found this. From this you have that the circle cannot be measured, but rather measures, namely, that eternity is not measurable, since it exceeds everything measurable, but rather eternity measures every duration. The infinite is not measurable, since the infinite is interminable. Therefore, it cannot be enclosed with the terminus of any measure, but rather is itself the measure of all.

Indeed, the infinite is the end and terminus of all, as also the absolute measure. It is not measurable through any contracted measure. And since no measure has its measure without that absolute measure, this is the true and most adequate measure for every contracted and nameable measure; just as whiteness cannot be measured through something white, but rather itself measures everything white, since everything white has that it is white from whiteness. It is from this therefore manifest, that God is incomprehensible through every creature, since He is immeasurable for every mind. Indeed, He is greater than every capacity. But if God should be attained, then He is not attained such that He is attainable in Himself, but rather as He is attainable in the attaining. And that means: in the equality of the measure of him who attains Him. Thus everyone who attains God attains Him according to the measure of his capacity; just as for a given straight and finite line a finite circular line is given, which is neither greater nor smaller.

And we name that equal, which is neither greater nor

smaller, although for this reason it is not something equal, as for example the equality, which befits substance. The one substance is indeed not more substance than the other, since quantity is not substance. But substance admits neither more nor less as does quantity. Nevertheless, not all substances are therefore equal. The one is indeed more perfect than the other.

One therefore concludes that although one and the same visible thing is seen by many, nevertheless this is not seen equally, since two cannot see precisely equally. Indeed, each one attains the visible through the angle of the eye peculiar and singular to him and measures it and judges that the visible is neither greater nor smaller than he attains it with his eye. Nevertheless, the visible is not attained by any eye as precisely as it is visible.

The same is true of the mind and its object, i.e., the truth or God. Indeed, that which is the angle, through which vision sees, is the capacity, through which the mind measures. However, between both there is the difference, that vision can neither alter the angle of vision nor make it greater or smaller, in order to see more truly and certainly, because that angle is not in vision itself, but rather in the organ. However, the capacity of the intellect is not in the organ; indeed it does not adhere to a corporeal organ as do the senses, but rather it is its possibility so actuated, that it can constantly be actuated more and more; as if the point, in whose possibility the line also lies, were led without terminus from potentiality to actuality, so that, were the educed line a foot long, also the mind, which measures with such a line, would measure everything by a foot length. If the flow of the point were now extended further, so that a two-foot-long line arose, then it would measure everything bipedally. The mind conducts itself in a contrary manner.

For united power is greater. Indeed, when the mind conceives first as some confused measure—as if a line of uncertain quantity, which is living—and contracts itself from confused incertitude to some certitude—as if the line were contracted towards the central point in order to become a line, called a rod, for measuring fields, since with it no more subtle measure could be attained—indeed everything measurable would not be attained except according to this gross measure. Now if the line were contracted more towards the center or point, so that a foot-length arose, it would measure everything measurable more subtly and certainly. And if it were thus to become continuously more united and simplified, its power of measuring would always grow and become more certain and approach precision more. From this you can elicit that the human mind is not the entelechy of the body, as vision is that of the eye, since its power does not depend on the organ, but rather it is as fire in potentiality, which, educed from potentiality through some motion, has in itself a motion, through which it is constantly more and more actuated.

One compares fire, however, with the effective intellect. However, that in which potentiality is latent is called possible intellect. The intellect, however, is educed from potentiality to some actuality by means of admiration, which moves it to inquire into that which it perceives with the senses. And on account of this it is in the body and the body is necessary for it. Indeed, otherwise, if it were in actuality, as the mind of the angel, it were not placed in the body. Indeed, the body is only given to the mind, so that the latter is excited through sensible admiration and perfected. And thus you apprehend that the mind is not dependent on the body, although it cannot come to perfection without the body.

For just this reason the mind is not corrupted through corruption of the body, although it sometimes abandons perfection on account of this corruption of the body. However, vision fails completely when the eye fails, without which it does not see.

The mind therefore measures acutely, the more it is placed in actuality, the more it separates itself from the body and closes the organs of sense and, absolving itself from the body, contracts to its spiritual and central being.

XII.

Thus as the circle measures all polygons, as eternity measures all duration, so also the eternal or infinite repose measures every motion and the unity of the object every potentiality. For this reason one should attend to how the transmutations of the figures occur with aid of the angle and by means of proportions, as this is reported extensively in the frequently mentioned booklet on complements. Likewise God Himself can also be considered as infinite angle, with whose mediation all transmutation of things occurs according to the proportion of imitation.

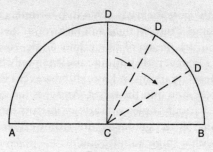

FIGURE 2

Indeed, God is as the maximum and simultaneously minimum angle. Let a semicircle be given and imagine the radius which stands orthogonally above the diameter, where it forms two right angles, and is moved continuously above the center in the direction of its coincidence with the diameter (see Figure 2). It is manifest that the one angle becomes continuously larger and the other always smaller. However, as long as the coincidence of the radius and diameter is not attained, no one absolutely maximum angle arises, since it can become still greater, nor an absolutely minimum, since it can become still smaller. However, supposing that the one angle is the simply maximum, then the other will also be the simply minimum. That, however, does not occur before the lines coincide. If you therefore notice that the two sides are resolved in a single straight line, then you see that the name angle does not apply to it. From this you elicit how what ascends to infinite God, seems more to approach nothing than something, as also the divine Dionysius says.

And thus see the wonderful God, who the less He seems to be, is so much the more, and the more impossible something seems to be for Him, so much the more necessary it is for Him. And see further how the infinite angle necessarily enfolds the opposites, the simultaneously maximum and minimum; and there can be no infinite or simply maximum quantity, and that the infinite being is completely absolved of everything that can be verified in respect to the finite.

However, that angle, which is infinite, will therefore be the true measure of all angles, because, as the minimum, it is neither greater than all others nor smaller, since the maximum. And if in geometry the potentiality is given to transmute curved figures by means of angles into straight and vice versa, then it lies in the power of God, by means of the infinite angle, to transmute all reciprocally. However, that infinite angle can only be God. God, therefore, effects by means of Himself whatever He wishes, also transmuting the one into the other. And it is not necessary that God possess various angles or various instruments for various transmutations, as the geometer must, but rather He transfers everything with a single infinite angle.

And since that angle is God, God is also the will of God. And thus that simply maximum angle is God's will. Consequently, God transfers and alters everything solely with His will. Therefore, this complement teaches that those angles, which are as incommensurable lines, are also deemed to be incommensurable; just as the side of the quadrate is incommensurable for the diameter, since if the one side is posited as an even number, the other cannot be as an even number, nor as an odd number. Therefore, because the habitudes cannot be numerated by all lines, we frequently fail in respect to chords and curves. But since the infinite number enfolds in itself the even as well as the odd number, everything is numerated by means of it.

Also consider how the mean of the second is not numerable by us. As soon as an approaching number is given, a nearer one can always be given into infinity. The infinite number is therefore precise. Hence the infinite number, which is neither more even than odd and not more number than not number, but rather is innumerable number, numerates precisely the mean of the second proportion and everything. In this way you see that the incomprehensible number is also the infinite and innumerable. It is simultaneously the maximum and minimum, which attains no rationality except in shadow and darkness, since it is in no proportion to all numerable numbers. And you see how God, who is named the number of all things, is thus number without discrete quantity, as He is also great without continuous quantity. And He, who is the infinite number, is also the infinite angle; so that He, as the simplest, numerates, measures, and transmutes everything in the simplest manner.

And when you consider this most subtly, you see very well, how no name can completely befit God, who is greater than one can think, namely, the absolutely Infinite; as also the name of the angle according to its imposed signification cannot befit the maximum and infinite angle, since it is more not-angle than angle. That is true of all names.

For every imposition of a name is done so that the name signifies something. However, that which is something, namely, this and not that, is finite and terminated. Consequently, it can in no way befit the infinite. Therefore, infinite Wisdom, which is nothing but absolute Infinity, is no more wisdom than not-wisdom, if we attend to the meaning of the name. Likewise infinite Life, since it is nothing but absolute Infinity, is no more life than not-life, according to the imposed name. Indeed, it appears that infinity, as soon as it is added to the name, is contracted from its absolute infinity to the rational sense of the word's signification. However, this cannot be, since absolute infinity is incontractible to any rational signification.

And although we say that God is wise and living and that He is wise according to one rational ground and living according to another, nevertheless that otherness of names of attributes cannot be seen in the simply infinite, although everything that we experience must befit the perfection of the causing. We conceive that in its cause it is simply maximum. Nevertheless, it cannot be there as the one and the other, but rather as all that which is enclosed under whatever diversity, according to the meaning of the name. By virtue of this meaning, we conclude, it is the infinite itself.

XIII.

You should not become fatigued and should again attend to the fact that no equal straight line can be given for a given circular line, unless one first finds how an equal circular line is given for the straight line. And then one comes from the proportion of the circular line by means of the known straight line and the proportion of the circular to the notion of the unknown straight line. Therefore, if you propose to measure that maximum truth, which cannot be other than it is, namely, not greater or smaller, as if a circular line, then you can only effect this such that you constitute some circular line as the measure for a given straight line. Therefore, for every proposed straight finite line a finite circular line will be its measure. Therefore, if an infinite circular line is proposed, which is the measure of all straight lines which can be given, then the infinite straight line will be the measure of this same circular line. However, the infinite straight line and the infinite circular line coincide, so that the infinite circular line is an infinite straight line.

Therefore, the measure and the measured coincide there. The infinite is therefore not measured through the finite, and between both there is no proportion. The infinite is rather the measure of itself. God is therefore His own measure. And it was already shown before that He is the measure of all things. Therefore, God is the measure of all things and of Himself. God is therefore immeasurable and incomprehensible for all creatures, since He Himself is the measure of Himself and all things. For the measure, however, there is no measure, just as there is no terminus for the terminus.

Therefore, the truth, which is itself the measure of things, is not comprehensible except through itself. And one sees that in the coincidence of the measure and the measured. Indeed, in everything this side of the infinite, the measure and the measured differ according to more or less. In God, however, they coincide. The coincidence of opposites is therefore like the periphery of the infinite circle. The distance of opposites is as the periphery of the finite polygon. Therefore, in theological figures the complement of that which can be known is to know this, namely, that in the infinite the difference of the measure and the measured is in God equality or coincidence. Hence, the measuring is there infinite rectitude. And the infinite circular line is measurable through infinite rectitude. And the measuring itself is the unity or the connection of both.

Complement in theology is therefore to behold the origin, in which what are opposites in the finite are coincidence. We cannot perceive something as white, unless it is white from whiteness. Likewise we do not conceive something as opposite unless it is opposite from opposition. Therefore, the opposition is the coincidence of the opposites and equality. We say that God, who is everything in everything, is the opposition of opposites. And that is nothing other than to say of Him, that He is the origin enfolding the absolute coincidence or the infinite equality.

In this way we make the infinite circulation rectilinear, when we conceive circulation as the coincidence of beginning and end. Then we conceive its rectilineal measure not as a line between point and point, beginning and end, closed and terminated, but rather as absolved from every terminus. Such a line, however, which has neither beginning nor middle nor end, measures the coincidence of beginning, middle, and end based on the fact that it is absolute equality. In the latter the beginning, middle, and end are not something other, but one and the same in equality.

And as everything which is in the finite circle, namely, that which is otherwise, different, or opposite—the part in the East is opposed to that in the West and that in the South to that in the North and everywhere each to each, which is distant through the diameter from the former; and the center, radius, and circumference are different, etc.—coincides in the equality of the infinite circle, so everything which is different in the straight line coincides in the equality of the infinite straight line. And because the infinite circular line is straight, the infinite straight is the true measure, which measures the infinite circle. And thus it is the equality or coincidence of all, that one sees in the finite as otherwise, different, or opposite. And that is the theological complement through which everything knowable—I say everything knowable—can be attained theologically in the most perfect manner in which it can be known by man in this world.

XIV.

However, everything which was hidden from the theologians until now and was not known by all inquirers, can be known through this circulation of the quadrate in the bespoken manner, in the manner in which it is knowable for men. If, for example, God is named *theos* from seeing and one asks how He sees, then one can respond: He sees in the manner in which He measures. For the infinite circle embraces all modes of expression. And all of theology is like that circle, in which everything is one.

To see is therefore not other than to measure in God. As God is therefore the measure of Himself and everything and each singular thing, so also is vision. Vision and seeing are the same in God. That God is the vision of the seeing means that He sees everything. If someone asked if He is otherwise when He sees Himself and otherwise when He sees creatures, one would have to respond: The infinite equality, which is the measure of things, does not befit otherness, but rather identity. Therefore, if He intuits Himself, He intuits simultaneously also everything created and sees Himself and the other in no way differently.

And in seeing, He sees the created and Himself simultaneously. Indeed, the created is not seen perfectly as created, except if the Creator is also seen. And the effect is not seen perfectly, since it is not seen as effect, except if the cause is also seen. The vision of God, however, is most perfect and by seeing Himself, since He is the cause, He also sees everything caused. And since He sees the caused as caused, He also sees Himself, since He is the cause. In God, to measure and to be measured coincide, since He is the measure and the measured. Likewise to see and to be seen coincide; and likewise to see Himself and to be seen by Himself and to see creatures and to be seen in creatures.

The same is true if one inquires about creation. Creation in God is indeed vision. To create, to see, to understand, to wish, to measure, to do, to work and such like, which we attribute to God, are to be understood as names of the infinite circle. Therefore, it is not more absurd to say: God creates Himself and everything, than to say: God sees Himself and everything; and that to create everything is to be created in everything. However, human names, since they are imposed for finite things, are not apt for the divinity.

Indeed, just as the finite circular line is called circular as to the difference with the finite straight line, so we name the infinite circular line similarly circular. And nevertheless it is not called circular according to the intention of the instituting of the name, for it is not circular, because it is not different from the straight line, etc.

Therefore, it is not necessary that you be confused by the meaning of the word. Rather, it is necessary to consider the coincidence and the highest equality and simplicity of that circle, where all names are one. And then what appears to be absurd becomes tolerable by means of another word, since this word is indeed another in respect to us, however, it is not other there, but rather in reality a synonym.

This is a brief explanation of the theological complement represented in the mathematical complements. It is written for the laud of God, be He always blest. Amen.

On Beryllus*

(1 4 5 8)

I.

Whoever has read what I have written in my various book-lets, will see that I was frequently concerned with the coincidence of opposites and that I have often endeavored to reach conclusions in accordance with the intellectual vision, which exceeds the vigor of rationality. In order to impart as clear as possible a concept to the reader, I wish to employ a mirror image and enigma as aid, so that thereby everyone may find assistance and direction in the extremity of the knowable for his weak intellect. I wish also to add a few important opinions and views of men who are learned in difficult questions, so that if one has applied a mirror image and enigma, one becomes a judge in intellectual vision, as to what extent the former have approached nearer to the truth.

And although this booklet appears to be short, it neverthe-less gives sufficient practical guidance as to how one can come from enigma to comprehensive and lofty vision. It will thereby be in the power of each individual, to apply and extend the underlying method to every investigation. However, the reason why both Plato in his letters, as well as the great Dionysius

*Beryllus is the name for the type of glass used for lens-making in fifteenth-century Italy.

the Areopagite prohibited those who are ignorant of intellectual elevation to communicate such mysteries, was that the latter find nothing more worthy of laughter than such lofty things.

Indeed, the man dominated by the animal does not perceive divine mysteries, but he whose intellect is practiced therein, will encounter nothing more desirable. If this appears to you at first sight as insipid nonsense, then you must know that the fault lies in you. However, if you continue a little in maximum desire for knowledge and accept meditation and practical guidance from someone who explains the enigma to you, then you come to the point that you place nothing in front of this light, and rejoice to have found an intellectual thesaurus. And you will experience this in the briefest time. Coming to the point, I now wish first to explain why I have given the booklet the name "Beryllus" and what my purpose is.

II.

Beryllus is a lucid, white, and transparent stone. It is given at the same time a concave and convex form, and looking through it, one attains to things which were previously invisible. If an intellectual beryllus, which has simultaneously the maximum and minimum form, is adapted to the intellectual eyes, one attains the indivisible origin of all things with its aid. However, how this occurs, I propose to develop with the greatest possible clarity. However, first I must premise some appropriate reflections.

III.

First, you should attend to the fact that the One is the first Origin and, according to Anaxagoras, it is called the intellect, from which everything advances into being, so that it manifests itself. Indeed, the intellect enjoys showing and communicating the light of its intelligence. Therefore, the Composer-intellect, who makes Himself the end of His works, in order to become manifest in His glory, creates cognitive substances, which are capable of seeing His truth. The Composer makes Himself visible to them in the manner in which they can grasp Him. This knowledge is the first, in which everything that can be stated is contained enfoldedly.

IV.

Secondly, you must know how that which is neither true nor verisimilar does not exist. However, everything which is, is different in another than in itself. Indeed, in itself it is as in its true being, in another as in its verisimilar being; just as the warm is in itself as in its true being, but in the warmed is through the similitude of its warmth.

However, there are three modes of knowledge, namely, the sensible, the intellectual, and the intelligential. These are called heavens according to Augustine. The sensible is in the senses through its sensible species or similitude and the senses in the sensible through their sensitive species. Likewise, the intelligible is in the intellect through its intelligible similitude and the intellect in the intelligible through its intellective similitude; thus the intelligential is in the intelligent and conversely. These terms should not confuse you, since sometimes the intelligential is also called the intellectible. However, I name it thus on account of the intelligent.

V.

Thirdly, you should take note of the dictum of Protagoras: Man is the measure of things. For with the senses man measures the sensible, with the intellect the intelligible and that which is beyond the intelligible he attains in the excess. And he does this on the basis of premises. For if he knows that the cognitive soul is the end of the cognizable, then he knows on the basis of the sensitive power, that the sensible must be just as it can be sensibly received. It is likewise with the intelligible, so that it can be understood; however, with the exceeding, so that it exceeds. For this reason, man finds in himself everything created, as if in the measuring rational ground.

VI.

Fourthly, pay attention to the utterance of Hermes Trismegistus: Man is a second god. For just as God is the Creator of real entities and of natural forms, man is the creator of rational entities and artificial forms. These are nothing other than similitudes of his intellect, just as the creatures of God are similitudes of the divine Intellect. Therefore, man has intellect, which is a similitude of the divine Intellect, in creating.

Therefore, he creates similitudes of the similitudes of the divine Intellect, so the extrinsic artificial figures are similitudes of intrinsic natural forms. Hence he measures his intellect through the power of his works and from this he measures the divine Intellect, as the truth is measured through its image. And this is enigmatic knowledge. However, man has a most subtle sight with which he sees that the enigma is an enigma of the truth, so that he knows that that is the truth, which is not figurable in any enigma.

VII.

Turning, therefore, after these few premises to the subject, we begin with the first Origin! Indeed, that Indian, whom Socrates interrogated, derided those who attempted to understand anything without God, since He is the Cause and Author of all things. However, we want to see Him as the indivisible Origin.

We want to apply the beryllus to our mental eye and see it as the maximum, beyond which there can be nothing greater and at the same time as the minimum, beyond which there can be nothing smaller. We shall see the origin before everything large and small, completely simple and indivisible for every mode of division, with which everything great and small is divisible.

If we intuit inequality through the beryllus, then equality will be the indivisible object, and through the absolute similitude we will see the origin, indivisible for every mode of division, with which the similitude is divisible or variable, namely, we will see the truth. For there is for that vision no other object than the truth, which is seen through each simultaneously maximum and minimum similitude as the first absolute Origin of all its similitude. Likewise the object will be the indivisible connection, if we see the division with the beryllus. It is exactly so with proportion, habitude, beauty and the like.

VIII.

If you wish to see an enigma of our art, then take a reed in hand and fold it in the middle (see Figure 1). Let the reed be AB and

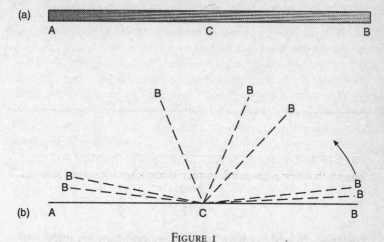

Figure i

its middle C [(a)]. I say that the origin of surface and angle is the line. Let the reed therefore be a line, which is folded in point C, let CB be movable and be moved towards CA. In this motion, CB makes all formable angles with CA [(b)]. But never will one be so acute that it cannot be more acute, so long as CB is joined with CA, and never so obtuse that it could not be still more obtuse, so long as CB forms a continuous line with CA. If you therefore see through the beryllus the angle, which is simultaneously the maximum and minimum of all formable angles, then the sight will not be terminated in any angle, but rather in the simple line, which is the origin of the angle, which is the indivisible origin of the plane angles for every mode of division, through which angles are divisible. Therefore, just as you see this, you see through a mirror image in the enigma the absolute first Origin.

IX.

Consider attentively that one advances to the indivisible through the beryllus. Indeed, so long as the maximum and the minimum are two, you have still in no way seen through the maximum and minimum simultaneously; indeed, the maximum is not the maximum and the minimum not the minimum. And you will see it clearly, if from C you make a movable line CD egress (see

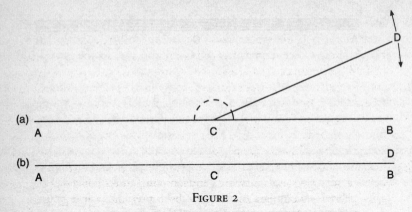

FIGURE 2

Figure 2). Indeed, so long as this line constitutes an angle with
CA and another one with CB, no one angle is the maximum or
the minimum [(a)]. Indeed, it can always be still greater. It can
be so much greater as the other exists, and therefore one angle is
no sooner the maximum, than the other is the minimum. And
this cannot occur, so long as there are two angles. If, therefore,
the duality of angles should cease, then you will see nothing other
than the line CD over the line AB, i.e., you will see no angle
[(b)]. And thus the maximum and simultaneously the minimum
angle must lie before the two and after the simple line. But it
cannot be represented. The origin therefore appears alone as
the maximum and minimum simultaneously, so that everything
originated can be nothing other than a similitude of the origin,
since there can be nothing greater or smaller than it. In the angles
for example: No angle can be so acute that it would not have its
acuteness from the origin, and none can be so obtuse that it
would not have its obtuseness from its origin. And because every
possible acute angle can be still more acute, it must lie in the
power of the origin, to create one still more acute; and it is
likewise with the obtuse. So the origin appears as the eternal,
that cannot be exhausted through everything originated.

X.

The great Dionysius, disciple of the Apostle Paul, summarizes
this elegantly in the eighth chapter of his book *On Divine Names*.

He says: "We do nothing which is alien to our institution, if, with the help of meager images, we ascend to the Author of all things and, with eyes entirely pure and superior to the world, behold everything in the Cause of all things and see the mutually contrary, uniformly and conjointly. Indeed, the origin of things, from which being itself and everything which is in any mode exists, is the beginning of everything and the end of everything." Shortly thereafter he adds: "All else, since it is, owes to being everything that it is." He also affirms of the same origin that it is finite and infinite, standing and progressing, and that it is neither standing nor moving. Indeed, one must concede, he says, that all exemplars of things subsist previously in a single supersubstantial conjunction in the Cause of themselves and all things. See how this divine man here and in various other locations affirms lucidly that the aforementioned is so.

XI.

Already on the basis of this enigma it is established, how you must understand the saying: The First is the measure of everything. Indeed, it has enfolded everything that can be. For the maximum and simultaneously minimum angle is as actuality every formable angle. It is not greater and not smaller, and before all quantity. Indeed, no one is so lacking in sense, that he would not see well enough that the simplest angle, which is at the same time maximum and minimum, enfolds in itself all formable, great or small angles, since it is neither greater nor smaller than any possible angle. The name of one angle befits it no more than that of all angles and of none. Therefore, one can call it neither acute nor right nor obtuse angle, for it is nothing of the kind, but rather the simplest cause of all. Therefore, Plato correctly rejects all assertions concerning the Origin itself, just as Proclus reports in his *Commentary on the Parmenides*. And likewise our Dionysius prefers negative theology to the affirmative.

XII.

However, it seems that the name One befits God more than another name. This is what Parmenides calls Him. And similarly Anaxagoras, who asserted, "it is better to call Him the One than everything together." You should not understand that as the numeral one, which is called the monad or the singular, but, namely, as the one indivisible for every mode of division, which is understood without all duality. After this, everything can neither be nor be conceived without duality, so that the already mentioned absolute One is first. Thereafter follows the one with addition, namely, the one entity, the one substance, etc. And it is likewise with everything, so that nothing can be said or conceived so simply, that it is not a one with addition, except only the superexalted One. Whence in what manner He should be named with the names of everything and with none of all names, as Hermies Mercurius said of Him, and everything concerning this you see clearly represented in the enigma.

XIII.

You should furthermore pay attention to how everything creatable is nothing other than similitude. For every possible angle says of itself that it is not the truth of angles; for the truth admits neither more nor less. Indeed, if the truth could be greater or smaller, then it were not the truth. How were it truth, if it were not that which it can be? Therefore, every angle says that it is not the angle-truth, because it can be other than it is. But it says that the maximum and simultaneously minimum angle, because it can be nothing other than what it is, is the simplest and necessary angle-truth. Therefore, every angle admits that it is the similitude of that true one, since it is the angle not as in itself, but rather as in another, namely in the surface. And therefore the true angle is in a creatable and designatable angle, as in its similitude. St. Augustine correctly tells all creatures to respond to the question, whether they are God: "No, for not we but rather He has created us."

XIV.

From this you can sufficiently see which knowledge of God we can have, if we, as the Apostle says, look through a mirror image in the enigma. It is no other knowledge than a negative one; since we know that whatever angle is designated this is not the simply maximum and simultaneously minimum angle. In every angle we therefore see the maximum in a negative manner, of which we know, however, that it is not designated one, and we know of this simultaneously maximum and minimum angle that it is the whole totality and perfection of all formable angles, and simultaneously all their innermost center and surrounding circumference. But we can form no concept of the quiddity of the simultaneously maximum and minimum angle, since sense, imagination, and intellect can feel, imagine, conceive, or think nothing that is similar to that which is simultaneously the maximum and minimum.

XV.

So Plato says in his letters that everything is in the King of all and that everything is through His grace and He Himself is the cause of all goods. And a little later: "The human mind endeavors to understand the content of things, by considering those things related to itself, of which none is sufficient. However, in regard to its King there is nothing of this kind." Quite correctly, he writes there that this should be kept a secret. Indeed, not without cause he names the first Origin the King of all. Every state is indeed ordered through the king and to him, and is ruled and exists through him. Therefore, what is found distinct in the state, previously and conjoined in him, is he himself and life. As Proclus adds: The commander, assemblymen, soldiers, judge, law, measure, weight, and everything of this kind are in the king as in the public person, in whom everything which can be in the state is he himself as actuality. His law written on parchment is in him living law; and so it is with everything whose author he is. From him everything in the state has being and name. Aristotle correctly names him therefore in the likeness of the ruler, to whom the entire army is ordered as to its end and from which the army has what it is. Just as the law written on the dead parchment is the living law in the ruler, everything is life in the First; in the First time is eternity, the creature creator.

XVI.

Averroes says in his commentary on the eleventh book of the *Metaphysics,* that all forms are as actuality in the first Mover. And in the commentary on the twelfth book of the *Metaphysics,* he says that Aristotle rejects the ideas of Plato and thereby places the ideas and forms in the first Mover. Albertus asserts the same in his commentary on Dionysius. He reports that Aristotle had indeed said, the first cause is tri-causal, namely an efficient, formal, and final cause; the formal cause is the exemplary cause— and that he does not rebuke Plato in respect to this understanding.

However, it is true that God has the exemplars of all things in Himself. However, the exemplars are the rational grounds. But the theologians call the exemplars or ideas the will of God, for "as He wished, so He did," says the prophet. However, the will, which is the rational ground itself in the first intellect, is properly called the exemplar; just as the will in the ruler supported through the rational ground, is the exemplar of the law. For what pleases the ruler has the vigor of law. All this, which Plato, Aristotle, or anyone else says, is nothing other than what the beryllus and the enigma show you, namely that the truth confers being on everything through its similitude.

Thus Albertus affirms in the above-cited location: One must somehow concede that in everything a single form flows from the First, which is a similitude of His essence, through which all the being dependent on Him participates. Furthermore, pay attention to the fact, that the truth, which is what it can be, is imparticipable; but in its similitude, which can be received to a greater or lesser degree, according to the disposition of the recipient, it is communicable. Avicebron says in the book *On the Fountain of Life,* that the varied reflection of entity would cause the difference of entities, since a single reflection beyond entity adds life, a double reflection intellect.

How this can be understood, you may imagine in the enigma (see Figure 3): Let the line AB be a similitude of the truth and stand between the first truth and nothing [(a)]. Let B be the end of the similitude in respect to the nothing. B should be folded over C in an enfolding motion toward A, and thus represent the motion, with which God summons from non-existence into existence. The line AB is fixed, so long as it egresses from the origin as AC does, and movable, so long as it is moved enfoldingly over C toward the origin. In this motion, CB with CA causes various angles, and CB unfolds by means of this motion different similitudes. First it causes in a less formal similitude an obtuse

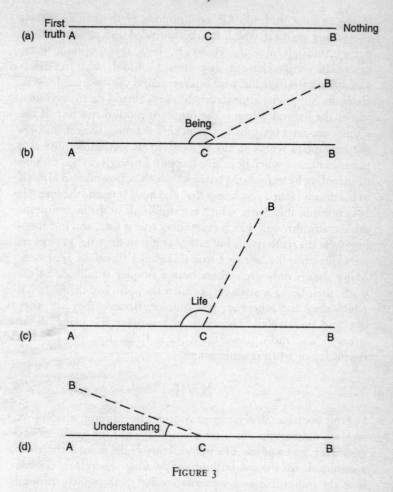

FIGURE 3

angle, which is its being [(b)]; then in a more formal similitude an angle, which is its life [(c)]; then in the most formal and most acute angle it causes its understanding [(d)]. The acute angle participates more in the activity of the angle and in its simplicity and is more similar to the first Origin.

And it is in the other angles, namely, in that of life and of being. Likewise the angle of life is in that of being. And what intermediate differences there are between being and life and understanding and what can be unfolded, you will see likewise in the enigma. Indeed, AB as similitude of the truth contains everything in itself which can be unfolded and this unfolding occurs through motion. However, how the motion occurs, where the simple element, as premised, unfolds what has originated from itself, is likewise represented in the enigma. Indeed, elemental simplicity exists from the movable and the immovable, just as the natural origin is the origin of motion and rest. If the Composer-intellect moves CB in this manner, then it unfolds the exemplars which it has in itself, in its similitude; just as a mathematician, when he folds a line into a triangle, in this motion of enfolding he unfolds the triangle, which he possesses in himself in his mind. Hence you know that one must imagine the line AB as communicable truth, which is a similitude of the incommunicable truth, through which everything true is true, and not absolutely, as the truth itself, but rather as it is in the true. However, we experience the being of true things in a threefold gradation: Many things only are; others bear a simpler similitude of the truth, their being is stronger, because they also live through that which they are; others are still simpler. Because they are, they live and understand. However, the simpler the being is the stronger and more powerful it is, and therefore the absolute simplicity or truth is omnipotent.

XVII.

For our doctrine, that we must consider the minimum when we seek the maximum, yet another enigma! The One or the monad is simpler than a point. The indivisibility of the point is therefore a similitude for the indivisibility of the One. Therefore, the one is as the indivisible and incommunicable truth, which through its similitude wishes to manifest and communicate itself, and the one indicates, forms, and manifests itself as a point. The point, however, as communicable indivisibility in the continuum, is not the One. Therefore, the point is communicated in the manner in which it is communicable, and has a body. For the point is indivisible in every mode of essential being of continuity and dimension. However, the modes of essential being of continuity are line, surface, and body; the modes of dimension are length, breadth, and depth. The line, therefore, participates in the indivisibility of the point, for it is linearly indivisible. Indeed, a line cannot be divided into not-line. It is also not divisible in respect to breadth and depth. The surface also partakes in the indivisibility of the point, for it is impartible into a non-surface. Nor is it divisible in respect to depth, since it is no body. Also the body participates in the indivisibility of the point, because it cannot be divided into not-body in accordance with its divisible depth.

In the indivisibility of the point all these indivisibilities are enfolded. Therefore, nothing other than the unfolding of the indivisibility of the point is found in them. Therefore, everything which is found in the body is nothing other than the point or the similitude of the One itself. Also the point is not found absolved from the body or the surface or the line, for it is the intrinsic principle, which gives indivisibility. However, the line participates more in the simplicity of the point than the surface and the surface more than the body. That is indeed quite apparent. Through this consideration of the point and the body elevate yourself now to the similitude of the truth and of the universe, and form for yourself in a clear enigma a conjecture of the stated.

XVIII.

You can receive a more truthful concept from man, who measures everything. In man the intellect is the highest level of his rational ground; its being is separated from the body and true per se; the soul follows it, thereafter nature and finally the body. I name the soul that which animates and confers animated being. The intellect, which on account of its simple universality and indivisibility is neither communicable nor participable, imparts itself in its communicable similitude, namely in the soul. Indeed, the sensitive cognition of the soul shows that it is the similitude of the intellect. Through the soul the intellect communicates itself to nature and through nature to the body. In that the soul is the similitude of the intellect, it perceives freely; in that it is united to nature, it animates. Consequently, it animates through nature and perceives through itself. Therefore, what the soul effects in the body by means of nature, it effects contractedly, so that, if it is actively discerning in an organ, it is contracted in correspondence to this organ. Therefore, we look to the body and all its formal members and to the law or nature, power, action, and order of each one, so that it is a single man. And whatever we find unfolded here, we find in the intellect as its cause, author, and ruler, in which everything is as in its efficient, formal, and final cause.

Indeed, everything is effective anteriorly in its power, just as the dignities and offices of the state are in the power of the commander. Everything is formally in it, which forms everything, so that the formed are insofar as they conform to its conception. Everything is finally in it, since it is for its sake and it itself is the end and desire of everything. Indeed, all members desire nothing other than inseparable union with it as with their origin, the highest good, and perennial life. However, how the soul, which is a similitude of the intellect, enfolds in itself everything vivifiable and communicates life by means of nature to everything, and how nature corresponds to an all-enfolding instrument, and has every motion and the nature of all members in itself beforehand—who shall explain this sufficiently? The intellect, with the help of its similitude, which is the sensitive soul in man, directs nature and every natural motion, so that everything conforms to its word or concept or will. Likewise in the universe, over which the Composer-intellect presides, nothing is found at all other than the similitude or the concept of its composer. Thus, if the Composer-intellect were sight and wished to show its power of seeing, then it would conceive everything visible, in order to show itself therein; and thereby it would have everything visible in itself and would form all the visible in conformity with the individual visible things existing in its conception. Indeed, in everything visible nothing were to be found other than conformity, and therefore the similitude of its Composer-intellect.

XIX.

Saints and philosophers have given very different enigmas. In his book on the *Republic,* Plato takes the sun and considers its power in sensible things. From their conformity he elevates himself to the light of the intelligence of the Composer-intellect. The great Dionysius imitates him, for this enigma is very pleasing, on account of the conformity of the sensible and intelligible light. Albertus takes the enigma of rectitude; just as if rectilinearity gave being to all wood, and in none can be participated in, as it is, but rather remains imparticipable and absolute. However, in contracted being, namely, in its similitude, in any piece of wood whatsoever, it is participated in variedly; for the one is knotty, the other curved and thus there are infinitely many differences.

Also he conceives warmth to be absolute. And just as everything warm participates in its similitude and has its being from it, he forms a concept of the Composer-intellect and the creature. Innumerable modes can be conceived; I have posited many others in *On Learned Ignorance* and other booklets. But no precision can be attained, since the divine mode is beyond every mode. And if you apply the eyeglass and see the origin of every mode through the simultaneously maximum and minimum mode, in which all modes are enfolded and which all modes cannot unfold, then you can make a truer mirror image of the divine mode.

XX.

Perhaps you will say that the use of the beryllus presupposes an essence, which receives more or less; otherwise its origin would not be seen through the simultaneously maximum and minimum. I respond that the essence according to itself indeed does not seem to receive a more or less, however, in comparison to the being and the peculiar actualities of the species, a more or less participates according to the disposition of the material of the recipient, to such an extent that, as Avicenna says, God appears in some: in those men, who have divine intellect and activity.

This mode of application of the beryllus was also not entirely hidden from Aristotle, who, in order to find the First, often proceeds through this argument: Where one finds participation in the One according to the more and less in the diverse, one must necessarily arrive at the First, in which the first itself is, just as in warmth, which is participated in in the diverse, one arrives at fire, in which the first is as in its font and from which everything else receives its warmth.

Thus in the use of that rule, Albertus also seeks the First, in which exists the fontal rational ground of entity, in which every entity participates. Likewise it is the origin of knowing. That is apparent, when he says: When intelligent, rational, and sensitive souls share in the truth of knowing, they must receive this nature from some One, in whom it first is as in a font, and that is God. However, it is impossible that they receive it equally from Him, for then they were equally near to the origin and had equal power in knowing. Therefore, it is first received in intelligence, which participates in the being of intelligence insofar as it participates in the divine ray. Similarly the rational soul participates in the cognitive power insofar as it receives the ray of intelligence, although the latter is overshadowed in it. Likewise the sensitive soul participates in cognition, to the extent that the ray of the rational soul is impressed upon it, although the latter is overshadowed in it. However, the sensitive soul is the last, beyond which the cognitive power does not flow.

However, as he said, the rational soul does not flow into the senses, unless the senses are conjoined to it; thus the first does not flow into the second, unless it is conjoined to it. That is not to be understood such that intelligence creates souls or the soul the senses, but rather in the first of them the ray of eternal wisdom is received as exemplar and as though a seed of the second. And because this ray is always received with diminished power, the soul does not receive the ray corresponding to intelligible being, nor does the vegetative receive the cognitive ray from the sensitive soul. Furthermore, in the cited commentary Albertus compares that divine ray, which illuminates cognitive nature, with the ray of the sun, which, considered in itself before it penetrates the air, is universal and simple. When it is received by the air it penetrates it deeply and illuminates it completely. Then it is received in the surface of terminated bodies, where it causes various colors according to their various dispositions. It is white and clear, if the surface is clear, black, if it is dark, and has median colors in accord with a median disposition.

Thus the first origin, namely, the wisdom of God or the divine cognition, which is the enduring essence of God and is incommunicable, in its ray, which is a cognitive form, is such that it illuminates certain natures, so that they know the simple quiddities of things. This cognition is in accord with the maximum brightness, which is possible to be received in creatures, as is the case in the intelligences. It is received in other creatures, where it effects no such cognition of simple quiddity, but rather of quiddity mixed with the continuous and time, just as in man.

For there cognition begins with the senses; therefore, one must compare one with the other to arrive at the simple intelligible.

For this reason, Isaac ben Salomon Israeli said that rationality arises in the shadow of intelligence, and the senses, in which cognition dies, in the shadow of rationality. Hence the vegetative soul arises in the shadow of the senses and does not partake of the cognitive ray, so that it could receive species and separate from the appendage of matter, so that a simple cognizability would arise. Avicenna again takes up the enigma of fire and its various modes of essential being, which come down from the aether and go to where it is completely overshadowed in the stone.

XXI.

All these and however many writers I have read lack the beryllus. And therefore, I believe that if they had followed the great Dionysius with constant perseverance, they would have seen the origin of all things clearly and would have composed commentaries on his works corresponding to the intention of the writer. But when they reach the conjunction of opposites, they interpret the text of the divine master disjunctively. It is something great to be able to adhere firmly to the conjunction of opposites.

For although I know that this must occur, nevertheless, we often stumble, when we revert to the method of discursive rationality; we attempt to render rational the mode of the most certain vision, which is beyond all rationality. And therefore we fall from the divine to the human and adduce unstable and meager rationality. This can occur to all, as Plato asserts in his letters, where he speaks about the vision of the first cause. Therefore, if you would see eternal wisdom or the cognitive origin, you can see it with the help of the beryllus through the simultaneously maximum and minimum cognizable. And in the enigma, for example in that of the angle, inquire into the acute, formal, simple, and penetrating cognitive natures as you inquire into the acute angles; other more obtuse, and finally the most obtuse, as you inquire into the obtuse angles. And you will be able to hunt down all possible gradations. And just as I have spoken about it here, likewise is it so for everything.

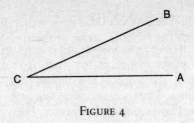

FIGURE 4

XXII.

Perhaps you doubt how the origin is seen as triune. I respond: Every origin is indivisible for every division, which is possible in that effected by it or originated from it. The first origin is therefore the simplest and most perfect indivisibility. However, in the essence of the most perfect indivisibility I see the unity, which is the font of indivisibility; I see the equality, which is the indivisibility of unity; and I see the connection, which is the indivisibility of unity and equality. I take up an enigma and intuit the angle ACB and consider point C as the first origin of the angle and lines AC and CB as the second origin (see Figure 4). Then the point C is the triune origin, for it is the origin of the line CA, which is an immobile line and the origin of the line CB, which is a distinction-forming line. And I see that point C is the connection of both and that point C is the innermost and nearest origin of the angle, namely, the origin and simultaneously the terminus of the angle. Indeed, it begins in point C and is terminated in the same. If I intuit the triune origin in C, then I see that it is the font, from which unity or necessity first emanates, which unites and constrains everything. Then I see the origin, from which equality emanates, which forms and equalizes everything, however varied. I also see with what motion this must occur. Thus, I see the origin C from which emanates the connection and conservation of everything constricted and formed. Therefore, I see the simplest, triune origin and find that its indivisibility is most perfect and is the cause of everything that cannot subsist in its indivisible essence without threefold indivisibility.

XXIII.

The philosophers have touched upon this trinity, of which they saw that it exists in the origin, in that they ascended from the caused to the cause. Anaxagoras and before him, as Aristotle reports, Hermotimos Clazomenius, were the first who saw the intellectual origin. Plato extolled the former. He read his books most frequently, for it seemed to him he had found a master. And what Plato said of him, Aristotle also said. For Anaxagoras opened both Plato's as well as Aristotle's eyes. However, both endeavored to find this origin through rationality. And Plato called the origin, by which everything is founded, the Composer-intellect and its father God and the cause of all.

And thus he said that at first everything is in the first, so that it is a threefold, efficient, formal, and final cause. Secondly, he stated that everything is in the Composer-intellect, which he called the first creature of God and of whom he asserted that his generation is from the first as that of a son from the father. The intellect, which the sacred writings also call the wisdom created from the beginning and before all time and the first-born before all creatures, he therefore designated as the composer—as though the mediator between the cause and the sensibly-caused, who executes the command or intention of the Father. Thirdly, he saw the spirit poured out through the universe or the motion, which connects and conserves everything which is in the world. Therefore, in God he saw everything in the first mode of essential being, in the first and simplest, thus everything is in the effective and omnipotent power. Secondly, he saw that everything is thus in the wisest executor of the commands. And this mode of essential being he calls the second. Thirdly, he saw that everything is as in an instrument of the executor, namely in motion. For through the motion everything which becomes is brought to completion.

These three modes of essential being Aristotle calls the world soul, although he does not use these terms. And he seems to say the same in respect to God, namely, that everything in Him is as in its triune cause and that all forms are in the heavenly moving intelligence and in the animated motion of noble souls. However, he multiplies the intelligences full of forms corresponding to the multitude of heavenly orbits, since he calls these orbits movers. Nevertheless, according to his rule, which extends to all moving intelligences, he shows that one must necessarily arrive at the first Mover. And he calls the latter the ruler or the first intellect.

But Plato, who considered the multitude of intelligences, saw the intellect as that through the participation in which all intelligences are intelligences. And because he saw that God is the first absolute, the simplest, imparticipable, and incommunicable Origin, he therefore believed that the communicable intellect, which participates and is communicated variedly in many gods or intelligences, is the first creature. Likewise he also believed that the world soul, which is participated in communicably in all souls, is before all souls and that all these are enfolded in it—as if anteriorly—as in their origin. I remember I have said something in respect to this in *On Learned Ignorance;* namely, how these three modes of essential being in their priority have received the names of fate.

However, you must merely note that it is not necessary, on account of the participation which moved Plato, that there be a universal created intellect or a universal world soul. Rather, for every mode of essential being the first triune origin is more than enough. Certainly He is absolute and superexalted, since He is not a contracted origin such as nature, which acts out of necessity, but rather is the origin of nature itself, which is therefore supernatural and free, because He creates everything through His will. However, what is made through His will, exists insofar as it conforms to His will. And therefore its form is the intention of the commander. However, the intention is a similitude of the intending, which is communicable and receivable in another. Therefore, every creature is the intention of the omnipotent will.

Neither Plato nor Aristotle knew that. Indeed, it is entirely evident that each believed that the Composer-intellect made everything out of the necessity of nature. And from this followed all of their errors. For although He does not act accidentally as fire through warmth—as Avicenna observes quite well, indeed no accident can occur in His simplicity—and therefore seems to act through His essence: He nevertheless does not act as nature or a necessary instrument through the command of a superior, but rather through the free will, which is also His essence. Aristotle saw very well in the *Metaphysics,* how everything in the first origin is He Himself. However, he did not attend to the fact that His will is not other from His rational ground and His essence.

XXIV.

However, which concept Plato had of this triune origin and how near he came to the mode of our Christian theology, Eusebius, student of Pamphilus, shows in his book *On Evangelical Preparations,* which he has compiled from the books of Numinius, who has recorded the secrets of Plato and Plotinus and others. Also Aristotle shows in his *Metaphysics,* which he himself calls theology, much rational, which conforms to the truth, namely, that the origin is intellect, which is completely in actuality, and understands itself. From this flows the highest delectation.

Also our theologians say that the divine Intellect, in that it understands itself, generates from itself and its essence and nature its most adequate intelligible similitude. Indeed, the Intellect generates the Word, in which it is substantially, and from this proceeds the delectation, in which is the consubstantiality of the generating and the generated. Truly, if you would have all possible knowledge about this origin, then consider in everything originated from it: whence it is, what it is, and the connection; and through the beryllus of the simultaneously maximum and minimum originated, reflect upon the origin in everything originated. In the origin itself you will find most perfectly in the divine mode the trinity as the simplest origin of all creatures triunely. And attend to the fact that in the simple concept of the originated, I express the trinity of the unity of essence through whence it is, what it is, and the connection. In the sensible substance this is commonly designated as form, matter, and composition; in man, for example, as soul, body, and connection of both.

XXV.

In that Aristotle brought all philosophers into concord, he said that the principles which are in substances are contrary. He named three principles: matter, form, and privation. I believe rather, that although he is held to be above all philosophers the most diligent and most acute, just like all the others he failed completely in one and the same. For if the principles are contrary, then they have not attained the absolutely necessary third principle, and have not attained this, because they did not consider it possible that opposites simultaneously coincide in the same, since they expel one another. Hence on the basis of the first principle, which rejects that contradictory opposites are simultaneously true, the philosopher shows that opposites cannot simultaneously exist.

Our beryllus makes us see more acutely, so that we see the opposites in the connective principle before duality, namely, before they are two contradictory things, just as if we see the minimum opposites coincide, as the minimum cold and the minimum warmth, the minimum slowness and the minimum velocity, etc., so that these are a single principle before the duality of both opposites, as I said in the booklet *On Mathematical Perfection,* in respect to how minimum arc and minimum chord coincide. Just as the minimum acute angle and the minimum obtuse angle are the simple right angle, in which the minima of both contrary angles coincide, before the acute and the obtuse are two angles, so is it with the principle of connection, in which the minima of the opposites coincide simply.

If Aristotle had understood the principle, which he named privation, so that this privation is the principle which establishes coincidence of opposites and is thus deprived of contrariety, because it precedes the duality which is necessary in opposites, then he would have seen correctly. The timidity, however, to acknowledge that opposites are simultaneously in the same, restrained him before the truth of this principle. And because he saw that a third principle is necessary and had to be this privation, he made privation into the principle without the position. Consequently he was able, so it seems, to evade the difficulties not otherwise than that he misplaced the beginning of forms in matter. However, if one examines it acutely, then it is a question of that connection, of which I speak. But he has thus neither known nor named it. And for this reason, all philosophers have not attained to the spirit, which is the principle of connection and, according to our perfected theology, the third person in the divinity; although most spoke elegantly concerning the Father and the Son, most of all the Platonics, of whom Saint Augustine says he found in their books the Gospel of our theologian John— "In the beginning was the Word"—up to the name of John the

Baptist and the incarnation. Nevertheless no mention of the Holy Spirit is found in this Gospel.

XXVI.

It very much behooves you to note what I have said about this third principle. Aristotle says, and justly, the principles are the minimum and indivisible in respect to the magnitude of quantity, however the maximum in respect to the magnitude of power. Therefore, neither the form nor the matter is divisible, since they have neither quality nor quantity. And also the connection is not divisible. Therefore, the essence, which subsists in them, is indivisible. Our intellect cannot conceive the simple, because it produces the concept in the imagination, which takes the principle or the subject of its image or its figure from the sensible. Therefore, the intellect is not able to conceive the essence of things. Nevertheless, it sees that it subsists indivisibly trinally, beyond its imagination and its concept.

If, therefore, the intellect is attentive, it sees that corporeal substance as substance is indivisible, but is divisible through the accidental. If, therefore, the body is divided, the substance is not divided, because it is not divided into not-body or into substantial parts, namely, into form, matter, and connection, which more properly are called principles rather than parts—for that would be to divide the indivisible from the indivisible as point from point, which is not possible. Rather, the continuous is divided in the continuous. That subject to it, namely, the quantity, can indeed receive a more or less. However, the potential-to-be-divided comes from indivisible matter, which is indivisible, not on account of unity, as perhaps form, or on account of smallness, as perhaps connection, but rather on account of formlessness as a not-yet-existing. Hence if the entity is through the form, which is deeply immersed in it and becomes greatly material, the quantity is divided on account of the matter. Therefore, you will be able through the enigma to investigate the differences of such forms, which are deeply immersed in the matter, and such which are less deeply in it and which are very simple. And because all corruption, mutability, and division is from matter, you see also immediately the causes of generation, corruption, and related such.

XXVII.

When Aristotle set to work writing his *Politics,* he turned to the minimum in the domain of the economy as well as in that of politics. In this minimum he saw how the maximum must be and said that one would have to do this similarly in others. In the *Metaphysics,* however, he said that the straight and the curved are contrary to one another by nature. Therefore, the one could not be converted into the other.

In the first case he spoke correctly. And I believe that if someone wants to know something maximum and he turns to the minimum of the opposite, he will certainly investigate the secret knowledge. In the second case, in respect to the straight and the curved, he has not considered well: for they are opposed and the one is the minimum of the other. Perhaps he has said this, in order to excuse his ignorance in respect to the quadrature of the circle, of which he often makes mention. However, you know, on the basis of the above, that the origin is indivisible for every mode of division which is possible in the originated. Therefore, the originated, which is divided oppositely, has an origin, which is indivisible in this manner. Therefore, the opposite is of the same genus. With the help of the beryllus and the enigma you can form knowledge concerning the origin of opposites, their difference, and everything attainable in respect to this. And in general, through the origin of the knowable you can form knowledge of knowledge and its differences, as you have heard it above in comparison. Indeed, the same mode of proceeding is valid for everything.

If, for example, you want to amplify and extend as far as it pleases you the intentions of the great Dionysius, who attributes many names to God, then through the beryllus and the enigma you can advance to the origin of every name and you will see, if God leads you always, everything that can be humanly said. Also you will attain the causes in nature more subtly; namely, why the generation of the one is the corruption of the other. Indeed, if you see an opposite through the beryllus, then you see that the origin of the other opposite lies in it; for example, if you see the simultaneously maximum and minimum warm, then you know that the origin of the warm is nothing other than the indivisibility for every mode of division of warmth, which is separated from all warmth. For the origin is nothing of everything originated; however, that which is originated from the origin of warmth is warm. Therefore, the warm is not the origin of warmth. However, that which is of the same genus and not warm I see in the cold, and it is likewise with other opposites. Therefore, if the origin of the other lies in the one opposite, then the transmutations are circular and both opposites have a common subject.

Thus you see how passion is transmuted into action. Just as the student undergoes instruction, in order to become a teacher or instructor, so is the subject, after the passion of warming, transformed into warming fire. And the senses undergo the impression of the species opposite them, so that they become actually sentient. Likewise the matter undergoes the impression of form, in order to be actual. When I speak of opposites, it is, however, necessary to observe how I denote that which belongs to the same genus and is divisible in like manner. Then, indeed, in the one is the origin of the other.

XXVIII.

After all these investigations, it seems to me, you will ask what according to my estimate is entity, namely, what is substance. I want to satisfy your wish, as far as I am able, although that which I am to say contains the greatest profundity.

Aristotle writes: All investigators of the truth have always asked this old question, and seek the solution to this problem still today. However, he himself reached the view that all knowledge depends on the solution to this question. For to know what-it-was-to-be, i.e., to know that a thing is therefore this—for example, a house, since the what-it-was-to-be-of-the-house is this—is to have attained the acme of knowledge. However, as he inquired carefully about this and sought high and low, he found that also substantial matter did not come into existence, since it is the possibility of essential being. For if it were from another, then this, from which it was, would have to have been the possibility of essential being, since nothing except the possible can become. Therefore, there is no possibility from possibility. Consequently, matter does not arise from another nor from nothing, since nothing arises from nothing. Consequently, he showed that the form does not come to be. Otherwise it were necessary that it would arise from entity into possibility and thus from matter. He offers as an example, how a spherical bronze ore does not form a bronze sphere, but rather that that which was always a sphere, is introduced into the matter of the ore. It arises therefore only from composition. Therefore, the form, which actually forms in composition, he calls the what-it-was-to-be. And if he perceives it separately, he calls it species.

However, what that substance is, which he calls what-it-was-to-be, he is in doubt. For he does not know whence it comes or where it subsists, whether it is the One itself, or entity, or the genus, or whether it is from the idea, which is the substance subsisting in itself, or whether it is educed from the potential of the matter, or how that occurs, if it were so. For every entity in potential must be led through entity in actuality into actuality. For if actuality were not prior to potentiality, how then should the potentiality come into actuality? For if it were to place itself in actuality, then it was in actuality even before it was in actuality. And if it were previously in actuality, then it was the species or the idea separately. And that seems not to be so. For then the same would have to be separate and not separate, since one can indeed not say that the one is a separate species and another substance—the what-it-was-to-be. For if it is another, then it is not what-it-was-to-be, and if the species are separate from the sensible, then they must be separate either as numbers or as magnitudes or as mathematical forms. However, if they depend on the matter and the subject, without which the mathematical does not have being, then consequently they are not separate. And if the species are not separate, they are not universal and there can be no knowledge of them.

He thought through most subtly much of such kind and, as it appears, could not commit himself fully, because of his doubt in respect to species and ideas. Also, as Proclus says, Socrates as a youth as well as in his old age had doubts concerning this; nevertheless he inclined more to the opinion that the species, although there are some substances separate from matter, nevertheless are not separate substances, as for example an artificial species, namely, a house, has no substantial being separate from matter. But this question occupied him frequently and he regarded it always as most difficult.

XXIX.

However, I pay attention to how Aristotle, even though he had found the species and the truth concerning them, nevertheless could not have attained the what-it-was-to-be, except in the same manner by which someone finds that this measure is a sixth, because it is the what-it-was-to-be-for-the-sixth. It is that, since it was constituted by the ruler of the republic to be a sixth. However, he did not yet know why it is determined so and not otherwise, except that when finally resolved, he said, because it pleased the ruler, it has the vigor of law. And thus I say with the sage, that there is no rational basis for all the works of God: namely, there is no other rational ground as to why the heaven is heaven and the earth earth and man man, than that He, who has created them, wanted it so. To investigate further is foolish, as Aristotle says also in a similar manner; for example, if one wanted to search for a demonstration for the first principle, "something is or is not." But if one attentively considers that no creature has a rational ground of essential being from elsewhere, than that it is created just so and that the will of the Creator is the ultimate rational ground of essential being and that God the Creator is the simple Intellect, which creates through itself, so that His will is nothing other than His intellect or rational ground, indeed the font of the rational ground, then one sees clearly how that which is made through His will, proceeds from the font of the rational ground, just as the law of the ruler is nothing other than the rational ground of the ruler, which appears to us as his will.

XXX.

In order to come nearer to the truth, we must therefore still consider how our intellect cannot free its concept from the imagination, to which it is connected, and therefore in its intellectual concepts, which are mathematical, posits figures which it imagines to be substantial forms. In them and the intellectual numbers it posits its considerations, since those are simpler than the sensible, because they are intelligible matter. And since it derives everything through the senses, it believes it apprehends everything attainable at least in similitude in these more subtle and incorruptible figures, which are freed from the sensible quality. Therefore, the one philosopher takes the substantial element as One and considers the substances as numbers, another considers them as point and draws therefrom the corresponding consequences.

By means of these intellectual concepts it becomes apparent that indivisibility is the origin prior to everything. For it is the rational ground as to why the One and the point and every origin is the origin: namely, because it is indivisible. And according to the intellectual concept the indivisible is the more formal and precise origin. Nevertheless it can only be attained negatively. Yet it is attained in everything divisible, as became clear above. For it is established that nothing remains of the substance, if one removes the indivisibility, and therefore all subsistence has only so much being and substance as it has indivisibility. Yet as Aristotle correctly says, this negative knowledge of the origin is obscured. For to know that the substance is neither quantity nor quality nor another accident, is not clear knowledge, like that which appears as positive.

However, we know here with the eye of the mind in the enigma through a mirror image the unnameable indivisibility, which can be named by us through no name and can be apprehended in no formable concept. We see it most truly in the excess and are not confused thereby, that our Origin exceeds all clarity and all accessible light; just as that one joys more, who has found an innumerable and inexhaustible thesaurus for his life, than the one who has found a numerable and consumable one.

XXXI.

After this we wish to recall to memory that which I have said above about the intention, namely, that the creature is the intention of the Creator, and we consider the intention to be His truest quiddity. For in a comparison: If someone speaks with us and if we attain the quiddity of the speech, then we attain nothing other than the intention of the one speaking. It is likewise, if we derive the sensible species through the senses. We simplify them, as much as is possible, so that we see the quiddity of the things with the intellect. However, to simplify the species is nothing other than to discard the corruptible accidents, which cannot be the quiddity. It is just as if we attain to the intention of the intellect of the Composer in running through the more subtle phantasmata in a speech or a writing, and indeed in the knowledge that the quiddity of that thing, which is contained in these signs and figures of the sensible thing as in the writing or vocal speech, is an intention of the intellect, so that the sensible is as it were the Word of the Creator, in which His intention is contained. And if we have apprehended it, we know the quiddity and find rest. However, because of the intention there is manifestation. Indeed, the speaking or creative intellect intends to manifest itself. Therefore, if we have apprehended the intention, which is the quiddity of the Word, then we have the what–it–was–to–be. For with the intellect the what–it–was–to–be is apprehended in the intention, just as in a perfect house the intention of the architect is apprehended, which was in his intellect.

XXXII.

You should also know that I, as I believe, have found yet another who has erred among the investigators of the truth. For Plato said, one could indeed consider the circle, as it is named or defined, drawn or conceived in the mind, but not have obtained therefrom the nature of the circle. But rather only through the intellect is its quiddity seen, which exists simply and incorruptibly without all opposition. And Plato asserts the same is true for everything. But neither he nor another author, whom I have read, paid attention to that which I mentioned in the fourth section. For if he had considered that, then he would have found that our mind, which forms mathematical things, has in itself in greater truth those things which are its official duties than those that are outside of it. Imagine a man who has mastery over mechanical art: He has the figures of this art in greater truth in his mental concept than they are figurable externally; just as a house, which arises through art, has a truer figure in the mind than in the wood. The form, which is made in the wood, is indeed a mental figure, an idea or exemplar. And thus it is with all such.

It is likewise with the circle, line, triangle, with our number and everything which takes its beginning from a concept of the mind and which lacks nature. But therefore the house, which is in wood or sensible, is not truer in the mind, although its figure is truer there. For it is required of the true being of the house, that it be sensible for the sake of the end for which it exists. Therefore, it can have no separate species, as Aristotle saw very well. Therefore, although the figures and numbers and every such intellectuality, which is an entity of our rationality and which lacks nature, is truer in its origin, namely, the human intellect, nevertheless, it does not follow from this that everything sensible, whose essence it is that it is sensible, is truer in the intellect than in the senses. For this reason, Plato seems not to have correctly deliberated, when he saw the mathematical things, which are abstracted from the sensible, in greater truth in the mind, and therefore believed they had yet another and truer being above the intellect. Yet Plato would have been able to say correctly, that just as the forms of human art are truer in their origin, namely, the human mind, than they are in matter, also the forms of the origin of nature, which are natural, are truer in their origin than externally. And if the Pythagoreans and others had considered that, then they would have seen clearly that the mathematical signs and numbers, which are produced by our mind and are in the mode by which we conceive, are not the substances or origins of sensible things, but rather only the rational entities, whose creator we are.

So you see how that which cannot arise through our art, is truer in the sensible than in our intellect, just as the fire has truer being in its sensible substance than in our intellect, where it is in the confused concept without natural truth. And that is true of everything.

But the fire has truer being in its author, where it is in its adequate cause and its rational ground. And although it is not in the divine Intellect with sensible qualities, which we perceive in it, nevertheless, it is for this reason no less true. Thus the dignity of a duke is truer in the regal dignity, even if the office of the duke is not here performed. Indeed, in this world the fire has its properties in respect to other sensible things by means of which it exercises its influence on other things. And since it has these properties in this world only in respect to others, they do not belong simply to its essence. Therefore, it does not require them, if it is freed from this activity and from this world. It also does

not desire them in the intelligible world, where there is no contrariety, as Plato has said it very well of the circle, which if drawn
on the pavement is full of contrarieties and corruptible according
to the condition of the location, but in the intellect is free thereof.

XXXIII.

It also seems good to me, to add some things concerning species.
They do not come into existence and do not perish, except in
respect to the accidental. They are incorruptible and similitudes
of the infinite, divine Intellect. How can this be understood,
namely, that the intellect is reflected in every species? This does
not occur as a face is reflected in many mirrors, but rather as an
infinite magnitude is in various finite magnitudes, and in each
totally.

I conceive this so that every species as, for example, a
triangle, is finite in respect to the surface magnitude. For it is the
first finite and terminated magnitude, in which the infinite angle
is reflected entirely. It is indeed the simultaneously maximum
and minimum angle, hence also the infinite and immeasurable,
since it receives neither more nor less. It is the origin of all
triangles. Indeed, it cannot be said that two right angles are
greater or less than the simultaneously maximum and minimum
angle (see Figure 5). For as long as the maximum appears smaller
than two right angles [(a)], it is not the maximum simply. However, every triangle has three angles, which equal two right
angles [(b)]. Therefore, the infinite origin of all angles is reflected
entirely in every triangle. And because the triangle has no angular, rectilinear, or terminated surface with one or two angles
before itself, but it is itself the first terminated surface, it is
incorruptible as species and first substance. Indeed, a triangle
cannot be resolved into a not-triangle; therefore also not into
another figure, whose three angles are greater or less. However,
there can be various triangles: some acute, others obtuse, and
others right angular and these can in turn be various. It is also so
in respect to the species. However, all species are perfect and
determined prime substances, because in them the entire first
Origin is reflected with its incorruptibility and magnitude in a
finite and determined mode.

And in order to make this clear to you, contemplate the

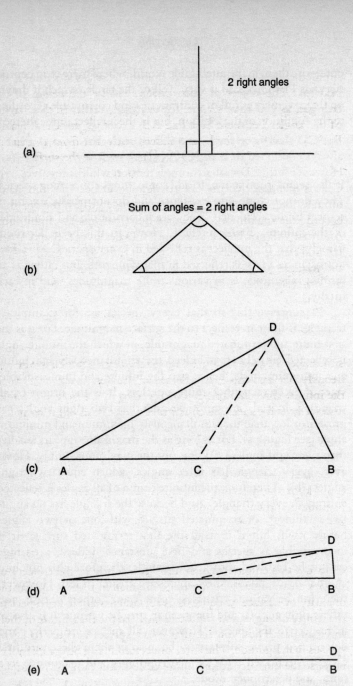

2 right angles

(a)

Sum of angles = 2 right angles

(b)

D

(c) A   C   B

D

(d) A   C   B

D

(e) A   C   B

FIGURE 5

simultaneously maximum and minimum triangle through the beryllus. The object of your vision will be the origin of the triangle, as you have seen it, for example, earlier in the enigma of the angle. Let there be a line AB. From its middle a mobile line CD shall issue forth, and indeed such that from D a line is always continued to B and to A, which enclose the surface [(c)]. However little CD varies through motion while it revolves over C, it is manifest that the one triangle never becomes the maximum as long as there is some other triangle [(d)]. If the one shall become the maximum, the other must become the minimum. And that will not be the case, until CD lies over CB and DA is BA and thus is one straight line, which is the origin of the angles and triangles [(e)]. Therefore, in this origin, which I see through the simultaneously maximum and minimum angle and thereby also through the simultaneously maximum and minimum triangle, which is the triune origin, I see simultaneously all angles and triangles enfolded, so that every angle, which is one and three, is the origin in it. And thus in every finite triangle, which is simultaneously one and three, the triune origin, which is simultaneously one and three, is reflected in the best manner in which the infinite three and one can be reflected in the finite. And thus you see how the species is constituted on the basis of the complete enfolding: namely, when it is reflected back completely over itself and connects the end with the beginning, just as the line AB is first folded over C into an angle; then CB is folded over D, so that B returns to A, and through this double reflection the triangle or the determined, incorruptible species arises, whose beginning and end coincide.

XXXIV.

Consider this enigma, which leads you subtly to the concept of species. A triangle, whether large or small in respect to sensible quantity or surface, is equal to every other triangle in respect to the trinity of angles and simultaneously to the magnitude of their three angles. Thus you see that every species is equal to every species in magnitude. The latter can certainly not be the quantity, because the quantity admits more or less, but rather it is simple, substantial magnitude before every sensible quantity. Therefore, when one sees a triangle in a surface, then it means that one sees the species in the subject whose species it is, and there I see the substance, which has come to be, which is the what-it-was-to-be of this, namely, it is an orthogonal triangle, because it is the what-it-was-to-be of the orthogonal triangle. It attains the whole through the species, which gives the to-be-thus.

And notice how it does not give only the general triangular being, but rather the right-angled triangular being or the acute-angled or the obtuse-angled or one differentiated from these. And thus the species is the specification of the genus through difference. The specification is the connection, which connects the difference with the genus. And thus the species gives the total being to the thing. Hence the species, which is one and the other, is not other from the subject, but rather has its essential origin in itself, through which it is substantially determined, just as a figure is held together through its terminus, just as in harmony and numbers.

The harmonious species are indeed various. For the general harmony is specified variedly through various differences, and that connection, through which a difference, for example, a high tone with a low one, is connected, which is the species, has in itself a proportionate harmony, which is distinctly determined from every other species through its essential origins. Therefore, the species is like a determined, harmonious habitude, which, although it is one, is nevertheless communicable to many subjects. Indeed, the habitude or proportionability is incorruptible and can be designated as species, which receives no more or less. And it gives species or beauty to the subject, just as proportion adorns beauty. For the similitude of the eternal rational ground or the divine Composer–intellect is reflected in harmonious or concordant proportion. And we experience this, because such a proportion, if it is perceived, is delectable and welcome to all senses.

XXXV.

Look how appropriate is the enigma, which is concerned with numbers, in that it conceives of numbers as proportion or as habitude. This habitude becomes sensible in numbers, just as the triangle in the surface or quantity. And just as the discrete quantity is simpler than the continuous quantity, so also the species is seen better in the enigma of discrete quantity than in the continuous one. As Aristotle correctly said, mathematics is indeed concerned with intellectual matter. But its matter is the magnitude, without which a mathematician grasps nothing. However, discrete magnitude is simpler and more spiritual and the species, which is completely simple, more similar than the continuous, even though the simplicity of the species, which is the quiddity, is before the simplicity of that discrete magnitude. For this reason, it can also not be grasped, since it precedes every magnitude which can be grasped. Indeed, no intellectual conception is possible without magnitude and one approaches it more subtly, if one approaches the mentioned, discrete magnitude, which is abstracted from every sensible discrete quantity. Hence the first substance, whose simplicity precedes every mode of the accidental, whether as it is in the sensible being or in the mathematical abstracted from the sensible, cannot be conceived by our intellect, which is united to the body or to quantity as an instrument which it conceives. Nevertheless, it sees it beyond every concept.

Consider also, how we have greater joy in a certain color; it is likewise with voice or song and the remaining sensory feelings. That is so because sensing is the life of the sensitive soul, which does not consist in sensing this or that, but rather in being in every sensible thing simultaneously. Therefore, it is more in that sensible thing, in which it apprehends more of the object in which therefore the sensible is in a certain harmonious union, just as if one color contains in itself many colors harmoniously or an harmonious song many different voices. It is likewise with the other senses. The same is true of the intelligible, where in one origin there are many different intelligible things. Therefore, it is for the intellect the highest life and immortal delectation to understand the first Origin, in which is the rational ground of all things. And thus the species is a determined whole of the one perfect mode of essential being of divine similitude, which enfolds in itself all particular contractions and is contracted in the subject to-be-this. Through the beryllus you can see, in the frequently mentioned manner, the Origin, and conceive how divine are all species which come from the substantial or perfect similitude of the eternal rational ground. And you can understand how the Creator-intellect manifests itself in them and that the species is the Word or the intention of this Intellect, which thus shows itself specifically; this is the quiddity of every individual. Therefore, every individual also reveres this species most and applies all diligence, so that it does not perish. His sweetest joy and highest desire is to hold fast to it.

XXXVI.

One thing still remains for us: namely, to see how man is the measure of things.

Aristotle says Protagoras said nothing profound thereby. Nevertheless, it seems to me that he expressed something very great thereby. First, I consider that Aristotle correctly said at the beginning of the *Metaphysics* that all men by nature desire knowledge. He explains this in respect to the sense of vision, which man has not only in order to work, but rather we prize it for the sake of knowing, since it manifests to us many differences. If, therefore, man has sense and rationality, then it is not only in order to use them to preserve his life, but rather also in order to know. Then sensible things furnish man with twofold nourishment, namely, such that he can live, and such that he can know. However, more significant and nobler is the knowledge, because it has a higher and more incorruptible end.

Above we have already presupposed that the divine Intellect creates everything, in order to manifest Himself, as the Apostle Paul writes in the Epistle to the Romans: that the invisible God is known in the visible things of the world. The visible things therefore exist, so that in them the divine Intellect is known, which has created everything skillfully. Therefore, as great as the power of the cognitive nature is in the human senses, which participate in the light of the rationality united with them, so great is the diversity of sensible things. Indeed, the sensible things are the books of the senses, in which the intention of the divine Intellect is described in sensible figures. And this intention is the manifestation of God the Creator. Therefore, if you are in doubt concerning anything at all, as to why it is one way or another, then there is only one response: because the divine Intellect wanted to manifest Himself to the sensitive cognition, in order to be known sensitively. If you ask, for example, why such a contrariety exists in the sensible world, you must say: because the opposites, placed side by side, shine forth all the more and there is for both only one knowledge.

So meager is the sensitive cognition, that it would not apprehend differences without contrariety. Therefore, each sense wishes contrary objects, in order to better discern, and therefore, those required for this are found in the objects. If you continue thus with touch, taste, smell, sight, and hearing and consider attentively which power of knowing each sense has, then you will find all objects in the sensible world and experience that they are ordered in service to cognition. Thus the contrariety of the first qualities serves the sense of touch, that of colors the sense of vision, etc. It is admirable how the divine Intellect shows itself in all these so various things.

When Anaxagoras saw that the intellect is the origin and cause of things, and yet in cases of doubt assigned other causes than the intellect, he was therefore rebuked both by Plato in the *Phaedo,* as well as by Aristotle in the *Metaphysics*. As if he had asserted that the intellect is the origin of the universe and not of singular things. I have been astonished at the philosopher princes, who saw that Anaxagoras is reprehensible in this and agreed with one another in regard to the origin, and have asked myself why they themselves sought another rational ground and, directly in that which they rebuked in Anaxagoras, are found to fall into a similar error. However, this comes from a false presupposition, namely, that they placed necessity in the first cause. If they had looked back in every inquiry to the true cause of the founding of the universe, which we have discussed, then they would have found the one true solution to their doubts.

For example: What does the Composer wish, when through the motion of the heaven and with nature as instrument, He educes from a thorn bush such a beautiful and fragrant sensible rose?

How otherwise can one respond, than that that admirable Intellect intended to manifest Himself in this His Word; that He wished to show how great His wisdom and His rationality are, which are the riches of His glory, when He so easily unfolds such beauty in the cognitive sense in such ornate proportion by means of a small, sensible thing, thereby exhilarating the whole nature of man in the motion of joy and sweetest harmony? He shows Himself gloriously in the vegetative life, from which the rose emerges. In even more glorious resplendence He appears in the intellective life, which illumines everything sensible. How glorious is that Ruler, who rules everything through nature as through a law. He preserves everything beyond time in the incorruptible species and temporally in the individual. And we see how everything arises through this law of nature, is moved, and does what the law of nature commands, in which law nothing else matters except that Intellect, who is the Author of all things.

XXXVII.

Aristotle also saw that, with the annulment of sensitive cognition, sensible things are also annulled, when he says in his *Metaphysics:* If there were no animated beings, there were also neither sensible things nor sensibility. There is more about this there.

Protagoras therefore correctly said that man is the measure of things. He knows from the nature of his sensitive knowledge that the sensible exists for the sake of the knowledge. He measures the sensible in order to be able to apprehend the glory of the divine Intellect in a sensible manner. And he does likewise with the intelligible, in that he refers it to the intellective cognition. And finally for the same reason he contemplates that immortal, intellective nature, so that the divine Intellect can show itself to him in its immortality. And thus the evangelical doctrine becomes more manifest, which places the end of creation therein, that the God of gods would be seen in Zion in the majesty of His glory. This is the revelation of the Father, in which everything is sufficient. And our Savior, through whom God has made time, namely, the Word of God, promises that he will show himself on that day and that those then will live the eternal life.

This revelation must indeed be understood as if someone were to see the intellect of Euclid with a single glance, and such that this vision were an apprehension of the art which Euclid unfolds in his *Elements*. Thus the divine Intellect is the art of the Omnipotent, through which He has created time and all life and all intelligence. Therefore, to have apprehended this art, when it shows itself naked on that day on which the intellect will appear naked and pure in the presence of Him, is to have acquired the filiation of God and the inheritance of the immortal Kingdom.

For if the intellect will have the art in itself, which is creative life and everlasting joy, then it has attained ultimate knowledge and felicity.

XXXVIII.

However, how cognition arises through the species of particular senses, which specify and determine the general power of the sentient, and how this passion, namely, the impression of the species, becomes action in the senses, and how the intelligence is full of intelligible forms, although it is one simple form, you will know, if you attend to how vision enfolds in itself the forms of everything visible and therefore knows them, when they are presented to it, from its nature and through its own form, which enfolds in itself the forms of everything visible.

It is likewise with the intellect, whose form is the simplicity of the intelligible forms, which it knows from its own nature when they are presented nakedly to it. And it is likewise, if one ascends up to the intelligences, which possess a more subtle simplicity of form, and see everything without it being presented to them in phantasmata. Finally, we see how in the first intellect everything is cognitive, such that the cognition gives being to the known, just as the causative exemplar of all forms makes itself into an example. We also understand why the senses do not attain the intelligible and the intellect the intelligences and that superior to them; namely because no cognition can attain to that which is simpler than it. To know is indeed to measure. However, the measure is simpler than the measurable; just as unity is the measure of number. Because all this is contained enfoldedly in the beryllus and in the enigma and many have written elegantly about it, to save time I do not wish to elaborate upon it.

Rather I wish to end the book with a saying of Plato's: that knowledge is most brief and is communicated better without any writing, if someone desired it and were disposed to it. Plato regards those disposed to it, who desire it with such avidity that they prefer to die than to do without wisdom. He regards as disposed to it those who abstain from corporeal vices and pleasures and have the mental aptitude therefor.

I concur with all that and add that one also must be faithful and devoted to God and must frequently, sincerely request to be illumined by Him. Indeed, He gives wisdom to those who, in firm belief, request as much as suffices for their salvation. This booklet, even if slightly digested, will give such men material for reflection. It will oblige them to track down secrets, to attain greater heights and, in laud of God, after whom every soul aspires, to always persevere; God, who alone works miracles and who is blest in eternity.

On the Origin

(1 4 5 9)

Who are you? Jesus responded to them: the Origin, as which I speak to you.

It is my intention, with God's help, to touch upon something concerning the origin for the exercise of the intellect. However, origin is in Greek of the feminine gender and is in this location in the accusative case. Hence Augustine interprets: "Believe in me, the Origin, as which I speak to you, so that you are not lost in your sins." Therefore, as the first point, we wish to investigate whether there is an origin.

As Proclus writes in the *Parmenides* commentary, Plato asserted that this world comes into being from an older cause. For something partible cannot subsist through itself. Indeed, what subsists through itself is that which it can be. However, the partible cannot be, because it can be divided. Now since it can be divided and cannot be, insofar as it is from itself, it is clearly not self-subsisting or auto-hypostatic.

Further: The visible acts effectively through the invisible power, as fire through warmth, snow through coldness. And thus in general the effecting or generating is invisible. However, in the self-subsistent, the effecting and the effected, the generating and the generated, are the same. Therefore, it is not visible. Further: If the divisible were self-subsistent, then it would simultaneously exist and not exist, just as the warm, if it were through itself what it is, would warm itself and thus would be warm and not warm. Indeed, how should it warm itself, if it were not warm? And how should it actually be warm, if it did not warm itself? Thus there cannot be something moved through itself.

Therefore, as all motion is from an immobile cause, so everything partible is from an impartible cause. However, since the body is divisible, this corporeal, visible world is certainly of a partible nature. It is therefore from an older, impartible cause. Our Savior expresses this when he said: "Which of you with his thought can add to his stature one cubit?" Indeed, he who is from a cause can add nothing in order to enlarge his being. Rather, that one gives increase, who has also given being, namely God. Thus Paul says in 1 Cor 3: "Neither the one who plants nor the one who waters is anything, but only God, who causes the growth."

From this it is clear, that alone the infinite and eternal is auto-hypostatic or self-existent, for this alone is impartible and nothing can be added to it. However, everything finite cannot resist an addition or subtraction. Therefore, it is not auto-hypostatic or self-subsisting, but rather is from an older cause.

However, that there is only one cause or one origin of all things, I say, is clear according to the teaching of Christ, who asserts: Only the One is necessary. Plurality, just as otherness, is disturbing and not necessary. In the above-mentioned location Proclus shows the reason for this as follows: Were there several origins, then they were certainly similar to one another in that they are origins. Therefore, they would participate in this One. That participated in is, however, prior to the participant. Therefore, there will not be several origins, but rather only the One before the multitude.

Even if you said there were several origins without participation in the One, then this assertion would destroy itself. For these many were certainly similar in that they did not participate in the One and dissimilar in that they did not participate in the One. Indeed they are similar, which participate in the One. Therefore they are dissimilar, which do not participate in the One. Therefore, it is clearly impossible that there be several origins.

For the same reason, it is clear that there are not several entities severed from the One. Indeed, if they did not participate in the One, then they were simultaneously and at once and in the same regard similar and dissimilar. And this is the subtle hypothesis of Zeno, who asserted: If there is a plurality of entities, then the similar is dissimilar. This hypothesis Proclus explains in the manner just described by me. Hence for the subtle observer only the One is necessary; if one abandons it, then rationality concludes that nothing can be. If we therefore pay heed to the necessity of being, we see that Parmenides has said the truth, namely, that there is nothing except the One. Thus, Christ also said only the One is necessary.

Therefore, if one does not see the One in the many, one sees in the multitude nothing but disturbance and formless infinity or non-termination. However, I believe that Christ has designated the One as necessary, because everything is necessitated or united or constricted in the One, so that if it is, it is not dissolved in nothing. However, some things are united, so that they are; others, however, are united more strongly, so that they are and live; others finally are united more firmly, so that they are, live, and understand. We indeed experience that the soul is united more strongly than the body. For it itself unites the body formed by it in its life and holds it, so that it does not dissolve.

We also see that power is generated from union. For the closer the union is, the stronger is the power. Therefore, the essential being has greater power, the more strongly it is united. Consequently, the infinite and simply maximum union, which is also unity, has infinite vigor. And therefore, were that unity, which is named the absolute One by Plato, not present in the possibility of the essential being, there were no possibility or material of the essential being. For this reason the entity in potentiality is no entity. Nevertheless it is seen in potentiality and is not seen without participation in unity, because it is not nothing or completely dissolved or not at all, since it can be necessitated or constricted. And therefore, before the entity in potentiality and the actual entity, one sees the One without which neither can be.

This necessary One is named God, as was said to the people of Israel: "Hear, O Israel, your God is One." And He is the Father of Jesus, who himself said to the Jews: "My Father, whom you name your God." He is Unity itself, the auto-One, namely, the One-through-itself, although He is better than everything nameable and, as is said below, auto-hypostatic. And we cannot deny that that One understands Himself, since to understand oneself is better. And therefore, He produces His rational ground or definition or Logos from Himself. This definition is the rational ground, in which the necessary One understands itself and everything which can be and is constricted through unity. And the Logos is the substantial Word or rational ground of the defined Father defining Himself, which enfolds in itself everything definable, since nothing can be defined without the rational ground of the necessary One.

Therefore, Christ says: "Just as the Father has life in Himself, so He also gave to the Son to have life in himself." However, in the divine, to have is to be. The Son is therefore the vivifying life, of the same nature and essential being as the Father. And so that you do not hesitate to believe that the Son is the Origin, pay heed to the fact that the Origin, because it is the Origin, is eternal. And because everything which one sees in eternity is eternity, you see that there cannot be the Origin in eternity without the originated in eternity. To see the originated in eternity is, however, to see it in the Origin, whence the originated is the originated Origin. You should also know that one may not consider eternity as some extended duration, but rather must consider it as a totally simultaneous essential being, which is also the Origin.

Therefore, if one considers eternity as the Origin, to say the Origin of the originated is not other than to say the eternity of the eternal or the eternity of the originated. And eternity cannot be other than the eternal. Indeed, eternity cannot be prior to the eternal in duration. Indeed, the eternal is the co-eternal of eternity. Thus the originated is co-eternal with the Origin. For if the Origin is the origin of the originated, and this is the same as if one says that eternity is the eternity of the eternal, it is clearly evident that the originated is eternal.

Therefore, you see the Origin without origin and the Origin from the Origin. However, if you see the Origin both without origin as well as from the origin in eternity, then you see also the originated of that Origin, which you see without origin and from the Origin and thus you see the Origin and the originated Origin. And you see that the originated of the Origin of both is the one essential being of eternity, which Plato called the One.

This does not seem incredible. For we see the origin without origin in temporal nature, namely in paternity, and the originated origin in filiation, and that originated from both, namely the connection of love, proceeding from the origin of both. Because the origin of generation without origin is temporal, the origin from the origin is also temporal. Similarly the first connection of love proceeding from both is also temporal. Indeed, the first friendship or the first natural connection of love is between father and son.

Therefore, we see that this is the case in time, so we believe, not without cause, that it is so in eternity most truly, for time is to eternity as the image to the exemplar; and in a similar manner, that which is in time to that which is in eternity. Hence it is clear that the Word, which spoke to the Jews—as our theme says—is the Origin from the Origin and has not received the name Origin from the created world, but rather was the Origin in eternity, before the world came into existence and has spoken after the constitution of the world in time.

You could say: It disturbs the listener, when you say that there is an Origin of the Origin. Indeed, no philosopher admits this, so that one does not in this way proceed into the infinite, and every search for the truth were sublated, because one could not come to a first Origin. However, I say: It is not at all unsuitable, that in eternity there is an Origin of the Origin. For as whiteness is the whiteness of the white, if the white were whiteness, then nothing were varied, if one were to name the whiteness the whiteness of the whiteness.

However, in eternity it is such that the eternal is eternity and the originated the Origin. Therefore, it is no more unsuitable to speak of the Origin of the Origin than of the Origin of the originated. Nor does the transition into the infinite impede this, since this is in infinite actuality. Indeed eternity, which is everything simultaneously, is nothing except infinite as actuality. However, where the contracted is not the same as the absolute, what the philosophers say is true, namely, that there is no terminus of the terminus, as for example there is no humanity of humanity; for because the infinite cannot be traversed, one can never come to an Origin.

This Trinity, in which the Christians believe, is also acknowledged by the Platonists, who put forth several trinities. And before all of these one eternal, as they indeed place the eternal before everything temporal, for example, the eternal before the temporal man. However, the Peripatetics also speak of a first cause, which they acknowledge is tri-causal. Likewise the Jews attribute to the eternal God the one, the intellect, and the spirit. And the Saracens similarly attribute to the eternal God the one, intellect, and the soul, as is clear from their books. I have indeed spoken about this elsewhere.

Perhaps you still hesitate in understanding our theme and ask yourself, in what way the Word is the Origin. I answer: It is, as you have heard, the essential and self-subsisting Origin from the Origin. And its eternity, which is its essential being, is the Logos or the eternal rational ground of eternity and all things which are enfolded in eternity. And there is nothing which can become possible, which is not the eternal rational ground of its essential being. Everything which does not subsist through itself, since it is not the cause of itself and is also not from chance and fortune, which are only accidental causes and not through themselves and not essential, must therefore be from a cause, which is the self-subsisting rational ground of the essential being of things. Thus the one absolute Exemplar, which is also the eternal rational ground, is the cause of all similitude.

Thus the rational ground of the circle is eternal and self-subsisting and absolute, because it cannot be contracted or sensibly designated. However, every circle can neither be nor be understood without it, and since it is the eternal, intellectual Exemplar of all sensible circles, so universally everything which can be is eternally in the rational ground of the essential being of everything as in the exemplary truth. And it is that which it is through just this rational ground of its essential being.

Hence if you pay heed, then these words of the Gospel, where Jesus says: "the Origin, as which I speak to you," are the light of intelligence itself. Indeed, the Word-Become-Flesh speaks, namely, this Word that is also God, the Origin, speaks sensibly. And it is not difficult to understand that the eternal rational ground of essential being speaks sensibly, in him who is sensible through the Word.

To speak is to reveal or to manifest. Therefore, everything subsisting is, because it is from that which subsists through itself, which is the rational ground of its substance. And its speech is the revelation or manifestation of itself. For example, since everything warmed has its being warmed originally from that which is warm from itself, namely from fire, the fire speaks or reveals itself in everything warmed, although variedly according to the variety of the warmed; more intensively in the pure flame than in the smoking, and more purely in the ignited wood than in the warm ash.

Thus the Logos speaks in everything rationally determined, revealing itself more purely in the seraphic spirits than in the angels and more purely in the angels than in men, and more purely in men whose conversation is in heaven, than in those whose conversation is on earth. However, in Christ, in whom the Logos is, it does not speak out beyond all gradations as in another, but rather as in the purity of the Origin, just as if the fire did not reveal itself in something warmed, but rather in the purest flame, which subsists in indissoluble union in the fire itself.

You could say: Since in the Gospel Christ speaks immediately from his Father, it is astonishing how he, who acknowledges himself as the Son, calls himself the Origin. I answer that, if he called himself the originated, then this expression were not appropriate. For since the Origin is nothing of the originated, in the divine nature, where the Father gives everything to the Son, the Father is not other from the Son. And the Son cannot in a proper sense be called the originated, since the originated is something other than the origin. But just as the Father is the Origin, so He also gives it to the Son to be the Origin. This is therefore the Origin from the Origin, just as Light from Light and God from God.

Furthermore, perhaps you ponder whether auto-hypostatic corresponds to the Word. It appears that it is so. Indeed, in the Gospel the words follow: "Then you will know that I am." However, only the self-subsisting can truthfully say: I am.

I say that in the divine, the human expressions are not precisely suitable. However, just as Christ has spoken concerning the divine in a human manner—for only in a human manner can his words be comprehended by man—we must presuppose that these words of the Gospel presented in a human way are more precise than all others, for here the Word of God speaks concerning himself.

Since the Origin is from no other, we say that it is self-subsisting. If we did not conceive that it is, then we were not capable of conceiving that something is at all. Indeed, the first that offers itself to conception is being, the second being-thus.

Indeed, since the Origin is nothing of the originated, the Origin of being is nothing of entity. Nevertheless we can form no concept for ourselves from this, if we do not conceive that there is the Origin.

However, Plato, who saw the one being, the one possibility of being, the one heaven, the one earth, and in all these saw the One as if passive, contracted, and altered, saw the One in itself and absolute, while he separated and removed everything from the One. And if one sees it thus, then it is neither being nor not-being, neither is it, nor does it subsist, nor is it a subsistent nor a self-subsisting nor the Origin nor indeed the One.

Indeed, the expression "the One is the One" were not even appropriate, because the copula *is* is not suitable to the One. And if one said, without the copula, "the One One," then it were also not an appropriate expression, since every expression, which cannot be produced without otherness or duality, is not suitable to the One.

If you attend to this, then the Origin of everything name-able is unnameable, for it can be nothing originated. And therefore, it can also not be named Origin, but rather the unnameable Origin of the nameable origin, which precedes everything what-ever nameable; thus you see better that the contradictory must be denied of it, so that it neither is nor is not, nor is and is not, nor is or is not. All these locutions do not touch upon the Origin, which precedes everything expressible.

Although this is the case and it is not appropriate to the origin to subsist through itself, since self-subsistence is not known without duality and division, and the One is before every otherness, nevertheless it is more truly suitable to no other than Him, who is the cause of everything subsisting, to subsist through Himself. For in respect to Him nothing caused subsists or is, whatever it may be, through itself.

Indeed, to whom could every signifying word whatever more truly correspond than to Him, from whom they have everything which they are and are called? What substance is truer than that which gives substantial being to every substance, although it is better than every nameable substance?

Plato saw how entity-through-itself exists before every other entity, for example, man-through-himself, the animal-through-itself, etc. Did he not see all that he saw as self-subsistent, not in another, but rather in itself notionally, as this was already treated in a preceding discourse? Thus what he saw in itself notionally, as if in the origin of the notional or the rational entities, which are the similitudes of the real entities, he also saw essentially beyond him in the Author of entities, just as it is in him notionally as in the author of notions.

Therefore, the latter is the universal intellect in itself, who is either the author or assimilator. The author gives essential being, the assimilator understanding. The author sees everything in himself that is, he sees himself as the causative or formative exemplar of everything. Hence his knowing is to create. The assimilating intellect, which is the similitude of the Creator, sees everything in itself. That is, it sees itself as the notional or figurative exemplar of everything. And its knowledge is to assimilate. Hence, as the causing intellect is the form of forms or the species of species or the location of formable species, so is our intellect the figure of figures or the assimilation of the assimilable or the location of figurable species or assimilations.

In order to exercise you further in these reflections, consider attentively, that Christ has said: "Before Abraham was, I am." And in another place: "Before the foundation of the world," and "before the world was" and "before everything," etc. For He is through Himself before all becoming. Indeed how would the self-subsisting be seen after the possible becoming? Who would have led the possible becoming into being? Anyone other than He, who is actual? Therefore, the actual self-subsisting is rightly seen before all possible becoming.

But how can it be seen before possible becoming? For was the future not always already the future? Therefore, the potential-to-become is always present to the self-subsisting. Now, however, since what becomes is temporal, then the potential-to-become temporally is present to the self-subsisting eternally. However, that which is seen eternally in the self-subsisting is certainly eternal. Nothing is before the eternal. Therefore, it is similarly self-subsisting.

Therefore, what becomes in time is self-subsisting in eternity. It is similarly the case, if we say that we will do something. Then this something, before it becomes visible to the others, is in us and we see it in us. And that which is mentally in the word or concept of the mind and is invisible to every other, becomes visible in time. Therefore, everything is clearly from the eternal, in the eternal everything is the self-subsisting eternal, from which everything is which has ever become.

Everything temporal is from the non-temporal eternal. Likewise everything nameable is from the unnameable, etc. Before all time is the eternal, before the before is no before, the absolute before is eternity. Before the world was, the before is seen, but in no way before the before. Therefore, in this before, before the world became, the world is seen not-made, therefore subsisting through itself. Therefore, the world, which is seen before it became, is the self-subsisting before. And the before itself is the self-subsisting world. Therefore, the self-subsisting world is the before, before the world became.

Therefore, from the before, which subsists through itself, everything is made which has been made. It is as if one says, "before the house became." The house which should become is, in any case, already named beforehand, if one says, "before the house became." Therefore, everything which has become, could become, and has been named beforehand. Therefore, it was before in the word, what it became, just as where it is said, "Let there be light and there was light."

The light that became, was already beforehand in the word, before it became, since its name was light. Also the light which has become, has no other name than that which it had before it had become. But before the light became, it was self-subsisting, because it was light, which had to become. Therefore, before everything that is made, is the self-subsisting, just as before the temporal is the eternal.

However, Proclus says that this name, auto-hypostatic, is suitable only to the first as to the cause of self-subsisting things, such as for example the cause of self-subsisting man, because the cause is eternal. Nevertheless, he names the One the King of everything or the God of gods. Indeed, he asserts of the species and the other, which he regards as eternal and hence self-subsisting, that it is enfolded and unfolded in the First as in the cause and in the font in eternity. Just as this is sensible and temporal in the sensible world, so it is eternal and intellectual in the eternal world. And just as he denies that the One, which he asserts is everything, as the cause of everything subsists through itself, but rather is better than and before everything self-subsisting, so he also denies everything other.

For, so he asserts, the One is not, but rather it is before everything which is, and it is not in a place or in time, but rather before everything spatial and temporal, likewise with everything else, because it is before all affirmation and negation. And in this he is right. It is before and better than everything of which one can make affirmative or negative locutions. However, he is not right in the assertion that there could be several co-eternal with it—excepting of course its three hypostases. The eternal and eternity are indeed the same and they cannot be plurified, any less than the One. As the One it cannot be participated in; therefore, it is not a smaller one and multiplicable.

Hence many seem to have been in error in respect to eternity, which they regard as a successive, although infinite, duration. But whoever considers the Origin as eternity and sees that in it, as in the origin and cause, everything is the one Origin itself, sees where the truth is. And he grasps what Parmenides concludes on the path of rational deliberation, namely, that everything must be denied of it and that of opposite expressions the one is no more affirmed than the other or than both, and that there are not many or several self-subsisting things. For either they did not participate in the One and were in this similar and, on the other hand, not similar, because they did not participate in the One; or if they participated in the One, then they would not subsist through themselves, but rather through the One, in which they participated. Therefore, there will not be several subsisting through themselves. For this reason, the many which has become, is that which it is from the self-subsisting. It therefore participates in the One, because the many cannot be without the One, in which it participates. For otherwise it would follow, as we have said previously, that contradictory opposites would be simultaneously true.

However, I have said above that no name is suitable to the self-subsisting, because it is unnameable, inexpressible, and ineffable. Also the name the One is not properly suitable to it. However, because there cannot be many self-subsistents, we form for ourselves concerning it the concept of the One. And the One is that with which we name it according to our concept; and we say that it is the one cause of the universe, which enfolds in itself the species of all things and is exalted above every contradiction, position and opposition, affirmation and negation, since these do not attain the inexpressible, but rather only among the effable divides the true from the false. However, there are no expressions concerning the One, because it is indeterminable. Therefore, Plato says that affirmations and negations are simultaneously untrue in the One.

The One is, therefore, incomprehensible for all senses, for all rationality, opinion, knowledge and all names. Nevertheless we say that God, who is the cause of all, is the more suitable name of the One and the Good, since indeed the One and the Good are desirable by all, just as nothing and evil are fled by all.

However, we name God the One, beyond which nothing better can be thought. And that something could be better than that which is desired by all does not enter into our cogitation. And therefore we say that the One and the Good is God Himself; in Him they are not diverse, but rather are the One itself, which Proclus names the auto-One. Also we do not name God the One as a known, since the One is desirable before all cognition.

Therefore, the comprehension of God is not as that of the cognizable, to which, if one has known it, one gives a name; but rather the intellect, desiring the unknown and, incapable of comprehending it, gives it the designation of the One, since it divines in some way its hypostasis from the unceasing desire of all for the One. However, that God is not acceded to intellectually, Proclus asserts, because then only the intellectual nature would be attracted to Him. For the non-intellectual things would not then strive after Him. However, since God is He, for whose sake all things are what they are, He must be desired naturally by all; indeed He is the One and the Good, after which all strive and which penetrates all entities.

Attend further: As has become clear, there can be no multitude which is deserted by the One. The One is, therefore, its hypostasis. However, the latter is not that one participated in and coordinated with the multitude, since this one does not subsist in itself, but rather in the other, namely in the multitude. However, everything in the other is from that which is in itself. For in-itself is prior to in-the-other, in which it is only otherwise. This otherwise, however, presupposes the in-itself. Therefore, the hypostasis, which is in-the-other, is from that which is in-itself.

Thus the coordinated hypostasis is from the exalted and the participable from the imparticipable.

Everything, therefore, which falls into consideration, is either the One exalted above the multitude or the one coordinated with it. The coordinated one, however, has its hypostasis only from the exalted One. Therefore, the exalted One is the Hypostasis of all hypostases; without its existence nothing would be and through its existence everything is that which it is; and through its existence and non-existence everything exists and does not exist.

Therefore, since the entities desire being, because it is good, they desire the One, without which they cannot be. However, what that is, which they desire, they cannot grasp, since each of the entities is one on the basis of participation in the participable unity, which has its hypostasis from the imparticipable. However, the participable is not able to grasp the imparticipable, just as the graspable cannot grasp the ungraspable, and the caused the cause; and that which belongs to the second is not able to grasp that belonging to the first. However, although it is not able to grasp it, nonetheless it is not fully ignorant of that which it desires so much. It knows most certainly that that exists which it desires.

And the intellectual nature, which knows that it is and that it is incomprehensible, is more perfect, the more it knows it is incomprehensible. For through this knowledge of ignorance one approaches the incomprehensible.

Parmenides attended to this and, in respect to the exalted One, he said that there is only one entity. Indeed, he saw that in the one entity is enfolded all multitude. And since the cause of multitude is the unity, without which it is not able to be, therefore, he put forth, in respect to the uniting cause of unity, that every multitude is the one entity, insofar as one considers the One.

Zeno, who saw in the multitude of entities only the one participated entity, said the many is not that which is entity. Indeed, as the many is not deserted by the one, it therefore subsists because of the one. Therefore, there are many only if the entities participate in the one entity. The one is, therefore, the hypostasis. And Zeno did not want to say the same as Parmenides. For he did not look to the exalted One as Parmenides did, but rather to the participated one. However, on his death-bed he came nearer to the assertion of Parmenides, in that he considered the multitude in the One according to the cause, whereby he could not uphold the one in mere multitude. The One is according to itself before the multitude, the multitude, however, is entirely on account of the One, that which it is.

However, whoever considers that every unity has some sort of multitude connected to it and that every multitude is contained by some sort of unity suitable to it, sees simultaneously the one and the many entities in the unity, the many, and in the multitude, the One, without which neither order nor species nor anything else exists, but rather confusion and formlessness.

It also does not matter if you speak of equality in the same way in which we have spoken of unity, as you have presented it in the foregoing discussion. For equality is unifying and can be called the cause of union. Just as it is with the One, so is it with the Good, justice and such things.

Furthermore, attend to how some philosophers speak concerning duality; they say that it is simultaneously unity and multitude. That is correct in the following way: Just as that which is the cause of union, as cause is one, so is duality as cause multitude. Duality is indeed in every respect the mother of multitude. However, duality is not deserted by the One. For everything which is after the One, participates in the One. Everything posterior participates in the prior and not vice versa.

Duality is not the first unity, which precedes everything and is exalted above everything, but rather it is participated unity. Indeed, it has from unity that it is unity and thus it is to some extent unity and duality. And thus unity appears to be multitude. But it is unity, insofar as it participates in the One, and multitude, insofar as it is the cause of multitude. Thus I understand what some said: Duality is neither unity nor multitude.

However, Plato posited two principles after the One, namely, that of the finite and that of the infinite; as for example number exists after the One from the finite and the infinite. If indeed you consider the unity of number separate from number, then it is the monad and it is not number, but rather it is the origin of number. If you consider multitude deserted by unity, then it is a kind of infinity. Number therefore appears to be constituted from unity and multitude, as if from the finite and infinite. This is the case for all entities. Now Plato takes infinity as the unterminated and confused, that is nevertheless apt to be terminated and defined; the finite, on the other hand, he understands as the form, which defines and terminates the infinite.

And if someone examines more subtly, then the position of the Melian is not so absurd, as Aristotle portrays it. For in every consideration one sees nothing other than infinity, namely, a defining infinity and a definable infinity. The defining infinity is the End, which has no end; it is the Origin subsisting through itself, which enfolds every end. And it is God before every entity. And the definable infinity, on the contrary, is the being free of every terminus and every definition definable through the infinite End. And it is after every entity.

Therefore, when the infinite First defines the second, then the finite entity arises from the infinite Origin, that is, from the First, which is more than the entity, because it precedes it. It does not arise from the second, since the latter is after the entity.

In the first infinite everything definable exists as actuality; in the second infinite everything definable exists in respect to the omnipotence of the first.

If we say, through Omnipotence everything is created from nothing, then that does not mean that in nothing everything is in potentiality—except of course if one refers potentiality to Omnipotence, where the potential-to-make coincides with the potential-to-become; as if you conceive nothing to be the matter of omnipotent form, which forms the matter as it wishes. However, you also conceive, that for the form of the not-omnipotent and finite power nothing is not the matter, but rather that a more formable or less resistant matter corresponds to it, as it is the possibility of essential being. This enables the form to form, as it were, suitable and obedient possibility, so that it merits such a form. This was said by Plato, who was of the opinion that the form was given to the matter according to merit.

And summarizing what has been touched upon, it is manifest that the Origin is triune and is the eternal itself. I say that this world is from the triune Origin what it is. As became clear, there are not many origins. The not-many can only be conceived as the One. Therefore, before this world and the many is the Origin, which is not-many; just as before the many is the not-many, before entity the not-entity, before intellect the not-intellect, and generally before the effable the ineffable.

The negative is therefore the Origin of every affirmation. The Origin indeed is nothing of the originated. But since everything caused is truer in its cause than in itself, therefore the affirmation is better in the negation, since negation is its origin. The Origin, therefore, is equally before the maximum and minimum of every affirmation; as for example the not-entity as the origin of entity. Thus it is seen before the entity, since it is seen superexalted by means of the coincidence of the maximum and minimum. Indeed, it precedes entity, because it is equally the maximum and the minimum entity, or is thus non-entity, so that it is maximally entity. The Origin of entity is not a completely non-existent entity, but rather a not-entity in the manner just explained.

If I look to the Origin of the entity, which is not originated, then I see that it is entity in the minimum degree. However, if I look to the Origin of the entity, in which the originated is better than in itself, then I see it as entity in the maximum degree. However, because the origin is ineffably above all oppositions and everything effable, I see it equally before the maximum and minimum and beyond everything which can be said. Consequently, everything which is affirmed of the entity is therefore equally denied of the Origin in the manner just described.

However, every creature is some entity. The not-many as Origin of everything, therefore, enfolds everything—just as the negative is called pregnant with affirmation, that is, as not-being it does not mean being, as it is signified through being, but rather a better being.

The ineffable Origin is therefore called neither Origin, nor many, nor not-many, nor the One, nor has it any other name, but rather before all that it exists unnameably. For everything that can be named, formed, or designated, presupposes otherness and multitude and is not the Origin. For the unity of every multitude is the Origin. The many cannot be eternal, since, as was said before, the eternal is eternity. The eternal Origin, however, cannot be multiplied. The Origin is neither alterable nor participable, because it is eternity.

There is nothing in this world, therefore, that has similitude with it, since it is neither designatable nor imaginable. The world is, however, the form of the unformable and the designation of the non-designatable. The sensible world is the form of the non-sensible world and the temporal world the form of the eternal and non-temporal. The formal world is the image of the true and unformable world. If I see the Origin by means of contradictions, then I see everything in it. For being and not-being embrace everything, since everything that can be thought or said, either is or is not. Therefore, the Origin, which is before contradiction, enfolds everything which contradiction embraces.

The Origin appears in the equality of opposites. The absolute equality of essential being and non-essential being is not participable, because the participating is other from the participated. Therefore, the equality which is only participable otherwise, is not the equality which is the Origin superexalted above the equal and unequal. Nothing of everything can, therefore, equally be and not be. Therefore, two contradictory expressions concerning the same cannot be verified equally.

Therefore, just as the imparticipable equality is in similitude, every creature participates in the imparticipable Origin in otherness. Since similitude with equality is not equality but rather just its similitude, it can neither be the maximum, in respect to which there can be none greater, nor the minimum, in respect to which there can be none smaller, because it were then not similitude, but rather either nothing or equality. Therefore, equality is participable in similitude, which can be otherwise and varied, greater and smaller.

Since the creature is nothing and has its whole being from the cause, it is the truth in the Origin. Indeed, the origin is the truth of all creatures. Therefore, this world, of which our Master says that He has constituted it, when He said "before the foundation of the world," is not the truth, but rather its Origin is the truth.

On this basis one finds nothing precisely true in the constituted world; here there is no precise equality or inequality or similitude or dissimilitude. The world can indeed not arrive at the precision of the truth, as our Master affirms concerning the spirit of the truth. In the Origin, therefore, which is the truth, everything is the eternal truth. Since the world constituted through the eternal world or the Origin is not constituted in the truth, but rather is posited in the fallibility of variety, it is posited not in the good, which befits God alone without the constituted world, but rather in the malignant.

Someone could say that the world enfolds everything, since it is seen before its constitution. And in fact the constituted world is seen before constitution. "In the beginning was the Word" and the constituted world is constituted through the Word, just as the Word before the designation and the designated Word. Indeed, when the intellect, in which it understands itself, wants to manifest its mental word, it does so through speech or writing or some other sensible designation. The Word before designation is therefore mental. Designated, however, it assumes a sensible species. And thus is the non-sensible constituted sensibly. However, the sensible has no proportion to the non-sensible.

The constituted world is also in a similar manner to the constituting. It is, therefore, clear, that the Origin of the universe is neither the same or otherwise in respect to its creatures, just as the undesignated Word is neither an other nor the same as its designated.

For the first Origin is before all otherness and identity. Likewise, one calls uncolored nature neither black nor white, not because it is deprived of them as material, but through its eminence, since it is their cause.

Thus we deny voice and silence in respect to the soul, not because it has neither voice nor silence, such as wood, but rather because the cause has nothing of the caused.

Indeed, the soul causes this in the besouled. Likewise we deny to the one Origin everything which proceeds from it. And the one Origin, which gives hypostasis to everything, is neither otherwise nor the same but rather superexalted through its eminence.

And in everything constituted by Him, the Creator is not the same as His creatures, just as little as the cause and the caused, however, also not so far removed that He is something other. For there would have to be some origin of Him and the creatures, who constitute a number, since for every multitude a unity is the origin and thus were the first Origin not the first Origin. The Apostle Paul expressed this, when he said: "God is not far from us, for we are in Him and we are moved."

And we name the very first monad a not-numerated—not because it underlies numbers as unterminated matter, but rather since it enfolds in itself all numbers and species of numbers and produces them from itself, and is neither the same nor an other from every species of number—we indeed form for ourselves, according to our capacity, a concept of similitude of the one Origin, although this is still far beneath precision. For it is indeed the one, non-multiplicable Origin, which enfolds and unfolds or produces all multitude; if you add something to it, if you say for example, the one entity, it does not remain the One simply and passes over into multitude.

The many entities have from the first Origin that they are many, from entity, that they are entities. And thus every multitude is a multitude from the One. And a contracted multitude has contraction from the contracted one, just as many entities have this from the One and from one entity.

The entity has from the One what it is. Indeed, if one sublates the One, then nothing remains. And if you pay attention correctly, then an addition to the One is not an addition to the superexalted One, but rather it is a mode of essential being, that is the entity of the entity of the one which is participable and contractible into variety. Likewise I have indeed spoken previously about the imparticipable equality and its participable similitude.

Thus entity is the universal mode of the essential being of participable unity, and life a more special and more perfect mode of the essential being of participable unity. And the intellect is a still more perfect mode. But contractible unity is the similitude and the image of absolute Unity, which is nothing other than its designatability or revelation. And it is to the simply undesignatable, namely to the absolute One, just as the designatable indivisibility of the point is to the indivisible. It is clear that the one entity is to the simply One just as the many, and that it is to the multitude of entities as the monad. In the unity of entity the One appears essentially contracted; and that is not possible without multitude.

But the One is the Origin exalted and expanded beyond all multitude. The one entity collects in itself the multitude of all entities, since no multitude of entities can be deserted by the one entity. And the unity of entity is unfolded in the multitude. The same is true for the life of the living and the intellect of the intelligent and for everything, because all multitude participates in the One and is united to its monad. The multitude of monadic unities, however, is enfolded in the very first One.

The Platonics believed that the one Origin is the very first God, the King of everything; and that there are other gods, who participate first among all entities in unity. Indeed, they ascribe to the very first God universal providence, to the other gods only a partial one. Similarly, we indeed read that angels are placed in command of the realms and that it is given to them to injure the earth and the sea. They even believed that gods preside over the mechanical arts, as for example Vulcan over the art of forging. However, they acknowledged that all gods, whether intelligential, celestial, or earthly possess nothing except that which is given them by the very first God, the King of everything. The ancients called him Jupiter; and in their time he was of all the king most named.

Hence they said everything would be fulfilled by Jupiter. They reduced everything to the one, because a multitude of rulers would be bad, if it is severed from unity. However, to every realm unity gives subsistence and division gives desolation, as the Ruler of all, our King, the Messiah teaches us.

Certainly if there were those gods, then they were new, recent, and created. They would not have been before the foundation of the world. They would exist on account of the world. And since the world is on account of God, we say with Paul, that there is none but one God.

For even if such exist, which are called gods, whether in heaven or on earth, just as there are many gods and many lords, so we nonetheless have only one God, the Father, of whom everything is, and in whom we are. And the one Lord Jesus Christ, by whom everything is and we by him.

And it is he of whom it is said in our theme, namely, the Origin, as which he speaks. To him is given all power which is in heaven and on the earth, to him are subjected all those created gods of whom the named speak, whether forces or powers, since he is the Word of the living God, through which everything is, in which all treasures of knowledge are concealed. Just as we have come through him alone into being and into time, so will we be able to be led through him alone to non-temporal being and to perpetual life on the road, which he has shown us in deed and word; through the Origin, which possesses dominion in everything, Jesus Christ, who be always blessed. Amen.

On Equality: The Life Was the Light of Men

(1 4 5 9)

For the exercise of your intellect, avid for the truth, and for the preparation of your comprehension of theological discourse, I have promised you, Peter, to compose something concerning equality. But my occupation as apostolic legate did not permit me to fulfill this promise more quickly and elegantly.

Therefore, please accept what, with the help of God, the theologian John the Evangelist has made known in the premised words; that God the Father through His consubstantial Word, or His Son, has given being to everything and that the being of everything is in the Word or His Son, who was the life and the light of the rational nature of man, since he was the light, which also is the Word.

He said this so that we would understand, that the Word of God not only brought us into being, but also illuminated us in our rationality. If we accept it, we can be illuminated by that true light and be brought to apprehension of this substantial light, which thus illumines us. Then we will be blessed and happy. For, since our understanding is the noblest life, if the intellect could understand the light of its intelligence, which is the Word of God, it would then attain its own Origin, which is eternal, and also His Son, through whom it has been led to the Origin. And this understanding exists in itself, since the understood and the understanding are not other and diverse things.

Therefore, the intellect will then be in the unity of the light, which is the Word of God; it will not be so unified as the Word of God the Father is united with God the Father, or the Son with the Father in the unity of substance, since the created intellect cannot be united to the uncreated God in the unity of substance, but man is very well unified with man in the unity of human essence. For this reason, therefore, the Word has become flesh, so that man, by means of the man who is the Word and the Son of God, is unified inseparably with God the Father in the realm of eternal life.

This maximum mystery of our Mediator and Savior Jesus Christ is made known to us in the Scriptures of both Testaments. Nevertheless, it is made known to us nowhere more clearly than in the Gospel of John the Theologian, whose mode, although it is inexpressible and incomprehensible, is nevertheless described in the form and enigma of the comprehensible.

However, for those who have wanted to enter faithfully into the joyful tidings and to somehow conceive the mode of this mystery according to human mental powers, it is necessary that they possess an intellect which is exercised maximally in respect to abstractions and the powers of our soul. Therefore, what occurs to me now in respect to this, I want to present to you as briefly as possible.

You have read in my writing *On Beryllus,* how the intellect wishes to be known. I now say that is true not only of the intellect itself but also of the other. And this means nothing other than that the intellect wants to know itself and the other, since its life and its joy exist in its knowing. However, the Master, who is the Word of God, has taught me that seeing and knowing are the same. He says indeed: Blessed are the pure of heart, for they shall see God. And otherwise: This is the eternal life, to know You, God. Furthermore: Who sees me, sees the Father, where seeing is knowing and knowing seeing.

We therefore wish to speak of vision, which coincides with human cognition. As introduction to that which I intend, I premise that otherness can be no form. Indeed, to alter is more to deform than to form. Therefore, that which is seen in the other, can also be seen in itself without otherness, since the otherness has not afforded it being. However, vision which sees the visible in itself removed from all otherness, sees that it is not other from the visible. This "itself" is therefore referred both to the seeing and to the visible, between which there is no otherness in essence, but rather identity. However, something can be seen removed from all otherness. However, that which is thus seen, lacks all matter. Indeed, the subject of alteration is neither nothing nor is it the form which gives being, but rather that which can be formed and which we call *hyle* or matter.

However, in the moment when the intellect sees the intellect in the one and the other intelligible thing and conceives the matter as the subject of alteration, since it sees through the intellect in itself, it also sees that it itself is separated from all matter. And it sees how the intelligence is intelligible through itself, on account of the absent matter, and that everything which is not without matter is not intelligible through itself, but rather must be abstracted from the matter, if it shall be understood. Hence the natural things are less intelligible, since they possess the underlying matter of otherness in greater degree, as is clear from their active and passive qualities. If the matter is abstracted from these, they are no longer natural entities. The objects of mathematics, however, are more intelligible, since their matter is not subjected to such great otherness. It is therefore not subjected to the active and passive qualities, but rather to insensible quantity.

Thus man cannot be seen absolved of all material and sensible quantitative and qualitative contraction. Thus the circle does not appear absolved of all material quantity, even though it is insensible. Only the absolute Entity or One can be seen separate from all quantity and quality, also from the intelligible.

One sees this man, who is Plato, and another, who is Socrates. Man is therefore seen separate from that individual otherness and this vision is not sensible, but rather is absolved of the sensible through the removal of individual contraction. And thus the man does not appear separate from all natural matter, but rather only from the individual, while the universal—namely that he is a man—remains. If I see him thus, absolved of this flesh and these bones, I nevertheless do not see him absolved of flesh and bones, since he were otherwise not a natural man. And hence the man whom I see in this way is universally absolved of the individual and the man is known in such vision through the higher cognitive power, in respect to the sensitive, however, through the inferior, in respect to the intellective part. And this is connected to the organs and is found also in animals. It is called imaginative.

We see indeed, that dogs know men in general and a certain man in particular. Likewise man sees this figure and that one separated from individual contraction, nevertheless not separated from all matter, since he does not see the figure except as extended. However, quantitative extension supposes matter. And this vision occurs by means of rationality, which is only partially contracted over to the organ.

One can also see the intellect of Plato and Aristotle in their books and it is an intellect separated from all contraction and quantitative or qualitative matter. This vision occurs through the supreme separated simplicity of the soul, which is called the intellect or mind.

However, everything that is seen otherwise in another, appears identical with the soul of the seeing through that which is in itself. However, man sees that the sense is another in vision, another in hearing, etc. He thus sees that the sense, which he sees existing in the other otherwise, is in himself without that otherness, identical with the rational soul. And so he sees the sense in the other through the sense in himself, which is universal and absolved of the individual contraction. In this way, he sees rectitude in the one, and the other upright through rectitude in itself, the form in the formed through the form in itself, and justice in the just through justice in itself, and generally the knowable-extrinsic through the consubstantial-intrinsic.

From this it appears how the intelligible-extrinsic comes into actuality through the intrinsic, although the intellectual presupposition or origin generates its word, its rationality, or its concept from itself. This were its consubstantial similitude, since it were the rational ground of the intellectual nature as well as the intellectual presupposition in which the form of its substance, i.e., the origin or the presupposition is clarified. Without such rationality it would remain the unknown presupposition in relation to itself and to everything. From this the love of both or the will proceeds. For love follows cognition and the known— nothing unknown is indeed a beloved—and love radiates in its rational works, i.e., in the syllogism, and here above all in the first mode of the first figure.

If, for example, the soul wishes to show that every man is mortal, it argues as follows: Every rational living being is mortal. Every man is a rational living being, therefore, every man is a mortal living being. The first proposition is the origin or the presupposition. The second, generated from the fecundity of the first, is the rational ground or the notion of its fecundity. From both follows the intended conclusion. As the first proposition is universally affirmative, so is the second also, so also the third. And none is more or less universal than the other. Therefore, the universality in them is equal without otherness. Thus it is also not contained more in the first substance than in the second or third. For the first embraces every rational living being. Likewise the second and third. Indeed, the second, which speaks of man, does not embrace less, even if only man is a rational living being. Therefore, those three propositions are equal in their universality, essence, and power. Hence they are not three universalities, nor three substances or essences or powers. Indeed, because of the total equality there is no otherness of substance in them, according to all our apprehension, although we know no other rational living being than man.

Nevertheless, the first proposition is the first and thus subsisting through itself. Likewise the second is the second and third the third, so that the one is not the other. However, the second unfolds the entire nature, substance, and fecundity of the first—just as the figure of its substance—so that, were we to name the first Father, the second would have to be named the only-begotten Son, since he, of equal nature and substance, in nothing inferior or unequal, was generated from the fecundity of the first. It is similar with the third proposition, which is the intended conclusion of both. The first proposition resembles memory, since it is the presupposed beginning, which precedes in the manner of the origin; the second resembles the intellect, since it is the notional unfolding of the first proposition; the third resembles the will, since it proceeds from the intention of the first and second as a desired end.

Therefore, in the unity of the essence this syllogism of three propositions, which are equal in everything, reflects the essential unity of the intellective soul as if in its logical or rational work. For by virtue of the premised rule, the rational soul sees itself in the syllogism as in its rational work in the otherness of this work.

It sees itself without that otherness in itself. And through this vision of itself in itself it sees itself in work. And thus you have the explanation how the soul advances through itself to everything other, and how it finds in all the variety nothing intelligible that it had not found in itself, so that everything is its similitude. And in itself it sees everything in greater truth than in the other, which is outside. And the more it egresses towards the other, in order to know it, the more it ingresses into itself, in order to know itself. And while it thus occupies itself through the intelligible peculiar to it sufficiently thereby to measure and attain the intelligible other, it thereby measures the intelligible peculiar to it or it measures itself.

The soul therefore sees the truth, which it sees in the other, through itself. And it is the notional truth of the cognizable, since as intellective soul it is true notion. In intuitive vision it illuminates everything through itself and measures and judges through its notional truth the truth in the other. And through the truth, which it finds otherwise in the other, it reverts back to itself, in order to intuit what it saw otherwise in the other, in itself without otherness truly and substantially, since it perceives everything notionally in itself as though in a mirror of truth and thus understands itself and the notion of all things.

The soul sees the terminus in everything terminated and since there is no terminus of the terminus, it sees itself without otherness as unterminated notional terminus. And thus it sees that it is neither extended nor divisible, therefore also not corruptible.

The soul is therefore interminable rational terminus, through which it terminates everything as it wishes, in that it forms a shorter or longer terminus, nearer or further from the first. And it thus makes the long line short and short long. And measuring, it forms concepts of length, breadth, depth, time, and of everything continuous. And it forms figures and such things, which cannot arise without a rational terminator. And thus it imposes termini or names on the terminated, and creates arts and sciences.

It unfolds all this from the notional power peculiar to it and judges everything through itself, as for example, when it passes judgment on the justice of causes on the basis of its notional justice, which is consubstantial with it, since it is the rational ground of justice, through which it judges between the just and the unjust.

If the soul sees that it has in itself the whole notion of the world, which enfolds the notions of the whole world, then it sees in itself that it is the Word or the notional concept of the universe and the name of all names, through which it forms a notion of every name. And it sees that all names unfold its name, since these names are nothing but the notions of things. And this is because the soul sees that it itself is named with all names.

The soul sees also that it is timeless time. For it perceives that time is in transmutable being and there is transmutation only in time. It perceives therefore, that time is always other in the temporal. Consequently, it sees that the time in it, removed from all otherness, is timeless. If it therefore sees that number is in the various numbers, it also sees that the all-numerating, innumerable number is in it.

And thus it sees that the time in it and the number in it are not other and diverse. And if it sees time contracted in the temporal and in itself absolved of contraction, then it sees that time is not eternity, which is neither contractible nor participable. Hence the soul also sees that it is not eternity, since it is time, although timeless. It sees therefore, that it is temporally incorruptible beyond the temporal in the horizon of eternity, however, not simply, as eternity, which is simply incorruptible, since incorruptibility precedes all otherness. Hence the soul sees that it is conjoined to the continuous and the temporal. Therein indeed are the operations which it effects with help of the corruptible organs, as for example perception, ratiocination, deliberation and the like, successive and temporal. And it sees, however, that it is absolved of the continuous in the work of the intellect, which is separate from the organ, since while it understands, it understands suddenly. And thus it finds itself between the temporal and the eternal.

However, it sees that the soul of the one, which is more strongly conjoined to the continuous and to time or to succession, comes to the intellect more slowly, whereas the soul of the other comes more rapidly thereto, since it is less immersed in the continuous. The latter frees itself therefrom more rapidly, and having organs better suited for its operations, attains it more precisely. Hence it sees that our soul, because of its imperfection, has need of organs and temporal succession, so that it can come from potentiality to actuality. Therefore, the more perfect intelligences, which are in actuality and are not subjected to the necessity of running to and fro, in order to attain actuality, come closer to eternity and are more strongly separated from temporal succession.

However, how it is with the vision of time, consider in the following: The Hebrews say that the beginning of time is the past, after which comes the present, and the future follows. If you look at the past as time gone by, you see that it is past in the present and in the future will be past. If you look at the present, you see that it was present in the past and will be present in the future. If you look at the future, you see that in the past it has been future and in the present is future and in the future will be future. And the soul, which is timeless time, sees all this in itself. It sees itself therefore as timeless triune time, as past, present, and future. However, the past time, which always is and will be past, is perfected time. Likewise the present time, which always was and will be present, is perfected time. Thus also the future, which always was and is future, is perfected time. And there are not three perfected times, but rather one perfected time, perfected in the past, perfected in the present, and perfected in the future.

This time will never be able to pass away. The past as past does not vanish, because it always is and will be past, just as little do the present and the future. Therefore, there is nothing new in that timeless time, where nothing is past that were not also present or future, although the past has indeed passed in the past and the future is not yet in the future, but rather only the present exists in the present; however, otherwise in the past and future time, as previously stated.

Therefore, the soul, which is timeless time, in its essence sees the past and future as present and names the past memory, the present intellect, and the future will. For that presupposed in the intellectual nature or the that-it-is, is the origin, which generates from itself the intellect or what-it-is of its presupposition or its that-it-is, which the intended end follows, which is called will or delectation.

Therefore, everything is in the that-it-is and that mode of essential being is called intellectual memory. Everything is in the what-it-is and that mode of essential being is called intellect, since it, as it is there, is in its rational ground and is understood. Everything is in the intended end and that mode of essential being is called will or desire.

This consideration of timeless time makes manifest that the soul is the similitude of eternity and that it intuits everything through itself as through the similitude of eternity, while it itself aims towards the eternal life, which it alone desires; just as the intellectual image of life or of eternal rest strives for its truth, whose image it is and without which it can find no rest. Indeed, the image of rest rests only in rest.

Therefore, what the soul finds in itself in respect to the perfection of its essence—namely the unitrinity of timeless time and the generation of the second, which succeeds the first time, and the procession of the third from both; the equality of nature in the three hypostases of timeless time and the existence of one hypostasis in the other, etc.—that it transfers to its Origin, which is eternal, in order to be able somehow to intuit this Origin in itself as though in a mirror and enigma.

And this intellect of the soul, through which it understands to enfold the world notionally in itself as if in the universal light of the rationality of the eternal light, which is the cause of itself and all things, is only organized to turn itself to the investigation of its cause and that of everything by means of itself in itself, in that it knows that everything is enfolded in it notionally or assimilatively and that its notion is not the rational ground or the cause of things, so that they are actually what they are. And it says: In my cause, which reflects in me, the caused, so that I am a notional enfolding of the world, the eternal, essential enfolding of all causable things is necessarily fully adequate, as in the rational ground of the essential being, and likewise the knowing of all things and each singular thing; in the similitude of this universal cause I participate through His Grace in the intellectual being, which consists in the universal similitude of the essential being and knowing of the universal cause.

In me the rational power of the universality and omnipotence of this cause is reflected, so that I can come nearer to it, intuit it in myself as its image, through the transcendence of myself in contemplation. Indeed, so that I see myself in everything, I separate the otherness from everything. However, in order to be able to see my cause, I must abandon myself as caused and as image, otherwise I would not attain the living rational ground of my rationality. However, as this is explained in the Gospel, the doctrine of Christ the Son of God, who upon this road promised us the revelation of His Father, aims at this, so that the soul, which pants for the vision of God and His rational ground, abandons this world and itself.

However, in response to some who said that the soul is harmony, we answer: In respect to harmony, which is seen in regard to much harmonic concordance, the soul sees that it is in it. And the consonance is seen first, then its rational ground. And from this the delectation is seen as consequence. One sees the harmonic consonance as the that-it-is and the presupposed and as that which generates from itself number or the rational ground, in which it understands or intuits itself as in the figure of its substance. The delectation arises from both.

Thus, for example, the rational ground of that harmonic consonance, which is called the octave, is a double habitude, in which proportion the octave, if it were intellect, would know and see itself as in its fully adequate and consubstantial rational ground, which is the figure of its substance, in which it knows what it is. For if one asked about the harmony of the octave, in which it is known, one would have to say that this occurs in the double habitude. In this the octave indeed knows itself as in its concept or its rational Word. Accordingly, if the octave were the practical intellect and wanted to make itself sensible in musical instruments, then it would do that by means of its peculiar and consubstantial rational ground, in which it knows itself, i.e., by means of the double habitude.

And what has been said of the octave is true universally of harmony absolved of every octave, fifth, and fourth contraction, as it is seen in itself. In this the harmonic concordance is memory, the rational ground of concordance intellect, and from both proceeds delectation, which is will.

The soul therefore attains all sensible harmony in otherness through itself, just as it attains the extrinsic through the intrinsic. That is to be said universally of all mathematical and other science.

Indeed, through the Word, by means of which it attains itself, it also attains everything else. And if the mathematical circle were the memory, which attains itself in its rational ground, namely, that it has a center equidistant from the circumference, then it would know itself in this rational ground and all formable circles, which one could form by means of this rational ground, whether iron or bronze, large or small.

Therein the soul sees as in an enigma, that the eternal Origin of creation creates everything creatable in eternity by means of the rational ground of its notion. Thus, if entity were the Origin of creation, then it would create every entity by means of the rational ground of its entity, as this is expressed by John the Theologian in regard to the Logos or the rational Word of the Origin, through which, as he asserts, everything is made.

And if you attend to how the rational ground of the quiddity of the entity is also the rational ground of every formable entity, and that that rational ground is before otherness, namely, where the universal and particular are not other and diverse, but rather coincide, then you see that the rational ground of things is in such a manner the universal, that it is also the rational ground of every particular.

Indeed, everything somehow formable is not formable outside of that rational ground and is nothing other in the rational ground than the rational ground. Therefore, conceive the rational ground of the formable and the formable as the same. Then you see how one and the same rational ground is the rational ground of everything formable, since just as it is the rational ground universally of everything and at the same time of every single formable thing, so also is it universally everything and at the same time any formable thing whatever, for in it they are the same. The creature, however, which goes forth from that rational ground, cannot be such that its rational ground and its formability are the same. For then it were not creature, but rather the Word of the Creator. Since, however, it takes its departure according to its rational ground and its peculiar formability, it is not the Word, but rather its similitude, in that it goes forth according to its peculiar rational ground and its formability, which are in the Word the Word.

It is thereby as if the absolute grammar were the intellect, which would know itself in its precise rational ground or definition. In it, it would also know everything that could be known or extrinsically said or made known through speech, because that rational ground universally and in particular would enfold in itself all such knowable and expressible things; so that nothing could be said grammatically, without it having to be said according to that rational ground and that expressibility, which coincides with the rational ground; every statement would therefore go out into the sensible world according to its peculiar rational ground and its expressibility, which were in the rational ground of the grammar of its rational cause, i.e., just as they were in the rational ground or the Word of the grammar. I say "as they were in the Word," since they could not go forth otherwise, i.e., through otherness, which is not the form of essential being, but rather, just as they were in the Word the Word. Produced in this way, it is the true Word, since it is in conformity with the inner or mental Word. Indeed, it has gone forth from the inner Word such that, as it was the inner Word, so also it is the produced Word.

However the Spirit, without which such a procession cannot occur, proceeds from the Father of the Word and from the Word. And it is consubstantial with them, since co-eternal. Indeed, it precedes the creature as the will precedes the extrinsic speech as the cause of this speech, which is tri-causal, efficient, formal, and final. About which elsewhere.

Concerning what has been said about the grammatical art, elevate yourself to the absolute Mastery, in which all art and science are enfolded. And you will see that it is similar with the rational ground of this mastery to what you have heard in regard to the rational ground of grammar. It is similar also in regard to the Spirit, without which there is no inner motion and consequently no expression of mastery in intelligible as in sensible creatures.

You say: How shall I see it, when the great Augustine says that the soul as the image of the Trinity has memory, from which the concealed intelligence is generated, and the will proceeds from both of these? I say that the intellectual memory is the origin of notions, but that it only appears, if it be known, just as it also does not become apparent that you have memory from the first principle—something is or is not—unless it were manifested in the rational light. For if it be manifested to rationality, then one sees at once that it has always been true and finds accordingly, that it had always been in the memory, but that it has not become apparent, except in self-manifesting rationality. Hence the memory as origin generates from itself its intellect, just as the memory from the first principle generates its notion from itself, i.e., that the soul is said to be the location or the folding together of the species.

However, the intellective memory is separated from matter. And on account of this immunity it can reflect upon the intelligible species and understand them. And because it knows what it understands, as befits the intelligence, it is followed by the will.

However, the peculiarity, which follows the soul, as far as it retains the intelligible species, is called memory. However, that, by means of which it applies itself to intelligible species in cognition, is called intelligence. But that, by means of which it strives for the intellectual species, is called will. Therefore, those who said that our learning is reminiscence did not speak wrongly, insofar as they could see this hidden intellectual memory.

To this I say: Do you not discover that the soul is memory, if you see in it the memory which you have seen in the one and the other memorable thing? The same is true of the intellect in the thought and in itself and of the will in the willed and in itself. You see in this way, that the soul is in itself memory, intellect, and will. However, if you see memory in its rational ground, in which it knows itself, then you also see that it knows everything memorable in the very same rational ground. It is therefore apparent that nothing is knowable unless it is remembered. Therefore, if memory knows itself and only the memorable is knowable, then it knows everything knowable, when it knows everything memorable in itself.

Therefore, the intellect reveals a hidden memory, since the intellect is nothing but the intellect of memory. And the will is nothing but the will of the memory and of the intellect simultaneously. Indeed, what is not found simultaneously in the memory and the intellect, can also not be in the will. But you say: It appears as if you now speak differently than above, where you have attributed the that-it-is to the memory and the what-it-is to the intellect. However, the that-it-is is seen sooner than the what-it-is. Therefore, how do you now say that the intellect reveals the memory?

I say: Because the that-it-is is seen earlier, but it is not understood except by means of the intellect. It is seen earlier in the memory, but as it is seen there, it is the that-it-is and not the what-it-is. However, one says that it is intellectually hidden as long as it is not seen in its rational ground, in which it alone is understood. Indeed, outside the light of intelligence one is ignorant of what everything is. And since the intellective soul lives in its intellect, as long as it does not understand it in itself, it does not find something vitally, but rather it is hidden from it, just as sensible vision, as long as it is only perceived audibly, remains hidden to the sight, until it sees it.

However, you must take heed not to let yourself be impeded by the variety of modes of expression. For the learned often name the intellectual memory intellect, as when they say that the intellect generates the concept of its intelligence, or the Word, from itself. You understand that the intellect is conceived as Father, who is the intellectual memory. The intellect is also understood as the intellect of someone, namely, of the memory, just as the Son is understood as the Son of someone, namely, of the Father. And thus the intellect is the Word of the intellectual memory, which is called Logos in Greek.

Do you not say that the Word understands itself? And if it thus understands itself in the Word or the Logos generated from it, will there then not be a Word, that generates the Word into infinity? I say: Just as the memory understands itself in its Word, the Word also understands itself in memory, so that the memory is not the Word of the Word. Likewise the Son also understands himself in the Father of the Son, not as generated from himself, but rather as in his Origin.

Therefore, the memory understands itself and everything in the Word generated from it. The Word, however, understands itself and everything in the generating, since it is the Word or the generated intellectual rational ground, which enfolds everything in itself—just as the Father knows Himself in His Son as Father and the Son knows himself in his Father as Son.

You are astonished at how the Word knows itself without the conception of itself or without the Word generated from it, since understanding is not possible without conceptions. However, if you attend to the fact that conception is common to the generating and the generated—indeed, the generating Father cannot know Himself as Father except in the concept of the Son generated from Him and the Son cannot know himself as Son except in the concept of the Father generating him—then conception in the Son does not bespeak generation as in the Father, but rather being generated. Hence the Father does not possess it from the Son, that He knows Himself, even though He does not know Himself as Father without the Son. However, since He knows naturally, He generates him naturally from Himself. Without him, He would neither understand Himself, nor anything else, nor could He be understood. Therefore, He generates from His intellectual substance the consubstantial Word, in which He understands Himself and everything. The Word is therefore that without which neither the Father nor the Son nor the Holy Spirit, nor angels, souls, and all intellectual natures can understand anything whatever. And it is sufficient for all intelligent beings that they understand. And the Word, which is sufficient in itself and everything, does not need to generate the Word from itself, since every Word that can be generated is equal to the generating, eternal, and infinite Father. The Word therefore knows everything in itself, since it is the Word of the Father, in which the Father knows Himself and everything. The Father knows Himself and everything in the Word, because He is the Father of the Word. The Word knows itself and everything, since it is the Word of the Father.

However, I say that it is sufficiently established from the aforesaid, that the one speaking, if he understands the Word, which he produces, understands the sensible, extrinsic Word by means of the insensible, intrinsic Word; and it is that intrinsic Word, which has been generated from its intelligence, i.e., the concept of rationally determined intelligence, in which the intellect understands itself and the extrinsic speech. Supposing now, the intellect of the one speaking is absolute equality, then the rationally determined Word of equality, in which it conceives itself, is the simple, i.e., inalterable concept, to which something can neither be added nor something subtracted. In this concept or Word, equality intuits its quiddity. And through this Word it understands all its extrinsic speech of equality and does all the work of equality. And although no nameable name can befit the first Origin, since it precedes all otherness—all names in fact are imposed to distinguish the one from the other and therefore distinction and name cannot advance to the Origin, which pre-

cedes otherness—equality is nevertheless the name of the first
and eternal Origin, if it is taken for the absolutely inalterable,
which precedes all otherness in being and potential, so that without it something neither is nor can be nor can it admit any
mutation whatever, whether in more or in less or otherwise,
since all this, which can be said or named or conceived, comes
after it.

However, we add on account of our infirmity, that it is
intellectual equality, although it is infinitely more than intellectual, and say that the most perfect Origin, which is equality,
certainly understands itself and what it does. Indeed, no one
doubts that this is the case for every rational worker. Indeed, the
house builder understands himself to be such and knows what
he does. Indeed, if the Creator of the creature did not know
Himself as Creator and what He creates, then the creature were
no more creature than not creature, the heaven were no more
heaven than not heaven, etc.

If, therefore, absolute equality is the same as the Creator of
heaven and earth, then it knows that it is equality and it knows
all that it makes. It will then be in fact necessary that the Word
of its knowledge, in which it knows itself, be the equality of
itself. Indeed, equality cannot form another Word or another
concept of itself than that of equality. Therefore, the rational
ground of equality, through which it knows and which we attempt to express as the inalterable, is nothing other than the
definition or figure of its substance. Therefore, its equality is the
equality of equality. It follows therefore, that equality is one,
which is equality and equality of equality. Therefore, equality
generates from itself the Word, which is its equality. From both
proceeds connection, which is equality. This connection we name
the Spirit of charity, since from the generating equality and the
generated equality only equality can proceed, which is called
connection or love. And if it is designated as absolute, then
equality is charity. Therefore, the intellectual charity generates
from itself the concept of its essence, which can be nothing except
the charity of charity, and from both nothing can proceed except
charity, which is the connection of both.

However, there cannot be three equalities, since if the one
were one and the other another, then the other were not before
otherness, where equality alone can be. Hence it is impossible

that there be several entirely equal things, since the many can only be otherwise and distinct in essence. Therefore, there will not be several equalities, but rather before all plurality there will be equality, which generates the Word, the generated equality, and the equality which proceeds from both.

And although the generating equality is neither the generated nor the proceeding, the generating is nevertheless no other equality than the generated equality and the proceeding equality. Therefore, the number with which we count the generating equality, the generated equality, and the proceeding equality, is no number intelligible to us, since it is before otherness; for we do not see number in the counted without otherness, unless we consider the number in itself and before the numerable-other, where the three precedes the three. Indeed, we name that three which we count through three, and we name the number three through which we count the three. The number is not dependent on the counted. Therefore, the number is in itself in relation to us nothing other than the soul, as mentioned above. The number in the absolute equality is nothing except the generating, generated, and proceeding equality. In equality they are the number, which is equality. And there are not three numerically equal things, but rather three subsistences or hypostases of equality.

Indeed, we see that it is first necessary that we affirm that the first, most perfect Origin before otherness is eternal, and that it therefore can never do without knowledge of itself and its work. And therefore, we necessarily affirm that it is triune and that, although it exceeds our entire concept, the one Origin is trine before otherness and the numerable. Hence it follows, that equality creates everything through its Word or its rational ground. Therefore, all things exist insofar as they participate in the rational ground of equality. However, that no two completely equal things are found, has its basis in the fact that two things cannot participate in equality equally.

There is therefore nothing that does not partake in equality, since the rational ground of equality is the form of essential being, without which nothing can subsist. The quiddity of everything that is is therefore equality, through which everything which is is neither more nor less, but rather that which subsists. It is the rational ground of essential being for everything equal. On this basis the quiddity cannot admit more or less, since it is equality.

Therefore, nothing of all that is is multiplicable, since everything is, insofar as it participates in the rational ground of equality, in which the many cannot participate equally.

Entity is therefore unmultiplicable equality. Likewise is substance, living being, humanity, every genus, every species, and every individual. Individuality is indeed unmultiplicable equality. And nothing is true except insofar as it participates in the unity or the rational ground of equality, nor in like manner is it just, virtuous, good, or perfect.

Every science and art is founded in equality. The rules of law or the rules of grammar or whatever else are nothing other than participation in the rational ground of equality. Indeed, reducing the diversity of stellar motions to equality is the science of astronomy. Reducing the diversity of grammatical connections to a rule is the science of grammar, etc. No name has any truth whatever in its signification, except in the equality of the signifying and the signified. Thus also every art is founded in equality, as for example the art of painting, in the equality of the sign and the signified of image and exemplar. Thus medicine looks to the equality of combination. Justice is founded in the rule of equality: "What you wish to be done to you, do to the other."

If one takes away equality, then prudence ceases, temperance ceases, and every virtue, since this consists in the mean, which is equality. Without equality truth is not understood, which is the adequacy of thing and intellect. Also there is neither life, nor being, nor time, nor motion, nor continuity without equality. Indeed, motion is nothing except the continuation of rest. And what is rest, if not equality? It is likewise the case with the now, since time is nothing other than the continuation of the now. And what is the now, if not equality, which can be neither greater nor smaller? Likewise the line is nothing other than the evolution of the point. What is the point if not equality? And so you see that, except in equality, nothing can subsist at all.

Indeed, in everything that is, insofar as it is, the rational ground of equality is reflected. And this rational ground is neither multiplicable, alterable, nor corruptible, since it is the adequate rational ground of all essential being, which were not the adequate rational ground, if it were not the rational ground of absolute equality. The rational ground or the adequate measure of everything is therefore one, namely, equality. This rational ground of equality is neither greater nor smaller than everything measurable; thus the one rational ground of the circle is the precise and adequate rational ground of all possible circles, wherefore they are neither more nor less than circles, whether they are among themselves equal or unequal in respect to quantity and other accidents.

Concordance, peace, and order are the equality, through which all things are and are preserved. Likewise beauty, harmony, delectation, love, and such things are equality. You cannot see several unequal things without equality. For, that they are unequal, in this they are in accord. However, concordance and similitude—what are they other than equality? Likewise delectation, friendship, and the like applaud the like on account of equality. And although unity appears to be the father of equality, since equality is unity taken once—as shown elsewhere—nevertheless absolute equality enfolds unity. For that which is equal is in one mode.

Indeed, in unity one sees nothing except equality. Thus the good, since it is the fullness of its diffusion, has this from nothing other than equality. And on account of equality it is desired equally by all. Everything is indivisible from itself on account of the indivisible equality of each thing to itself. And each thing is a mode of participation in equality, as is manifest, if it is said that quantity participates in absolute magnitude, that the quantitatively extended line is such a mode of participation in magnitude, namely, according to length, that the surface is such according to width, the body according to depth, and the figure according to the externally limiting surface, and the circle according to the circular figure, and the sphere according to the spherical figure, and the cube according to the cubic figure; and it is the case for infinitely varied such things participating in magnitude by means of quantitative extension. Now this magnitude is nothing other than participation in equality. Therefore, man is similarly nothing other than a certain mode of participation in living being. Likewise are the lion and the horse. Living being is participation in equality. Equality in fact enfolds equally every mode of essential being, whether the elemental, vegetative, animal, rational, or intellectual. However, it is participated in in the other otherwise, since equal participation is impossible. Therefore, equality is equally present to all, but it is not received equally, just as the solar ray is equally present in a meadow to all grasses, however, is not received equally, so that the grasses are nothing but various modes of reception of the vigor of the solar ray, which is participated in by them.

Is it not so, that if one removes equality, nothing is understood, nothing is seen, nothing subsists, nothing endures? Indeed, the more equal a combination, the more sound, the more perfect, the more durable it is. Equality itself is eternal duration. Equality, which is life, is eternal life. The intellect of the intellect is life, life consists of equality. Therefore, if the soul, which examines all, sees that nothing remains with the removal of equality, it concludes that everything is from it, through it, and in it.

If you exercise your intellect in such deliberations and apply yourself not to the words but rather to the mental intention, you will penetrate more precisely much that was always previously hidden from you. For that which you read concerning the Trinity in the Holy Scriptures and among the learned, who explain the latter—that the Son and the Holy Spirit are as the Father and that the Son is equal to the Father, and similarly the Holy Spirit, and that the person of the Father is one, of the Son and of the Holy Spirit others—you will certainly grasp with better and firmer faith, if you reflect upon what has been said concerning equality. Also you will better see what is the most difficult of all difficult things, namely, to understand how there will be a Trinity before all otherness, if you attend to how three equal persons are not equal through something accidental, but rather through essence, since they are equal without otherness. Thus, they are nothing except the same unmultiplicable equality. Since this is not accidental to the persons or participated in by them, it is that which each person is essentially. And where nothing is other than unmultiplicable equality, there can be no otherness.

Hence, when one reads that one person is that of the Father, another that of the Son, another that of the Holy Spirit, then one cannot understand that as were it another on the basis of the otherness, which that Trinity precedes. And if we want to see that through which the person of the Father is one, of the Son another and of the Holy Spirit another, we find nothing except the equality, which stands before otherness. Hence if I say: The equality, which is the Father, is the Father; the equality, which is the Son, is the Son; and the equality, which is the Holy Spirit, is the Holy Spirit, I say one and the same. Nevertheless, I have spoken about nothing except the one, unmultiplicable equality. For it is not true that the equality, about which I first spoke when I said, "the equality, which is the Father, is the Father," is another, or is not that of which I said secondly, "the equality, which is the Son, is the Son," and of which I said thirdly, "the equality, which is the Holy Spirit, is the Holy Spirit."

And since I see that these propositions are true before otherness, where the Father is not other than equality, and likewise nor is the Son, nor the Holy Spirit, it is the same as if I said: The equality, which is the Father is the Father, as also: The equality is the Father, since it is the Father. And I see then that that proposition, "equality is the Father, since it is the Father," is true. And I see that that proposition, "equality is the Son, since it is the Father," is not equal to the prior one or equally true. And on this basis I affirm that the Father is neither the Son nor the Holy Spirit, even though they are one and the same equality before all otherness. And I help myself with a concept, which I have gained from that equality, which I have advanced in respect to time, the soul, and the syllogism.

Therefore, with an intellect exercised in the ideas advanced, direct yourself to the most sacred Gospel and consider how John the Evangelist wrote his Gospel for the purpose of strengthening the faith, that Jesus is the Son of God and that those who believe in his name have life; and that he heard Christ say to God the Father: Father, glorify me, with Yourself, with that glory, which I had with You before the world was made. Furthermore: If you knew me, you would know my Father also. And again: Who sees me, sees the Father. And elsewhere: Whatever the Father has, is mine, and everything which is mine is yours and everything which is yours is mine. And: I am in the Father and the Father is in me. He also said: I am come a light into the world, that whosoever believes in me, should not abide in darkness. And elsewhere: I proceeded forth from the Father and came into the world. And again: The speech which you hear is not mine, but His who has sent me, the Father's. And to the Father he said: Your word is the truth. He said also that he is the way, the truth, and the life and that no man comes unto the Father but by him;

and that the Father gave him power over all things of the flesh, that he may give them life. And that which He gave him is greater than everything; He placed everything in his power and gave him all power of judgment, since he is the Son of man. He called himself the Son of God and said that the Father, abiding in him, does the works which he also does and which no one before him has done, and that his works give witness that the Father has sent him. That he is the life and the resurrection and the living bread, which gives eternal life, and still more of the like, John heard and wrote down.

Before this narration, John advanced his all-resolving theology, showing how all this can be seen as true, by saying: "In the beginning was the Word." For in the beginning, even before God the Father made something, that had to be, without which nothing has been made. But nothing has been made by God, the wisest Father and Creator of all things, without the Logos, which is the rational ground or the Word. The Logos was therefore in the beginning, even before anything whatsoever was made. And it was nowhere else but with God. And since it was nothing other, it was also not with God as something other, but rather it was the same: God and the Word.

Hence the necessity is evident, that God the Father and Creator did not have another rational Word, but rather one consubstantial with Him, i.e., the consubstantial Word or rational ground or notion, in which the cognition of Himself and everything creatable was. And since this Word was consubstantial and of the same nature with the Father or Creator from whom it was, just as the notion of the thing from the thing, it was therefore the Son. Indeed, that generated in the same nature with the generating is the Son. And this explains what Christ said to the Father: Glorify me with that glory which I had with You, before this world was made, i.e., may it become clear, that I am Your consubstantial Son. This Word was, as the Evangelist says, in the beginning with God, since God was the Word with God, such that it was God. And thus he concludes that the Logos has been with God before every creature. Indeed, the pure intellect is never without its notion. Likewise the eternal God the Father was never without this consubstantial Son.

It follows: Everything has been made through him, since the intellectual work does everything through the rational ground, which is its Word. As stated above, it is one and the same rational ground, in which the Creator creates and knows Himself and everything else. I have given the example of the circle therefor. And everything has been so made that without it nothing has been made, since this Word is the most precise rational definition and determination of everything creatable and intelligible, so that if something had been made or were to be made by God without the Logos, this were not made rationally. To say this of God, the wisest, were a blasphemy. Thus, for example, everything regal is effected through the order of a most wise king, which is disclosed through word or speech. And this speech is nothing other than the rational ground—the word of the wisest king does not therefore participate in the rational ground, but rather is itself the rational ground and truth. Thus also the heavens are established through the Word and nothing through the silence of the Lord.

However, since everything creatable was necessarily in the consubstantial Word as in the vivifying, concluding rational ground; moreover, since the rational ground is the living life, so also everything which has been made through it was in the Word, since the Word was life. Hence the rational ground of everything lives in eternal life. For through the rational ground, through which the circle is the circle, the circle was and will always without defect be the circle. The creatures which have been made, even if they did not live in themselves, therefore lived eternally in that Word, even though they are not this Word, which is God. And this life was not only the Word of God, through which it creates everything, but rather also the Word, through which in its light it leads the man, who is strong in the light of the rational ground. The Word of God is indeed the lamp for the feet of those who strive for eternal life.

And the light was shining in the darkness of ignorance and the darkness did not comprehend the light, which is the Word or the speech of God, through which God has spoken multifariously and in many modes naturally and through prophets. Finally, after all the prophets, a man was sent by God, whose name was John. The latter came as witness, in order to bear witness to the brilliance of the light of the Word of God, which had then appeared. John was not that Word, which was the light, but rather he came, in order to bear witness to the brilliance of the light. The true light, however, was the Word of God, which light illuminates every man who is vigorous in his rationality and comes into this world.

The Logos or that speech was in the world and the world has been made through it, since God the Father spoke and everything has been made. And the world knew him not. He came unto the place peculiar to his Father, i.e., unto the Holy Land and his own received him not, although he was the Word of God. However, to all of them and all the peoples, who received him and obeyed him as the Word of God sent by God, he gave power, although they were men, to become the sons of God through grace, just as he was by nature. And those who received him were generated in the spirit of the Son of God, not in that generation which causes men to be born according to this world out of blood and the will of the flesh and out of the will of man, but rather in celestial generation out of God, who is spirit, they are born in the spirit. This Word, therefore, which enables and effects all this, is the Logos or the Son of God. This Word has become flesh, since the Son of God has become the Son of man. And he has dwelt among us and we have seen his glory; the glory of the light, not as that of some adoptive son of God, as many were seen, but rather as that of the only-begotten of God the Father, who possessed from the Father everything that is the Father's; i.e., the Word, which is full of all grace and truth.

That is the fullness of the Gospel according to the intellect of John the Theologian. And explaining this, he amplifies and proves it through the testimony of God the Father, John the Baptist, the Apostles, the miracles, through the evidence of the teaching of the Word of the truth, the voluntary sacrifice up to the most ignominious death for the salvation of all the faithful and the resurrection from the dead. Through all this he showed most manifestly that Jesus is the Son of God, who has spoken the words of his Father, who is truthful, and did his works. His words are firmer than heaven and earth and bear the maximum promise, namely, the resurrection to immortal life, which only God possesses and to which possession Christ is heir, and those who believe in him with heart and work are co-heirs. And all this occurs in man through the Holy Spirit, which proceeds from the Father and from the Son; which is the spirit of the Son and also the charity of God. If the latter is poured in the hearts of the faithful, it makes these agreeable to God on account of the inhabiting Holy Spirit. And it unites them in indissoluble connection with Christ, the head, the heir, and the possessor of immortality, so that they are, in the unity of the body of Christ through the spirit of Christ, living co-heirs of the kingdom of immortality and most happy possessors of eternal life.

This is the sum total of the Gospel, which I have explained variously in various sermons set forth here, as grace was accorded me; at first it seemed more obscure, when in adolescence I began and was a deacon, then clearer when I ascended to the priesthood, and finally it seemed to become yet more perfect, when I performed priestly duties in my Brixen parish and was active during my apostolic legation in Germany and elsewhere. May God grant that in the years still remaining to me, I make further progress and finally embrace the truth face to face in eternal joy. That God grant this, pray, you most beloved brother. And if something in the already given or the following sermons or writings is found that deviates from Catholic truth, I correct and revoke it herewith.

Prologues to an Examination
of the Koran

(1 4 6 1)

To the Supreme and Most Holy Pontiff of the Universal Christian Church, Pius II.

Most holy Father, accept this booklet, which your humble servant has collected with zealous faith, so that when, in the manner of your predecessor, the thrice-holy Pope Leo, who condemned the Nestorian heresy in the apostolic spirit, with angelic genius and divine eloquence, you demonstrate with the same spirit and equal genius and fluency that the Mohammedan sect, which arose from the former, is erroneous and reprehensible, you will have the rudiments, which it is necessary to know, quickly and simply at hand. To your judgment, you who are the first in the episcopate of the faith, I submit this booklet and everything which I have written and shall write, and my whole self, as it befits the faithful, and shall deviate in no point at any time from your apostolic throne.

Prologue

I have attempted diligently, as best I could, to understand the book of law of the Arabs, which I have obtained in Basel in the translation procured for us by Peter, Abbot of Cluny, together with a disputation of those noble Arabs, of whom the one, a follower of Mohammed, attempts to persuade the other, who was a scholar and important man among the Arabs; the latter, however, shows that it would be better to hold the Christian faith, which he served zealously.

There were also other writings therein on the generation of

Mohammed and his twelve successors in power and on one hundred questions concerning his doctrines. I left this book behind with Master John of Segovia and went to Constantinople, where among the Minorite Brothers who reside in the Church of the Holy Cross, I found the Koran in Arabic, which the brothers explained to me in certain points to the best of their knowledge. However, in Pera, in the convent of St. Dominicus, there was a copy translated in the same manner as the one I had left in Basel.

I inquired whether any Greeks had written against these follies and found no one except John Damascenus, who lived shortly after the initiation of this sect and had written the few things which were on hand.

In Constantinople there was a merchant, Balthasar de Luparis, who, seeing that I solicited the above mentioned, told me that a very learned and important man among the Turks, after he had been secretly instructed in the Gospel of St. John, proposed to go with twelve distinguished men to the Pope and to be fully instructed, if I wished to provide for their escort in secret. From the report of the brothers I learned that it really was the case and arranged the escort, as they requested. However, because that great man was the director of hospitals, he wanted first to visit the latter and then proceed to the place where the ship awaited them for the journey to Rome. However, during this visitation the plague carried him away.

Lord Balthasar, who now abides in military service in Bologna, has often told me that all their scholars love the Gospel very much and prefer it to their own book of law.

Later I have prompted the Carthusian Brother Dionysius to write against the Koran, which he did and sent his great work to Pope Nicolaus. After this I saw in Rome the booklet of Brother Ricoldi of the Order of Preachers, who occupied himself in Baghdad with Arabic science, and that pleased me better than the others. I also saw the Catholic writings of other brothers on this theme, especially those of St. Thomas *On the Rational Grounds of Faith* to the Cantor of Antioch, and lastly the writing of the Most Reverend Lord Cardinal of St. Sixtus, who had refuted the heresies and errors of Mohammed with vital proofs.

I have, however, also applied my thinking to showing the

Gospel to be true even from the Koran. So that this can occur easily, I shall set forth my compendious conception in a few words.

We experience that there is in us a certain appetite, which on account of the motion which is in it, is called spirit, and that the basis of this motion is the Good. Our appetite is moved on the basis of the Good. So we see that the Good through its own strength attracts our spirit, and that there is no other reason that the Good is desired than that it is good. The end of desire is therefore the Good.

Also our spirit cannot have this appetite for the Good except from the Good. Therefore, the Good is the creator of our spirit for itself and is equally its origin and end. Therefore, our spirit does not rest except in its origin. And because our intellectual spirit is not itself the Good that it desires, because that Good is not in it—for were the Good in the intellect, then it would be intellect, just as in our knowledge the known is our knowledge—therefore, our intellect does not know what that Good is. The intellectual spirit in its nature desires to comprehend that Good. For although it can be lacking to no thing which is, since to be is good, nevertheless, unless the intellect understands it, it is without it and can find no rest.

Since the intellect does not know what this Good is, the existence of which it does not doubt, it also does not know its name. It can form no concept of that which it does not doubt is greater and better than every concept. And since we experience that nothing is comprehended in our intellect that does not enter into it through our senses—for example, a man blind from birth has no knowledge of color—we know that that Good is not of the region of this sensible world and that our spirit does not come to rest in this world. Nevertheless, because we know that the appetite for that Good is not possessed by us in vain, we are also certain that our intellectual spirit is of the sensible world, but that its appetite can attain rest only when it has put the sensible life aside.

But unless this world were to come to the help of our intellectual nature, we would enter it in vain. Therefore, we must confess that in this world we can be made fit or unfit for finding rest or lack of rest in the future age. However, the way which we must travel in this world, in order to be made fit for apprehension of the desired Good, should be only a good way. One which leads astray will be an evil way.

It is clear to everyone who is in possession of his intellect that this is the case. However, since there can be many ways which appear good, the doubt remains as to which of them is the true and perfect way, which leads us with certainty to cognition of the Good; this Good we name God, in order to understand each other, when we speak concerning it. Moses described one way, but it is not accepted and understood by all.

Christ illuminated and perfected it, and yet many still remain unbelieving. Mohammed endeavored to describe this way as easier, so that it would be accepted by all, even idolaters. These are the most famous descriptions of the aforementioned way, although the sages and prophets have given many others. However, all the above-mentioned descriptions have as their foundation that this frequently-mentioned Good is the maximum, and therefore One, which One all name God. They designate their descriptions of the way as good because they are revealed to them by the same good God. But because no mere man can conceive God, it is clear that we have no certitude that some mere man can make known to us the way to an end which is unknown to himself. Therefore, if neither Moses nor Mohammed, as long as they were in this world, ever saw this oft-mentioned Good—indeed a man has never seen God—how could they then make known to others the way to Him? However, even if they had proclaimed some words infused in them, which symbolized or signified God and the way to Him, neither they nor another man could explain them. And if some man had been able to or could manifest this way, then he would necessarily have had to be the greatest of all men, as all people acknowledge the Messiah to be. If this man were not the omniscient divine Wisdom, through which God effects everything, he could not reveal what were unknown to him.

But Jesus, the son of the Virgin Mary, that Christ whose coming Moses and the prophets prophesied, appeared, and since nothing was unknown to him, he revealed to us the oft-mentioned way most manifestly. Even Mohammed attested to this. It is therefore certain that whoever follows Christ and his way, attains to comprehension of the desired Good. If, therefore, Mohammed in any point deviated from Christ, he must have done this either out of ignorance, because he neither knew nor understood Christ, or out of perverse intention, because he did not intend to lead men to that end of rest, to which Christ showed the way, but rather sought his own glory under the guise of that end. A comparison of the law of Christ with his law will teach that both must be believed to be true. Therefore, we believe we must hold that ignorance is the cause of the error and the malevolence. For no one who knows Christ dissents or detracts from him.

Our intention now is to examine the book of Mohammed under the presupposition of the Gospel of Christ and to show that even in this book things are contained, through which the Gospel, if it required corroboration, would be fully confirmed. And where there are contradictions, this has occurred out of ignorance and consequently out of the perverse intention of Mohammed himself. Christ sought not his own glory, but rather that of God the Father and the salvation of men; Mohammed, on the other hand, sought not God's glory and the salvation of men, but rather his own glory.

Second Prologue

That noble Christian Arab, whom I mentioned above, reports that the monk Sergius came to Mecca after he had been ejected from his monastery. There he found two peoples, idolaters and Jews, and there he preached the Christian faith as Nestorius held it, in order to placate his brothers belonging to this sect. He converted all idolaters to his faith and among them was Mohammed, who, converted from idolatry, died a Nestorian Christian. But three very crafty Jews attached themselves to Mohammed in order to avert him, lest he become perfect. And they convinced him of various evils. However, when after the death of Mohammed all reverted to their own sect, these Jews approached Alis, the son of Abitalip, to whom Mohammed had bequeathed his collection of writings. And they persuaded him, just like Mohammed, to elevate himself to a prophet. And in respect to the book of Mohammed they added and deleted what they wanted. It seems therefore that Mohammed was firmly grounded from the beginning by Sergius, so that he was a Christian and observed Christian law. The Jews could not move him away from this way. But in order to hold him back as much as possible, they added those passages through which he appears as the prophet of his own sect, which gives credence to the Old Testament no less than to the Gospel.

However, Sergius got him, as the above-referenced authority reports, to put in the Koran that Christians, especially the religious and priests, are better friends than the Jews. And, although he says this, nevertheless being later induced, he derides the Christians, who venerate their prelates and priests in place of God. This is because Christians call them by the name by which God alone is called, namely "lord." This name befits no one except God, for it is said in Exodus: "The Lord Himself is God." He also mentions at times ten names of God, among them Adonai, which is translated as Lord. And by Adonai the inexpressible name is written, read, and expressed. Therefore, in the Koran he gives no one except God this name, not even Christ or the Virgin Mary. And because the Christians call Jesus Christ Lord and Mary lord, he says that they are venerated in place of God. And just as he is careful never to give someone the name Lord except God, he is also careful never to give God the name Father, for he says that God creates everything as He wishes. Therefore, the act of generation does not befit Him.

Therefore, when he says something good about Christians, he understands it in respect to those clothed in white—for thus he names the disciples—and in respect to the believers in Christ, as he regards the Nestorians, of whose error he was ignorant. Nor did he know other Christians. But Nestorius accepted everything which is in the Gospel, and that body, soul, and divinity were in Christ. However, he erred in respect to the mode of the union. He acknowledged that body and soul were united in a natural union, so that Christ was a true man. But he said this man was united with divinity through grace, but not through the common grace, through which good men are united with God, but rather through the fullness of grace, because of which the Will of God and the will of the man Jesus were one. Because of this most excellent grace, it is true to say of Christ that he is the Son of God. But he did not admit that Mary is the mother of God, because that which is found in Christ as received from his mother does not befit God. Thus he wanted the human nature in Christ to be deified. And because the Gospel says that the Word of God became flesh, but not that the flesh became the Word of God, the Church in the third and fourth universal councils condemned this interpretation and gave the mother of Jesus the name *Theotokos,* which is the begetrix of God.

The Nestorians, however, do acknowledge the eternal generation. Therefore, it seems that Mohammed did not wish to write against the most Holy Trinity and eternal generation, but rather only condemned the plurality of gods, as will be discussed. If someone had asked Mohammed, in what form God had sent to men a legate, who would be greater than an angel, he would certainly have said that God, were He to send an angel as legate to men, would clothe him with human form. And he would respond similarly, if He had sent one who were greater than an angel. According to his own words, however, He sent Christ, whom he calls the Word of God and the son of Mary. Therefore, since the Word of God is of the same nature as God, whose Word he is—everything which is of God, is God on account of His most simple nature—therefore, when God wanted to send the highest legate, He sent His Word, than whom no greater legate can be conceived. And because He sent the Word to men, He wanted him to put on the cleanest human nature. This he did in the Virgin Mary, as is frequently read in the Koran.

Therefore, it will not be difficult to find the truth of the Gospel in the Koran, although Mohammed himself is very far removed from a true understanding of the Gospel. We also may not overlook that the chapters of the collection of the aforesaid book of law of the Arabs do not cohere with one another, but rather that each exists by itself alone. Each is its own rhythm or is a fully measured poem. The compiler indeed took the greatest pains to entice and amaze all by the charm of his speech, in order in this manner to make the expressions appear divine. Therefore, one must pardon me if I nowhere seem to follow an appropriate order, when I discuss the contents of this most confused book.

I have divided my booklet into three parts and will cite the chapters of each one below.

The chapters of the first part of my book are as follows:

I. On the Koran, and that the true God is not its author;
II. What the Koran contains according to its praisers;
III. What it contains according to the judgment of the perfect;

393

The chapters of the second part of this book are the following:

The chapters of the third part:

X. That Mohammed constantly varies his views, as in examples;

XI. Against the assertion that the law of the Koran is the law of Abraham;

XII. The Koran unjustly calls Abraham an idolater, and the true history is reported;

XIII. On the promise made to the faithful Abraham;

XIV. The covenant of God and Abraham excludes the Ismaelites and it concludes in Christ, the Mediator;

XV. Only a Christian who adores the Trinity in unity is able to be a son of Abraham;

XVI. The Arabs do not know the law of Abraham at all and they are persecutors of it;

XVII. A recommendation that the Sultan mandate that the Virgin Mary be believed in as the *Theotokos* and the light of the Gospel be embraced;

XVIII. To the Caliph in Baghdad: the Jews have made additions in the Koran concerning Abraham;

XIX. A demonstration that no one can be made happy without Christ;

XX. A demonstration that Christ has merited immortality for Christians;

XXI. An explanation of the similitude of Christ and Adam.

On the Not-Other

(1 4 6 2)

The Most Reverend Father in Christ and Lord Nicolaus of Cusa, Cardinal of St. Peter in Chains, commences a little book, which is inscribed for the direction of observers. The interlocutors with the Cardinal are Abbot John Andrea Vigevius, Peter Balbus of Pisa and Ferdinand Martin of the Portuguese nation.

I.

ABBOT: You know that we three, who have dedicated ourselves to study and whom you have permitted to speak with you, are occupied with lofty things. I am indeed occupied with Proclus' *Commentary on the Parmenides,* Peter on the other hand with the *Platonic Theology* of the same Proclus, which he translates from Greek into Latin, and Ferdinand for his part examines the genius of Aristotle. You, however, devote yourself, when you have time, to the theologian Dionysius the Areopagite. It would joy us now to hear whether perhaps a briefer and clearer way does not occur to you, to that which is treated by the writers already named.

NICOLAUS: In every respect we are occupied with profound mysteries. And I do not believe that someone has expressed them more briefly or more simply than the men whose writings we often read, although it sometimes seems to me that we neglect just that which could bring us closer to that which is sought.

PETER: We ask you to explain this.

FERDINAND: We are all so affected by the truth, that we long to be able to find it in every respect in consciousness, to have that as guide, which places it before our mental eyes. However, you prove yourself indefatigable therein in your already declining age and if one requests you to speak about it, you seem to become young again. Therefore, speak with us about that which you have considered before us.

NICOLAUS: I will speak with you, Ferdinand, on the condition that you reject as unimportant everything that you hear from me, unless your rationality compels you.

FERDINAND: The philosophers, my preceptors, taught me to do so.

NICOLAUS: I ask you first therefore: What is it that causes us to know in the first place?

FERDINAND: Definition.

NICOLAUS: You respond correctly, for definition is speech or rationality. But whence is the definition expressed?

FERDINAND: From the defining, since it defines everything.

NICOLAUS: Very rational. If therefore a definition defines everything, does it therefore also define itself?

FERDINAND: Certainly, since it excludes nothing.

NICOLAUS: You see therefore that a definition defining everything is not other than the defined?

FERDINAND: I see, since it is the definition of itself. However, what this definition should be, I do not see.

NICOLAUS: I have expressed it to you most clearly. It is that which I said we neglect, in passing by that sought for in the course of our hunt.

FERDINAND: When have you expressed it?

NICOLAUS: Just now, when I said the definition defining everything is not other than the defined.

FERDINAND: I do not yet comprehend you.

NICOLAUS: The little that I said is easily examined. In it you will find the Not-other. And if you direct yourself with all the acumen of your mind to the Not-other, then you will see with me that it is the definition defining itself and everything.

FERDINAND: Instruct us how that occurs, for what you affirm is great and not yet believable.

NICOLAUS: Therefore answer me: What is the Not-other? Is it other than not other?

FERDINAND: In no way other.

NICOLAUS: Therefore the Not-other.

FERDINAND: That is certain.

NICOLAUS: Therefore, you define the Not-other!

FERDINAND: I see well indeed: how the Not-other is not other than not other. And this no one can deny.

NICOLAUS: You say the truth. Do you not see most certainly, that the Not-other, since it cannot be defined by something other, defines itself?

FERDINAND: I see that for sure, but it is not yet firmly established that it defines everything.

NICOLAUS: Nothing is easier to know. What indeed do you answer, if someone asks you what is the other? Do you not answer: not other than the other? Thus you answer to the question what is heaven: not other than the heaven.

FERDINAND: Thus I could certainly respond truthfully concerning everything which is required to be defined by me.

NICOLAUS: Since, therefore, without doubt this mode of definition, in which the Not-other defines itself and everything, is the most precise and truest, nothing remains other than to persist in it attentively and to find that which can humanly be known.

FERDINAND: You say and promise something wonderful. First I am eager to hear if any of all the contemplators has expressed this explicitly.

NICOLAUS: Although I have read it in none, it seems to me that Dionysius has come closer to it than others. For in everything which he variously expresses, he illuminates the Not-other. When he indeed comes to the end of *Mystical Theology,* he affirms that the Creator is neither something nameable nor something other. However, he says it such that he appears thereby not to reveal something great. For an attentive reader, however, he expresses thereby the secret of the Not-other, which he has explained in many places and in sundry ways.

II.

FERDINAND: While all name the first Origin God, you seem to want it to be signified by the Not-other. One must indeed acknowledge that as the first, which defines itself and everything, for since there is nothing earlier than the first and it is absolved of everything posterior, it can certainly not be defined except by itself. Since on the other hand the originated has nothing that it is from itself but rather from the Origin, its origin must indeed be the rational ground or the definition of its being.

NICOLAUS: You understand me very well, Ferdinand. For although many names are attributed to the first Origin, of which none can be adequate to it, since it is the Origin of all names and things and is nothing originated and precedes everything, it is nevertheless seen more precisely by the acumen of the mind through the one mode of signifying than through the other. Nor indeed have I experienced until now that anything signified has better directed the vision of man to the first. For as far as everything signified is terminated in something other or in the other itself, and since everything other is from the Not-other, it certainly does not lead to the Origin.

FERDINAND: I see that that which you say is indeed so. For the other, the terminus of vision, cannot be the origin of the seeing. For since the other is not other than the other, it certainly presupposes the Not-other, without which there would be no other. Therefore, everything signified, which is an other from the signification of the Not-other, is terminated in something other than in the Origin. That I know certainly as true.

NICOLAUS: Very good! However, since we cannot reveal our vision to another except through the signification of words, nothing occurs to us more precise than the Not-other, although it is not the name of God, which is before every nameable name in heaven and on the earth, just as also the road, which leads the wanderer to the city, is not the name of the city.

FERDINAND: It is just as you say, and I behold this clearly, when

I see that God is not other than God and that something is not other than something and nothing is not other than nothing and not-being is not other than not-being; and it is thus the case with everything which can somehow be said. Thereby I see indeed that the Not-other precedes all such, because it defines this, and that this is the other, since the Not-other precedes it.

NICOLAUS: The promptitude and vivacity of your mind pleases me, since you comprehend both well and rapidly what I intend. Therefore, in respect to the Not-other you now see clearly on this basis, that its signification serves us not only as the road to the Origin, but rather it also represents for us in greater proximity the unnameable name of God, so that in it, as in a more precious enigma, He reflects on the searchers.

III.

FERDINAND: Although it is apparent that you see the Origin of being and knowing through the Not-other, nevertheless I do not perceive it, unless you show it to me more clearly.

NICOLAUS: The theologians say that, since we climb to the intelligible through the sensible, God reflects upon us more clearly in the enigma of light. In fact, that light, which is God, is before every other light, howsoever nameable, and before everything other simply. However, what one sees before the other, is not the other. Since that light is therefore the Not-other itself and no nameable light, it shines forth in sensible light. But one comprehends that the sensible light, compared with sensible vision, is as the light of the Not-other to everything which can be seen by the mind. However, we know from experience that sensible vision sees nothing without sensible light and that visible color, as the rainbow shows, is nothing except the termination or definition of sensible light. And thus sensible light is the origin of the being and the knowing of the visible-sensible. Thus we conjecture that the Not-other is the Origin of being and knowing.

FERDINAND: A clear and agreeable guidance! For it is just the same in the case of sensible hearing. Sound is indeed the origin of the being and knowing of the audible. Therefore, God, whom we have signified through the Not-other, is the Origin of being and knowing for everything. If someone removes Him, then nothing remains, neither in respect to the thing nor in cognition. Just as after the removal of the light, neither the rainbow nor anything visible exists or is seen, and after the removal of sound, nothing audible exists or is heard, so if one removes the Not-other, nothing either exists or is known. I am fully convinced that this is so.

NICOLAUS: You have this conviction correctly, but I entreat you to heed this also: When you see anything whatever, for example, a stone, you see it only by means of the light, although you do not consider it. And when you hear something, you hear it, although you do not attend thereto, only by means of sound. Therefore, the Origin of being and knowing, without which one endeavors in vain to see or to hear, presents itself anteriorly. Moreover, because your attention is directed to an other, which you desire to see and to hear, you do not concentrate in consideration of the Origin, although it is the beginning, middle, and end of that which is sought. Pay attention to the Not-other in the same way. For since everything, whatever it may be, is not other than itself, it does not have this from somewhere else; it therefore has it from the Not-other. Therefore, it neither is, nor is the being that it is, known, except through the Not-other. For that is its cause, its most adequate rational ground or definition, which presents itself anteriorly, because it is the beginning, middle, and end of that which is sought by the mind. However, it is in no way considered in the manner of being, as far as that which is sought, is sought as something other. For then one does not actually seek the Origin, which always precedes that which is sought and without which that which is sought cannot be sought in the least. Everyone who seeks seeks, however, to attain the Origin insofar as he is able to, as Paul says. Since this cannot be attained just as it is in itself, the one seeking it before the other, since he is himself an other, indeed seeks it in the other; just as the light, that in itself, as it is expressed in the purity of solar light, is invisible to the human eye, is sought to be seen in the visible. For it is also not necessary to seek the light, which displays itself in the visible, since it were otherwise incomprehensible; one would have to seek the light with the light. The light, therefore, is sought out and is thus seen at least approximately in the visible, where one perceives it.

IV.

FERDINAND: You have urged us to dwell on the Not-other. And since you have made such great promises, in no way will I hasten to leave it. Tell me, therefore, what you understand through the Not-other?

NICOLAUS: What I understand it as cannot be expressed otherwise through the other. For everything that is after it is another exposition and indeed less conformable to it. How should that which the mind attempts to see through it, be otherwise expressed, since it precedes everything that can be thought and expressed? All theologians have indeed seen that God is greater than He can be conceived. And therefore they have affirmed Him as supersubstantial, above every name and the like, and they have not expressed to us something other in God through "above," "without," "in," "non," and "before." For it is the same to say it is supersubstantial substance, as it is substance without substance or insubstantial substance, nonsubstantial substance, and substance before substance. However you may express it, since that which you say is not other than the same, it is evident that the Not-other is simpler and earlier and cannot be stated or expressed through an other.

FERDINAND: Would you say the Not-other is an affirmation or a negation or something of this kind?

NICOLAUS: Not at all. Rather it is before everything of this kind and is that which I have sought for many years by means of the coincidence of opposites, as the many booklets which I have written on these investigations show.

FERDINAND: Does the Not-other posit something or does it take something away?

NICOLAUS: It appears before every positing and ablation.

FERDINAND: It is therefore neither substance nor entity, nor the one nor any other.

NICOLAUS: Indeed I see it thus.

FERDINAND: Thus it is also neither not-being nor nothing.

NICOLAUS: And indeed I see it thus.

FERDINAND: I follow you, Father, as much as I can. It seems to me most certain that the Not-other can be comprehended neither through affirmation nor through negation nor in any other way; it seems rather in a wonderful way to aspire toward the eternal itself.

NICOLAUS: The stable, firm, and eternal seem to participate greatly in the Not-other, since the Not-other can receive no otherness or mutation. Since the eternal, however, is not other than the eternal, it will certainly be something other than the Not-other. And thus I see that the Not-other is beyond all comprehension before the eternal and before all time.

FERDINAND: Everyone who has the same perception as you must speak thus as soon as he applies himself to that which precedes everything which can be said. But I am truly astonished at how the one, entity, the true, and the good exist after it.

NICOLAUS: Although the one, when it is used to denote every-thing either as one or as other, seems to be rather close to the Not-other, so that it appears as though the Not-other, nevertheless the one, since it is nothing other than the one, is nonetheless an other, which is from the Not-other. Therefore, the Not-other is simpler than the one, which has from the Not-other that it is one and not the converse. Certainly some theologians, who take the One for the Not-other, understand this one before contradiction, as it is found in Plato's *Parmenides* and in Dionysius the Areopag-ite. However, since the one is other from not-one, it does not lead to the first Origin of everything, which can be an other neither from the other nor from nothing, because, as you will see below, it stands in opposition to nothing.

Consider entity in the same way. For even though the

Not-other is seen to shine forth clearly in it, since of that which is, it in no way seems to be other from anything, nevertheless the Not-other precedes it. It is likewise with the true, which similarly is denied of no entity, and with the good, in which nothing is non-participating. Therefore, all these are taken as revealed names of God, although they do not attain to precision. Nevertheless, one cannot actually say they are after the Not-other. For if they were after the Not-other, how then could each of them be not other than that which is? Thus, therefore, the Not-other appears before these and others, which are not after it, but rather through it. You are therefore correctly astonished at those things which the Not-other precedes; if they are after it, and how this is possible.

FERDINAND: If I understand you correctly, the Not-other is seen before everything, such that it can be lacking to none of the things appearing after it, even if they are contradictory to one another.

NICOLAUS: I certainly regard this as true.

V.

FERDINAND: I entreat you, Father, to grant to me that I express that which I, led in this manner to the Not-other, intuit, so that if you sense that I err, you show me the correct way in your manner.

NICOLAUS: Speak out, Ferdinand.

FERDINAND: If I intuit the Not-other separately before everything other, then I see it such that I intuit everything in it which can be seen. For outside of it something can neither be nor be known. Even the other from being and being known cannot flee from it. Indeed, it is not even possible for me to imagine being or understanding outside of the Not-other. It is so impossible that if I even attempted to see nothing and not-knowing without the Not-other, I would attempt to see mistakenly and in vain. For how were the nothing nothing visible except through the Not-other, through which it is not other than nothing? It is likewise with not-knowing and all the rest. For everything that is, is only insofar as the Not-other is; and everything that is understood, is understood only insofar as one understands that the Not-other is; and everything that is seen as true, is seen as true only insofar as one perceives the Not-other. And finally, whatever appears as other, appears as other only insofar as the Not-other appears. Therefore, just as after the sublation of the Not-other nothing remains nor is something known, so in it indeed everything is and is known and seen. For the Not-other itself is the most adequate rational ground and distinction and measure of everything that is, that it is; and of everything that is not, that it is not; and of that which can be, that it can be; and of that which is so, that it is so; and of that which is moved, that it is moved; and of that which stands, that it stands; and of that which lives, that it lives; and of that which understands, that it understands; etc. That it necessarily is so, I see therein, that I see that the Not-other defines itself and consequently also everything which can be named.

NICOLAUS: You have directed your eye correctly to God, who is signified through the Not-other, so that you see everything humanly visible in the Origin, cause, or rational ground, which is not other or diverse, as much as it is conceded to you now. It is, however, conceded to you as much as the Not-other, namely, the rational ground of things, is revealed or exhibited visibly to your rationality or mind. However, by this means, through the Not-other, since it defines itself, He has revealed Himself now more clearly than before. In what way He earlier presented Himself visibly to me, you can read in many books; now, however, He appears above all, because He defines Himself, in this enigma of the significance of the Not-other, more fruitfully and clearly and indeed so much so, that I am able to hope God will reveal Himself to us once without enigma.

FERDINAND: Although in that just said everything is enfolded that we are able to see, nevertheless, in order to become more strongly stimulated, we want to advance certain doubts, so that through their invalidation, the vision for which we constantly exerted ourselves, becomes easier.

NICOLAUS: I am in agreement that you proceed so.

FERDINAND: The one eager for knowledge asks first of all, where is the rational ground to be found for the fact that God is signified three and one through the Not-other, although the Not-other precedes every number.

NICOLAUS: On the basis of that said, since the Origin signified through the Not-other defines itself, everything seems to subsist in a unique rational ground, which you have indeed seen. We therefore intuit its unfolded definition that the Not-other is not other than the Not-other. If, therefore, the same repeated three times is the definition of the first, as you see, then it is in fact triune and this for no other reason than that it defines itself. For it were not the first, if it did not define itself. If, however, it defines itself, it appears as threefold. You see therefore, that the Trinity results from perfection. Since you see it, however, before the other, you cannot count it nor affirm that it is a number, for this trinity is not other than unity and this unity is not other than trinity, since trinity like unity is not other than the simple Origin signified through the Not-other.

FERDINAND: I see very well, that the necessity of the perfection of the first—since it defines itself—requires that it nevertheless be triune before the other and number, because that which presupposes the first contributes nothing to its perfection. However, since you have often endeavored in sundry ways elsewhere, above all in *On Learned Ignorance,* to explain this divine fecundity with other expressions, it will be sufficient if you now only add a little.

NICOLAUS: The secret of the Trinity, received only in faith through a gift of God, although it far surpasses and precedes every sense through that means with which we investigate in the presence of God, cannot be expressed otherwise nor more precisely than you have heard it above. Those, however, who designate the Trinity as Father, Son, and Holy Spirit, indeed approach less precisely, however, make use of these names suitably on account of the conformity to the Scripture. Those, however, who name the Trinity unity, equality, and connection, would come nearer, if these expressions were found inserted in the Holy Scripture. Indeed, these are that in which the Not-other shines forth clearly. For in the unity, which bespeaks indistinction from itself and distinction from the other, the Not-other is surely perceived. Likewise it manifests itself to the observer in equality and in connection. Yet simpler are the expressions this, that, and the same. They imitate the Not-other yet more clearly and precisely; however, they are less in use. Thus it is therefore evident, that in the Not-other and Not-other and Not-other—even though it is employed least of all—the triune Origin is revealed most clearly, beyond, however, all our apprehension and our capacity. Indeed, when the first Origin, signified through the Not-other, defines itself, then the Not-other arises in the definitive motion from the Not-other, and from the Not-other and the arising Not-other the definition is concluded in the Not-other. The one who contemplates it will intuit it more clearly than it can be expressed.

VI.

FERDINAND: Indeed, that is enough about this. Now continue further and show us the Not-other in the other.

NICOLAUS: The Not-other is neither other, nor other from another, nor is it another in another, and for no other reason than that the Not-other can in no way be another, as though something were lacking to it as to another. Indeed, the other, since it is another from another, is without that, in virtue of which it is another. However, the Not-other, just because it is an other from none, is not without anything nor can something be outside it. Whence just as without it something can neither be said nor thought, which is not said or thought through it, without which it is not possible that something is or is discerned, since it precedes all such, so does one now see that it in itself is anteriorly and absolutely not other than itself, and one perceives in the other, that it is not other than the other. If I, for example, say that God is nothing visible, because He is its cause and creator, I also say that He is in heaven not other than heaven. Indeed, how should the heaven be not other than the heaven, if the Not-other were in it something other than heaven? However, since the heaven is other from not-heaven, it is therefore something other. But God, who is the Not-other, is not the heaven, which is something other, even though in it He is not other and not other from it; likewise the light is not color, although it is neither another in it nor from it. You must be attentive to how everything that can be thought or said, for this reason, is not the First signified through the Not-other, because all this is another from its opposites. However, God is the Not-other, since He is the Not-other from the other, although the Not-other and the other seem to be opposed. The other is, however, not opposed to that from which—as we have said before—it has that it is another. Now you see how the theologians have correctly affirmed that God—although nothing of everything—is everything in everything.

FERDINAND: There is no one who would not see this with you, if he were to apply his mind. Hence it is established for everyone that the unnameable God names everything, that the infinite defines everything, the interminable terminates everything, etc.

NICOLAUS: Correct. For since in the cessation of the Not-other, everything that is and is not necessarily ceases, one perceives clearly how in it everything anteriorly is it itself and it itself is everything in everything. Hence, if I intuit it in the other and the other in it itself, then I see anteriorly how through it itself everything without anything other is what it is. Indeed, it does not create the heaven from an other, but rather through the heaven, which in it is it itself. Likewise is it, if we name it intellectual spirit or light and consider it in the intellect as the rational ground of all being. For then it is in it anteriorly the rational ground—why the heaven is heaven and not something other—through which the heaven is constituted and which in heaven is heaven. The sensible heaven, therefore, is not that which it is from another or something other from heaven, but rather it originates from the Not-other from anything which you see before the name, because it is everything in every name and nothing of everything. For with the same rational ground with which I named that rational ground heaven, I could name the same rational ground earth or water. And it is equally true of every single thing. And if I see that one can name the rational ground of heaven not-heaven, because the cause does not bear the name of the caused, so I see from the same rational ground, that He is nameable with no name. I do not see Him therefore as unnameable, as though He were deprived of a name, but before any name.

VII.

FERDINAND: I understand that and perceive also that it is true. For if the cause ceased, the effect would also cease; and therefore, with the cessation of the Not-other, everything other would cease and everything nameable and thus even the nothing itself, since it is named nothing. Show me, I entreat, how I may examine this.

NICOLAUS: It is certain that if the coldness ceased, also the ice that is seen multiplied now in Rome would cease. But on that account the water, which is prior to the ice, would not cease. However, were entity to cease, both the ice and the water would cease, so that the latter would not actually be. And nevertheless the matter or the possibility of the being of water would not cease. Indeed, this possibility of the being of water can be called one possibility. But were the one to cease, the ice and water and also the possibility of the being of water would cease. But nevertheless not every intelligible thing would cease, which through Omnipotence could be required for the possibility of the being of water, as in the case that the intelligible nothing or chaos would not cease. This is certainly further removed from water than the possibility of the being of water itself, which, although most remote and confused, is nevertheless compelled to obey Omnipotence. However, the vigor of Omnipotence over that would not cease with the cessation of the one. However, if the Not-other were to cease, everything which the Not-other precedes would immediately cease. And thus not only the actuality and potentiality of entity would cease, but rather also the not-entity and the nothing of entity, which the Not-other precedes.

FERDINAND: You have satisfied my doubt. Now I see that the nothing, that is not other than the nothing, has the Not-other before itself, from which it is farther removed than from actual-being and potential-being. Indeed, it appears to the mind as the most confused chaos, which through the infinite power, which is the Not-other, can be held fast, in order to become determined.

NICOLAUS: You have said that the Not-other is infinite power as actuality. How do you see that?

FERDINAND: I see that the power which is united and less other is stronger; therefore, that one which is completely Not-other will be infinite.

NICOLAUS: You speak very well and especially rationally. I say rationally. For just as sensible vision, however acute it may be, cannot be without all sensation or sensible motion, so also the mental cannot be without all rationality or rational motion. And although I see that you intuit correctly, nevertheless, I still wish to know whether the Not-other is seen by the mind in everything such that it cannot not be seen.

FERDINAND: I turn back to the Origin, which defines itself and everything that can be expressed, and I see how to see is not other than to see, and I see further that I behold the Not-other itself both through seeing as well as through not-seeing. If, therefore, the mind can neither see nor not see without the Not-other, then the Not-other itself cannot not be seen, just as it cannot not be known, because it is known through knowledge and ignorance. In the other the Not-other itself is perceived, because if one sees the other, one sees the other and the Not-other.

NICOLAUS: You say that well. But how do you see the other, if you see it neither in the other nor in the Not-other?

FERDINAND: Because the positing of the Not-other is the positing of everything and because its sublation is the sublation of everything, the other is neither outside the Not-other nor is it seen there.

NICOLAUS: If you see the other in the Not-other, then you certainly do not see that it is another being there, but rather the Not-other, since it is impossible that the other is in the Not-other.

FERDINAND: That I see the other in the Not-other, I say because it cannot be seen outside of it. But if you ask me, what is the other in the Not-other, I will answer the Not-other.

NICOLAUS: Correct.

VIII.

FERDINAND: It were good to say something concerning quiddity.

NICOLAUS: I will do that. You do not hesitate, I believe, to say that the quiddity of the Not-other is the Not-other itself. Therefore, the quiddity of God or of the Not-other is not other from any quiddity, but rather in every other quiddity the Not-other is no other quiddity. Therefore, the others from the quiddity of the other happen as accidents to the other, because the other which is without the other, were the Not-other. Those others, therefore, which are consequent to the quiddity of the other, are reflections of the quiddity of the other, which reflections sink down into the shadow of nothing. Therefore, the quiddity, which is the Not-other, is the quiddity of the quiddity of the other, which is a reflection of the first quiddity. There are others that happen as accidents to it, in which the quiddity, to which they happen as accidents, shines forth.

 The quiddity, which I see in the mind before quantity, since it cannot be imagined without quantity, receives various images in the imagination, which cannot be without various quantity. And although quantity is not from the essence of quiddity, which the mind contemplates beyond the imagination, and that quiddity which the mind sees, is not other from the quiddity which the imagination imagines, the quantity is consequent to the quiddity of the image in such a manner that the image cannot be without it. In the same way, I speak of magnitude, which is seen in the mind beyond the imagination before the imagined quantity. But in the imagination quantity is discerned. The more absolved its imagination is of the gross and shady quantity and the more subtle and simple it is, the more simply and certainly the quiddity of magnitude shines forth in it and the truer it is as the imagined magnitude. For quantity is not anything which were necessary for the quiddity of magnitude, as if it were constituted from it, since the maximum simplicity or indivisibility is great without quantity. However, if the magnitude shall be imagined or appear imaginable, then quantity is immediately necessary, as if the former would not be possible without the latter.

Quantity is therefore the reflection of magnitude imaginable in its image, but it shines forth more certainly in intelligence. Indeed, we speak of great intellect and of great knowledge. There magnitude shines forth, however, intellectually, namely, separated and absolved prior to corporeal quantity. But it is known most truly beyond all intellect, namely, beyond and before all cognitive modes. And thus it is comprehended incomprehensibly and cognized incognizably, as also seen invisibly. Because this is a cognition beyond every cognition of man, it is only negatively touched upon in the humanly known.

For we do not doubt that the imaginable magnitude is not other than imaginable, that the intelligible is not other than intelligible, and thus we see also that the magnitude, which is imaginable in the imaginable and intelligible in the intelligible, is not that which is the Not-other itself and stands before the other, or without whose existence the intelligible would also not exist. Indeed, the imaginable magnitude presupposes the magnitude which is before the imaginable contraction, and the intelligible magnitude that which is before the intelligible contraction, which shines forth in this and that manner in a mirror and enigma, so that it, which is before the other, measure, and everything effable and cognizable, is known as that magnitude of God which has no end; a magnitude which can be comprehended through no cognizable terms. Thus quiddity, which is the Not-other, defines itself and all quiddities of things universally, just as it was said of the quiddity of magnitude. Therefore, just as the Not-other is not multiplicable, because it is before number, the quiddity, which is the Not-other, even though it is an other in other things and other modes, is also not multiplicable.

FERDINAND: You have opened my eyes, so that I begin to see how it stands with the truth of the quiddity. And in the enigma of the quiddity of magnitude, you have led me certainly to a most agreeable vision.

NICOLAUS: Well, and with clear mind you see now that the Not-other is presupposed and known in every cognition and that what is known is no other from it, but rather is that unknown, which shines forth in the known in the manner of the known, just as the clarity of the sun, which is sensibly invisible, shines forth visibly in the visible colors of the rainbow variously in various clouds.

IX.

FERDINAND: I entreat you, say something about the universe, so that I, following you, attain to a better vision of God.

NICOLAUS: I shall say something. If I see the heaven and the earth and what is in these with my corporeal eyes, and—in order to imagine the universe—collect that which I have seen, I behold intellectually every single part of the universe in its place and in corresponding order and peace. I contemplate the beautiful world and see that everything has been made with rationality. I experience that this rationality shines forth in everything, both in that which only is, as well as in that which simultaneously is and lives, as well as in that which equally is, lives, and understands; and indeed in the first more obscurely, in the second more vitally and clearly, however in the third most lucidly, and in the particular modes variously in various ones. Then I turn to the rational ground of the things themselves, which precedes the world and through which I see the world constituted, and I discover that it is incomprehensible. Indeed, I do not hesitate to say that that rational ground of the world, through which everything has been rationally made, underlies every cognition, and that it comes to light in everything created, since nothing is created without rational ground. However, I do not comprehend it itself at all. For if I were to comprehend it, I would truly know why the world is thus and not otherwise, why the sun is the sun, the moon the moon, the earth the earth, and everything whatsoever is what it is and not something other; why it is not larger, not smaller.

Therefore, if I knew that, I were not a creature and a part of the universe, since in that case my rational ground were the creative art of the universe and its own creator. For this reason, I comprehend the Not-other, when I see that the rational ground of the universe is not comprehensible, since it precedes everything comprehensible. Therefore, I behold it as the incomprehensible itself, since it shines forth in the comprehensible incomprehensibly.

FERDINAND: It is difficult to comprehend what precedes being.

NICOLAUS: Form gives being and being known. Hence, what is not formed, because it precedes or follows, is not comprehended, just as God and *hyle* and nothing and such things.

When we touch upon that in the vision of the mind, we touch upon it beyond or on this side of comprehension. However, because we cannot communicate the vision without words, we cannot without being explain what is not, since otherwise, those who hear would not comprehend. Therefore, just as that mental vision is beyond comprehension, so is it also beyond expression. And all speaking about it is improper and is without precision, as when we say, matter is matter, *hyle* is *hyle,* nothing is nothing, etc. Therefore, the observer must act as someone who sees snow through a red glass. He sees the snow and attributes its red appearance not to the snow, but rather to the glass. The mind, which sees the in-formed through the form, does likewise.

FERDINAND: How can I see that as true, which the theologians say: Everything is created through the will of God?

NICOLAUS: The will of God is the Not-other; for the will determines. However, the more perfect the will is, the more rational and ordered it is. Therefore, the will, which is perceived before the other as the Not-other, is not other from rationality nor from wisdom, nor any other nameable thing. If you, therefore, see that the will is the Not-other, then you will also see that it is rationality, wisdom, and order, from which it is not other. And thus you see, that through the will everything is determined, caused, ordered, established, strengthened, and preserved, and that this will shines forth in the universe; just as the will of Trajan, in which there is wisdom and power, shines forth in his column. For since Trajan wished to show posterity his glory, which could not be shown except in the sensible enigma to sensible beings, to whom the presence of his glory was impossible to exhibit, he did it through the column, which is named after him; the column is what it is through his will. And the column is not other from his will, even though the column in no way is his will, but rather that which the column is, it has from the will, which defines and determines it. But in this will one perceives the wisdom and order, which shine forth in the figurative representations of the happily completed war; the power of Trajan shines forth also in the preciousness of the work, which could not have been completed by an impotent person.

With this enigma you may help yourself, in order to see that the King of kings, who is signified through the Not-other, has created the universe and all its parts through His wise and powerful will, in order to show His glory. This will shines forth triply in everything, namely essentially, intelligibly, and desirably, as we experience in our own soul. For here it shines forth as the Origin of the being, from which the soul has its being, as the Origin of the knowing, from which arises its knowledge, and as the Origin of the desiring, from which it also has its will. And contemplating therein its triune Origin, the soul ascends to its glory.

FERDINAND: I see very well that this is so, and I see that the will, which is the Not-other, is desired by all and named as the creative good.

For what do all desire, who are? Not other than to be; and those who live? Not other than to live; and those who know? Not other than to know. Therefore, everything desires that, because it is from the Not-other. Since, however, the Not-other is not other from anything whatever, it is desired by everything in the highest degree as the origin of being, as the means of preservation, and the end of resting.

NICOLAUS: You direct your course correctly towards the Not-other, in which everything comes to light.

X.

FERDINAND: Many theologians said the creature is not other than
a participation in God. I wished very much to hear your
opinion of this.

NICOLAUS: First you see that the Not-other is unnameable, since
no name attains to that which precedes everything. However, every name is that which it is, through participation
in it. It is therefore named the by-no-means-nameable.
Thus it is participated in in everything as the imparticipable.
There are things which participate in the Not-other only
obscurely, because in a confused and general manner; there
are things which participate more specifically, and many
which participate most particularly therein, just as in the
life of the soul, some members participate obscurely, some
more clearly, but some most particularly. Thus also of the
powers of the soul, the one participates more clearly, the
other more obscurely in intelligence. Also those creatures
which are less other from the others, as for instance pure
intelligences, participate more in it; however, those which
are more other from the others, as for example corporeal
things, which are not able to be together with one another
in one location, participate less in its nature, which is not
other from anything.

FERDINAND: I see that it is as you have said. But let it not, I
entreat, displease you to add, in what way it appears true,
that the essences of things are incorruptible.

NICOLAUS: First: You do not hesitate to state that the Not-other
is incorruptible. Indeed, if it were to be corrupted, then it
would be corrupted in an other. However, as soon as the
other is posited, the Not-other is posited; therefore, it is
not corruptible.

    Furthermore: It is certain that the Not-other defines
itself and everything. All essences of things do not exist,
therefore, except as essences of the Not-other. Therefore,
since the Not-other is in them, how shall these essences be
corrupted, as long as the Not-other endures? Indeed, just
as the Not-other precedes the essences and everything

nameable, so the essences precede mutability and fluxability, which are rooted in the alterable matter. The Not-other is therefore no essence, but rather, because it is the Essence in the essences, it is named the Essence of essences.

The Apostle said: What one sees is temporal, what one does not see is eternal. That which is perceived with any of the senses is indeed material and, corresponding to the nature of matter, is fluxional and unstable. However, what is not seen sensibly and nevertheless is, is not seen to exist temporally. Rather it is eternal. If you see the essence in another, as for example the humanity in Socrates, then you see it in the other as other and come to the insight that it is corruptible in the corruptible Socrates through the accidental. If you see it, however, separate from the other and in the Not-other, indeed according to its nature, in which you see it, you see it as incorruptible.

FERDINAND: You seem to denote that essence, which the Not-other precedes and the other follows, as idea or species.

NICOLAUS: Thus Plato saw the exemplar of things before the thing and after God. For the rational ground of the thing precedes the thing, since it comes into existence through it. However, the variety of things requires various rational grounds, which must be after the source from which, according to Plato, they emanate. But, because the Not-other, which is the most adequate cause as to why everything is what it is, is before the things, the Not-other is, however, not multiplicable; therefore it is the rational ground of things, which precedes the other and precedes number and plurality, and is enumerated innumerably corresponding to the things which participate in it.

FERDINAND: You seem thereby to say that there are no essences of things, but rather only the one, which you assert to be the rational ground.

NICOLAUS: You know that the one, the essence, the idea, the form, the exemplar, or the species does not attain to the Not-other. When I therefore intuit the things, in which I see their essence, since the things are through them, then I assert, when I contemplate them anteriorly through the intellect, that they are now this and now that. However, when I see them beyond the intellect and before the other, then I do not see now this and now that essence, but rather nothing other than the simple rational ground of essences, which I contemplated in the things. And I call it the Not-other or the Essence of essences, since it is what is perceived in all essences.

FERDINAND: You say therefore that the essences are one single essence. Aristotle did not want to admit that, lest there would ensue a progression into the infinite and one would then never come to the First and all knowledge would perish.

NICOLAUS: As far as quantity is conceived by the mind, Aristotle said correctly that one could not pass over into the infinite. Therefore, he excluded it. However, as the infinite is before quantity and everything other and is everything in everything, he did not reject it, but rather led everything back to it, as from the first Mover, which, as he found, is of infinite power. And he saw that this power is participated in in everything. I now refer to this infinite as the Not-other. The Not-other is therefore the Form of forms, or the Form of form and the Species of species and the Terminus of terminus. Thus it is true in the same way of everything, without there occurring thereby a further progression into the infinite, since one has indeed already attained to the infinite defining everything.

XI.

FERDINAND: I would like you, dear Father, to lead me by means of some enigma to vision of the aforesaid, so that I might intuit better what you mean.

NICOLAUS: Willingly. Do you see this carbuncle stone, which rustics are wont to call ruby? You observe that in the third hour of the night, at a time and in a location which is completely dark, one needs no candle, because there is light in it. If the light would be propagated, it does so by means of the stone, because it is invisible in itself to the senses. Indeed, it would not occur to the senses and therefore would never be perceived, for the senses know only what meets them. Therefore, that light which flashes in the stone, brings to the light which is in the eye, what is visible of that stone.

However, I consider how the one carbuncle shines more, the other less, and that the more perfect it is the more strongly it shines, and that a stone of greater quantity but of less brilliance is more ignoble. I know therefore that the measure of its preciousness is the intensity of its brilliance, not the mass of the body, unless it causes an increase of the intensity of the brilliance. Therefore, I do not look at the quantity of mass as the essence of the carbuncle, since a small stone is just as much a carbuncle as a large one. Therefore, I perceive the substance of the carbuncle before the large and small body. It is likewise with the color, the figure, and its other accidents. And therefore everything which I attain through sight, touch, and imagination concerning the carbuncle, is not its essence, but rather everything which is accidental to it, in which, in order to become sensibly perceptible, it shines forth, because it cannot be sensible without this.

That substance, which precedes the accidental, therefore has nothing from the accidental, but rather the accidents have everything from the former, because they are its accidents or shadows and images of its substantial light. Therefore, that substantial light of the carbuncle shows itself—in closer similitude—more clearly in the shining of its clearer brilliance. However, the color of the carbuncle or ruby, namely, red, is nothing except the terminus of the substantial light; it is not, however, the substance, but rather the similitude of the substance, since it is extrinsic or sensible. Therefore, the substantial light, which precedes the color and everything accidental which can be apprehended in the senses and imagination, is more intimate and stands nearer to the carbuncle and is invisible to the senses. However, through the intellect, which separates it anteriorly, it is perceived. It sees entirely that the substance of the carbuncle is not other than the substance of the carbuncle and that, therefore, this is also another from everything which is the substance of the not-carbuncle. And this it experiences in now this and now that operation, which follow from the power of the substance of the carbuncle and not from some other thing. Because the intellect, therefore, sees the invisible, substantial light of the carbuncle as one, the substance of the magnet as another, substantial, invisible light, that of the sun as another, that of the lion as another, etc., it sees that the substantial light in every visible thing is indeed now this and now that and it sees that before all sensibly perceptible things stands the intelligible, since the substance, which one sees before the accidental, is not seen except by the intellect, which alone sees the intelligible.

Now if one of sharper mind penetrates into the universe and its single parts, he sees that, just as the substance of the carbuncle is not other from its quantity, color, hardness, etc., for these are its accidents and it is everything in them which they are, although it itself is neither that quantity nor that quality nor anything accidental, but rather it itself is in them that which is now this and now that, since one accident is the quantity, another the quality, etc. (in like manner I see necessarily, that the Not-other, since the substance of the carbuncle is one, that of the magnet another, of man another, of the sun another, must precede all these different substances), the Not-other is not other from everything that is, but rather everything in everything, namely, that which subsists in everything. Thus John the Evangelist calls God the light before the other, namely, the darkness, since he says of Him, He is the light in which there is not any darkness. If you therefore call that light, which is the Not-other, then the creatures of darkness will be other. Thus the mind discerns the origin of light beyond the intelligible, substantial light of singular things as the Not-other, because it is not other from the single substances.

XII.

FERDINAND: It seems to me that I truly understand you: However, in order to test it, tell me: Do you not admit that this small carbuncle is an other from that larger one?

NICOLAUS: Why should I not admit that?

FERDINAND: Since both are carbuncle, the substance of the one seems to be no other from that of the other. How, therefore, are they other from one another?

NICOLAUS: You direct your view to the absolute substance, which can be no other in the other things substantified by it. However, in order to become sensibly perceptible substance, it requires substantifiable matter, without which it cannot be substantified. For how could it be substantified without the possibility of sensible being? Since, accordingly, that carbuncle is an other from this one, this one must necessarily come forth from the possibility of being in one otherwise than in the other. Since, therefore, sensible matter is necessary for sensible substance, substantial matter will be in the sensible things. Hence the two carbuncles differ substantially according to this substantial matter, which is other in the other carbuncle. In respect to the intelligible substance, however, which is understood as the form of being of the possible and sensible substance, the two carbuncles are not one and another.

FERDINAND: Therefore, the substance of the carbuncle or the ruby is not an other from any substance of any carbuncle, even if its extreme accidents follow it, since it is sensible and material.

NICOLAUS: You understand very well. For in the diverse carbuncles there is a substance, which is not an other from the substance of any carbuncle, even if on account of the variety of its substantial possibility and the accidents consequently occurring, it is nevertheless the substance of neither of these carbuncles. Therefore, the first substance, which the intellect sees separated, is the substance or specific form. The other, however, which one calls the sensible, is specified through the first and specifiable matter.

FERDINAND: That is completely clear; but do you not see that the Not-other is one intelligible substance at one time and another at another?

NICOLAUS: Precisely.

FERDINAND: Therefore, will the one universe not be as though this one carbuncle?

NICOLAUS: Why this?

FERDINAND: Because its substance were not other from the substance of any of its parts; for example, its substance is not other from the substance of the carbuncle or that of man; just as also the substance of man is not other from the substance of his hand, although it is not hand, which is another substance.

NICOLAUS: What follows from this?

FERDINAND: In fact something absurd! For the Not-other would be the substance of the universe and thereby it would be the universe itself; however, I see that that is impossible, since I behold the Not-other before the universe and the other. That universe, however, I see completely as something other.

NICOLAUS: You do not err or deceive yourself, Ferdinand. For since everything is ordered to God or the Not-other and in no way to the other, which is after Him, the universe is not to be regarded as though the end of the universe; for then God were the universe. Since, however, the universe is ordered to its Origin—through order the universe indeed shows itself as being from God—it is ordered to Him as to the Order of the order in everything. For He orders everything, so that the Not-other or the Order of the order shines forth more perfectly in the perfection of the things ordered to Him.

XIII.

FERDINAND: If I collect what I have already understood, the intellect perceives something in the plurality of carbuncles, which effects their membership in the same species. And although it is contained in all carbuncles, as specifying, one nevertheless intuits it anteriorly as the similitude of the Not-other before that plurality of carbuncles; it indeed causes every carbuncle to be a carbuncle; it is the inner substantial origin of every carbuncle, without which the carbuncle would not endure. Therefore, this specific origin specifies the specifiable possibility of the being of the carbuncle and gives this possibility actual being; when it makes the potential-to-be of the carbuncle through its actuality into the actual carbuncle; when we experience the confused possibility of being determined and specified as through the specific act. And then you see what you previously have seen intellectually detached, in the singular carbuncle as the actuality of the possibility, because it actually is a carbuncle. It is as if someone observing ice considers that what he now looks at, as concrete and stable ice, formerly was a flowing rivulet.

If he contemplates the cause, he will find that the coldness, which he sees intellectually separated, is a species of the being, which hardens and binds the freezable matter of every rivulet into concrete and stable ice, so that every rivulet, in consequence of the presence of this its actual cause, is actually ice, as long as it is prevented by it from flowing out. And although one finds no coldness separated from the cold, the intellect nevertheless intuits coldness as the cause of the cold before the cold, and perceives that in the cold, the coolable was made actually cold through coldness, and that in this way ice, hoarfrost, hail, and others of their kind, corresponding to the variety of the coolable, can arise and be found. But because coolable matter is also warmable, the coldness otherwise incorruptible in itself on account of the matter, without which it is never actually found, since this is altered just as the warmable through warmness, falls through the accidental into corruption. Thus you yourself seem to me to have said.

I understand also, how the accidental is consequential to the specific substances. Just as there are some accidents which follow the one piece of ice as well as the other, so also there are others which follow the snow, the hoarfrost, the hail, the crystal, and any other stone. From these wide and open-lying works of nature, I find clearly enough that also the more deeply hidden accidents are not other than you yourself have briefly touched upon; namely, that the specific and substantified forms are seen through the intellect as separate and attained in the specified and the substantified in the aforesaid manner. However, I elevate myself from the sensible substance to the intelligible through similitude.

NICOLAUS: I see that you have lucidly explained my concept with help of a most apt example from nature and I rejoice; by this mode of consideration, you will indeed ascertain everything. For the fact that a small quantity of heat does not dissolve a crystal, such as ice, because of the victory of the congealing coldness over the fluxibility of the congealed water, shows clearly that where the form places all fluxibility of matter into actuality, as in heaven, its corruption does not follow. From this it is evident that corruption, which is in sensible things, is impossible in the intelligent, which are separated from matter which is suited to alteration.

Now because in the intelligent warmth does not alter the intellect, so that it becomes warm—as in sensible perception, where it alters the sense—it is evident that the intellect is not material or alterable, because the sensible things, the characteristic of which is alteration, are in it not sensibly but rather intellectually. If you consider attentively and sharply, that the intellect is before the senses and therefore not attainable by the senses, then everything whatsoever which is in the senses you will find anteriorly in the intellect. However, I say anteriorly, i.e. insensibly. Just as coldness is in the intellect and the cold in the senses, coldness is in the intellect anteriorly relative to sensibly perceptible coldness; for coldness is not sensed, but rather understood, whilst the cold is sensed. Just as warmth is not perceived, but rather the warm, likewise water is not found, but rather the watery, nor fire, but rather the fiery, in the realm of the sensible. This must be stated similarly concerning everything composite, because the simple, which is of the realm of the intelligible, precedes every such thing of the sensible world. And the Not-other, the simplicity of the intelligible-simple, precedes one and the other intelligible. For this reason, the Not-other is not at all understood in itself, but rather simply in the simple, compositely however in the composite. These are, if I may say so, its Not-othered, namely, the things from which the Not-other itself is not other. I see, therefore, how of those things which are found in the realm of the sensible, whichever is perceived is preceded by its simple, which is understood. No less does the

Origin, which we call the Not-other, precede everything in the realm of the intelligible. Its cause, which defines it to be not other than coldness, certainly precedes intellectual coldness.

Just as the intellect through intellectual coldness understands everything sensibly cold without alteration of itself and without becoming cold, so the Not-other through it itself, or the Not-other without mutation or alteration of itself, brings it about that everything intellectually existing is not other than what it is. And as the sensible cold is no intellectual coldness, although it is by no means other from coldness, so intellectual coldness is not the first Origin, although the first Origin, which is the Not-other, is not another from it.

XIV.

FERDINAND: First, I see most clearly, that all this is just as you say. And I find furthermore, that in the intellectual the Not-other shines forth intensely as the Origin, because although the intellectual is not sensible, it is nevertheless not other from the sensible. Indeed, coldness is, as you have said, not other from the cold. Indeed, if one took away coldness, there would neither be nor be understood to be anything cold. The intellect is thus relative to the senses. Similarly, I see that every agent produces a resemblance, because it has everything that it is from the Not-other. Therefore, warmth endeavors to make warm and coldness to make cold, and thus it is with everything. However, these are thus sufficient for now! Indeed, I entreat you to introduce me, in accord with your promise, very briefly to that great theologian Dionysius and to others concerning this Origin.

NICOLAUS: I shall comply with your wish as briefly as possible. Dionysius, greatest of theologians, presupposes that it is impossible for man, except through the guidance of sensible forms, to ascend to the intelligence of the spiritual, wherefore, for example, he holds visible beauty to be an image of invisible grace. Therefore, he calls the sensible the similitude or image of the intelligible; however, he asserts that God, as the Origin, precedes everything intelligible. And he says he knows that God is nothing of everything that can be known or conceived. Therefore, he believes one can only know about Him, whom he designates to be the being of everything, that He precedes all intellect.

FERDINAND: If it is not a burden to you, tell me his words.

NICOLAUS: The different translators rendered his words differently into Latin. I shall append in succession what will be seen to serve my purpose from the newest translation of Brother Ambrose, General of the Camaldolese.

[*a*]

From the first chapter of *The Celestial Hierarchy:* "It is impossible for man to ascend to intelligence of the spiritual unless he is led by the forms and similitudes of the sensible, so that he holds visible beauty to be an image of invisible grace."

From the second chapter: "Since the simple substance of divine things in itself is unknown to us and escapes our intelligence. . . ." From the same: "When we say, it is nothing of the things which are, we surely say the truth, although we are completely ignorant of its supersubstantial, incomprehensible, and ineffable measure, since it is undefined."

In the fourth chapter of *The Celestial Hierarchy:* "Therefore, whatever subsists is governed by the rationality of providence, which flows from the highest deity, who is the Author of all things. Indeed, none of these things would exist, unless they participated in the origin and substance of things. And all the inanimate things receive from Him what they are, since the being of everything is the Divinity Himself, who surpasses the measure of every essence." From the same chapter: "The secret of God—whatever it may finally be—no one has ever seen, nor will he see it."

In the thirteenth chapter of the same: "Therefore, the Theologian was admonished, from what he perceived, that, according to every substantial eminence, God is incomparably loftier than all visible and invisible powers."

[*b*]

From the first chapter of *The Ecclesiastical Hierarchy:* "In order to say it in the true and proper sense: The One is that which all

desire, who prefer the species of the One; but they do not participate in one manner in that which is the one and the same, but
rather as the divine and most equal pair of scales distributes to
each its merited lot." In the same chapter: "The Beginning is the
Font of life, the Essence of goodness, the one Cause of all things,
the most blessed Trinity; from this one cause of goodness all
things receive the fact that they are and that they are good.
Therefore, this all-transcending, trine and one divine Beatitude,
in which alone being is truly inherent, in a manner unknown to
us, but clearly known and manifest to itself, is the wish for the
rational welfare of all human and celestial substance."

[*c*]

From the first chapter of *The Divine Names:* "As the carnal beings
are not able to perceive and to inspect the spiritual, as those who
cling to figments and figures do not aspire to what is simple and
devoid of figures, as those which are formed according to the
lines of the body never attain to the formlessness of incorporeal
things, which are subject neither to figures nor to sense of touch,
according to the same rational ground of truth the supersubstantial infinite surpasses all substances, the unity which is loftier than
the senses excels all the senses, that One, which is higher than
the mind, is inconceivable for all minds, and the good, which
surpasses the word, is ineffable for all words." In the same: "It
itself reports concerning itself in the Holy Scriptures that it is the
cause, beginning, substance, and life of everything." In the same:
"You will find, that all, I should have said almost all, laudation
of the theologians forms divine names for exhibiting and lauding
the beneficent progress of the Divinity. Hence we find in almost
every sacred book, that the Divinity is praised in a holy manner
as singular and unique on account of the simplicity and unity of
that excellent indivisibility, from which by means of its unifying
power we climb up to unity; and after our divisible othernesses
are pressed together into one in a supramundane manner, we are
gathered together into a divine monad and union imitating God,
etc." In the same: "In it all termini of all sciences pre-subsist more
than ineffably. And we can neither understand nor express nor
intuit it in any way, because it is excepted from everything and
is eminently unknown." In the same: "If all sciences are occupied
with the substance of things and end in the substances, then

He, who exceeds all substances, must be superior to all science. Although He perceives, comprehends, and anticipates everything, He nevertheless remains completely incomprehensible." In the same: "According to the testimony of the Scriptures, He is everything in everything. He is praised most truly as indulger and consummator of substance, the preserving custodian and domicile, the converter to Himself and all this conjointly, uncircumscribedly, and excellently."

In the second chapter of the same book: "Also the ineffable is proclaimed with many words: ignorance; what is understood through everything; the positing of everything; the ablation of everything; what transcends all positing and ablation; the Divine is known only through participation." In the same chapter: "It is not part and not the whole and is part and the whole, for it comprehends everything, the part and the whole in itself, and has everything excellently, before it has it. It is perfect in imperfection, since it is the beginning of perfection, but also imperfect in the perfect, since it transcends perfection in excellence and time." In the same: "It is the measure of things, it is time, and beyond time and before time." In the same: "He is not one and does not participate in the one, and far beyond this He is the One beyond that one which is in the substances."

In the same book of *The Divine Names* in the fourth chapter: "The theologians apply particularly goodness from among all things to the highest deity, calling, I think, the divine substance goodness." In the same: "The one which is is counted among the things which are. Furthermore number participates in substance. However, that supersubstantial One determines both the one which is, as well as every number." In the same: "Since the substance, which is goodness, can neither be augmented nor diminished, etc." In the same: "The light is from that Good and is the image of goodness. Therefore, the Good is praised in the appellation of the light, just as the original form, which is expressed in the image." In the same: "It illuminates all things which admit the light, it creates, vivifies, preserves, and perfects, it is the measure of substances, the time, number, and order, etc." Note the example of the sun. In the same: "The Good is denoted as intelligible light, since it fills every supercelestial spirit with spiritual light, expels all ignorance and drives away error from every soul, in which it has insinuated itself, etc." In the same: "Therefore, that Good, which, as original ray and exuberant effusion of light, surpasses every light, is called intelligible light." In the same: "This Good is also proclaimed by the holy theologians as the Beautiful." In the same: "Since it has the original beauty of everything beautiful most excellently in itself before time. . . ." In the same: "The Beautiful is seen to be the same as the Good." In the same: "In the substances of things there is none which would not participate in some measure in the Beautiful and the Good, indeed we even venture to assert in our discussion that also that which is not, participates in the Beautiful and Good. Then indeed, etc. . . ." In the same: "In order to briefly summarize: Everything which is, is from the Beautiful and Good, and everything which is not, is supersubstantially in the Beautiful and the Good; it is the beginning and end of everything, etc."

In the same in the eighth chapter: "He is not. But for the things which are, He is being itself. And not only the things which are, but rather also their being is from Him, who is before all time. Indeed, He is the time of times, who is before all time." In the same eighth chapter: "In summary, we can say: All things which are and all times have their being from Him, who is before; every age and time is from Him." In the same: "Everything participates in Him and He departs from no existent." In the same: "If anything whatever exists in any manner, then it exists and is thought and preserved in Him who is before, and this precedes every other participation." In the same: "God has before, so that He is before and exists most eminently and has being excellently. He prescribed that in Himself all things are being itself, and through His own being He caused to subsist everything which in any way exists. Finally, through participation in His being all the origins of things are, and are origins; first they are, then they are origins. And if you want to call life itself the beginning of the living as living, and similitude the beginning of the similar as similar, etc." In the same: "You will find, that these things participate first of all in His being and remain at first in this being, and then by participating they are the origins and essences of this or that being and as such are participated in. However, if the essences exist through participation, then it is all the more the case for those which participate in them." In the same: "Goodness is celebrated as the first of the participations."

In the same: "He is neither in any subsisting things nor is He any of them."

In the same in the ninth chapter: "Nothing is opposite to Him."

In the same in the tenth chapter: "He, who is discovered from all things, the theologians call the incomprehensible and the impenetrable." In the same chapter: "We should not wish to understand divine things in a human manner, but rather we must entirely pass beyond ourselves and pass over absolutely into God." In the same chapter: "God does not have one peculiar knowledge of Himself, and another universal one, which comprehends everything. For, if the Cause of all things knows Himself, why should He not know the things which are from Him and whose cause He is?" In the same chapter: "God is known in everything and divided from everything and God is known through knowledge and ignorance." In the same chapter: "He is everything in everything and nothing in nothing."

In the same in the eleventh chapter: "God is power and the author of all power." In the same chapter: "The infinitely powerful, divine distribution extends itself to everything that is. And among all things there is nothing which is not suitable for receiving any power." In the same chapter: "Something which is supported by absolutely no power, neither is, nor is it something, nor is there any positing of it." In the same chapter: "All things which exist, He has excellently and before all time in His supersubstantial power, and to all things which exist, He bestows from the fullness and the exuberant profusion of His excellent power, that they can exist and are this."

In the same book in the twelfth chapter: "God is called great on account of His own magnitude, which He imparts to everything great in partnership with Himself and which is extended extrinsically upon every magnitude and is expanded beyond, containing every location, transcending every number, and passing over every infinity." In the same: "This magnitude is both infinite and it is without quantity and number." In the same: "Indeed, He is called small or slight, because He transcends every mass and distance, because He advances to everything without impediment, and yet, the cause of everything is certainly tiny; nowhere do you find the incommunicable species of this tininess." In the same: "This tininess is without quantity, no quality contains it, it is infinite and indeterminate, comprehending everything and comprehensible to none." In the same: "Because it cannot be augmented or diminished. . . ." In the same: "Further, God is called the other, because He is present to everything by reason of Providence and for the well-being of all becomes everything in everything, while remaining in Himself and His own identity!" In the same: ". . .the power of divine similitude, through which all things that are produced are converted toward their Author; these things must be called godlike and created according to the image and similitude of God. However, God must not be said to be similar to them, since man is not similar to his own image." In the same: "Theology itself describes Him as dissimilar to and not in agreement with everything, since He is other from everything. What is still more astonishing is: Theology says there is nothing similar to Him. And certainly this is not opposed to the similitude with God, for to God similar and dissimilar things are the same. Similar, because according to their power they imitate Him, who cannot possibly be imitated clearly." In the same: "However, this is because the caused is far inferior to its author and is in infinite and unconfused measure divided from Him."

In the same in the thirteenth chapter: "He produces everything from Himself as from an omnipotent root." In the same: "He does not let it fall from Him. . . ." In the same in the thirteenth chapter: "He is for everything duration and time and before the days and before duration and before time, although we can name Him appropriately time and day and moment and duration; He, who by every motion is incommutable and immobile, and although there is always motion, persists in Himself as the author of duration and time and days." From the thirteenth chapter: "The life of all that live and the cause of life itself; being itself, life itself, and the deity itself we have named the One, which principally, divinely, and according to cause excels all beginnings."

In the fifteenth chapter: "He terminates every infinity and is extended beyond every end, and is conceived and comprehended by none; rather He extends Himself simultaneously to everything." In the same: "And this One, the cause of everything, is not one of many, but rather before the one, etc." In the same: "It is the definition of everything one and of the multitude." In the same: "If someone places everything conjointly with everything, everything will be totally one." In the same: "The One is, as it were, the element of everything." In the same: "If you take away the One, neither the whole will exist nor any part nor any other thing. For the One has uniformly contained and enfolded everything anteriorly in itself." In the same: "The One is before the finite and the infinite, etc." In the same: "It determines everything that is and also being itself." In the same: "What is beyond the one, determines that which is the one." In the same: "The one that is, is counted among the things which are. Number, however, participates in substance. The supersubstantial One determines the one that is and every number."

[d]

Toward the end of *The Mystical Theology:* "He is not anything other from that which is known to us or to anyone else in the world, nor is He anything which does not exist nor anything which exists." In the same: "There is no positing of Him, nor any ablation."

[e]

In a *Letter to Gaius:* "If someone seeing God understands what he sees, then he does not see Him, but rather something; not being known and not existing, He exists supersubstantially and is known beyond the mind. Our knowledge of Him, who is above everything which is known, is perfect ignorance."

XV.

FERDINAND: I see that the expressions of the Theologian are ponderous and profound and such that they lead one's view to the ineffable divinity in the manner it is conceded to man.

NICOLAUS: Have you noticed how he has spoken concerning the Not-other?

FERDINAND: I have not yet clearly perceived it.

NICOLAUS: You have surely considered how he speaks concerning the first cause, which he shows now one way, now another, as everything in everything.

FERDINAND: So it seems. But I entreat you to lead me, so that I can look into it more clearly with you.

NICOLAUS: Have you not considered how, where he names the Origin the One, he says thereafter that the supersubstantial One determines the one that is and every number?

FERDINAND: I have considered it and it has pleased me.

NICOLAUS: Why did it please you?

FERDINAND: Because, although the One comes close to the Not-other, nevertheless he also says that the supersubstantial One is before the one. And this is certainly the One before the one, which is one. And you see this as the Not-other.

NICOLAUS: You have comprehended very well! Hence, if A were what is signified by the Not-other, then A were that of which he speaks. However, if, as he says, the One is before the finite and infinite, terminating every infinity, simultaneously extending to everything and remaining incomprehensibly away from everything, the definition of everything one and every multitude, then surely A, which defines the one, precedes the one, which is another. For since the one is not other than the one, the one would cease to exist with the removal of A.

FERDINAND: Correct. For since he speaks of how the One, which is beyond the one, determines that one, which is one, then he certainly spoke previously of this One beyond the one as the One before the one. Therefore, A determines the one and everything, since, as he says, this One is the definition of every one and every multitude.

NICOLAUS: You could also see how the Theologian converts the mind to this "before," saying that God has a "before," so that He exists "before" and exists most eminently. Nevertheless, one sees the A before the "before," since the "before" is not other than the "before." Now since the "before" is understood only before something which it precedes, the A is the "before" most eminently, since it precedes everything other. However, "before" can be said of an other, so that the one is what precedes and the other, what follows. If, therefore, as the Theologian maintains, everything which is found in the posterior exists eminently or

anteriorly in the anterior, then we perceive everything most
eminently in A, since it is before the "before" itself.

FERDINAND: You remember very well. Indeed, I notice how the
Theologian says that He, who is before time, is the time of
times. And I think that he would like to speak similarly of
Him in respect to all things. Therefore, because I see God
anteriorly as A, I see that in Him everything is He Himself;
however, because I perceive God posteriorly in the other,
I perceive that He is everything in everything. If I see Him
before time, I see that in Him the duration is God; to be
sure, in its own origin or rational ground time is seen before
time. If I see Him in time, then I see Him as time. For what
I saw beforehand as God, I see afterwards as time; the time,
which I saw in God as God, I intuit in time as time; that,
however, is not other than if the posterior is seen in the
prior; then it is indeed the prior. But if the prior is seen in
the posterior, then it is the posterior.

NICOLAUS: You penetrate everything with the help of that which
you have conceived about the Not-other. And as much as
the origin A affords you light, you will intuit that which is
otherwise hidden from you. But tell me one thing more:
How do you apprehend the assertion of the Theologian,
that God could be most appropriately named duration,
time, day, and moment?

XVI.

FERDINAND: I understand it according to the vision of the Theologian. Namely, he saw that in time everything temporal is
moved temporally, nevertheless, time itself always remains
immutable. Therefore, in time the Not-other shines forth
very cognizably. In an hour time is indeed hour, in a day
day, in a month month, in a year year, and as it is seen
before all this, so is this in it, it itself, as it itself is everything
in everything. Although in everything that participates in
time it is everything and extends to everything and remains
inseparably with everything, defines, and terminates everything, it nevertheless remains no less firmly and immobilely
in itself and is neither augmented nor diminished, although
time seems to be greater, with longer duration, in a month,

for example, greater than in a day. However, that comes to pass only on the basis of the other, which participates in it more or less. Therefore, while remaining unable to be participated in, it is participated in in various ways.

NICOLAUS: As I see, nothing remains hidden to you; yet you must pay attention to all the words of the Theologian. Indeed, he says nothing in vain. He says God could most appropriately be named moment.

FERDINAND: Indeed, he says so. But why do you admonish that this should be keenly attended to?

NICOLAUS: The moment is the substance of time. For if it were sublated, nothing would remain of time. The moment, therefore, because of its most simple indivisibility and inalterability, participates to a very great degree in A. It seems indeed to be substantiality itself. If this had been named duration, it would be easily discerned how in eternity it is eternity, in time time, month in month, in a day day, in an hour hour, and in a moment moment. The same is true for everything that participates in duration. And duration is not other from everything that endures. Most of all that is true for the moment, or the now, that endures steadfastly. Therefore, duration is everything in everything, even though before everything which participates in it. Hence, because these things which participate in it, are other and it itself not other from the participating, it is thus evident that the Not-other is participated in by eternity, or more truly, by duration and the moment.

FERDINAND: I believe that by moment you wish to say the present.

NICOLAUS: I regard the now, the moment and the present to be the same.

FERDINAND: I already see clearly that the present is the origin of being known and being of all differences and varieties of time. Indeed, through the present I know the past and the future. And whatever these are, they are through it, indeed the present is in the past past, however in the future it is future, in the month month, in the day day, etc. And although it is everything in everything and proceeds to everything, it is nevertheless incomprehensible by everything and remains constantly without otherness.

NICOLAUS: You have penetrated it perfectly and therefore it is also in no way hidden from you, that the A is the present of the present. For it precedes the present itself, because the present, which is not other than the present, presupposes the Not-other, because in the Not-other the present is Not-other. And because the present is the substance of time, you see correctly that A is the substance of substance. For if the present is removed, then time no longer persists. But if A is removed, then neither the present nor time nor anything else could possibly remain.

FERDINAND: You have admonished well, Father, and now I see clearly that all the statements of this theologian are illuminated through the A. Moreover, it pleases me very much that Dionysius affirms, the theologians had celebrated goodness as the first participation in God. I see from this that all divine names signify participation in the imparticipable. However, since with the removal of A all these names lose their significance and participation, because A is participated in in everything, I am happy to be situated, and indeed first of all, according to the theologians, in goodness. For, since that which all desire, is desired under the rational ground of the Good, then A, without which everything ceases, is correctly named goodness. Moses says the Creator was moved to create everything, because He saw that it was good. If, therefore, the Origin of things is good, then certainly everything exists insofar as it is good. Just as the Good is not other from the Beautiful—as Dionysius asserts—so it is not other from every existing thing. However, it has this from A. Therefore, the latter shines forth very well in it. Indeed, if A shines forth in something optimally, then certainly this both is and is said to be good.

NICOLAUS: You discern quite clearly, because you survey everything correctly with the help of A. But have you also considered how the Theologian says the One is, as it were, the element of everything, in *The Mystical Theology,* nevertheless, he denies that God is one?

XVII.

FERDINAND: I have indeed considered that he spoke just as you assert. But I entreat you to explain to me what he wishes to express by this.

NICOLAUS: I believe he wanted to say the following: Just as, if the one were sublated, singular things would cease, and just as, if the element were sublated, things which arise from the element would desist, so likewise, if A were removed, all things would cease. For it is more intimately and inwardly related to everything than the element is to what has arisen from the element.

FERDINAND: Therefore, David of Dynant and those philosophers whom he followed did not err, when they designated God as *hyle, nous* and *physis,* and the visible world as visible God.

NICOLAUS: David calls *hyle* the origin of bodies, *nous* or mind the origin of souls, but *physis* or nature the origin of motion, and saw that insofar as they are in the origin, these do not differ among themselves; therefore, he spoke in this way. But you have already seen that A defines these and is these in them, even though it is none of them. Therefore, don't let this and similar propositions, namely, the fact that the Theologian calls the One, as it were, the element, disturb you, but rather you will not err if you always return to the A and to the aforementioned.

FERDINAND: You instruct and inform me scrupulously. Also what the Theologian wrote to Gaius is quite pleasing to me. It is lucid and in accordance and consonant with what you said.

NICOLAUS: What is it?

FERDINAND: When the Theologian asserts: "If someone, seeing God, understood what he saw, then he did not see Him, but rather something other." If, therefore, David of Dynant saw that God is *hyle* or *nous* or *physis,* he certainly saw something other and not God.

NICOLAUS: You are marvelous, Ferdinand; but still more marvelous, if you have considered in the words mentioned that which is loftier.

FERDINAND: I ask what that should be?

NICOLAUS: When he says: "Since everything that is understood
is something, it is not God." Something, however, is something other. Therefore, if God were understood, then He
would be understood not to be other. Therefore, if He
cannot be understood to be that which is signified through
other and something, and something cannot be understood
which is not signified by something, then if God were seen,
He would have to be seen beyond and before something
other and beyond the intellect. However, before the other
nothing can be seen except the Not-other. From this it
therefore follows, that the Not-other leads us to the Origin,
which excels and precedes the intellect, the other, something, and everything intelligible. The Theologian explains
this in this location, and also how knowledge of the Not-
other can be named perfect ignorance, since it is the knowledge of that which is beyond everything which is known.
Now those are the words of our admirable Theologian.
They indeed suffice for our purpose also in respect to whatever else has been said by him in this manner.

XVIII.

FERDINAND: If you now have the time, we wish by means of this
principle of ours to explore some perhaps not unworthy
writings of Aristotle, the greatest and most sagacious Peri-
patetic. Since he is not altogether unknown to you, I entreat
you to tell me what the Philosopher, who was full of such
solicitude, wanted to show us.

NICOLAUS: I believe, certainly, that which he discovered concerning the notion of the true.

FERDINAND: What therefore did he find out?

NICOLAUS: To confess honestly, I do not know. However, he
says that quiddity, the object of the intellect, is always
sought and never found. Thus he asserts in *The First Philosophy:* "The most difficult question for all and the one that
has the greatest uncertainty is whether or not one and entity,
as the Pythagoreans and Plato said, are not something other
but rather the substance of entity; or whether this is some
other subject, for which Empedocles names friendship, an-

439

other fire, another water, another air." And in another location in the same book he says: "In times past as now and always it is asked and is always drawn into doubt, what entity is, i.e., what is substance." Indeed, some say it is one, others that it is many.

FERDINAND: These words of the great Philosopher are surely to be esteemed. Therefore, prepare us so that we may explore with acute vision these remarks of the Philosopher.

NICOLAUS: I will attempt it to the best of my abilities. Indeed, I consider how he asks whether one and entity are not anything other, but rather the substance of entity, to be as if he sought the substance of things through the Not-other. For he saw that the substance of things is not anything other and therefore he doubted concerning entity, concerning the One, concerning friendship, concerning air and water and everything, whether any of them were the substance of things, since he ascertained all of them to be something other. He therefore presupposed that the substance of things exists and that it is not plural. Like all others, however, he was in doubt as to what this would be. And as he inquired, he concurred with all those who had named it variously, in investigating whether it had been named well by anyone. And finally, it seemed to him that no one named it well, since whoever had given a name to it, had named something other or another thing, but not the most simple quiddity of things, which he saw could not be anything other. And in this he did not err; yet he stopped there, like the other men. For he saw that no manner of rational hunting suffices for grasping this so-desired and nourishing knowledge.

FERDINAND: I see that that has happened to the Philosopher of which you previously made mention.

NICOLAUS: What was it then?

FERDINAND: Since he, who endeavors to see what the substance of a visible thing is, seeks it with his eyes among visible things, he does not attend to perceiving anteriorly the light, without which he could neither seek nor find the visible. But if he attended to the light, he would desist from seeking anything other; surely it occurred thus to the Philosopher.

When he sought the quiddity of things with his mind, the light, which is signified through the Not-other, struck him as that, without which he could make no discovery at all. Otherwise, he did not attend to the fact that the light, as the Not-other, is not other from that which is sought. However, because he sought the other by means of the Not-other, he only found what is other from the others, and therefore he discovered with his searching only what is very remote.

NICOLAUS: You speak truly. For if he had attended to the fact that this light, which he saw in the mind to be the means of arriving at the sought-after Origin, is also the end, then he would certainly not have deviated and would have cut short so many labors. If indeed he had said: I see clearly that the quiddity of things can be no other thing—for how would it be the quiddity of things, if it were other? The other indeed itself denies that it is that which is sought. Indeed, if it must not be other, then it must surely be the Not-other from every other. However, that which must not be other from every other, can certainly not be named otherwise. Therefore, it will correctly be named the Not-other. Therefore, if A is now signified by the Not-other, then A will truly be that which is sought.

XIX.

FERDINAND: If only Aristotle had been attentive, as you say! He would have handed down this secret in the simplest, clearest, and fewest words and thereby spared himself and us a lot of labor. He would have needed to avail himself of neither laborious logic nor the difficult art of definition, which that man, although he investigated with great labor, nevertheless was not able to lead to perfection. Also in regards to species and ideas, all difficulties and diversity of opinion would have disappeared and he would have gloriously consummated the knowledge of man.

NICOLAUS: You show an extraordinary affection toward the exceptional Philosopher, who indeed seems to have been gifted with the most lucid rationality. Certainly the same could perhaps be said of all speculative philosophers. For this is a facility with difficulties, which directed all speculative philosophers to the indubitable truth for mental vision. According to my opinion no briefer and conciser facility than this can be handed down or apprehended; it is alone perfect and no man can possibly add anything to it. Indeed, it directs vision to the Origin, so the one contemplating it is delighted and is continuously nourished and thrives. Also no other instruction is discoverable which were perfect, absolute, and complete. Indeed, everything which the sight of the mental eye does not see, but rather rationality investigates, does not achieve ultimate certitude, even if it seems to come near to the true. However, the certitude, which is ultimate and altogether perfected, is vision.

FERDINAND: Surely everything that you say is so. That philosopher seems to have attempted throughout his life to elicit on the basis of rationality the way or the art of achieving the substance of things and to have found none which sufficed. For even rationality cannot advance to that which precedes it; and even less can the arts produced by rationality provide a way to that which is unknown to all rationality. That philosopher regarded it as most certain, that every affirmative assertion contradicts a negative one and that both cannot simultaneously be said of the same thing, inasmuch as they are contradictions. He said this, however, by means of rationality concluding this as true. But, if someone had asked him what is the other, he certainly could have responded truly: It is not other than other. And if the questioner consequently added: Why is the other other, he would certainly have been able to say correctly as before: because it is not other than other. And thus he would have seen that the Not-other and the other do not contradict themselves as contradictions. And he would have seen that that, which he named as the first principle, does not suffice for showing the way to the truth, which is contemplated by the mind beyond rationality.

NICOLAUS: I laud your remarks and add that also in another manner he has precluded himself from the road to intuiting the truth. Indeed, he asserted, there is no substance of substance and no origin of origin, as we have considered it above; likewise he would also have denied that there is contradiction of contradiction. And had someone now asked him whether he saw contradiction in the contradictories, then he would have responded that truly he did see it. Had someone asked him further, if he saw that which he saw in contradictories anteriorly—just as he would see the cause before the effect—did he not then see a contradiction without contradiction, he would certainly not have been able to deny this is so. For just as he saw that the contradiction in the contradictories is a contradiction of the contradictories, so before the contradictories he would have seen the contradiction before the named contradiction, just as the theologian Dionysius saw God as the opposition of the opposites without opposition. For before the opposites nothing is opposed to the opposition. Although this philosopher failed in the first or mental philosophy, he has nevertheless written much in the rational and moral philosophy that is most worthy of all praise. However, because this does not belong to our present speculation, let what has been said about Aristotle suffice.

XX.

PETER BALBUS OF PISA: I have listened to you, Father, discussing with Ferdinand many things most pleasing to me. However, most of all I admired the quotations from the books of the greatest theologian Dionysius. Indeed, during recent days when I translated Proclus, the Platonist, from Greek into Latin, in his book on the theology of the divine Plato, I found the same things in almost the same mode and tenor of expression. For this reason, I would also like to hear from you something about *The Platonic Theology*.

NICOLAUS: It is certain, Peter, that your Proclus was later in time than Dionysius the Areopagite. But whether he saw the writings of Dionysius is uncertain. However, report more particularly, in which assertions they agree.

PETER: Just as Dionysius says that the one which exists is posterior to the simply One, so Proclus also asserts in referring to Plato.

NICOLAUS: Perhaps all wise men wanted to say the same concerning the first Origin of things and various of them expressed it variously. However, Plato, whom Proclus extolled so much, as if he had been a god in human form, attempted in always looking to what is anterior to see the substance of things before everything nameable. Therefore, since he saw that the corporeal and divisible thing cannot subsist from itself and can also not preserve itself on account of its debility and fluxibility, he saw the soul before it, before the soul, however, the intellect, and before the intellect the One.

The posterior subsists through participation in the prior. Therefore, the First, through participation in which everything is what it is, appears before the intellect, since in no way does everything participate in the intellect. Therefore, in order to use his words, the intellect does not attain to what is earlier or older than itself. On this basis, I believe Plato has perceived the substance or the Origin of things in his own mind by way of a revelation in the manner in which the Apostle tells the Romans that God has revealed Himself to them. I grasp this revelation in the similitude of the light, which through itself pours itself into vision. Other than that it reveals itself, it is neither seen nor known, since it is invisible, because it is before and beyond everything which is visible. That this is so, Plato expresses in his letters very briefly, when he says, God manifests Himself to him who seeks most vigilantly and constantly. Proclus also repeats this in his *Commentary on the Parmenides*. Therefore, while he supposes this as true, he says that the soul, which in contemplating itself enfolds in itself in the manner of the soul everything posterior, inspects as in a living mirror everything which participates in its life and which lives through it and subsists vitally. And since these things are in it, it ascends upward in its similitude to the prior, just as Proclus recites this in his theology.

PETER: Declare, I ask, whether what you have said means the same as what you have advanced concerning the Not-other.

NICOLAUS: To him who considers it, this easily becomes evident. As he himself said, the cause of everything must be participated in by everything. Therefore, the One, which, as he says, is before the one which is one, is not other from the latter, since it is its cause. Therefore, he names the cause of the one that is, the One, in order thus to express the Not-other. Hence, just as he names the cause of the one which is, the One, he names the cause of entity Entity, that of substance Substance. And he does likewise with everything. Thereby we can understand that everything which is and is named has that which it is and is named from the cause of everything, which in all existing things is that which they are and are named and not other. Therefore, you see that all names which he says precede the names of the named, just as the One which is before the one that is and is named one, he has for that reason attributed to the cause, in order to designate that the cause is not other from the caused. Therefore, in all names the Not-other is what is signified.

PETER: I see, Father, that this is not to be doubted. However, when I turn to the Not-other, I cannot mentally conceive what it is.

NICOLAUS: If you could conceive it, then it were by no means the Origin of everything, which signifies everything in everything. For every human concept is the concept of some one thing. However, the Not-other is before the concept, because a concept is not other than a concept. Therefore, the Not-other is called the absolute Concept, which is seen mentally, but is otherwise not conceived.

PETER: Since, therefore, the Not-other is not other from anything, but rather is everything in everything, is it then not everything in every concept?

NICOLAUS: Yes, indeed. Since every concept is not other than a concept, in every concept the Not-other is whatever is conceived, but to be sure the concept, which is the Not-other, remains inconceivable.

XXI.

PETER: When you say in a definition, the earth is not other than the earth, the "than" certainly disturbs me. Therefore, I'd like you to explain this.

NICOLAUS: Clearly you see that this definition of the earth, which says the earth is not other than the earth, is true, but the one that says, the earth is other than the earth, is false.

PETER: I see.

NICOLAUS: On what therefore does the truth of the definition depend?

PETER: I perceive clearly that the "than" is both in the true and in the false definition. Accordingly, I cannot say that the truth depends on this "than"; but rather on that Not-other.

NICOLAUS: Very good. The "than" therefore does not define. It should not perturb you.

PETER: Why therefore is the "than" added?

NICOLAUS: Because it directs the vision. For, when I say the Not-other is not other than the Not-other, then the "than" directs the vision simply to the Not-other, as it is before the other. However, when I say the other is not other than the other, then it directs the vision to the Not-other, as it is other in the other. And when I say the earth is not other than the earth, then it directs the vision to the Not-other, as it is earth in the earth and it is similar concerning everything.

PETER: Very good! Now I see that the answer to the question, what is the earth: the earth is not other than the earth, unfolds the acute vision of the mind, by which the mind sees that the Origin of all things signified through the Not-other defines the earth, i.e., that the Not-other is the earth in the earth. For if it were asked, why the earth is earth? one must answer: because it is not other than earth. The earth is indeed earth, because its Origin or cause is in it, it itself. And if it were asked thus: whence does the earth have it, that it is earth? one would surely have to answer that it has it from its Origin or from the Not-other. Indeed, from that, from which it has that it is not other than earth, it has that it is earth. Wherefore, if it is asked: from what does the good have that it is good? one can answer: from that which is not other from the good. For, since the Good does not have that it is good from another from the Good, it is indeed necessary, that it has this from the not other from the Good. Thus the earth has that it is earth from the not other from earth and the same is true for all things. In this way I see everything anteriorly in the Origin, which is the Not-other. It is signified most simply and absolutely by the Not-other, because A is not other from anything. Therefore, the names cause, exemplar, form, idea, species, and the like were attributed to it by the philosophers, just as you made me see heretofore.

NICOLAUS: You have explored this, Peter, and you see that the Origin of everything is signified through the Not-other; consequently it is not other from anything and is everything in everything. But now turn back to Plato, whose intention it was to intuit the Origin, which is everything in everything. He saw that everything that can be otherwise, such as figure, name, definition, rational ground, opinion, and the like in no way shows quiddity, since the essence and quiddity of things precedes all these. Therefore, anteriorly to that which is other, unstable and variable, he saw that that which precedes the other is the Substance of all substances and the Quiddity of all quiddities, which, since it is everything in everything, is that which is signified through the Not-other. In this First, therefore, he saw everything and that everything emanates from it and its grace as from a font or a cause.

PETER: Plato writes this quite clearly in his letters. But he adds that everything exists first in the first King, secondly in the second and thirdly in the third.

NICOLAUS: He saw the diverse modes of being of things. For before the other he intuited everything as the simplest Origin, in which everything that exists otherwise in another is discerned as the Not-other. For when I transfer my attention from the earth, which with the eye of rationality I see to be something other from not-earth or heaven or fire, to intuiting it in the Origin, I do not see it there as other from the not-earth, for I see it as the Origin, which is not other from anything. I do not intuit it in a more imperfect mode than before, but rather in the most precise and true mode. For everything is then seen most precisely, when it is discerned as the Not-other. Indeed, whoever sees the earth, so that he sees it as the Not-other, intuits it most precisely.

And this is to discern the quiddity of its quiddity and of all things. Another mode of seeing is the vision of the quiddity of the earth, which is seen by the intellect to be other from the quiddity of water or of fire; it follows the Not-other, because it is other from the others. And this is the second or intellectual mode of being of quiddity. But there is yet a third mode of being, as is attained by the soul in distinguishing this from that in the manner of the soul, according as the thing or the quiddity of a thing is sensed. Plato wanted to say this or perhaps something higher. Indeed, Plato disclosed this, his hidden secret, timidly and briefly and with his few words has excited the most acute mental powers of many.

XXII.

ABBOT JOHN ANDREA: I have often heard you, Father, both formerly and especially now, bringing to us the vision of your mind, which you direct to the First, which is everything in everything; prior to which something cannot be conceived and which you name the Not-other. And, nevertheless, you assert that the First is seen before everything nameable. That seems to me to be truly a contradiction.

NICOLAUS: Father Abbot, you remember well what you have heard. But I certainly do not say that the Not-other is the name of that, whose name is beyond every name. With the Not-other I make known to you rather the name of my concept of the First. No more precise name occurs to me expressing my concept of the unnameable, which is other from none.

ABBOT: I would truly be astonished at how that which you see before and beyond everything other, is not other, since the other seems to be opposed to the Not-other, except that Plato said nearly the same in the *Parmenides,* and his commentator, Proclus, clarified this uncertainty. Although Plato as well as Proclus discuss the One and the other there, saying that the One could not possibly be other from other, you, however, cause me, through the more precise expression of your concept, to intuit clearly by means of the Not-other, that the Not-other cannot be other from any other, whether nameable or unnameable, since the Not-other defines everything, so that it is everything in everything. Dionysius the Areopagite indeed says that God is called the other, which is denied, however, in the *Parmenides*.

NICOLAUS: You remember, I believe, that Plato denies that the definition attains the what of a thing, since as Proclus also explains, the definition circumscribes the quiddity. That is, however, not the case, when the Not-other defines itself and everything. Indeed, it does not define the quidditative principle, as someone who determines or defines a triangular surface by the circumscription of lines, but rather as if someone constituted the surface, which is called a triangle. However, you see from the following that Plato and Dionysius are not incompatible with or opposed to one another: Dionysius asserts that God is the other—just as we commonly identify a friend as another I—indeed not on account of a separation, but rather on account of an agglutination, and in regards to an essence, so to speak, He is everything in everything, as he explains. And Plato intends nothing other.

ABBOT: I certainly see that this definition, which you assert to be the only true and quidditative one, is not that which Plato calls defective and incomplete and I am exceedingly amazed, when I direct greater attention to it, at how the more known, the more clear and easy this mode is, the more distant and free it is from all obscurity and doubt. For this reason, since no one can doubt that these definitions of yours are so true that they cannot be truer, in them the quiddity of things shines forth truly. But what do you say to the Gospel, where it is read that John the Baptist, than whom no one among those born of woman is greater, asserts that no one has ever seen God and that the Son of God, who is named the Truth in the same Gospel, has revealed this?

NICOLAUS: I indeed assert the same; namely, that God is invisible for every mode of vision. For if someone asserted that he had seen Him, then he could certainly not express what he had seen. For in what sense is He visible, who is before the visible and the invisible, except in the sense that without

Him nothing is discerned, since He excels everything visible? Hence, when I see that He is not heaven, nor other from heaven—and universally—is neither another nor another from another, then I do not see Him, as if I knew what I see. Indeed, that seeing, which I refer to God, is not a visible-seeing, but rather a seeing of the invisible in the visible. As soon as I see that it is true, that no one has seen God, then I see God truly beyond everything visible, as the Not-other from everything visible. However, that actual infinity, which exceeds all vision, the Quiddity of all quiddities, I in no way see as visible, since the visible or the object is another from the power. God, however, who cannot be other from anything, exceeds every object.

XXIII.

ABBOT: It is not astonishing that God the Creator is invisible. For although we see the wonderful works of the intellect in civic buildings, ships, works of art, books, paintings, and innumerable other things, nevertheless we do not attain the intellect with our sense of vision. And thus we discern God in His creatures, although He remains invisible for us. Thus heaven and earth are indeed the works of God, whom no one has ever seen.

NICOLAUS: Vision does not see itself, although in the other, which it sees, it attains itself as seeing. That vision, however, which is the Vision of vision, does not attain to its own perception in an other, since it is before the other. Therefore, since it discerns before the other, in this vision the seeing, the visible, and the vision proceeding from both are not other. Therefore, it is evident that God, who is called *theos,* which is from *theoro,* or *I see,* is this vision before the other, which we cannot see perfectly except as trine, and that to see the infinite and interminable in the other is to see Him, who is the Not-other from anything. Therefore, the wise men say that God sees Himself and everything in a single and indescribable look, since He is the Vision of vision.

ABBOT: Who would not see that as true, which you have shown

that you already see! Surely, no one except he who lacks mental acumen, denies that God, who is the origin before the other and before everything and who is certainly before all privation, is not deprived of vision. But if He is not deprived of vision, but rather is called *theos* from vision, God has the most perfect vision, which perfects or defines itself and everything in the manner which you have previously explained. However, what God possesses is before the other. The vision, which is the triune *theos,* certainly does not see itself in the one vision and the other in another, but rather with the same vision, in which it sees itself, it simultaneously intuits everything. This seeing is defining. For this seeing does not have its motion from another—as in us an object moves the power; but rather His seeing is constituting, as Moses says: God saw that the light was good and it was made. This light is therefore not other than the light which is seen as light through the vision, which is the Not-other. Hence, I see from one rational ground that all things are not other than that which they are; namely, because the vision, which is the Not-other, sees nothing other from itself. Yet it remains for me to hear from you concerning the good, which Moses mentions, when he says: God saw that it was good and thereupon He created it.

NICOLAUS: You have read in the *Commentary on the Parmenides* that God is called similarly the One and the Good. Proclus proved them to be the same, since they penetrate everything. It is as if he wanted to say: Because God is everything in everything, we must attribute to Him this name, which we discern to be present in everything centrally. But the Good shines forth in everything. Everything loves its own being, because it is good, since the Good is of itself lovable and estimable. Therefore, when Moses wished to describe the constitution of the universe, in which God manifested Himself, he said that in its constitution each single created thing is good, so that the universe is a perfect revelation of the glory and wisdom of God. Therefore, that which He saw as good in itself before the other, because it was good, came into the constitution of the universe. But since God saw the Good before the other, He Himself was not other from this. If someone could intuit the Good alone, as it is the Not-other, before every other, he would certainly intuit that no one is good except God alone, who is before the not-good. All things other, because they are other, are able to exist otherwise. Therefore, the Good itself, which because it is Not-other, cannot exist otherwise, is not at all verified from these. But pay attention to how the Good befits the Origin, because it precedes the not-good and how the Not-other precedes the other and befits the Origin; and how the Good, which is expressed from the Origin, is the Not-other. Nevertheless, the Not-other is more precise, since this defines itself and the Good.

ABBOT: Attend to whether it is so, that the Good precedes the not-good; for according to Plato, the not-existing precedes the existing; and generally, the negative precedes affirmation.

NICOLAUS: When it is said that the not-existing precedes the existing, then—according to Plato—this not-existing is certainly better than the existing and likewise the negative, which precedes affirmation. For it precedes because it is better. But the not-good is not better than the Good. Hence, according to this the Good precedes and only God is the Good, since there is nothing better than the Good. However, the Good, because it is seen as other from the not-good, is not the precise name of God. And therefore, like all other names for God, it is rejected, since God is not other from the Good, nor from the not-good nor from any nameable thing. On this basis, the signification the Not-other directs more precisely to God than does the Good.

XXIV.

ABBOT: Now I see most clearly why the Teacher of the truth asserted that only God is good. However, I entreat you, Father, to add still one more thing and then we shall cease being burdensome to you: For what reason does this same Teacher call God spirit?

NICOLAUS: He says God is a spirit because, since He is incorporeal, He is not enclosed by space, like a body. Indeed, the incorporeal is before the corporeal, the non-spatial before the spatial, the incomposite before the composite. What indeed is discerned in everything composite except the simple and the incomposite? The composite indeed says about itself that its own origin is incomposite. For if in the composite a composite were seen, and in that composite again a composite, then the one would have to be more composite and the other less. And finally one would come to the incomposite, since the composing is before the composite. Indeed, nothing composite has composed itself. Therefore, the composing, which is before the part and the whole, and before the universe and everything in which everything exists anteriorly or incompositely, will be incomposite. Therefore, in the composite only the incomposite is seen.

Thus the mind contemplates the incomposite point before the composite line. The point is a sign, the line, however, the signified. But what is seen in the signified except a sign, indeed a sign which is a sign of the signified? Thus, the sign is the beginning, middle, and the end for the signified, or the point is such for the line, rest is for motion, the moment is for time, and universally the indivisible for the divisible. But I do not see the indivisible in the divisible as its part, since the part is a part of the whole. Rather, in the divisible I see the indivisible before the part and the whole, and I see it as no other from it. For if I did not discern it, I would see nothing at all. Furthermore, when I see the other in it, I see nothing except the Not-other. God is therefore the Spirit of spirits, who is seen by means of the Not-other before every spirit. If He were sublated, then neither spirit, nor body, nor anything nameable could remain. Just as, if coldness, which can be called spirit on account of its invisibility and its activity, which is sensed in the cold or ice, is sublated, the ice ceases to exist (indeed if the spirit, which effects the congealing and glaciation of the ice, is removed, then the ice also ceases), thus also if the connecting spirit in the composite ceases, the composite also ceases; and likewise if the spirit of being ceases, the entity ceases. And if the discerning or distinguishing, or if I express myself more precisely, the Not-othering, spirit ceases, everything ceases at the same time.

The Spirit, which effects everything in everything, through which each thing is not other than it is, is indeed named the Not-other. It is the Spirit of spirits, since every spirit is not other than spirit; that Spirit is not seen in truth except in the spirit or mind. For only the spirit of the rational creature, which is called "mind," can intuit the truth. But in the truth it sees the Spirit, which is the Spirit of truth, which truly effects that everything is what it is. And just as it sees it, it also adores it, namely, in spirit and in truth.

ABBOT: You have led me, Father, to the Spirit, which I see as the Creator of all things, just as the Prophet saw, who said to the Creator: Send forth Your Spirit and they will be created; just as if one, who desired ice, were to ask that a spirit emit a glaciating breath; and thus with everything desired. You have also led me to see that the mental spirit is an image of that Spirit. And that spirit, which advances from its own power to everything, examines everything, and creates notions and similitudes of everything. I say it creates, since it does not make the notional similitudes of things from something other, but rather—just as the Spirit, which is God, also does not make the quiddities of things from the other—from itself or the Not-other. Therefore, just as God is not other from something creatable, so also the mind is not other from something intelligible through it. I also see well that in a mind, which is more absolved of the body, the creator-spirit shines forth more perfectly and creates more precise notions. But because it is only your purpose to carry us away with you and to lead us to the path of the vision of the First, which is everything in everything, and because the one person comes more quickly to comprehension on this pathway than the other, I shall now let you rest at more length. Your direction, through which you have attempted to direct us to the Origin, which defines itself and everything and which was hitherto sought by all and will always be sought in the future, is indeed sufficient for us. We are content with the path which you have revealed to us by means of the Not-other. On behalf of all, I give you today and we shall always give you immortal thanks until in Zion we see the always blessed God of gods face to face.

Propositions of the Same Most Reverend Father,
Lord Cardinal Nicolaus, on the Power of the Not-Other

I. The definition, which defines itself and everything, is that which is sought by every mind.

II. Whoever sees that it is most true, that the definition is not other than the definition, also sees that the Not-other is the definition of the definition.

III. Whoever sees that the Not-other is not other than the Not-other, sees that the Not-other is the definition of the definition.

IV. Whoever sees that the Not-other defines itself and is the definition defining everything, sees that the Not-other is not another from every definition and from everything defined.

V. Whoever sees that the Not-other defines the origin, since the origin is not other than the origin, sees that the Not-other is the origin of the origin; thus he sees it also as the middle of the middle, the end of the end, the name of the name, the entity of entity, the not-existing of the not-existing; and thus of each and every thing which can be said or thought.

VI. Whoever sees how, by virtue of the fact that the Not-other defines itself, the Not-other is the not other of the Not-other, and how, by virtue of the fact that it defines each and every thing, it is everything in everything and each in each, sees that the Not-other is the other of the other and sees that the Not-other is not opposed to the other. That is a secret, with which there is no comparison.

VII. Whoever sees how, if the Not-other is removed, neither the other nor nothing remains, since the Not-other is the nothing of the nothing, sees indeed that the Not-other is everything in everything and nothing in nothing.

VIII. It is impossible that anything can come into human cognition without the Not-other, since it is the cognition of cognition. And although the Not-other is not other from the cognition, which cognizes concerning itself, it is nevertheless not cognition itself, since cognition is not the simply Not-other, but rather not other than cognition; nor does the Not-other exist otherwise in everything which can be said.

IX. What the mind sees, it does not see without the Not-other. For it would not see the other, if the Not-other were not the other of the other. Thus, it could not discern an entity if the Not-other were not the entity of entity, and it is thus with everything that one can say. Thus the mind sees every other through that other which is the Not-other; therefore, everything other also thus. It sees for example the other truth through the truth, which is the Not-other; the other rational ground through the rational ground, which is the Not-other. It therefore sees every other anteriorly as the Not-other. And in the same way it sees that everything has its name, its quiddity, and whatever else it possesses from the Not-other.

X. Whoever sees that the finite is not other than the finite, the infinite not other than the infinite, and that it is likewise with the visible and invisible, with the numerable and innumerable, the measurable and immeasurable, with the conceivable and the inconceivable, the imaginable and the unimaginable, the intelligible and the unintelligible and everything of this kind, sees that God, who is signified through the Not-other, is definable neither through the finite nor through the infinite, is measurable neither through the measure of the measurable nor through that of the immeasurable, is numerable neither through a numerable nor through an innumerable number, is likewise not conceivable, not imaginable, not intelligible, and is nameable neither with a nameable nor with an unnameable name, although He is another from none of all of these and others which can be named, nor is He another in them.

XI. Whoever sees how the Not-other in defining itself defines everything, sees that it is the most adequate measure of everything, a larger measure of the larger, a smaller one of the smaller, an equal one of the equal, a beautiful one of the beautiful, a true one of the true, and a living measure of the living, etc.

XII. Whoever sees that the Not-other is the definition and the defined of itself and everything, sees in everything which he sees only the Not-other defining itself. For what does he see in the other except the Not-other defining itself? What other in the heaven than the Not-other defining itself? And thus it is with everything. The creature, therefore, is the revelation of the Creator defining Himself or of the light, which is God, manifesting itself; the announcement as it were of the mind defining itself, which is made to those present through living speech, to those remote through a messenger or writing. In these manifestations of the mind there is nothing other than the mind defining itself, which manifests itself most clearly and vividly through its own speech to the listeners, to those remote through delegated speech, and to those most remote through writing. Thus, the Not-other, the Mind of the mind, shows itself in the first creatures more clearly, in the other ones more obscurely.

XIII. Whoever sees how the Not-other, which is the Not-other of the Not-other, shines forth in the eternal, where it is the eternity of the eternal eternity and likewise in the true, where it is the truth of the true truth, and in the good, where it is the goodness of the good goodness, etc., sees that God, who defines Himself, shines forth in everything triunely. For in the one the triune Not-other is the unity of the one unity, in an entity the entity of existing entity, in a magnitude the magnitude of the great magnitude, in a quantum the quantity of the quantitative quantity, etc.

XIV. Whoever sees that in the other the Not-other is the other, sees that in the affirmation the negation is affirmed. And whoever sees God before affirmation and negation, sees that God in the affirmations which we make concerning Him, is not a negative expression which is affirmed, but rather the affirmation of affirmation.

XV. Whoever sees that in the other the Not-other is the other, sees that in the warmed the not-warmed is the warmed, in the cooled the not-cooled is the cooled, in the formed the not-formed is the formed, in the made the not-made is the made, in the divisible the indivisible is the divisible, in the composite the incomposite is the composite, and generally in the affirmed the not-affirmed is the affirmed. And he sees the negative expression as such a principle of affirmation, that if it is sublated, the affirmation is sublated. Negations, therefore, direct the vision of the mind to the "what," affirmation, however, to the "what of such a kind."

XVI. Whoever sees how the negations, which direct the vision of the mind to quiddity, are prior to the affirmations, sees that every name signifies a "what of such a kind." For the body does not signify a quiddity which is incorporeal, but rather a quiddity of such a kind, namely, corporeal; just as the earth signifies an earthly, the sun a solar quiddity, etc. Therefore, all names have signification imposed on the basis of some sensible signs, which signs follow the quiddity of the things. They therefore do not signify quiddity, but rather one of such a kind. The mind, however, which contemplates it anteriorly, denies that the name is proper to the quiddity which it sees.

XVII. The mind sees how the Not-other is the actuality of actuality, the maximum of the maximum, the minimum of the minimum. And consequently it sees that the pure actuality, which cannot be purer, has never been in potentiality, for otherwise it would have come into actuality through a purer actuality. On this basis, it sees that everything which could be other, can always be other and that therefore, in that which admits of more or greater, one is never able to arrive at an actual maximum, in respect to which there cannot be a greater; and that that which can be other, can always be other, since it never attains to the Not-other.

XVIII. Whoever sees how the Not-other, which is the other of the other, is not an other, sees the other of the other, which is the other of other things. Likewise he sees the equal of the equal, which is the equal of equal things, and the good of the good, which is the good of good things, etc. He indeed sees how the Not-other, which is the other of the other, is not participated in through the other, because it is not other from it, but rather in it is it; however, the other is participated in by others. It is likewise with the equal, the good, etc. Therefore, the Good, from which the Not-other is not other, is participated in by all other goods and in others otherwise. There will therefore never be two equally good or equally equal things, which could not be better or more equal. It is likewise with similar things. Indeed, everything other must necessarily be other from another, since only the Not-other is not other from every other.

XIX. Whoever sees that God is not other from everything which understands nor from everything which is understood, sees that God grants to the intellect that it is not other than an intellect which understands, and to the intelligible, that it is not other than understandable by the intellect, and that the intellect which understands is not other from the understood. The Not-other, therefore, shines forth more clearly in the intellect, which is not other from the understood—just as knowledge is not other from the known—than in the senses. Indeed, seeing is not as clearly not other from the seen and hearing from the heard. However, the intelligences, in which the Not-other shines forth more clearly, understand the intelligible, from which they are less other, more rapidly and clearly. Indeed, to understand is to make the intelligible not other from itself; just as light, when it is more intense, more rapidly makes the illuminable not other from itself. The Not-other is seen to shine forth in everything, since it is certain that everything strives to define itself in everything. Just as warmth endeavors to make all things so warm that it is not other from them and that it defines itself in all things, thus the intellect endeavors to bring it about that everything is intellect and that it defines itself in everything. The same is true of the imagination and everything else.

XX. When the mind considers the not-warm becoming warm and the cold becoming warm, then through the intellect it attains the not-warm, through the senses the cold, and it sees that they are not the same, since it attains them through diverse powers. And when it considers that the not-cold is seen through the mind just as is the not-warm, and that the not-warm can become warm and the not-cold can become cold, and that the cold can become warm and the warm can become cold, then it sees how the same thing is the not-warm and the not-cold. And it is called not-warm, because, although not actually warm, it nevertheless can become warm, and likewise it is called not-cold, because, although not actually cold, it nevertheless can become cold. Therefore, when it is actually warm, the potentiality for the cold remains, and when it is actually cold, the potentiality for the warm remains. However, the potentiality does not come to rest, unless it is in actuality, since actuality is its end and perfection, otherwise the potentiality would be in vain. Therefore, there would be no potentiality, because nothing is in vain. Since, however, the potentiality does not bring itself into actuality—indeed this would be inconsistent—a Mover is therefore necessary, who moves the potentiality into actuality. Thus the mind sees nature and natural motion and the Not-other as the nature of nature shining forth in itself.

On the Hunt for Wisdom

(1 4 6 3)
Prologue

Since I do not know if a longer and better time will perhaps be conceded to me for reflection, and indeed I have passed beyond my sixty-first year, it is my intention to leave to posterity, briefly summed up, my hunts for wisdom, which up to this age through mental intuition I regarded as ever more true.

A long time ago I put in writing my concept on searching for God. After this, I made further progress and again wrote down my conjectures. But since I have now read in Diogenes Laertius' book, *On the Life of the Philosophers,* about the various hunts for wisdom of the philosophers, I was impelled to devote my mind entirely to this so-pleasing speculation, than which nothing more delightful can occur to a man; and what I have found through the most diligent meditation, I wish, although it is but little, as a sinful man, to disclose modestly and timidly, so that the more acute are moved to better deepen their minds. I will proceed in the following manner.

We are roused by an appetite placed in our nature not only for knowledge, but also for possessing wisdom, or tasteful knowledge. First I will mention a few things concerning its rational ground, then I will describe to him who wants to philosophize—which I call the hunt for wisdom—regions and certain locations in these, and I will lead him into the fields which in my opinion are exceedingly full of the quarry which he seeks.

I.
Wisdom Is the Sustenance of the Intellect

Since our intellectual nature lives, it must necessarily be nourished. But similar to the manner in which every living being is nourished through the food which is appropriate to its life, it cannot at all be refreshed with any other food than that of intelligible life. For because the vital spirit moves delectably (which motion is called life), the power of the spirit of life, unless it is restored through its natural refreshment, becomes weak and expires.

The Pythagoreans asserted that the vital spirit subsists potentially in the vapor of the seed, the body in its body. The Stoics, whom one also denotes as adherents of Zeno, concurred with that, and said that the substance of the fruit-bearing seed is in the vaporous spirit. If this expires in the grain or in another seed, it does not bear fruit. Indeed, we see that the fire diminishes and expires, if its nourishment runs out.

Hence, the ancients also called the heavenly bodies spirits, because they are in motion. Thus, for example, wise Philo and Jesus, son of Sirach, affirmed that the sun is a spirit; and for that reason they also said, the sun is nourished by the vapor of the ocean, and in a similar manner, they affirmed that the moon was refreshed by the vapor of other waters, as were the planets, which they believed to be filled with divine life. And believing that the other gods delighted in vapors, they appeased them with incense and pleasant odors. Indeed, claiming the spirit of ethereal or celestial life to be in them by the nature of the purest fire, they offered them the vapor of the sweetest odors.

However, because all living beings have a natural understanding, a firm recollection of their sustenance, and a sense of their similitude, and sense which beings are of the same species, Plato says this must necessarily stem from the idea, since nothing endures except ideas. From this you elicit that the ideas are thus not separated from individuals, as if they were extrinsic exemplars. For the nature of the individual is united with the idea, from which it has everything in a natural manner.

Laertius said that Plato affirmed that the idea establishes and moves the one and the many. For in that which is incorruptible species, it is intelligible and one, but in that which is united out

462

of many individuals, it is called many. Likewise, he said, that it is firm and stable in that which is inalterable and intelligible, but in that which is connected to the mobile, it is moved.

Proclus explains more fully how the essential principles are intrinsic and not extrinsic and how the individual, by means of that contact in which the individual is joined to its idea, is connected through this intelligible idea to the divinity, so that according to its capacity it exists in the best manner in which it can be and be preserved.

Laertius also reports that Plato said the ideas are the origin and the beginning of things which are formed by nature, so that in this way they are what kind they are. And if they are correctly understood, perhaps they are not so opposed to the truth, as his bad interpreters have suggested.

Also Epicharmos said that all things which live participate in notions and wisdom. Indeed, a hen does not bring the living young into the world, but rather first incubates the eggs and animates them through her warmth. However, nature alone knew by means of wisdom how that occurs, for the hen is educated by her. He says further: It is truly nothing astounding—if I may say so—that they please each other and are mutually supportive and appear beautiful. Indeed, a dog is seen by a dog to be beautiful and an ox by an ox and an ass by an ass and likewise a pig by a pig, is seen to surpass all others in loveliness.

Behold, if every living being has the cognate capacity for understanding those things which are necessary to the necessity of his preservation in himself and, because he is mortal, in his descendants, and has industry in hunting down his sustenance, and suitable eyesight and the organs appropriate for his hunt (as for example the congenital good eyesight of animals which hunt by night), and if he knows that which is found, selects it and unites it with himself, certainly our intellectual life cannot at all do without these things; therefore, the intellect is given logic by nature, so that the intellect runs through everything with its help and makes its hunt. For as Aristotle said, logic is the most exact instrument both in the hunt for the true and also for the verisimilar. Hence, when the intellect finds something, it knows it and embraces it avidly.

Therefore, it is wisdom which is sought, since it nourishes the intellect. Since it is immortal food, it therefore nourishes in an immortal manner. It shines forth, however, in various rational grounds, which participate in it variously. Indeed, the intellect seeks the light of wisdom in various rational grounds, so that it imbibes and is nourished from thence; just as in varied sensible things, in which life has at some time been nourished, this sensible life seeks its sustenance in a rational manner, the intellect hunts for intelligible food in sensible notions, in that it applies rationality. Hence, the intellect is refreshed in the one food better than in the other; but it is more difficult to find what is more precious.

And because man, in order to nourish his animal existence well, requires a greater industry than another living being, and because it is necessary that he make use of his naturally endowed logic in the hunt for corporeal food, he is not so dedicated and attentive to the intellectual as nature demands.

When this occupation is too much, then it alienates from the speculation of wisdom. For this reason, it is written that philosophy, which is contrary to the flesh, mortifies the latter.

Also among the philosophers one finds a great difference, and this occurs above all, because the intellect of one is a better hunter; because it is exercised, because logic is more promptly at its disposal and it uses it more carefully. Also the one knows better in which region one will find more quickly the wisdom which is sought and in what manner one can detain it. For the philosophers are nothing other than hunters of wisdom, each of whom investigates in the light of the logic cognate to him in his manner.

II.
With which Principle I Inquired Carefully into the Rational Grounds of Wisdom

The first among the wisemen, Thales of Miletus, said that God is the oldest, since He is unbegotten, and that the world is the most beautiful, since it is made by God.

These words pleased me in the highest degree, when I read them in Laertius. I see that the most beautiful world, in which the highest good, wisdom and beauty of the highest God are reflected, is united in admirable order.

I am moved to inquire after the Artist of this so admirable

work, and I say to myself: Since the unknown cannot be known through something more unknown, it behooves me to grasp something most certain, undoubted and presupposed by all hunters and to seek the unknown in its light. For the true is consonant with the true.

When my mind within me avidly and carefully inquired into this, the assertion of the philosophers occurred to me, which Aristotle also assumes at the beginning in his *Physics,* and which reads: "That which cannot possibly become, does not become." And in accordance with this assertion, I inspected the regions of wisdom as follows.

III.
On which Path Rationality Hunts

Since that which cannot possibly become, does not become, nothing has become or does become that could or cannot become. However, what is and was neither made nor created, could and can neither become nor be created. For since it has neither become nor is it created, nor can become other, it precedes the potential-to-become and is eternal.

However, everything that has become or becomes, since it neither has become nor becomes without the potential-to-become, has one absolute Origin; this is the origin and the cause of the potential-to-become and it is that eternal, which precedes the potential-to-become, and is the absolute and the uncontractible Origin, since it is everything which it can be, and that which becomes is produced from the potential-to-become, since this potential-to-become actually becomes everything which becomes.

However, everything that has become out of the potential-to-become is either that which can become, or it is after that and never is that which can become, but rather follows and imitates the potential-to-become, since the latter has been made neither from itself nor was it made from another. For how shall the potential-to-become, become itself, since the potential-to-become precedes everything that has become?

However, since it is after that which is everything which can be, namely, after the eternal, it has a beginning. Nevertheless, the potential-to-become cannot cease. If it indeed ceased, then that could occur. Therefore, the potential-to-become does not cease.

Therefore, the potential-to-become, which has begun, remains eternal and is perpetual. And because it has not become and nevertheless has begun, we call it created, for it presupposes nothing except its Creator, from whom it is taken. Everything, therefore, which is after it, is produced by the Creator from the potential-to-become.

However, that which has become what it can become, is named the celestial and intelligible; however, that which is, but is not that which it can become, is never fixed and passes away. Therefore, it imitates the perpetual, but never attains it; it is therefore the temporal and is called earthly and sensible.

Therefore, when I turn toward contemplation of the eternal, I see it simply as actuality, and in the mind I intuit everything in it enfoldedly in the absolute cause.

When I intuit the eternal and perpetual, then I see the potential-to-become intellectually and in it itself the nature of all single things, just as they should become in accordance with the perfect unfolding of the predestination of the divine Mind. When, on the contrary, I intuit time, then I comprehend in a sensible manner that everything is unfolded in succession through the imitation of the perfection of the perpetual. For the sensible imitates the intelligible. Therefore, in the created potential-to-become, everything created is predetermined, so that this beautiful world became just as it is; more concerning this below.

However, to show how this can be conceived, I wish to subjoin some kind of example, even though it is remote.

IV.
How the Intellect Assists Itself with the Example of the Art of Logic

The intellect of the master wants to create the syllogistic art. For it itself precedes the potential-to-become of this art, which art is in it as in its cause. It therefore founds and secures the potential-to-become of this art.

For what that art requires it can become. Indeed, these are

name and word and the propositions from these and the syllogism from these, which comes into existence from three propositions, of which two are advanced, from which the third ensues as conclusion. It is also required that the subject and predicate of all three propositions have only three terms. Hence one idea, which is called the middle term, must be contained twice in the premises. This is the case, when in the first premise, which is called the major, it is subject, and in the minor premise the predicate, or where it is in both the predicate or subject.

And thus three figures arise. Also various modes of the individual figures arise out of the various and useful combinations of propositions, after one has rejected the unuseful combinations, as, for example, the unuseful combinations of three negations or of three particular propositions, or others in accordance with the figure. One names the first syllogism, which consists of three universal affirmative judgments, in the first figure "Barbara." The second, which consists of a universal negative major, and an affirmative minor, and of a negative conclusion, one names "Celarent," etc. And these specific forms of the syllogism are grounded and abide in rationality. Every syllogism expressed in sensibly perceptible speech must imitate these. And thus the potential-to-become of this art is explained. The master, who has invented this art, transmits it to the obedient student, and commands that he syllogize everything according to the modes proposed to him.

Perhaps to some degree the artwork of the world also is likewise.

For when its master, glorious God, wanted to constitute the beautiful world, He created its potential-to-become, and in this enfolded everything that was necessary to the constitution of this world. The beauty of the world, however, required not only that which exists, but also that which lives and that which understands, and also that of these three there were various species or modes of beauty, which are the effective, predetermined, rational grounds of the divine Mind and the useful and beautiful combinations, suitable to the constitution of the world.

God handed this divine work of art over to obedient Nature, which was concreated with the potential-to-become, so that it would unfold the potential-to-become of the world in accordance with the mentioned, predetermined rational grounds of the divine Intellect; it unfolds, for example, the potential-to-become of man in accordance with the predetermined rational basis of man. And thus it is with all, just as the syllogizer in syllogizing looks to the predetermined rational grounds, which are called Barbara and Celarent.

V.
How the Intellect Makes Progress in the Example of Geometry

However, when the geometer forms a circle, he seems to imitate nature. For he looks to the predetermined rational basis of the circle, according to which he endeavors to operate, as much as the potential-to-become of the sensible subject permits. For the one is better suited thereto than the other and that rational basis is nothing other than the equidistance of the center of the circle to the circumference, which is the true rational basis or cause of the circle, which admits neither more nor less.

However, no sensible circle can become so perfect that it attains that rational basis precisely. For the potential-to-become of a sensible circle is after that fixed and stable, intelligible, rational basis, which it follows as the image of the truth. It imitates the potential-to-become of the circle in the sensible matter. Since this is variable, a circle which is described will never be everything that a sensible circle can become, since it can become truer and more perfect and more similar to the intelligible circle mentioned, than every sensible circle given.

Thus, when a geometer wishes to form a right angle, he looks to its intelligible, rational basis, which is that which an intelligible right angle can be and which no sensible angle can precisely imitate; and when he makes an acute or obtuse angle, he looks to no other species than the right species, than which the acute is smaller and the obtuse larger. The acute can indeed always be more similar to the right; and likewise the obtuse; and if one of them were the minimum of its kind, such that it could not be less, it were a right angle. Therefore, both are enfolded in the rational basis of the right angle, because they are right, when they are that which they can become.

Thus, Nature does not look to another species than the

human, when it produces the masculine or the feminine, although the rational basis of man is neither masculine nor feminine, which befit the sensible. The species is indeed the median which unites in itself that which diverges from it to the right or to the left.

That it is so, you will see very well, when you observe that the intelligible are or have nothing of that which is found in the sensible. For it has neither color nor form, which is attained by sensible vision, nor hardness nor softness nor something that is perceived by touch; likewise neither quantity nor sex nor anything that the senses apprehend. Indeed, all those follow the intelligible as the temporal the perpetual.

Thus nothing intelligible is in eternity, which precedes everything intelligible, just as the eternal precedes the perpetual. However, everything precise and permanent is more beautiful than the imperfect and fluid. Thus the intelligible is more beautiful than the sensible, which is only beautiful insofar as intelligible species or beauties are reflected in it.

VI.
The Elucidation of the Potential-to-Become

Whoever has read this will undoubtedly occupy himself with conceiving the potential-to-become, and that will be difficult, because the potential-to-become is not terminated, except in its Origin. Therefore, how can a concept be formed of that which is interminable? Nevertheless, so that you do not go completely astray, I will help with a rough example.

Imagine that the eternal light is called God and that the world is entirely invisible, which is judged by vision not to exist, since vision judges nothing to exist unless it is seen by itself. The light, however, disposes that it wishes to make the world visible, and since the potential-to-become of the visible world is color, the similitude of the light (for the light is the hypostasis of color), light therefore creates color, in which everything which can be seen is enfolded. Indeed, just as, if color is sublated, nothing is seen, so by means of color through the light everything visible as such is brought from potentiality to actuality.

Hence since color is reflected in colored things variously, color appears closer to the light in certain ones, and those are more visible and for this reason more noble, as, for example, the color white; but nevertheless, no colored thing participates in any color so perfectly that it could not participate more perfectly. Only the cause of color is the terminus of this potential-to-become.

Some things, such as the celestial, remain stably and perpetually in the same color, others, such as the terrestrial and whatever else is of this corruptible world, remain unstably and temporally. Therefore, color is the visible potential-to-become; for everything that is seen is only seen because it is colored and is seen and distinguished discretely from all other colored things on account of its own discrete and singular color.

And because the sense of vision, which is a lucid spirit, participates in the distinguishing and discerning light, and, although it judges concerning every color, is itself in no way colored, therefore color is not its potential-to-become. Thus, the intellect is also more lucid than vision. For it discerns most subtly what is invisible: for example, the intelligible abstracted from the visible. For this reason, color is not the potential-to-become of the intellect, but rather, the potential-to-become of the lucid and beautiful world and of all things which are in it, even color itself, is simpler than color, which is called the similitude of the eternal light, enfolding in its own passive potentiality everything lucid that is, that lives and understands, just as a seed participating in the light and the beautiful.

The lucid in the animal seed shows the participation in this seed in some way, since it is the potential-to-become of the animal that is, lives, feels, and understands in its mode. It would not have this capacity, if it did not participate in the similitude of the potential-to-become of the world and of the mentioned seed of seeds, and were not its image.

Hence, the seed of the existing, living, and understanding seeds is the participable similitude of God, which we name the potential-to-become. From this, the eternal light produced this beautiful and lucid world and constituted everything that becomes. For since it is the participable similitude of the eternal light, it is good, because it endures in its plentiful diffusion, it is great, because its strength is in no way terminable, it is true, delectable, and perfect and above all laudable; its works are laudable and glorious, as we shall narrate below.

VII.
That the Cause of the Potential-to-Become of All Things Is One

The point at which the conjectures of my hunts come to rest, is the knowledge that there is only one cause of everything, the Creator of the potential-to-become of all things, and that that precedes all potential-to-become and is its terminus.

This is not nameable nor participable, but its similitude is participated in in all things.

And because the varied participating things are in everything which participates according to the same species of similitude in the similitude of that cause, one must come to the one which is maximally one such. It is the first or the preeminence or the origin of that specific participation and, in connection with the others of the same species, maximally such, and through itself of such a kind, in whose specific similitude the others of this order participate.

Thus we call the light a similitude of the first cause, which in maximum lucidity, as for example the sun, radiates back first and principally, as in lucidity per se; in other lucid things, however, as sunlight in participating things. However, the cause of the sunlight has nothing in common with the light of the sun, but rather it is the cause of everything; therefore, it is nothing of everything.

So that you understand and can judge both the aforementioned as well as what follows, I will now reveal according to which method of thinking I have undertaken my hunts.

It is certain that the first Origin has not become, since nothing becomes from itself, but rather first from it. However, what has not become, can neither cease nor perish. And we call this eternal.

And because the potential-to-become cannot bring itself into actuality (for production is from actuality), it is therefore confused to say that passive potentiality brings itself into actuality. Hence actuality exists before potentiality. Therefore, the potential-to-become is not the eternal Origin.

A holy doctor correctly said, it is a heresy to affirm that passive potentiality has always existed; it therefore follows the first cause. But the great Dionysius asserts in the ninth chapter of *On Divine Names,* that that first eternal is inflexible, inalterable, unmixed, immaterial, most simple, not indigent, inaugmentable, irreducible, has not become, is always existing.

Whoever attends to the fact that the First precedes the potential-to-become, sees that this and everything similar is so. For flexible, alterable, material, augmentable, reducible, and makeable, and everything similar, indicate the passive potentiality and never precede the potential-to-become; hence, they are to be rejected with respect to the eternal Origin.

I take two of these, namely, the inaugmentable and the irreducible, and hasten with them to the hunt, and I say that the inaugmentable cannot be greater; therefore, it is the maximum. The irreducible cannot be smaller; it is therefore the minimum. Hence, because it is equally the maximum and the minimum, it is in no way smaller, since it is the maximum, and in no way greater, since it is the minimum, but rather the most precise, formal, and exemplary cause and measure of everything great or small.

As I have shown in the booklet *On Beryllus,* in the enigma of the angle, the maximum and at the same time minimum angle is necessarily the most adequate formal cause of all angles which can become. And it is not only the formal cause, but also the efficient and final cause (as Dionysius shows, where he writes concerning beauty). For Beauty, which is that which it can be, is inaugmentable and irreducible, since it is at the same time the maximum and the minimum, is the actuality of all potential-to-become-beautiful, effecting everything beautiful, and as far as its capacity admits, conforming and converting it to itself.

It is likewise with the Good, which is that which it can be, and with the True, with the Perfect, and everything which we laud in creatures. We see that when they are that which they can be, they are the eternal God in God. And hence we laud God as the efficient, formal, and final cause of all things.

Above all it is still to be revealed, how the potential-to-become cannot be terminated by anything which follows it or that can become, but rather, its beginning and end are the same. More concerning this below.

VIII.
How Plato and Aristotle
Have Conducted their Hunt

Plato, a wonderfully circumspect hunter, considered that the superior is in the inferior participatively; the inferior, on the other hand, in the superior excellently. When he saw that many are named good by reason of participation in the Good and likewise just and honorable, he attended to the fact that the name is obtained from that participated in, and directed his attention to that which is good and just per se and to the fact that, if the participating are good and just, that which is such per se is such to the maximum degree and is the cause of the others.

And in this, Aristotle, the most acute leader of the Peripatetics, consented. When he saw that there is much in nature that is warm through participation, he affirmed that one should come to the warm per se, which is the maximum such and is the cause of warmth in everything, as for example in fire. And in this way one came to the first cause per se of all causes, thus to the entity of the entity, the life of the living, and the intellect of the intelligent.

However, Plato hunted for the universal cause of all things through the ascent of the participating good to the Good per se in the following manner: Indeed, he considered that all entities— both the actually existing as well as the potentially—by reason of participation in the one Good are called good. Indeed, the progress from potentiality into actuality and everything existing in actuality does not do without participation in the Good. Therefore, that which is maximally such, namely, the one Good per se, is desired by all. For everything eligible is eligible by reason of the Good. Therefore, since the terminus of the eligible and the desirable is the Good, that which is the Good per se will be the cause of everything, since everything is directed to its own cause and desires that from which it has everything that it has.

He therefore named the first Origin the one and good God per se and the origins of the others, namely, of entity, life and the intellect, etc., existence per se, life per se, intellect per se, and he affirmed that they are the origins and causes of being, living, and understanding. And Proclus named these composer-gods, through participation in which everything which exists exists, everything which lives lives, and everything which understands understands; and since everything that lives and understands, neither lived nor understood unless it existed, after the first God of gods, whom he, as I have said, called the one Good, he therefore affirmed the cause of entity as the second god, namely, the composer-intellect. Proclus believed the latter was Jupiter, the king and ruler of all.

Proclus thus posited celestial and earthly and various other eternal gods, as he has expressed it extensively in the six books *On the Theology of Plato*. However, he placed at the head of all the God of gods, as the universal cause of all, and he seemed to regard as diverse gods, on account of the diverse rational grounds of the attributes, that which we attribute to the good God, which are only the rational grounds, and by no means a different thing. He was moved by the thought that nothing is intelligible, except if it actually exists, since being is necessarily participated in by the intelligible. Therefore, he affirmed that everything exists which is understood. Thus he asserted, that an intelligible man and lion and everything that he saw abstracted and separated from matter, exists intellectually as is posited above.

The Peripatetics, who saw that the being of the rational ground is constituted by our intellect and the being does not attain reality, do not agree with him in this, nor did they agree that the good is older than entity. They say that the one and entity and the good are exchangeable.

Hence, if the cause of entity is the first cause and the composer-intellect of everything, then those who say that the one and entity and the good are exchangeable, also concede that the cause of the one and of entity and the good is the same. Nevertheless, Aristotle, who like Anaxagoras asserts that the first cause is the intellect, which is the principle of motion, does not attribute to it the administration of the whole universe, but rather only that of the heavens. However, the celestial, he says, governs the earthly.

Epicurus, on the other hand, attributes the whole administration of the universe to God alone without any assistance.

But our divine theologians learned from supernal revelation, that the first cause—according to the assertion of all, this is tricausal, namely, an efficient, formal, and final cause, which is named by Plato the one and good, by Aristotle intellect and the Entity of entity—is one in such a way that it is trine and trine in such a way that it is one. Insofar as it is an efficient cause, it is called unity after Plato; insofar as it is formal cause, it is called entity after Aristotle; and insofar as it is final cause, it is called the Good after both of them. However, how this most sacred trinity in unity, which precedes everything intelligible and all continuous and discrete quantity, all number and otherness, can be seen here in an enigma by the faithful, I will annotate below, as God will give it.

IX.
How the Sacred Writings and the Philosophers Have Designated the Same Differently

If someone first turns with these premises to the genesis of the world described by holy Moses long before the philosophers, then he will find there what I have said above concerning origins. For Moses said: "In the beginning God created heaven and earth," then the light.

By this he is pointing to the potential-to-become of the world, which is contained in heaven and earth, as created in the beginning. For afterwards, like Dionysius, he expresses that which has actually become heaven, as the firmament, that which has become earth, as the arid, and that which has become light, as sun.

For everything, of which one later reads about as made and unfolded, is created confused and enfolded in the potential-to-become. Hence, when Moses says, "God spoke, let there be light and there was light," he says that in respect to the nature of the potential-to-become. For God saw the light in the potential-to-become and that it is good and necessary for the beauty of the visible world, and He spoke to the nature of the light in the potential-to-become, so that the light would become as actuality—and the light of the potential-to-become-light was created.

At the command of the Creator's Word the light has come

into existence naturally. This motion, through which potentiality is moved, so that it would become as actuality, is called natural. For it is created in the potential-to-become by nature, which is the instrument of the divine precept, so that it becomes naturally and delectably without all labor and fatigue as actuality, what it can become.

However, that Word of God, to which nature looks so that everything comes into existence, is God; for nothing is God's which is not itself God. However, this Word the Platonics called the Composer-intellect, which they also called the only-begotten and the Lord of the universe, as Proclus believes. For they called God the One, therefore the Composer-intellect the only-begotten.

Some call it the first Intelligence. Anaxagoras, however, names it the Mind, the Stoics the Word, which they, as can be read in Laertius, also call God. And these have followed the prophet David very well, who said: "Through the Word of the Lord the heavens are established," and in another place, "He spoke and it arose, He commanded and it was created."

Take note of what the philosophers thought in respect to these principles.

Anaxagoras says that the mind has been added as the origin of motion to matter, in which everything was in confusion, and has composed the singular discretely. Thus Plato calls God and matter the two origins of things. Aristotle resolves everything into actuality and potentiality; Pythagoras assimilates the principles of the monad and duality, in that he says that duality is subjected as undetermined matter to the monad as its author. The Stoics say that God, whom they also call Mind or Jupiter, is the architect of this immense work; to them there appeared to be two principles of all things, the active and passive. The passive is substance or matter without quality, the active, however, is the Word, which they say is God. However, Epicurus said that at the order of God everything has arisen from matter, which he believed to be an infinity of atoms. One finds this more extensively in Laertius.

If you consider this well, they all intend nothing other than the aforesaid, namely, that God, who is the purest actuality, makes everything from the potential-to-become. But Moses said more expressly that the potential-to-become is a creation of God.

Thales does not dissent when he says that the world is a work of God, whom he firmly believes is the most ancient. Therefore, God, who has preceded the world, which is made, is also the Origin and Creator of the potential-to-become of the world. In Him the world was the potential-to-become, which Moses said was made, since nothing has become actual which could not become.

Thus Plato also holds that the world has been generated or created. For he constantly says, that everything sensible is necessarily from an older origin and that there could be no time before the founding of the world, since when it was composed, time was simultaneously present.

Aristotle, however, denies that the potential-to-become has a beginning; thus he does not believe that motion and time have been made, having been deceived by the following reasoning: The world, which has become, could become and the potential-to-become does not become actual without motion. Thus he concluded that motion and time have not been made. If he had paid attention to the fact that the eternal is before the potential-to-become as actuality, he would not have denied that the potential-to-become originated from that which precedes it. Indeed, the succession, which is in the motion whose measure is time, reveals from itself that time, motion and what is moved are not eternal, since eternity as actuality is simultaneously that which can be; therefore, it is before succession; indeed the succession comes from the eternal.

For this reason, Plato, who sees better, said correctly that time is the image of the eternal; for it imitates the eternal and follows the potential-to-become. How indeed would succession come into existence, unless it could become?

Anaxagoras posited a beginning of things and an end of time. To the question, whether the ocean will at some future time be where the Lampsaceni Mountains were, he responded, certainly, unless time runs out. He believed therefore that time at some point would come to an end.

Thus also the Stoics, who affirmed that the world is corruptible, agree better with us, to whom the truth has been revealed through faith.

X.
How the Sages Have Named the Potential-to-Become

Thales of Miletus assimilated water to the potential-to-become, when he saw that from its vapor it becomes air and through its subtleness fire and from its grossness earth and that therefore everything living is nourished and arises from it. For from that from which the living exist, they are nourished.

But from the following can be seen that the water is not the potential-to-become of the world and all things, although much thereof is reflected in it. Indeed, God, as Thales correctly says, is the most ancient, He therefore is before everything made or created. The water therefore, since it is after Him, has become. The potential-to-become therefore precedes it.

Zeno, the Stoic, said that God converts the substance of fire by means of air into water, and just as the seed is contained in the fruit, the rational ground of the sowing resides in the moisture, namely, as the material which is most suitably prepared for the work, from which everything else can later be brought forth.

It is necessary for you to understand that our origin, namely, the potential-to-become, precedes the water and all elements and everything that has become, whether it exists, lives or understands. And this moisture, of which Zeno speaks, is not pure water, even if it is watery. For since there is always some water that is purer and simpler than other water, all water that there is can be still purer and simpler. The potential-to-become of the sensible and corporeal must therefore not be attributed to one element, but mutually to everything composed.

That the Stoics had also thought likewise, Laertius reported in the life of Zeno of Citium; speaking about the sensible and corruptible world, he says that the world was made, when the substance of fire was transformed by way of the air into moisture, whereas the denser part of the same was made into earth, next the more subtle remained air and, after the latter had become more and more rarified, passed over into fire. From the mixture has arisen the living beings and the trees and all other genera of earthly creatures.

It is obvious enough that the latter and their followers have spoken about the sensible and terrestrial world, in which no simple elements, but rather only mixed elements are found, since thus the one could arise from the other and also everything living from all. For if there were a simple and pure element, if it were that which it can become, there were in it no potentiality for something other, as it is the case in the fire, which Dionysius calls inalterable in *On the Celestial Hierarchy*. And in another place, in the book *On Divine Names,* in the chapter on evil, he affirms that nothing in respect to its nature and substance is destroyed, even if some are destroyed with respect to their accidents.

But the Stoics affirmed that parts of this world are corruptible. They concluded that this world is both generated and also corruptible. The Peripatetics, on the other hand, asserted that it is restored by means of a circulation. Because this circular motion always perseveres, they say it can never cease and is without beginning.

Nevertheless, this is most certain: The whole world can never cease. For the intelligible things, which are their principal parts, are that which they can become, as we said above.

XI.
On the Three Regions and Ten Fields of Wisdom

However, in order to unfold our proposition, we state that there are three regions of wisdom. In the first it is found as it is eternally. In the second it is found in perpetual similitude. In the third it shines forth from afar in the temporal flux of similitude.

However, I regard ten fields most suited for the hunt for wisdom.

The first I call learned ignorance; the second actual-potential; the third the Not-other; the fourth the field of light; the fifth the field of laud; the sixth the field of unity; the seventh the field of equality; the eighth the field of connection; the ninth the field of termini; and the tenth the field of order.

XII.
On the First Field,
Namely, of Learned Ignorance

When I enter the first field, I direct my attention to how the incomprehensible is comprehended incomprehensibly.

Eusebius, the student of Pamphilus, reported that an Indian had come to Athens. Socrates met with the latter and asked him whether anything could be known, if one does not know God. The latter was astonished by the question and responded, how is this possible? For the Indian did not want to know nothing nor also to be fully ignorant concerning God. For because everything exists, it attests that God also is, or rather: because God is, everything is.

Because everything which is known can be known better and more perfectly, nothing is known just as it is knowable. Therefore, just as the *because-He-is* of God is the cause of the knowledge of the *because-they-are* of all things, so the *because-God* in respect to what it is, as it is knowable, is not known; the quiddity of everything, as it is knowable, is also not known. Aristotle says concerning it that it is always sought just as he himself seeks for it in the first philosophy, but does not find it.

It was seen by Proclus how what that is, which is the origin of all and the most difficult to find, is not other than the one many, the one in essence and the many in potentiality. But one does not know through this, what constitutes the one many. More concerning this below.

It is impossible to know that which precedes the potential-to-become. Therefore, God, since He precedes it, cannot become comprehensible, and because what the potential-to-become is, is not comprehensible, thus its cause preceding it is also not, for the quiddity of nothing (of unknown cause) is actually comprehended, just as it is knowable.

Therefore, the better someone knows that this cannot be known, the more learned he is. For if he who denies that the magnitude of the sun's brightness can be comprehended by vision, is more learned than he who affirms that it can, and he who denies that the magnitude of the ocean can be measured with any measure of liquidity, is more learned than he who affirms that it can, then certainly he who denies that both the absolute magnitude, which is contracted to the brightness of the sun or to the amplitude of the ocean or of another thing, and the completely unterminated and infinite measure of the mind, which is contracted to the mind, are measurable, is by far more learned than he who affirms that they are.

I have answered this question as well as I could in the book *On Learned Ignorance*.

It is wonderful! The intellect desires to know; nevertheless, this natural desire of the intellect is not related to knowing the quiddity of its God, but rather to knowing its God is so great that there is no end to His magnitude; that He is therefore greater than every concept and everything knowable. For the intellect would not be content with itself, if it were the similitude of a creator who is so small and imperfect that he could be greater or more perfect. For He is certainly greater than everything knowable and comprehensible, of infinite and incomprehensible perfection.

Every creature recognizes Him as its God and itself as His similitude and in no way as that of anything less. For every creature, as Epicharmus said, is content with its species as with the most perfect, because it knows that it is a similitude of the infinite beauty of its God and is a perfect gift. Therefore, Moses wrote: God saw everything that He had made, and it was very good. Therefore, every thing rightly rests in its species, which is created from the best and is very good.

Notice how God, in exceeding the potential-to-become, precedes everything that can become. Therefore, nothing can become so perfect that He does not precede it. He is therefore everything that can be, everything perfectible and perfect. For this reason, He is the Perfect itself, that is the perfection of everything perfect and perfectible.

The intellect therefore rejoices to have such a perfecting and never consumable food, by which it sees it can be nourished immortally and perpetually, live most delectably and always be perfected, grow, and be enlarged in wisdom. Likewise, he rejoices more, who finds an infinite and innumerable, incomprehensible and inexhaustible treasure, than he who discovers a finite, numerable, and comprehensible one. This was recognized by Pope Leo the Great, who in a sermon, in which he lauds the ineffable God, says, "We want to feel in ourselves, that it is good that we are overcome. No one comes nearer to cogitation of the truth than he who understands that in the divine things, even if he has already discerned much, something always remains which he must seek."

You see now that the philosophical hunters, who attempted to hunt the quiddity of things (without knowledge of the quiddity of God), and who attempted to make the quiddity of God always knowable and known, have engaged in a useless labor, because they have not entered the field of learned ignorance.

Only Plato, however, who saw somewhat more than the other philosophers, used to say that it would astound him if God could be found and astound him even more if, found, He could be communicated.

XIII.
On the Second Field: Actual-Potential

The intellect, which enters the field of actual-potential (i.e., where the potential is actuality), hunts down food most sufficiently.

God, whom Thales of Miletus rightly called the most ancient, is indeed older than everything nameable, because He is not made or generated. For He is before the something and the nothing, the effable and the ineffable, and also the potential-to-become and the has-become; and therefore He cannot become what is not eternal as actuality.

Indeed, even if humanity is that which humanity requires, it is nevertheless not that as actuality which it can become. For it is after the potential-to-become and under the omnipotent power of the Creator of its potential-to-become.

Nothing, therefore, of all that follows the potential-to-become, is absolved at any time of the potential-to-become other than it is. God alone is the actual-potential, because He is as actuality what He can be. Therefore, God may not be sought in another field than that of the actual-potential. For whatever is described is not God, because it can become other. God is not small, because the small can be larger, and not large, because the large can be smaller, but rather He is before everything that can become otherwise and before everything that differs.

Indeed, He is before every distinction, before the distinction of actuality and potentiality, before the distinction of the potential-to-become and the potential-to-make, before the distinction of light and darkness, also before the distinction of being and not being, something and nothing, and before the distinction of indistinction and distinction, equality and inequality, etc.

Hence, if you look at everything which is after Him, everything is distinct from the other, and also that which is in agreement with the other in genus of being or according to species, is different through number. However, God Himself is before every distinction of distinction and agreement, because He is actual-potential; and because He is before the distinction of the one and the other, He is one no more than another, and because He is before the distinction of the small and the large, He is not larger than one and smaller than another, and not more equal to the one and more unequal to the other.

The most delectable hunts are in this field, because the actual-potential is every potentiality as actuality; therefore, everything that follows the potential-to-become, so that it becomes actual, is only actual insofar as it imitates the actuality of the actual-potential, which is the eternal, unmade actuality, according to which everything that becomes actual, must become. For since the potential-to-become and the being actual are different, and the eternity, which is God, precedes this distinction, in eternity—in which the potential-to-become and the actual being do not differ—you look at everything that has become and can become as actuality, and you see that there everything is itself eternity. Therefore, everything which has become or becomes, necessarily follows the created potential-to-become and also its actuality, which is eternity.

Likewise, the one and its potentiality differ. For the one as actual, for example, as the principle of number, is after the potential-to-become, because it is multiplicable, and as actual is not what it can be. However, as potential, the one is every number. Therefore, the one and its potentiality differ.

Therefore, look at the actual-potential before that distinction, and you will see that in eternity the one and its potentiality before distinction are eternity as actuality.

You see, therefore, that every number which can actually be constituted from the potentiality of unity after the potential-to-become, is eternity as actuality, and the actuality of number, which becomes or can become as an image of the truth, follows this eternal actuality. For just as the monad in eternity is one so that it is as actuality everything that one can become, thus the two in eternity is two, such that it is everything that two can become. And thus it is with everything. You see therefore that the actual two after the potential-to-become imitates the actuality of the two in eternity. The proportion of the two after the potential-to-become to that two, which is eternity, is as that of the numerable to the innumerable or the finite to the infinite.

It is clear how the philosophers who have not entered this field have not tasted these most delightful hunts. However, that which frightened them away from entering this field was that they presupposed that also God, like everything other that follows the potential-to-become, is to be sought on this side of the distinction of opposites.

For they did not believe that God is found before the distinction of contradictory opposites. Since they therefore wanted to limit the hunt for Him to the ambit of the principle that "something is or is not," they did not seek Him, who is older than this principle and whose ambit excels this principle, in the field of the actual-potential, where the potential to be and to be in actuality are not different. I have written extensively elsewhere on the actual-potential in a trialogue. Therefore, those things touched upon here should suffice.

XIV.
On the Third Field, Namely, the Not-Other

Aristotle writes in his *Metaphysics,* that Socrates first devoted his genius to definitions. Definition indeed generates knowledge. For it expresses the generic agreement and the specific difference of the defined, which the word enfolds in its signification.

That which is sought is therefore seen in its definition in that manner in which it can be known. The intellect, which hunts that which precedes the potential-to-become, must therefore attend to how it also precedes the other.

For that which precedes the potential-to-become, cannot become another, because the other is after it. And because this is the case, it cannot be defined through other terms, namely, through its genus, nor be specified or determined through distinctions, which it precedes.

It is therefore necessary that it be the definition of itself and this is also clear from the aforementioned, since it precedes the distinction of definition and the defined. Not only this, but it is also necessary that everything be defined through it, because everything can only exist, if it exists and is defined through it.

This is seen very well by Dionysius, who in his book *On Divine Names,* in the chapter on "The Perfect and the One" says: "This One, which is the cause of everything, is not one of many, but rather before every one and all multitude, the definition of every one and of all multitude."

But the field on which the most jocund hunt occurs for that which defines itself and everything, I name: the Not-other. Indeed, this Not-other defines itself and everything.

If I ask, for example, what the Not-other is, then the most suitable response is: The Not-other is not other than the Not-other. And if I ask, what then is the other, one answers properly: The other is not other than the other. And thus the world is nothing other than the world; and the same is true of everything that can be named.

You see now that that most ancient eternal can be sought in this field in the most delightful hunt. For since it is the definition of itself and of all others, it is not found in any other more clearly than in the Not-other.

Indeed, in this field you touch upon the most ancient three-and-one, which is also the definition of itself. For the Not-other is not other than the Not-other.

The intellect is astonished by this secret, when it directs its attention to the fact that the trinity, without which God does not define Himself, is unity, because the definition is the defined; God therefore, as three-and-one, is the definition defining itself and everything.

The intellect experiences therefore that God is not something other from the other, since He Himself defines the other. If, indeed, the Not-other is sublated, the other does not endure. Indeed, it is necessary that the other, if it shall exist, be not other than the other. Otherwise, it were other than the other and thus would not exist. Since the Not-other is therefore before the other, it cannot become other and is in actuality everything that can exist simply.

However, you notice how the Not-other does not signify only the same. But since the same is not other than the same, the Not-other precedes everything which can be named.

Therefore, although God is named the Not-other, because He is the not other of any other, He is nevertheless not the same as another. For just as He is not other from the heaven, so He is not the same as the heaven.

All things are therefore such that they are not other than they are, since God defines them. And from the Not-other they have the characteristic to generate nothing other in the species, but rather to effect a resemblance to themselves. Goodness therefore produces good, the white, white and so it is with everything.

The philosophical hunters have not entered this field, in which alone the negation is not opposed to affirmation. For the Not-other, since it defines and precedes it, is not opposed to the other.

Outside of this field, the negation is opposed to the affirmation, as, for example, the immortal to the mortal, the incorruptible to the corruptible, etc. The Not-other alone is excepted. To seek God in another field, in which He is not found, is therefore a futile hunt. For since God is before all difference of oppositions, He is not opposed to anything. God is therefore called living, to which not-living is opposed, and immortal, to which mortal is opposed, in a more imperfect manner than He is called the Not-other, to which neither other nor nothing is opposed, since He also precedes nothing and defines it. Indeed, the nothing is not other than nothing.

The divine Dionysius said most subtly that God is everything in everything and nothing in nothing. However, I wrote extensively on the Not-other in a tetralogue in the past year in Rome. Therefore, this is enough now on this.

XV.
On the Fourth Field, Namely, the Light

Now I want to enter the field of light and seek in the light given us the light of wisdom. Indeed, as the prophet says, the light of the countenance or the knowledge of God is marked upon us, and in it there is a very joyful and jocund hunt. Now, I say this because everyone who sees snow affirms that it is white. To contradict this assertion is to act crazily. Thus, one cannot deny that to be true, of which everyone thinking intelligently says that it is true.

Since, however, that which defines everything is a definition, the definition which defines itself and everything, is certainly very good and is great; this definition is beautiful, it produces wisdom, it is delectable, it is perfect, it is clear, it is equal and sufficient. Every intellect acknowledges that all these and similar things are said most truly of that definition. Therefore, these are in the definition the definition and in the defined the defined. Therefore, if I define the world to be not other than the world, then I see that all the aforementioned are in the defined world the world, and in that definition the definition, which is verified from all these.

Therefore, goodness, magnitude, truth, beauty, wisdom, perfection, clarity, and sufficiency are in the defined world the world, in the defined earth the earth. Likewise, they are in the defined God God and in the Not-other they are the Not-other, as also in the other the other. Therefore, when in the sun, which is another, they are sun, then they are sun, which is called another (namely sun). Therefore, as they are in God not other than simply the Not-other, so in the sun they are not other than the other, which is called sun. The goodness of the sun is therefore not the Not-other in its simplicity, but rather the solar Not-other, because it is in the sun the sun. And it is thus with everything.

The intellect hunts down admirable and most delightful knowledge, when it intuits with maximum certainty, that everything in the eternal and most simple God is God Himself, who defines Himself and everything; and hence is also the defined in everything defined. From this it knows that nothing of all that exists, can be completely lacking in the good, the great, the true, the beautiful, and consequently in each one of the aforementioned.

And because nothing of everything is lacking in sufficiency, everything is founded most sufficiently, since each thing possesses as much sufficiency, as is sufficient for it. Thus nothing of everything is lacking in wisdom and clarity or light, but rather each has as much thereof, as is sufficient for its nature, so that it is not other than in the relatively best manner in which it can be.

O marvelous wisdom of God, which, when it saw everything that it had created, said that it is very good! To obtain admiration of eternal wisdom through every hunt is to come close to it, since as the wise Philo says, it is the vapor of the power and majesty of God. The hunter admires its sweet and fresh scent, which completely refreshes the intellectual capacity, and he is inflamed by unspeakable desire, to hasten in that scent in order to attain that which he does not doubt is near.

This joyful hope strengthens and accelerates the course of the hunter; nevertheless, he is retarded by the arduous burden of the body, which he must bear with him, and unable to comprehend the rapidly fleeing wisdom, which extends from one end to the other, he longs to be released from the body and renounces that friendship which ties him to the body, than which none is greater according to nature, and does not fear death, in order to comprehend and taste the immortal food of God, namely, wisdom. In no other way—as the incarnate wisdom of God taught us—is it possible for any hunter to come to its comprehension, which no one except the worthy apprehends. However, he alone is worthy, who knows that it is to be preferred to everything, even his own life, and who is so inflamed by love for it that he abandons himself and everything in order to gain it.

XVI.
On the Same

The intellect rejoices in this most delightful hunt. For this hunt is good, great, true, beautiful, savory, delectable, perfect, clear, equal, and sufficient.

Indeed, the intellect sees that when the good is defined, all the aforementioned, the great, true, etc. are this good; and when the great is defined, in it the good, true, etc. are the great; and thus in each one of these all others are it itself; and since in the Not-other they are the Not-other itself, the good is here not other from the great and true, etc. And the great is not other from the good and true, etc. For the Not-other makes everything into the Not-other. Thus, the other makes everything into the other.

The good is indeed in the other the other, and likewise the great and the true. Since, therefore, each one is an other, the good will then not be not other from the great or the true. But, just as it is in the Not-other the Not-other, so is it also in the other the other. Hence, if the sun is another, its goodness is not not other than its magnitude or truth, etc., but each one of them, if it is solar, is an other from the other. The solar goodness contracted to the sun is indeed not that absolute goodness, which is the Not-other. Consequently, it is an other from solar magnitude and solar truth, etc.

For those were not in any other, which is called sun, this other itself, if each of them were not an other themselves. For the sun is in one way good, in another way great, and in another way true. And thus it is with each of these. For this reason, the other, which is on this side of the simplicity of the Not-other, in respect to the Not-other, is not without composition. However, the other, in which the Not-other is reflected less, is more composed, so that it is more composed in the sensible than in the intelligible other. Also in the solar goodness, in which magnitude, truth, etc. are contained, goodness and magnitude are not the Not-other, but rather other from the truth; and each is other from each other, if they are in solar goodness, which itself is another, namely, solar goodness. It is therefore necessary that solar goodness fall into composition, since it is contracted from the simplicity of the Not-other, or God, into solar otherness.

Therefore, the goodness, magnitude, truth, etc., which are in the composed the composed, must necessarily be other and composed. As they are in the most simple God Not-other but rather as uncomposed the simple God Himself, so the caused in the cause are the cause. However, all things that the intellect can conceive, are either the Not-other or the other. In the Not-other, since it is that which it can be, the most simple and most perfect, variety does not occur. Therefore, the intellect sees that all variety falls to the other.

Hence, the variety of the modes of being of the other is allotted now this and now that name. Therefore, goodness, magnitude, truth, etc. constitute, according to one mode of combination, that which is called to be, according to another, that which is called to live, according to another mode, that which is called to understand, etc. All things which exist, live and understand are not other than the varied receptions of the Not-other, which defines everything.

From this it follows that its varied reflection is in the one clearer, in the other more obscure; clearer and more durable in the intellectual, obscurer and more corruptible in the sensible and differently in these.

XVII.
On the Same

Proclus reports in the first book of the *Platonic Theology*, that Socrates, in whose mouth Plato placed his views, says in the *Alcibiades*, that the intellective soul, if it looks into itself, observes God and everything. Indeed, it sees that those things which are after it, are shadows of the intelligible. However, what is before it, it sees, he says, in the depths as it were with closed eyes. For he says everything is in us in the mode of a living being.

Behold Plato's divine judgment! Thus I believe that everything is in everything, namely, in its own mode. In our intellect, therefore, everything is contained according to its own mode of being. For goodness, magnitude, truth, and all those ten are in everything everything, in God God, in the intellect intellect, in the senses sense. If, therefore, these are in God God, in the intellect intellect, and in everything everything, then everything is in the intellect intellect. Therefore, everything there is in an intellectual or notional or cognizable manner. And because the intellect is good, true, beautiful, wise, and the rest of the ten, it sees, if it intuits itself, that it is thus—as I have said—and it is maximally content, since it sees that it is perfect and sufficient.

And because the intellective soul is in an intellectual mode, it is capable, by means of its intellectual goodness, of understanding both absolute goodness as well as contracted goodness. Likewise, by means of its intellectual magnitude, truth, and wisdom, it forms notions of wisdom absolved of everything and contracted to everything and intuits the order of things in wisdom and contemplates the ordered.

Hence because cognition is assimilation, it finds everything by means of the intellectual life in itself as in a living mirror. Looking into itself it sees everything as assimilated in itself. And this assimilation is the living image of the Creator and of all things. However, since this is a living and intellectual image of God, in which God is not other from anything, the intellect, if it enters into itself and knows that it is such an image, observes in itself the quality of its exemplar.

Indeed, without doubt it knows this its God, whose similitude it is. For in its notional goodness it knows that the goodness of God, whose image it is, is greater than it can conceive or think. Thus it knows in the intuition of its own magnitude, which embraces everything intellectually, that the exemplary magnitude of its God, whose image it is, exceeds its ambit, because it has no end. And that is true of everything. It also sees intelligences beyond itself which are more lucid and more capable of divinity, and after itself it sees sensible cognition, which is more darkened and less capable of divinity.

How sufficient this intellectual hunt is, when it proceeds within itself without ceasing to pour itself forth, is demonstrated by the discoveries of the theologians, philosophers, and mathematicians, which are disclosed to us multiply in their writings. However, in what manner Dionysius made his chosen hunt in the field of light, is certainly found in his book *On the Divine Names*.

XVIII.
On the Fifth Field, Namely, Laud

After I had wandered through the field of light, the most lovely field of God's laud immediately appeared.

For when I had stored everything in the pantry of the mind which I have hunted down in the field of light—the aforementioned ten, namely, goodness, magnitude, truth, etc.—I found that they all and still more are planted in the field of God's laud and said: Since this flowering and happy field produces only these ten and what is similar to them, these ten are therefore the lauds of God.

And looking inside myself, I observed how the intellect, in affirming that the definition defining itself and everything is good, great, true, etc., attempts to express its laud. Indeed, it lauds that definition which is God, since it is good, great, true, etc. What therefore are those ten, other than the laud of God? What is lauded through them, if not that laud which is God? Are not these all lauded? Goodness is lauded, magnitude is lauded, truth is lauded, etc. Therefore, these ten and others, which are lauded by everyone who is in possession of his intellectual power, are cited in the laud of God and are well said of Him, because He Himself is the font of the laud. Therefore, they are all, on account of the lauds of God and benedictions, that which they are.

Hence, the prophet Daniel, looking at all of God's work, sang: "Bless the Lord, all works of the Lord, laud and exalt Him forever." And one by one he enumerates the angels, the heaven, the earth, the water and everything else created, which laud God. For they all are nothing other than a becoming and jocund laudation of God. For as Dionysius attests, the divine is known only through participation. However, in what manner it is in its origin and in its foundation, no intellect can attain.

Furthermore, we know—whether we now call the concealed super-substantial light or life or word—nothing other of it than the participation and strength emanating from it to us, through which we are assumed into God and which give us subsistence, life, and wisdom. Thus Dionysius.

Rightly, therefore, everything created by God lauds God, because He is good; for it acknowledges that through His gift it itself is good and laudable, great, and true, etc. All prophets, seers, and elevated intellects made their most devoted hunts in the field of laud, which the sacred writings and the works of the saints attest to, in which everything is referred to the laud of God.

In the treatment of divine names, Dionysius called those names the laud of God; and in lauding God through them, he explained them as in His laud. Thus in the chapter "On Wisdom," intellect and rationality are lauded. And he says that God is lauded by all that subsists.

I therefore discovered that in this field of laud the most delightful knowledge consists in the laud of God, which from His lauds constitutes all things into His laud. Indeed, just as the varied hymns of lauds contain various harmonic combinations, so each species, such as man, the lion, the eagle, etc., is a special hymn of the lauds of God and is composed in His laud.

The celestial hymns are more festive and fecund in lauds

than are the terrestrial. For the sun is a wondrous combination of lauds of God, and each hymn is in itself beautiful and singular, because in its singularity it has something which the other hymns lack. Hence they are all accepted by God, who blessed and called everything good which He created, through participation in His laud.

From this I elicited that a living and understanding man, the best composed of hymn of the lauds of God, possesses more than all other visible things of the lauds of God, so that he lauds God more incessantly than the others, and that his life consists therein alone, that he gives back to God that which he, in order to be, has received, namely, lauds. If he does that, he hastens toward his end and gains the most blissful merit of immortal lauds.

XIX.
On the Same

Everything, therefore, lauds God through its being.

And since everything is so perfect and sufficient, that it is not lacking in respect to laud, it lauds its Maker from whom alone it has that which is lauded.

Therefore, by nature all created things laud God, and when a creature is lauded, then this laud is not for the creature, which has not created itself, but rather for its Composer in it. Idolatry, in which the lauds belonging to God are bestowed on a creature, is therefore the insanity of a weak, blind, and seduced mind. For to revere in place of God that which, according to its nature, lauds its Creator, is certainly to be insane.

There is no creature which recognizes another God than Him whom it lauds as its Composer, than whom it knows nothing more excellent. Every creature therefore knows that and, as far as suffices it, knows its omnipotent Composer. It lauds Him, and hears and understands His Word, and obeys. If He, for example, were to command a stone to come alive, so it will hear Him, understand, and obey. Indeed, even the dead will hear the Word of God and live. Just as Lazarus, who was dead for four days, and others heard and lived, as Christians know.

From this it is certain that when a man, who has freedom

of decision, desists from lauds of God and does not hear the Word of God, which speaks in him and his conscience, nor wants to understand and obey Him, so that he acts justly, it is inexcusable, since he is rebuked by his own nature. And he is not worthy of the community of the blessed, who laud God perpetually.

Moreover, I have found in hunting in this field that the perpetual and most jocund laudation of the Lord by the sacred spirits is unutterable. As they love Him, so they proclaim Him, and the more they laud Him, the more laud do they themselves achieve and come ever nearer to the infinitely laudable, even though they never attain equality with Him. For just as finite time can never be so augmented that it becomes similar to infinite perpetuity, so the initiated perpetuity can also not ever be equal to the uninitiated eternity.

Also just as little can the perpetual damnation of rebellious spirits ever become temporal and finite.

However, what kind of laud men attain who are perfect praisers of God, is taught by the always observed respect, which exalts them to community with God and the saints and brings divine lauds to them. However, those who have achieved perfection laud God in the highest and lay aside what could impede this laud, such as self-love and love of this world, and put themselves aside, in that they enter into the religious faith, which mortifies the impeding love of self and the world. They imitate the teacher of truth, the Word of God incarnate, who in laud of God taught to take upon oneself voluntarily through word and example the most terrible of all terrors, namely, the most disgraceful death. Following him, an infinite number of martyrs have achieved immortal life through death and today most religious aspire by dying to the world and becoming free for these lauds of God to be perfect praisers of God.

XX.
On the Same

The prophet commanded to play the laud of God on the ten-stringed psaltery.

Attending to this, I have taken only these ten strings of laud: goodness, magnitude, truth and the others aforementioned.

However, the psaltery is a work of the intelligence, so that man would have an instrument on which he can play sweet and delectable modes. For he makes those modes sensible and audible, which he bears in himself in an intelligible manner, and since these modes are in the intellect, those who have intellect enjoy hearing what they have insensibly in the soul, by means of the ear and sensibly in the sounds. Hence, if these sounds agree with the vital harmonic measures of the soul, then they laud the singer; if they do not agree, they vituperate against him.

Three things are necessary, if one wishes to play the psalter: a psaltery, which is composed of two parts, namely, the vessel and the strings; and a player of the psalter: that is intelligence, nature and subject. The psalter player is the intelligence, the strings are the nature, which is moved by the intelligence, and the vessel is the subject appropriate to the nature.

These are in the microcosm, man, just as in the larger world. In him there is intelligence, human nature, and the body appropriate to the latter. Thus man is a living psaltery, who unites everything in himself for singing lauds to God, which he recognizes in himself. In the psaltery and cithara, in the euphony and jubilation of the cymbals, every spirit lauds the Lord.

Our intellectual spirit has all these instruments living in itself. However, it is astonishing whence a man of vigorous intellect has by nature this knowledge of laud, the laudable, and the reprehensible. For if this knowledge were not necessary to that nature for its own nourishment and preservation, man would not have it more than the ass. For just as divine providence is not lacking in the necessary, so it also does not abound in the superfluous.

And because we are also nourished and fed by that from which we are, every living creature seeks its nourishment, which when it finds it, it also knows on account of the conformity of the food to that from which it is. Hence if man, in accordance with his intellectual soul, knows the laudable by nature, and embraces and rejoices in it as in a nourishment conforming to his nature, he knows that he is in a natural manner from that which, on account of natural conformity to his being, he lauds and embraces.

Through the gift of divine providence the intellect therefore possesses in itself all the knowledge necessary for it of the origins, through which it hunts down that conforming to its nature; and this judgment is infallible. And since its origins are laudable—just as those often-mentioned ten—and man himself is originated from them, so that as laud of God he lauds his Creator, man is not fully ignorant of his God, whom he knows is laudable and glorious forever.

No other knowledge is necessary for him, since he knows as much as suffices him, in order to do that for which he is created. Therefore, by lauding God, because He is good, he knows that goodness is laudable. It is likewise with the truth, wisdom, etc. And although he does not know what these are, he is nevertheless not completely ignorant of them, when he knows that they are laudable and enfolded in the laud of God and in such correspondence to the laud of God, that without them man is not able to laud God or anything else.

Man also knows that he should determine his free decision by means of the laudable, so that he is laudable by election just as by nature. For goodness, virtue, truth, honesty, equality, etc. are laudable and they or their contrary can be elected through a free decision.

If they are elected, then the whole man is laudable both by nature as well as by the election of his decision, and lauds God perfectly. If, however, he elects vice and the opposite of the laudable, he is not laudable, but rather contrary to himself and God. How then could he laud God, if he himself were contrary to laud? However, whoever always lauds God advances constantly, as the cithara player citharizing, and he becomes always more similar to God.

And this is, as Plato quite rightly said, the end of man, namely, to become more similar to God. For the more he lauds God, the more pleasing he is to God. Therefore, he is also more laudable and more similar to the divine laudability.

The wise Socrates rightly discovered that we know nothing more certainly than that which is laudable, and he admonished us to direct our efforts exclusively thereto and to dismiss everything else as superfluous and uncertain. He also advised sweating after laudable morals, the knowledge of which we can draw from ourselves, to acquire from usage a perfecting habit and thus to become constantly better.

XXI.
On the Sixth Field, Namely, Unity

When Aurelius Augustinus endeavored to hunt for wisdom, he wrote in the booklet *On Order,* that the consideration of all philosophers revolves around the question of the One. After him, the most learned Boethius declared in his writing *On Unity and the One,* that one must undertake the hunt for wisdom in the same manner as it has occurred there. Both follow Plato herein, who calls the One the first and eternal principle. Earlier Pythagoras of Samos, who investigates everything in respect to the property of number, affirmed that the monad is the principle of all things. For unity is prior to all multitude.

Therefore, we want to traverse this field of unity in the mind for the sake of our hunt. Indeed, even though the Notother precedes unity, nevertheless the latter seems quite near to it. For the one and the same seem more than all others to participate in the Not-other.

Plato supposed that the One is eternal. For he saw nothing that was not after the One. It is, as Dionysius, who imitated Plato in this, says, before the finite and the infinite. Consequently, as Proclus reports, Plato placed the principles of the finite and the infinite after the first principle, because everything existing is compounded of these, in that it has its essence from the finite and its strength and potentiality from the infinite. And since the One is that which it can be, and indeed is completely simple and unmultiplicable, it seems to enfold everything in itself that, as long as it is remote from the One, in no way endures.

Indeed, everything exists only insofar as it is One. However, it embraces both that which actually is, as well as that which can become. The One is therefore more capacious than entity, which only is if it actually is, although Aristotle said that entity and the One are interchangeable.

However, that which moved Plato to prefer the One to everything and to designate it as the origin of everything, was that, since the initiated has nothing from itself, but rather everything from its origin, by the fact that the origin is posited, everything initiated is posited. Since, however, with the positing of entity, entity as potentiality is not also posited—this is something completely other—with the positing of life, entity without life is not posited, and with the positing of the intellect, non-understanding entity is not posited, and since to be, to live, and to understand are found in the world, the origin of the world will be neither entity, nor life, nor intellect, but rather that which enfolds them in itself and what those can be, and this he called the One.

Indeed, the One is verified in regard to potentiality as one potentiality, and in regard to actuality as one actuality. The same is true of entity, life and intellect. Also, there can be no multitude which does not participate in unity. For if there were such multitude, the similar, by not participating in unity, would be dissimilar. Everything multiple would be similar and similarly—because it does not participate in unity—dissimilar. Therefore, everything multiple and plural, every number and everything that can be called one, would cease, if this One were sublated, as this is demonstrated with wonderful subtlety in the *Parmenides* of Plato.

Therefore, the One cannot be what is made, since it precedes it. And it cannot be destroyed nor altered nor multiplied, since it precedes the potential-to-become and is everything which it can be. Truly, as Dionysius says, "the One, which is, is said to be multiplied, in that it produces many substances from itself." Nevertheless the One, which is God, remains One in multiplication and connected in proceeding.

Therefore, through participation in invariable and unmultiplicable unity, all things which can become, can become and actually do become. And because there can only be one unity, which as Dionysius says, is more eminent than the senses and incomprehensible to the mind and precedes it, therefore it is the One which unites everything, so that anything whatever exists only insofar as it is one.

Only the eternal One is before the potential-to-become. Hence, that postulation is not true, that there are gods before the potential-to-become, which participate in the One, as in a divine species. For since the eternal One is unmultiplicable, since it is before the potential to be multiplied, there cannot be many gods in the One, as if united in the first, eternal God as in a divine species. For if it were so, there would be many gods. Therefore, they would participate in various ways in the divine nature in eternity, which is impossible, since it is the eternal, and the most simple eternity is completely imparticipable.

Therefore, Proclus took completely superfluous pains, in wishing to investigate in the six books of the *Theology of Plato* on the basis of uncertain conjectures, the differences between those eternal gods and their relation to the one God of the gods, since there is only the one eternal God, who is the administrator of this whole world and who is the most sufficient God for everything, for which Proclus postulates the former.

Proceeding from this sensible world and from that which is necessary for it, so that it is that which it can become, in the best possible way, the philosophical hunters appear in all their running to and fro concerning God, gods, the heavens, their motion and fate, concerning intelligent spirits, ideas, and nature itself, to undertake inquiries, just as if all those were necessary for the earthly world, and this world were the end of all those works. Thus Aristotle, like Plato, posited that God administers the heavens through His providence, however, the heavens exist only for the sake of this world and are moved through intelligences, so that the generation and everything necessary to the preservation of the world occur and are continued in a natural manner, according to the order and motion of the heavens. However, they did not attend to the fact that so many innumerable stars, greater than the inhabitable earth, and so many intelligences, are not created as the end of the earthly world, but rather for the laud of the Creator as touched upon above.

Therefore, the omnipotent God, who creates everything for His laud and governs with complete providence, is One, as Epicurus correctly stated. Even though he does not deny that there are gods, he nevertheless said that that which is said and written about them is completely alien to the truth.

Attention should be paid to this: No one has ever affirmed that there is a plurality of gods, who has not preferred the one God to this multitude of gods. Therefore, he makes enjoyable hunts in this field of unity, who, as Augustinus has done in the book *On the Trinity,* sees the fecund unity, which generates equality from itself, and the connecting love, which proceeds from unity and equality, so in eternity, that they are the most simple eternity itself. What I could conceive thereof, I have set forth elsewhere in *On Learned Ignorance,* in *On the Vision of God,* and in many other booklets.

XXII.
On the Same

When Plato diligently examined the field of unity, he found the One, which as cause of everything is before potentiality and the actuality arising from potentiality, but also at the same time—in order to be the cause of everything—is nothing of everything. In order to be the cause of plurality, it is not plural. Hence, in denying all things of it, he saw it ineffably before everything.

However, how he made his hunting for the One by means of logic, he shows in the book *Parmenides.* Proclus summarizes it in the second book of his *Theology of Plato,* and says that Plato believes it abides in negation. For an addition to the One contracts and diminishes the excellence of the One and through it the not-one is shown more than the One.

Dionysius, who imitates Plato, makes a similar hunt in the field of unity and says that the negations, which as privations show excellence and are pregnant affirmations, are truer than affirmations. Proclus, however, who cites Origen, comes after Dionysius. Following Dionysius, he denies of the first that it is the One and the Good, even though Plato named the first so, because it is entirely ineffable. Because I think one must follow these admirable and laudable hunters, I refer students to their writings, bequeathed to us with diligence.

And since in the field of unity there is a singular meadow, where the most singular quarry can be found, we now wish to visit this meadow for the sake of our hunt. Moreover, it is called singularity.

For since the One is not other than the One, it appears singular, since it is in itself undivided and divided from the other. Indeed, the singular embraces the whole. For all are singular and each is unpluralizable. Therefore, since the singular are everything and unpluralizable, they show that the One is maximally such, which is the cause of everything singular and which is the singular and unpluralizable through essence. For the One is that which it can be and the singularity of everything singular.

Hence, just as the simplicity of everything simple is per se so simple that it cannot be simpler, so the singularity of everything singular is per se so singular that it cannot be more singular. The singularity of the One and the Good is therefore the maximum, because everything singular is necessarily the One and the Good, and thus is enfolded in the singularity of the One and the Good. Just as the singularity of the species is more singular than that of its individuals, also the singularity of the whole is more singular than that of the part and the singularity of the world more singular than that of all singular things.

Hence, just as the most singular God is maximally unpluralizable, so after Him the singularity of the world is maximally unpluralizable, then that of the species and finally that of individuals, of which none is pluralizable. Each one, therefore, rejoices concerning its singularity, which is in it so great that it is not pluralizable, not in God, nor in the world, nor in the angels. Indeed, all rejoice to participate in the similitude of God and when a chick emerges from the egg, although the singularity of the egg ceases, nevertheless not the singularity itself, since the chick is just as singular as the egg, nor is the one an other singularity than the other, but rather there is one cause of all singular things, which singularizes everything. The latter is neither the whole nor the part nor a species nor an individual, neither this nor that nor everything nameable, but rather the most singular cause of all singular things.

Since the singular has been singularized from an eternal cause, it can never be resolved into the not-singular. For by what should that which is singularized from an eternal cause be resolved?

Because every singular thing is good, the singular never desists from the good. Thus, the singular entity never ceases to be this, since everything actual is a singular entity and however much a singular body is divided, it always remains a singular body. Likewise the line, the surface, and the whole as singular is not divisible, except in singular parts, which were comprehended in the singularity of the whole.

Therefore, all variety is not in respect to the singular, but rather in respect to that which is accidental to the singular, which makes a singular one way or another, so that this singular continues to subsist in the same manner as in the celestial bodies, when the variety in it is not of quality and quantity. Thus Dionysius also said that nothing with regard to nature and substance is corruptible, but rather only in respect to the accidental.

Therefore, the singularity, which forms and preserves all, is incorruptible and all seek with the most natural desire for the cause of their singularity as for the sufficient, perfect, and most singular good.

I want to add one thing for you, which I see as marvelous above all others, in which you will judge that all simultaneously bear the similitude of God. Dionysius correctly said that the opposite should simultaneously be affirmed and denied of God. Thus if you turn to the whole, you will discover that everything is uniform. For if everything is singular, then it is simultaneously similar, just because it is singular, and dissimilar because it is singular, and also not similar and not dissimilar, because it is singular. It is likewise with the same and the diverse, the equal and unequal, the singular and the plural, one and the many, the even and odd, with the different and concordant, etc., even though it appears absurd to those philosophers, who even in theology hold fast to the principle that each thing either is or is not.

Also attend to the fact that the potential-to-become is singular. Therefore, everything is singular, which was or is made, because it arises from the potential-to-become. Therefore, the imitable singularity is the potential-to-become itself, in the potential to be singular of which everything singular is singularly enfolded and from which it is unfolded.

For singularity is not other than the similitude of eternal light. Singularity is indeed separation. However, it is for the light to separate and to singularize. About this see above and in the booklet *On the Form of the World,* which I compiled recently in Orvieto.

XXIII.
On the Seventh Field, Namely, Equality

We wish to enter the field of equality, which is full of possibilities for our hunt.

Certainly nothing is multiplicable just as it actually is. Indeed, the equality, which is that which it can be, since it is before the other and the unequal, is not found except in the region of eternity. However, equality, which can become still more equal, follows the potential-to-become. Hence, equality, which is as actuality what it can be, is unmultiplicable. For eternal unity brings it forth in eternity.

Therefore, several things cannot be precisely equal; they were then not several things, but rather the equal itself. Indeed, just as goodness, magnitude, beauty, truth, etc., which in eternity are eternity itself, are also so equal, that they are the equality which is eternity, they are therefore not several, just as there cannot be several eternals, since the eternal is the actual-potential itself, namely, that which can exist simply. And thus everything eternal is not a plurality of eternals, just as eternal goodness, eternal magnitude, eternal beauty, eternal truth, and eternal equality are not a plurality of eternals; likewise, there is also not a plurality of equals, because they are equals in such a manner that they are the most simple equality itself, which precedes every plurality. And thus the equality of every actually existing thing is not multiplicable.

Indeed, the precision which exists in the indivisible, is not just as number multiplicable, nor just as four or five. Hence, humanity is not plurified in several men, just as unity is not in several ones. Nor can the humanity from several men, to whom it gives the name "men," be participated in equally. Indeed, they are men by participation in unmultiplicable humanity and by unequal participation, which causes them to be many. And just as humanity, as it is, is unmultiplicable, thus also each man and all others are unmultiplicable.

Also everything composed is composed out of unequal parts; thus a composed number also cannot be composed except out of even and odd numbers, and an harmonic song out of high and low tones. It is clear that everything equal, which is not the absolute equality, can become still more equal and that this potential-to-become of all things cannot be defined and determined except through an equality preceding the potential-to-become. It alone is the Not-other from everything; everything else is in an unequal manner unequal among themselves, even though nothing of everything is excluded from the equality, through which everything existing in an equal manner is that which it is, because it is not more and not less and above all not other than that which it is.

For equality is that Word of the Not-other, namely, of the Creator-God, who names and defines Himself and everything.

Therefore, all things unequal among themselves participate in equality as in the form of any being and in this are equal; and since all things participate in it unequally, they are unequal. Therefore, all things are simultaneously in concord and differ. Just as every species is the unity, which unites everything of its species in itself, it is also the equality, which in an equal manner forms the united. In a similar manner it is also the connection of everything.

And since I have already written earlier in Rome at length on equality, let this suffice.

XXIV.
On the Eighth Field, Namely, Connection

Now, in making our hunt in the field of connection, we observe that connection is constituted before every division.

Therefore, from here we see that the indivisible eternity is that which it can be, that it precedes the potential-to-become and proceeds most directly from the eternal unity and its equality. For just as division proceeds from plurality and inequality, so the connection of love proceeds from unity and equality. Since the latter are before plurality in the indivisible, most simple eternity, their connection will similarly also be eternal. The unity, the equality generated from it, and the connection of both are therefore the simple eternity before the potential-to-become and divisive plurality.

For the eternal unity, its eternal equality, and the eternal connection of both are not several, divided eternals, but rather the unpluralizable, completely indivisible and inalterable eternity itself, and although the generating unity is not the equality generated from it and the connection proceeding therefrom, nevertheless unity, equality, connection are not other, since they are the Not-other, which precedes the other. Therefore, just as the eternal unity, which is that which it can be, enfolds everything in itself in a unifying manner, and the equality enfolds everything in an equalizing manner, the connection of both connects everything in itself.

Therefore, I see that everything which exists, because it is from this eternal Trinity, which is so called, although not entirely appropriately, is that which it is and imitates this Trinity. Indeed, in everything whatever I see unity, entity and the connection of both, so that it is actually that which it is.

Entity, which is the form of being, is the equality of unity. The unifying unity indeed generates its equality from itself. The equality of unity is nothing other than the species or form of being, which is called entity, because this word entity in Greek is derived from the term for one. Therefore, everything existing is not other than unity and its equality, which is also entity, and the connection of both. Unity is the constriction of fluxability, equality the formation of the unified and the constricted, the connection of both is the connection of love. Unless the potential-to-become is constrained from its confused fluxability by the unifying, it were not capable of beauty, neither of the species nor of the form. And because it is constrained by the unity, which conveys everything to an end, therefore, the form is generated from the unity, which such a constriction requires or merits. Hence, the connection of love proceeds from them both.

XXV.
On the Same

Now you see that love, which is the connection of unity and entity, is most natural. For it proceeds from unity and equality, which are its most natural origin. Indeed, from them is exhaled the connection, in which they are connected most ardently.

Therefore, nothing is destitute of this love, without which nothing can persist. The invisible spirit of this connection therefore penetrates everything. All parts of the world are preserved among themselves through this spirit and are connected with the whole world. This is the spirit, which connects the soul to the body and in whose expiration vivification ceases. The intellectual nature will never be deprived of this spirit of connection, since it is itself spiritual nature.

Since the unity and entity of the intellectual nature are

intellectual, they are constrained through an intellectual connection. The connection of intellectual love cannot become feeble nor expire, since the understanding is nourished by immortal wisdom. The natural connection of the intellectual nature, which is inclined to wisdom, therefore preserves this intellectual nature, not only just as it is, but rather, it also adapts to that which it by nature loves, so that it is connected with it.

The spirit of wisdom therefore descends into the spirit of the intellect as the desired into the desiring, according to the fervor of this desire, and converts the spirit of intelligence towards itself, which is connected to it in love, like to fire, as Dionysius says, which assimilates the singular things united to it according to their aptitude; in this connection of love the intellect is made happy and lives happily.

Few philosophers recognized this. Indeed, they appear not to have grasped the principle of connection, without which nothing subsists and all intellectual nature must do without happiness. But because they lacked it, they did not attain true wisdom. Elsewhere I have spoken in various sermons and written a lot on this and therefore that recapitulated here should suffice.

XXVI.
On the Same

Now I would like to subjoin a mathematical guide, so that you see that the aforementioned Trinity, since it is unity, is that which it can be, even though it precedes all intellect and is not comprehended except incomprehensibly by every human mind. In the latter, God is seen as much before the potential-to-become as before the impossible, as if He were that something which the impossible follows.

I suppose that the straight line is simpler than the curved, since the curved, which diverges from the straight, cannot be conceived without the concave and convex.

Then I presuppose that the first rectilinear figure is defined as a triangle, to which all polygons are resolved as to the prior and simpler, before which there is none to which it could be resolved. However, since there is no line without length, then the line which is not so long that the length could not be greater

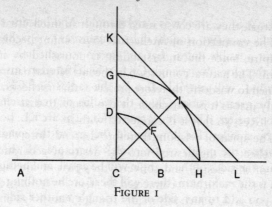

FIGURE I

in respect to it, is imperfect. Therefore, if the first Origin could be figured, it were the perfect triangle with three perfect sides. The intellect sees this in the potential-to-become of the sensible triangle in the following manner (see Figure 1):

Let AB be a straight line. Describe above a point C of this straight line a circular quadrant, whose radius is CB. Draw the other radius CD. Let the arc DB be the quadrant whose middle point is F. Draw the chord DB, then continue CD and CB to infinity. Beyond C describe the quadrant of the larger circle, which is GH, whose middle is I. As before, draw the chord GH and draw the circumscriptive straight line of the arc GH, which is KIL.

It is certain that the triangular figure CDFB has a right angle in the middle point and two angles at the arc, of which each, insofar as it falls beyond the chord and inside the arc of the angle, is greater than a half-right angle. And because in the greater circle, namely CGIH, the angles at the arc are greater than in the smaller circle—the angle of incidence which falls above the chord GH is indeed greater than the angle of incidence above the chord DB—it is certain that these angles, which are formed from the radius and arc, can always become greater, when it is a question of the arc of a greater circle.

If it were therefore possible to designate the arc of the maximum circle which could not be greater, then those angles at the arc would necessarily be that which acute angles could be. And thus they were right angles. Indeed, when the acute angle cannot be greater, then it is a right angle. And because the arc, which falls over two straight radii, constitutes two right angles, this is not possible unless that arc were a straight line.

So therefore that triangle CKL, which I intuit in this manner in the mind, will certainly also be the radius line CK, which cannot be greater, since CK is the radius of that circle which cannot be greater. The same is true of CL. The arc KL, however, cannot be smaller, for how would the arc of the quadrant be smaller than the radius of the circle? Therefore, all those lines which are the sides of the triangle will be equal, and because each of them is the maximum, there will therefore be nothing greater, even if you add to any side of the triangle another side or two others. Each side is therefore equal to any one, both and all simultaneously. Consequently, the outer angle, namely KCA, is equal to the two inner angles opposite it, and the two right angles, CKL and CLK, since ACK is as KCL, will be as KCL.

And because every triangle has three angles, which are equal to two right angles, and any angle for the reason stated is equal to two right angles, any angle is therefore equal to all three angles. Thus any angle is equal to the other one, and equal to the other two, and equal to all three angles and this triangle were the enfolding as well as the origin and resolution, as well as the end and most precise measure of all figurable figures.

It is certain that if the potential-to-become were so perfected that it were brought entirely into actuality and were the actual-potential, these would thus be the necessary consequences. However, I am most certain that if I see these somehow necessary consequences, they are incomparably more truly actuality in the actual-potential. For something cannot be seen in a rational manner, which lacks the actual-potential itself, since this represents everything comprehensible and everything which exceeds comprehension in the most perfect actuality. The Blessed Anselm says the truth, when he asserts that God is greater than He could be conceived, and Saint Thomas says it more clearly in the booklet *On the Eternal World,* where he wrote thus: "In respect to the omnipotence of God, who exceeds every intellect and capability, it can be said that he derogates the omnipotence of God, who asserts that in the creature something could be understood that cannot be made by God."

Therefore, I see that in the actual-potential the maximum

triangle is in eternal actuality, just as was said. The actual-potential is therefore before every corporeal quantity, because in corporeal quantity, whether discrete or continuous, the actual-potential
cannot be found. Rather, it is before everything sensible, intelligible, and everything finite. In all things which can be conceived,
one does not find the trinity which is unity or the unity which is
trinity.

You see that the potential-to-become of one nature is not
terminated in the same, because the actual-potential and the potential-to-become are of different natures. The warmable, for
example, if it shall be that which it can be, will not be the
warmable, but rather the warming. Wood can be warmed more
and more. However, when it is warmed so much that it cannot
be warmed further, then fire arises as actual out of the potentiality. This cannot be warmed further, but rather merely warms.
And if in one warmable thing the point is reached for warming
more rapidly than in another, it is because the one comes to the
terminus of its warmability more rapidly than the other. And
that one, which never becomes so warm that it could not become
still warmer, never comes to the terminus, so that it would
become fire. The warming is only in the warmable the warming
in potentiality. When it therefore comes from potentiality to
actuality, nothing essentially new arises. For the same passes over
from the one mode of being into the other.

Therefore, in everything warmable, since it is fire in potentiality, it appears that fire is latent in everything of this world,
even though in the one less and in the other more. Indeed,
everything is either warming fire or warmable. However, since
fire cannot be cooled, even though it can be extinguished or
suffocated in its actuality, water is therefore not in fire in potentiality, and it is, as Dionysius says, inalterable.

That is the rational ground of the rule of learned ignorance,
that one never attains to the simply maximum or simply minimum in that which admits of more or less, although possibly to
the actual maximum and minimum.

When the warmable has indeed attained to the simply maximum, it is no longer warmable, but rather the warming. For the
warming is the maximum warmable, just as the cooling is the
maximum coolable and the naturally moving the maximum
movable and in general: the effecting in nature the maximum

effectible. The effectibility is not the effecting potentiality, but rather, in the effectibility the effecting is in potentiality. The effectible indeed never becomes the effecting, but rather, the effecting potentiality in the terminus of effectibility passes over into actuality.

Hence, the warmable never becomes warming fire, although the fire, which exists in potentiality in the warmable, passes over in the terminus of the warmable into actuality, and likewise the effecting intellect is seen in the terminus of the intelligible. The terminus of the intelligible, however, is its actuality; thus the intelligible in actuality is the intellect in actuality, and the sensible in actuality is the sense in actuality. Thus in the terminus of the illuminable is the illuminating light, and in the terminus of the creatable the creating Creator, who can be seen in the creatable. But as actuality, He cannot be seen except in the terminus of the creatable, which is the unlimited or infinite terminus. Indeed, great is the hunt with the net of this frequently mentioned rule.

XXVII.
On the Ninth Field, Namely, the Terminus

The field close to that of connection, which I call terminus, is full of the desired quarry most suited to our hunt. It is very large and interminable, because there is no end to its magnitude. It has no beginning and no end, but it holds the beginning, middle, and end of everything terminable in itself, just as the root of omnipotence contains everything in its power, unfolds all and determines the universe.

Individual things subsist in their precision, so that they are not other than that which they are. But the interminable terminus is the end of everything terminable and the precision and terminus of all precision.

The terminus, which is everything that can be, is before every terminus of that which can become. It therefore determines the whole and defines the individual. For it is certainly the interminable terminus of the potential-to-become, which bears in itself in advance in a determined manner everything which can become. It is the terminus therefore of all things and all knowledge.

However, what is it that posits the terminus, if not mind and wisdom? Indeed, the mind, as Anaxagoras saw very well, determines the confused possibility, and discerns and moves all things, so that they attain to their terminus, which it predetermines for them. The mind defines the exemplars of things, which—as Dionysius saw quite well in writing *On Divine Names*—are the rational grounds of the things preexisting in it, according to which divine wisdom predestined or predetermined and produced everything. What else therefore are those exemplars mentioned above, than the termini determining everything? It is certain that the divine Mind of all these things is the terminus. For it itself determined the former in itself in a rational manner.

When you look back before the potential-to-become, and in a human manner consider that God has conceived from eternity the will to create, when still nothing was created, neither heaven nor earth, nor angels, nor anything other, certainly they were no more creatable than others, which have nothing in common with them and of which we can form no concept. But God Himself determined within His concept that He would create this world or this beautiful creation, which we see. Therefore, everything receives its terminus of being thus and thus from the determination of the mind in itself.

And creating according to this eternal concept, He determined the potential-to-become for the world and its parts, which He had preconceived in eternity. Indeed, the potential-to-become is not vague and indeterminate, but rather it was created to the end and terminus, that the world became this and not other. Therefore, that concept, which is also called the mental word or wisdom, is the terminus, of which there is no end. For no other mind, which would have determined it to creating this world, precedes the divine Mind.

However, since the eternal Mind is free to create and not to create, or to create one way or another, He has determined His omnipotence from eternity in Himself, just as He wanted. Indeed, the human mind, which is an image of the absolute Mind, is free in a human manner and posits termini for all things in its concept, because it is a mind which measures everything notionally. Thus it gives a terminus to lines, which it makes long or short, and establishes in them as many punctual termini as it wants. And anything it proposes to make, it first determines in itself and it is the terminus of all its works, and all the things that it makes do not terminate it, such that it could make nothing more; in its manner it is an interminable terminus. I have written about this in the book *On the Mind*.

XXVIII.
On the Same

Therefore, it is clear that divine wisdom is latent in this field and can be found through a diligent hunt.

For it is divine wisdom, which gave the terminus to the ocean, the arid land, the sun, the moon, the stars and their motion, and determined a law for every creature, which can not pass away. It determined specific orbit or location of each individual, it placed the earth in the middle, and determined it to be heavy and to move to the center of the world, so that it always subsists in this middle and deviates neither upward nor laterally.

It determined for every creature its measure, its weight, and its number. And thus the divine Mind determined everything in the wisest manner, such that nothing does without the rational grounds as to why it is so and not otherwise. And if it were otherwise, everything would be confused. Therefore, the divine Mind is the measure and terminus of everything, since it is the rational ground and definition of itself and all things. The potential-to-become of the perfection and terminus of the species is therefore not terminated in these, but rather in their interminable terminus. Hence they have no other exemplar than the divine Mind, through which they are that which they are and in consequence of which they are terminated.

For it itself is the rational ground, which cannot be greater and more perfect, and therefore is the mind itself. The rational ground is indeed perfect insofar as the mind or intellect is reflected in it. Therefore, it shines variedly in the various rational grounds, in the one more perfectly than in the other.

The rational ground therefore, which cannot be more perfect, since it is all that which can be, is the eternal Mind itself. Therefore, the rational grounds or exemplars of all things look back to that eternal rational ground, in which they are terminated most perfectly, because they are not powerful and perfect except insofar as they participate in that which is the eternal Mind, through whose participation they are what they are.

The variety of exemplars is therefore based only on the varied participation of rational grounds participating variously in the eternal rational ground. Therefore, all things which are determined through their exemplars specifically are content, because their potential-to-become is determined in their species. In these species they participate in the eternal rational ground, the divine Mind, the best Creator of all things.

Therefore, since the species is a specific determination of the potential-to-become, it shows that those are of the same species, whose potential-to-become, if it came into existence, is terminated in the same. Thus all men are of the same species, since, if each man became that which man can become, then the perfection of the potential-to-become of each one would be determined in the exemplary rational ground or in the intelligible man. It is likewise with all circles: If each of them became as perfect as a circle can become, then it were determined in that exemplary rational ground of the equidistance of the center from the circumference. Thus it is with all things of the same species. And those who did not pay attention to this were often deceived, since they denied those being of the same species which were and affirmed those which were not.

XXIX.
On the Same

Since our mind is not the Origin of things and also does not determine their essences (for the divine Mind does that), but rather is only the origin of its own actions, which it determines, and since everything is notionally enfolded in its power, most hunters wearied themselves in vain, who sought to apprehend the essences of things. For the intellect apprehends nothing that it does not find in itself. However, the essences and quiddities of things are not in it in itself, but rather only the notions of things, which are the assimilations and similitudes of things.

Indeed, it is the power of the intellect, to be able to assimilate all intelligible things. Thus, the species or the assimilations of things are in it. Because of this it is called the location of the species. But it is in no way the Essence of essences.

Therefore, he seeks superfluously in his understanding for the essences of things, which are not there. For just as the sense of vision has nothing in its power and potentiality except the visible species or forms, and the sense of hearing nothing except the audible, so also the intellect has nothing in its power and potentiality except formal species.

Indeed, God alone contains in His power and causal potentiality the essences and essential forms of all things. Therefore, although everything is in the sense of vision in a visible manner, the sense of vision can nevertheless not attain the intelligible, which precedes and exceeds its power, and likewise that is not directly audible, which is not included in the power of the sense of hearing. Nevertheless, sometimes it attains it indirectly in signs and visible writing. But in no way does it attain the intelligible directly or indirectly, since it is after it and has insufficient power to apprehend it. Thus the intellect can never so attain the essential forms and quiddities of things, since they are before its notional power and exceed it, that it understands them, although it can form conjectures about them through that which it understands.

God alone, the Creator and Giver of these essential forms, intuits them in Himself. Indeed, He does not in the proper sense understand, but rather gives essence and this is to be the terminus of everything. For the potential-to-become of intelligence is not terminated except in the intellect, which is what it can be. Hence His intelligence does not arise from things, but rather the things are from it. Indeed, our intellect understands, when it assimilates everything to itself. For it could understand nothing, if it did not assimilate the intelligible to itself, so that it can read in itself, namely, in its word or concept, what it understands.

Also the intellect cannot attain its own quiddity and essence within itself, except in the same manner in which it understands something other by forming, if it can, an intelligible assimilation of itself. Thus even the sense of vision does not see itself. For how should the sense of vision see itself, unless it became visible? But from the fact that man sees something other, he attains to the realization that the sense of vision is in him. Nevertheless he does not see the sense of vision. Likewise man understands, if he knows that he understands, that the intellect is in him, although he does not understand what it is. This was already touched upon above, where the response of the Indian was recited.

Indeed, since the divine essence is unknown, consequently, no essence of things can be comprehended through cognition. Also direct your attention to what I have said above about how the notions of things follow the thing. The intellective power therefore extends itself up to the notions of things and therefore follows the essences of things. But the essence of this power is prior to its power and to the more ignoble sensuous essences, which are after it. For the essence of the intellective soul is not its power and potentiality. This indeed can only be true in God, who is before the difference of actuality and potentiality, as has been satisfactorily shown above.

Indeed, we do not know everything that can be known by man. You are not a grammarian, orator, logician, philosopher, mathematician, theologian, technician, and everything else, which nevertheless, you as man can become. Even though the human potential-to-become is actually determined in you in such a way, as you are, and this determination is your essence, the potential-to-become of man is nevertheless in no way perfected or finally determined in you. Hence in respect to this infinite and interminable potential-to-become, the Platonics, as Proclus reports, used to say that everything is from the finite or determined and the infinite, finite in respect to the determined essence, infinite in respect to potentiality and potential-to-become.

XXX.
On the Tenth Field, Namely, Order

After these Dionysius—more acute than all the others—found in his search for God, that in God the opposites are verified conjointly and that privation is excellence. Indeed, the substance of everything exceeding every substance is called insubstantial. In the chapter "On Wisdom" he speaks at length as follows: "We must ask, how do we know God, who is neither intelligible nor sensible nor anything else of the intelligible? Perhaps we shall correctly say that we cannot know God from his own nature (because He is unknown and surpasses all rationality and sense), but rather we climb from the most ordered disposition of all creatures, which is produced by Him and which bears certain images and similitudes of divine exemplars, in accordance with our powers, by means of a path and order, to that which transcends everything, in the most eminent privation and in the cause of all things. Therefore, in everything and apart from everything God is recognized and God is known through knowledge and ignorance. To Him belongs intelligence, rationality, notion, touch, sense, opinion, imagination, name, and everything else and nevertheless, He is neither understood nor expressed nor named nor is He anything else of that which is, nor is He known in some creature, and He is in everything everything and in nothing nothing, and from all He is known by all and from none by no one."

Indeed, "And we say these things about God most correctly and He is therefore also celebrated and lauded by all substances in consequence of the analogy and rationality of all things, of which He is the Author. On the other hand, the most divine cognition of God is known through ignorance, in accordance with that union which is beyond the intellect, when the intellect, receding from all entity and letting go of itself, is united with supersplendid rays and therefore is illuminated by the unfathomable depth of wisdom. It must be distinguished from all things, as I have said. For according to the eloquence of all, it is that which creates, which binds everything harmoniously, the indissoluable cause of all harmony and order, which always connects the end of the first with the beginnings of the following and effects the union and the harmony of the beautiful universe."

These things seemed great to me and to contain in the highest degree the completed hunt of that divine man. Therefore, I decided to set them forth in this location.

The Apostle Paul, the teacher of this same Dionysius, said that the difference between that which is from God and the other consists in the fact that what is from God is ordered. And Dionysius himself correctly confesses in another location that God is the order of everything ordered.

Therefore, in the terminus of that which can be ordered,

one sees the Author of order. For since this world had to be beautiful and its parts could not be precisely alike, but rather varied, so that immense beauty is more perfectly reflected in its variety (since everything, however varied it may be, would not be destitute of beauty), it pleased the Creator to create together with the variety, such an orderability that the order, which is absolute beauty, is reflected simultaneously in everything; through it the supreme of the lowest is connected with the lowest of the supreme and is united to the one beauty of the universe. Through this order, everything, content with its place in respect to the universe, enjoys the peace and quiet, than which nothing is more beautiful.

Indeed, the foot as the lowest in man is content that it is the foot and the lowest; likewise the eye is content to be the eye and to be in the head. Both see that they are necessary members for the perfection of man and his beauty and thus stand in their determined location. However, if they are found outside these locations, they are neither beautiful nor necessary and see neither that the beauty of the whole body is perfect, nor that they contribute to its self-completed beauty, but rather if they themselves are deformed, they make the whole body deformed. Therefore, in them the magnitude is so ordered that it is beautiful, so that from them and the other members, the magnitude of the body ensues as beautiful. Therefore, the proportion of every single member to the other and to the whole is ordered by the Orderer of all things, who has created man beautiful. Indeed, it is that proportion, without which the one habitude of the whole and of its parts related to the whole would never appear beautiful and most ordered.

XXXI.
On the Same

For you to see order in eternity, consider the following. Since all things, in order to exist in actuality from the potential-to-become, presuppose the order through which this possible becoming becomes, the order, which is all that can be, is certainly eternal. For if the order were made, and one came through order from the possibility of becoming to actuality, thus it would have been before it was. The order therefore has no beginning and no end; the order is therefore eternal.

But how is the order in the simplest Origin of things, unless it is itself this Origin, and indeed just as much an Origin without origin as an Origin from the Origin and even an Origin proceeding from both? Indeed, without that, the order cannot be seen in the origin, since from the essence of the order comes the beginning, the middle, and the end. If in the simplicity of the eternal Origin, which is also the eternal order, they are denied, the order itself is denied. If it is sublated, nothing remains, for nothing can exist without order and beauty.

Indeed, how could a being which is without order and beauty attain to actuality from potential? And if the Origin lacks order, whence shall the originated have order? I now see that whence the Origin without origin and the Origin from the Origin and the Origin proceeding from both arises, so also will the originated without prior origination and the originated from the originated and the originated proceeding from both arise.

The originated without prior origination is the essence, the originated from the originated is the power, and the originated proceeding from both is the action.

These are to be found in all things, so that everything participates in the divine order and this entire world consists of the intellectual, the vital, and the existing. The intellectual nature is the highest and has before itself nothing previously originated. The vital nature is the middle and has before it the intellectual nature, which is its hypostasis. The existing nature, however, proceeds from both.

In the first the succeeding are enfolded, for it understands, lives, and exists.

The second lives and exists. Therefore, in it, just as in the first, is enfolded the third, which only exists. For the first to exist and to live is to understand, for the second to exist and to understand is to live, and for the third to understand and to live is to be.

The divine Dionysius describes in what way the hierarchy of angels and the hierarchy of the church participate in the divine order. The studious person sees and admires the participation in order in all species and in each species, in the celestial and temporal bodies, and in the motion of living creatures, and in everything that arises from the human mind, in the powers, in the authorities and in the governance of states and of private lives, in technical sciences and in liberal arts, and he admires the most ordered rules and modes in which everything beautifully proceeds, is found, composed, and communicated.

The slave of Meno could respond correctly to all geometrical questions, just as if this knowledge were cognate in him with order, because he who questioned him adhered to the order of questions, as Plato reports in the book *Meno*. Indeed, whoever knows to reduce everything to order, accomplishes that for which he strives and searches.

No one can be an orator or another expert, if his manner of speaking lacks order, for one to whom order is foreign neither understands himself nor is understood.

Indeed, order is the reflection of wisdom, without which nothing would be beautiful and clear nor wisely engaged in.

A memory reduced to order remembers with ease, just as it is clear that in the art of remembrance everything is firmly established in the order of succession of places. So that the lecturer remembers and comprehends, he distinguishes that which he is to say and orders the distinction. Likewise, it is clear that order participates greatly in the light of wisdom.

XXXII.
On the Same

Therefore, the highest wisdom placed order in heaven and earth and in everything, in order to manifest in the relatively best way, of what the creature is capable.

Indeed, the order of an army shows the prudence of its chief orderer more than all his deeds. The order of the universe is therefore the first and most precise image of the eternal and incorruptible wisdom, through which the whole machine of the world persists in a beautiful and peaceful manner. How beautifully it located man as the connection of the universe and as the microcosm in the highest of sensible nature and in the lowest of intelligible nature, in that it connected in him, as in a middle, the inferior temporal and superior perpetual!

It placed him in the horizon of time and perpetuity, as it demanded order of perfection.

We discover in ourselves, in whom the senses are common with the other living creatures, that beyond that we have the mind, which knows about order and lauds it, and in this we know that we are capable of the immortal wisdom of the Orderer of all and of being the connection with God and the intelligent. For just as in that part, in which we are bound to other living creatures, we have acquired their nature, so in that part, through which we are bound to the intellectual nature, do we participate in the intellectual nature. Therefore, the spirit is not extinguished in us through the mortality of the animal, for it is connected to the intelligent, which is perpetual.

What is more, we know that the mortal nature, untied from the possibility of dying because of the connection by which it is connected to the mortal, can be resurrected to the life of immortal spirit in the power of God's Word, through which everything is created and which is incarnate in the man Jesus Christ. In Him, humanity is not only the middle of the connection of the inferior and superior natures, the temporal and perpetual, but rather also of God the Creator and eternal immortality, if we ourselves shall have become like our Mediator, which occurs through faith and love. What is more beautiful than this marvelous order of regeneration, through which we attain to the resurrection of life, which is described in the most sacred Gospels?

I have said some things concerning the fields of the hunt for wisdom, but here Wisdom incarnate has made clear by example its way, through which the dead attain to the resurrection of life, which is what is sought.

We strive after wisdom, in order to be immortal, but since no wisdom liberates from this sensible and horrible death, the true wisdom will be that through which the necessity of dying is turned into a virtue and a certain and secure path to the resurrection of life is created for us, which befalls those alone, who hold fast to this path through Jesus and his strength. Therefore, we must apply the greatest zeal to this, and in this way alone there is a secure hunt, which the most certain possession of immortality follows.

XXXIII.
On the Meaning of a Word

If you ponder everything in deep meditation, you will find that hunters have paid attention diligently to the meaning of a word, as if a word were the precise figuration of things. However, since words were imposed by the first man on things, on the basis of the rational ground which the man conceived, the words are not so precise that the thing could not be still more precisely named by a word. For the rational ground, which man conceives, is not the rational ground of the essence of the thing, which precedes every thing.

If someone knew the name of this rational ground, he could name everything properly and would have the most perfect knowledge of everything. Hence, the dissension is not in the substantiating rational ground of things, but rather all diversity of opinion among disputants is in the words attributed variedly to things on varied rational grounds and in the configuration of the essence of the thing, which is likewise varied. Thus Plato also writes most elegantly in his letter to the tyrant Dionysius, that the truth precedes the words, speeches, or definitions of words and sensible figurations, as he exemplifies with the depicted circle, its word and speech and concept. Therefore, Dionysius the Areopagite recommended to pay more attention to the intention than to the meaning of a word, although he himself in the *Divine Names* adheres exactly like Plato very much to the significance of the name.

No one inquired into the meaning of a word more attentively than Aristotle, as if the imposer of all names were the most capable of expressing that which he knew in words, and as though to attain to his knowledge were to achieve perfection of the knowable.

Therefore, he affirmed that the light of knowledge is in the definition, which is the unfolding of the word. I believe this is so in human knowledge, which at first and in an excellent manner the first Adam or the one called man is believed to have had. And for this reason, the knowledge which is established in the meaning of the word, is most gratifying to man, as if conformed to his nature. However, whoever hunts for this divine wisdom, must reject such human words in respect to God, just because they are an imposition of man. For example, the life, which extends to all the living, does not pertain to God, who is the cause of all life. And thus it is with all words.

Also, the distinctions which are made by the hunters who interpret words, must be diligently attended to. For example, in his commentary on Dionysius' book *On Divine Names,* St. Thomas indicates that three substances of the existing are to be considered. The first, the singular, which Plato in himself actually is, embraces the principles of the extreme and the individual. The second is the species or genus, such as man or animal, in which the extreme principles are comprehended in actuality, the singular however in potentiality. For he is called a man, who has humanity without the precision of individual principles. The third is the essence itself, such as humanity, in which word the principles of the species alone are comprehended. Indeed, nothing of the individual principles pertains to the rational grounds of humanity, since humanity signifies precisely that through which man is man. None of the individual principles is of this kind. Hence in the name *humanity,* neither actuality nor potentiality is included according to some individual principle. And to this extent, one speaks about nature as well.

Behold how this most learned man has elucidated many things through this distinction of a word, which otherwise are found to be obscure.

Also his *Metaphysics* reveals how much Aristotle labored to distinguish words.

Hence, through the distinctions of words, many varieties of writers, with whom many of the most learned occupy themselves, are brought into concordance.

But this inquiry of ours into the ineffable wisdom, which precedes both the imposer of words and everything nameable, is sooner found in silence and vision, than in loquacity and hearing. One presupposes that those human words which one employs are not precise, nor angelic, nor divine. But one employs them, since one cannot otherwise express the concepts in connection with which it is nevertheless presupposed that one does not wish these to signify something on account of which they are imposed, but rather, since one wishes to express eternity through them, that for such reason the word belongs to no time.

XXXIV.
On the Quarry Taken

After I have thus traversed the ten fields, it now remains for me to assemble what I have caught.

I have certainly undertaken a great hunt, in order to bring home a great quarry. For, not content with anything great which could still be greater, I have investigated the cause of the magnitude which cannot be greater. Indeed, if that could be greater, it could become greater through that caused by it. Thus the posterior would be before the prior.

The cause of magnitude is therefore necessarily that which it can be. For now, however, we name the cause of magnitude Magnitude. Therefore, Magnitude precedes the potential-to-become, since it cannot become other, because it is all that can be. Magnitude is therefore the eternity, which has no beginning and no end, since it was not made, because before everything that was made is the potential-to-become, which Magnitude precedes. And because it is verified by God and all creatures, as is found above in the field of laud, we therefore wish to apply that to the sensible and intelligible, then also to the laudable, so that we see if we are able to show it as grasped by the senses or the intellect.

For this reason, I draw a line AB and say that this line AB is great, because it is greater than its half, and that it can be greater through its extension or augmentation. But it does not become Magnitude, for this is what it can be. If a line became so great that it could not be greater, thus were it that which it can be, and it were not made, but rather it were eternal, preceding the potential-to-become, and it were no line, but rather eternal magnitude. Thus I see that everything which can become greater, since it is after the potential-to-become, never becomes that which can be. But because Magnitude is that which it can be, then it cannot be greater, nor can it be smaller.

Hence it is not greater nor smaller than everything great and everything small, but rather the efficient, formal, and final cause of everything great and small and their most adequate measure. In everything great and small it is simultaneously everything and none of everything, because everything great and small is after the potential-to-become, which precedes these. Hence, because surfaces, bodies, continuous and discrete quantity or number, quality, sense, intellect, heaven, the sun, and everything that is made, is not destitute of Magnitude, in them all the actual-potential, which I call Magnitude, is that which they are and none of everything. It is therefore conjointly everything and nothing of everything; it is also true, that the great is great through Magnitude. Because it precedes the potential-to-become, the name Magnitude, which is the name of the form of the great, does not befit it, for it is no form, but rather the absolute cause of forms and all things. Therefore, no name, of everything that can be named, befits it, even though its name is not other from every nameable name, and in every name is named what remains unnameable.

XXXV.
On the Same

Since I see that the good is great and that it can become still better, when a good is given that is better than an other, therefore that good which is so good that nothing can be better than it, is the cause of magnitude, since it is the actual-potential itself, as follows immediately from the aforementioned. Thus the beautiful which cannot be more beautiful is the cause of magnitude, and thus the true which cannot be truer is the cause of magnitude, likewise the wise that cannot be wiser is the cause of magnitude, and it is so with all ten laudabilities. And likewise the great which is so good that it cannot be better, is the cause of goodness, and the beautiful that is so good that it cannot be better, is the cause of the goodness, etc. Therefore, I see that the actual-potential is the cause of goodness, of magnitude, beauty, truth, wisdom, delectation, perfection, clarity, equity, and sufficiency.

And the terminus of the potential-to-become of the nine others shows the actual-potential as the cause of the tenth. For the terminus of the potential-to-become of magnitude itself, of goodness, beauty, truth, etc. shows the actual-potential as the cause of magnitude; and the terminus of the potential-to-become of goodness, beauty, magnitude, truth and the others shows the actual-potential as the cause of the goodness. So the nine always show the actual-potential as the cause of the tenth.

Therefore, if I see that the actual-potential is the cause of all laudabilities and all ten laudabilities are laudabilities through participation in laud, I call the actual-potential the laud, which is that which it can be, because it is the font and cause of all laudabilities. Therefore, I do not inappropriately laud the actual-potential as laud, since the great prophet Moses says in his song: "The Lord is my laud." And because I see that God is the essential cause of all laudabilities, I also see, as Dionysius alleged above, that the essences or subsistences of all things, which have or will become through participation in the laudabilities, are that which they are.

This therefore is what I have captured in my hunt: My God is that one, who is laudable through all laudabilities; not as one who participates in laud, but rather as the absolute Laud He is through Himself laudable and the cause of all laudabilities, and for this reason prior to and greater than everything laudable, because He is the terminus and the actual-potential of all laudabilities. All the works of God are laudabilities, because they are constituted through participation in the laudabilities, through which God as the cause, and everything laudable, as the caused, is lauded. And I know that my God, greater than all laud, through no laudability can be so lauded, as He is laudable; to all who seek to laud Him ever better, He reveals Himself, so that they see that He is laudable, glorious, and superexalted in eternity.

They laud Him not only in the goodness in which He communicates Himself to everything, or in the magnitude which He distributes to everything, or in the beauty which is bestowed on everything, or in the truth of which nothing does without, or in the wisdom which orders all, or in the delectation through which everything delights in itself, or in the perfection in which everything glories, or in the clarity which illuminates everything, or in the equity which purifies everything, or in the sufficiency in which everything finds rest and contentment, or in other modes of divine participation, but rather they laud the God of gods in Zion, contemplating Him in His revealed light.

XXXVI.
On the Same

If you consider it correctly, the truth, the true, and the verisimilar are everything that is seen with the eye of the mind.

The truth is all that it can be; it can be neither augmented nor diminished, but rather endures eternally.

The true is the perpetual similitude of the eternal truth, in which it participates intellectually. And because one true thing is truer and clearer than another, the true which cannot be truer is the absolute and eternal truth. Indeed, the verifiable action is the eternal truth, which verifies itself and everything in the action.

However, the verisimilar is the temporal similitude of the intelligibly true.

Thus the sensible is a similitude of the true, because it is an image of the intelligible, as Dionysius correctly said and Plato before him saw. Therefore, the actual intellect is true, just as it is also good and great and it is likewise with the other ten, since it is the intellectual participation in these. In addition it is also true in the understanding, when it is compared to understood things. An intelligible thing is understood then truly, when its intelligibility is so purified of everything extraneous that in actuality it is a true, intelligible species or the rational ground of the thing, and then the intellect is true in actuality, because the intellect is the same as that understood.

The corruptible is not understood except through its incorruptible species. For the intellect abstracts the intelligible species from the sensible.

Indeed, the species or the intelligible rational ground of the warm is not warm, and that of the cold is not cold, etc., but rather it is absolved of all alterability, so that it truly represents the form of the thing as its true exemplar. And since only that incorporeal and immaterial species or the rational ground of the thing is actually intelligible and transformable into actual intellect, it is evident that the intellect is higher than everything temporal and corruptible and is purer and by nature perpetual.

You perceive this most clearly, when you see that the matter purified of everything corruptible, which requires no abstraction, is more rapidly understood. Thus according to Proclus, the absolute One is intelligible through itself and conformed to the intellect as the light to vision; and thus the other intelligible things, which are the principles of mathematics and the other sciences, are known through themselves. They are indeed the species of themselves or their intelligible rational ground.

XXXVII.
Explanation

I now repeat something which I have already often said, because it is the rational ground of our entire hunt: That which has become, because it succeeds the potential-to-become, has never become such that the potential-to-become is completely terminated in it.

For even if the potential-to-become, so far as it is actuality, is terminated, it nevertheless is not so simply; if in Plato the potential-to-become of man is terminated, the potential-to-become of man is nevertheless not completely terminated in Plato, but rather only that terminating mode, which is called Platonic, and still innumerable other, more perfect modes remain; also in Plato therefore, the potential-to-become of man is not terminated. Man can become much which Plato was not, for example, a musician, geometer, and technician. Hence the potential-to-become is not determined simply except in the actual-potential, which, according to Dionysius, is equally its beginning and end.

Thus, number is terminated in the monad, which is equally its beginning and end. For the beginning of every number is the monad, and likewise its end is the monad. As actuality, the potential-to-become is nevertheless terminated in the world, which, as actuality, is not more perfect nor greater. Thus the rule says: in that which admits a greater, one does not attain to the simple maximum, but rather only to the actual maximum.

Thus one does not come in the quantity which admits a greater, to the maximum quantity which cannot be greater, for this maximum that cannot be greater precedes quantity. Nevertheless, one comes to the actual maximum quantity, as it is the quantity of the whole.

However, that which has become is always singular and unpluralizable, like every individual. But it is not always incorruptible, except if it is a first. Indeed, that which imitates a first, just because it is that which it is through participation in the first, is corruptible. For it cannot participate in its incorruptible singularity, which is unmultiplicable.

And the fact that first things, whose being does not depend on participation in something which has previously become, are incorruptible, is because the potential-to-become is specifically determined in them. For this reason, the intelligible and celestial things are incorruptible, just as are the intellectual natures, the sun, the moon, and the stars. However, since the sun, the moon, and the stars were at first created, Moses declares clearly in Genesis, that they are created by God, so that they always shine. Therefore, this is always and without interruption necessary for the visible world, if its visibility shall not cease. The things which are created, in order to shine, must therefore always remain so. For this reason they are not made after something previously made, through whose participation they are that which they are.

Consequently, the potential-to-become of the sun, the moon, and the stars is determined in those individuals which we see. The individuals of sensible nature, however, imitate the intelligible exemplars, and are, as Dionysius says, their images, even though they are not multiplicable according to their singularity. Since they are images of the intelligible, through whose participation they are that which they are, and because the intelligible cannot be precisely imitated through the sensible, they nevertheless participate variably and temporally in that which is perpetual. For this reason they cannot be perpetual.

XXXVIII.
Recapitulation

In order to express more clearly what I would like to say, by means of recapitulation of the aforesaid, I now add the following. It is certain that the potential-to-become refers to something that precedes it and therefore, since it precedes the potential-to-become, and since nothing has become which could not become, this can neither become nor have become: Therefore, what has become follows the potential-to-become. However, because that precedes the potential-to-become, to which it refers and which it presupposes, it is necessarily the eternal.

Hence since the eternal cannot become, it will be necessary that the eternal be not other from that which is affirmed in the potential-to-become. The eternal is therefore not other from all that which becomes, even though it itself does not become. Therefore, it is the origin and end of the potential-to-become. Hence, that which has become is the representation of the eternal which cannot become.

Hence, it is clear that the potential-to-become of the world refers to the archetypal world in the eternal mind of God. And because eternity is neither pluralizable nor multiplicable nor can signify another possibility, since it precedes the potential-to-become, just as it is not intelligible nor sensibly perceptible, it is likewise not completely representable, imaginable, nor assimilable.

The potential-to-become is therefore not terminated ultimately in something which follows it, but rather its terminus precedes it. I therefore see that everything which can become, possesses only that most simple exemplar, which, since it is the actuality of every potential, is not other from everything that can become. Since this is the actuality of every potential and can be nothing other, neither greater, nor smaller, nor otherwise, nor in another mode, then it is not other from anything, neither greater nor smaller than anything, nor otherwise, nor in another mode. Therefore, it is the cause, exemplar, measure, mode, and order of everything which is, lives, and understands. And in everything and each, nothing is discoverable that was not from it as from its cause and did not proceed from it.

And because everything is nothing other than the representation of that alone, everything is converted to this, everything desires it, proclaims it, lauds it, glorifies it and declares that this is the infinite good reflected in everything, through whose participation everything is that which it is. Therefore, from everything that actually is, I obtain that itself, which is the interminable terminus, graspable through no terminus or actuality of any intellect, since the intellect and all things are its image and similitude. I see indeed that everything which is actual bears the image of this its exemplar, in comparison to which it is neither actual nor its perfect image, since every image of everything can be more perfect and more precise. Nevertheless, I see it in the terminus in which the perfection and precision of the image is terminated, which is infinitely remote from it.

Thus I see that the actuality of life is a nobler image of it. However, since life can be more perfect and purer, without admixture and shadows, I see from far off in the terminus of simplicity and precision the eternal life, which is the true life and creates all life, as the exemplar of all life, compared to which everything of this life is less than a painted fire in relation to a true one.

Then I contemplate the actuality of the intellect, which is a similitude of its divine and eternal exemplar; I see the terminus of this living and intelligent similitude, which shows the precise similitude of God, infinitely distant from every actuality of the intellect, and I say that of all that which can be, and can be and live, and can be, live and understand, there is no image of the eternal exemplar so precise, that it demands similitude with it. Then I see God in the excess above everything which is or can become, and indeed, just as much in the excess of being as in the excess of life and of the understanding of all things, since He is greater than everything which can be or live or understand. And as much as the truth surpasses His image and similitude, He is more lofty and also more perfect than all this. For the truth is the hypostasis of His image and similitude, from which He is not other. Indeed, things are from it as their exemplar, in that they only subsist and participate in the truth of their exemplar, insofar as they imitate and represent it.

All this that I thus see, and that can never be expressed or written as I see it, I can briefly express thus: The terminus of the potential-to-become of everything is the potential-to-make everything. Thus the terminus of the potential-to-become-determined is the potential-to-make-determined, just as the terminus of the potential-to-become-warm is the potential-to-make-warm.

The fire, which is called the terminus of the potential-to-become-warm, can indeed make warm. Thus the potential-to-become-light is terminated in the potential-to-make-light; this is called the sun in the sensible, and in the intelligible, the divine Intellect or the Word, which illuminates every intellect. And the terminus of the potential-to-become-perfect is the potential-to-make-perfect, and the terminus of the potential-to-be-moved is the potential-to-move. Hence, the desired which all desire, since it is the terminus of the desirable, is the cause of all desires and the terminus of everything eligible and the cause of every election.

Hence, it is patent that the Omnipotent, since He—having the power to make everything—is the terminus of every potential-to-become, can also make the potential-to-become itself. And thus He is the terminus of that, whose origin He is, and the potential-to-become is not before the Omnipotent. Just as in everything which has become, the potential-to-become is previously seen, and indeed both the potential-to-become simply, the beginning and end of which is the Omnipotent, as well as the potential-to-become, contracted to that which becomes, in which the potential-to-become itself is terminated, when something becomes actually that which it can become.

And this determination is from the Creator of the potential-to-become, who, because He is Omnipotent, alone can determine that the potential-to-become become one way or another. And since the potential-to-become is terminated only through the Omnipotent, every determination of the potential-to-become in that which becomes, is no termination of the potential-to-become, since the Omnipotent could not then make of it anything He wanted, but rather, it is the determination of the potential-to-become in a particular case, contracted to that which is the nature and the substance of that which has become thus.

XXXIX.
Epilogue

Since nothing has become that had not been able to become and nothing can make itself, it follows that the potential is threefold, namely, the potential-to-make, the potential-to-become, and the potential-to-have-become.

Before the potential-to-have-become is the potential-to-become, before the potential-to-become is the potential-to-make. The origin and terminus of the potential-to-become is the potential-to-make. The potential-to-have-become has been made through the potential-to-make from the potential-to-become.

The potential-to-make, since it is before the potential-to-become, has neither been created nor can it become something other. It is therefore everything that it can be. Therefore, it cannot be greater and this we call the maximum, nor smaller and this we call the minimum, nor can it be other. Therefore, it is the efficient, formal or exemplary, and final cause of everything, since it is the terminus and end of the potential-to-become and for that reason also of the potential-to-have-become. Therefore, everything which can become and which has become is previously in the potential-to-make as in the efficient, formal, and final cause, and the potential-to-make is in everything as the absolute cause in the caused.

The potential-to-become, however, is in everything which has become, that which has become. For only that has actually become, which also could become, but in another mode of being, in a more imperfect mode in potentiality and in a more perfect one in actuality.

The potential-to-become and the potential-to-have-become are therefore in their essence not different, but the potential-to-make, although it is not other, nevertheless, because it is the cause of essence, is not the essence. For the essence is that caused by it.

However, since the potential-to-become is not the potential-to-have-become, the potential-to-become has not been made out of the potential-to-become, but before the potential-to-become there is nothing except the potential-to-make; therefore, it is said that the potential-to-become has been made out of nothing. Thus we say the potential-to-make precedes the nothing, but the potential-to-become does not.

We therefore say that the potential-to-become, since it has been produced and not made through the potential-to-make, is created from nothing.

However, since we name the absolute potential-to-make the Omnipotent, we say that the Eternal-Omnipotent has neither become nor is created; and since He can neither be annihilated nor become otherwise than He is—since He is before the nothing and the potential-to-become—we reject all things which are nameable concerning Him, since they follow the potential-to-become.

Indeed, the nameable presupposes the potential-to-become, with which it is named. Also the potential-to-become is not terminated except in the potential-to-make. Therefore, this cannot be annihilated. For if this were to occur, it could not occur—how then could the potential-to-become be annihilated? It is therefore perpetual, since it has a beginning and cannot be annihilated, but its terminus is its beginning.

However, because, among those which can become, some are first, others are after the first and imitate the first. In first things, since their potential-to-become is actual and complete, they are therefore perpetual, just like the potential-to-become. In the subsequent ones, the potential-to-become is not complete and perfect, except in respect to the imitation of the complete; consequently, these are not perpetual, but rather imitate those which are perpetual. However, that which is not perpetual and stable, but rather only imitates this, is unstable and temporal. This is a brief recapitulation of the aforesaid.

But because we are strengthened in the art of this general hunt for wisdom through particular examples, we apply this form of the hunt to something sensible, for example, to warmth.

And we wish to say that the potential is threefold, namely, the potential-to-make-warm, the potential-to-become-warm, and the potential-to-have-become-warm. We wish to proceed contractedly in the manner in which we proceeded above absolutely, and say: The potential-to-have-become-warm has the potential-to-become-warm before it, but the potential-to-become-warm cannot actually make itself warm. Therefore, the potential-to-make-warm is before the potential-to-become-warm; and because the potential-to-make-warm precedes the potential-to-become-warm, it is all that which can be warm and can thus not be greater nor smaller nor something other.

Therefore, in respect to everything warm it is the creator of the potential-to-become-warm and produces from the potential-to-become everything warm in actuality. It is the efficient, formal, and final cause of everything warm and is in everything warm as the cause in the caused. And everything warm is in it as the caused in the cause; and it will be in respect to the warm without beginning and end, never the essence of the warm, but rather the cause of the essence, unnameable through all names of the warm. The potential-to-become-warm therefore has begun and is without end, and there is something warm, in which the potential-to-become is completed and which endures always.

Some other things follow this. They are unstable and the warmth declines in them. And although certain men designate the sensible fire as that warmth which is everything that the warm can be, it is nevertheless not this, for all warmth of any sensible fire is not the end of every potential-to-become-warm, because every sensible warmth can be greater. However, that which we name fire is, according to Plato, only the firelike or the fiery and not so fiery as it can become fiery.

Therefore, the fire per se precedes everything combustible and fiery, whose cause it is. It is completely invisible and unknown before all sensible fire. For this reason, it is the similitude of the first cause (as Dionysius explains this in detail), which that saint saw, who said that God is a consuming fire. However, before this sensible fire is motion and light. For through motion the combustible is ignited and the light accompanies it. The same is just as true of the lucid as of the warm, of light as of fire. Neither the sun nor anything sensible is the light, which is the cause of the lucid, but all these are lucid, and not the light itself. It is likewise with the cold, the humid and everything that participates in something according to the relation of more or less.

Indeed, the unity of every multitude is the origin, as Proclus says, and of all such the maximum such, as Aristotle believes, and of all such through participation the such per se, and of all such per se the simple per se, as the Platonics believe; and what is per se without addition is the cause of everything that is per se with addition. And this per se, as that above, is the cause of all causes and of everything singular, which on account of the varied diversities of the participants is named variously the principle of all, even though it precedes everything nameable. Those are the expressions of the Platonics and the Peripatetics, which one must correctly understand in respect to the origin and cause.

For there is only one causal origin, which I name the actual-potential, in which all potential-to-become is determined. Although the first is also called in the ordered sequence the origin of the others, which follow it, and is called the maximum such, which the others are through participation in it, nevertheless, it is not called the maximum simply, but rather only the maximum such.

From this you could also hunt down the order of priority

and posteriority. For the per se precedes all participants, as the warm per se, for example, precedes the fiery, the warm air, the warm water, the warm earth, and all potential-to-become-warm. And thus the fire can also not become humid or cold or earthly or dry; indeed, it precedes this. And because the water is cold per se, it is prior to the earth, which can become cold. Likewise it also is not after the air, because the air can similarly become cold. So the air is prior to the earth, since it is humid per se and the earth can become humid. Also it is not after the water, which can similarly become humid. Thus the earth is the last among the elements and fire is the first.

However, the air and water simultaneously hold the middle and the one is not in order prior to the other, but rather simultaneous with the other. Hence, just as water is connected to the earth without a median, so also is the air to the dry earth, although the friendship of the fire with the air and that of the water with the earth is greater. And because the water is converted into air and the air into water and both can be mixed variedly and are able to participate in the warmth of the fire and to be made solid in the earth, the things which are generated from these must consist of them; and consequently, because earth, water, air, fire, the moon, and stars participate in light, the light per se will be the cause of everything lucid, which some call the sun, because among sensible lucid things it is the maximally lucid.

Hence in that which is sensibly lucid it is called the cause of everything participating in light. However, since it is not the light, but rather a lucid thing, as was already said, the light is the cause of it and all lucid things. The light is indeed nothing of all these. Hence the sun, the maximally lucid, is neither dry nor cold nor humid nor warm, neither of the nature of the moon nor of Venus, Mercury, Jupiter, Saturn, nor any other star or any visible thing, but rather the origin of all light, whether of the elements, the minerals, vegetation, or the sensible. Thus wisdom per se, which is the intelligible light, is before everything which can partake of its light, whether it is called the senses, the imagination, estimation, rationality, the intellective soul, intelligence, or whatever name it is named, and before everything sensible and intelligible and all separation and order, of all of which it is the cause.

However, the sun is sensible, since it is visible. The senses therefore precede it. But because the visible light per se is the material cause of the visible and because the sense of vision in actuality is the visible in actuality, thus vision is the formal cause of the visible, since the cause of the potential-to-be-seen is the potential-to-see. And thus it is patent how in the sense of vision the sensible light is connected with the intelligible light just as two extremes, namely, the supreme of the inferior and corporeal nature, with the inferior of the superior, cognitive nature.

Not undeservedly, all laud the great Plato, who ascended with the help of similitude from the sun to wisdom. Likewise proceeds the great Dionysius, who ascends from fire to God and from the sun to the Creator, with the help of the similitude of properties which he enumerates. Gregor the Theologian also recommends the same in his theological sermons against Eunomianos. In this world, where we know in part and in part prophesy, we must ascend in a mirror and enigmatically, as the divine Paul reports.

Thereby, I believe, I have unfolded the rough and not completely purified concepts of my hunts, as far as it was possible to me and submit everything to him, who is better able to contemplate these lofty things.

Compendium

(1 4 6 4)

I.

Accept a short compendium touching upon matters which must engage your consideration.

If you want to make progress, first hold firmly to that as true to which the sound mind of all men attests: that the singular is not several and the one is not the many. Consequently, the one cannot be singular in the many or as it is in itself, but rather in the mode of communicability for the many. Accordingly, it cannot be denied that the thing is earlier by nature than it is cognizable. Therefore, neither the senses, nor the imagination, nor the intellect attains to the mode of being, since it precedes all these. Rather, everything which is attained by some mode of cognition only signifies this prior mode of being. And therefore this is not the thing itself, but rather its similitude, species, or sign. Therefore, there is no knowledge of the mode of being, although we have a mental vision which looks into that which is earlier than all cognition. Whoever is eager to find in cognition that which he sees of this sort, endeavors in vain—just as one who attempts to touch with his hand the color which is only visible. The vision of the mind is therefore to that mode of being as sensuous vision to the light, which it indeed sees as most certainly at hand, but does not know. The light indeed precedes all that which can be known by a vision of this kind. Likewise also that which can be known with its help is the sign of light. The colors, which can be known through vision, are the signs and termini of the light in reflection. Therefore, take the sun as the father of sensuous light and according to this example conceive God, the Father of all things, as the light, which is inaccessible to all cognition; however, conceive all things as the splendor of this light, to which the vision of the mind is as the sensuous vision to the light of the sun. And stop there in consideration of that mode of being which is placed above all cognition.

II.

Should a thing be observed, it must be received in signs. Therefore, it is necessary that you seek the various modes of cognition in various signs.

Since no sign designates the mode of being as sufficiently as it can be designated, if one should attain to cognition in the best possible mode, this must occur through various signs, so that one can obtain a better cognizance from these; just as one knows a sensuously visible thing better from five visible signs than from one or two.

However, the perfect being of a thing requires that it can know. Since, for example, a perfect animal is not able to live without nutriment, it is necessary that it know its food. Since this is not found in every place, the animal must be of such a kind that it can move from place to place and seek it. It follows from this, that it has all senses in order to obtain the food suitable to it through vision, hearing, smell, taste and touch. Because animals of the same species mutually support and help themselves in order to be able to live better, they must know their species and must mutually hear and understand themselves in proportion as perfection of the species demands it. With a certain call the rooster calls the hen when he has found feed, and with another one he warns her so that they flee before the hawk, which he saw lying in wait in the shadows.

And since the more noble an animal is the greater the cognition required is for its well-being, man must have the greatest cognizance of all. For without technique, liberal arts, moral science, and theological virtues he does not subsist well and happily. Since, therefore, cognition is more necessary for man than for all others, all men desire to know by nature. Thereby the transmission of knowledge comes to their aid, so that the unlearned and the not-knowing are informed by the learned.

Now since this cannot happen except through signs, we apply ourselves to the cognition of signs. All signs are sensuous and designate things either by nature or on the basis of their institution. They exist naturally as the signs through which an object is designated in the senses. They exist on the basis of an institution, as names and writings and all signs which are perceived by hearing and vision, and which designate the thing according as it has been instituted. Natural signs are known by nature without any other master, for example, a sign that designates a color and is noted by all onlookers; and a sign that designates a sound is noted by all listeners. This is also true in respect to the other senses. There is a sound of joy noted as laughter, a sound of sorrow as sighs, etc.

Other signs, however, which are instituted arbitrarily for designation, are known to those, to whom this institution is not known, only through art or instruction. And because all signs through which knowledge should be passed on, must be known to the teacher and the student, the first part of instruction will be about the knowledge of such signs. This is therefore the first part, because without it nothing can be passed on and because everything which can be passed on is included in its perfection.

III.

However, our first parents, who had been created perfect, had to have had from God not only the perfection of nature, but also of the knowledge of these signs, in order thereby to make known their thoughts mutually to one another and to be able to pass on this knowledge to their children and posterity. Hence we see that children as soon as they can speak are capable of the art of speaking, since this is the first and extremely necessary knowledge for a good existence. It also does not seem absurd to believe that the first human art of speaking was so rich in many synonyms that all the later separate languages were contained in it. For all human languages are from that first language of our father Adam, i.e., of man.

And as there is no language which man does not understand, so also Adam—which means the same as man—would be ignorant of no language if he heard it. Indeed, one reads that he himself has given things their names. Therefore, no word of any language was originally instituted from another. Also we must not marvel at all about Adam, since it is certain that he acquired knowledge of all languages suddenly through a gift of God. For man there is no more natural and simple capacity than that of speaking, since no perfect human lacks it. We can also not doubt that our first parents had the art of writing or designating words, since this art confers a great assistance upon the human species. Through it the past and the absent become present.

Therefore, as the first knowledge is designating things with names, which the ear perceives, so the second knowledge is in the visible signs of names, which confront the eyes. This knowledge is by nature remote; children learn it more slowly and also only when the intellect begins to become vigorous in them. Hence it takes a greater part in the intellect than the first. Therefore, between nature and the intellect, which is the creator of art, these two arts fall, of which the one stands nearer to nature, the other to the intellect.

However, the intellect forms in man this first art in a sensuously audible sign, i.e., in sound, because the animal endeavors by nature to make known its affections in this sign. Hence, art articulates the formless sign and modifies it in order to communicate better the various desires. Thus it comes to the aid of nature. And because that sign in which this art is laid down, disappears after its emergence and slips from memory and does not extend into the distance, the intellect adds a remedy in another art, namely, in the art of writing, and sets it forth in the sign visible to the eyes.

IV.

If someone considers how from the object sensible signs come to the senses, then he will find that corporeal things shine forth actually or conditionally; actually as lucid, potentially as colored things. Also no corporeal thing is entirely without a part in the light or the color, which comes from the light. However, the color, unless it is helped by the light, can send forth from itself no splendor perceptible by our vision. A ray of light is propagated suddenly and in a straight line from a great distance. The sense of vision is naturally adapted to perceive it. However, a sound diffuses itself from the distance circularly. The sense of hearing is created for its sensation. Vapor, however, diffuses itself a shorter distance and is perceived by the sense of smell. By the sense of touch the more proximate tangible object is indeed perceived. And by the sense of taste the interior taste is perceived. These are thus ordered by the marvelous providence of nature to the well-being of animals. For since no thing, as it is in itself, is multiplicable, and yet its well-being requires the knowledge of things, the things which do not by themselves enter into the knowledge of another must enter through their designations.

For this reason there must be a mean between the sensible object and the sense, through which the object can multiply its species or its sign. And since this does not occur except through the present object, unless these signs can be retained so that even were the objects removed the designated would remain, the knowledge of things would not remain. Therefore, through these designations of signs the things remain designated in the interior imaginative power, just as words remain written on a piece of paper, although mention of them ceases. This remaining can be called memory.

The signs of things in the imagination are therefore signs of the signs in the senses. For nothing is in the imagination which has not previously been in the senses. Therefore, someone who is blind from birth on, has no mental image of color and cannot imagine color. Therefore, although the sensible signs are more abstract than the sensible matter, they are nevertheless not completely separate. Hence vision is also a little colored, but the mental image of color lacks color altogether. Therefore. the signs of things in the imagination or mental image are more removed from the matter and more formal; in respect to the sensible less perfect, and in respect to the intelligible more perfect.

Nevertheless, they are not completely abstract. For although the mental image of colors has nothing of the quality of the colors, nevertheless that which is perceived does not lack all connection to it. Namely, one can imagine nothing which is neither moved nor rests and has no extension, i.e., were large or small, although it is without that termination which is found in sensible things. Nothing can be so small that the imagination cannot attain its mean, or so large that its double could not be imagined.

However, in all perfect animals one attains to those imaginative signs which are the signs of the signs of the senses, so that the knowledge suitable to them is not lacking. Indeed, only man seeks a sign which is free of all material connection and entirely formal and which represents the simple form of the thing, which gives being to it. And although this sign is very remote in respect to the sensible thing, it is nevertheless very near in respect to the intelligible.

V.

However, you must pay attention to the fact that the sensible sign is at first indistinct and generic rather than proper and specific. Thus, the sign for a word is at first only the sign for a sound, when a voice is heard from afar; then, when it is heard nearer, it becomes the sign of an articulated sound, which is called a voice. If it comes still nearer, it becomes the sign of the voice of a certain language. Ultimately it becomes the sign of a specific word. And this is the case for all.

And although one often does not perceive the intervals of time, because of their astonishing celerity, the sign can nevertheless not be perfect unless it attains to the specific from the indistinct. For one and the same unmultiplicable thing there are therefore various signs, i.e., generic and specific, with which it is noted. Among these some are more generic and the others are more specific. However, since perfection of the signs admits of more or less, no sign will ever be so perfect and specific that it could not be more perfect. Hence it is not possible to give a sign for singularity, which does not admit of more or less. And therefore such is not cognizable through itself, but rather only by accident. For example, Plato, who does not admit of more or less, is not seen except by accident in the visible signs, which supervene in respect to him.

Therefore, since everything which is attained by the senses or the imagination is not known except in the signs which admit of more or less, it is not attained without quantitative signs. Therefore, the signs of quality, which attain to the senses, cannot exist without signs of quantity. However, signs of quantity are not per se in sensible things, but rather by accident, since quality cannot exist without quantity. Indeed, the signs of quantity do not require signs of quality; therefore, they can exist without them. For this reason a quantitative thing comes into knowledge through the sign of quantity. And thus that which is unknowable through itself becomes known through the accidental.

Therefore, when one takes away magnitude and multitude, no thing is known. To repeat this seems useful: The sign or the natural species of a singular quantity cannot be singular, since nothing singular is multiplicable or pluralizable, whether it is substance, quantity, or quality. For although it is the species and the sign of quantity, nevertheless, it is not so for this quantity.

Therefore, quantities are designated and known as singular with a sign of general quantity, the singular red with the sign of universal redness. Therefore, since no thing is of the same quantity and quality as another and each singular thing has a singular quantity, the quantity is not something general in the thing, but rather in the cognition or species and in the sign. Therefore, the small and the large have species, although not this small or this large thing, which are singular quantities. But through the species or the sign of largeness this large thing is known and through that of smallness this small thing.

Therefore, the natural signs are species of singular designated things. For these species are not forming forms, but rather in-forming forms. Indeed, the in-formed as such admit of more and less. The one is better in-formed than the other, and the same is now less and later more. Such forms can be in many, since it is not required that they be in them in the same mode of being. For the mode of being cannot be multiplied, but rather is in the varied variously, just as the one art of writing is varied in the various writers.

Hence it follows that a determinate number, for example, three, ten and others, have only indeterminate species, since on account of their singular determination they do not admit of more or less. Thus through the species of indeterminate multitude, which can be called enumeration, a determinate multitude can be known. And in the species of magnitude and multitude a large, determinate number is known; likewise a small number through the species of multitude and smallness; and similar colors are known through the species of similitude and of color, dissimilar colors through the species of dissimilitude and of color; and concordant voices through the species of concordance and of voices and discordance through the species of discordance and voices, etc.

However, since knowledge of a thing is formed in us in this manner from signs and notional species, a thing, which is thus known, cannot then be distinctly known in contrast to another except if the knowledge is formed through distinct marks and species. As each thing is singular, so its notion is also something which is not found in that of another. Therefore, if one has a word with six letters and another likewise with six letters, although they agree in number, they need not necessarily agree in figure and position, so that they are diverse just as are the things of which they are the words. The diversity of notional species leads us to knowledge of the diversity of things. And although two individuals seem to agree in many species, it is, however, not possible that they not also disagree in others.

VI.

Consequently, you should attend to the fact that it is not required that a mole possess the capacity to see; since he finds what he seeks in the dark earth, he does not need cognition of visible signs. One can state the same about everything: namely, that all living beings take in so many species of sensible things as are necessary to them for a good life. Therefore, not all perfect animals agree in the number of species and in signs, although they agree in the number of senses. The ant takes in other species, the lion others, the spider others, the cow others; just as diverse trees take in diverse aliment from exactly the same earth, each according to its nature. The power of imagination of every single animal forms another imagination than another animal, out of the species received through the senses, and gives another estimation of friendship and hostility, of agreement and disagreement, than another.

Therefore, man perceives from the sensible signs those species which correspond to his nature; since this is a rational nature, he receives those species corresponding to this nature in order with their help to be able to ratiocinate well and in order to find suitable nourishment, both corporeal for bodies as well as spiritual for the spirit or intellect. These are the different species of the ten categories, the five universals, the four cardinal virtues and many of that kind, which suit a really rational man.

Man receives more species through vision than a brute animal. Originally, for example, because the sense of vision receives the species of color, through which it attains differences of the colored as colored; consequently, because the sense also receives the species of magnitude, longitude, latitude, figuration, motion, rest, number, time and place. Only man, who uses his mind, receives so many species through vision. Thus through hearing he receives the species of different sounds, the low, high, middle, of songs, of notes and so forth, and the nine other species of common feeling which we have already named. The same is true also of the other senses.

From all these sensuous species the power of ratiocination obtains in addition species of various arts by means of which it compensates for the deficiency of the senses, members, and corporeal infirmities. Also, it helps itself thereby to resist corporeal injuries, to expel ignorance and dullness of the mind, and to strengthen the mind so that man advances and becomes an observer of divine things. He also possesses innate species of insensible power, justice, and equality, so that he knows what is just, right, laudable, beautiful, delectable, and good and the contrary of these. And he elects the good and becomes good, strong, prudent, chaste, brave, and just.

To someone who considers all this, what is discovered by man in the mechanical and liberal arts and in moral science becomes apparent. For man alone has discovered how a burning candle compensates for the lack of light, so that he can see, and how one remedies bad sight with glasses, how one corrects optical illusions through the art of perspective, how one makes raw food suitable to the taste through cooking, how one drives away stinking fumes with pleasant smells, relieves the cold through clothes, fire and a house, tardiness with vehicles and ships, aids defense through weapons, memory through writings and the art of memorizing.

Of all this and much more the brute animal is ignorant. Man is as man to animal as a learned man is to an unlearned one. A learned and an unlearned man see the letters of the alphabet. But the learned man assembles syllables from their various combinations, words from the syllables and sentences from the words, while the uneducated man is not able to do that, because he lacks the art, which, acquired through the exercise of his intellect, is in the learned man. From the power of the intellect man has the capacity to assemble and divide the natural species and from them to make intellectual and artificial species and notional signs. In this he excels animals; and a learned man excels an unlearned one, since his intellect is exercised and reformed.

VII.

It is not to be wondered at that a man can advance and can have advanced so much through long exercise of this kind, that from various combinations he elicits a species, which enfolds in itself many arts, through which he comprehends and understands much simultaneously; for example, the variety of natural things through the species which he calls motion, when he sees that without motion nothing occurs and that natural motion is distinguished from a violent one, and that therefore the motion of nature comes not as in the case of violent motion from an extrinsic principle, but rather from an intrinsic cause. And thus also for others.

Another could find a still more precise and fecund species, just as the one who has endeavored to extract from the nine species of principles a single species of the general art of everything knowable. However, beyond all others, he who has embraced everything intelligible with a single species, which he named the Word, has achieved the most precise point. It is, namely, that species of art which forms everything.

What enables one to conceive, speak or write outside of this species? It is the Word, without which nothing has been made or can be made, since it is the expression of the expressing and the expressed, just as the Word is the speech and what is spoken of speaking. Also the conception and what is conceived of the conceiving is the Word. And the writing and what is written of the writing is the Word. And the creation and what is created of the creating is the Word. And the formation and what is formed of the forming is the Word. And in general the making and made of the making is the Word. The sensible Word makes itself and everything sensible. It is also called the light, which makes itself and everything visible. It is also called equality. Namely, it is equal to everything, since it is no more the one than another, giving to all equally that they are what they are, no more, no less.

Therefore, since knowledge and the known of knowing is the Word, he who converts himself to the Word quickly finds what he desires to know. If, therefore, you would like to obtain the species of the mode according to which all occurs, then reflect upon how a vocal word arises.

First reflect upon the fact that without air it cannot become audible. The air, however, as air is attained by none of the senses. Vision does not see air, but rather colored air; we experience it when a ray of sun penetrates a colored glass and we see colored air. The sense of hearing does not attain air unless it is resounding. The sense of smell does not unless it is smelling. The sense of taste does not unless it is tasted—as when one grinds down wormwood and consequently tastes the strongly bitter air. The sense of touch does not unless it is warm or cold or in another manner is altering the sense of perception. Therefore, the air as air is attained by none of the senses, but rather it comes by accident to the notice of the senses. Nevertheless, it is extremely necessary for hearing, since without it nothing can become audible.

Therefore, it is necessary that in like manner you consider that everything which should be as actuality, whether sensible or intelligible, presupposes something without which it does not exist, since it is neither sensible through itself nor intelligible. And because it lacks sensible or intelligible form, it cannot be known unless it is formed. And it has no name. However, it is called *hyle,* matter, chaos, possibility, or potential-to-become, or subject or other names. Then one should attend to the fact that although without air sound would not become sensible, nevertheless air is not of the nature of sound; thus *hyle* is not of the nature of some form and also not its origin; but rather the origin represents its former.

Although sound is not able to arise without air, it is not therefore of the nature of the air. Indeed, fish and men perceive sound outside the air in water, which would not be the case if it were of the nature of the air.

Then one should direct one's attention to the fact that man

is the former of vocal words, that he does not, however, form the word as does a brute animal, but rather as one who possesses a mind, which the brute lacks. Since, therefore, the mind, the former of the word, does not form the word except in order to manifest itself, the word is nothing other than a self-revelation of the mind. Thus the variety of words is also nothing other than a manifold revelation of the one mind.

The conception, however, with which the mind conceives itself, is the word generated by the mind, i.e., the cognition of itself. The vocal word is, however, the revelation of this word. However, everything which can be said is nothing except the word. From the Former of everything make yourself in the same way a concept as from the mind: namely, that it knows itself from the word produced by itself and reveals itself variedly in various signs in the creature, which is a sign of the uncreated Word. And nothing can be which were not a sign of the revelation of the generated Word.

And just as the mind, not wanting to reveal itself further, ceases with the vocal production of the word, and if the mind does not incessantly produce it, the vocal word cannot endure, so it is with the creature in respect to the Creator. However, all others, without which a vocal word cannot be well made and which are called Muses, are ordered to the end of the vocal word and serve the manifestation of the mind. They are likewise creatures who are marks and revelations of the inner word; they are creatures who serve the former as their end.

VIII.

A perfect animal, in which the senses and intellect are inherent, one can therefore consider as a cosmographer, to whom belongs a city with five gates, of the five senses, through which messengers from the entire world enter bringing news of the whole disposition of the world in the following order: Those who report something new of light and its color, enter through the gate of vision; those who report of sound and voice, through the gate of hearing; those who tell of odors, through the gate of smell; those who speak of taste, through the gate of tasting; and those who report of warmth, cold and other tangibles, through the gate of the sense of touch. And the cosmographer is enthroned therein and writes down everything which has been reported to him, so that he has designated in his city the description of the whole sensible world. Indeed, if any gate of his city remains permanently closed, for example, that of vision, then, because there is no entrance for the messenger of the visible, the description of the world will be defective. For the description will make no mention of the sun, stars, light, colors, figures of men, of beasts, of trees, of cities and of the greater part of the beauty of the world. Likewise, if the gate of hearing remains closed, the description will contain nothing of speeches, songs, melodies and such. The same is true of the remaining senses.

The cosmographer therefore strives with all means to have all gates open, and constantly to hear reports of new messengers, and to make his description ever more true. At last, when he has completed the whole description of the sensible world in his city, then he puts it down well-ordered and measured proportionately on a map and turns towards it. He dismisses the messengers. He closes the gates and now turns with his inner vision to the Composer of the world, who is nothing of all this which he has understood and retained concerning the messengers, but rather who is the Artist and the Cause of all these things. Concerning Him, he thinks that He is anteriorly to the total world, as he himself as cosmographer is to the map.

On the basis of the relations of the map to the real world he beholds in himself as cosmographer the Creator of the world in likeness, since through his mind he contemplates the truth in the sign of the designated. With this observation he perceives that no brute animal, although it seems to possess a similar city, gates and messengers, could make such a map. And so he finds in himself the first and more nearly related sign of the Composer, in which his creative power shines forth more than in any other known animal.

Namely, the intellectual sign is the first and most perfect of the Composer of all, the sensible, however, the last. He therefore withdraws, as much as he can, from all sensible signs and turns to the intelligible, simple, and formal signs. And as the light, eternal and inaccessible for all sharpness of mental vision, shines forth in them, he turns his entire attention on them, so that he sees that the incomprehensible cannot be seen other than in an incomprehensible mode of being, and that he, who is incomprehensible for every comprehensible mode, is the form of being of all things which are, which in all things that are remains incomprehensible in intellectual signs as the light shines forth in the darkness. From these it is by no means comprehended, just as one face appearing variedly in diversely polished mirrors is not observed, incorporated, or materialized in any mirror, however well polished, so that from the face and the mirror one composite of both were made, whose form were the face and whose matter the mirror.

But remaining in itself the one light shows itself variously, just as the intellect of man manifests itself visibly in its various arts and the products of these various arts variously, but remains in itself one and invisible, although it remains perfectly unknown in all that to all of the senses. Through this observation the contemplator attains in the most pleasant manner to the cause, origin, and end of himself and all things, so that he concludes happily.

IX.

These few words are easily understandable and sufficient for your consideration, since you yourself are simple. If you would like to inquire into it more acutely, then look back from the elements to the parts of sound and to the letters, which designate these parts, of which some are vowels, others consonants—still others semi-vowels and liquids. Observe further how from these the combination of syllables and words arises, from them speech, and that finally speech is the intent. Thus what is by nature, proceeds from the elements to that intended by nature. Speech is the designation or definition of things. Through this quaternary one attains to the perfect from the imperfect. And what of this can be treated philosophically, can be hunted down sufficiently in the progress of this art. For in nature combinations, beautiful and graceful and pleasing to men, are found; likewise, in the art of speaking and in the concordance of voices. Many are in a contrary manner in both.

Man therefore conducts his consideration of such things and forms his knowledge of the things from the signs and words, just as God forms the world out of things. Beyond that he adds ornament and concord, the beauty, vigor and virtue of the art of speech to the words, in that he imitates nature. Likewise he adds to grammar, rhetoric, poetry, music, logic and the other arts, which arts are all signs of nature.

For just as the mind finds sound in nature and adds art, in order to place all signs of things in sound, so he adds the art of music to the concordance in sounds which he finds in nature, in order to designate all harmonies. Thus it is with everything.

The considerations which calm wise men have found in connection with nature, they have sought to bring forth into general art by means of the equality of the rational ground; just as when, based on habit, they have experienced that the harmonies of certain notes correspond to sounds, which black-smiths produce as soon as they strike the anvil with the hammer. As a result they found the same proportionally in organs and chords, in great and small, and deduced the harmonies and dishar-monies of nature in art. And this art, because it clearly imitates nature, is more pleasing. It incites the impulse of nature and helps in the vital motion, which is the motion of agreement and comfort, which is called joy. All art is therefore founded in the conclusions which the wise man has found in connection to nature, which he presupposes, since he does not know the cause, for whose sake it is. To that discovered he adds art, in that he extends it through the species of similitude, which is the rational ground of art, which imitates nature.

X.

Now inquire further: If you have found any art and endeavor to transmit it in writing, you must see to it to advance words appropriate to the purpose and to explain their meaning in accord with your mind. This is the fundamental condition.

And because the word designated in these words is the art which you would like to expound, your whole effort will have in view that, as precisely as it is possible to you, you teach through the words what you have conceived in your mind. The definition, namely, which effects knowledge, is the unfolding of that which is enfolded in the word.

Consequently, direct your principal attention in every study of books to achieving the interpretation of the words in accordance with the mind of the person writing. Then you will easily apprehend everything and you will bring the writings which you thought contradicted each other into agreement.

Hence distinctions of terms contribute much to the agreement of different writings, if the distinguishing does not err. And he will then deviate least if he endeavors to reduce these to equality.

I wish to add the result of a consideration, which I have made in respect to the species of knowledge of the origin. The origin must be that in respect to which there is nothing prior and nothing more powerful. Only the power which generates its precise equality cannot be greater. For it unites everything in itself.

I therefore take four terms: potential, equal, one, and similar. Potential I call that in respect to which nothing is more powerful. Equal is that which is of the same nature; one that which proceeds from them; and similar that which is representative of its origin.

Nothing can be before potential. For what could precede, if it could not precede? Therefore, the potential in respect to which nothing can be more powerful or prior, is the omnipotent Origin. It is before being and not-being. For there is nothing, if it could not be, and there is not nothing, if it could not not be. And it precedes to-make and to-be-made. For nothing makes that cannot make and nothing is made that cannot be made. So you see the potential before being and not-being, before to-make and to-be-made, etc.

However, nothing of everything which is not itself the potential can be or be known without it. Therefore, whatever either can be or be known, is enfolded in the potential and belongs to it.

The equal, which cannot be unless it belongs to the potential, must be prior to all things, as the potential to which it is equal. In its equality it shows itself as the most powerful potential. For to be able to generate itself out of itself is the highest power. The potential therefore, which stands in an equal manner to the contradictory, so that it cannot be one more than another, acts equally through its equality.

From the potential and its equality proceeds the most powerful union. For the united potency or strength is more powerful. The union of the most powerful and its equality is therefore not weaker than that from which it proceeds. And thus the mind sees that the potential, its equality, and the union of both is the single, most powerful, most equal, and most united Origin. This shows clearly enough that the potential equally unites, enfolds, and unfolds everything. Therefore, whatever it makes, it makes through equality. And if it creates, it creates through it, and if it shows itself, then it shows itself through it. However, the potential does not create itself through equality, since equality is not prior to it itself. Also it does not create the dissimilar through equality. For equality is not the form of dissimilitude and the unequal.

Therefore, that which it makes is similar. Therefore, whatever is and is not the Origin itself, must necessarily be its similitude, because equality, which does not admit of more and less, cannot be multiplied, varied or altered; just as little as the singular. Indeed, singularity is nothing other than equality. The object of all cognitive power can therefore be nothing other than equality itself, which can show itself in its similitude.

Hence the object of sensitive cognition is nothing other than equality, likewise the object of the imaginative and the intellective. By nature the power of cognition knows its object. Cognition is indeed effected through similitude. Hence equality, whose similitude actualizes all cognitive powers, is the object of cognitive powers. By nature those gifted with intellect see that there is equality, whose similitude is in the intellect; just as the colored vision, whose similitude or species is in vision. However, all similitude is the species or the sign of equality. Equality confronts vision; it is seen in the species of colors, etc.

However, equality is nearer in the imagination, because it is not imaginable in the species of quality, but rather in that of quantity. And this species has a similitude closer to equality. Indeed, in the intellect equality is not attained by means of the similitude involved in the species of quality or quantity, but rather by means of the simple and pure intelligible species or bare similitude. And equality appears as one, which is the form of the being and knowledge of all things, which appears variously in varied similitude. And its singular appearance, which we call the singular thing, the human mind naturally intuits in itself in its splendor—just as its living and intelligent appearance.

Indeed, the human mind is nothing other than the sign of that coequality, just like the first appearance of cognition, which the prophet calls the light of God's countenance, which is impressed upon us. Hence man knows by nature the good, equal, just, and right, because these are the splendor of equality. Therefore, he praises that law: What you want to be done to you, do to the other, because it is the splendor of equality. Indeed, the food of intellectual life consists of such virtues. Therefore, it is not unknown to him that that represents restoration with regard to his sustenance. As the sensible vision is to the sensible light, so is the vision of the mind to this intelligible light. For the sensible light, the image of that intelligible light, bears the similitude of equality, since nothing unequal is seen in the light.

It is certain that as the sensible vision senses nothing except the light and the appearance of light in its signs, and forms the judgment that there is nothing other, yes, indeed, constantly affirms that nothing is left when one takes away the light—indeed its vision is nourished by it—and thus the vision of the mind perceives nothing other than the intelligible light or equality and its appearance in its signs, and certifies with the greatest truth that without this light nothing can be or be known. For how shall the intellect, whose understanding consists of assimilation, which would entirely cease to exist through the sublation of equality, endure if equality were removed? Would the truth not be sublated, which is the assimilation of things and the intellect? Therefore, nothing would remain in the truth, if equality were sublated, since there is nothing other to be found in the truth itself than equality.

XI.

So that you see that the sensitive soul is not the intellect, but rather its similitude or its image, attend to how the form in an act of seeing is double. The one is the in-forming form, which is the similitude of the object, and the other is the forming, which is the similitude of mental understanding. Forming and in-forming are kinds of action. However, since nothing is done without a rational ground, the intellect is the principle of the actions, which are directed to an end.

However, everything occurs either through itself or by nature. Therefore, the work of nature is the work of mental understanding. Therefore, when an object in-forms by means of its similitude, then it occurs naturally, i.e., through the mental understanding by means of nature. However, when the mental understanding forms, then it does this through its own similitude.

Therefore, in the act of seeing, there are two similitudes: The one is that of the object, the other that of the mental understanding; without both of these vision does not occur. The similitude of the object is superficial and extrinsic, the similitude of the mental understanding is central and intrinsic. The similitude of the object is the instrument of the similitude of the mental understanding. The similitude of the mental understanding, therefore, perceives or knows by means of the similitude of the object.

To sense therefore requires a sensitive soul, which is the similitude of the mental understanding, and the species of the object, which is the similitude of the object. For this reason the sensitive soul is not the intellect, since it does not sense without the similitude of the object. Namely, the intellect is not dependent on something in order to know the intelligible and requires nothing other than itself as an instrument, since it is the origin of its own actions. It understands this relationship, "Something is or is not," without any instrument or means, likewise everything else intelligible.

It does not know the sensible, because it is sensible and not intelligible. Therefore, intelligible things must first exist, before they are understood; just as also nothing sensible is perceived unless it becomes sensible.

XII.

In order to consider equality in the sensible: Is the one surface not level, the other round, and a third of an intermediate kind? And if you observe either the level or the round in your mind, then they have nothing that were not equal. What is the level other than equality? Likewise, roundness is also equality. For a round surface is equal from the center and is necessarily equal on all sides and is nowhere otherwise. The level is likewise equal on all sides. If you look at that levelness, in respect to which there can be none more equal, then this will certainly shine forth maximally, as far as all level surfaces shine. And thus the round will shine forth and be moved, as it is revealed in the book *On the Game of the Spheres.*

However, the intermediate surfaces cannot be completely alien to all equality, since they fall between the level and the round surfaces. Likewise, no line which does not participate in equality, can fall between the straight line and the circular line, each of which is equal. It is the same with number, of which none does not participate in equality, since only the progression of unity is found in them and there is none which were variable or could be greater or less.

This can certainly only be so from equality. Furthermore, is there really nothing other than equality found in health or life and things of this kind? If one takes it away, then neither the senses nor imagination nor comparison nor proportion nor intellect will remain. Thus neither love nor concord nor justice nor peace will exist nor will anything whatever be able to endure.

XIII.

After the consideration of the first Origin I want to add something else concerning the soul on the basis of the aforesaid.

From the aforementioned you can elicit, that air is attained by none of our senses except insofar as it is qualitative. Hence it is certain that the air, if it would live a sensitive life, would sense in itself the species of quality. The air, however, is either subtle or gross or it is in an intermediate mode. Aether is subtle. Therefore, the sensitive soul must vivify the air connected to it in order to be able to sensibly perceive the species of the object in the vivified air; for example, in the living air, which is transparent and subtle, the species of the visible; in the common, the species of sound; in the thickened and altered, the species of other senses.

Therefore, the sensitive soul is neither earth, nor water, nor air, nor aether or fire, but rather the spirit, which vivifies the air in the manner discussed. It perceives from the conjunction of spirit and air, which has been placed into actuality through the sensible species. Therefore, the air represents the body of the life of our sensitive spirit, with whose aid it vivifies the total body and perceives objects. And it is not of the nature of some sensible object, but rather of a simpler and higher power.

To sense is a kind of suffering. Therefore, the species becomes active as a result of the aforesaid organic body. Hence the species, although it acts in the body, is not corporeal, but rather is the forming spirit in regard to that organic body. And because it is perceived, that living body must be pure and free of every species.

However, the soul, which vivifies it and to which perceiving belongs, and which in every respect is simpler and more abstract than all bodies and species, does not know except if it attends to it. Therefore, it is an ever vivifying and cognitive power, which is utilized, when it is moved, in order to be attentive. There is therefore in the sensitive soul beyond the vivifying power a cognitive power, as it were, an image of intelligence, which is bound in us with this intelligence.

You see how a solar ray penetrates a colored glass and consequently a species of color appears in the air. For in that splendor, which is the splendor of the color of the glass, you see the colored air in similitude with the glass. However, the color of the glass is as the body and the color of the air is as the intention and the spirit in relation to it. However, the species of this intention is even more subtle and spiritual, because it is its splendor. And it is perceived in vision, i.e., in the living, transparent air of the eye.

Therefore, the sensitive soul, which vivifies the transparent, is so spiritual that it perceives the splendor of the splendor in its purest transparency. For it perceives the completely colorless surface of its transparency to be colored in the similitude. And turning itself to the object from which the splendor comes, it knows the object by means of that splendor, which it senses in the surface of the body of its transparency.

Since no vision occurs unless the seeing attends to the splendor or intention, for we do not see the transient if we are not attentive, it is clear that vision arises from the intention of color and attention of the seeing. And if you consider it well, you will find in the example of this colored air a similitude for man. For he is body, soul and spirit. The body is as air, the soul as the species of color which totally penetrates, forms, and colors the air. The spirit, however, is as the ray of light, which illuminates the color.

For if our rational soul did not have in itself the spirit of discrimination which shines in it, then we were not men and we would not perceive clearly in comparison with all other animals. However, that light which shines in us is given us from above and is not mixed with the body. However, we experience the light to be discriminating. Therefore, we know most certainly that we have every gift of discrimination and illumination and perfection of our vivacity from that insensible light. If it did not shine in us, we would have to fail completely, just as when the solar ray ceases to penetrate the colored glass, nothing of the colored air remains visible.

However, heaven is as a glass, which contains in itself the zodiac or the circle of life. However, the power of the All-Creating is as the ray. From these few words take upon yourself the material for your reflections, which you can amplify as you wish. Still remaining is the consideration of our sweetest faith, which surpasses everything through its certainty and alone brings happiness; engage yourself in it firmly and frequently.

Conclusion

What else we think more extensively on this you have in many and various little works which you can read after this compendium. And you will find that the same first principle has appeared to us everywhere variedly and we have depicted its varied revelation variously.

Epilogue

The total direction tends to the unity of the object, in respect to which the Apostle Philip, led by Christ, the Word of God, has said: "Lord, show us the Father and that will be enough for us." Above we have called the Father of the Word and of equality the potential, because He is omnipotent; the object of the vision of the mind and of the vision of the senses is one. The mental vision is as it is in itself, the sensible vision as it is in the signs. And it is the potential-itself, in respect to which there is nothing more powerful. Since this is everything which it can be, and also all things which can be, it is itself without variation, augmentation, or diminution. Therefore, since all things are nothing other than that which they can be and the potential, in respect to which nothing is more powerful, is the potential-to-be of everything, there is for everything which is no cause except this potential-to-be itself. Namely, the thing is, because the potential-to-be itself is. And it is this and nothing other, because the highest equality is. And it is one, because the highest union is.

Therefore, nothing presents itself to the vision of the mind in everything and through everything except that in respect to which there is nothing more powerful. For this vision does not desire many and various things, because it is not inclined to the many and the varied. But rather it is drawn by nature to that in respect to which nothing is more powerful, in whose vision it lives and finds rest. And because the power, in respect to which nothing can be more powerful, is the most unified power, it names this unity itself, in respect to which nothing is more powerful. The things, however, which can be, it calls numbers.

The object of the vision of the mind is the omnipotent, invariable, and unmultiplicable Unity. It is not number, since in number there is nothing which it desires to see except unity itself, which is all that which every number is, can be, or can unfold. For it looks to that which is enumerated in every number and not to the number.

However, nothing in whichever and whatever large or small, even or odd number is able to be, except that power in respect to which nothing is more powerful, which is called unity. The object of the vision of the mind is therefore nothing other than the potential, in respect to which there is nothing more powerful, since this alone without its alteration can be everything, and also is that without which nothing can be. How indeed should something be without the potential–itself, since it could not be? And if something could be without it, then it could be without the potential.

However, the object of the vision of the senses is some sensible thing, which, since it is only that which it can be, is nothing except the same object of the vision of the mind. It is, however, not such as it in itself confronts the mind, but rather as it is represented in a sensible sign to sensible vision. Therefore, because the potential–itself, in respect to which nothing is more powerful, wishes to be seen, this is the case for everything.

And this is the cause of causes and the end for the sake of which everything exists. As a result the causes of all things are ordered in being and being known. And thus I close this very short and concise direction, which men with purer and more acute and subtle contemplating vision will elaborate more clearly to the praise of the Almighty, who be always praised. Amen.

On the Summit of Vision

(1 4 6 4)

*The interlocutors: The most reverend Lord Cardinal of
Saint Peter, and Peter of Erclencz, Canon of Aquensis.*

PETER: For some days now I have seen you enraptured in some
profound meditation; and indeed so much so that I fear being
too much of a bother to you, if I turn to you with the questions
occurring to me. Now, however, it seems to me that you are
less intent, as if you had discovered something great and were
happy about it; therefore, I hope that you will pardon me, if I
interrogate you beyond the usual.

CARDINAL: I shall be happy to. For I have often been astonished
at your long taciturnity, especially because you have listened to me for more than fourteen years, when I have
spoken a lot publicly and privately about the discoveries
made in my studies, and you also have collected several of
the little works I have written. Now, since you, through
the gift of God and through my assistance, have obtained
the divine position of the most sacred priesthood, the time
has come that you begin to speak and question.

PETER: I am indeed shy because of my inexperience, but your
kindness encourages me to ask: What is the new thing
which has come into your meditation during these Easter
days? I believed you had completed all speculation, which
you have explained in so many of your books.

CARDINAL: If the Apostle Paul, enraptured into the third heaven,
does not yet comprehend the incomprehensible, then no

one will ever be so satisfied by Him, who is greater than all comprehension, that he did not always persevere in order to comprehend Him better.

PETER: What do you seek?

CARDINAL: You assert correctly.

PETER: I ask you and you deride me. If I ask what you seek, then you say "you assert correctly," although I assert nothing, but rather I inquire.

CARDINAL: When you say: "What do you seek," you have spoken correctly, since I seek "what." Whoever seeks, seeks "what"; for if he did not seek something or a "what," then he would not seek at all. As all inquirers, I therefore seek the "what," for I would very much like to know what this "what" or the quiddity is, which is sought so much.

PETER: Do you believe that it can be found?

CARDINAL: Quite certainly. For the motion which is given all inquirers is not in vain.

PETER: If no one has found it until now—why do you strive beyond all the rest?

CARDINAL: I am of the opinion that many have seen it in some manner and have left behind a vision of it in their writings. For the quiddity which was sought, is sought, and will always be sought—how should it be sought, if it were completely unknown and if it remained unknown even when found? Therefore, a certain sage said that it is seen by all although only from afar.

Since, therefore, I have seen in the course of many years that one must seek it beyond every cognitive power, before all variety and opposition, my attention was directed to the fact that the quiddity subsisting in itself is the invariable subsistence of all substance, and therefore can be neither multiplied nor plurified, and that consequently there is not now one and then another quiddity of other entities, but rather the same hypostasis of all. Thereupon I saw that one must necessarily concede that the hypostasis or subsistence of things could be. And because it can be, it can in no case be without the potential-itself. For how could it be without potential? Therefore, the potential-itself, without which nothing can be, is that without which nothing can be subsistent. Therefore, it is the sought-after "what" or the quiddity itself, without which nothing can be. And with this vision I have occupied myself during these feast days with enormous delectation.

PETER: Because, as you assert, without the potential nothing can be, and I see that you say the truth, and because without the quiddity nothing is at all, I see well that the potential-itself can be called the quiddity. Since, however, you have previously spoken a lot about the actual–potential and have explained it in a trialogue, I wonder why that should not suffice.

CARDINAL: You will see below that the potential-itself, in respect to which nothing can be more powerful or earlier or better, names more aptly that without which nothing can be, live, or understand than the actual–potential or some other designation; for if it can be named at all, then it were better named the potential-itself, beyond which nothing can be more perfect. And I do not believe that there can be another name, which were clearer, truer, and easier.

PETER: How do you say easier, when I believe there is nothing more difficult than a thing which is always sought and never completely found?

CARDINAL: The clearer the truth is, the easier it is. I once believed that it would be found better in the dark. The truth is of such great power, the potential-itself shines forth in it powerfully; indeed it cries out loudly in the streets, as you have read in the booklet *On the Laity*. It is found everywhere very surely and easily. Which boy or adolescent does not know the potential-itself, since each says he can eat, can run, and can speak? And none who is in possession of a mind is so ignorant, that he did not know without a teacher, that nothing is without being able to be, and that, without the potential, something can neither be nor have, do nor undergo; if one asked an adolescent whether he could carry a stone and, as soon as he had answered that he could, asked further whether he could also do it without the potential, who would not then answer: in no case? For he regarded that as an absurd and superfluous question; for no one in his right mind would ponder over whether one can make something or whether something can come into existence without the potential-itself.

Indeed, every potential presupposes the potential-itself as necessary, so that nothing at all can be without its presupposition. Indeed, if something can be known, nothing is more known than this potential-itself. If something can be easy, nothing is easier than the potential-itself. If something can be certain, nothing is more certain than the potential-itself. Likewise nothing is earlier or stronger or more solid or more substantial or more glorious, etc. However, if the potential-itself is lacking, neither being nor the good nor anything else can be.

PETER: I see nothing which is more certain than this. And I am of the opinion that the truth of these words can remain hidden from no one.

CARDINAL: Between you and me exists only the difference of attention. For if I ask you what you see in all Adam's posterity, who were, are, and will be, although they were infinitely many, would you not respond at once, if you pay attention, you saw in all nothing other than the paternal potential of the first father?

PETER: It is entirely so.

CARDINAL: And if asked further, what you see in the lions and eagles and all species of animals, would you not answer in the same way?

PETER: Certainly not otherwise.

CARDINAL: And in everything caused and originated?

PETER: I would say that I saw nothing except the potential of the first Cause and the first Origin.

CARDINAL: And if I asked you still further: Since the potential of all these firsts is completely inexplicable, whence does this potential have such strength? Would you not answer at once: from the absolute, uncontracted, and completely omnipotent potential-itself, in relation to which nothing more powerful can be sensed, imagined, or understood? For it is the potential of every potential. Nothing can be earlier or more perfect, and if it did not exist, nothing at all could endure.

PETER: Thus would I indeed answer.

CARDINAL: Therefore, the potential-itself is the quiddity and hypostasis of everything; in its power all things must necessarily be contained, both those which are as well as those which are not; would you not say that one must affirm this as entirely certain?

PETER: I would say so entirely.

CARDINAL: Therefore, the potential-itself is named light by some saints. It is not the sensible or rational or intelligible light, but rather the light of all that which can shine forth, for there can be nothing more lucid, clear, and beautiful than the potential-itself. Turn yourself therefore toward the sensible light, without which there can be no sensible vision, and attend to how there is no other hypostasis in every color and in everything visible than the light, which appears variously in the various essential modes of the colors. And consider also that, were the light removed, neither color nor the visible nor vision could remain. However, since the clarity of the light, as it is in itself, excels the power of sight, it is not seen as it is, but manifests itself rather in the visible, in the one more clearly, in the other more obscurely; and the more clearly something visible represents the light, the more noble and beautiful it is. However, the light enfolds in itself and excels the clarity and beauty of everything visible; nor does the light manifest itself in the visible, in order to show itself as visible, but rather in order to manifest itself as invisible, because its clarity cannot be grasped in the visible. Indeed, whoever sees the clarity of the light in the visible as invisible, sees it more truly. Do you grasp that?

PETER: I grasp it more easily, since I have heard such already frequently from you.

CARDINAL: Now transfer this sensible condition to the intelligible, for example, the potential of light to the simple potential, or the absolute potential-itself, and the being of color to the simple being. For the simple being, which is only visible for the mind, is to the mind, as the being of color to the sense of vision. Observe more closely what the mind sees in the various entities, which are nothing other than that which they can be, and can only have that which they have from the potential–itself, and you will see that the various entities are nothing other than various modes of appearance of the potential–itself, that their quiddity, however, cannot be various because it is the potential–itself, which appears variously. Also nothing other can be seen in that which is, lives, and understands than the potentialitself; the potential to be, the potential to live, and the potential to understand are its manifestations. Indeed, what else can be seen in every power than the potential of allpower?

Nevertheless, the potential–itself cannot be grasped most perfectly in all the power either of being or knowing, just as it is. Rather, it appears in them and indeed in the one more powerfully than in the other; more powerfully in the intellectual potential than in the sensible; and indeed as much more powerfully as the intellect is more powerful than the senses. However, the potential–itself is seen in itself more truly beyond all cognitive powers by means of the intelligible potential, when one sees that it excels every power of the capacity of the intelligible potential—that which the intellect grasps and understands. Therefore, when the mind in its potential sees that the potential–itself, on account of its excellence, cannot be grasped, then it sees by means of vision beyond its capacity; just like a boy, who sees that the quantity of a stone is greater than the fortitude of his potential is able to carry.

The potential to see of the mind, therefore, excels the potential to comprehend. Hence the simple vision of the mind is not comprehensive vision, but rather it elevates itself from the comprehensive to see the incomprehensible. If it sees that one comprehensive is greater than another, then it elevates itself, in order to see that, beyond which there can be nothing greater. And this is the infinite, which is greater than everything measurable or comprehensible. And this potential to see of the mind beyond all comprehensible strength and power is the supreme potential of the mind, in which the potential-itself manifests itself maximally and it is not terminated this side of the potential-itself, for the potential to see is so much ordered to the potential-itself, that the mind can foresee whither it tends; just as a pilgrim foresees the terminus of his motion, so that he can guide his steps to the desired terminus. Therefore, if the mind is not able to see from afar the terminus of its repose and desire, its joy and its felicity, how should it then hasten in order to comprehend it? The Apostle rightly admonishes us to run, so that we comprehend it. Therefore, collect all this, in order to see that everything is so ordered to this, that the mind can run to the potential-itself, which it sees from afar, and comprehends the incomprehensible in the relatively best way. For the potential-itself, if it appears in the glory of its majesty, is alone able to satisfy the desire of the mind. Indeed, it is that "what" which is sought. Do you see what I have said?

PETER: I see that what you have said is true, although it excels the capacity. For what could satisfy the desire of the mind other than the potential-itself, the potential of every potential, without which nothing at all can be? Indeed, if something other than the potential-itself could be, how could it be able without potential? And if it were not able without potential, then it would have what it could entirely from potential. The mind is only satisfied if it comprehends that, beyond which nothing better can be. And that can be nothing other than the potential-itself, the potential, namely, of every potential. Therefore, you see correctly that alone the potential-itself is that "what," which is sought by every mind. It is the origin of mental desire, since it is that, before which there can be nothing earlier. And it is the end of the same mental desire, since nothing more can be desired beyond the potential-itself.

CARDINAL: You now see very well, Peter, how much the frequent discussions with me and the reading of my works help you to understand me easily. Whatever I see, I do not doubt in the potential-itself. And if your mind is ready, you will also soon see it. For since every question concerning whether something can be presupposes the potential-itself, no doubt can be raised about this; indeed, no one advances to the potential-itself. Indeed, whoever asks whether the potential-itself exists, if he pay attention, sees immediately that this question is impertinent, because without potential no question can be raised concerning the potential-itself; and he sees that even less can it be asked, whether the potential-itself is this or that; for the potential to be and the potential to be this and that presuppose the potential-itself, and hence it is certain that the potential-itself precedes every doubt which can arise. If, therefore, the doubt cannot other than presuppose it, then there is neither something more certain than the potential-itself, nor can one imagine something more sufficient or perfect. Likewise nothing can be added to it and nothing can be separated or removed from it.

PETER: Now tell me one thing please: Will you reveal something still clearer than before concerning the First? For you have already often and extensively said much concerning it, although not as much as can be said.

CARDINAL: Now I propose to open to you a facility, which I deemed most secret and have previously not communicated openly. Thus I want to show you, for example, that all precision in this speculation is to be assigned only to the potential-itself and its appearance, and that all who saw correctly have attempted to express this. Indeed, those who affirmed the One, looked thereby to the potential-itself; those who spoke of one and many, looked to the potential-itself and the many essential modes of its appearance; those who said there could be nothing new, looked to the potential-itself before every potential to be and to become; those, however, who affirmed the novelty of the world and things, turned their mind to the appearance of the potential, just as if someone turned the vision of his mind to the potential of unity. He would without doubt see in every number and plurality nothing other than the potential-itself of unity, in relation to which there were nothing more powerful, and he would see that every number is nothing other than the appearance of the potential-itself of innumerable and infinite unity. Indeed, the numbers are nothing other than special modes of appearance of the potential-itself of unity. And this potential appears better in the odd ternary than in the even quaternary, and better in the perfectly certain numbers than in others. Likewise the genera and species and all such are attributable to the essential modes of appearance of the potential–itself.

Those who said there are not several forms which give being, looked to the potential–itself, in relation to which there is nothing more sufficient. However, those who said there are several specific forms, attended to the specific essential modes of the appearance of the potential–itself. Those who said God is the font of ideas and there are several ideas, wanted to say the same that we say: namely, that God is the potential–itself, which appears in various and different essential modes according to the species. Those who deny ideas and such forms, looked to the potential–itself, which alone is the "what" of every potential. Those who say nothing could pass away, look to the eternal and incorruptible potential–itself. Those who say death is something and who believe that things perish, turn their vision to the essential modes of the appearance of the potential–itself. Those who say God, the Almighty Father, is the Creator of heaven and earth, as we do, say that the potential–itself, in relation to which there is nothing more all-powerful, created heaven, earth, and everything through its appearance; for in everything which either is or can be, one can see nothing other than the potential–itself; just as in everything made and to be made, nothing other than the potential of the first making and in everything moved and to be moved, nothing other than the potential of the first Mover is seen.

Therefore, through such resolution you see that everything is easy and that all difference passes over into concordance. Therefore, my dear Peter, turn the eye of your mind with acute intention to this secret and enter with this resolution into our writings and whatever else you read. And exercise yourself well in our books and sermons, but especially in the book *On the Gift of* [the Father of] *Lights,* which, if one understands it well in respect to the aforesaid, contains the same as this booklet. You should also keep in your memory the booklets *On the Image or the*

Vision of God and *On Searching for God,* so that you are better habituated in these theological matters. And in addition to these writings occupy yourself with the memorial *On the Summit of Vision,* which I want to add now as briefly as possible. I hope you will be a welcome contemplator of God and incessantly pray for me in the holy rites.

The summit of vision is the potential-itself, the potential of every potential, without which no one can contemplate something; indeed, how could someone without the potential?

I. To the potential-itself nothing can be added, since it is the potential of every potential. Hence the potential-itself is neither the potential to be or the potential to live or the potential to understand or any other potential with some addition, although the potential-itself is the potential of the potential to be, of the potential to live, and of the potential to understand.

II. Only that is which can be. Being, therefore, adds nothing to the potential to be. Thus man adds nothing to the potential to be man and the young man nothing to the potential to be a young man or an old man. And because the potential adds nothing with addition to the potential-itself, he who contemplates acutely sees nothing other than the potential-itself.

III. Nothing can be prior to the potential-itself. For how could it without the potential? Therefore, in relation to the potential-itself nothing can be better, more powerful, more perfect, simpler, clearer, better known, truer, more sufficient, braver, more stable, easier, etc. And because the potential-itself precedes every potential with addition, it can neither be nor be named, neither be sensed nor imagined nor understood. Indeed, what is signified with the potential-itself precedes all this, although it is the hypostasis of all, just as the light is that of color.

IV. The potential with addition is an image of the potential-itself, in relation to which nothing is simpler. Hence the potential to be is an image of the potential-itself, the potential to live an image of the potential-itself, and the potential to understand an image of the potential-itself.

Nevertheless, the potential to live is a truer image of it and the potential to understand a still truer image. Therefore, the contemplator sees the potential-itself in everything. Thus the truth is seen in the image and thus the image is the appearance of the truth; thus everything is nothing other than the appearance of the potential-itself.

V. Just as the potential of the mind of Aristotle manifests itself in his books (although these books do not show the potential of his mind perfectly, even though one book is more perfect than another), and as also the books were only published for the purpose of the mind showing itself—although the mind was also not compelled in the publication of the books, because the free and noble mind wished to manifest itself—the potential-itself is thus in all things. The mind is in reality like an intellectual book, which sees in itself and everything the intention of the writer.

VI. Although in the books of Aristotle nothing is contained other than the potential of his mind, nevertheless the ignorant do not see this. And although in the universe nothing is contained other than the potential-itself, nevertheless those lacking mind cannot see this. However, the living intellectual light, which is called mind, contemplates in itself the potential-itself. Thus everything exists on account of the mind and the mind exists in order to see the potential-itself.

VII. The potential to choose enfolds in itself the potential to be, the potential to live, and the potential to understand; it is the potential of the free will, which by no means depends on the body as the potential of concupiscence depends on the desire of the animal. Hence it does not follow the infirmity of the body. For it never grows old and declines as do concupiscence and the senses in old people, but rather always remains and dominates the senses. Indeed, it does not always allow the eye to look out when it is so inclined, but rather averts it, so that it does not see vanity and scandal. Likewise it prevents the hungry from eating, etc. The mind, therefore, sees the laudable and the scandalous, and sees virtue and vice, which the senses do not see. And the mind can compel the senses to stand by its judgment and not by their own desire. And in this we experience that the potential-itself appears strong and incorruptible in the potential of the mind and has a separate being from the body. He is less astonished by this who experiences that the powers of certain herbs, separated from the bodies of these herbs, are in the vital sap; namely, when he sees the same operation of the vital sap, which the herbs had before they were immersed in water.

VIII. That which the mind sees is the intelligible, which precedes the sensible. Therefore, the mind sees itself. Because, since there is much that is impossible for it, it sees that its potential is not the potential of every potential, it sees that it is not the potential-itself, but rather the image of the potential-itself. Since it sees that in its potential the potential-itself is nothing other than its potential to be, it sees that it is a mode of appearance of the potential-itself. And it sees that similarly in everything that is. Everything which the mind sees is therefore the mode of appearance of the incorruptible potential-itself.

IX. The being of the body, although it is the most ignoble and the lowest, is seen only by the mind. Indeed, what the senses see is the accidental, which is not, but rather is present. This being of the body, which is nothing other than the potential to be of the body, is attained by none of the senses, since it is neither quality nor quantity. Therefore, it is neither divisible nor corruptible. When I divide an apple, then I do not divide the body. The part of the apple is indeed as much body as the whole apple. A body is long, wide, and deep, without which it is neither body nor perfect dimension. The being of the body is the being of a perfect dimension. Indeed, the length of the body is not separate from its width and depth, just as little as the width is from the length and depth or as the depth from the length and width. Also they are not the parts of the body, since a part is not the whole. The length of the body is body, just as the width and depth. And also the length of the being of the body, which is body, is no other body than the width and depth of this being of the body; but each of them is the same indivisible and unmultiplicable body, although the length is not the width or depth. Nevertheless, it is the origin of the width, and the length is with the width the origin of the depth. Thus the mind sees the potential-itself appear incorruptibly in the triune being of the body. And because it sees it thus in the lowest being of the body, it sees it also in every nobler being. It sees that it appears more nobly and powerfully and in itself yet more clearly than in the living or corporeal being. However, how the triune potential-itself appears clearly in the remembering, understanding, and willing mind, the mind of Saint Augustine has seen and revealed.

X. In operation or action the mind most certainly sees the potential-itself appear in the potential to make of the making, and in the potential to be made of the makeable and in the potential of the connection of both. There are not three potentials, but rather the same potential is that of the making, the makeable, and the connection. Likewise it sees in sensation, vision, taste, imagination, intellection, volition, election, contemplation, and in all good and virtuous actions the triune potential as reflection of the potential-itself, beyond which there is nothing more active and perfect. However, because the potential-itself does not shine forth in them, the mind experiences corrupt acts as inane, bad, and dead and as something that darkens and destroys the light of the mind.

XI. There can be no other substantial or quidditative origin, whether formal or material, than the potential-itself. And those who have spoken of various forms and formalities, ideas, and species, did not look to the potential-itself, as it shows itself according to its will in the varied, general, and specific essential modes. And that, in which it does not shine forth, is lacking hypostasis; just as vanity, defect, error, vice, infirmity, death, corruption and such like. All these lack entity, because they lack the appearance of the potential-itself.

XII. With the potential-itself the three-and-one God is signified, whose name is the Omnipotent or the potential of all power. In Him everything is possible and nothing impossible. He is the strength of the strong and the power of power. His most perfect appearance, beyond which there can be none more perfect, is Christ, who leads us to the clear contemplation of the potential-itself through word and example. And that is the felicity, which alone satisfies the supreme desire of the mind. This is only a little, but it can suffice.

Bibliography of Works Cited

I.

Nicolaus of Cusa's Works: Texts and Translations

Texts

Nikolaus von Kues, *Philosophisch-Theologische Schriften,* edited by Leo Gabriel, translated by Dietlind and Wilhelm Dupre, Latin-German, 3 vols. (Vienna, Austria: Herder & Co., 1964, 1966, and 1967).

English Translations

Anonymous, *The Idiot.* Reprinted in 1940 with a preface by W.R. Dennes (San Francisco: California State Library Occasional Papers. Reprint Series No. 19, 1940).

Dolan, John P., Ed. *Unity and Reform: Selected Writings of Nicholas de Cusa* (South Bend, Indiana: University of Notre Dame Press, 1962).

Hopkins, Jasper, *A Concise Introduction to the Philosophy of Nicholas of Cusa* (Minneapolis: University of Minnesota Press, 1978). Contains a translation of *On Actualized-Possibility.* I have referred to this work in my introduction as *On Actual-Potential,* because the Latin title *De possest,* which is a combination of *posse* and *est,* is in the present rather than in the past tense.

———, *Nicholas of Cusa on God as Not-other* (Minneapolis: University of Minnesota Press, 1979).

———, *Nicholas of Cusa on Learned Ignorance* (Minneapolis: The Arthur J. Banning Press, 1981).

———, *Nicholas of Cusa's Debate with John Wenck: A Translation and an Appraisal of De Ignota Litteratura and Apologia Doctae Ignorantiae* (Minneapolis: The Arthur J. Banning Press, 1981).

———, *Nicholas of Cusa's Metaphysics of Contraction* (Minneapolis:

The Arthur J. Banning Press, 1983). Contains a translation of
The Gift of the Father of Lights, with Latin text.

————, *Nicholas of Cusa's Dialectical Mysticism* (Minneapolis: The
Arthur J. Banning Press, 1985). Contains a translation of *On the
Vision of God.*

————, *Nicholas of Cusa's De Pace Fidei and Cribratio Alkorani: Translation and Analysis* (Minneapolis: The Arthur J. Banning Press,
1990).

Miller, Clyde Lee, *The Layman: About Mind* (New York: Abaris
Books, 1979).

Sigmund, Paul E., *The Catholic Concordance* (Cambridge: Cambridge
University Press, 1991).

Watts, Pauline Moffitt, *On The Game of Spheres* (New York: Abaris
Books, 1986).

II.

Other Primary Sources

Aquinas, St. Thomas, *The Summa Contra Gentiles,* 5 vols. (Notre
Dame, Indiana: University of Notre Dame Press, 1975).

————, *The Summa Theologica,* The Great Books, 2 vols. (Chicago:
Encyclopedia Britannica, Inc., 1952).

Augustine, St., *On Christian Doctrine,* translated by D.W. Robertson,
Jr. (Indianapolis: Bobbs–Merrill Educational Publishing, 1984).

————, *The Trinity,* translated by Stephen McKenna (Washington,
D.C.: The Catholic University of America Press, 1981).

Cantor, Georg, *Foundations of a General Theory of Manifolds,* translated by Uwe Parpart, *The Campaigner,* Vol. 9, Nos. 1-2 (New
York: Campaigner Publications, Inc. 1976).

Cassirer, Ernst, *The Individual and the Cosmos in Renaissance Philosophy,* translated by Mario Domandi (Philadelphia: University of
Pennsylvania Press, 1963).

Feuerbach, Ludwig, *The Essence of Christianity* (New York: Harper
& Row, 1957).

Gestrich, Helmut, *Nikolaus von Kues 1401-1464, Leben und Werk im
Bild* (Mainz, Germany: Verlag Hermann Schmidt, 1990).

Hamerman, Nora, "The Council of Florence: The Religious Event
that Shaped the Era of Discovery," *Fidelio,* Vol. 1, No. 2
(Washington, D.C., Schiller Institute, Inc., 1992).

Janelle, Pierre, *The Catholic Reformation* (Milwaukee: The Bruce
Publishing Company, 1948).

à Kempis, Thomas, *The Imitation of Christ,* edited by Harold C. Gardiner, S.J. (New York: Doubleday, 1955).

LaRouche, Lyndon H., Jr., *The Science of Christian Economy and Other Prison Writings* (Washington, D.C.: Schiller Institute, Inc., 1991).

———, "The Science of Music," *Fidelio,* Vol. 1, No. 1 (Washington, D.C.: Schiller Institute, Inc., 1992).

———, "On the Subject of Metaphor," *Fidelio,* Vol. 1, No. 3 (Washington, D.C.: Schiller Institute, Inc., 1992).

———, "The Mozart Revolution," *Fidelio,* Vol. 1, No. 4 (Washington, D.C.: Schiller Institute, Inc. 1992).

———, "On the Subject of God," *Fidelio,* Vol. 2, No. 1 (Washington, D.C.: Schiller Institute, Inc., 1993).

Leibniz, Gottfried Wilhelm, *Monadology,* translated by George Montgomery (La Salle, Illinois: Open Court Publishing Co., 1990).

Olvera, Ricardo, "Columbus and Toscanelli," *Fidelio,* Vol. 1, No. 2 (Washington, D.C.: Schiller Institute, Inc., 1992).

Plato, *The Collected Dialogues,* edited by E. Hamilton and Huntington Cairns, Bollingen Series 71 (Princeton: Princeton University Press, 1961).

Pope John Paul II, *On Social Concern* (Boston: St. Paul Books and Media, 1987).

———, *Centesimus Annus* (Boston: St. Paul Books and Media, 1991).

Pope Paul VI, *Populorum Progressio* (Boston: Daughters of St. Paul, 1967).

Proclus, *Commentary on Plato's Parmenides,* translated by Glenn R. Morrow and John M. Dillon (Princeton: Princeton University Press, 1987).

Pseudo-Dionysius, *The Complete Works,* translated by Colm Luibheid (New York: Paulist Press, 1987).

Wertz, William F., Jr., "Why St. Thomas Aquinas Is Not an Aristotelian," *Fidelio,* Vol. 2, No. 1 (Washington, D.C.: Schiller Institute, Inc., 1993).

Zepp-LaRouche, Helga, "Nicolaus of Cusa and the Council of Florence," *Fidelio,* Vol. 1, No. 2 (Washington, D.C.: Schiller Institute, Inc., 1992).

———, "Why We Need an International Coalition for Peace and Development," *Fidelio,* Vol. 1, No. 3, (Washington, D.C.: Schiller Institute, Inc., 1992).

About the Translator

William F. Wertz, Jr. was born on July 28, 1945 in Summit, New Jersey. He received an academic scholarship to attend Wesleyan University in Middletown, Connecticut. While at Wesleyan he was enrolled in the College of Letters. During the first semester of his sophomore year he studied abroad in Vienna, Austria and at the University of Cologne in West Germany. He graduated from Wesleyan University in 1967 Magna Cum Laude, Phi Beta Kappa, with a Bachelor of Arts degree. He received a National Education and Defense Act Fellowship to study English at Harvard University, but left Harvard before receiving a graduate degree.

In 1971 he joined the political movement founded by Lyndon H. LaRouche, Jr., because he agreed with LaRouche that world peace could only be established on the basis of a commitment to eliminating the underlying causes of war, through the economic and cultural development of all mankind.

In 1984 he began to coordinate a project for the Schiller Institute to translate the works of the German poet Friedrich Schiller into English. He has since then been the editor and primary translator of three books of translations of the works of Schiller published in paperback form. These works include translations of the dramas *Don Carlos, Wilhelm Tell,* and the *Virgin of Orleans,* numerous poems, and such aesthetical writings as *On the Aesthetical Education of Man.*

He is currently the Editor-in-Chief of *Fidelio,* a journal of poetry, science, and statecraft, published quarterly by the Schiller Institute beginning in 1992.

HELP MAKE A NEW GOLDEN RENAISSANCE!

Join the Schiller Institute!

Every renaissance in history has been associated with the written word, from the Greeks, to the Arabs, to the great Italian 'Golden Renaissance.' The Schiller Institute, devoted to creating a new Golden Renaissance from the depths of the current Dark Age, offers a year's subscription to two prime publications— *Fidelio* and *New Federalist,* to new members:

FIDELIO is a quarterly journal of poetry, science and statecraft, which takes its name from Beethoven's great operatic tribute to freedom and republican virtue.

NEW FEDERALIST is the national newspaper of the American System. As Benjamin Franklin said, "Whoever would overthrow the liberty of a nation must begin by subduing the freeness of speech." *New Federalist* is devoted to keeping that "freeness."

Join the Schiller Institute and receive NEW FEDERALIST and FIDELIO as part of the membership: $1,000 Lifetime Membership
$500 Sustaining Membership
$100 Regular Annual Membership

All these memberships include: ● 4 issues FIDELIO ($20 value) ● 100 issues NEW FEDERALIST ($35 value)

Sign me up as a member of the Schiller Institute.

☐ $1,000 Lifetime Membership   ☐ $ 100 Regular Annual Membership
☐ $ 500 Sustaining Membership   ☐ $ 35 Introductory Membership
(50 issues NEW FEDERALIST only)

Name _____

Address _____

City _____

State _____ Zip _____ Phone ( ) _____

Copy or clip and send this coupon with your check or money order to:

SCHILLER INSTITUTE, INC.

P.O. Box 66082, Washington, D.C. 20035-6082